GW00569819

SEA OF ITALY

WHITE STAR PUBLISHERS

ITALY SEA OF

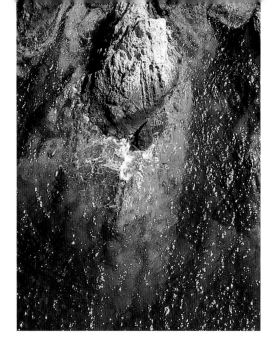

PHOTOGRAPHS
Antonio Attini
Marcello Bertinetti

TEXT
Alberto Bertolazzi

Contents

2-3 Punta Mezzogiorno and Punta Vardella are the tips of this white tufa arch that plunges into the turquoise sea off Palmarola (Latina), Pontine Islands.

4-5 Waves breaking on the coast near Camogli (Genoa). The delicate relationship with the sea is expressed in the origins of the town's name: "Cà de mugee," meaning "where the wives lived," referring to the women who stayed behind when the men were far away, fishing.

6-7 As early as the late 1800s, Portofino (Genoa) was a famous tourist resort. First the Germans came to appreciate the enchanting bay's beautiful nature, then British. The Italians came later and turned the village into an exclusive jet-set rendezvous.

8 The clear waters around the Pontine Islands, off the Lazio coast, make this stretch of the Tyrrhenian Sea one of the cleanest of all Italian waters.

9 The waters around Capo Passero (Siracusa), Sicily's southernmost tip, are a paradise for sailing and snorkeling fans.

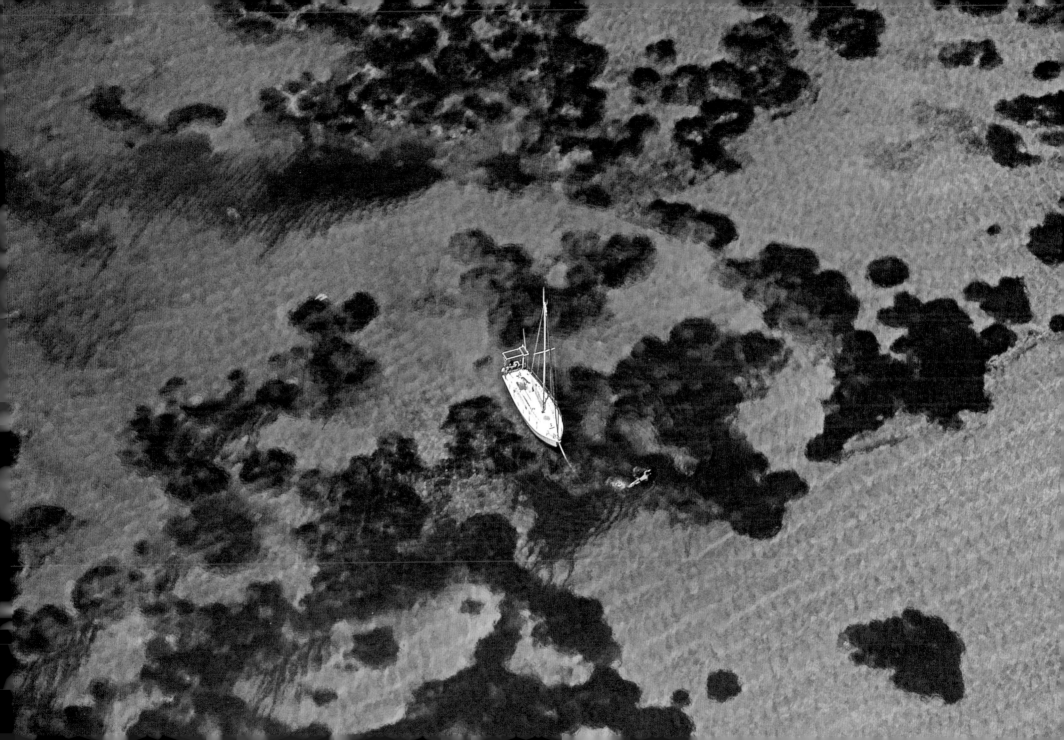

"The sea has never been friendly to man. At most it has been the accomplice of human restlessness." Probably Joseph Conrad, author of seafaring and adventure stories, was gazing at the Mediterranean when he wrote these words. A somber, foaming Mediterranean that the gentle Tcodor Józef Konrad Korzeniowski discovered in his youth, as a sailor, leaving Marseille for his future as a great, enthralling narrator.

The Mediterranean coasts are essentially restless. Geologically, the Mediterranean was the protagonist of the last great transformation of the earth's physiognomy, which indirectly brought about human evolution.

About five million years ago the sea that lapped our coasts evaporated completely and left a blanket of salt, 3280 ft (1000 m) thick, on its bed. The phenomenon was the consequence of the Gibraltar edge being lifted and the cutting off the Mediterranean from the Atlantic Ocean, reducing it to a lake that then dried out through evaporation.

This episode caused an extensive change to the climate which, among other effects, oriented prehominids to the forms that developed into modern humans. This radical change in the Mediterranean landscape lasted about a million years, then the Gibraltar edge descended and allowed the waters of the Atlantic to flow back into the basin and swiftly fill it up.

The tectonic plates, massive blocks of rock that move deep below our feet and slowly collide to release incalculable energies, have made the Mediterranean a workshop where nature has suffered unimaginable catastrophes (the explosion of Santorini, the eruptions of Vesuvius) and produced fabulous beauty.

The Mediterranean's history is also restless: it is rare to find a place where the bond between humanity and the sea is as close as it is in the Mare Nostrum. Millenary cultures have alternated over the centuries, forging various relationships with the coastlines.

The Egyptians ignored the sea, the Phoenicians and the Greeks colonized it, the Romans and the Normans exploited it without loving it, Italy's maritime republics made it their source of wealth.

10 On Ponza's (Latina) southernmost tip, a lighthouse clutches the Cape Guardia rocks, almost concealed by a veil of clouds.

In this great sea, the Italian peninsula stretches north to south, reaching out toward Africa – which is not so far away if the truth be told.

Strategic as a great natural aircraft carrier, our country owes part of its history to the sea, as well as much of its wealth and its clear geographical boundaries. Over 5600 miles (9012 km) of coast, including that of Sicily and Sardinia, which alone account for almost half the total length, separate the land from the water, and Italy from the rest of the world.

The Italian seas reach the coasts of continents and islands. The long, long coasts reach from the fliparin Sea to Dalmatia, outlining bays and coves, promontories and beaches, reefs and cliffs that gaze out onto seas shimmering through cobalt to turquoise.

They may be rocky coasts, wedged between tall mountains and sheer cliffs, as is the case in much of Liguria, or rolling shores that are the continuation of gentle hill slopes, fostered by thousands of years of river silt that has created deep, wide beaches, as on the Adriatic.

Adventurers and pioneers like Christopher Columbus and Giuseppe Garibaldi set sail from the Italian coasts; occupying and liberating army vessels landed on the peninsu-

12 left The silhouette of San Fruttuoso di Capodimonte (Genoa) abbey dominates the bay of the same name, tucked into the heart of the Portofino promontory. The waters in front of the abbey house the statue of Christ the Redeemer, a destination for divers, set about 30 ft (9 m) underwater.

la's shores. In those same coves where Phoenicians and Greeks, Normans and Americans disembarked, pleasure craft now drop anchor.

All islands are unique, but this is especially true in Italy where the symbols and meanings that concentrate have little to do with geography. Greek mythology, the heritage acquired by the Latins and then by all the peoples of the peninsula, have associated the island with a concept of peace and asceticism. Peace in the isolation; asceticism, as few are capable of enjoying its precious treasures. Yet by a strange twist of fate, the Italian islands have become more famous as prisons than refuges: Ustica was the place of exile for Antonio Gramsci, fierce antagonist of Fascism; Ponza imprisoned the partisan Sandro Pertini, later President of the Republic, and also Benito Mussolini, the Fascist leader; Caprera was the refuge of Giuseppe Garibaldi, in a sort of voluntary exile that he maintained until his death. Elba was where Napoleon Bonaparte sojourned, but not by choice. Capraia and Pianosa are or were the sites of high security jails. Yet for the person on the street, these 40 or so islands that form a crown encircling the Italian coasts are splendid fragments of paradise.

Leaving aside Venice, which is an island only geologically, and in fact is a city-state and city-of-dreams defying all definition, leaving aside Sicily and Sardinia, whose historical, anthropological and administrative underpinning make them out and out cultural "continents," leaving aside the reefs and myriad rocks that are set into many sections of coastline (for instance each single, uninhabited rock fragment that makes up the Maddalena Archipelago), there are 34 Italian islands: the Tuscan Archipelago, the Sardinian, the Pontine, Ventotene, Ischia and Capri, Ustica, Lipari, the Egadi, Pantelleria, the Pelagian and the Tremiti islands.

Each archipelago, each island, for its own reasons, unique and unlike any other, each worthy of being loved: flat, and deserted like the Tremiti, wind-shattered and scarred like Sardinia's islands, barren and harsh like the Pelagian Archipelago, colorful and verdant like the Tuscan Archipelago, disturbing and mysterious like volcanic Lipari, puffing steam like hell's kitchen.

12 center The tiny uninhabited island of Palmaiola (Livorno), in the Piombino Channel, has all the typical elements of a Mediterranean island: vegetation, hard rock, cobalt sea.

12 right The mouth of Vulcano's crater (Messina) gapes skyward: an abyss of petrified lava and ash. In the distance, beyond the luxuriant green hillside, beyond the houses on the slope, is a stretch of the turquoise Tyrrhenian Sea, with Stromboli, Vesuvius and Etna.

We say that the continent's coasts and the islands have opened the way, on various occasions, to wealth, histories, adventures. However, where the seas meet the earth there are also magical places: the sun that sets behind the Maddalena crags, in a fiery seas fragmented by a thousand islets; the Adriatic Riviera's long, endless beaches, deserted in winter; seagulls that allow themselves to be carried by the wind and glide through the sky until they skim the foamy waves that beat against the Cinque Terre; a long string of villages hugging the sheer Sorrento cliffs; the subtle vertigo that lurks for those who lean out from the Capo Caccia overhang in Sardinia, seeking to embrace the entire promontory with a single glance. The spell we describe is cast by all this splendor: breathtaking beauty. A hamlet, a tiny beach, a stretch of rocky shore, a lonely islet set in the sea, any one of them can seem like a corner of paradise to us. For sailors it was the flight of the seabirds that warned of land ahoy; for us, enamored of beauty, the flight of the albatross proves there is a marvelous way to cross the expanse of waters and land in distant countries: gliding into the sky astride the wind, free to choose a route or an altitude, dominating the horizon and letting the sea below ripple past.

Those of us who travel crowded roads everyday cannot do that in person. So the photographers who shot the images for this book did it on our behalf. They flew in tiny planes or in hot air balloons, in gliders and helicopters, at high altitude or skimming the ground, to show us in the most spectacular way how lovely, how unique, and how unspoiled most of our coasts and islands are, and how clear the Mare Nostrum can still be.

15 Duino castle (Trieste) rises on the rock spur of the Carso, that tumbles directly into the Gulf of Trieste. Only a 16th-century tower survives of the ancient building, whose origins date back to the 11th century. The castle, owned by the princely house of Thurn und Taxis, is the starting point for a splendid stroll dedicated to the German poet, Rainer Maria Rilke, who stayed at Duino in the early 1900s.

18-19 Cala Rossa and Punta dello Zenobito are the two most evocative points on Capraia (Livorno), in the Tuscan Archipelago.

20-21 Conigli Island is just a few yards from Lampedusa Island's southern coast (Agrigento). The name Coniglio, the Italian word for rabbit, derives from the wild rabbits that once lived on the island, but are now extinct.

22-23 This spectacular stretch of coastline was photographed near Arbatax (Ogliastra), the main town on the Costa Rei, in eastern Sardinia. The town is surrounded by a natural wealth of coves and bays that render it unique and fascinating.

Sea of Italy
key data

- The Italian peninsula and its minor islands have a coast extending 3000 miles (4828 km). Add in Sicily and Sardinia's coasts and the total is over 5600 miles (9012 km).

- The Ionian is the deepest sea, at 16,550 ft (5044 m). Next there are the Tyrrhenian Sea (12,300 ft/3750 m), the Ligurian Sea (9265 ft/2823) and the Adriatic Sea (4000 ft/1219 m).

- Italy has 34 major islands, of which the ten largest are Sicily, 15,900 sq. miles (41,180 sq. km); Sardinia, 14,900 sq. miles (38,590 sq. km); Elba (Tuscany), 140 sq. miles (363 sq. km); Sant'Antioco (Sardinia), 68 sq. miles (176 sq. km); Pantelleria (Sicily), 52 sq. miles (137 sq. km);

San Pietro (Sardinia), 32 sq. miles (83 sq. km); Asinara (Sardinia), 32 sq. miles (83 sq. km); Ischia (Campania), 29 sq. miles (75 sq. km); Lipari (Sicily), 23 sq. miles (60 sq. km); Salina (Sicily), 16.5 sq. miles (42 sq. km).

- Main ports:
  Genoa, Savona, La Spezia, Trieste, Ravenna, Livorno (Leghorn), Piombino, Fiumicino, Naples, Taranto, Milazzo, Augusta, Siracusa (Syracuse).

- Fish catch per shore/per year:
  Upper Tyrrhenian: 496 tons (450 tonnes); Lower Tyrrhenian:1302 (1000 tonnes); Upper Adriatic: 1110 tons (1007 tonnes); Lower Adriatic: 653 tons (592 tonnes); Ionian Sea: 1.6 tons (1.45 tonnes).

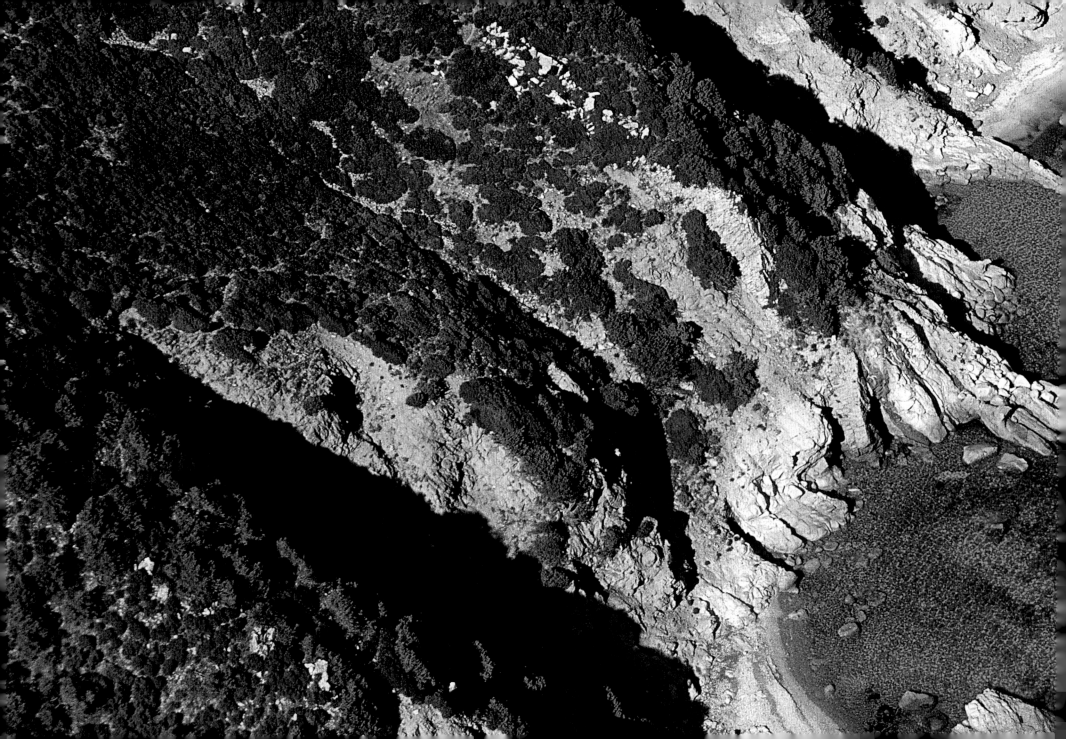

THE UPPER TYRRHENIAN SEA

The two seas that lap the northwestern coasts of Italy take their name from the ancient races who, in different measure, wrote the history of this country: the Ligurians and the Tyrrhenians, better known as the Etruscans.

"The convex part of the Alps – which are very tall mountains that form a curve – faces the Celt plains already mentioned, and Monte Cemmeno; the concave part faces Liguria and Italy. Many peoples live in these mountains, all Celts except the Ligurians: this is a different race, but with a similar way of life; they inhabit the part of the Alps that meets the Apennines and they also occupy part of the Apennines . . . ." In his Geographia, the Greek historian Strabo thus described the people that came from France.

The Ligurians were not sailors, they did not colonize, they did not travel, they did not invent, but they were fortunate enough to occupy for centuries, until the Roman conquest, one of North Italy's the most fascinating regions. The Etruscans, on the other hand, arrived from far-off Lydia (in Turkey),

led by a legendary prince: Tyrrhenian. Herodotus suggested they fled toward the Italic coast to escape years of famine. Fate was good to them and offered them a sea full of fish and fertile land: Tuscany. So Etruscan thalassocracy was born, characterized by centuries of undisputed reign from the Gulf of La Spezia to the Iolfa mountains. Nonetheless, the Etruscans were also forced to surrender to the Romans, who gave the name Tyrrenum to this part of the Mare Nostrum.

Now the Ligurian Sea and the Upper Tyrrhenian are biological havens and despite the huge number of ferries and cargo ships that sail the waters, corals grow there and dolphins and whales are resident. This is the location of the Cetacean Sanctuary: a vast protected area of sea set amid the territorial shores of Levante, Ponente and Corsica, with a major point of interest just off the Riviera di Ponente. A flight over these waters often offers some spectacular sightings: in the deepest blue, amid the reflections, the light and shadows of the lengthy high sea waves, spurts of water, then backs ap-

24 left Riomaggiore (La Spezia), set at the eastern tip the Riviera di Levante, is the nearest of the Cinque Terre villages to La Spezia. A path dug in the rock, steep over the sea, connects Riomaggiore to the nearby village of Manarola.

24 right Giglio Island (Livorno), an enchanting Mediterranean postcard view, derives its name from the word aegilium, a Latinized version of the Greek for "goat."

25 Capraia (Livorno), the island of stones or island of goats, is perhaps the most fascinating of the Tuscan Archipelago's "Seven Sisters." Capo dello Zenobito and the vermilion maquis of Cala Rossa, two of the striking localities that can be reached by boat, seen in the picture bottom right.

26 From the Portofino (Genoa) promontory, the village of San Rocco dominates thye Gulf of Paradiso. The city of Genoa is visible in the distance.

pear, in small groups or alone, moving slowly or chasing fast. The route the whales follow takes us into a journey of almost 200 miles (320 km), from west to east, along the curve of land that belonged to the Ligurians.

The two shores, Ponente (the western stretch) and Levante (the eastern stretch), are a lovely sequence of cliffs, beaches, Mediterranean maquis and pine groves, broken up by small bays, gulfs and ancient coastal settlements.

From Ventimiglia, whose hinterland of narrow valleys is reminiscent of rivers that brought water gushing down from the Apennine peaks, to Genoa, the Riviera di Ponente is less rugged and more colorful that the eastern basin, thanks to the flowers, grown in hundreds of greenhouses along the coast, but also to the greater shelter afforded by the curving coastline against the inclement weather and currents that roll in from the west.

There is no lack of narrow, multicolored houses, typical of Riviera architecture, an element that renders the Ligurian coastal panorama unique in the world. These former fishermen's dwellings, leaning into one another and separated by narrow lanes, are now holiday homes for city folk on the run from the metropolis. Their façades owe the eye-catching colors to the need to be identifiable at many miles from dry land: a comfort for those sailing on fishing boats and dreaming of the return home. Set into the rock, hugging the Riviera di Lev-

ante mountain slopes, the fishing villages lie all along the narrow western beaches; the occasional alluvial plains that typify this part of Liguria have always been settled, and towns like Albenga and Luni still offer evident traces of the customary ancient Roman urban plan.

The built-up areas are separated by nature, testified by the presence of parks like Bergeggi and Gallinara. A luxuriant Mediterranean maquis with maritime pines, which grow even in the most impervious and sterile terrains, stretches across the Riviera di Levante, to the east and inside the Portofino reserve, to alternate with various botanical species that cover the rock faces sheer down to the sea. The promontory is dotted with elegant homes, the legacy of an era when the protection of nature lay in human hands.

Portofino and the Cinque Terre are perhaps the most enchanting subject to photograph from the sky: a green stain reaching out to sea, with rocks that plunge into waters said to be the cleanest in the Mediterranean, proved by the presence of colonies of corals.

The Tuscan coast starts in Versilia, after the Gulf of La Spezia and the magical Portovenere promontory. The northern part of the coast offers a splendid sequence of wide, sandy beaches, stretching from the mouth of the River Serchio to the threshold of Pisa, as far as the Cinquale canal, the boundary between Lucca and Massa Carrara. This stretch of riviera has

29 Capodimonte Bay (Genoa), in front of San Fruttuoso (on the right) is delineated by Punta della Torretta, a rocky ridge which stretches from Monte Portofino down into the sea.

some of Italy's richest landscapes, scented by the Mediterranean maquis and, in particular, by the pine grove that runs the entire length of the sandy shore.

Versilia, with the Ligurian rivieras, was the cradle of seaside tourism that drew hordes of foreign visitors to Italy as the 1800s drew to a close, all seeking experiences that were not simply artistic. There are still clear traces of that era in Viareggio, Forte dei Marmi and even in the smaller towns, both in the urban layout, easy to spot from the sky, and in the buildings. The stretch of coast known as the Costa degli Etruschi, found between Livorno (Leghorn) and Piombino, is characterized by a superb

landscape, with the coasts plunging sheer into the sea, dotted with fishing villages, and surrounded by the greenery of the hills. The Tuscan shore, from here down to the Lazio (ancient Latium) border, is an alluvial formation and therefore has long, sandy beaches, which set the pine groves and inland hills back from the foreshore.

The slow, small streams that head into the Tyrrhenian often open into pools and small lagoons: parts of the coast, like the Maremma, were once unhealthy swamps but were cleared and are now protected areas. The Uccellina mountains, a promontory, the Argentario, and endless rocks, are the prelude

30 left Monte Argentario (Grosseto) reaches its highest altitude at Punta Telegrafo (2083 ft/635 m), in the center of the photo. Originally an island surrounding the mountain of the same name, the Argentario is linked to the Tuscan coast by two strips of land, the Giannella tombolo (sandbar) and the Giannutri tombolo, which form the Orbetello Lagoon.

to the Tuscan Archipelago, describing an edgier shoreline, with bays and inlets alternating with sandy beaches. A southern Mediterranean landscape, with high temperatures, a bright sky, little rain, reflecting in a crystal sea, nuanced with turquoise. The typical areas of this coast are the Uccellina Park and the Argentario, with the Orbetello lagoon: the former is a huge thicket of maritime pines, furrowed by water courses that flow to the sea with a play of currents, a long beach of fine sand, embraced by tall peaks and different-sized pools; the latter is a mountainous island, almost circular, connected to the mainland by three slim filaments of ground that enclose two lagoons. Two milieus unique both for their beauty and the biological magnificence, a stopover for many migrating birds.

From the Argentario it feels as if Giannutri and Giglio are at our fingertips, two of the "Seven Sisters" that form the Tuscan Archipelago.

Or as classical mythology would say, two of the seven pearls in the necklace of Venus. Giannutri, the southernmost, has a distinctive half-moon shape. Its coastline is steep and rocky, like mighty buttresses to protect the wild beauty of the inner territory, overrun with juniper and oleaster. From the aircraft, to the north, we can see the remains of the villa owned by the distinguished Roman, Domitius Ahenobarbus. It was built in the first century A.D.

Giglio also has rugged cliffs and a dense vegetation covering its entire surface. Human presence is well-defined in the port and the hamlets of Castello and Campese. The fascinating medieval village of Giglio Castello, with its fortifications, has narrow alleys that lead to the fortress. Its position on the ridge that cuts across the island provides a marvelous panoramic position.

Mule tracks and paths wind through extensive vineyards, as far as Giglio Campese, the settlement that was built on the north-west side, hallmarked by a mighty tower set on a large sandy cove. Montecristo is a solitary granite rock, an unmistakable mushroom shape, and the archipelago's island that is the farthest away from dry land. It is protected by a special environmental provision because it hosts some extremely rare endemic species. The Council of Europe has declared this rock to be a Biogenetic Nature Reserve. It was of course made

30 center The beaches near Punta Ala (Grosseto) open along narrow strips of sand, against a pinewood backdrop. The Punta Ala promontory closes the Gulf of Follonica to the south, a particularly characteristic stretch of the Tuscan Coast.

30 right Giglio Castello (Livorno) is surrounded by imposing walls, broken by towers, and was built by the Pisans in the 12th century. Its narrow streets, often surmounted by arches and the Rocca Aldobrandesca, dominating from on high, makes it a splendid example of a typical medieval fortified village.

famous by Alexandre Dumas in his The Count of Monte Cristo; Dumas was responsible in part for creating its special appeal and air of mystery. The island is not accessible to the general public and visits must be authorized.

Like Pianosa, the "flat" island, farmed since the most ancient times and now an unspoiled nature reserve, Capraia and Gorgona are heavenly wildernesses where both land and sea fauna and flora live in delicate equilibrium with humankind. Seen from above they are easy to recognize: Capraia has a characteristic elliptical shape and big, reddish coastal cliffs that betray its rich ferrous composition; Gorgona, however, is small and round, and completely mountainous, covered in dense vegetation.

Two towers are easy to see in the aerial photographs: Torre Vecchia, of Pisan origin, and Torre Nuova, erected by the Medici family.

Elba, known as early as Ancient Greek times by the name of Aethalia, has played an important economic role over the centuries, thanks to its endless iron deposits, exploited successfully by the Romans, who loaded the raw mineral at the wharf in Portoferraio, the name of the port clearly deriving from its strategic significance at that time. Like the Romans, Napoleon also left a legacy, exiled here after his defeat at Leipzig: the majestic Villa dei Mulini and Villa San Martino, both at Portoferraio.

Apart from the iron, however, and recorded history, the island's real treasure is its landscape: steep red-tinged cliffs, furrowed by green inlets and white beaches, lapped by the crystal-clear sea; mountain slopes, covered with scented Mediterranean maquis and dense woods; gentle, vineyard-smothered slopes and sunny plains, where agaves and prickly pears reign; the seaside villages, that often retain the atmosphere of fishermen's ancient refuges, hugging the higher slopes, speak of pirates attacking in bygone times.

33 Capo Enfola and the nearby Gulf of Viticcio, on the island of Elba (Livorno), are well-known to birdwatchers: a large colony of herring gulls that can be observed during spring on the granite cliffs that plunge almost sheer into the sea. Capo Enfola offers a very evocative environment, particularly at sunset when its white rocks, beaten by wind and sea, acquire magical shapes and pinkish hues.

34 The tip of Capo Varigotti (Savona) closes the vast inlet to the north, where the Ligurian village of Varigotti lies. Of its beaches, those around the point are the most admired and unspoiled; strong currents keep the water crystal-clear.

35 This view of Varigotti shows both the new quarters (on the left), and the old quarters (on the right), with characteristic small colored-washed houses hugging ancient alleys.

36-37 Heavy seas rage on the Ligurian Riviera, at the Gulf of Paradiso, near Camogli (Genoa.) The small town of Sori can be made out in the background.

38 and 39 Exceptionally high waves break on the castle that towers above Camogli harbor (Genoa), wind-driven water and spray washing up as far as the rooftops.

40-41 The colors and outlines of the farthest tip of the Portofino promontory make this photo unique, with its view of the village, castle and lighthouse.

42 and 43 left The turreted villas set amid the greenery of the Portofino (Genoa) promontory are typical of the Ligurian Riviera and of the aristocratic tradition of building homes on higher ground, above the villages, and surrounding them with plant life brought from every corner of the world.

43 right The villas overlooking Portofino, set in their dream gardens, often suggest medieval castles, sometimes authentically old, sometimes more modern, but all offer superb views.

44 Punta Mesco is a narrow promontory overhanging the sea, which leads into the Cinque Terre (La Spezia). Beyond the point, the landscape opens onto Monterosso, the only village with a beach. The whole promontory is important for its wildlife, especially for the coral that grows in the deep waters close to the cliffs.

45 Punta Baffe, near Riva Trigoso, presents an extraordinary scene of wind and wave-beaten cliffs plunging into the waters of the Gulf of Sestri Levante. The vegetation covering the promontory is slowly recovering from the devastating fire of 2004.

46 left Levanto (La Spezia), lying in a delightful bay surrounded by Monte Spezzini's greenery, is an entry point for the Cinque Terre. The town has been a popular seaside resort since the early 20th century.

46 right Sestri Levante (La Spezia), sheltered by a narrow peninsula, is a paradise for amateur sailors, who love to moor in its marina and stroll along the alleys of the old quarter.

47 Vernazza (La Spezia), one of Cinque Terre's most fascinating villages, seems almost trapped in this narrow coastal inlet. The past economic importance of Vernazza, founded in about A.D. 1000, is revealed by its loggias, arcades and portals.

48-49 Like Vernazza, Manarola (La Spezia) also has ancient roots, lost in time. Originally a fishing village, today it survives of on the overflow of the heavy tourism in the Cinque Terre, curbed only by its difficult access, clearly visible in this photo, where terraced vineyards seem to besiege and isolate the small village.

50 Clear waters bathe a natural wharf at Riomaggiore (La Spezia). The famous "Lovers' Walk," a suggestive and panoramic trail that links the Cinque Terre, starts from Riomaggiore, the easternmost village.

51 Vernazza's marina harbors (La Spezia) a fleet of colored boats moored in narrow rows. Some of them have had outboard motors, the sole concession to modernity.

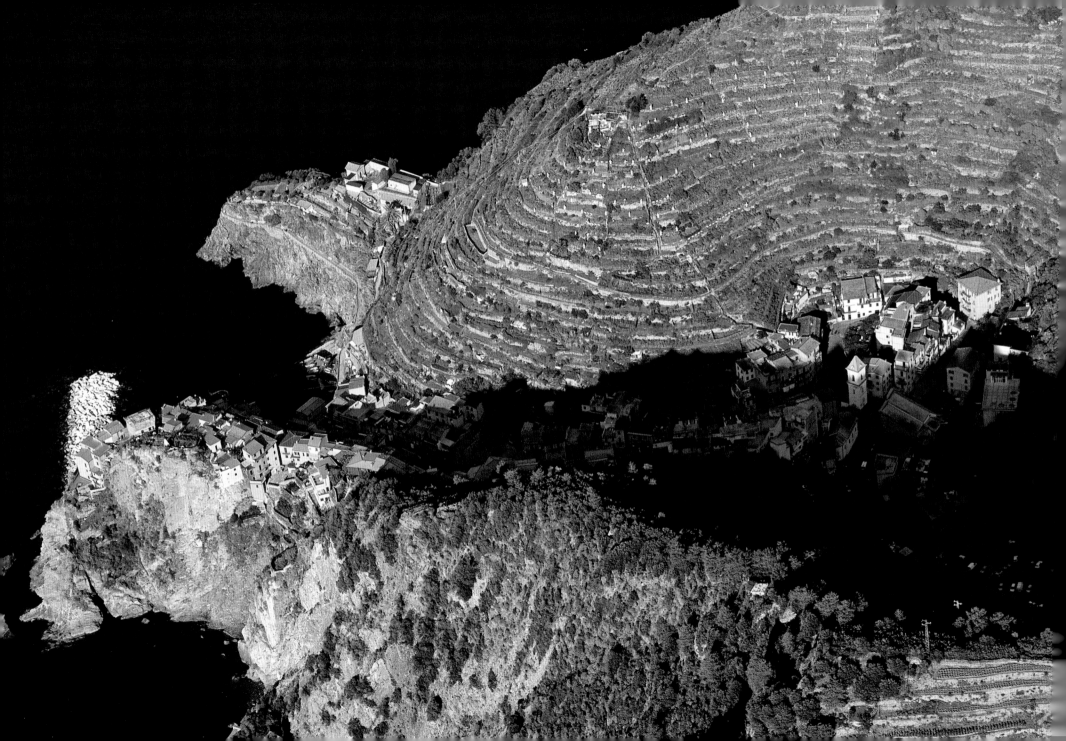

52 Manarola (La Spezia), one of the Cinque Terre, is a small harbor enclosed by mountains where renowned vineyards are cultivated.

53 The Ligurian Riviera offers numerous landing places for sailing fans, as this promontory near Sestri Levante (Genoa) shows.

54 Gorgona (Livorno) seen here from the south, is the smallest island of the Tuscan Archipelago. Called Urgon in ancient times and once inhabited by Etruscans and Romans, it is frequently visited today by sailing enthusiasts and scuba divers.

55 Gorgona is also a protected natural haven. Some stretches of its shores are famous: the Costa dei Gabbiani, for instance, or Cala Scirocco whose Grotto del Bue Marino was once a breeding ground for monk seals.

56 Elba (Livorno), a predominantly mountainous island, has few beaches. One of them is Fetovaia beach, at the tip of a narrow inlet visited by numerous sailing enthusiasts, many of whom go ashore.

57 Steep sea and wind-struck crags unfolding along the Elban coast shelter migrating birds who often nest there. The island of Napoleon's exile is a pole of attraction for tourists all over the world, enchanted by its rocky coasts and clear waters.

58 This white sand and pebble beach captured at low tide on Elba (Livorno), with a pine grove backdrop and lapping deep blue waters, recalls the crescent of an isolated moon.

59 The impact of wind and rain is evident on this cliff on Elba's west coast, also chiseled and sculptured by the sea.

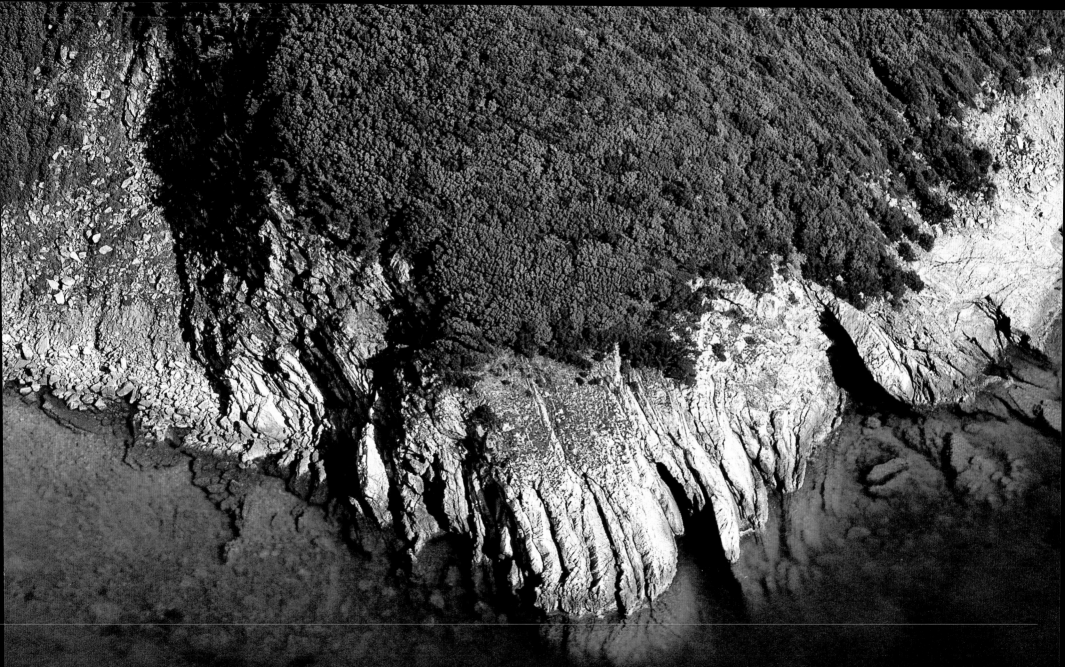

60 Pianosa (Livorno), fifth in size of the Tuscan Archipelago's islands, lying on a resistant shelf of calcareous rock and molded by tossing waves, is practically uninhabited. It has retained part of the thick vegetation that characterized it before medieval deforestation, and is furrowed by a network of tracks.

61 Pianosa's penitentiary, a square 19th-century square block, is the island's only important building. The prison is closed, but a few guards still live there to safeguard the building.

62 A splendid aristocratic residence, probably dating from the 19th century, built to replicate a medieval castle, overlooks the ever restless sea that beats against the rocks of Monte Massoncello (Livorno), on the Piombino promontory.

63 Cerboli (Livorno), an islet situated in the middle of the Piombino channel, appears from above like a calcareous shelf covered in patches of marine cistus, garrigue and lentisk. A few miles ahead, Elba rises in the open sea, facing toward the Gulf of Follonica.

64 The tower that dominates Giglio Campese's small harbor (Livorno) and bay was erected between 1670 and 1705 by the Medici family as a defense against pirates. Giglio Campese, one of Giglio Island's small inhabited centers, is popular with scuba divers, who leave from here on excursions to nearby seabeds.

65 This turreted construction, with its large square yard, was built on the island's hard granite, not far from Giglio Campese. The building, which resembles a rural manor, is situated on a panoramic vantage point, bathed on three sides by the sea.

66-67 Splendid inlets and beaches with very fine sand and cobalt-blue sea make the whole Riviera degli Etruschi (Livorno) a coveted destination for international visitors. The path that unwinds toward the beach from the hinterland follows a dry riverbed. These are numerous and contributed to shaping the landscape in this stretch of Tuscan coast.

68 The yellow-orange of the cultivated farmland near Populonia (Livorno) strikes an amazing contrast with the green Mediterranean maquis and the blue sea. The farthermost offshoots of the Piombino promontory can be seen in the distance.

69 This combination of shapes and colors results from a northward-focused shot of the Piombino promontory's vertical face. Note the pattern of farmland near Populonia in the foreground and the long strip of sand and pines that stretches up to Cecina in the distance.

71 Cecina beach (Livorno) is about 66 ft (20 m) deep and at one time the tide reached the margin of the cultivated land. Grand Duke Leopold of Tuscany had a pine grove planted along the coast, still there today, to protect the farmlands from sea salinity.

72-73 Along the coast between San Vincenzo and Populonia, in the Livorno (Leghorn) area, it is not unusual to find farmhouses like this, set on a rise amid maquis, at an arm's length from the sea, The turret, a common feature in this land teeming with rural traditions, is a sign of the owner's noble origins. Landowners usually lived on higher grounds so they could overlook and control their property

THE LOWER TYRRHENIAN SEA

As our southbound journey along the Italian coast proceeds, the Mediterranean gradually takes the upper hand. Windswept beaches, limy promontories, maquis scented by rosemary and myrtle: the route down to the lands of Magna Graecia skirts the coast of Lazio, with the wide, sandy shore that attracts the Romans fleeing from town. Ladispoli, Fregene, Lido di Ostia and then Torvaianica and Anzio, as far as the Pontine countryside, below the Tyrrhenian, which glimmers in the flat countryside southwest of Rome. A sea for bathers, not as crowded as the Romagna Adriatic, but nonetheless popular and busy.

Nature then takes command, as the coast rises to Monte Circeo's 1625 ft (495 m): a paradise that has been awarded national park classification for its specific environmental features. A green terrace offering a marvelous vista of the Campanian Archipelago reigns over the great lands of the reclaimed Pontine Marches, where entire communities of emigrants from northeast Italy worked and were struck down with malaria.

On Circeo National Park's boundaries, Terracina is rather more than just a port for setting sail toward Ponza: it is the gateway to the south, echoing with a Roman past that Sperlonga so elegantly preserves. The four-sided area whose farther points are Circeo, Ponza, Ventotene and Gaeta is a portion of the Tyrrhenian coast where nature plays with history, and vice versa: from above the sheer seas there are not infrequent glimpses of the traces left by passing centuries, just as the bather can swim among amphorae and ancient relics. The Gulf of Gaeta is the door into northern Campania, the land of volcanoes and sea-lapped hills. Eruptions buried in the mists of time have carved out the coasts, plunging sheer into the seas, and have tinged the landscape with the black of lava rock and the yellow of tufa stone. Land of sailors and fishermen, who still live in the tiny villages set on the sea, overlooking the small fishing boats bobbing in the Gulf of Naples.

The coasts of Campania are where the ancient Greeks landed. The earliest colonizers arrived in Ischia and called it

74 left The town of Capri (Naples) overlooks the Marina Grande. The panorama is closed off by Monte Tiberio, fading down into the Tyrrhenian at Punta del Capo.

74 right Bathers on one of Costa Viola's sandy beaches, in Calabria. This stretch of coast takes its name from the violet sea.

75 The landscape of central Ponza Island (Latina), between Cala Feola and the Monte Guardia area, is typically verdant, with terraced cultivation.

77 The Amalfi Coast (Salerno) is marked by villages and inlets: visible here, Atrani (foreground), Minori and Maiori, then Scala and Ravello on the slopes.

Pithecusa, in other words "the island of vases," because clay was used here. Ischia is the island of greenery and fire. Hundreds of thermal springs provide water to the countless spas and gardens that ramble up the hillside from the sea, amid exotic plants and flowers, olive and lemon groves.

This is the Neapolitan sea: villages against a backdrop of hills, where for centuries the womenfolk of fishermen and sailors have flocked to the tiny white church set over the sea, to pray to the Madonna that the waves restrain their fury until their loved ones are safely home. The nearby islands of Vivara and Procida, one next to the other, are separated only by an old,

sea-flooded crater. The tiny island of Vivara is a cascade of rare vegetation reflected in the clear sea; Procida is the island of fishermen, with pastel-colored houses that look out onto the small bays looped in solidified tufa and lava. Corricella, the most famous and prettiest village, is a maze of tiny houses weaving through arches, stairs and lanes. A haven seemingly not of this world, light years away from modern life.

Opposite the Campanian islands the coast again presents a landscape of surreal outlines, scarred by eruptions. Cuma is tufa, from which trees spring, just a step from the sea, or lava rock like that under the Acropolis. Capo Miseno is an impres-

78 left Deep, narrow coves are met with on the Sorrento peninsula (Salerno); little fjords like this one between Nerano and Positano.

sive rock: legend has it that here the great rocks fell with such force that they dug out the bays that the sea later smoothed into small and large craters that interweave among the grottoes. The surrounding area bears vestiges of an important past – a Roman theater, walls of Roman villas – and volcanoes that have never quite gone to rest. Nearby, Baia is dominated by a castle that was built over the relics of the Caesars' villa. This is where the most luxurious of spas of ancient Rome were built; here, Horace wrote, was the world's most entrancing gulf.

Naples is close by. Its calling card is the magical bay of Porto Paone and Posillipo's tall tufa cliff. Vesuvius commands the gulf. From the great crater's height our gaze will melt into a spellbinding panorama: Naples, its sea, the Sorrento coast, the islands. Tall on the horizon stand the towering chimneys of the Bagnoli steelworks, now closed and awaiting a radical program for conversion to tourist use, with the recovery of one of the loveliest stretches of coastline. To the south, the Sorrento peninsula: a tall, narrow rock that plunges into the Tyrrhenian, reaching out toward the island of Capri. On one side the charm of the Sorrento coast, on the other, the precious Amalfi Coast. Then, farther south, beyond the Gulf of Salerno, Punta Licosa, the Sirene promontory. The Cilento coast, also rugged and irregular here, offers small bays and golden beaches at the foot of the greenest pine groves.

The section of coast south of Naples is mountainous and falls sheer into the sea. The settlements are fishing villages hugging hairpin bends: tiny centers whose intricate fabric consists of steps and lanes, labyrinths of blind alleys, but also towns that have left their mark on history. Amalfi was merely a hamlet locked in a stone casket, without roads, just an infinite threshold onto the sea: it became a powerful maritime republic, like Genoa, Venice and Pisa. Its ships ruled the world and, setting forth from that isolated village with its tall slopes, encountered distant cultures, returning to transform the few existing houses into an increasingly rich and lovely city.

A seafaring land, but also of farmers who succeed in persuading the harsh terrain to yield narrow terraces, nowadays visible from the air. The crops that ramble up the hillsides and

78 center Capri (Naples) is known for its stunning cliffs, like the one from Monte Tiberio down to Punta del Capo; there is also the eroded cliff recaptured in the famous Faraglioni stacks (left). Some of the sea-sculpted grottoes (of which more than 60 are known) can be picked out.

78 right Tyrrhenian Calabria, toward Capo Vaticano, presents landscapes like this, with small sandy beaches nestling between rocky promontories.

slope down to the sea create a landscape of fierce colors: the yellow of the lemons and the broom, the green of the olives and the darker shades of the vines, the deep blue of the deep sea that embraces magical islands. The island of Capri, the backdrop to the imperial sojourns of Augustus and Tiberius, is now a venue for VIPs who crowd the medieval quarter's lanes as far as the famous "piazzetta," between the church of Santo Stefano and the tower with its majolica clock. The island, as is quite clear from the sky, is a calcareous rock, whose rugged landscape is marked by tall spurs and spectacular stacks, soaring from the sea depths. Then steep coasts and grottoes everywhere, opening onto the sea.

Farther along, the coast bends back onto itself and here, in the great Gulf of Salerno, the temples of Paestum form the gateway to the Cilento. This is where the province of Salerno, the largest in Campania, slides south to reach the slim strip of Lucania, with Maratea looking out over the Tyrrhenian, just a stone's throw from Calabria.

A landscape of lovely lands that blend into the sea: from Agropoli toward Punta Licosa, and straight to the south, toward Capo Palinuro. The outline of coast around the small port called Palinuro – in memory of Aeneas' helmsman who drowned here – is once more formed by crags that rise out of the sea. The shore is woven through by old villages and new seaside resorts, and we have now passed the Gulf of Policastro and reached Calabria.

Here, like in many of Italy's regions, the sea speaks of history: from town to town the traces of the most ancient colonies come to light, whether Greek or Roman, against backdrops that clear, clean waters (whose purity is confirmed each year by experts and environmentalists) render even more lovely. The names are those of modern tourism that seeks beaches and reefs that are still unfettered: Riviera dei Cedri (with towns like Scalea, Diamante, Cetraro), the Gulf of Sant'Eufemia, down as far as Tropea and Capo Vaticano, on a spur of Apennine rock, and the Costa Viola, down to Reggio Calabria and its shoreline, which D'Annunzio defined as "the most beautiful kilometer of Italy."

81 Capri's superb Faraglioni (Naples), towering over a lapis-lazuli sea, rise beyond the Punta di Tragara promontory. There are three Faraglioni: the one nearest to the coast is the "Stella" (350 ft/106 m) high; the most distant is named "Scopolo" and is 310 ft (94 m) high; the "Faraglione di mezzo," in the center, is 265 feet 81 m) high, with a 200-ft (61-m) tunnel through it.

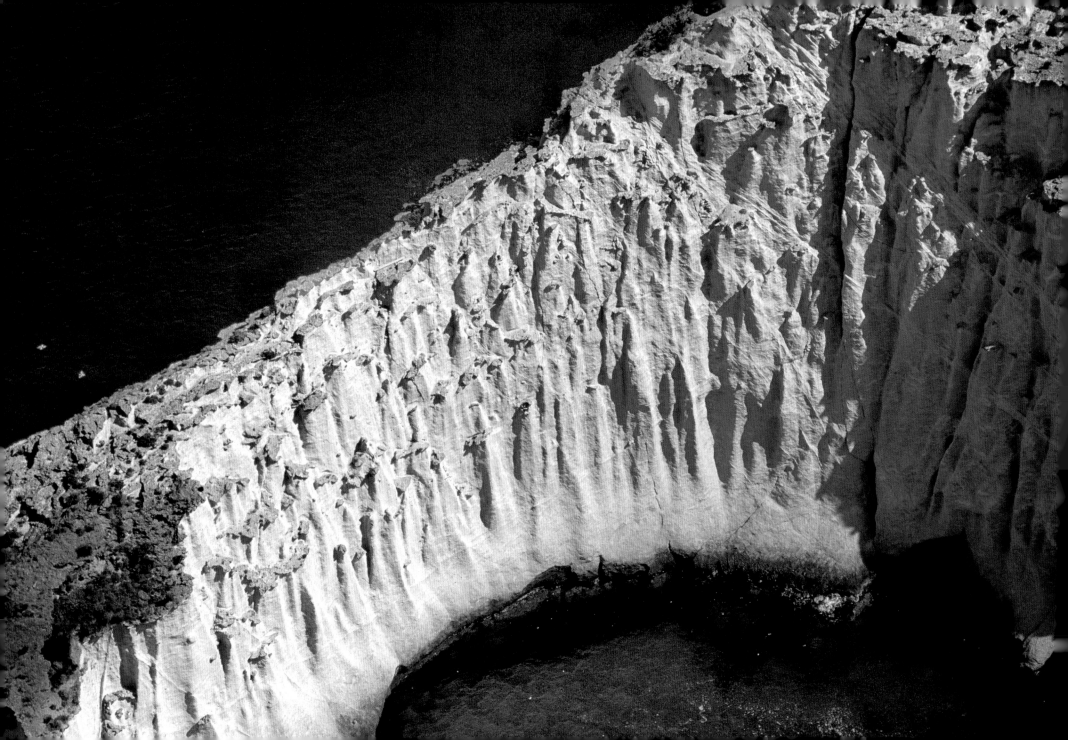

82 and 83 Ponza's (Latina) rocks of volcanic origin have been molded into coves and stacks and grottoes and outcrops, like the famous and charming Capo Bianco. Circe's Island – as it was known in Classical mythology – watches over a clear and restless sea that over the centuries has sculpted fascinating grottoes; among the most famous is the grotto through Capo Bianco.

84-85 Ponza's beauty is not just in its white tufa cliffs: the rugged part of the island is never trite, and arouses powerful emotions. Take, for instance, the Piscine Naturali, a scenario of rocks caressed by waters whose color varies from intense blue to turquoise.

86 and 87 Zannone (Latina), 6 miles away from the main Pontine island, resembles Ponza in that it has a big, single rock plateau and cliffs of volcanic origin. Zannone, a small strip of land – about 675 sq. yards (564 sq. m) – surrounded by the clear waters of this part of the Tyrrhenian, and is one of the few places that still preserves typical Mediterranean flora and fauna in full. Because of its natural beauty and deep blue sea rich with fish, it has been included in the Circeo National Park.

88 Palmarola (Latina), comprised of rocks, grottoes and stacks that produce a spectacular environment, is a sort of appendage to Ponza, with a similar morphology.

89 Palmarola, an island of volcanic origin, still shows signs of ancient explosions and fractures, like those that form the vitrified lava arc between Punta Mezzogiorno and Punta Vardella, here seen from the north.

90 Palmarola (Latina) is made up of lava rocks and tuffs produced by volcanic powders, ash and lapilli, deposited in layer upon layer over the centuries. Sea erosion has sculpted these rocks, creating the island's characteristic cliff, grottoes and stacks.

91 Deep blue reflections and colors enhance the sea that laps Zannone (Latina), where thick Mediterranean maquis clings to the rocky land.

92 The islet of Santo Stefano (Latina), with sparse vegetation and lacking in natural landing places, is a "satellite" of Ventotene, visible at top. The photo clearly shows the former Bourbon prison, a semicircular,18th-century fortification.

93 Ventotene (Latina) is a long arc-shaped strip of land that rises from the waters of the Lower Tyrrhenian halfway between Ponza and Ischia. The sickle-shaped rock and cement harbor, which closes the northern part of the island at Punta Eolo, is shown from above.

94-95 Procida's (Latina) name derives from the Greek *prochyo*, meaning "erupted." The island's volcanic origins show in the tuffaceous nature of the coast overhanging the sea. Its regular conformation makes it appear like a big terrace overlooking the sea; it reaches its highest point at the Terra Murata acropolis, visible here in the foreground.

96 Capo Miseno (Naples) owes its name to the Greek hero Misenus, the friend of Aeneas who was hurled into the sea by a Triton. The capital town of the same name is an important seaside resort at the north end of the Gulf of Naples. The islands of Procida, Vivara, Ischia and Capri, farther out, stand in front of Capo Miseno and its beach.

97 The islet where the Aragonian castle stands is linked by an isthmus to the ancient sea village of Ischia Ponte (Naples). Legend has it that the castle, which is reached from the island, was commissioned by Alfonso V of Aragon in about 1438 on the remains of an ancient fortress thought to date to the 4th century B.C.

98 From atop Monte Solaro, on Capri (Naples), the remains of the "Fortino di Bruto" can be seen, built at the beginning of the 19th century, when the English and French were at war; the San Giacomo charterhouse, Punta di Tragara and the Faraglioni can be pinpointed.

99 Monte Solaro is Capri's highest point and its peak provides a spectacular view of the entire island and the village of Anacapri, built on its slopes. The mountains of Calabria, the Apennines and the Amalfi Coast can be made out in the distance; beyond are Sorrento peninsula and the Gulf of Naples.

100 Positano (Salerno) is blessed by its location in the heart of an area among Italy's wealthiest in history and natural beauty. Positano, closed at north and west by high ground of over 4500 ft (1370 m), has a crystal-clear sea to the south and east, and a view that unfurls to embrace Punta Licosa and Capri.

101 Along the Amalfi Coast, a corner of paradise on earth, history and legend entwine with natural beauty: the result is an endless sequence of inspiring views, as in this photograph, which shows an old lookout tower now converted into a private residence.

103 Terraced land, scattered houses clinging to the slopes of Monte San Costanzo, rocky inclines that slide into a cobalt blue sea: the coast near Punta Campanella, one of the most beautiful stretches of the Mediterranean littoral, occupies the tip of the Sorrento peninsula (Salerno). Capri is just a few miles away, opposite the promontory

104-105 Artificial terraces and natural steps
alternate on the high ground between Amalfi
and Maiori (Salerno.) Thick vegetation has grown
over the unusual stratification, and here the
houses of Ravello, a pearl of the Amalfi Coast,
have been built.

106 Sirenuse's (Salerno) two coves, on the south coast of the Sorrento peninsula, are a paradise for the few yachtsmen who drop anchor there. The Amalfi Coast begins few miles ahead, to the north, and the shore becomes steeper, a precipice over the sea.

107 The Sorrento peninsula is viewed here from atop Marina di Puolo, on the north coast. Massa Lubrense and Capri, on the right, can be seen looking farther out, toward Monte San Costanzo.

108-109 The fortifications that can still be found along the coasts of the Sorrento peninsula (Salerno) often have very ancient origins: even before the need to signal invading Saracens, the people living along the coast had to cope with Roman ships drawing near. The watchtowers, where fires were lit and burned all night long, also served as primitive lighthouses, warning ships of the most dangerous stretches of the coast.

110 and 111 The Sorrento peninsula (Salerno) is a superb natural environment of verdant hills, deep valleys, majestic mountains and rock terraces that descend gradually down to the sea. In these lands apparently hostile to humanity, not only have oranges, lemons, olive and vines been planted, but aristocratic villas and rural houses have been built.

112 The Cilento coast, south of Salerno, with its coves and grottoes, today presents the same scene as when Aeneas' helmsman Palinurus was induced into deep sleep by Morpheus, causing him to fall into the sea and drown. According to the myth, the Sibyl had promised him that the place – Capo Palinuro – would be named after him.

113 The Cilento (Salerno) offers enchanting views near the fishing village of Marina di Camerota. Coastal woods seem to reach out to meet the waves and the rocks that outline the tortuous shores.

114 The Lucanian and Calabrian coasts, between the gulfs of Policastro and Sant'Eufemia, alternate low, sandy stretches and tall, crags, as seen here, dropping sheer into the waves. It is a region of mountains and sea, with places of an extraordinary nature such as the Pollino Park – north, toward Basilicata – and the coastal chain farther south.

115 Between Scalea (Cosenza) and San Nicola Arcella, along Calabria's Tyrrhenian coast, captivating views greet us: small beaches between ancient coastal lookout towers, deep bays and wind-hollowed rocks.

117 Seaside resorts and lidos alternate along the sandy shores that are typical of this part of Italy, from Tropea (Vibo Valentia), beyond Capo Vaticano, on the stretch called Costa degli Dei, and farther south, in the Gulf of Gioia Tauro. In fact, Tyrrhenian Calabria ends with the Costa Viola, the stretch of shore that opens from Palmi down to Villa San Giovanni, and which owes its name to the violet color of its clear, transparent waters,

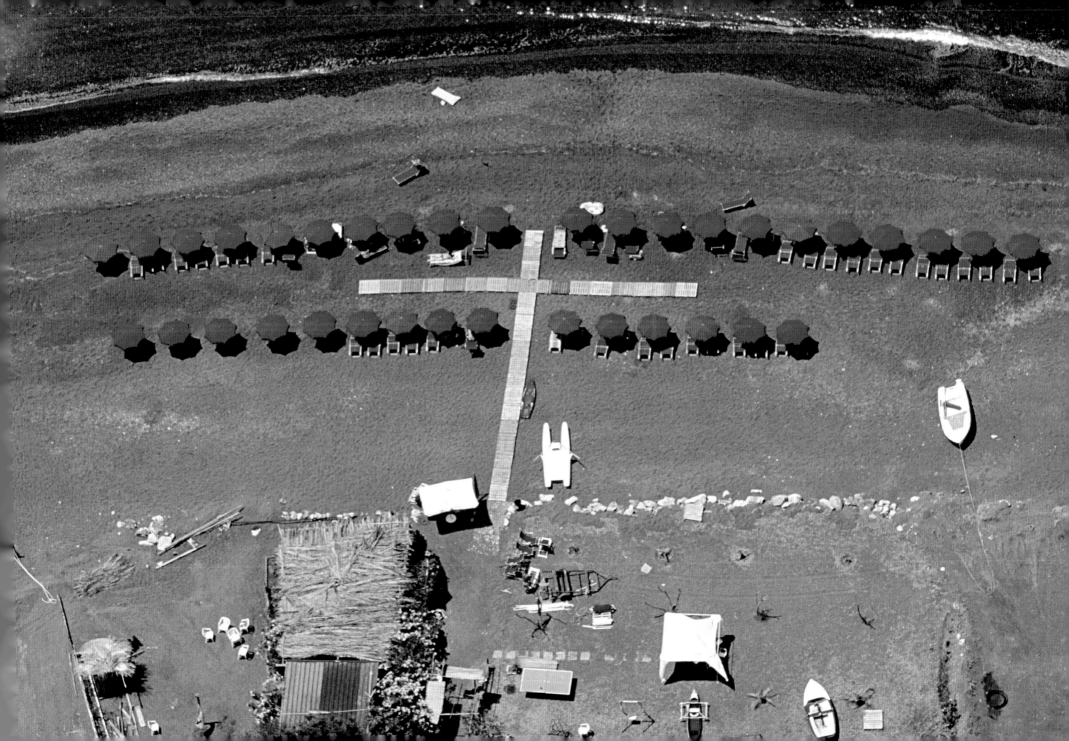

THE GREAT ISLANDS

The great Italian islands are subcontinents that are difficult to classify as "archetypal islands," both for historical and morphological reasons. In any case, whether referring to Sardinia or considering Sicily, the sea is always the key to understanding the past and the future, and perceiving their essence. The sea that is never just a stretch of blue in these islands: it is small bays, a beach with wooden fishing boats and nets; a thousand white lights on the boats stacked with crescent-shaped lampara nets; sand, stone peaks, terraces, hills that slope down to the rocks; little beaches, hamlets of white houses.

The first impact from the coast of Sardinia is the scent of eternity: broom, rosemary and countless other essences, long before our eyes have focused on the cliffs, the long tongues of sand and sequence of colors that tinge the water from blue to turquoise. There is something unique, unmistakable: it is the rapport of the sand with the rocks and the water and the wind. The island's ancient name, Ichnusa, means "imprint": in no other place are the signs – imprints, obviously – of the sea's hustle and bustle on an ancient land quite so evident.

The journey into the blue begins to the north, along Gallura and the Costa Smeralda, Sardinia's most famous stretch of shoreline: about 40 miles from the Gulf of Cugnana at Liscia di Vacca. This quintessential resort was opened in 1962, when a group of operators headed by the Aga Khan Karim, formed the Costa Smeralda Consortium to exploit the tourism potential of an area that at that time was still unspoiled. So, buildings were erected that were a homage to the local rural architecture; they were installing them in the territory without spoiling it; this was the onset of the Smeraldo style that has inspired some of the most famous complexes worldwide.

Opposite the Costa Smeralda, the Maddalena Archipelago includes the most famous granitic islands in the Mediterranean. It is a paradise of sails and sea, amidst wind-smoothed boulders and cliffs, small bays and natural pools that call to mind the Caribbean. To the west, we find one of the Mediterranean's stormiest places, where the western basin's current weaves between the Sardinian and Corsican coasts before rushing into the Tyrrhenian Sea.

118 left Capo Falcone (Sassari) defines the Asinara gulf to the west and is itself one of Sardinia's most western outcrops.

118 right The stretch of Sardinian coast between San Teodoro (Olbia-Tempio) and Olbia is characterized by coastal lagoons fed by small seaward corridors.

119 Capo Caccia (Sassari), a few miles away from the Gulf of Alghero in western Sardinia, is an imposing promontory with stacks that rise sheer from the sea. A lighthouse stands over the Nettuno grottoes, a geological complex of stalactites and stalagmites reached by a long flight of steps.

121 A fisherman's net traces out an original spiral on the flat expanse of waters surrounding Punta d'Aligi, opposite the island of San Pietro (Carbonia-Iglesias).

In this windswept kingdom other granitic islands provide a land habitat for colonies of sea birds and singular vegetable species, as well as countless life forms in the fertile, oxygen-rich seabeds. This is the Bocche di Bonifacio International Park, which protects one of the most primitive areas in Europe.

Farther west, the natural extension of the Stintino promontory, the large island of Asinara, teems with vegetation and has many miles of unspoiled beaches and cliffs. Turing south, the coast begins at Capo Argentiera and continues in the Porto Ferro inlet, with limy faces at Capo Caccia, as far as Monte Ruiu and Monte Mannu massifs, where the landscape seems to have been torn away from the Atlantic. Solemn, solitary, stormy: the tall, rocky coast at Argentiera, north of Alghero, stands in an area that has suffered little human intervention. The Gulf of Alghero is closed off by the Punta Cristallo promontory, distinguished by lovely sea grottoes and covered with dense vegetation. The area is home to one of the last colonies of griffon vultures, who fly over the coast and the garrigue (scrubland vegetation) in search of food.

Southwards, near the Phoenician remains and fishermen's shacks, the Sinis offers lovely beaches, rocks cloaked in flowering maquis and salt pools teeming with fish, the refuge of

122 left The Sardinian coast frequently presents views of beaches like this: in front, segments of tropical sea, crystal waters with turquoise and sky-blue reflections; behind, fragrant Mediterranean vegetation, rich with ilex and rosemary, myrtle and maritime pines.

thousands of water birds. The island of San Pietro, a little corner of paradise for the colony of rare Eleonora's falcons, lies beyond Costa Verde, at the far southwest tip of Sardinia and not far from the lovely sandy dunes of Capo Spartivento. Tuna processing plants and *salinas* (salt pans) lend interest to the landscape here, a former Ligurian colony.

On the outskirts of Cagliari the saltwater pools and the *salinas* of Molentargius and Santa Gilla are endowed with an astonishing environmental wealth, and break up the Gulf of Cagliari landscape, closed by mounts Sulcis and Carrabus.

Beyond Capo Carbonara, the farthest strip of Monte Abu, we fly along Costa Rei, as far as Arbatax, following a sandy shore that is closed by rocky reliefs, still safe from the attack of construction work and mass tourism. Then the Gulf of Orosei appears, beyond the Gennargentu outcrops, and stretches from Santa Maria Navarrese to Cala Gonone, one of the last surviving refuges of the rare monk seal which loves grottoes with underwater entrances and the white sandy beaches that open here and there in the rock bastions.

We near the end of our journey and we can glimpse the long white beaches, with the costal pools of San Teodoro, leading to the islands of Tavolara and Molara, and then to the Golfo Aranci. From here the gateway to the Costa Smeralda and its jet-set villages come to the fore once again.

If Sardinia, geographically, is a real island, so far from the mainland and so different from neighboring Corsica, conversely Sicily is separated from the tip of the "Boot" only by a narrow channel, so narrow in fact, that it is called a strait.

Our circumnavigation of Sicily begins in Messina, the departure point for the army of emigrants that has become the arrival point for hordes of visitors. The first stop is Taormina, the Pearl of the Ionian Sea, with its Isola Bella and fairytale castle on the citadel; then Capo Taormina, crowned by its stacks; Mazzarò, with its bay and Sirene beach; Capo Sant'Andrea and the Gulf of Naxos, with its gorgeous sea. Intensely blue waters surround Catania, passing in the mouth of the Fiumefreddo and from the Riviera dei Limoni, gradually tingeing with emerald green as we move away from the volcanic rock.

The Ionian's encounter with the great River Simeto creates fabulous landscapes: sand dunes, reed-beds and ponds. Siracusa seems to have changed little since it was an ancient

122 center Budelli, with its secluded coves and rugged offshoots is the gem of the Maddalena Archipelago National Park (Olbia-Tempio). Renowned since Roman times, the Sardinian island is famous for its Spiaggia Rosa (Pink Beach), whose atypical color is due to coral fragments and unique type of seashell.

122 right Capo Milazzo, the Sicilian promontory in the Messina area, stretches for three miles, a strip of land in the Tyrrhenian Sea. A web of hiking trails breaks the continuity of the Mediterranean maquis that covers its surface.

Greek city, and leads to the Maddalena peninsula and the Gulf of Noto, dominated by the Avola vineyards and stretches of Pachino tomatoes.

Toward Capo Passero and Capo delle Correnti, the Malta Channel muddies the waters rich in tuna and fish life, which biologists believe actually come from the Red Sea. Skirting around the first of Trinacria's tips we find ourselves on the southwestern coast, practically facing Africa. This is the Hyblean Sea, with Marina di Modica, and beyond Punta Braccetto and the *maccuni* – sand dunes that change shape depending on the wind – it reaches Porto Empedocle, with its sea-sculpted rocks called Scala dei Turchi.

The flight continues to Siculiana, with the white beach of Eraclea Minoa, and on the sea facing Sciacca, looking for a glimpse under the surface of the ghost island that appeared in 1831, only to vanish underwater six months later.

We pass Selinunte and Capo Granitola, then Mazara and its fishing boats, Capo Lilibeo, Marsala, the saltpans that are a coastal feature as far as Trapani. This might be the starting point for another journey toward the fragments of Sicily that are gathered in the Egadi Archipelago, or scattered on the distant southern routes: Pantelleria, Lampedusa, Linosa, Lampione . . . . Routes to another world, set south even of Tunisia and Malta, from which we would return with Africa in our eyes.

The final stretch of Sicilian coast begins after Trapani, at Capo San Vito: the Gulf of Castellammare reaches as far as magnificent Scopello della Tonnara. Here a sea of oranges faces a real sea of the deepest blue. It is the same sea that just 30 miles out (48 km) laps the coast of solitary, wild Ustica. This is the Conca d'Oro, with Monte Pellegrino, evoking the magnificent Gulf of Palermo.

The Imerese coast, abounding with art and history, a sequence of entrancing localities of which the most interesting are Santo Stefano di Camastra, with its radial layout reminiscent of 1700s royal gardens, and Tindari, with its archaeological remains, toward Capo Milazzo.

From here we can chase after volcanic impressions, heading north toward the Lipari Islands. In the triangle formed by Stromboli, Alicudi and Vulcano, a primordial energy is still overt, able to generate rock from open sea. With a touch of melancholy we leave the craters gaping skyward and return to Capo Peloro, the spur curving toward Calabria and closing the Strait of Messina.

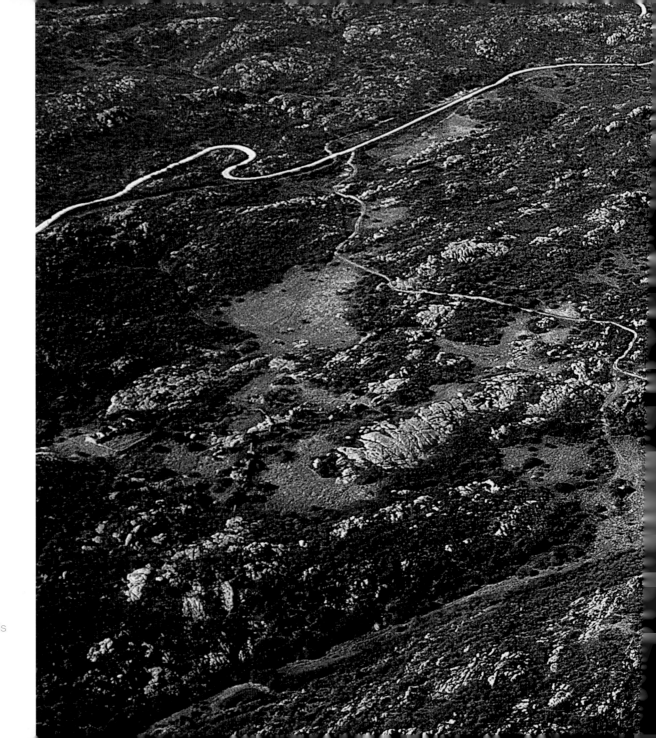

126-127 Sardinia's northeast coast, with little vegetation but rich in rocky caves and sandy coves carved by a constantly transparent sea, is a Caribbean corner in the heart of the Mediterranean.

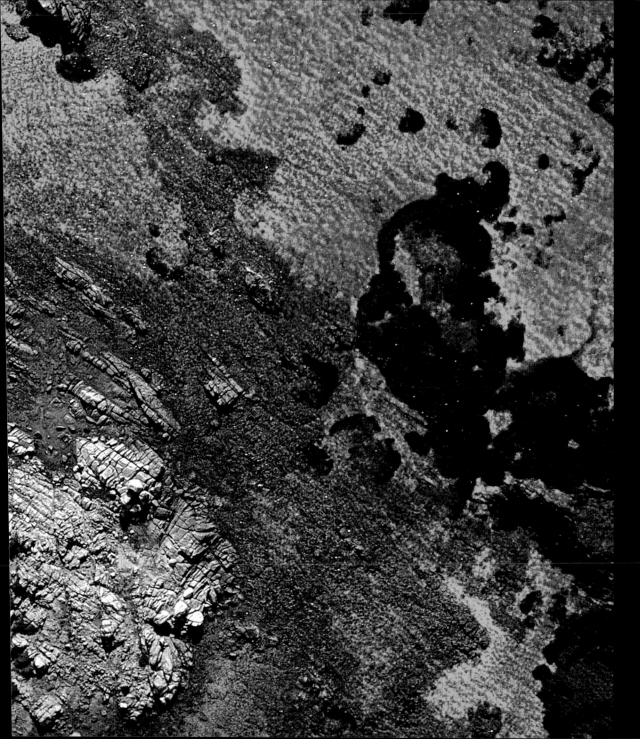

128-129 Rocks scarred by wind and waves plunge into the Costa Smeralda's deep blue sea, in northeast Sardinia.

130-131 The plains of Sardinia's east coast, near Oristano, are studded with pools, at one time the cause of malaria, but today an attraction today for scholars and tourists.

132 The island of Tavolara (Olbia-Tempio), just south of the Gulf of Olbia, is an imposing calcareous massif rising high over the sea. The green of the Mediterranean maquis softens the sharpness of the granitic rock's rifts and protrusions.

133 Mortorio (Olbia-Tempio) is one of Maddalena National Park's little pearls, even though it is geographically set southeast of the archipelago itself. The island has unspoiled beaches and views: it is uninhabited and can be reached only by privately-owned boats.

135 Like a splash of pastel tempera, the coral sand beach of Lu Portu de li Coggi (Olbia-Tempio), on the Costa Smeralda, stretches between the rocks that enclose it seaward, sheltered from the waves, and among the shrubs that surround the mainland side. The beach named Lu Portu de li Coggi is also known as Spiaggia del Principe (the Prince's Beach). The prince in question is said to be the Aga Khan, Karim, whom the locals explain was beguiled by this corner of paradise.

136-137 A pool of turquoise water, low Mediterranean vegetation, a short frame of rocks encircling the sandy beach: this cove, photographed at Capo Testa (Sassari), at the far north of Sardinia, sums up the natural beauty of the island in few square feet.

138 and 139 Capo Testa (Sassari), overlooking the Bocche di Bonifacio, is Sardinia's northernmost tip. A lighthouse dominating Cala di Luna, also known as Valle della Luna, has been built to signal the many dangerous rocky outcrops in the waters surrounding the promontory.

141 The gigantic block of jutting rock that forms the Capo Testa (Sassari) promontory has some openings on the seaward side, with small inlets that conceal enchanting and inaccessible little beaches.

142-143 The rugged coast that unfolds toward the Bocche di Bonifacio shatters into myriads of wind-beaten islets and rocks.

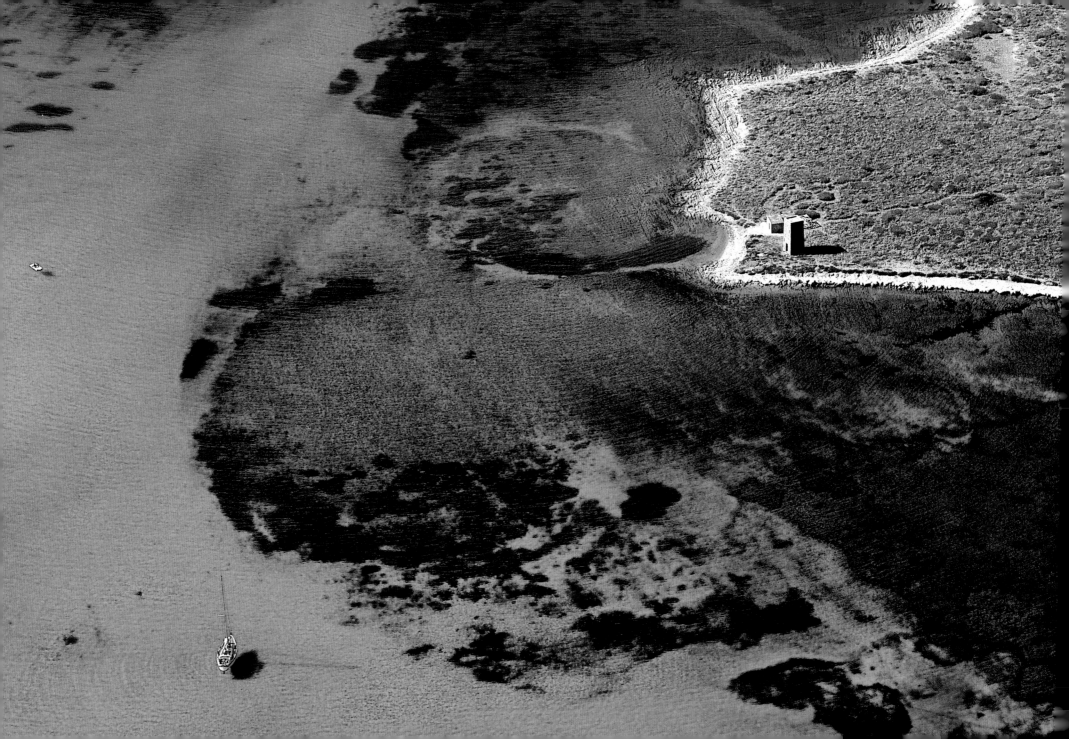

144 and 145 Ancient towers built by different peoples, silent witnesses of the Sardinian coastline's eventful past, rise on the farthest reaches of the Gulf of Asinara (Sassari) mainland.

146-147 A sailboat moored off Stintino (Sassari) seems enshrouded by the blue of the sea. The dark patches are colonies of posidonia, anchored close to the rocks – lighter in color – that plunge into the depths, but seemingly nearby in the transparent waters.

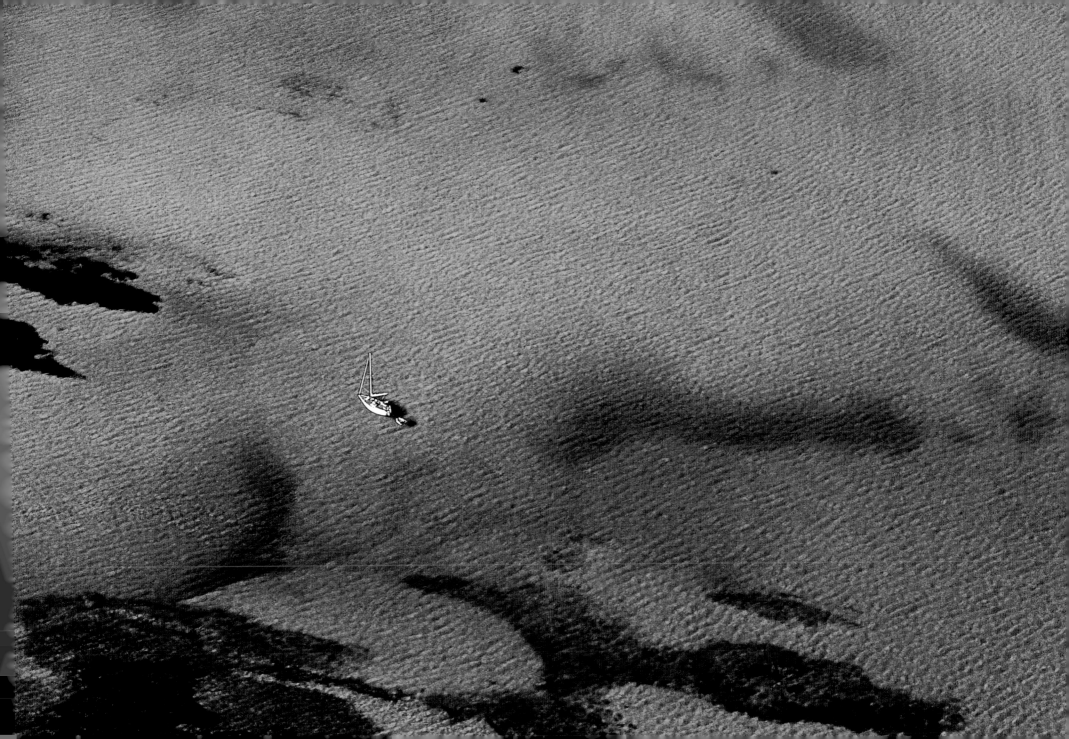

149 We are in the Nurra, the most northwest coast of Sardinia. Superb beaches of fine white sand are caressed by Stintino's fresh waters (Sassari), and sandy islets linger in a turquoise and blue scenario. By the shore, fishermen draw strange patterns with their nets.

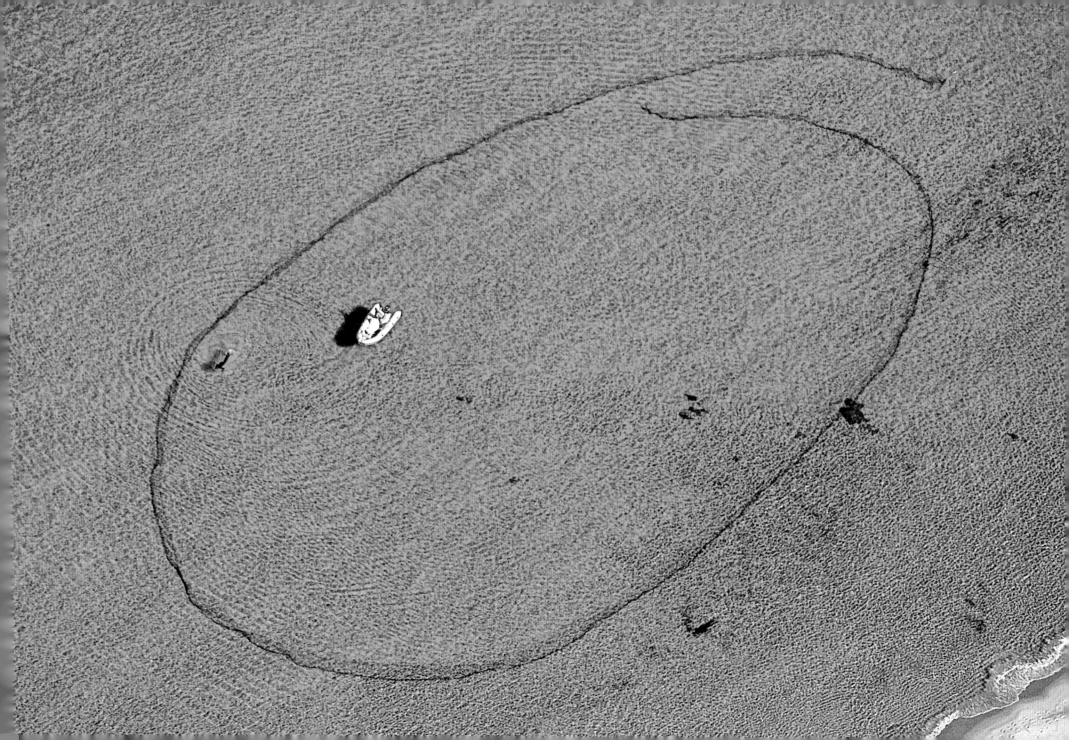

150 Capo Caccia (Sassari) lighthouse stands atop a sheer overhang, the southern boundary of the Gulf of Porto Conte, in western Sardinia. Its lantern, positioned on an 80-ft (24.4 m) tower, not only aids navigation but is also a landmark for aircraft landing at nearby Alghero airport.

151 Waves that break on the Capo Caccia rocks, together with the action of the elements, have shaped many natural forms, including these red pinnacles, reaching skywards, as if they were defending the land from the sea.

152 In some spots, Sardinia's southwest coast shows lunar landscapes like this, on the coast north of Buggerru in the Iglesias area, where the colors of sand and earth are punctuated with the colors of sea and vegetation.

154 Freeclimbers today are particularly fond of the "Pan di Zucchero" (Carbonia-Iglesias) rocks, and the Porto Flavia cliffs opposite, which in the past were mined for metals.

155 Cala Domestica beach (Carbonia-Iglesias), a "fjord" of crystal-clear water, winds inside Sardinia's rugged southwest coast, guarded for centuries by an ancient Spanish tower.

156 A granitic promontory unfolds like a claw in the coastal waters of the Iglesias area. The tall cliffs on this coast attract not only sea but mountain lovers also, especially climbers..

157 The "Pan di Zucchero," a stack formed of metalliferous limestone, widespread in the Iglesias area, stands out against the waters of Sardinia's west coast. Apart from its remarkable height – approximately 430 ft (131 m) – this islet's great appeal comes from the contrast of its white rocks against the dark blue of the surrounding sea.

158 This scene reveals the variety of nature along Sardinia's south coast, where the vegetation's shady greenery, the white sand's aridity and the sapphire-colored seawater blend in total harmony. Rare human settlements have not contaminated the wild beauty of this stretch of coast between Capo Teulada and Sant'Antioco (Carbonia-Iglesias).

160-161 Olive terraces and patches of shrubs spread over the steep volcanic slopes of Alicudi, the most westerly of the Lipari Islands (Messina), allowing glimpses of the few houses.

162-163 Surrounded by Salina's (Messina) rich vegetation, this lime and volcanic-stone house, built to Aeolian tradition, overlooks the sea-dominating cliff.

164-165 The crater of Vulcano (Messina), Lipari's biggest island, is close to the village of Piano del Porto. Here, a small isthmus connects the main island to Vulcanello, what remains of a now dormant ancient crater.

166-167 The island of Salina (Messina) in the Lipari Archipelago is characterized by two volcanic cones that outline its contours, and by the spontaneous vegetation that almost completely covers its surface.

168-169 The profile of Stromboli (Messina), Lipari's most northerly island, stands out against a blue sea backdrop. The cloud emerging from the crater reveals that the volcano is active. Sciara del Fuoco, a sloping face where the volcanic lava slides down into the sea, can be observed in the foreground.

170 Punta del Perciato, a rocky promontory, at the southern tip of Lipari (Messina), the archipelago's largest island, stands firm in the sea facing the Pietralunga stack, which is about 200 ft (61 m) in height.

171 An ancient defensive fortress used as a prison in Bourbon times, stands on Punta Troia, on the Marettimo (Trapani) promontory, the most westerly of the Egadi Islands.

172 A now disused tuna processing plant, heritage of an era drawing to its close, stands on the islet of Formica, opposite the port of Trapani.

173 A catamaran anchored near Favignana Island (Trapani) in the Egadi Islands, in the far west of Sicily. The island is famous for its tuna-processing plant, one of the last still in use. The island's flat surface and scant vegetation make a striking contrast with the transparent blue of the sea.

174-175 Levanzo (Trapani), ancient *Phorbantia*, is the smallest of the Egadi Islands. Mostly mountainous nature, it has rocky coasts without beaches, and numerous grottoes, the most famous being Grotta del Genovese, where graffiti have been found dating back to 9200 B.C.

176 and 177 On the coast of Favignana (Trapani), the biggest of the Egadi Islands, rocky stretches alternate with sandy beaches. A tall cliff in tuff, a stone that is particularly abundant on Favignana, emerges in the flat eastern area of the island.

178 A square fortress, built for the Emperor Charles V in the 16th century, can be seen on the island of Capo Passero, off Portopalo (Siracusa), at the southern tip of Sicily. Behind the fortress a 65-ft (20-m) plinth supports the bronze statue of Holy Mary on the Holy Stair to Paradise, a monument unveiled in 1959, in honor of the "Protector of the Sicilian Sea."

179 An outcrop of volcanic origin along Sicily's southern coast near Sciacca (Agrigento), in the province of Agrigento, indicates the presence of intense telluric activity in this part of the coast. In fact, in July 1831, earthquakes and underground eruptions brought a "ghost" islet to the surface, which was then engulfed by the waters six months later.

180 and 181 White calcareous rock and clay cliffs can be encountered along the stretch of coast between Porto Empedocle and Sciacca, in the province of Agrigento. The wind and waters have worn the rocks, carving the evocative vertical and horizontal streaks that are discernible in the photograph.

182

182-183 At Sicily's southeastern end, a short distance separates the island of Capo Passero from the Portopalo coast (Siracusa), which was once joined by an isthmus of sand. The imposing fortress of Charles V, which dates back to the 16th century, is clearly visible in this aerial photograph.

184 Capo Sant'Andrea is one of the rocky spurs that marks the stretch of coast near Taormina (Messina). Together with Isola Bella, it is one of the two extremities that borders the small bay of Mazzarò, famous for its beach and superb waters.

185 A small isthmus of sand connects Isola Bella to the mainland, bringing to life one of Taormina's most evocative panoramas. Once private property, the island is now a World Wildlife Fund (WWF) Nature Reserve.

186-187 In Sicily the Greek theater of Taormina (Messina) (rebuilt in the Roman era) is second in size only to that of Siracusa. Built on high ground with a commanding view of the coastline and Etna, the theater is still used for events and performances.

188 The *dammusi*, traditional stone dwellings with vaulted ceilings found along the volcanic stone coast, are characteristic of Pantelleria (Trapani). A modern tarmac road runs around the entire perimeter of the island.

189 The island of Pantelleria's northeast coast draws a jagged line, broken by numerous promontories and inlets, overlooked by small villages and farmed terraces that make a verdant landscape.

190 Traces of past lava activity can be observed on the slopes of Monte Nero, an ancient volcano directly overlooking the sea near Cala Pozzolana di Ponente, on Linosa (Agrigento). Sulfurous mineral outcrops tinge the black and reddish volcano rocks yellow.

191 The small island of Linosa, in the Pelagian Archipelago, has volcanic origins, as revealed by the island's highest rock formations, which are often the remains of ancient craters. The town of Linosa is situated on the island's plains, between mounts Nero and Bandiera.

192 The island of Lampedusa's (Agrigento) northwest coast appears like an unapproachable cliff of calcareous rocks, dropping steeply into the sea. The ochre yellow streaks marking the rocks are also visible on this stack in the Capo Ponente area.

193 Capo Grecale, at the northeast end of Lampedusa, the southernmost of the Pelagian Islands, where the coastline becomes less steep and high, is where the island's main lighthouse is located.

194-195 Conigli Beach at Lampedusa, where the *Caretta caretta* (loggerhead sea turtle) nests, looks out over a small bay delineated by a promontory and Conigli Island, a small, flat rocky spur.

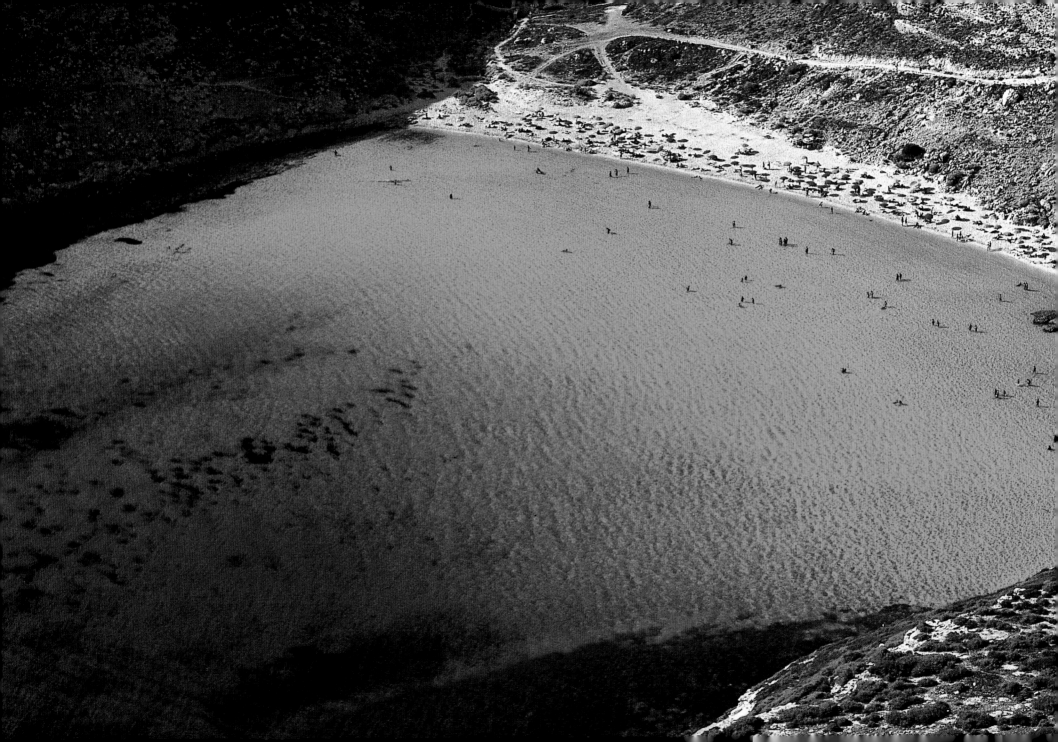

197 The streaks of the calcareous rocks that form Lampedusa's (Agrigento) surface emerge in this low and jagged stretch of coast, in the island's south. Lampedusa, together with Linosa and Lampione, form the Pelagian Archipelago. It is Italy's southernmost offshoot, south of Pantelleria and west of Malta, nearer to the North African coast than to Sicily.

THE ADRIATIC SEA

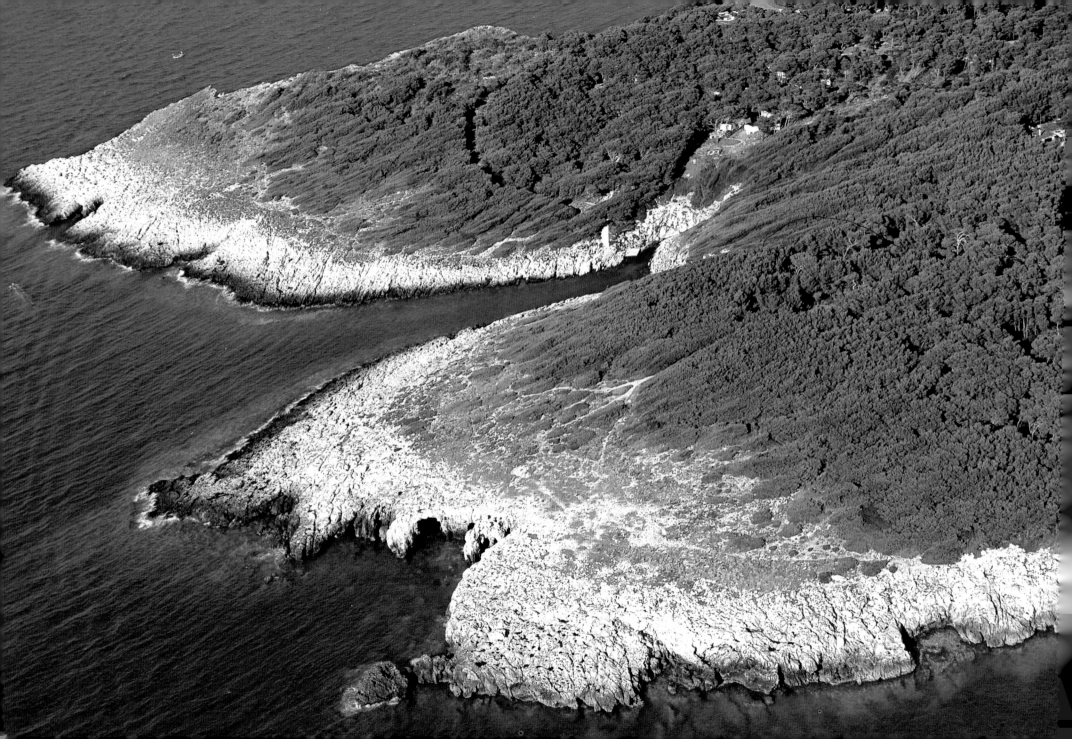

Ionian Calabria is acquainted with History: the dominant powers of the Classical Mediterranean, in other words the Phoenicians and Greeks, landed on the region's southern coasts. These colonizers built towns that still bear the signs of their origins. Setting off from Reggio Calabria and working our way north along Calabria, we will meet several sea towns where ancient Greek is still spoken: Condofuri, Bova, Palizzi.

The increasingly blue sea contrasts with the white sands that are the scenario of resorts like Brancaleone, Bianco, Bovalino. We are on the Ionian coast: Locri and Monasterace, ancient Kaulon, where the air is still redolent with Magna Graecia. Between these two seaside towns that are also archeological sites, Marina di Gioiosa Ionica, Roccella Ionica, Caulonia and Riace offer a fusion of history and spellbinding nature. This is the province of Catanzaro, where we discover the beauty of Soverato, of the cliffs at Copanello, and the remains of the "Roccelletta" (Little Rock) di Borgia. Continuing north, beyond Catanzaro, we will see Simeri Crichi, Sellia, Isola Capo Rizzuto, then arrive in Crotone. In the province of Cosenza, the Ionian

echoes with ancient history and bathes the lovely towns of Rossano, Corigliano, Greek Sibari, and then pushes on to Villapiana Lido, Trebisacce, Roseto Capo Spulico and, lastly Rocca Imperiale, with its impressive castle. With the Metaponto Plain to the west and the Gulf of Taranto to the east, we cross the region of Basilicata. The ruins of Metaponto glitter in the mouth of the Bradano, on an extensive sandy shore that points our gaze out to Greece.

Not far north: Apulia. From Marina to Leuca a giddy journey begins toward the east, taking in over 75 miles (120 km), added to the other 450 (725 km) required to reach the Gargano promontory. Apulia is an offshoot of the Italian peninsula that plunges into the Adriatic and the Ionian seas, abounding with steep cliffs, grottoes, quiet coves and long, sandy shores. A coastline of many colors, edged with Mediterranean maquis and whose history speaks mainly of Oriental influence. Numerous traces were left by the arriving Mycenaeans, Iapygians, Daunians, Peucetians, Messapians, and by the Spartan colonizers who founded Taranto and other Magna Graecia

198 The Venetian Lagoon symbolizes a heritage of beauty and poetry. Every island is a jewel: from San Clemente (left), formerly the site of a mental hospital, to the monastery of San Francesco del Deserto (right), where St Francis is said to have landed on his return from the Orient, in 1220.

199 Zagare Bay's two stacks (Foggia), along the Gargano promontory, stand out from the backdrop of the crystal-clear Apulian sea.

200 Punta del Diamante marks the northern limit of San Domino, Tremiti's largest island (Foggia). The thick pinewood covering this island off the Gargano coast, has earned it the title of "Garden of Paradise." It spreads as far as the cliffs, sheer over the sea.

colonies on the Ionian shore, as well as by bloody Saracen attacks, traveling crusaders, pilgrims and merchants. The Ionian coast reveals bays of white sand and Mediterranean maquis, with peeks at dreamlike sites: Torre Vado, Lido Marini, Torre Mozza, Torre San Giovanni, where the pines are just a few steps from the shore, and from what remains of the ancient Roman port of Usentum. Gallipoli, the capital of the section of coast from Taranto to the Otranto Channel, is a melting pot of art and history, which conceals a maze of streets in the old center – nestling on an islet connected to the rest of the city by a bridge – with buildings set in oriental-style gardens, Baroque churches, kiosks, a castle, a merchant port. Just slightly further

ahead, beyond Lido delle Conchiglie, the coast wends out to the Santa Maria al Bagno and Santa Caterina inlets, and the cliffs at the Porto Selvaggio Nature Park, with lookout towers and grottoes that preserve evidence of prehistoric settlements.

Capo di Santa Maria di Leuca, the extreme tip on the heel of Italy, called *finis terrae* by the ancient Romans, is bathed in the magic of the South's most beautiful locations: olive groves and prickly pears, closed by dry stone walls, form a backdrop to the sanctuary built over a pagan temple to Minerva and, according to legend, a compulsory path for reaching paradise. Returning northwards, here is Otranto, certainly the loveliest medieval town in the Salento, the ideal place to set up a base

202 left A stretch of rock stretching between Leuca and Otranto (Lecce), in Apulia, this spur is visited by few visitors who enjoy its crystal-clear waters.

for visiting the rest of the peninsula. Nearby we skirt the slightly salty waters of the Alimini Lakes, a wildlife oasis with populations of baldicoot and grey heron.

Toward Lecce and, farther north, Brindisi, the heel of the boot-shaped peninsula is called the Salento, and is Italy's most eastern section, a frontier land, always a rendezvous point for the East and the West. The Salento bears the signs of a history that began in Neolithic times; here the Messapians established their settlements, fortified by gigantic walls; this was the location of centers that became tiny capitals of Magna Graecia. The Salento is still an Arab context, with lookout towers and multicolored villas that enjoy balanced Islamic beauty, blending in with Byzantine traces. Lastly, the coast here is fascinating, with cliffs, luxuriant pine groves, fertile plains abounding with olive groves and vines, small ports and light-filled old town centers. White stretches of sand slip into the Adriatic seabeds: Savelletri and Rosa Marina, two famous seaside resorts, are the prelude to Ostuni, the white town. Looking out for the vast Gargano promontory, we cover the Murge coast, with its long line of sandy beaches: Levante, Ponente, Boccadoro, Verde, Lido Bella Venezia and Colonna, between Barletta and Giovinaz-

zo. We will encounter sandbanks, treasures left by Frederick II (1194-1250), villages pointing out to sea, and the Saline plain, a suggestive puzzle of basins, pools, draining pumps, canals, sluices, banks and mountains of salt crystals; an area favored by flamingoes, mallards, avocets, cranes, cormorants and many other species of aquatic birds than come to winter here, in this tiny artificial, pink-tinged sea.

Northwards, the Apulian coast appears with the Gargano cliffs, a unique place, where the mountains meet the sea. It is an enormous calcareous island that reaches out toward the Balkans, with a sequence of rocky points dominated by stacks, bays, shingle beaches, and white towns that are mirrored in the blue of the sea. The magic of the "spur of Italy" lies chiefly in its flint-veined cliffs, casting light from Vieste on the most easterly rock spur of the promontory, called Testa del Gargano, with the fantastic Pugnochiuso bay, set on an inaccessible and wild coast, and Zagare bay, with the Mergoli stacks.

A Mediterranean paradise lingers in the lakes of Lesina and Varano, two bird-life oases at the foot of the promontory's northern slope, separated from the sea by a long strip of sand dunes.

202 center Two solitary boats anchored in a beautiful inlet of Caprara, an uninhabited island in the Tremiti Archipelago (Foggia).

202 right Fresh water entering the brackish waters of the Venetian Lagoon creates this play of forms and colors, near Lake Ripola.

We fly out toward the Abruzzo coast, jagged to the south, low and sandy to the north. From Vasto to Ortona, the tiny coves are smothered in broom and vines, alternating with sandbanks and beaches framed with dense Mediterranean vegetation.

In the Teramo area, on the other hand, from Martinsicuro to Silvi Marina, the beaches of Pescara and Montesilvano Marina, as well as Francavilla al Mare, offer panoramas not so different from those of the Romagna coast, with no lack of bathing facilities. The Marches coast offers a gentle, suggestive landscape. The beaches stretch straight to the endless sandy shores of the North Adriatic, interrupted only by the great Conero rock. From here we are in Romagna. An aerial view of the coast shows an endless sequence of beach umbrellas and deckchairs, waves muddied by the crowds.

The impact of the Riviera dei Sogni slackens as we approach the Po Delta and the Comacchio valleys, populated by many bird species and by rather less welcome mosquitoes. A similar panorama is also to be seen in parts of the Venetian Lagoon.

Now we have come to the end of our journey: with Venice, the Jesolo Riviera and the Caorle "fjord" behind us, we can finally plunge into the last two Adriatic jewels: the lagoons of Marano and Grado, and the Gulf of Trieste.

The former are unequalled worldwide for the astonishing, untouched habitat, and for the traces of Roman Grado, accompanied by the *casuni*, primitive constructions with straw cupola roofs used by fishermen. The most typical feature of the lagoon's landscape is the changing air and color in the canals, the innumerable islets rising from the sea, in the stretches of water.

The Gulf of Trieste is the mirror that reflects the capital: Trieste, an ancient and noble city of middle-European heritage with the ambitions of a capital, an authentic jewel set in a rugged crown of Carso territory and the blue of the waters. The culmination of our itinerary is not, however, the undoubtedly splendid sea terrace called Piazza Libertà, but charmed Miramare Castle, where it is still possible to look out onto the great loop sketched out by the Gulf of Venice and, finally, over the Upper Adriatic.

205 The modern Terrazza a Mare dominates the beach at Lignano Sabbiadoro, one of the Upper Adriatic's most renowned resorts. Lignano, located at the tip of a peninsula overlooking the Marano Lagoon, in the province of Udine, is famous for its fine sandy beach, some 5 miles (8 km) long.

206 A rugged stretch of Apulia's Ionian coast, embracing a small inlet with green scrub overlooking it.

207 The lighthouse on Sant'Andrea Island, opposite Gallipoli (Lecce), was built in 1866 to help fishermen navigate in storms. The 200-ft (61-m) lighthouse is built on the island's flat calcareous surface, where traces of human occupation dating back to the Bronze Age have come to light.

208 Numerous *trulli* (stone-built farmhouses) and *pagghiare* (dry-stone walls marking field boundaries) and traces of Salento's ancient agricultural civilization can be found along the rugged coast that begins with the Santa Maria di Leuca (Lecce) promontory.

209 The white Santa Maria di Leuca lighthouse is at Apulia's southernmost point, indicating the meeting of the Adriatic and Ionian seas. Behind the lighthouse, on the promontory, is the sanctuary of Santa Maria de Finibus Terrae. The small Apulian town with its harbor is visible in the background.

210 Torre dell'Alto, near the Ionian resort of Santa Caterina nel Salento (Lecce), used to be part of a coastal defense system against Saracen incursions, which Emperor Charles V ordered to be built in the 16th century. The tower, which stands on a crag known as the Dannata that rises sheer from the sea, is reached by a flight of steps supported by three arches.

211 This farm occupies a splendid location along the stretch of coast between Monopoli (Bari) and Polignano a Mare. Dry stone walls, called *gisure* or *cisure*, can be seen clearly in the vicinity.

212 and 213 Near Polignano a Mare, in the province of Bari, tracks running along the coast map out geometric patterns around the farm fields, occasionally dotted with typical trulli cottages.

214-215 The flat, straight Apulian coastline on the Adriatic changes near the Gargano promontory. Here, the thick woods that cover the inland high ground sometimes extend down to the shore.

216 Pizzomunno's white stack on the Gargano coast, south of Vieste (Foggia), enhances the view of a lido packed with beach umbrellas and deckchairs.

217 A few *trabucchi*, old fishing structures typical of the Gargano area, overhang the sea at this rugged spot near Peschici (Foggia). The wooden poles support a big fishing net that is lowered into the waters by a winch system.

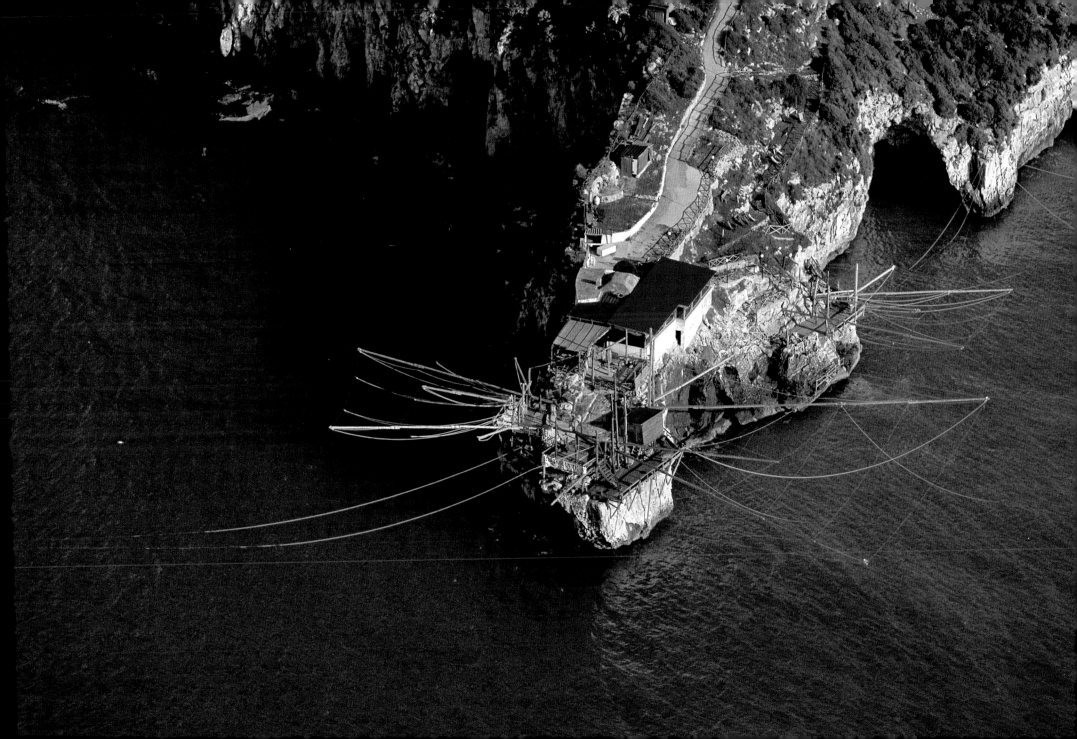

218 Uninhabited Caprara, in the Tremiti Archipelago (Foggia), is covered in caper bushes – which give it the island its name. In the background is an old flashing-lantern lighthouse, near Punta del Grottone.

219 Set in the background of Punta Diamante, the north end of San Domino Island, we can see the Cretaccio and tip of San Nicola Island, with its harbor. The three islands make up the Tremiti Archipelago.

220-221 From the top of a rocky cliff, hollowed by the force of the waves, San Domino lighthouse overlooks the south end of the largest of the Tremiti Islands (Foggia). Numerous grottoes can be seen along the coast, some of which are famous: in the south-east stretch of the island, Grotta del Sale and Grotta delle Viole, with its violet reflections in the early hours of the morning; to the west, the Grotta del Bue Marino, approximately 230 ft (70 m) deep, where monk seals were seen in the past.

222 and 223 Breakwaters safeguard this stretch of the Adriatic coast bordering the Marches. These artificial barriers are used to defend sandy beaches from the erosive currents. The countryside still reaches the shore in areas that have not been developed.

224-225 Cattolica beach (Rimini) with its long rows of beach umbrellas. The Romagna Riviera, with its wide beaches of fine sand, shallow waters and usually calm sea, has become a popular summer holiday destination for Italian and foreign families.

227 The blue waters of the open sea and the muddy waters of the coast converge and mingle off Emilia Romagna's Adriatic coast. River waters that flow into the sea and sand from current-worn beaches compete to tinge the waters with earthy nuances.

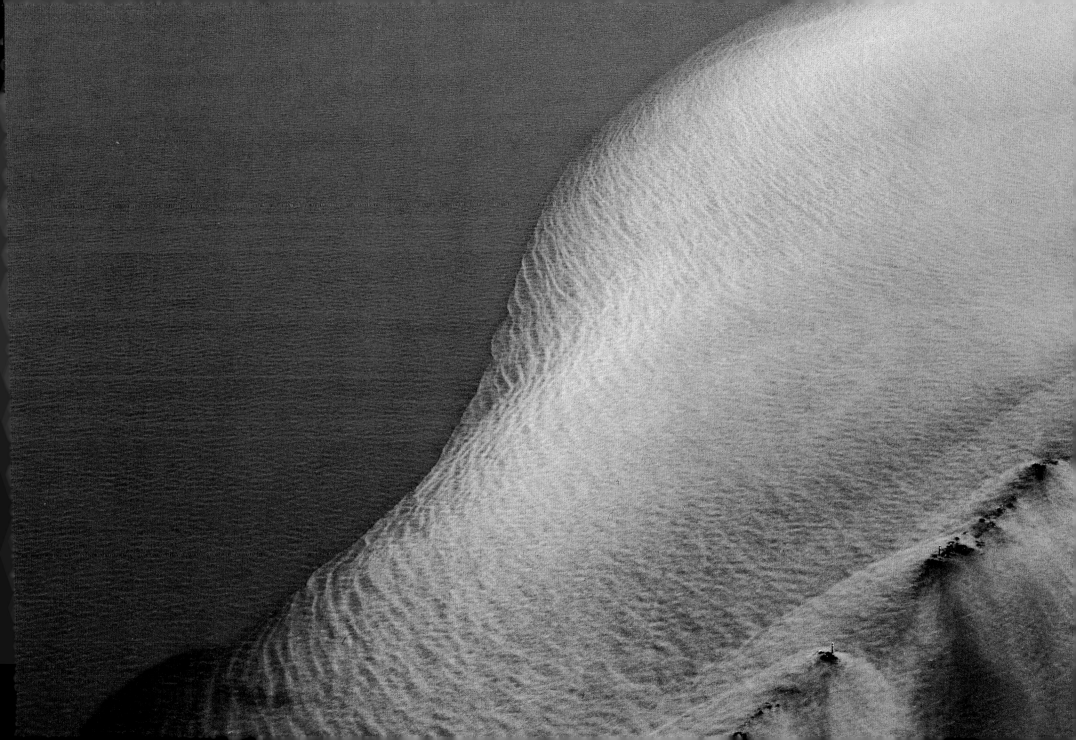

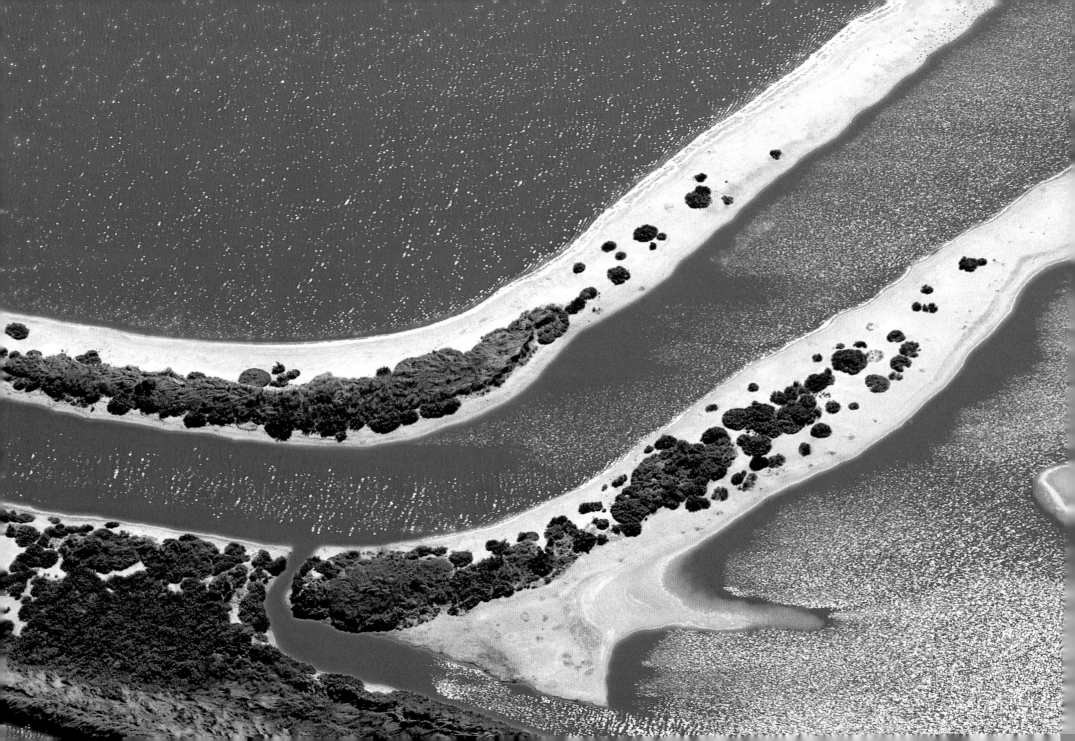

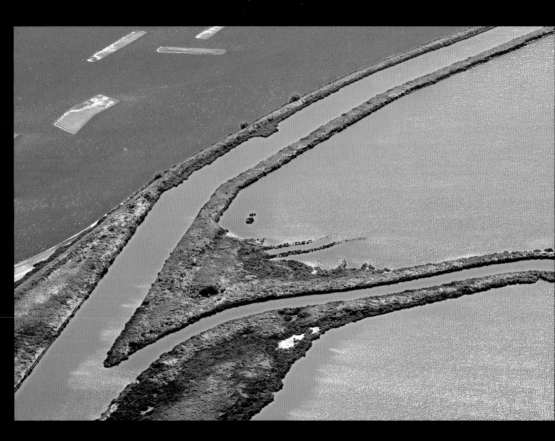

228 and 229 Valli di Comacchio lagoon system, enclosed between the mouths of the Po and the Reno, is a brackish water environment that covers over 70 sq miles (180 sq. km), in the provinces of Ferrara and Ravenna. The valleys are linked to the Adriatic by several channels and they provide a habitat for numerous bird species and halophilous plants. Embankments, canals, rises, strips of sand, all break the huge expanse of water, livening up the landscape.

230

230-231 Poveglia, one of the numerous islets that speckle the Venetian Lagoon is situated in front of the Lido, near the small town of Malamocco. The island preserves an old octagonal fortress and the bell tower of the ancient San Vitale church.

232-233 Fish farming in some areas of the Venetian Lagoon is done using the traditional fish valley system. Fish are farmed inside broad sheets of water, separated from the lagoon by banks of earth and protected from the tide in environments where the salinity is constantly controlled by a system of sluice gates called *chiaviche.*

234 Burano, approximately six miles northeast of Venice. The island's built-up area rises on four different islets connected to one other by bridges. Apart from its colorful pastel buildings, the island is famous for its handmade lace.

235 In the 16th century a military fortress, designed to protect Venice, was built on Sant'Andrea Island, opposite the entrance that connects the Venetian Lagoon to the Adriatic. Recently restored, the fortress is today a military barracks.

236 and 237 Miramare Castle (Trieste) with its unmistakable white profile, stands on the Gulf of Trieste promontory, near Grignano Bay. It was commissioned by Archduke Maximilian of Austria in honor of his wife, Charlotte of Belgium, and was built between 1856 and 1860. Behind the castle there is a big botanical park directly overlooking the sea. The Archduke was enamored of seascapes and made an explicit request that all the building's windows be placed to maximize the views of the gulf.

Index

Index

239

Photographs
Antonio Attini
Marcello Bertinetti

Text
Alberto Bertolazzi

Editor
Valeria Manferto De Fabianis

Editorial coordination
Maria Valeria Urbani Grecchi

The publisher would like to thank:
Valentino Benvenuti, Elio Rullo,
Emo, Francesco and Fabio Bientinesi of Volitalia

© 2007 White Star s.p.a.
Via Candido Sassone, 22/24
13100 Vercelli, Italy
www.whitestar.it

TRANSLATION: ANGELA ARNONE

ISBN: 978-88-544-0193-8

REPRINTS:
1 2 3 4 5 6   11 10 09 08 07

Printed in China

THE HORNBY GAUGE 0 SYSTEM

Chris and Julie Graebe

FRANK HORNBY
1863–1936

New Cavendish Books

LONDON

First edition published in Great Britain
by New Cavendish Books – 1985
Reprinted 1988

FOR NARISA
The real fire
in a wondrous partnership
that created this and
other masterpieces

B.

SPECIFICATION: 336 pages, over 500 illustrations
including 423 in full colour.

The Hornby Companion Series

Design – John B. Cooper
Text production and supervision – Narisa Levy
Editorial direction – Allen Levy

Phototypeset and mono integration, Wyvern Typesetting Ltd, Bristol.
Colour separation and film planning, Aragorn Colour Reproduction, London.
Printed in Spain by Jerez Industrial, S. A.

New Cavendish Books, 23 Craven Hill, London W2 3EN.
Distribution: ABP, North Way, Andover, Hampshire.

ISBN 0 904568 35 0

Contents

Acknowledgements

One of the pleasures of assembling a work like this is the willingness of fellow enthusiasts to lend a hand. We have been lucky to have had the help and cooperation of a very large number of friends from far and wide. These are some of the people who have made a useful contribution to the finished result, and to whom we are most grateful.

We are also deeply indebted to the National Westminster Bank.

The Hornby Railway Collectors' Association Committee have saved us a great deal of time studying archival material. Many other people have given us valuable information and support during our researches, for which we offer our thanks. In particular we would like to mention Jack Steer (whose pioneering work in analysing publishing literature gave an excellent framework on which we have built), and Michael Foster, who helped to preserve copies of archive material from the Binns Road Works, the use of which has been most valuable. Nicholas Oddy has taught us a great deal about the subject; his assiduous studies have made him an unrivalled expert, particularly in the history of early Hornby. Both Nicholas Oddy and Bruce Baxter saw early copies of the manuscript and made many valuable suggestions.

Even in a generous volume such as this, it has proved impossible to illustrate more than a representative selection from the Hornby range. Even so, only a small proportion of the trains in the photographs come from our own collection, and we are very much obliged to the many people who let us photograph their items. Some of the trains are in less than perfect condition, since they are toys that have been used and enjoyed as such, and the present owners quite properly prefer not to over-restore them.

Richard Atkins	Alan Daniels	Roy Hallsworth	Clive McTaggart (Australia)	Eric Rogers
Ted Austin	Sylvain Denis (France)	John Hardy	Mike Mallett	Don Roberts
Mark Bailey	Brian Dicker	Lester Harrison	Len Mathews	David Salisbury
Douglas Baldock	Nat Donnelly	Dennis Higginson	John & Stuart Metcalfe	John Schofield
Bill Baker (Australia)	Robin Doust (Zimbabwe)	Brian Hollins	Brian Methley	Gordon Selby
Peter Berlanny	Keith Downer	John Hopkinson	Rod Moore	David & Pursey Short
Anthony Bianco	Ted Doyle	Gerry Horner	Tim Morris	Angus Souter
Bob Boorman	Peter & Joan Dunk	Friedenstern Howard	David Moss	Ian Standfast
Ian Braggins	Alan Ellis	Keith Lewis Hall	David Nathan	Joe Swain
Joe Brown	Archie Napier-Ewing	Dave Howel	Jim Osbourne	Alan R. Taylor
Alan Brown	Bob Field	Basil Hutchinson (New Zealand)	Richard Packham	Doug Taylor
Mike Brown	'Fin' Finlayson	Dave Jowett	Don Palmer	Geoff Taylor (Australia)
Ron & Angela Budd	Peter Flataus	Mike King	Roy Paton	Ron Truin
David Burt	David Gale	John Kirk	Stan Peachey	David Uttley
Ian Button	Jim Gamble	John Kitchen	Henry Pearce	Tatchell Venn (South Africa)
Pierce Carlson	Chris George	Dave Lambourne	Bruce Perrott	Ken Vernon
Royston Carss	Peter Gomm	Ted Lane	John Pentney	Harry Walker
Len Champion	Bruce Gosbell (Australia)	Ian Layne	Barry Potter	Richard Welsbey (France)
Ian Cook	John Goulden	Richard Lines	Jim Powis	Patrick Whitehouse
Peter Corley	Ken Grace	The London Toy & Model Museum	John Proctor	Jim Whittaker
George Cornwell	Colin Gregory	Bert Love	Peter Randall	Chris Willis
Nigel Cotton	George Grisby	Eduardo Lozano (Argentina)	Mike & Sue Richardson	Peter Wray
Derek Cox	Christopher Groom	Nigel Macmillan	John Ridley	F. Zachayus (France)

Preface

The best toy trains in the world came from Frank Hornby's Liverpool Factory. That at least is the opinion of the band of enthusiasts all around the world who keep alive an interest in them.

Part of the reason for this sustained enthusiasm has been the lack of any definitive list of the products of Meccano Ltd, and the resulting excitement of not knowing what is going to turn up next. Although a wealth of catalogue and advertising material was printed, it was not always an accurate reflection of the products which were available; even when this information has been collected and collated, it can still be misleading. So a large part of the fun is the detective work of piecing together what changes were made, why they happened, and when. There are still regular surprises when previously unknown variations appear!

Another strong part of the appeal is that, paradoxically, rare Hornby items are extremely common. Very many items were produced in small batches, numbering only hundreds and sometimes less; consequently practically every collector has desirable items that provoke great envy and admiration. But there are so many different rare items that for one person to assemble a complete collection of 0-gauge Hornby Trains is a practical impossibility.

By some omission, collecting Hornby Trains is not listed as one of the seven deadly sins. It does, however, give splendid scope for enjoying them. Of the seven, I have always particularly prided myself on my sloth; if I had systematically recorded details of all trains seen over the last few years, the information in this volume would be more complete. In many cases there is scope for argument or debate on the facts presented, and I hope none will be accepted uncritically; where Hornby Trains are concerned no rule applies without exception. It will be interesting to look back in a few years time to see how many of the 'facts' are changed in the light of new information that is bound to be uncovered. History does not stand still!

Chris Graebe

A Historical Survey

1900 to 1919

The closure of the Binns Road Meccano factory in 1980 came at a time when a general slump in trade had affected Liverpool more seriously than almost any other part of England. By contrast, at the turn of the century, the City of Liverpool was a very prosperous deep sea port, carrying the traffic of an Empire to and from a wide area of central England. Its prosperity through the nineteenth century was based on seafaring trade, and the volume of shipping was second only to that of the Port of London.

Frank Hornby was employed by one of the shipping companies in Liverpool when in 1901 he had the inspired – and patentable-idea of making the new toy 'Mechanics Made Easy', which was soon to become world-famous as 'Meccano'. The patentable feature was the perforation of metal strips with equidistant holes, enabling different models to be built, changed and dismantled at will. It was one of the very first and the very best of the constructional toys that are now a commonplace. With such a good idea, and a plentiful supply of workers and of business premises, success was virtually assured. Parents proved to be keen to buy this novel and adaptable toy for their children's enjoyment and education. The Meccano factories grew, and were outgrown. The premises moved from James Street and Duke Street to West Derby Road, and finally in August 1914 to a six-acre site at Binns Road in the 'Old Swan' district of Liverpool.

The first important attempt to diversify the range of Meccano products was an educational Meccano set, the 'Hornby System of Mechanical Demonstration', first sold circa 1909. There were special parts to enable the principles of mechanics – leverage, mechanical advantage, pulleys etc. – to be demonstrated in the classroom. Although not a best-seller, it is of note as being the first Meccano Product

to bear the 'Hornby' trade name, predating the Hornby trains by a decade.

Further diversification was planned during the war; the 'Model Engineer' for 10 June, 1915 reported the British Industries' Fair, and said of Meccano Limited that 'The firm are now entering the steam engine and general model world, and were showing some splendidly finished vertical steam engines and boilers, model clockwork trains, and model saw benches and churns'. The trains were probably only trade samples, shown as examples of what the firm intended to produce after the war, rather than as finished products. At the time, production of Meccano was restricted because of the munitions work carried out at Binns Road, and the production of model railways was shelved for a more propitious moment. By early 1918 Meccano boys were being told that 'All our machines which are suitable are devoted to Government work . . . we are still manufacturing Meccano on machines which cannot be used for Government work, but we cannot hope to provide sufficient . . .'

The 1915 Model Engineer report continued: 'Another novelty is Raylo, a complete model railway table game, which will no doubt provide considerable interest and amusement.' The Raylo game was the first Toy Train to be marketed by Meccano Limited; it was the subject of an early patent application, although it was the track and not the locomotive that had the patentable features. The locomotive was rather unusual (by later Hornby standards) in having the front axle at an angle to the rear, to make it run more easily round the sharply curved track!

The complete game, with locomotive, was shown in the Book of Prize Models published in 1915. The description said that 'This is a new and complete railway game, consisting of track, switches and crossings, and a neat and well-made

clockwork engine. The game is to keep the engine on the outer track by operating the levers at the proper moment. It is beautifully decorated, is of excellent workmanship, and forms a splendid game of skill for the family circle. In leather-bound carton, attractively finished'. It was by no means a cheap toy, with a price of 25s in the UK and 40s overseas.

There is a certain irony in the possibility that if the Great War could have been avoided, the Hornby Train might never have been put into production. But this terrible war, with its tragic waste of life, gave rise to the conditions that made possible the success of Hornby Trains. After the war there was no spirit of reconciliation between the parties to the armistice of 1918. The Treaty of Versailles imposed on Germany harsh and unfair reparation terms that could not possibly be met. An attempt was made to recover from Germany the whole cost of the war, and to ensure that German industries (among them the toy trade) were so heavily shackled as to render their competition ineffective. An indication of the feelings of the nation was the famous speech of Sir Ian Geddes: 'The Germans . . . are going to pay every penny. They are going to be squeezed, as a lemon is squeezed – until the pips squeak. My only doubt is not whether we can squeeze hard enough, but whether there is enough juice'. There was scarcely a home in the country that had not felt the loss of relatives or of close friends, so even had the Government made no attempt to cripple Germany's postwar recovery, the loathing of the man in the street for anything connected with Germany would have been sufficient to give British goods a competitive edge – even in the toy trade that had been dominated by continental manufacturers before the war. Meccano Ltd was already a major manufacturer of British toys, and the Government was naturally anxious to encourage the company to take advantage of the new chances that were arising.

27,533. Toys. HORNBY, F., 274, West Derby Road, Liverpool. Nov. 26. [*Classes* 132 (ii) *and* 132 (iii).*]

A toy, shown as being of the clock-work engine and railway type, but which may be made of the tilting-board and rolling-ball type, has an intertwined continuous set of rails 1 with sidings 4 normally kept open by spring-controlled points 5. The points are operated by hand-levers 6 and linkwork 8 so that an engine or the like can be kept running continuously round the track. Difficulties are created by making some levers work oppositely to others and by providing a derailing catch 19 which can be depressed by means of a button 20ᵇ. A counting-wheel 18 is set in the track to count the number of circuits made by the engine.

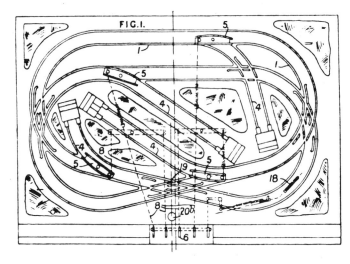

FIG. 1.

Part of the 'Raylo' patent.

'Raylo' instructions.

RAYLO. The Great Railroad Game

INSTRUCTIONS: To be Read Carefully

Each player must wind up the engine himself, which is prevented from running by the small brake at the back. The engine must then be placed with the front in line with the word "Start."

The engine is started by operating the starting lever, which is the first lever to the right. This releases the brake, and at the same time the "Wreck Stop" must be depressed, also the lever controlling Siding No. 7. The next lever to be operated is the one controlling Siding No. 8, followed by Nos. 9 and 10. This completes one round of the double track, and this will be recorded on the indicator, which should be set at 0 before the commencement of the run.

At the commencement of the next and each succeeding round, the "Wreck Stop" and the No. 7 Siding Lever must be operated together.

The object of the game is to keep the engine running as long as possible.

Each complete run round the entire track represents 113 points, two runs 226 points, and so on. With care and skill the engine may be kept running round the track several times.

If the engine comes to a stop on the track, the number immediately in front of it is added to the score. If it runs into a siding, the number indicated on the sleeper in the siding must be deducted from the score. The last numbers before the sidings are : 8, 33, 56, and 85.

Only one switch lever at a time may be operated, and the player is not allowed to touch any other switch lever than the one which he is operating, on penalty of forfeiting the run.

If the engine is wrecked through not operating the "Wreck Stop," or from any other cause, the entire run is forfeited.

Any number of players may take part in the game, and the one scoring the largest number of points in five runs wins the game.

The game should be played on a level table, and the track must not be moved by any player whilst a run is in progress.

MANUFACTURED BY MECCANO LTD., LIVERPOOL.

The diminutive Raylo locomotive, more or less of OO gauge. No tender was provided. Probably made by Marklin in Germany; similar locos were marketed independently by Marklin.

The 'Raylo' mechanism, seen from below.

The 'Raylo' set, illustrated in the Meccano Book of Prize Models, circa 1915.

An LNWR-livery Tinprinted Train Set, first advertised by Meccano Ltd in 1920. Probably the first gauge O trains made at Binns Road.

But all these factors on their own would not have combined to make the Hornby Trains a long-term success for Meccano Ltd if the product had not been up to standard. As we shall see, Hornby created two ranges of toy trains – a cheaper 'Tinprinted Train' set which was a copy of a German design, and the more expensive 'Hornby Train'. It was the quality and the original design of the Hornby Train that turned it into a best-seller, while the less original 'Tinprinted Train' ultimately failed.

1920

'The builders are hard at work erecting great new factories for us, and soon the Meccano works will be double their present size. We want to find employment for as many British workpeople as possible, and to play our part in the national movement for providing British boys and girls with British-made toys.'

'Before next winter I shall be able to announce that we have ready for delivery the finest series of clockwork Railway Trains ever made, all designed on a new principle.' (March–April 1920 MM)

THE 'NEW FACTORIES'

After the war, the change from munitions work to production of Meccano was swift and sure. In the May–June 1919 Meccano Magazine (MM) the Editor had reported that 'Since the Armistice our factory has been working night and day on Meccano, and many thousands of new and old Meccano boys have been made happy by being able to obtain their outfits. It has been a hard struggle to meet the remarkable demands which you boys have made on us, but by the time this number of the Meccano

Magazine reaches you, our output will be so big that there need be no further waiting for any of you. Full steam ahead is our motto from now on.'

The extensions to the Meccano works which were put in hand in 1920 were the biggest yet undertaken by the company, and much of the new area was reserved for production of the new toy trains, which had been designed between 1915 and 1920. The factory extensions had not been completed when toy train production started in the spring of 1920, so the new building which was to have been the works canteen was pressed into temporary service as the birthplace of the first Hornby Trains – to the dismay of some of the workers. But Frank Hornby defended his decision in 'Meccano News', a small leaflet issued to employees and friends of Meccano Ltd in November 1920: 'It has been a matter of considerable regret to me that we have been unable to get our new canteen going. The building was finished some time ago and everything ready, when we were faced with the difficulty of lack of space for the production of our new goods. The choice lay between clockwork trains and meals in greater comfort, and clockwork trains won the day. I believe this was a right decision, as any delay in pushing along with our new lines would have meant loss of valuable time, and would have been a highly dangerous proceeding in my opinion, and when the progress which we have made is taken into consideration, together with the additional employment which we have provided for so many girls, I do not think any of us has any cause to regret the course adopted. At the present time we have well over 1,200 employees in the works, and I have every hope that this number will greatly increase in the future.'

'I am looking forward to the time when the whole of this work will be transferred to the new building, and I can assure you that it will be a real pleasure to see the new canteen in full swing. It is a splendid building with 16,200 sq. ft. floor space. We have had the floor specially laid in order to make it suitable for dancing, and at one end we propose erecting a stage so that concerts and other entertainments may be held. . . . I hope that it will be ready for occupation next year.'

P. G. Wodehouse wrote that the Great War was fought 'to make the world a safe place for the working man to strike in.' Frank Hornby concluded his article: 'As we all know, there is considerable unrest in the labour world at the present time, due to a variety of causes over which no-one appears to have control. I am happy to think that these troubles have so far touched us but lightly, and I believe that this is due mainly to the fact that our workers recognise and understand the spirit of fair-mindedness and sincerity with which we have dealt with those questions that concern their welfare. If this understanding continues in the future . . . there is every reason to believe that whatever misunderstandings or differences of opinion may arise in the future will be dealt with in a friendly and satisfactory way.'

THE FIRST HORNBY TRAINS

'I want to warn you that supplies of foreign made trains have found their way into this country, and your only protection is to insist that what you buy has been actually made in this country' (Editorial, September–October 1920 MM)

'We knew that demand would be very large, but we did not know it would be quite so big as has proved to be the case . . . More machines and more workpeople are being added to the Company's Train Department, and very soon I hope all demands will be filled' (November–December 1920 MM)

The name of the 'Hornby Train' is so much a part of the language that it is now impossible to imagine that they could have been called anything else. It was quite a common and a pardonable conceit for a manufacturer to sell his goods under his own name; we are lucky that 'Hornby' is passably mellifluous. Think of going into a toyshop and asking for a 'No. 1 Ramsbotham Passenger Train, please.'

The first public announcement of the new trains was in the June–July 1920 MM: 'For a long time now we have been urged by the Government and by the public to produce clockwork trains to replace those which used to be imported from the continent. We have spent much time and thought on these goods, and we are now ready to supply a range of beautiful trains which will add much to the fame of our factories. The clockwork mechanism is excellent, and every train set has the Meccano guarantee behind it.'

'We are very proud of this fine clockwork train system, and it will be a great favourite amongst boys. It is built on the Meccano principle, and any damaged part may be instantly replaced by the user himself. Like all Meccano products, it is strong and durable, superbly finished and absolutely reliable.'

A confidential 'Book of help for the Meccano Dealer,' issued in July 1920 and titled 'Increased Sales and Profits', described the system further: 'With the introduction of this line commences a new era in clockwork train construction. Engine, tender and trucks are put together on the Meccano principle. The whole system may be built up by the boy from standard units, and if one of the parts is lost or damaged, a new part may be purchased and fitted by the user himself. The engines and trucks are supplied in complete outfits, ready built up for instant use, but

the boy derives much additional pleasure from being able to take them all in pieces and refashion them. The standardisation is the same as in the Meccano system, and boys will look upon the Hornby Trains as Meccano models of a new and altogether delightful type.'

The Meccano Products catalogue, and advertising leaflets, added that the trains were available in 'One size only, Gauge O, in three colours to represent the London and North-Western, Midland and Great Northern Railway systems. Each set contains Engine, Tender and one Truck, set of Rails, including a circle and two straights. The engine is fitted with reversing gear, brakes and regulators. Complete in strong attractive box, 27/6 each.'

LOCOMOTIVE and TENDER

The Hornby Locomotive was a novel design, on the constructional principle, to be made with what were in effect special purpose Meccano parts. The limitation was that there was no possibility of putting the train together in different ways – only one design was possible. The train was supplied assembled rather than in kit form, which was an advantage for the user; many of the early Hornby Trains show no sign of ever having been taken to pieces and re-built! Three liveries were available, with the loco enamelled in green, red and black for the GN, MR and LNWR companies respectively. But although the colours were different, none of the locos bore any crests or company lettering to identify the railway company – perhaps to eliminate the need for special liveries for export versions.

The boiler was fitted with a polished brass dome, and a cast chimney. An embossed brass plate bearing the locomotive number 2710 was clipped to the cabside. Although a single short splasher was fitted beside the cab, there was unfortunately none over the front wheel. This gave an even more ludicrous appearance to the tiny wheels fitted to the first mechanism. The top of the wheels came not just below the splasher, but below the running plate and valance as well! Piston and connecting rods were fitted to the rear wheels, one of the nicer features of the loco being the outside cylinders; but there were no coupling rods. The buffers were in turned brass, as were the couplings (with wire links) which on these early trains were fitted to both front and rear of the locomotive and the tender.

The tender was a four-wheeled constructional design. It came in two main parts, the base (which was like a short version of the Truck base), and a three-sided top with embossed lining and a pierced coal-rail. There was no embossed imitation coal as fitted to the cheaper Tinprinted Train Tender, and no tank for the water.

WAGONS

The wagons in the Hornby Train Set were made in three main pieces. The base had deep sides, and small plain trunnions which held the axles. The axles themselves were of the same diameter as Meccano rod, and on the earliest wagons the wheels were spaced by split pins through holes drilled in the axles. Brass buffers and couplings were fitted. The base was fitted with two identical pieces each forming one side and one end of the wagon.

Although the locomotives were not finished with the lettering and crests of any particular railway company, the Hornby TRUCK was prominently marked, by pressed metal letters clipped by lugs onto the wagon sides. The Trucks for the GN, LNWR and MR companies were designed in January and February 1920. A further selection was made in December 1920, when the London, Brighton and South Coast Railway and Caledonian Railway wagons were drawn. French companies were

A gauge O Hornby LNWR Train Set, made late in 1920.

represented by wagons with 'Nord' and 'PLM' (Paris, Lyon & Mediterranee) letters; both these were produced in reasonably large quantities, but although the tools for producing Etat lettering were designed, no complete examples have come to light. Similarly the British South Eastern and Chatham Railway (SECR), and Great Eastern Railway (GE) wagons were designed, but not catalogued.

The Great Northern, Midland and London and North Western Railways were obvious choices for the first Hornby Trains. A glance at the route-mileages for the major pre-grouping companies (excluding most joint lines) indicates their relative prominence at the time:

Great Western Railway	3005 miles
London and North Western	2667 miles
(Including L & YR, merged in January 1922)	
Midland Railway	2170 miles
North Eastern Railway	1757 miles
North British Railway	1378 miles
Great Eastern Railway	1191 miles
Caledonian Railway	1114 miles
Great Northern Railway	1051 miles
London and South Western Railway	1039 miles
Great Central Railway	852 miles
South Eastern and Chatham Railway	637 miles
Highland Railway	506 miles
Glasgow and South Western Railway	493 miles
London, Brighton and South Coast Rly.	457 miles

The list probably overstates the importance of the minor Scottish lines (which were apt to ramble round for miles without serving more than a few scattered settlements). Furthermore the indubitable prestige of the LBSCR is not apparent merely from mileage. But the list serves to show the importance of the MR, GN and LNWR chosen for the first Hornby Trains. It also shows the outstanding omission – the Great Western Railway. This was all the more surprising, because the 'G' and 'W' letters had already been designed for use on the first issues. Furthermore, the Hornby advertising leaflet printed in June 1920 (for inclusion in Meccano sets) listed Great Western as the alternative to LNWR and MR livery, although this was altered to Great Northern in the August 1920 and subsequent lists. There are rumours that the GWR discouraged the production of models by threat of legal action, but there is no

evidence available; indeed, it seems unlikely in view of the value the GWR placed in self-publicity in later years. Whatever the reasons, GWR enthusiasts had to wait until 1926 before Hornby remembered them.

RAILS

The design of rails for the early Hornby train sets was based on the rails sold by Bing (a famous Nurnburg manufacturer) in similar sets, such as their 'Hercules'. Four curved rails formed a circle of about 9 inch radius measured to the centre, or 25 cm measured to the outside of the curve. A pair of straight rails was included to make up an oval – an oval as understood by all but the pedantic. The length of the straight rail was about 10¼ inches. Presumably these sizes were adopted because there was no particular reason to change from the Bing precedent; the rails were after all reasonably convenient for packing, and were suitable for the small mechanisms of the early locos. Each sleeper was stamped with the Meccano name, and the centre sleeper (there were only 3 on each rail) was marked with the gauge. The paucity of sleepers, the light gauge of metal used and the small rail section contributed to a general flimsiness. There was no method of locking or clipping the rails together, the owner was merely instructed to 'push the rails together with care, and as close up as possible'. Extra rails were available at 6s per dozen, straight or curved.

THE TINPRINTED TRAIN SET

The poor relation of the Hornby Train, the TIN-PRINTED CLOCKWORK TRAIN SET, appeared in the June 1920 and subsequent advertising leaflets and in the 1920 catalogue, but it did not share the frequent publicity in the Meccano Magazine accorded to its big brother. The train set lacked the constructional features of the Hornby Train, and the finish was (as the name suggests) printed rather than enamelled.

There is no doubt that the Hornby Train Set was a 'hit' with the customers from the start. The sets were soon to be produced in prodigious quantities, and their sturdy construction and good workmanship ensured that they worked well and that they stood the test of time. The same cannot be said of the

Tinprinted Train Set, which (being based on an inexpensive German design) lacked the obvious sales appeal of the Hornby Train. The locomotive was reasonably proportioned, but the tender and carriages looked delightfully undersized; the carriages have been compared to telephone boxes! With this obviously toy-like train set 22s 6d, and the proper Hornby Train with its constructional features at only 27s 6d, most customers made the obvious choice. Thus the Tinprinted Train is less well known than the Hornby Train.

It has frequently been claimed that these Tinprinted Trains were actually manufactured by Bing for Meccano Limited, or that the tools used to produce them at Binns Road had come from Germany. The main ground for this suspicion is that the design is superficially identical to trains produced by Bing and carrying the Bing trademark. Close examination shows, however, that none of the pressings were made with the same tools. There are differences in the sizes of the lugs and slots, and components such as the handrails and chimneys are also quite different. The tinprinting of the Meccano Ltd version is distinctive, and both loco and carriages are clearly marked 'Made in England'. The Meccano Ltd trademark is embossed on each item, and also on the mechanism (which is itself distinctly different from the German version). The early catalogues clearly stated that this trademark '. . . is printed on all the toys described here, and it indicates that they have been manufactured by Meccano Ltd.' The cataloguers proved themselves in later years to be masters of circumlocution, and this direct claim must be accepted as genuine in view of the importance of the 'Buy British' philosophy to Hornby's production.

In addition, a number of the original design drawings have survived, which would not have been required if the loco had been produced abroad. It is most likely that the drawings were made by copying one of the Bing locos, by flattening it out (what an agreeable task!) and measuring up the dimensions. What is beyond doubt is that the quaint appearance and controversial origin of the Tinprinted Trains have made them of greater interest today than they ever were to the customers for whom they were intended.

A Great Northern Hornby No. 2 Train of 1921. The Lattice Girder Bridge was the first Hornby accessory, also dating from 1921.

1921

'A Hornby Train lasts for ever!' (November–December 1921 MM)

'The smartest looking and smoothest running clockwork train you ever saw; delightful to handle and to watch as it dashes busily round its track' (May–June 1921 MM)

1921 was a busy year for Hornby developments. The March–April MM talked about new Hornby Trains in preparation: 'This successful clockwork train system is being very rapidly developed. Bigger engines, passenger coaches, new trucks, larger radius lines, crossings, switches etc., are all designed and decided upon, and are already in the hands of skilled men in the Meccano works. Nothing could exceed the charming finish and beauty of these goods, and there is no doubt that they will create a sensation in the world of toys next winter.'

The original Hornby Train Set was improved in a number of ways during 1921; the engine was fitted with a new larger-size mechanism, with longer wheelbase and larger wheels, giving longer runs and

better pulling power as well as improving the appearance. The couplings and buffers were also improved. The bad news was a small increase in price to 30s for the Hornby set, while the price of the Tinprinted Train fell to 20s.

The rails were re-designed (or rather, re-copied from another German design) to suit the new mechanism. The new rails had a larger 1 ft radius, a more sturdy rail section, and had five instead of three sleepers on each curved rail. The straight rails had four sleepers instead of three. Locking wires were provided to clip the new-style rails together. Six rails instead of four were needed to form a 1 ft radius circle. The new-style Hornby rails were capable of being converted to electrical operation, and conversion accessories were advertised once only in the November–December 1921 MM. This was probably envisaged as a means of running Meccano model trains rather than commercially available models. Clockwork points, crossings, half rails and quarter rails were all made available during 1921.

The new-style loco and rails were sold in a striking new box, covered in brown leather paper

and embossed in gold. The new presentation was shown in the May–June 1921 MM; it made for better display in the shop since the sides of the tender and wagon were now visible. The set was now called the 'No. 1 Hornby Train Set' to distinguish it from the larger sets in preparation. Sets were also advertised for the first time in Caledonian Railway livery (with a dark blue loco), and for the first and only time LBSCR sets were mentioned. Although LBSC wagons on their own are quite common, no examples of boxed sets are yet known, so the colour of the engine can only be conjectured. It is more likely to be the same as one of the other four colours than to be in a prototypically correct shade.

The first van in the Hornby system appeared in the same May–June 1921 Meccano Magazine. The COVERED LUGGAGE VAN, price 6s, was built on the same base as the Hornby Truck; 'Like the Hornby Train it is built of standardised parts, and may be taken to pieces and rebuilt. Any damaged parts may be renewed at any time.' The constructional features soon proved to be impractical when it was found necessary to fit stays across the body above and below the hinged doors, to prevent the sides bowing inwards. MR, LNWR and GN-lettered Vans were offered in the May–June 1921 MM only, but the version with clip-on MR letters is the only one of these known to have been made.

The catalogues and leaflets issued around September 1921 listed the No. 2 HORNBY PASSENGER and GOODS TRAIN SETS. The No. 2 Locomotive was a 4–4–0 similar in style to the 2710, and numbered (with stunning inspiration) 2711. Both the sets were constructional, and available in CR, GN, MR and LNWR colours. The appearance of the No. 2 Loco was quite impressive; although it lacked the outside cylinders of the No. 1 type, it at least had convincingly shaped splashers. The wheels had more spokes and were of larger diameter. The motor was altogether a larger and more powerful affair, the design being based very closely indeed on the mechanisms used by Bing for their Great Northern style locos. The No. 2 Loco could be reversed from the track, unlike the No. 1 which at that time could be reversed only by a lever in the cab.

The No. 2 Tender was also similar in style to the smaller No. 1 version, but had a longer six-wheeled

14 *The Meccano stand at the British Industries Fair, White City, in 1921.*

base, and a crosspiece at the front to prevent the fireman shovelling any of the non-existent coal into the clockwork. Once again the designers did not recognise that tenders are supposed to carry water as well as coal. The only consolation with this glorified coal-cart was that at 5s it cost only 6d more than the No. 1 Tender.

The No. 2 Goods Set had two Trucks instead of the one supplied with the No. 1 Goods Set. The No. 2 Passenger Set included two bogie saloon-type coaches, with non-opening doors at each end. The coaches were constructional, like the other components of the set, and finished in a pleasant livery (albeit unrepresentative of the prototypes) of green

with a cream or very pale green band above the bottom of the windows. There were two versions in each set – one a Pullman Car with 'Pullman' transfers and two fine Pullman Company crests, and the other a Dining Saloon, with 'Dining Saloon' transfers and also the crest of the appropriate railway company – LNWR, GN, MR or CR, the crest being the only difference between them. Both Goods and Passenger Sets were supplied with a circle of twelve curved rails of 2 ft radius – one of which was the Brake and Reverse rail. No straight rails came in the No. 2 sets.

The new No. 1 PASSENGER TRAIN SETS included the No. 1 Passenger Coach. This showed a common provenance with the Covered Luggage

Van, but was fitted with non-opening end doors and with windows. Unlike the bogie coaches they were painted in different colours for the different railway companies – Great Northern coaches being brown with red-lined windows, London and North Western in brown and white with white window surrounds, and the Midland Railway coach in maroon. Each carried the railway company crest on the side. The Caledonian Railway coach was quite unrealistically finished, in the same colour as the Great Northern coach but with a different crest. There was no lettering on any of the coaches except for the 1st and 3rd class brass letters clipped to the doors – despite the fact that there were no compart-

No. 2 MR and LNWR Locos, and No. 1 MR and GN Locos. The No. 1 Passenger Coaches and the Covered Luggage Van were new in 1921.

ments to separate the hoi polloi from the high-born. The roof colour was dark grey in each case. The windows of the No. 1 Coaches were glazed in plain sheet celluloid, and are the only ones in the whole Hornby range to survive well. The Pullman Car celluloid windows were coated with a layer of gelatin to allow them to be printed with black and red details of blinds. The gelatin coating was the undoing of the windows, since it rendered them liable to all manner of ills from shrinkage to severe curling, yellowing and cracking. As a result, hardly any Pullman Coaches (or others with similar windows) have survived with perfect celluloids.

The No. 1 Coach base was a new design, with detachable axleguards secured by nuts and bolts and having details of springs pierced and embossed. This added to the interest as a constructional item, but the wagons were not fitted with the new base, presumably on grounds of expense. The No. 1 and No. 2 Coach bases were both embossed with the Registered Design numbers.

The other major introduction of 1921 was the LATTICE GIRDER BRIDGE, which appeared in the November–December MM at 10s 6d. Although the bridge was constructional, and was the only Hornby accessory to be built on the Meccano principle, all the parts were special-purpose items. None were identical to existing Meccano parts, although they were compatible with the Meccano system, and Meccano parts could be added to represent signals for example.

1922

'Hornby Clockwork Trains – the trains with a guarantee' (October 1922 MM)

The first good news of the 1922 season was a reduction in Hornby Train prices from March 1922. For example, the No. 2 Pullman Train Set was reduced from 80s to 70s, and the No. 1 Goods Train from 30s to 25s 6d. The prices for the recently-introduced coaches were unchanged, but the Covered Luggage Van went down from 6s to only 4s 6d. Perhaps the most surprising change was the Tinprinted Train Set, the price of which was nearly halved to 12s 6d.

Another price alteration was for the Hornby TIMBER WAGON, introduced in January 1922, which was reduced from 7s 6d to 5s 6d. The Timber Wagon was a substantially built bogie vehicle made from the No. 2 Coach base, with riveted stanchions retaining the load of five wooden planks. It was suitable only for the 2 ft radius curves.

A new group of wagons for both the No. 1 and No. 2 Trains was shown in the May–June 1922 Meccano Magazine. These important introductions included a SHELL PETROL TANK WAGON, two different BRAKE VANS, a CEMENT WAGON, and a GUNPOWDER VAN. The Gunpowder Van was based on the existing Luggage Van, but had a bright red finish. Instead of the clip-on MR letters, LNWR letters were applied by stencil spraying. One Brake Van was a single-ended type in grey for the LNW, and the other a double-ended version in brown for the GN. These were also of the constructional type, with stencilled lettering. The Shell tanker and the Cement Wagon were the first wagons to abandon completely the constructional principle, being held together with lugs rather than nuts and bolts.

The MM illustrations show all the wagons (except the Petrol Tank) on a new-style wagon base introduced in 1922. From the side this looked like the No. 1 Coach base, but was formed in a single piece, with axleguards incorporated in the pressing rather than being separate pieces bolted on. Thin axles like those of the Tinprinted Train were used on these new bases, and on some wagons with the 1920-style base, for instance the Shell Petrol Tank Wagon. Thin axles were also adopted for the No. 1 Coaches.

Another introduction was the Spring Buffer Stop, an essential accessory for any layout with points, to stop trains falling off the ends of the sidings!

The failure of the Tinprinted Train Set had become evident, and since Hornby needed a second string to his bow, a new range of lower-priced trains was introduced and shown in the May–June 1922 MM. These were sold not as Hornby Trains, but under a different – and rather odd – trademark; ZULU CLOCKWORK TRAINS. The Meccano Magazine Editor commented that 'The new Zulu Trains derive their name from a well-known Great

Western train that runs between Paddington and Birkenhead. I agree that sometimes trains have peculiar names. . .' The choice of a euphonious name is essential for sales appeal, and one cannot help wondering why such a bad choice was made. The trains themselves were in every way satisfactory, being similar in style to the existing No. 1 Hornby Sets. The difference was that they were non-constructional, and the Zulu Loco was non-reversing, with a simplified – but no less powerful – mechanism. The buffers and the handrail knobs were cast instead of being turned brass, giving a small saving in cost. Only LNW livery was available, the loco being finished in black even on the dome. The cab windows and embossed lining were nicely picked out in red paint. The wagons were similar to the Hornby type, but looking a touch more realistic with stencil-sprayed 'LNW' lettering instead of clip-on letters. Loco, tender and wagon were assembled using eyelets instead of nuts and bolts. The Zulu Coaches were also similar to the Hornby type, except that the non-constructional base was used and no window celluloids were fitted.

The Zulu sets were not markedly inferior to the Hornby trains in appearance, and were substantially cheaper at 18s 6d for the Goods Train Set, and 25s for the Passenger Set.

Another very important 1922 introduction was the ZULU TANK LOCOMOTIVE. It was advertised as a non-reversing loco at 12s in the May–June 1922 MM, but it was quickly decided that the locomotive should be reversing and it was advertised as such at 12s 6d in the next MM; a tank loco which did not reverse would have been rather unusual!

Electric rails were first advertised in March 1922, and a wider range of clockwork points including Double Symmetrical and Parallel Points became available later in 1922. Half and quarter rails reappeared in the 1922 lists, together with a new style of 9 inch radius rails and points. To help with the design of layouts, a 'Rail Formations' booklet (2d) was printed in 1922, which gave dozens of more or less useful layouts, together with a list of Hornby Rails and Accessories. These lists were soon outdated by the rapid expansion of the Hornby range, however, and customers were advised to write to the factory for the latest lists.

A late introduction in November 1922 was the four-wheel Timber Wagon, for use with No. 1 trains. This was of very simple construction, the stanchions being pressed upwards out of the base rather than attached as separate parts. A timber load was provided. The price of only 2s made it the cheapest wagon in the range.

A personal honour given to Frank Hornby in 1922 was his election as the President of the British Toy Manufacturers' Association, in recognition of his contribution to the industry. The Hornby Trains were by no means the last of his bright ideas, though. The 1922 MMs devoted a lot of space to the radio craze that was sweeping the nation. The up-to-date Meccano enthusiast of 1922 should have been 'listening in' to Marconi House on an 'efficient and inexpensive' Meccano Crystal Receiving Set, complete with Meccolite crystal. Regrettably the plans to introduce a Meccano Valve Radio Receiving Set came to nothing, since the sales of the crystal sets were rather disappointing!

1923

'To use cheap-looking rolling stock or a foreign-looking station with a Hornby Train completely spoils the effect.' (November 1923 MM)

'In view of the recent re-grouping of the railway system we do not consider it advisable to elaborate too much on individual colours.' (June 1923 MM)

HORNBY TRAIN LIVERIES IN 1923

The grouping of the Railway Companies in January 1923 under the 1921 Railways Act produced four major groups. The largest was the London Midland and Scottish, which absorbed the Midland Railway, the London and North Western, the Caledonian Railway, and many others. There appears to have been some rivalry between the Crewe works and the Derby works, with the result that LMS passenger engines appeared either in red, or in lined black, but the Caledonian Railway blue disappeared quite rapidly.

The Great Northern and Great Central Railways, again with many others, were merged to form the London and North Eastern Railway. A green livery was adopted for the passenger locomotives of the group.

No. 1 Locos in LMS livery, with 16 wagons that were first advertised in 1923.

The principal companies forming the Southern Railway were the London, Brighton and South Coast, the South Eastern and Chatham, and the London and South Western. The Great Western Railway alone was hardly affected by the grouping, absorbing only a few minor lines.

The approximate route mileages (and other statistics) for the groups were as follows:

	MILEAGE	LOCOS	COACHES	WAGONS
LMSR	7,500	10,300	27,000	325,000
LNER	6,700	7,400	20,000	299,000
GWR	3,800	4,000	10,000	100,000
SR	2,200	2,200	10,000	40,000

The LMSR had over 20,000 miles of lines, including sidings – enough to go most of the way round the world. The actual mileage of track produced in the Binns Road works was equally impressive; in 1930 alone, 9 million sleepers were made, enough for 500 miles of rail! Over the years the Meccano factory also produced many millions more locomotives than the real railway companies had ever owned.

L&NER livery No. 1 and No. 2 Locos of the 1923–24 season.

18
L&NER livery No. 1 and No. 2 Locos of the 1923–24 season.
Some wagons were also issued with L&NER lettering, although quite soon the ampersand was omitted.

From 1923 the changes in the real railway companies were reflected in the Hornby range by the progressive adoption of two of the four group liveries, only the LMS and LNER being represented. The changeover was gradual, and some rolling stock in pre-group liveries continued to be made in 1923. Passenger sets in 1923 still contained pre-grouping coaches, but some locomotives were produced with LMS and LNER lettering. The Hornby Wagons in the No. 1 and No. 2 Goods Sets were also changed to LMS and LNER lettering, using transfers rather than clip-on letters as before.

The 1923–24 season post-grouping locomotive liveries are particularly confusing, but this is not surprising since the real railway companies took a while to settle down to a standard practice. The Hornby locomotives carried 'L&NER' lettering long after the LNER had dropped the ampersand. A few Hornby locomotives with 'LM&S' letters also appeared. The Hornby loco colours were still GN green to represent the L&NER, and LNWR black or MR red to represent the LMS; Caledonian Railway blue disappeared. To confuse matters further, some remaining stocks of pre-group sets in the factory appear to have been updated to the new liveries. Thus it is possible to find LMS and LNER sets with a 'tested' date as early as 1921! For good measure, the wagons and tenders were sometimes changed to the most recent types. A few locos were produced with the company lettering on the tender instead of – or as well as – on the splasher.

Both the Zulu Loco and the Zulu Tank Loco were produced for the 1923–24 season with LMS lettering on the sides, and with the 'Zulu' transfers on the smokebox doors. The wagons supplied in the Goods Sets were usually LMS types after the remaining stock of LNW wagons was used up. But the Tinprinted Trains continued to be sold (with the new name of George V Trains) in the pre-grouping liveries, since no post-grouping versions were printed.

Many of the 1923–24 season LMS and LNER

19

wagons were fitted with the obsolete 1920-type wagon base, rather than the open-axleguard 1922 type which had been used for the later pre-grouping wagons. Old stocks of constructional wagon, coach and loco parts were frequently used up in this way between 1923 and 1925. For example, the 1921 van parts were used up on MR Refrigerator Vans made in 1923.

Most shops were stocked with a mixture of trains in pre- and post-grouping liveries, and the catalogues of the period said that the No. 1 Trains were 'In colours to represent the principal British railway Co.'s rolling stock', a carefully chosen formula of words to avoid any difficulty from shopkeepers trying to palm off old stock onto unsuspecting customers.

HORNBY DEVELOPMENTS IN 1923

1923 was another year of rapid and significant expansion of the Hornby product range. New items of rolling stock were produced at a prodigious rate, and 1923 would have been an exhilarating (and exhausting!) time to have worked in the drawing office or the tool room at Binns Road.

No. 1 and No. 2 LUMBER WAGONS were produced. Only the bogie version was provided with a load, beech dowels looking more like telegraph poles than lumber. SIDE TIPPING and ROTARY TIPPING WAGONS were produced, to represent types used by public works contractors. A HOPPER WAGON was also introduced, fitted with bottom doors; all these wagons had a strong appeal for lads wishing to simulate permanent way operations by discharging suitable loads all over the floor. The new GAS CYLINDER WAGON proved to be a consistently good seller, as did the CRANE TRUCK and the bogie BREAKDOWN VAN and CRANE. Also on offer for the first time in 1923 was a 'NATIONAL BENZOLE' PETROL TANK WAGON, as an alternative to 'Shell'. Another popular introduction was the MILK TRAFFIC VAN – well worth the extra 6d on the price of a Luggage Van, because of the milk cans provided as a load. Unlike the Luggage Van it had sliding doors instead of hinged, and the body was slatted for ventilation. A similar wagon with only the upper slats cut out was sold as the No. 1 CATTLE TRUCK, at the same price as the Luggage Van. A pair of bogie equivalents to the Luggage Van and Cattle Truck, the No. 2 LUGGAGE VAN and the No. 2 CATTLE TRUCK, were also produced.

From the collector's point of view, one of the most popular 1923 introductions was the COLMAN'S MUSTARD VAN. This first in a series of private owners' vans was based on the Gunpowder Van body, painted in an appropriate mustard yellow, and with a splendid transfer applied on the van side and doors.

The REFRIGERATOR VAN was advertised for the first time in 1923. Except for the colour it was identical to the MR Luggage Van. It was finished in white, with black clip-on MR letters. The other major introduction was a 50-ton TROLLEY WAGON. This bogie vehicle was available from early 1923, and was one of the first wagons to appear with post-grouping lettering. Certain versions packed as early as May 1923 have 'NE' letters.

1923 also saw the introduction of the new No. 2 TANK LOCOMOTIVE. This 4-4-4 loco was similar in style to the No. 2 tender locos (although not constructional), and had the same mechanism.

HORNBY PRESENTATION SET B.

No.	£	s.	d.	No.	£	s.	d.
1 No. 2 Hornby Pullman Set		3 10	0	1 Rotary Tipping Wagon		3	6
2 Goods Wagons	3/9	7	6	1 Hopper Wagon		4	0
1 Luggage Van		4	6	1 Cement Wagon		4	6
1 Brake Van		4	6	1 Windsor Railway Station		12	6
1 Milk Traffic Van		5	0	1 Turntable		4	6
1 No. 2 Cattle Truck		7	0	3 Telegraph Poles	3/-	9	0
1 Refrigerator Van		4	6	1 Loading Gauge		1	9
1 Colman's Mustard Van		4	6	1 Double Lamp Standard		4	0
1 Breakdown Van and Crane		7	0	3 Signals	2/6	7	6
1 Trolley Wagon		6	6	2 Spring Buffer Stops	2/-	4	0
1 Petrol Tank Wagon		3	6	1 Lattice Girder Bridge		10	6
1 Gas Cylinder Wagon		4	0	Extra Rails, Points and Crossing to make figure 23L		1 1	0
1 No. 2 Lumber Wagon		5	6				
1 No. 2 Timber Wagon		5	6	Total cost of Hornby Equipment B £11 9 9			
1 Side Tipping Wagon		3	6				

Hornby Locos and Tenders are enamelled in three colours—Black, Chocolate and Green, and the colour desired should be specified when ordering.

MECCANO LTD.   LIVERPOOL

Hornby Presentation Set B.

As on the Zulu Tank Loco, there was no partition to separate the bunker from the rest of the cab!

The range of accessories was also greatly expanded, with the TELEGRAPH POLE, SIGNAL, SINGLE and DOUBLE LAMP STANDARDS, LOADING GAUGE and TURNTABLE all advertised for the first time. Also issued was the largest-yet tinplate product of the Binns Road factory, the WINDSOR STATION. The platform, complete with fenced ramps, supported a fair-sized building tinprinted with a busy scene. One feature which was never advertised was the provision of the two candle-holders fitted into the base, to light the inside of the building. The windows on several doors were punched out to allow for ventilation – the chimneys being non-functional. Severe scorching of the tinprinting was the disadvantage of actually using the holders!

Although the station was quite a respectable offering, it was spoilt by lack of the most recognisable feature of most English stations – the canopy. Happily this omission did not seem to spoil the enjoyment of the users.

If you were rich, and could not make up your mind which Hornby Trains to buy, PRESENTATION SETS A and B were offered in 1923. These were selections from the normal Hornby range, but the prices of £6 19s 9d and £11 9s 9d allowed no discount on the normal list prices despite the quantities involved. Presumably there were few customers, as the outfits were advertised for one year only.

FRANK HORNBY'S BIRTHDAY PRESENT SCHEME

To celebrate the fifteenth year of Meccano Ltd's 'unbroken success and progress' since it was formed in 1908, Frank Hornby ran a promotion to give a birthday present to the lucky lads whose birthday fell on the same day as his own. Like most free gifts, there were strings attached; to find out if you qualified, you had to buy a Meccano Outfit or a Hornby, Zulu or George V Train Set. A form was included with every outfit and train set sold in late 1923 and early 1924; the purchaser had to fill in the form, stating his birthday, then get the form witnessed. If

his birthday was the same as Frank Hornby's, and the form had arrived by the closing date of 15th May 1924, the lucky chap received a 'handsome wallet in Morocco leather'. Frank Hornby's birthday, (2nd May, if you are interested) was published in the June 1924 MM. Since wallets were offered as prizes in later Meccano model-building competitions, perhaps there were plenty left over when the scheme closed!

1924

'If you are not yet the proud possessor of a Hornby Train, choose one for you next Birthday present – you will never regret it!' (September 1924 MM)

The 1924 catalogues were able to show the completion of the changeover to post-grouping LMS and LNER lettering. Many goods wagons which had previously not carried any company letters now had them, and some of the remaining stocks of 1923 wagons were converted to LMS and LNER by the addition of company letters. This can be proved in a few cases where the seals on the boxes were broken to remove the wagon, and new labels put on top of the old when the updated wagon was put back. The 1924–25 loco liveries became more standardised, and company crests and lining became the norm. LNER locos in black began to be produced, in addition to the three liveries already available. Nonetheless the catalogues remained unhelpful and evasive on all matters of colouring. The 'L&NER' transfers already produced continued to be used for the green engines while stock lasted, but the black LNER locos were actually lettered 'LNER', with no ampersand.

An important event in 1924 was the adoption of the 'Hornby Series' tradename, not just for the Hornby Trains but for the Zulu Trains as well. In fact, the Zulu Tank Loco was renamed the Hornby No. 1 Tank Loco, although the tender engines were described as 'Hornby Series' Zulu Locos. 'Hornby Series' transfers sprouted on nearly every item of rolling stock, and on accessories; even on a few boxes. Another distinctive feature of the 1924 and later productions was the application of a thick coat of protective varnish over the paintwork, making a sleek, glossy finish (a light varnish may have been

A Morocco wallet, presented to Norman Bell by Frank Hornby. These wallets were given as prizes in Frank Hornby's Birthday Present Scheme.

used previously, but did not give the same depth of finish). Even mundane items like the Turntable were affected; such was the enthusiasm for the new finish that some wagons were varnished after final assembly – over the wheels, couplings and all! This varnish coat is a boon to collectors as it still protects the trains from damage by damp and rough handling after several decades. It also gives a false impression of some colours, particularly the plain dark grey enamel used for the roofs of Cattle Trucks, which when varnished becomes a rich green-grey.

For the 1923–24 season the coaches had only been available in pre-grouping livery. It is not clear quite why no LMS or LNER Dining Saloons were produced after the crests were made for the 1924 locos, and labels were certainly produced in 1924 for LMS Dining Saloon boxes. Instead the Dining Saloon was only given a 'Pullman' crest.

New tinprinted LMS and LNER No. 1 Passenger Coaches were supplied in the 1924 No. 1 Passenger Train Sets. They were fitted with what are commonly called 'clerestory' roofs, although the Hornby versions lacked any representation of windows or ventilators. The coaches were longer than the constructional type, but narrower, and with three opening doors on each side. A new and rather odd design of tender for the 2710 loco was also produced, built to the same narrow beam as the coach. The Hornby Wagon was redesigned to fit the long thin base used for the new coaches. All these new designs were non-constructional, being clipped together by lugs. The constructional aspects of the Hornby Train were no longer advertised from 1924,

and although it was still true to say that the parts were standardised and that damaged parts could be replaced, this could now only be done in Meccano Ltd's Repair Department. Most references to taking the trains to pieces and rebuilding them had disappeared from the advertisements in 1923, and from 1924 set boxes no longer carried instructions for constructional use. Indeed some 1924 sets had to have the old instructions on the box lid covered by pasting over an extra sheet!

There is no disguising the fact that the long thin pattern was one of the silliest and most impractical designs to have been produced by Meccano Ltd. The short wheelbase, high centre of gravity and general

flimsiness gave a cheap appearance and a poor performance. The fact that Bing used a base of very similar dimensions for some of their range gives no excuse whatever for its adoption by Hornby!

A clerestory Guard's Van was also offered in 1924, but the No. 1 Passenger Sets were sold with a pair of coaches, rather than with one coach and a brake. Presumably this ensured that, having exhausted Father's resources in buying the set, there was still something vital left for Sonny to buy from his pocket money.

The other introductions announced in 1924 were mainly accessories; a double track LEVEL CROSSING was offered, although a single track version

By 1924 most wagons were in LMS or LNER livery. The Zulu trademarks began to disappear from the No. 1 Tank and No. 0 Locos as they became part of the Hornby Series during the 1924–25 period.

would have been more useful for most railways. The narrow spacing of the tracks did not match either the old 1 ft radius Parallel Points, or the 2 ft radius Parallel Points which were new in 1924. The Level Crossing was not even the length of a standard straight rail. Also announced was a FOOTBRIDGE, a non-constructional type for those who could not afford a Lattice Girder Bridge. It was available with or without detachable signals. A JUNCTION SIGNAL and a tinprinted SIGNAL CABIN were catalogued. Three sets of PLATFORM ACCESSORIES were produced, these being No. 1 LUGGAGE AND TRUCK, No. 2 MILK CANS AND TRUCK, and No. 3 PLAT-

FORM MACHINES ETC. These helped to fill the platform of the Windsor Station, but it was to be some years before any Hornby figures were made. A tinprinted TUNNEL was also produced in 1924; although of unlikely appearance (what engineer would have driven his railway through such a small hill and not round it?) it was a nice toy, with imposing portals. Equally disappointing compared with the real thing was the new so-called VIADUCT; this would have been put to shame by most small bridges, and could only have spanned a couple of small ditches. The shallow slope of the ramps was nonetheless enough to halt most clockwork trains as effectively as a brake rail! Other new

accessories were HYDRAULIC BUFFER STOPS, and a large WATER TANK.

The most important new wagon to be advertised was the SNOWPLOUGH. This was fitted with a most convincing rotary fan, operated by a spring drive belt from the front axle. Bing had produced a very similar toy, on the long narrow base, but the Hornby version was more solid and satisfactory. It was nicely finished in grey, with black lining and a bright red fan. The other new wagons required no new tooling, being a new series of private owners' vans which required only new colours and a new series of transfers – CARR'S BISCUIT, JACOB'S BISCUIT, CRAWFORD'S BISCUIT and SEC-

1924 introductions included the Snowplough, Viaduct, Hydraulic Buffers, Level Crossing, Junction Signal, Signal Box, Footbridge and Tunnel. The Station was updated, with opening doors, and Platform Accessories became available. Clerestory No. 1 Coaches and Guards Vans replaced the early coaches.

COTINE VANS. They replaced the Colman's Mustard Van.

A new straight Brake Rail was catalogued, along with the 1 ft radius Brake Rail and 2 ft radius Brake and Reverse Rails which had previously been sold only in sets.

1925

'Finest fun in the whole world' (June 1925 MM)

'Boys! You don't know what fun you are missing until you have a Hornby Train!' (Boys' Own Paper, October 1925)

'Real Trains are made of steel and painted in their correct colours – so are Hornby Trains. Real trains pull heavy loads over long distances – so do Hornby Trains. You can build a REAL railway system in miniature – complete to the smallest detail – if you like. That's why Hornby Trains are such good fun – they're so real that you don't just play at trains – YOU OWN AND RUN A REAL RAILWAY.' (September 1925 MM)

The most important news for the 1925 season was the introduction of the HORNBY ELECTRIC TRAIN. This was a model of one of the Metropolitan Railway locomotives that had become famous as an exhibit at the Wembley exhibition. Indeed there were few other electric locomotive prototypes which Hornby could have chosen. As it was, the Hornby loco was a respectable model, albeit four-wheeled and not mounted on bogies like the prototype. However, the deep sideframes made this omission reasonably inconspicuous.

Frank Hornby had travelled to the United States very regularly in connection with his American interests – with patent and copyright lawsuits to pursue, and later with the operation of the Elizabeth NJ Meccano factory. It is probable that he carefully inspected the American toy train market on these trips, and the Metropolitan train set shows evidence of an influence from Lionel Trains, instead of the German design influence that had been evident in the clockwork range. The style of the loco, with brass-work surrounds to the windows, brass handrails and knobs, and lamps at each end, certainly shows more

Four new private owners vans replaced the 1923–24 Colman's Mustard Van. Black LNER Locos became available from 1924.

than an echo of Lionel. The new-style electric rails, which were almost certainly designed with a view to this new set, were a straightforward copy of the Lionel sleepers designed for connection by rail connecting plates instead of locking wires. The Hornby electric crossings were also redesigned on a single solid base, almost identical to the Lionel pattern. Having admitted to so much Lionel influence it should be added that the coaches were purely British, being similar in shape to the No. 2 Pullman Cars. They were tinprinted in two styles, to represent a 1st Class coach, and a 3rd Class brake coach; the windows were smaller and more numerous than on the Pullman Cars. The roofs were almost identical to those of the No. 2 Pullmans spoiling the accuracy of the model somewhat since the ends were rounded. Nonetheless, it was Hornby's first attempt at a true-to-life model, and it was a creditable effort; but at the shocking price of 110s.

The shocks, however, were not confined to the price; the locomotive was designed to run on a lethal high voltage system. The rheostat provided in the set reduced the mains voltage through a light bulb and resistances, but still left enough volts lying around to give rather more than a nasty jar. The resistance coils were switched by a lever (economically made from the blank of the No. 2 Loco coupling rod) wiping over contact studs which were fully exposed to finger poking.

Having exhausted themselves with this new electric toy, the design staff must have put their feet up for a while, as there were few other new introductions. The tanker was enamelled as a PRATTS PETROL TANK WAGON, in green livery, representing the Anglo American Oil Company's brand – hence the 'Angloco' tradename incorporated in the transfer. An ELECTRICAL VIADUCT was offered, and also separate CENTRE SECTIONS for both clockwork and electric viaducts. During 1925 the Zulu sets were re-named HORNBY No. O GOODS and PASSENGER TRAIN SETS, removing the last trace of the old trade name. Wagons in the long thin 1924 style were deservedly unpopular, an operational disaster, and in the 1925–26 season new tabbed versions of both the No. 0/1 Tender and the Hornby Wagon were designed to the same proportions as the rest of the range, to replace the unsuc-

Pratt's Petrol Tank Wagons, and the CO2 Crossover Points, were among the few new items in 1925. Note, incidentally, the Cattle Truck lettering used on the Brake Van.

cessful types.

The new CO1 and CO2 CROSSOVER POINTS were of 1 ft and 2 ft radius respectively. Both were available only in left-hand versions, and neither had the same spacing as the double-track Level Crossing or the Parallel Points! Also available for the first time in 1925 were electric 2 ft radius parallel points.

Three new clockwork train sets were offered in 1925 – the No. 1 TANK GOODS SET, with the Tank Loco, Hornby Wagon, 'Shell' Tank Wagon and Brake Van; a No. 2 TANK GOODS SET with the No. 2 Tank Loco, the same three wagons plus a No. 1 Cattle Truck, and a No. 2 TANK PASSEN-GER SET with three clerestory coaches and a Guard's Van. These were the first sets to contain tank engines.

1926

'The most efficient locomotives ever produced.' (November 1926 MM)

'The remarkable development of Hornby Trains represents a feat of model engineering that has not been equalled since the invention of Meccano twenty five years ago. From the day of their introduction, Hornby Trains have always represented the latest model railway practice, and their popularity has grown to such an extent that their name has become a household word. And now another Hornby 'thrill' – the Hornby Control System!' (December 1926 MM)

The January 1926 Meccano Magazine made the usual far from subtle attempts to encourage young lads to

A full range of Great Western Railway Hornby Trains was available for the 1926–27 season; this scene shows a few of them. The Passenger Platform and Island Platform were also new.

spend any left-over Christmas cash on their Hornby railways. The difference was that in addition to the usual LMS and LNER liveries, GWR sets were also listed. By the time the 1926 catalogues and leaflets were printed, the complete range of GWR locos, coaches and wagons was available. The wagons were identical to the LMS types except for the lettering, and the clerestory coaches were of the usual type but tinprinted in GWR chocolate and cream. The locomotives were made in only one colour, the passenger livery of green lined in yellow or gold. As a concession to the real world, although none of the locos was a scale model, the GWR locos were fitted with cast safety-valve covers instead of domes as on the other types. It is hard to believe that it was really worth representing this feature, since it meant producing two versions of each loco housing. No wonder the introduction of GW items had been delayed!

Smallest and cheapest of the 1926 range of locos was the new SERIES M No. 1 LOCOMOTIVE. This was a simple tinprinted loco, with a tiny boiler, and a diminutive mechanism fitted with a fixed key for the benefit of the younger user. This loco was packaged with the new M PULLMAN COACH in the M1 and M2 Passenger Sets, which had 2 and 3 coaches respectively. There was no goods set with this loco, instead the M3 Goods Train set contained the SERIES M No. 3 LOCO-

MOTIVE. This was identical to the loco in the tinprinted 00 Train Set, which was withdrawn from sale in 1926. The tenders with the M1 and M3 Locos were of the narrow pattern no longer used for the '2710' locos; the finishes were tinprinted. The M3 wagons were also in the obsolete long thin style, at a price of 1s 6d, and were very similar to the 1924–25 No. 1 Wagons that had been sold at 2s 6d.

As well as these M-series sets at the bottom of the range, a new locomotive was introduced at the upper end. The RIVIERA 'BLUE TRAIN' SETS were a major innovation. They were sold in No. 1 and No. 2 versions, with electric or clockwork locos respectively. The importance of this train set was that, although it was a model of a French train, produced primarily to develop the French market, it was also saleable in Great Britain as a model of the famous train patronised by wealthy travellers on their way to the South of France. The Hornby Riviera 'Blue Train' also proved to be a firm favourite in the Colonies.

The Loco was based on the famous Pacific locomotives of 'la Compagnie des Chemins de Fer du Nord,' but was spoilt a little by the absence of one pair of driving wheels, being a mere 4–4–2. It was nonetheless larger than any of the previous Hornby locos. The bogie tender was a more satisfactory model than any of the preceding 'coal-cart' types, and the difference in price was not exceptionable.

The 'Blue Train' coaches were built on the same imposing scale as the loco, and were bulkier than previous Hornby No. 2 Pullmans. They were painted in royal blue with cream roofs, and lettered in the style of the 'Compagnie Internationale des Wagons-Lits et Des Grands Express Europeens'. Such coaches could be seen until quite recent years working ferry services into Victoria. There were two coaches in the Hornby set, a sleeping car (with plain windows) and a restaurant car with windows printed with lamps for the tables, and frosted glass in the kitchen section. Both were of the end-vestibule type, and for the first time on Hornby Trains, corridor connections were fitted between the vehicles, and corridor end-plates were supplied to prevent passengers falling out of the ends of the train.

Unfortunately the 'Golden Arrow' versions of the Pullman Car produced for sale in France were never sold in this country, although they would have been popular. The Riviera 'Blue Train' Set was only sold with the brown Nord loco, never with the maroon PLM loco which was offered as an alternative in the sets on sale in France.

The No. 1 Electric Riviera 'Blue Train' was sold with a new type of motor, wound for 4 volt operation from an accumulator, instead of the high voltage motor used for the previous year's Metropolitan set. The High Voltage Metropolitan was actually withdrawn from the UK market for the

1926–27 season, and it appears in none of the season's catalogues or leaflets. The reason for this was a nation-wide scare on the safety of such sets, and the withdrawal is said to have been the result of a Home Office request. But the HV Metropolitan remained available for export customers, since the Home Office had no objection to killing off the children of mere colonials and foreigners!

Since the HV version was no longer sold, the Metropolitan Sets were made available in 1926 with the 4 volt (Low Voltage or LV) No. 2 Metropolitan Locomotive. There was also a clockwork No. 3 Metropolitan which (like the clockwork Riviera 'Blue Train' Loco) had a mechanism of new design, fitted for operation by the new HORNBY CONTROL SYSTEM. This was a means of remotely operating Control System signals and points by a system of wires, from LEVER FRAMES which could be fitted into the Signal Cabin. Locomotives like the clockwork versions of the Riviera 'Blue Train' and the Metropolitan could be remotely reversed, or braked and subsequently re-started, by operating the special CONTROL RAIL from the Lever Frame. The No. 2 Loco and the No. 2 Tank Loco were available either in the normal version or fitted for control; the No. 3 Locomotives were available only fitted for control.

1926 was a year of industrial strife, not least the general strike which took place from the 4th to the 14th of May. Although Frank Hornby was genuinely interested in the happiness and welfare of the lads who used his toys, and of his employees, his company was not insulated from the eternal struggle between capital and labour. It was necessary to make an apology in a March 1927 trade booklet to the effect that 'Unfortunately, last year, we were unable to deliver all the Hornby Control Sets ordered and there was much disappointment in consequence. Unless there is a recurrence of the industrial strikes that made manufacturing so difficult last year, there will be ample supplies this year. . .'

The PASSENGER PLATFORM was a new accessory for lengthening the platform of the Windsor Station. As an alternative to a through station, a terminus could be created by connecting the Passenger Platforms to new connectors provided in the front platform edge of the Windsor Station. A length

of PALED FENCING was supplied, which could be fitted to the Passenger Platform by Meccano nuts and bolts, and extra lengths of fencing could be bought separately. The new ISLAND PLATFORM was the same as the Passenger Platform, but instead of the fencing it had a canopy, supported by two latticed posts and carrying a Windsor nameplate. It was supplied with a pair of PLATFORM RAMPS, which could also be bought separately. They were like the Windsor Station ramps, but without the fencing.

The GOODS PLATFORM was another useful new item. It was fitted with a canopy similar in style to the one used on the Island Platform. One end of the platform was fitted with steps, and with a revolving crane for loading and unloading operations.

Another change that was made during 1926 and 1927 was the gradual replacement of 'LNER' lettering on wagons by more correct 'NE' letters. Requests for this change had been made in the Meccano Magazine's 'In Reply' pages, and the August 1926 MM confirmed that 'Goods rolling stock bearing the initials NE only will be available in the near future.'

1927

'Ask Dad to buy you a Hornby Train for Christmas. Nothing could possibly give you greater pleasure!'
'Realistic in every detail. Make friends with your dealer – he can help you.' (December 1927 MM)

The major introduction in the 1927/28 season was the series of No. 3 PULLMAN TRAIN SETS, with either the 4 volt electric motor or the No. 3 clockwork motor fitted for Hornby Control. The No. 3 Locomotives were named after the most famous engines of the major railway companies – Royal Scot, Flying Scotsman, and Caerphilly Castle. Even the most naive observation would have revealed a small discrepancy in the number of wheels when compared with the prototypes; these were not in any sense scale models, simply the 4–4–2 Riviera 'Blue Train' Loco modified to the extent of leaving off a dome here and there, and adding a few splashers to give somewhere to put the nameplate transfers. They were finished in more or less the correct

liveries. Instead of anglicising the No. 3 Nord Tender, the No. 2 type with appropriate new transfers was substituted.

Both the loco and the coaches required minimal extra effort in design and manufacture, the new No. 3 PULLMAN COACH being based very closely on the Riviera 'Blue Train' coaches. They had recessed end-vestibules and corridor connections as before, but with larger windows similar to those of the No. 2 Pullmans. The finish was chocolate and cream, with 'Pullman' transfers as on the smaller and cheaper No. 2 Pullman Cars, which were still available and included with the No. 2 sets.

Like the Metropolitan and Nord locos, the clockwork No. 3 was only sold fitted for Control. From early 1927 the No. 1 and No. 1 Tank Locos and Sets became available with the choice of Control System or normal working. There were also No. 2 Goods and No. 2 Tank Goods sets fitted for Control. The Control Rail became available in No. 1 and No. 2 versions, and for locos not fitted for Control there was also a new straight BBR1 BRAKE AND REVERSE RAIL, operated by a lever of the type fitted to the pointwork. The usefulness of this rail was increased by the adoption of the 1927-type No. 1 Mechanisms, which for the first time allowed reversing from the track as well as from the cab, for both the normal and the Control versions.

There were further attempts to woo the customers in 1927, with price reductions (for example the price of the No. 2 Tank Loco dropped from 30s to 22s 6d) and with the introduction of new, brighter colour schemes for many wagons and accessories. Examples are that the Cement Wagons came out in red, Crane Trucks and Breakdown Vans and Crane in blue and brown, Trolley Wagons in brown, Cattle Trucks and No. 2 Luggage Vans in blue and grey, Snowploughs in green and grey, Side Tipping wagons in blue, Rotary Tipping Wagons in orange, the Hopper Wagon in green, and the Milk Traffic wagons in blue and green. In the accessories, the fashion colour changed from black to blue for the Signals, Lamp Standards, Telegraph Poles and Loading Gauges, all with blue bases and white posts. Some difficulty had been experienced with the white lettering on wagons and vans, and from 1927 large company letters in gold shadowed red and lined in

LNER wagon lettering was altered to NE only during 1926 and 1927. These wagons from 1926 are shown with the newly-introduced Goods Platform.

LNER No. 2 and No. 2 Tank Locos in 1927 styles. The BP and Nord wagons were first catalogued in 1927.

In 1927 the nut-and-bolt constructional vans were replaced by non-constructional versions. These GW items are from the 1927–28 period. (From the middle of 1927 GW locos were fitted with brass safety valve covers).

black replaced the large white letters previously used on the open Wagons, Brake Vans, Luggage Vans, No. 2 Cattle Trucks, and the Gunpowder Van.

The HV Metropolitan was back in the 1927 catalogues, the scare on its safety having abated somewhat. The Ferranti TRANSFORMER became available for LV trains. A new BP PETROL TANK WAGON was to be another popular introduction, together with two wagons for use with the Nord locomotive – the FRENCH-TYPE WAGON and FRENCH-TYPE BRAKE VAN. A new PLAT-FORM ACCESSORIES set, No. 4, was simply a combination of the contents of sets 1, 2, and 3. A start was made on a series of simplified accessories at budget prices, the first of which was the WAYSIDE STATION, which was similar to the Windsor Station but lacked the ramps, fences, chimneys and opening doors. There was also a SMALL TURN-TABLE, which could just accommodate an M-series loco and tender, or a No. 1 Tank engine!

In 1927 the Meccano factory in the USA produced an interesting series of 'Hornby Lines' train sets, but they were not marketed in the UK.

1928

'You can't help being thrilled when you see a Hornby loco dashing along the track.' (January 1928 MM)

'Every hour spent playing with a Hornby Railway is brimful of thrills and enjoyment.' (Hornby Train Catalogue, 1928)

Apart from the early and short-lived LBSC wagon, Hornby had been content so far to ignore the needs of purchasers in the bottom right hand corner of the country. The 'In Reply' pages of the MM had admitted in 1926 that 'There appears to be a growing demand for SR finishes', and asked to hear from all readers who were in favour of their introduction; the

response to these replies and other requests was such that the April 1928 MM stated that 'It has been definitely decided to introduce Southern Railway colours into the series.' These SR finishes were soon put in hand, and the 1928 catalogues and leaflets advertised the full range of SR sets, locos, carriages and wagons.

The Southern Railway locomotives were available in two colours – green with white lining for passenger trains, and black lined in green for goods trains. The Southern Railway No. 3 Loco was named 'Lord Nelson', and the No. 3 Train Set was advertised as the 'Dover Pullman' at first, although the October 1928 MM announced a change of name to 'Continental Express'. It was to be changed yet

again in 1931 to 'Golden Arrow'! The Hornby SR loco liveries were quite reasonable representations of SR practice at the time, in that for instance the loco numbers were on the tenders, not the cabside. The smokeboxes were black, and the domes were green or black instead of shiny brass, in line with the standard styles recently adopted for all Hornby locos.

Before the introduction of the SR wagons, the goods rolling stock had been finished in the same colours for all three companies (with the exception of the Brake Van). But presumably in an effort to be true to life, the new SR wagons were made more interesting by the choice of different colours, predominantly brown. A dark chocolate brown was used for the open Wagon, Trolley Wagon, Cattle Trucks, Luggage Vans, and for the base of the Breakdown Van and Crane which had a lighter brown body. The Lumber and Timber wagons were usually in the lighter brown, as was the Brake Van. The Refrigerator Van came out in an extraordinary shade of pink, with gold SR letters. The SR Gas Cylinder wagon was green instead of red, and the SR Hopper Wagon red instead of green! The Milk Traffic Wagon was green with a black base, but the remaining wagons – Snowplough, Cement Wagon, Crane Truck and Gunpowder Van, were all in the same colours as for the other groups.

Another new exception to the normal colour rules was the GW Gunpowder Van, which became grey (with a red cross on the door) instead of the usual red of the LMS, LNER and SR.

Apart from these new Southern wagons, there was also a REDLINE PETROL TANK WAGON, finished in dark blue with an appropriate red-lined transfer, and also a double barrel WINE WAGON for French-type trains.

The most significant change in the rolling stock was the improvement of the No. 3 Pullman Coaches introduced the previous year. The revised No. 2–3 PULLMAN COACH and COMPOSITE (which were later to be called the No. 2 Special Pullman Coaches) were of considerably improved appearance, and at remarkably low prices compared with the old types. According to the 1928 Hornby Book of Trains they were 'the most realistic gauge 'O' Pullman cars that have ever appeared on the market at anything like the price'. The names of the coaches were 'Iolanthe' and 'Arcadia'. The SR versions of the four-wheeled No. 1 Coach and Guard's Van were issued in 1928, and like all the 1928 series No. 1 Coaches they had rounded roofs without the raised clerestory. Also new in 1928 were the No. 1 PULLMAN COACH and COMPOSITE which were of completely new design. The Coaches were named Cynthia, Corsair and Niobe, and the Composite was named Ansonia.

The range of accessories was increased both at the bottom end of the price scale, and at the top. The new No. 1 and No. 2 ENGINE SHEDS were amongst the finest pieces of tinplate craftsmanship ever to have been designed at Binns Road, with their

GW Locos in 1928.

Signal Gantries and Double Track Rails were introduced in 1928, as were the improved No. 2–3 Pullmans, the Wine Wagon and the Redline Petrol Tank Wagon. Most 1928 locos had black smokeboxes, and domes were of the same colour as the boiler.

large size and attention to such details as the guttering and ventilation. They showed a sophistication utterly lacking in the Windsor Station. Even this effort was surpassed, however, by the magnificent SIGNAL GANTRY. This was designed to straddle a double track, and was fitted with an imposing set of four signal posts, bearing a somewhat unlikely arrangement of arms, these being operated by an impressive array of levers, bellcranks and wires. Unhappily no control system version was ever produced. The platform, accessed by a serviceable ladder, was surrounded by a well-modelled handrail. The amount of work that went into the design and manufacture of the gantry was also impressive, and perhaps inappropriate for this class of toy. It shows all the best characteristics of the new models of 1928 and 1929; an attention to detail, and an apparent disregard of effort and expense in manufacture. Also new for the 1928–29 season was a No. 2 DOUBLE ARM SIGNAL. The Goods Platform was improved in 1928 by fitting a tinprinted building which had sliding doors. The revised crane was fitted with a worm-gear drive for the rotary movement, and the same revised crane (fitted to a simple base) was also catalogued as the PLATFORM CRANE.

These new accessories were appropriate for the aim of making the Hornby range as complete and accurate as possible. But it was also necessary to cater for the more juvenile (or less affluent) customers, and the range of budget price accessories was increased by the introduction of a simplified No. 1 SIGNAL CABIN, which lacked the hinged roof, open windows and steps of the No. 2 type. There were also pairs of No. 1 SIGNALS, HOME and DISTANT which did not have the ladder, transparent spectacle glasses, dummy lamp or finial of the No. 2. There was also a No. 1 DOUBLE ARM SIGNAL, and a new No. 1 LEVEL CROSSING, for single track and equivalent in length to a straight half rail.

The No. 2 Level Crossing was also substantially re-designed for the 1928–29 season, to fit the new DOUBLE TRACK CURVED and STRAIGHT RAILS. These were the answer for those who wanted to make tidy-looking up-lines and down-lines, which had previously been difficult to arrange with the existing curved rails. The spacing of the track

was based on that of the 2 ft radius parallel points introduced some years earlier. There were also new right-hand and left-hand CROSSOVER POINTS COR2 and COL2, in the new double track spacing, which replaced the 1 ft and 2 ft radius versions that had been available only in left-hand versions. Also new were the most elaborate (and, of course, the most expensive) clockwork points; the POINTS ON SOLID BASE, with ground disc & lamp. Although fitted for Hornby Control, these also had levers for manual operation.

For those kids who had only a few coppers to spare, there was still a new temptation in the form of the SHUNTER'S POLE at 4d, or for 6d the No. 1 OIL CAN or a bottle of MECCANO LUBRICATING OIL. The wealthy could probably afford 2s 6d (the price of a new wagon!) for a No. 2 'K' TYPE OIL CAN. The MANSELL WHEELS used for the

No. 2–3 Pullmans could be bought for 4d a pair. There were also TARPAULINS lettered for each of the four railway companies. Still in the lower price bracket, the new RAILWAY ACCESSORIES No. 7, the Watchman's Hut complete with Brazier, Shovel and Poker, was to become a firm favourite. RAILWAY ACCESSORIES No. 5 was a very useful set of Gradient Posts and Mile Posts, at 2s, but the RAILWAY ACCESSORIES No. 6 at 4s, a set of notice boards and station name boards (with names chosen from major stations on the LNER East Coast main line) was to prove rather less than a best-seller, before it was split the next year into separate sets Nos. 8 and 9.

The contents of some boxed sets were revised in 1928, giving more sensible trains. Brake Vans were added to the Nos. 1 and 2 Goods Sets (but not to the No. 0 Goods, which was given two open wagons

Simple accessories added to the range in 1928 included the No. 1 Signals, Watchman's Hut, No. 1 Level Crossing, No. 1 Signal Box and Platform Crane. Shunter's Poles, Notice Boards, Station Name Boards and Gradient/Mile Posts were also listed.

34   *LMS locomotives of the 1929–30 season. Front to back, left to right, they are No. 3E, No. 1 Electric Tank, No. 1 Special Tank, No. 3C, No. 2 Special, No. 1, No. 0, No. 1 Special, No. 1 Tank and No. 2 Special Tank. The Engine Sheds No. 1 and No. 2 were introduced the previous year.*

instead of only one). A Guard's Van was added to the two coaches in the No. 1 Passenger Set, and the No. 0 Passenger Set now had a Coach and a Guard's Van instead of two Coaches. The No. 2 Tank Passenger Set was given one of each of the four new No. 1 Pullmans, instead of the clerestory No. 1 Coaches. These improvements were made without any increase in price; in fact certain prices were reduced.

1928 also saw the launch of the HORNBY RAILWAY COMPANY, a 'world-wide organisation formed for the sole purpose of enabling all Hornby railway owners to obtain 100% fun,' by showing them how to plan and to run their railway on real railway-like principles, and to obtain 'the utmost possible fun and enjoyment'.

1929

'The year 1929 will be an outstanding year in the history of Hornby Trains, for it marks the introduction of a range of new locomotives that are the last word in efficiency and realism.' (November 1929 MM)

'The big railways have been making improvements and additions – so also has the Hornby Railway. Boys, it's your turn now! Bring your Hornby Railway up to date. This year Hornby Trains are better than ever.' (December 1929 MM)

1928 had been an exceptionally good year with availability of new accessories and of SR trains; 1929 was to be still more memorable for the new range of improved locomotives.

Most important of these was the series of No. 2 SPECIAL LOCOMOTIVES, four true-to-life models of 4–4–0 tender locomotives run by the major railway groups. They were a Midland Compound, an LNER D49 loco 'Yorkshire', the Great Western 'County of Bedford', and an SR L1 class loco. They were designed to replace the '2711' Locomotives, but were a very much more ambitious undertaking. The expense of manufacturing them, with the massive amount of new tooling required for both locos and tenders, was far greater than anything that the company had undertaken in the past; indeed it may not even have been fully appreciated before

the project was started late in 1928. The locomotives were fitted with mechanisms that were bulkier and more powerful than any of the previous types, and they were fitted with large twenty-spoke driving wheels. The initial price of 22s 6d for the loco, compared with 20s for the old 2711 type, was amazingly low. The No. 2 SPECIAL PULLMAN TRAIN SETS included the No. 2 Special Loco, Tender and the No. 2–3 Pullman Coach and Composite.

There were also new No. 1 SPECIAL and No. 1 SPECIAL TANK LOCOMOTIVES, which were substantially bigger and more detailed than the old types. They had much larger radius boilers, and lower-profile cabs, chimneys and domes; the boiler backs were embossed with details of firebox doors etc. Outside cylinders were fitted, with steam pipes above the footplate leading to the smokebox; there were more realistic coupling rods, and fluted piston rods. Also, for the first time, the tank engine was

fitted with a plate dividing the bunker and the cab. Like the No. 2 Special Locos they featured lamp irons with detachable headlamps, to give correct headcodes for the class of train. Although the design drawings had been labelled 'No. 1 Locomotive, 1929 type', as the No. 2 Special locos had been headed 'No. 2 Loco, 1929 type', in the event they did not replace the existing No. 1 types – probably because of the very much higher production costs. Instead, they were sold as the No. 1 Special and the No. 1 Special Tank Locos. The prices were higher than for the No. 1 types, for example 16s 6d for the No. 1 Special Tank instead of 12s 6d for the No. 1 Tank.

The No. 0 and No. 1 tender engines were also revised in 1929 by replacing the ridiculous short splasher above the rear driving wheel by a longer splasher above both drivers. The mechanism was also improved to give a longer run.

A No. 1 ELECTRIC TANK LOCOMOTIVE

SR No. 1 Special and No. 1 Special Tank Locos double-heading a Pullman train.

was produced, fitted with a permanent magnet motor designed for operation on a direct current supply of 6 volts. The only modifications required to the locomotive body were cutouts to take the brush-holders, which protruded from the tank side. The advantage of the permanent magnet motor was that it allowed remote control of the locomotive by the two-lever SPEED and REVERSE CONTROL SWITCH, whereas the existing universal motors could only be reversed by a lever in the cab. The drawbacks were an undeniable lack of power, despite a hefty current consumption, and regrettably a very high price of 32s 6d, compared with 12s 6d for the clockwork type. However the price did include a Terminal Connecting Plate, the two-lever Speed and Reverse Switch and 3 ft of flex. The loco could only

be driven from an accumulator, not from the mains supply.

The 4–4–4 No. 2 Tank Loco disappeared in 1929, to be replaced by the 4–4–2 No. 2 SPECIAL TANK LOCOMOTIVE at the same price of 22s 6d. Unlike the other 'Special' locomotives, however, there was really nothing very special about this loco. It was based on the No. 3 frame, boiler and firebox, and given a cab stolen from the 4–4–4, still spoiled by the lack of a partition for the bunker. The early versions did not even have the 'Special' lamp brackets and detachable lamps, but had fixed lamps as fitted to the other early engines. But the powerful and efficient No. 2 Special motor and wheels were fitted, with coupling rods only since there were no cylinders. The bogie and pony truck were identical to the

No. 3 type.

The same No. 2 Special mechanism with large diameter driving wheels was also fitted from 1929 to the clockwork No. 3 locomotives (although the electric locos continued to have the smaller diameter wheels for some years). This change was possible because in 1929 the failure of the Hornby Control System as originally envisaged was tacitly admitted, by the withdrawal of all Control System loco-motives, sets and Control Rails. This meant that the Control System could no longer be used for the remote control of locomotives from the Lever Frame, but the other components of the system continued to be advertised as a means of remotely controlling Signals and Points from the Signal Cabin. Thus none of the 'Special' locos were ever

A GW No. 2 Special Tank pulls out of Windsor Station with the latest No. 2–3 Pullman Coaches. In the background are the No. 0, No. 1 Special, No. 1 and No. 1 Special Tank Locos of the same period, and a (transitional) earlier No. 0 loco.

SR electric locos of 1929–30. No. 3E (6 volt) and No. 1 Electric Tank Locos.

An LMS No. 1 Special Loco, with United Daries Tank Wagon and Robert Hudson Side Tipping Wagon, each first catalogued in 1929.

LNER locos of 1929–30. The Level Crossing had, by 1929, been altered to the standard double track spacing.

available fitted for Hornby Control.

The clockwork locos were not the only ones to receive attention. As well as the No. 1 Electric Tank engine already mentioned, all the 1929 electric locos, the No. 3 Trains and the LV Metropolitan, were wound for 6 volt operation instead of 4 volt as before. A new style of low voltage mechanism was produced, with brush-holders similar to those used for the No. 1 Electric Tank Loco. Changes in the loco housings to clear the brush caps became necessary. The new type of brush-holder made changing worn brushes an easier job than it had been with the earlier motors, and also gave more reliable contact. Associated with the change to 6 volt working was the change from 4 volt to 6 volt Meccano Accumulators. The HV Metropolitan did not appear in the 1929 catalogues, and it re-appeared after this only as obsolete stock.

All this work on locomotives seems to have been at the expense of the rest of the Hornby range, but there were a few important wagon introductions. The MILK TANK WAGON based on the United Dairies prototypes, and the BITUMEN TANK WAGON 'COLAS', were new wagons of the highest standard seen from the Binns Road works. The other important new wagons were a FRENCH-TYPE COVERED WAGON and a SINGLE WINE WAGON, which continued the series of new products in the late 1920s aimed mainly at the French market, but also sold in the UK. There was also a new ROBERT HUDSON SIDE TIPPING WAGON, offered as an alternative to the McAlpine version until stocks of the latter were sold out. Both were finished in blue, and they were identical except for the different transfers.

There were some more changes in the contents of Hornby train sets. An MO Passenger Train Set was introduced, containing the M locomotive and a single M Pullman Coach. The M3 Goods Train Set was withdrawn, and an M Goods Train Set with the M1 Loco and a pair of M Wagons replaced it. Other new sets included the No. 1 SPECIAL GOODS SETS, with the No. 1 Special Tender Engine, an open wagon and a Brake Van; also the No. 1 SPECIAL PASSENGER SET with the No. 1 Special Loco, two No. 1 Pullmans and a Composite. The No. 2 Special Tank Loco was sold in two goods sets,

one the No. 2 MIXED GOODS TRAIN SET with Open Wagon, Cattle Truck, Shell Petrol Tank Wagon and a Brake Van and the other (sold for one season only) the No. 2 SPECIAL GOODS SET with two open wagons and a Brake Van.

The No. 0 Goods Set was changed again to include the new No. 0 HORNBY WAGON and a Timber Wagon, instead of two opens. The No. 0 Wagon introduced in 1929 differed from the No. 1 in having tinprinted sides; the No. 1 Wagon continued to be enamelled. The No. 0 Passenger Set was given a pair of M Pullman Coaches instead of the No. 1 Coaches. These changes made the No. 0 sets considerably cheaper than the No. 1 sets.

Now that the range of electric locos was being enlarged, ELECTRIC DOUBLE TRACK STRAIGHT and CURVED RAILS were catalogued; but electric crossover points were not yet available.

The range of Hornby accessories was virtually unchanged in 1929, except for the splitting of the Railway Accessories No. 6 into sets Nos. 8 and 9. The height of the No. 1 and No. 2 Buffers was changed to suit the lower buffer height of the Special series of engines. Their colour was also changed from green to blue. Other colour changes began to occur, such as the progressive adoption of a yellow-cream for the platforms of the Station, Goods Depot, Island and Passenger Platforms, and the base of the Platform Crane.

1930

'Right away for Happy Days!' (April 1930 leaflet)

'Only the finest materials obtainable are used. . .' (March 1930 MM)

'The magnificent new models of LNER, LMSR, GWR and SR Locomotives are fitted with double-power mechanisms for longer runs and bigger freights . . . the thrill and fascination of a Hornby Railway are real and lasting because a Hornby Railway is A REAL RAILWAY IN MINIATURE.' (April 1930 MM)

The export market in Canada was the next to get serious attention from Meccano Ltd, with the production in 1930 of a No. 3 electric train set in

Canadian Pacific livery. The set was illustrated in the 1930 Canadian editions of the Meccano instruction manual. The loco was identical to the Nord loco, but with the addition of a cow-catcher and a headlamp at the front, and a bell fitted to the firebox. The tender was lettered 'Canadian Pacific', and the cabside number was 2800. No clockwork version was mentioned. The coaches were of the No. 2 Special type, in maroon with black roofs, and with impressive 'Canadian Pacific' lettering above the windows.

The biggest surprise with this 1930 train set was that it was available not for 6 volt operation as in the UK, nor for 4 volt operation as the French Hornby trains had remained, but for 15 volt working. There was a transformer in the set to supply 1 amp at 15 volts, for operation from the electric light main. A few production drawings for this short-lived experiment in medium voltage motors survive in the archives – for example the 15 volt Motor Brush drawn in August 1930. This interesting Canadian set shows that the shortcomings of the 6 volt system were already apparent, and that other options were being pursued – even if not destined for the UK as yet. The MM for July 1926 had said that Meccano Ltd were 'unable for the present to introduce rolling stock and accessories modelled on the Canadian railways,' and even in 1930 no effort was made to sell the set in Great Britain.

The other trains offered in the 1930 Canadian Meccano manuals are of equal interest, since they were the train sets produced in the former Meccano factory in the US, that had been sold out to A. C. Gilbert in 1928. This explains what happened to the remaining stocks of US produced Hornby Trains, but since the August 1929 MM had firmly stated that 'At present we have no intention of manufacturing an American train set, as we do not consider it would be popular enough to justify its cost,' it was perhaps inevitable that the American-type Pullman Cars and freight cars were catalogued in the UK in 1930! Although a very limited number of these vehicles may have been imported from the USA in a finished state, the majority were assembled in the UK. The AMERICAN TYPE PULLMAN CARS were offered with two names, Madison or Washington, each in either yellow or green livery with a grey roof. The wagons were the BOX CAR, CABOOSE and

In 1930 a revised standard wagon base was adopted. An LNER No. 1 Special Tank marshals Petrol Tank Wagons of the period, while a No. 1 Tank Loco passes with a train of Saloon Coaches, introduced in 1930. The Platelayer's Hut was also new.

TANK CAR. All were of the same pattern that had been previously made and sold in the USA.

None of the American-type locos were disposed of in the UK, having been reserved for Canada; but the new M1 LOCOMOTIVES made in England in 1930 show a distinct similarity in style to the US loco. They were based on a simple one-piece body pressing of boiler and cab on a narrow frame, which made them very suitable for use with the American-type rolling stock. In fact, they look suitable for little else in the Hornby range! The M1 loco had a new-style mechanism with patented features that gave it a very long run for its size, and very good pulling power. The M1 Tender was the same as the previous M type, but tinprinted in green or red to match the new locos. The M1 was sold in the M1 GOODS SET with a pair of M1 open Wagons, and in the M1 and M2 PASSENGER SET with 2 or 3 M1/2 Pull-man Coaches respectively.

The M0 LOCOMOTIVE was an even smaller and simpler engine, again built in the style of the American loco. The mechanism was smaller than that used for the M1, and was non reversing – the motor design was similar to that of the old style M Locomotive (which remained in the catalogues, now as the M2930 LOCOMOTIVE AND TENDER). Unlike the new M1 Loco, the M0 had no cylinders or rods. The winding key was fixed to the shaft. Because of the short wheelbase, the M0 Loco could run on 9″ radius rails, and special M0 RAILS of this radius were introduced in 1930, including curves, straights, brake rails and points. These rails used special small sleepers for economy, and could not be clipped to the normal Hornby rails.

The M0 rolling stock consisted of M0 PULL-MAN COACHES Joan and Zena in the M0 Passen-ger Set, or two M0 WAGONS in the M0 Goods Set. The couplings on these M0 vehicles were part of the base pressing, and could only be used with other M0 rolling stock. Unfortunately they were very prone to breakage, both the hook and the loop having weak spots. Suprisingly these faults were never corrected, despite the fact that these trains were intended for the younger user. The prices however were remarkably low, with sets starting at only 5s. Wagons were 7d, and the Coaches 10d.

These new M series trains were accompanied by a series of M accessories, the M STATION SET comprising M Signal Box, two M Signals, M Station, M Wayside Station, and two M Telegraph Poles. These models were all very simple pressings from tinprinted material. For economy, the build-ings had no backs! Nonetheless the M Signals and M Telegraph poles were in a more suitable scale for use with the ordinary Hornby Trains than the standard products, and MM publicity photographs often used the M Series types when creating their evocative studio photographs.

The range of electric railway items was extended in 1930 by the addition of the No. 2 ELECTRIC TANK LOCO, the 4–4–2 tank loco body provided with the 6 volt motor of the No. 3 types. Extra electrical accessories included a No. 2E TURN-TABLE, a No. 2 ELECTRICAL LEVEL CROSS-ING, and interestingly a new series of CENTRE RAIL CONVERSION ACCESSORIES. From 1930 to 1935 the clockwork rail sleepers were slotted to enable centre rails to be clipped on at a later date by customers changing from a clockwork to an electric railway. Only the straight and curved rails could be converted, not the points or crossings. Another new electrical item was the 2 volt 20 amp Accumulator, to enable those who already had suitable 4 volt accumulators to run 6 volt trains.

Other new accessories in 1930 included the TUNNEL ENDS, similar to the tinprinted ends of the metal Tunnel, but pressed differently to allow tunnel framework to be made from Meccano. There was a new No. 1A FOOTBRIDGE, which was like the No. 1 Footbridge but supplied with detachable tinprinted signals in the M series style. A very popular introduction was the PLATELAYER'S HUT, a nicely modelled lineside building, with a spring-loaded opening door, and a chimney stack complete with pot, at a very reasonable 2s 6d. The COMBINED RAIL GAUGE, SCREWDRIVER and SPANNER was catalogued at 3d – an essential item for the electric train operator, and included with most train sets and locos. Another oddment announced in 1930 was the MECCANO RAIL ADAPTOR for joining Hornby rails to Meccano strips.

Rolling Stock changes in 1930, apart from the introduction of the US rolling stock, included the introduction of a CASTROL OIL TANK WAGON. The Pratt's 'Angloco' tanker was repla-ced by a different brand, PRATT'S 'HIGH TEST', and the colour of the wagon changed from green to orange. The creation of the Special series of loco-motives, and the introduction of Southern Railway Hornby items had expanded the range that Meccano Ltd had to keep in stock, despite the withdrawal of the Control System locos and sets. The desirability of cutting down the number of different items that had to be catalogued led to a decision in 1930 to remove company lettering from a number of wagons that had previously carried it; the Cement Wagon, Lumber and Timber Wagons, Snow-plough, Milk Traffic Van, Crane Truck, Gas Cylinder Wagon, and Trolley Wagon. Confusion was caused by the continued production for a while of one or two of these items in SR colours, but without the SR lettering; the unlettered brown No. 1 Lumber Wagon is a good example. In other cases the existing lettering was overpainted, as on one SR-lettered No. 1 Timber Wagon that was given a coat of green over the old finish, and left unlettered.

Further confusion was caused later in the same year by the revision of virtually the entire series of goods rolling stock to the buffer height of the Special locomotives, one inch in height from the rail run-ning surface. If the decision to remove company letters from certain wagons had not already been taken, lack of space on the revised base would have forced the change at least on the Crane Truck, No. 1 Timber, No. 1 Lumber, and Milk Traffic Wagons. 'Tommy Dodd' described the new base in the October 1930 MM: 'A change that cannot fail to meet with the approval of all miniature railway owners is to be made to many wagons in the range. This will be found in the provision of a new design of base. In this the buffer height is lowered to match

There were some odd liveries in 1930 for No. 0, No. 1 and No. 1 Tank locos, as transfers for the old-style housings ran out. This GW loco has no splasher lining. Some SR wagons appeared in the SR colours, but without any SR lettering.

that made standard in the "Special" series of loco-motives, axleguards of realistic design are provided having embossed springs and a tie-bar connecting the lower end of the axleguards. This latter feature is often seen on present day wagons. Between the solebar and the tie-bar a dummy brake V-hanger is found, while provision is also made for the addition of axleboxes should these be desired by the owner. These are available separately at a cost of 6d per dozen and may be obtained through any Hornby Train dealer.' The upper part of the new base formed the base platform of the vehicle and was shaped at the ends to form the buffer beams, and the lower part formed the axleguards. The axleboxes were the same type used on the No. 2 Special Tenders and Pullman Coaches, and could only be obtained by special

order.

Reality finally struck home in 1930, when it was concluded that labour-intensive products like the No. 2–3 Pullman Coach and Composite could not be made and sold profitably at only 11s 6d. The name was changed to the No. 2 SPECIAL PULLMAN, and the prices were accordingly raised to 15s for the Coach and 16s for the Composite. To soften the blow, a No. 2 PULLMAN COACH was intro-duced which was identical except in detail to the No. 3 Pullman of 1927. The lower price of 11s 6d was possible because they were simpler to build than the No. 2 Special Pullmans. The Special loco-motives, which had been similarly underpriced (especially the No. 2 Special), were also priced at more realistic levels in 1930.

The No. 2 Pullman Coach body was also used for the SALOON COACH, available finished in LMS and LNER liveries. Bogie coaches in the col-ours of the four groups had been one of the major unfilled gaps in the Hornby Series. Even when the Metropolitan coaches were introduced in 1925, apparently no thought was given to producing any other versions, whether by enamelling or tinprint-ing, despite the fact that the extra manufacturing costs would have been minimal. All the more strange that even this belatedly introduced Saloon Coach was not made available in SR or GW colours! Pullman Coaches were, after all, only a minor ele-ment in the stock of most railway companies.

1930 also saw the start of the PART EXCHANGE SCHEME, under which you could

41

In 1930 the GW No. 1 Special Tank loco was numbered 5500. The Brake Vans (each different) are from the 1930–31 season. The No. 1 Tank Loco is unusual in having LMS-type lining! The No. 2 Luggage Van has lowered bogies to match the 4-wheel stock.

return your old loco through a Meccano dealer, and get an allowance of half its original cost against a brand new engine. Even some of the obsolete types were accepted for exchange, at somewhat lower rates.

1931

'"Switch her, Dad!" Dad will be prepared for all kinds of commands when he has given you a Hornby Train. . .' (August 1931 MM)

'Still better Hornby Trains this year! New locomotives with stronger mechanisms that give longer runs . . . every item exhaustively tested – every part one hundred per cent efficient. Always the leaders, always the best, Hornby Trains are better than ever now. They are supreme!' (September 1931 MM)

One of the most interesting happenings at Binns Road during 1931 was the designing (for the French

market only) of a new electric FRENCH-TYPE LOCOMOTIVE, based on those serving the Paris–Orleans lines. Although not a scale model, it was at least representative of the style of the actual locos, even if it did suffer from the usual shortage of wheels, having only four driving wheels. But the wheel arrangement was nearly hidden by outside framing with embossed detail of springs, and the sides of the loco were embossed with windows, louvred panels, and (unusually for a Hornby loco) rivet detail. The roof was fitted with two pantographs that could be raised or lowered – but for show only, since the loco was for normal centre-rail operation. The interesting point about the motor was that it was the first type to be wound for 20 volt operation, a system which was not adopted until a year later in the UK. There is much evidence in the design drawings that this loco was designed in Great Britain, although the manufacture may have been shared with the Paris works. A clockwork version was also planned.

Also in 1931, a range of new wagons was offered in the UK – a BARREL WAGON (advertised as a European-type wagon), a COAL WAGON with imitation coal load, a FIBRE WAGON, a FYFFES BANANA VAN, and an OPEN WAGON B. All these types had been on sale in France the previous year, although with some differences of finish, and in France they had all been issued on the open-axleguard base. Clearly the French market continued to be the dominant driving force behind the introduction of new wagon types; in the late 1920s half the new wagons issued in the UK had been French-types. The 1931 French-type Loco appears to have been the last occasion on which the initiative for new French-market designs came from Binns Road; from then on the French works became sturdily independent, capable of designing and making their own products from start to finish. During the 1930s the quantity of goods made in the UK for sale in France fell, as the French manufactured more products for themselves.

The locomotives that had been designed in 1929 to replace the No. 1 Locos had, in the event, been sold as No. 1 Special Locos. The old style No. 1 Loco and No. 1 Tank Loco clearly still had to be replaced with more modern-looking engines, but at a more modest manufacturing cost than the Specials. As a result new No. 1 LOCOMOTIVE and No. 1 TANK LOCOMOTIVE designs were produced for the 1931 season. The designs chosen were shorter, simpler and generally on a smaller scale than the No. 1 Specials. Certain parts, such as the cylinders, were common between the No. 1 and the No. 1 Special Locos. Lamp irons for detachable lamps were provided, but the No. 1 Locos did not have the cast safety valves, steam pipes, steps or (on the tank loco) the bunker back. The mechanism was a further improvement on the previous 1929 type, giving 'longer runs with heavier loads'. This was the last major re-design of the No. 1 motor, which was used for another thirty years with little alteration.

There was also a new No. 0 mechanism, made with cheaper pressed metal frames, but fitted with reversing gear not available on the old-style No. 0 Locos. The reverse could only be operated from the cab, as the motor was not fitted for reversing from the track. This new mechanism was another successful design, and was long-running, although not as powerful as the No. 1 type. Again it was little modified over the next three decades.

The new No. 0 LOCOMOTIVE that used this motor was a cheap version of the revised No. 1 type. Different cabside numbers were used for the No. 0 Locos, and cylinders were not fitted to the new No. 0 (although the wheels were coupled). The handrail knobs were still castings, instead of turned brass as on the No. 1, and there were no handles on the smokebox door. Lamp irons were fitted, however, and a front coupling was provided now that the No. 0 was capable of reversing.

The tank engine equivalent, the M3 TANK LOCOMOTIVE, was an anomaly in many ways. Although nominally in the M series, it was available in four alternative tinprinted finishes, passenger liveries for the LMS, LNER, GW and SR. The GW loco was fitted with the appropriate cast safety valve, and like the No. 0 and No. 1 Locos was usually fitted with a taller chimney than the other types. Compared with the No. 1 Tank Loco body on which it was closely based, there were minor differences: there were no cylinders, no smokebox door handles, and no knobs on the handrail wires, and the wheels were not coupled. But the quality of the loco was head and shoulders above that of the rest of the M series, and the M3 Loco looks much more at home with the normal Hornby rolling stock than with the M series. The price of 7s 6d, not much more than half the 13s 6d charged for the No. 1 Tank Loco, made it a very attractive buy, and indeed it became very popular. It was available either separately or in the M3 GOODS TRAIN SET, which was also budget priced at 15s against 25s for the No. 1 equivalent. The three wagons supplied were an M3 Wagon, an M3 Timber Wagon and an M3 Petrol Tank Wagon. The M3 Wagon was a special version of the M1/2 open wagon, with a crimped section along the length of each solebar to reduce the coupling height; not the buffer height, as no buffers were fitted to the M3 wagons, in the interests of economy! Unlike normal Hornby practice none of these M3 wagons could be bought separately.

The reason for the adoption of the lower coupling height was that this set, and all the other new locos and wagons, were being fitted with Frank Hornby's patent AUTOMATIC COUPLINGS. These devices operated by a hook and a wire that

Revised No. 0 and No. 1 Locos were made from 1931 onwards. There were also 9 new types of goods wagon.

were supposed to couple on impact when the vehicles were shunted together. They were adopted for all new production, except the M0, M1 and Metropolitan trains. The front couplings of the locomotives remained as the drop-link type, probably because the automatic couplings were so large and ugly. This led to interesting consequences when propelling the Snowplough, which for no logical reason was fitted with the automatic couplings!

The crimped base used for the M3 open wagon was also used for the No. 1 Coaches and Guard's Van, and for the Barrel Wagon. Certain wagons which still appeared on the old 1922-type open axleguard base (notably French-types such as the Wine Wagons) were fitted with a special stepped or cranked version of the automatic coupling which reduced the coupling height while the buffer height was unchanged.

The No. 0 PULLMAN COACH was a new version of the M1/2 Pullman Coach fitted with automatic couplings, and costing 3d extra. There were also new coaches for continental trains, the German-style MITROPA COACHES No. 0 and No. 3. The No. 0 Mitropa Coaches were based on the American-type Pullman Car, and the No. 3 on the Riviera 'Blue Train' Coaches. Each was produced in Dining Car (Speisewagen) and Sleeping Car (Schlafwagen) versions. Both were enamelled in red, with gold transfers, and the No. 3 had the eagle crest of the Mitropa company.

Other new rolling stock for the 1931 season included a MOBILOIL OIL TANK WAGON, finished in grey, and the first three of a series of vans for perishables traffic: the GW No. 0 MILK TRAFFIC VAN, the NE FISH VAN and the LMS MEAT VAN. These were tinprinted with a reasonable degree of realistic detail, and were fitted with sliding doors. The price at 2s 6d was 6d less than the enamelled No. 1 series vans.

There were also new accessories for the M Series enthusiast: an M LOADING GAUGE and an M LEVEL CROSSING (complete with an M Straight Half Rail, not sold separately), and the M2 TELEGRAPH POLE, which was a taller version of the M1 type.

The new MODELLED MINIATURES No. 1, STATION STAFF were an interesting and significant new product, the first of the range that became known as Dinky Toys. Another die-cast product was the STATION or FIELD HOARDING; to this were attached posters from a magnificent series of gummed colour-printed contemporary advertisements, which could also be bought separately as a set of 51 POSTERS IN MINIATURE. These posters could also be used on the new POSTER BOARDS, designed to clip onto the paled fencing; but most people seem to have preferred to stick them at random on every available flat surface!

The Hornby Control System's fortunes had declined since the locomotives and sets were withdrawn in 1929, but 1931 saw a revival of interest from Meccano Ltd, with the introduction of the first new items for a while, including the RODDING TRAVERSE. This allowed control of accessories on either side of the track by a single Lever Frame. There were also 2-LEVER FRAMES and 4-LEVER FRAMES, which were identical to the six lever frame except for having fewer levers fitted. Extra LEVER ASSEMBLIES were offered so that levers could be added to the frame as the railway system grew.

For the owners of electric railways, there were few new delights in 1931. The MM for May 1931 said that Meccano Ltd were ' . . . considering the application of electric motors to several existing locomotives, but no definite decision has yet been reached.' Interestingly, the works drawings for the permanent magnet motor show that in December 1930 its use with the 1931-style loco bodies was considered, but this did not happen. The new 20 volt motor developed for the French-type loco was more promising, so the electrification hung fire for another year. The No. 1 and No. 2 ELECTRICAL LAMP STANDARDS were the first of a full range of electrically lit accessories, for use with new transformers still not announced. The No. 1 ELECTRICAL LEVEL CROSSING was another novelty in the 1931 lists.

1932

'Almost every operation in modern railway practice can be carried out with a Hornby Railway. The locomotives are the best in the world . . . the rolling stock includes every type in general use and the accessories provide the final touch of realism. There is an endless variety to choose from.' (October 1932 MM)

The new trains announced in 1932 included a few of the smaller 0–4–0 locomotives operating on the 20 VOLT SYSTEM. The plans to use the 6 volt DC

GW No. 1 Tank and No. 0 Locos, 1931.

The No.1 Tank Loco was also redesigned in 1931. Other new introductions included the No. 1 (not shown) and No. 2 Electrical Lamp Standards. The Station or Field Hoardings were another novelty.

LMS No. 1 Tank and No. 1 Special Tank Locos . The No. 3 Mitropa Coach was new in 1931, as were the Modelled Miniature Station Staff.

motor for the new No. 1 types had been shelved, and the 20 volt motor designed for the French-type loco was chosen instead. The LST1/20 ELECTRIC TANK LOCOMOTIVE was the electric equivalent of the No. 1 Tank; the clumsy LST1/20 designation was necessary to distinguish it from the No. 1 ELECTRIC TANK, PM type, which continued to be sold with the old style body – probably because of large unsold stocks. The initials LST denote 'Locomotive, steam' to distinguish it from the LE1/20 LOCOMOTIVE, 'modelled on the type in use on the Swiss Federal Railways' according to the catalogues, but actually based on the French-type loco made the previous year, adapted by the removal of the side frames and air cylinders and by the addition of steps. The transfers used were also different from those used on the French loco.

The LSTM3/20 TANK LOCOMOTIVE was the electric version of the M3 Tank Loco, at 22s 6d against 25s for the LST1/20. No cylinders or coupling rods were fitted to the LSTM3/20, but like the LST1/20 there was a bulb-holder in the smokebox door.

The other 20 volt loco new in 1932 was the LE2/20 LOCOMOTIVE, the big brother of the LE1/20 Swiss-type loco. This was nothing but the Metropolitan in disguise, again with the outside frames cut away below footplate level, and with pantographs fitted.

These new 20 volt trains could be run from the T20 and T20A TRANSFORMERS, which were an important new development. The cost of the power supply, whether by accumulators or from transformers, was a very significant part of the expense of setting up an electric Hornby railway. Clearly Meccano Ltd preferred to see this money spent on a product built by themselves, rather than on one bought in from outside suppliers like Ferranti. These transformers were a new departure for the electrical department at Binns Road, and similar electrical products were to become an important source of revenue for the company; although sales were not particularly large in volume, they were high in value.

The T20 Transformer gave an output of 20 volts at 1 ampere, suitable for running any of the locomotives. A 5-speed resistance controller was built in.

The T20A was similar in style, but was larger to accommodate the 35 watt windings. The 20 volt output could be obtained either direct, or via the 5-speed regulator. A third pair of output sockets gave an output of 17 volts, for use with the wide range of ACCESSORIES FITTED FOR ELECTRICAL LIGHTING announced in 1932. The slightly lower voltage was intended to make the 20 volt bulbs last longer.

This range of accessories was announced for the first time in the May 1932 MM. Most of the important accessories were available fitted with electric lights, to be connected to the transformer by any of three lengths of FLEXIBLE LEADS – 9, 18 or 36 inches – which were fitted with plugs at one end and sockets at the other. A number of accessories could be run from the same transformer by use of the DISTRIBUTION BOX. The Lamp Standards 1E and 2E had been available the previous year. In 1932 the new items included the ENGINE SHEDS E1E and E2E, each with a single light inside, and the 2E STATION, ISLAND PLATFORM E and GOODS PLATFORM E each with a pair of lamps illuminating the platform. The SIGNAL BOX 2E was originally planned in a version with two lamps; one over the steps, and the other inside. In the event, only a single-lamp version was produced, and the light over the steps was not fitted; but the double-lamp version did creep into one or two illustrations. Also available was the WATER TANK E, a very handy item for the locomotive depot.

The signals fitted for electric lighting were the SIGNAL No. 2E, the No. 2E DOUBLE ARM SIGNAL, the JUNCTION SIGNAL E, and the GANTRY SIGNAL E. The lampholders were fitted behind the transparent spectacle glasses. LEVEL CROSSINGS E1E and E2E were catalogued in addition to the existing electrical versions, not as replacements; lamps with red aspects were fitted on the gates. The BUFFER STOPS 1E and 2E also had red warning lamps.

The COUNTRYSIDE SECTIONS were the other major introduction in 1932. This was an ambitious system of sections of scenery for Hornby Layouts with 2 ft radius curves; the sections were of standardised sizes that could be laid inside or around the tracks. The sections were made of stout card-board, covered with a printed representation of green pastureland; the square sections also had instructions printed on the reverse. The road sections were particularly successful in capturing the atmosphere of a country lane, with well-modelled diecast gates leading into the fields. Two things prevented the system becoming a success. The first was the sheer expense; even a simple 2 ft radius circle required twelve sections to fill the inside area, at a total cost of 21/–! The second was the rather ludicrous appearance when used on a large area, because of the regularity of the pattern of hedges, gates and trees. The hedges were green-dyed loofah, fixed to the edges of the sections by glue and protruding nails (imagine that being sold as a toy today!), but Frank Hornby's original patent specification for the countryside sections showed 'detachable and flexible hedges, secured by clips and by rubber suction cups'; these suction cups were also to be used for fixing down the trees and haystacks! Unfortunately these ideas were never put into production, although detachable hedges could have helped to make the system more realistic. The haystacks did not appear at all, and the trees supplied were only of the standard type plugging into cardboard tubes set into the sections. Other features of the patent not put into production included the plans to produce ploughed land as an alternative to pasture. Perhaps the idea of a detachable cover for the square sections contoured with hills and a pond was a bit far-fetched – but this and other ideas were patented, and copyright was also secured.

Still concentrating on scenery, there was also a new range of cuttings and tunnels in 1932. For straight track the smallest was the No. 0 TUNNEL, then there was a slightly larger No. 1 TUNNEL, and the largest was the No. 2 TUNNEL. The No. 3 TUNNEL was a curved version suitable for either 1 ft or 2 ft radius curves, the larger No. 4 TUNNEL being suitable only for 2 ft radius lines. All these were made from a wooden frame covered by strawboard, with fabric glued on top with puckers formed; the fabric was then covered with green-dyed sawdust, and hand-finished with other colours, mainly yellows, reds and purples, to give it more life. Some of the colours used were extraordinarily vivid, but unfortunately they were also fugitive

A system of electrically lit accessories became available in 1932. These were connected to the transformer via a Distribution Box and Flexible Leads. The LST1/20 Tank Loco was new in 1932.

colours and most examples exposed to light and air quickly become faded.

The two other large tunnels were the No. 5 TUNNEL (LEFT-HANDED, CURVED) and No. 6 TUNNEL (RIGHT-HANDED, CURVED). The distinction between a left-handed and a right-handed tunnel may seem a little abstruse, unless it is realised that the bases of these rectangular tunnels were equivalent to the shapes of the countryside sections – in one case sections G1 and L1, and for the other G2 and L2. This made the tunnels suitable for use with the countryside sections. The ends were also shaped to match the end of the No. 1 CUTTINGS (END SECTION).

Like the Tunnels, CUTTINGS No. 0 to No. 4 were strawboard on a wooden frame, finished in the same way. The No. 0 and No. 4 Cuttings were complete units, with embanked sections each side of the track, the No. 4 being a much larger version. Cuttings No. 1, a pair of end sections, were designed to go with the No. 2 Straight Section and the No. 3 Curved Section, by means of which cuttings of any length could be built up. The curved sections were said to be suitable for either 2 ft radius or 1 ft radius curves, but the idea was not a particular success. The No. 3 Cuttings were not actually curved, but the ends were cut off at an angle, so that long curved sections looked like regular polygons.

The trees supplied with the countryside sections were also included in FENCING WITH FOUR TREES, the trees being supplied with special tinplate sockets for attachment to the paled fencing.

To go with all this extra scenery, there were also some very useful new Modelled Miniature figures; the new sets were No. 2 FARMYARD ANIMALS, No. 3 PASSENGERS, No. 4 ENGINEERING STAFF, No. 5 TRAIN AND HOTEL STAFF, and No. 13 HALL'S DISTEMPER ADVERTISEMENT.

Another series of cheap and useful accessories were the TRAIN NAME BOARDS, which could be used in clips fitted to the roofs of the No. 2 Special Pullmans. There were also ROOF CLIPS for TRAIN NAME BOARDS No. 2, for use with Metropolitan, Saloon and No. 2 Pullman Coaches; also No. 2S ROOF CLIPS for use with the older No. 2 Special Pullmans made without clips already on the roof.

Countryside Sections were a noteworthy 1932 introduction. The No. 6 Right-Handed Tunnel was one of a range of 7 Tunnels. The Cuttings (one No. 1 end section is shown) were also new. Modelled Miniature Farmyard Animals and the Hall's Distemper Advertisement were among the new figures. The latest vans (now including Cadbury's Chocolate) had sliding rather than hinged doors.

There were no developments in rolling stock during 1932, except for some colour changes, and the issue of a new private owner's wagon, the CADBURY'S CHOCOLATE VAN. This was fitted with sliding doors, which were also adopted in 1932 for most of the other vans, instead of the hinged doors used before.

There was also a new transfer for the REDLINE GLICO PETROL TANK WAGON, which replaced the previous Redline tanker.

1933

'A perfect miniature railway . . . No others run so smoothly. No others pull such heavy loads. No others haul trains so far on a single winding.' (November 1933 MM)

1932 had been a fairly dull year for everything except accessories – the Countryside Sections and electrically lit accessories being bright spots in a quiet year. But in 1933 there were still fewer innovations. An M FOOTBRIDGE was added to the range of M accessories, most of which were included in the new M10 COMPLETE MODEL RAILWAY set, a delightful outfit with the M0 Loco and Pullmans, M Signals, M Telegraph Poles, M Station and M Wayside Station, M Signal Box, 3 Trees with Stands, 6 figures, No. 0 Cutting, No. 0 Tunnel, M loading Gauge, M Footbridge and the M Level Crossing.

The trees were now sold separately, as POPLAR TREES at 2s dozen or OAK TREES at 2s 6d dozen; the DIECAST STANDS were 1s dozen. Alternatively, ASSORTED TREES WITH STANDS were 3s dozen, 6 Oaks and 6 Poplars. HEDGING was sold in lengths equivalent to a straight rail, at 3s dozen; the hedges were the same as the countryside type, but mounted on wooden bases.

There were further additions to the range of electric locomotives; the LST2/20 TANK LOCOMOTIVES were electric 4–4–2 tanks with 20 volt motors, and the E3/20 LOCOMOTIVES were 20 volt versions of the No. 3 tender engines. Electric light bulb holders were put in the smokebox doors of all these locos on both the 20 volt and the 6 volt 1933 models, so that all the electric locos with the exception of the PM tanks now had the light fitted. The first 20 volt train sets, the LST1/20 and LST2/20 TANK GOODS TRAIN SETS, were introduced in 1933.

Many Hornby Train colours were changed in 1933. Green was widely used, both for wagons and for platforms. The E3/20 Loco and LST2/20 Electric Tank loco were the first 20 volt electric 4–4–2s.

The range of transformers was once again transformed, the Ferranti types being replaced by a choice of the T6 TRANSFORMER, 20VA with a 5-stud speed control, the T6A TRANSFORMER, 35VA with additional uncontrolled 9 volt and 3.5 volt circuits, or the T6M TRANSFORMER, 20VA with a single non-controlled output. The T20A Transformer was altered to give a 3.5V lighting circuit instead of 17 volt, which ensured compatibility between the lighting systems, and increased the number of bulbs that could be lit from a single transformer; 14 in the case of the T20A, 18 bulbs for the T6A. The T20 transformer was still available, and there was a new T20M TRANSFORMER with a non-controlled 20 volt output that was intended primarily for use with Meccano motors, since no Resistance Controller was yet available for 20 volt use. All these transformers were made by Meccano Ltd at Binns Road, and were available for three standard voltages – 110/120V, 200/225V and 225/250V, all at 50 cycles. Transformers could be specially ordered for other power supplies, usually at no extra cost.

Although there was little innovation in 1933, that is not to say that there were no changes. Hornby Trains had never been colourless or drab, the private owners' vans and petrol tank wagons in particular being available in a profusion of cheerful colours. 1933 however marked a brief period when this colourfulness infected virtually the whole Hornby range, and was carried to an exuberant excess. There had been a prelude in 1932 when a few colour combinations varying from the choice to the obnoxious had begun to creep in (notably the red-based No. 1 Cattle Trucks). This was just a beginning, for in the 1933–34 season the old paint pots were flung away, and most of the colours appeared in brighter and more virulent forms. Even the grey used for sober-sided wagons like the Brake and Luggage Vans was changed to a cleaner, lighter shade. The reds, blues and greens were similarly lightened, and even the Pratts High Test tanker appeared in a brighter orange. The Snowplough and the Tipping Wagons burst out into blues and yellows; the Fyffes Banana Van, always conspicuous in its yellow and green coat, now became an even more prominent yellow and red. Fashion colours for bases

An LNER No. 1 Loco hauls No. 1 Pullman Coaches, while the No. 1 Tank Loco pulls a train of private owners' vans.

were green and red, and green bases spread even to the relatively realistic tinprinted No. 0 vans. Timber and Lumber Wagons became conspicuous in bright reds, yellows and greens.

The Signals, which had previously been a rich blue, caught the disease and appeared either in green or in a lighter blue, with red levers. For the first time the customer was offered a choice of colour in both the No. 1 and No. 2 types, although curiously the choice was never mentioned in the catalogues. The platforms of the stations, goods depots and so on, were turned green, whether from envy or indisposition it is hard to say.

Even the No. 1 Coaches were affected, and appeared with red or green bases, and the roof colour was changed from grey to cream. Perhaps the worst hit were the No. 1 Pullman Cars, which appeared with red, green or blue bases and roofs; luckily only one colour per coach!

This plague of colours swept through almost the whole range, but stopped short when it came to the locomotives. Admittedly the M0 and M1 Locos were issued with green or red bases, in garish colour combinations, but sadly none of the larger types were thus afflicted. It is true that the 'Modelled Miniature' boxes of figures showed an artist's impression of the 'Yorkshire' in bright red, with bright red No. 2 Special Pullmans; and very lovely it would have been. Unfortunately this pleasure was denied to future generations, as no such locos have yet come to light. Instead the wagons and coaches in lively (not to say jarring) colours had to be hauled around the tracks by locos in the usual carefully distinguished shades of SR, LNER, or GW green, or LMS maroon. Only the Swiss-type locos appeared in sensibly extravagant creams, reds, blues, yellows and greens.

Despite this imperfection in an otherwise explosive concatenation of colours, the 1933–34 Hornby range captures what one sincerely hopes was the confident spirit of the age. Running a Hornby railway certainly became a more exciting experience; whether this was a step upwards or downwards from the late '20s, when Hornby was striving to create increasingly realistic models to be run on strict railway-like principles, can only be a matter of opinion. But the temporary abandonment

of the pursuit of realism, to make a series of splendidly attractive and enjoyable toys was an interesting change of direction, and seems if anything to have improved trade. What a lovely year it would have been to have been let loose in a toyshop, with unlimited pocket money!

1934

'The last word in realism and efficiency. . .' (Clockwork Hornby Train folder, 1934)

'This year is a notable one in the history of the Hornby Electric Railway System, for it is marked by the introduction of a series of new electric train sets, and the development of a perfect system of remote control. . .' (Electric Hornby Train Folder, 1934)

Although the electric trains had at first been only a tiny part of Meccano Ltd's total sales, they had been growing steadily in importance. In 1934 there was a dramatic increase in the number of electric trains offered; no fewer than 28 electric train sets were catalogued in 1934, compared with only 5 sets the year before!

The new electric locomotives were all versions of existing clockwork types, so there was not an overwhelming amount of extra tooling required for the loco housings, although the mechanisms, which were mostly of improved design, required careful preparation. One of the improvements was the AUTOMATIC REVERSE 20 VOLT MECHANISM produced to a design patented by Frank Hornby. This reversing gear operated when full voltage was applied suddenly; to facilitate this, the T20 and T20A transformers were revised so that

Among the enlarged electric loco range of the 1934–35 season were these LMS E220 Tank Locos, and the E020 Loco. The Dinky Toy Shepherd Set, the Flat Trucks (with or without Cable Drum) and the revised No. 1 Coaches were also new.

their switching sequence was off–max–min instead of off–min–max as on previous controllers. The newest of the 20 VOLT RESISTANCE CONTROLLERS introduced in 1934 were also of this type.

The locomotives available with the automatic reverse mechanisms were the E120 SPECIAL, the E120 SPECIAL TANK, the E220 SPECIAL, the E220 SPECIAL TANK (replacing the LST2/20 Tank Loco), the E320 Locos (replacing the E3/20, the oblique distinguishing the non-automatic versions) and the LE220 Loco which replaced the LE2/20.

The smaller 0–4–0 engines were not available in the UK with the automatic reversing equipment (although interestingly enough they were in France – French-built, of course). Instead they had a modified version of the previous motor, with a slim-line brush-holder unit which did not require protruding brush caps. (The larger new-style mechanisms used

a similar flat brush-holder.) Although this meant that there was no need to provide holes in the housings for the protruding caps, the frames and boilers still had to be cut away to take the wider parts of the electric mechanisms, and a lot of work was put into design and tooling for these modifications.

The smaller-type electric locos included the EM320 Tank Locomotive (replacing the LSTM3/20), the E120 Tank Locomotive (replacing the LST1/20 Tank), the E120 LOCOMOTIVE and the E020 LOCOMOTIVE; the LE120 Locomotive replaced the LE1/20. The M series was extended to include the EM120 LOCOMOTIVE, with a small and simple non-reversing mechanism unique to the type. To coincide with the introduction of these smaller types, the 1 ft radius ELECTRIC POINTS EPR1/EPL1 and DOUBLE SYMMETRICAL POINTS EDSR1/EDSL1 were re-introduced, having been discontinued in 1925. The 1 ft radius rails were suitable for the EM320 Locomotives as well as

the EM120 Locos. Also new in 1934 were the SWITCH RAILS EMC6 and EMC20, which were straight rails incorporating the equivalent of a Terminal Connecting Plate, with a switch lever added – at the same price as a Connecting Plate on its own! The usefulness of the switch was somewhat reduced by the fact that it switched the supply to the outside rails, not to the centre rail.

The new large range of 20 volt locomotives did not replace the 6 volt system, as might have been expected; but probably less than half the homes in the UK were connected to the 'electric light', so for many the use of accumulators was Hobson's choice. In 1934 an enlarged range of 6 volt locos was also made available; Nos. EM16, EM36, E06, E16 TANK, and E16 LOCOMOTIVES were offered, and also the E26 Special Tank (replacing the No. 2 Electric Tank Loco), the E36 Locomotives (replacing the E3/6) and the E36 Metropolitan. The mechanisms were similar to the 20 volt types, without the protruding brush-caps, but reversing was only manual; the voltage was too low for successful automatic reversing. The No. 1 Special, No. 1 Special Tank and No. 2 Special Locos were not available in 6 volt versions except by special order; nor were the Swiss-type locomotives. There was no technical reason for this, presumably a line had to be drawn somewhere on the number of items that the dealers could be expected to hold in stock.

The 6 volt permanent magnet motor was now installed in the EPM16 SPECIAL TANK LOCOMOTIVE, instead of the ancient No. 1 Electric Tank Locomotive housing. The motor was revised by fitting extra-long brackets to suit the No. 1 Special Tank housing; the brush-caps remained, and clearance holes had to be provided in the loco body. The mechanism looked particularly out of place in the EPM16 Loco, because of the small diameter 8-spoke wheels and the unusually short wheelbase. The 1934 catalogues were also able to announce the availability of TRANSFORMER–RECTIFIER TR6, to power the EPM16 Loco. Its modest output of only 1.5 amps at 6 volts DC was barely sufficient.

The rolling stock included in the new 1934/35 season electric train sets was the same as for the equivalent clockwork sets. The new range of sets available in both 6 volt and 20 volt versions included:

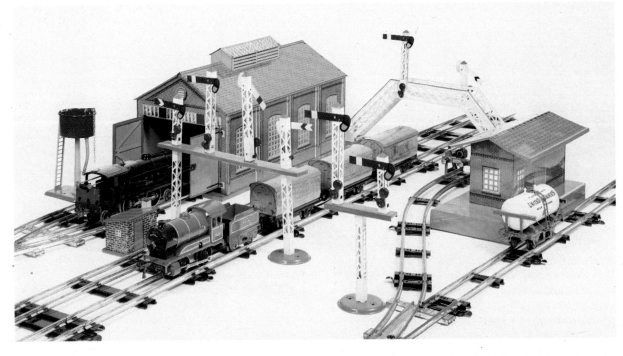

Simple accessories added to the Hornby series in 1934 included the No. 1 Water Tank, No. 2A Engine Shed (also No. 1A, not shown), No. 1 Signal Gantry and No. 1 Junction Signal, and the No. 1 Goods Platform. The Platelayers Hut and the UD tanker were simplified, and the No. 1A Footbridge had No. 1-type signals instead of tinprinted.

LNER E120 Special and E120 Tank Locomotives of 1934–35, at a country goods depot. The No. 0 Rotary Tipping Wagon was a new model, despite its old-fashioned design.

EM16·and EM120 Goods and Passenger Sets
EM26 and EM220 Passenger Sets
EM36 and EM320 Goods Sets
E06 and E020 Goods and Passenger Sets
E16 and E120 Tank Goods Sets
E16 and E120 Goods and Passenger Sets
E26 and E220 Special Tank Mixed Goods Train Sets
E36 and E320 Riviera 'Blue Train' Sets, and the
E36 and E320 Pullman Train Sets.

The sets available in only one of the two voltages included:

E36 Metropolitan Train Set

E220 Special Pullman Train Set
E120 Special Goods and Passenger Train Sets.

There were still no train sets with the E120 Special Tank or No. 1 Special Tank Locos.

The No. 1 Passenger Train Sets included a completely different No. 1 Passenger Coach; the 1924 style was clearly outdated despite several minor revisions, and it is suprising that a new coach was not ready when the 1931 series of locos was produced. The new coach designs were actually completed in 1932; the reason for the delay before they were actually made is uncertain. Despite the lack of opening doors the new tinprinted style was attractive, and the shape of the coach much more satisfactory.

The 1934–35 Hornby Book of Trains is particularly interesting, since most of these sets are illustrated (excepting those with the larger 20 Volt locos, which were however included in the Meccano Products Catalogue of the same year). No wonder the HBT needed 46 pages to illustrate the trains against only 33 pages the year before!

The only new clockwork train sets were three new COMPLETE MODEL RAILWAYS, M8, M9 and M11. The M8 set had a particularly interesting tunnel, hewn from a solid block of wood, and finished in dyed sawdust as for the normal types. This tunnel was very short, to fit the shallow M8 train set box! It was not sold separately.

Apart from the extraordinary increase in the range of electric trains in 1934, the other memorable events were in the field of the simpler accessories. In 1934 some of the more over-elaborate toys were modified and reduced in price, to put them into the hands of a larger number of children. The Platelayer's Hut was a good example of the simplifications that were carried out; the sprung, opening door was no longer fitted, and the separate chimney-pot was replaced by a plunged hole in a single-piece pressing. These changes helped to reduce the price of the hut from 2s in 1933–34 to 1s in 1934–35.

The No. 2 Signals were also simplified, the finials being replaced by flat caps on all except the electrically lit versions and the Signal Gantry. The sides of the revised 1934-style No. 1 Signals were shaped to form a pyramid-shape cap, and a smaller round base replaced the rectangular base used before. The range of No. 1 Signals was also increased to include a No. 1 JUNCTION SIGNAL, Home or Distant, and a No. 1 SIGNAL GANTRY, built on the same lines and sold at budget prices.

The No. 1A Footbridge was given No. 1 style signals, instead of the tinprinted M type, and the No. 2 Footbridge was withdrawn, as was the No. 3 Lattice Girder Bridge. There was also a completely new No. 1 WATER TANK, nearer to the correct scale for Gauge 0 than the old version now known as the No. 2 Water Tank. The No. 1 GOODS PLATFORM had a smaller platform than the old type, now called the No. 2 Goods Platform. The No. 1 Goods Platform had no crane, and the doors of the shed did not open. There were two new ENGINE SHEDS, No. 1A and No. 2A. The No. 1A Engine Shed had doors at only one end, and there were no chimneys or ventilators. The No. 2A Engine Shed had doors at each end, but again had no chimneys, and only a single central ventilated skylight.

The range of Dinky Toys now included the No. 6 SHEPHERD SET, with a Shepherd and Dog, three white Sheep and one black. Also issued was a second series of the popular POSTERS IN MINIATURE, with up-to-date advertisements including several for the latest Meccano products – Elektron and Kemex Sets, and the Motor and Aeroplane Constructor sets.

The range of rolling stock was little changed in 1934, except for the deletion of the Seccotine Van, and the addition of the FLAT TRUCK and the FLAT TRUCK WITH CABLE DRUM. The cable drum could also be purchased separately. Less interesting was the No. 0 ROTARY TIPPING WAGON, an over-simplified design that had little to commend it except the price of 1s 6d.

1935

'Fine fun on the line – with a Hornby!' (February 1935 MM)

'This is the dawn of the electric toy age, and the new Hornby Electric Trains reach the pinnacle of perfection. . .' (December 1935 MM)

On odd occasions, the Meccano Magazine had carried advertisements offering a few items of obsolete stock; but in early 1935 there was an exceptionally large clear-out of the store rooms, and the list of old stock in a full-page advertisement in the January 1935 MM ran to about 100 different items. Many were offered at true bargain prices, for example only 5s for a Signal Gantry with a current catalogue price of 10s; but postage was charged extra, since these special offer items could only be bought direct from Meccano Ltd and not through dealers. Several items on the list had been out of production for six or seven years – like the 1 ft radius Crossover, and Control System engines including the No. 2 Tank Loco. The list also included a very diverse range of obsolete wagons, on the 1922 open-axleguard base. Several sets were offered, including the short-lived No. 2

The Signal Gantries were changed in 1935 to all home or all distant, instead of a combination. No. 2 Passenger Coaches were introduced; also the LMS Banana Van.

Special Tank Goods Set, and (for the last time) the High Voltage Metropolitan Set. Understandably most of these items were quickly sold out, but there was a further short list of the remaining items in the February MM.

Having cleared the decks for action, so to speak, suprisingly little action actually took place. There was an important new range of bogie coaches, the No. 2 PASSENGER COACHES, FIRST/THIRD and BRAKE/THIRD. These double-length versions of the No. 1 Passenger Coaches were a highly satisfactory – if belated – answer to the prayers of those who had been looking forward to seeing the first Hornby SR and GW bogie coaches; they were of course also available in LMS and LNER colours. They were fitted with lamp brackets, and the Brake/3rd coaches were supplied with DETACHABLE TAIL LAMPS; both these and the Detachable Head Lamps were catalogued from 1935, so that a special order would not be necessary in case of loss.

Another new tinprinted item was the LMS No. 0 BANANA VAN, the fourth in the series of vans for perishables traffic. This van was not fitted with sliding doors, and the other three wagons in the series were also issued in new printings and without the sliding doors. The NE Fish Van was changed from grey to bauxite, and the GW Milk Traffic from grey to brown. The only other significant addition to the rolling stock was the new series of MO wagons – the MO ROTARY TIPPING WAGON, MO CRANE TRUCK, MO SIDE TIPPING WAGON, and MO PETROL TANK WAGON. The owners of MO sets had never previously had any choice of wagon, and the new additions gave them a chance to run a mixed goods train.

A new pair of points for clockwork trains was produced in 1935. The POINTS ON SOLID BASE SPSR2/SPSL2 were similar to the PSR2 and PSL2 Points on Solid Base, but were not fitted for Hornby Control and did not have the ground disc and lamp – only the normal operating lever. The price of 5s per pair was well above the 3s per pair for the normal points, with no obvious operational advantages; the 2s difference was a lot of pay for the extra strength of the bases, so not surprisingly they were a commercial failure.

The No. 2 Special Locomotive for the LNER

In 1935 the LNER E220 and No. 2 Special Loco name was changed to 'Bramham Moor' instead of 'Yorkshire'.

Train Sets was changed to 'Hunt' class loco No. 201 'Bramham Moor', instead of 'Shire' No. 234 'Yorkshire'. There were certain accompanying changes of detail to correspond to the prototype.

The range of Hornby products was very large in 1934 and 1935, and clearly the pace of innovations and introductions of the early years could not be sustained indefinitely. There was an increasing number of deletions of the less successful products in the late 1930s, which balanced the smaller number of new products. In 1935 these deletions included the Single Wine Wagon, and the Accumulators. The 1934 range of sets was unnecessarily large, and the 6 volt system was losing ground to the 20 volt; so the EO6 and E16 Locomotives were withdrawn, together with the corresponding sets. The other sets withdrawn included the EM16, EM26 and EM220 Passenger Sets, the EO20 Goods Set, the E120 Passenger Set, and the E26 Goods Set; but the contents of these sets could still be bought separately.

Both the No. 1 Special Goods Train Set and the E120 Special Goods Train Set were replaced by the first sets with the Special Tank Locomotives, a 'Shell' Petrol Tank Wagon taking the place of the tender; these new No. 1 SPECIAL TANK GOODS SETS and E120 SPECIAL TANK GOODS SETS making very attractive trains.

The accessories fitted for electric lighting were simplified in 1935, to enable them to be sold at more realistic prices. The new system used a common return through the rails; henceforth the lighting circuit of the transformer was connected by a single wire to a screw terminal on the accessory, instead of the previous plug and socket arrangement, while the return to the transformer was connected to the track by a BONDING or EARTHING CLIP. For accessories such as the Buffers, Level Crossings and Engine Sheds which were connected to the track, no further connection was necessary; for others, such as the Signals, the second screw terminal was connec-

The No. 0 Silver Jubilee Train.

of his death was full of schemes for new products.'

One of the last of the new Hornby Train developments under Frank Hornby's direction was the No. 0 'SILVER JUBILEE' CLOCKWORK TRAIN SET, an exciting train for the younger enthusiast. The LNER had run the special 'Silver Jubilee' train service between King's Cross and Newcastle, commencing on the 30th September 1935; it was the first fully streamlined train to run in Great Britain, and was also advertised as the fastest timetabled service. The four locomotives on which the service devolved were Nos. 2509 'Silver Link', 2510 'Quicksilver', 2511 'Silver King' and 2512 'Silver Fox'; of these it was 'Silver Link' that was modelled by Meccano Ltd, although to say modelled is perhaps to stretch a point, since the new train was in the MO style despite the official No. 0 designation. The MO mechanism was used, with a brake lever extended through the cab roof because of the close-coupled tender; the delicate MO-type couplings were used.

The streamlined loco was a delightful representation of the A4 Pacific Locos, the tinprinting managing to complement the simple, clean lines of the body. There were only four driving wheels, but the rear wheels were at least fitted with a boss to allow rods to be fitted – like the M1 rods they were designed to look like a combination of piston and coupling rods. These revised wheels and the rods were also fitted to the MO Locomotives from 1936 onwards, the locos being provided with M1-type cylinders; the change was made without any increase in price.

The details on the Silver Link tender included an embossed representation of coal, while the water filler and the tender corridor connection were included in the tinprinting. The coach was an articulated unit, consisting of a four-wheeled front car supporting the 2-wheeled rear unit closely coupled to it by a pivot rod. The coaches were tinprinted with lively detail (the 'Silver Jubilee' train name boards included) to match the loco and tender.

The set was a little short of rolling stock, having only this single coach unit, but the coaches and other components of the set could be bought separately. Even the LNER were short of coaches, since only a single rake was available to run the service!

ted to the outer rails of the track by another Bonding Clip, supplied with each accessory. Many electrically-lit accessories were simplified from double to single flex internal wiring, with the return through the tinplate body, a change that had in fact already been made for some plug-and-socket accessories.

There were two new TRANSFORMERS, T26M for 6 volt trains and T22M for 20 volt trains, each with high-power 50 VA windings to allow two trains to be run from a single unit. In 1935 they were available by special order, although they were not catalogued until 1936.

1936

'Designs are continually being improved and new items added so that the system is complete in practically every detail.' (May 1936 MM)

Meccano boys were saddened by the announcement in the November 1936 MM of the death of Frank

Hornby. His son Roland took over, in the Binns Road works that had been Frank Hornby's greatest achievement; the MM obituary said that 'To the end of his life, the Factory was Frank Hornby's great pride, and he was delighted to welcome to it the thousands of Meccano Boys who visit it every year . . . The addition of Hornby Trains to the range of products of the Meccano factory is another romance of the toy trade. The idea originated in a little Meccano locomotive, and from this developed first the clockwork trains and later the electric trains which, with their accompanying range of track, rolling stock and accessories, have reached world-wide fame. Most men would have been content with these two phenomenal sucesses . . .', the other being Meccano, '. . . but Frank Hornby's active brain was always searching for new ideas. The result was the rapid development of the many other Hornby products – constructional motor car and aeroplane outfits, chemical and electrical outfits, and the most fascinating of all miniatures, the famous "Dinky Toys". He never lost enthusiasm and up to the time

This set was one of the most evocative toys made by Meccano Ltd, representing in miniature (however simply) the most modern railway practice, and at a competitive price of only 7s 6d. Even the youngest enthusiasts were now being offered railway-like toys at pocket-money prices. The only qualification to the success of the set was that the King had died so soon after his Jubilee celebrations had begun.

The Countryside Sections had not been included in the 1935 Book of Hornby Trains and Meccano Products or the other catalogues, but they were listed in the 'How to Plan Your Hornby Railway' booklet of October 1935, at prices well below those of 1934, which in turn had been much lower than the

1932 prices. All except the Road and Support sections remained in stock to be offered (as items 'no longer included in the range of Hornby accessories', in limited supply only, at the same low prices) in the September 1936 MM; their deletion after only four years showed their limited success. The No. 5 and No. 6 Tunnels disappeared at the same time. The Oak and Poplar Trees were offered in dozens with stands, instead of without. The accessories fitted for electrical lighting by the old system of plugs and sockets, which had been offered in the 1935 catalogues as an alternative to the newer types, were no longer listed in 1936; nor was the Distribution Box. The French-type Brake Van was another casualty.

The 1934 range of 6 volt trains was cut back

further, with the 20 volt trains predominating in the market place. The E16 Tank Loco and E16 Tank Goods Set, E36 Locos and the E36 'Riviera Blue Train' and Pullman Train Sets were withdrawn; but the Swiss-type locos LEC1 and LE120 and the LE220 also left the lists because of the lack of sales appeal on the home market.

Apart from these deletions there were few significant changes to the range of locomotives. The LNER locos began to appear in a darker shade of green than had previously been used; although the exact shade of the LNER green had varied perhaps more than the others, this was a marked change of hue. The 'Lord Nelson' and 'Royal Scot' locos began to be shown with smoke deflectors in the catalogues

Wembley, 1936. A No. 1 Special Tank Loco with the latest LMS High Capacity Wagon, and a No. 2 Special Compound Loco arriving with Saloon Coaches and Pullman stock.

57

and the MM, each deflector different in shape from those used on the 'Nord' loco from 1934. Their adoption reflected prototype practice.

Accessories for the centre-rail conversion of clockwork rails were withdrawn in 1936, and slots to take the clips were no longer punched in the sleepers. The reason for the change was probably that the part-exchange scheme was extended in 1936 to cover rails as well as locos – clockwork rails could be swapped for their electric equivalents, with an allowance of half the current list price of the clockwork rail. This was actually a better scheme for the user, since he got brand new rails, and could exchange points and crossings which could not be converted. The cost of exchange for full straight and curved rails was exactly the same as for the conversion accessories; and the exchange scheme cost only a few pence more than the conversion for half and quarter rails.

The points on solid base were finally produced in an electric version, the ESPSR2 and ESPSL2 POINTS ON SOLID BASE. They differed from the original 1927 design (never produced) in having no ground disc or control fittings. Unlike the clockwork SPSR2/SPSL2 they were not offered as an alternative to the ordinary type, they actually replaced the EPR2 and EPL2; in fact the following year they were renamed EPR2/EPL2. Reading from the catalogues, it seemed that the customer had no choice but to pay 7s 6d per pair instead of 6s 6d for the older type. But many dealers seem to have realised that the special order Reversed Switch and Control System points could still be obtained, at the old prices, because they were not made with the solid base (although there was later to be an electric control system solid base point). So these special types had a wider sales appeal than perhaps Meccano Ltd intended!

The automatic CIRCUIT BREAKER was a very useful accessory for the 6 volt or 20 volt electric railway, preventing damage to the windings of the transformer in the event of a short circuit (a frequent occurrence with the electric bogie locos, as the pony trucks and bogies fall off the rails at the slightest unevenness). The Circuit Breaker was much more effective in this respect than fuse wire. Also catalogued in 1936 were the T22M and T26M TRANS-FORMERS that had been special order items in 1935.

As far as rolling stock was concerned, there were some important new wagons; foremost among these were the HIGH CAPACITY WAGONS No. 2, which were as the name implied high-sided bogie versions of the open wagon, to carry coal in the LMS and GW versions, or bricks in the NE type. The sides were tinprinted, and fitted to a base of about the same size as that of the No. 2 Passenger coach. The GW wagon was tinprinted in dark grey to represent the GWR 40 ton loco coal wagons, and it differed from the other two in having the centre section pierced to represent the trussing of the underframe. The NE brick wagon was tinprinted in a bauxite colour to represent its prototype, of 50 ton capacity. There was no SR version, probably because the SR had fewer wagons of this type in service.

The CONTAINER was a new and up-to-date load for the flat truck, representing the containers that were in increasingly widespread use on the British railways. Although much smaller than their present-day 'Freightliner' counterparts, they nonetheless had a useful capacity, and served a wide variety of purposes. Originally 13 different types were planned, but in the event only the LMS Furniture, LNER Goods, GWR Insulated and SR Ventilated versions were produced. Curiously, they were made in the same style as the cable drums, in solid wood with colour-printed paper sides; although common practice for other manufacturers, it is surprising that the masters of mass-produced tinplate trains chose not to make the container in the tinprinted plate that might have been expected.

Containers could be bought separately, or as the FLAT TRUCK WITH CONTAINER. The 1936 catalogues also offered a loaded TROLLEY WAGON WITH CABLE DRUMS, with two of the British Insulated Cable Co. drums secured to the well by string, making a convincingly weighty-looking load. From the 1936 season, the Trolley Wagon and the Breakdown Van and Crane, like the High Capacity Wagons, were fitted with axleboxes on the bogies, and diecast spoked wheels replaced the tinplate wheels; an unfortunate change in view of severe 'fatigue' problems with the mazac castings used for many Hornby wheels from early 1936. The No. 2 Pullman and Saloon Coaches also had the axleboxes fitted, but were given Mansell pattern solid wheels. The axlebox slots (but not the axleboxes) appeared on the No. 2 Lumber, No. 2 Timber, No. 2 Cattle and No. 2 Luggage Vans from the same time.

The obsolete Pratt's tanker was replaced by a buff 'ESSO' PETROL TANK WAGON No. 1. The new 'ROYAL DAYLIGHT' OIL TANK WAGON replaced the 'Shell' Petrol Tank Wagon, both in the train sets and in the range of separate wagons; it was coloured in the same cheerful red. The BP tanker was replaced by the 'SHELL-MEX & BP' PETROL TANK WAGON No. 1; the cream livery was similar to that of the MO Petrol Tank Wagon.

The MO Petrol Tank Wagon, with the Rotary and Side Tipping Wagons were included in the MO CLOCKWORK MIXED GOODS TRAIN SET, an attractive and colourful set, but at 6s 11d the appeal was bound to be less than that of the 'Silver Jubilee'!

1937

'Hornby Trains – the name spells magic to thousands of boys of all ages. . .' (September 1937 MM)

1937 was to see the last important additions to the Hornby Gauge O system, in a glorious Indian summer (or perhaps an 'Old Swan' song?) before the harder years ahead. Most notable of these fine new models was the 'PRINCESS ELIZABETH' LOCOMOTIVE. After years of responding to requests in the MM for locos with 6-wheel mechanisms with an inventive catalogue of replies to the effect that it was both technically and economically impossible to produce one, the actual appearance of the 'Princess Elizabeth' made a fitting climax to the story of the Hornby Series; it was unfortunate that Frank Hornby did not live a few more months to see it produced. The quality of finish and design was in some respects superior even to the No. 2 Special Locomotives – in the chromium plating of some of the fittings, for example – and the tapered boiler was fitted with a soldered smokebox door, with none of the usual Hornby slots and lugs, or overlap over the boiler diameter. No clockwork version was made –

Bristol Station, 1936. Two local trains wait to depart, behind E120 and E120 Special Locos.

only a 20 volt electric loco with automatic reverse. Compared with its predecessors the 'Princess' was an imposing product, with the loco and tender supplied in a lined wooden presentation box; unlike the other Hornby locos the tender was not sold separately. The price of 105s should have been enough to deter all but the most well-to-do customers, but the less well off were offered temptation by the new SCHEME OF DEFERRED PAYMENTS; the Meccano Magazine and the 1937 Catalogues invited those interested to apply for details of never-never terms for the more expensive purchases.

The other new locomotives of outstanding interest were the Southern Railway 'Schools' Class E420 'ETON' LOCOMOTIVE, 20 volt with automatic reversing, and the No. 4C 'ETON' LOCOMOTIVE. These were cleverly designed to use various parts from the existing No. 2 Special Locomotives, so they did not require the inordinate expense of a full new set of tools. Despite this economy they were most successful evocations of the Southern's smart and efficient 4–4–0s, altogether more attractive to the enthusiast than the L1 Class loco could have been. It was classified as a No. 4 rather than as a No. 2 Special type, as the L1 remained in production, and in any case a higher price had to be charged; 42s 6d for the E420 and 35s

for the No. 4C, against 37s 6d for the E220 Special and 27s 6d for the No. 2 Special. Despite this price differential they sold very successfully.

Neither the 'Eton' loco nor the 'Princess' was sold in sets; nor did the electric versions have the lamp-holders in the smokebox doors that had characterised the previous electric Hornby locos. Indeed the ordinary E220 Special Locomotives became available by special order with the clockwork-type smokebox doors, for those who preferred a more realistic appearance. There are no recorded cases of special order 'Eton' or 'Princess' locos with lampholders!

These locomotives were not the only important

Margate, 1936. An E320 Lord Nelson hauls No. 2 Passenger Coaches, while a No. 1 Tank Loco struggles with a goods train, including the new Trolley Wagon with Cable Drums. The HRC Coal, Trinidad Lake Asphalt Rotary, ShellMex & BP, Royal Daylight and Esso Wagons were all new in 1936.

new Hornby items; a set of No. 2 CORRIDOR COACHES was also produced for use with these new engines and the existing types. They were similar in design to the No. 2 Passenger Coaches, but fitted with the corridor connection as used on the Pullman Coaches, and with tinprinted sides representing the stock of each of the four railway groups in both 1st/3rd and Brake/Composite versions (or in the case of the SR, Open-3rd and Brake/Composite). Roof clips were fitted to the LNER, GW and SR coaches, to enable the Train Name Boards to be fitted; the LMS coaches had the clips on the sides rather than on the roof. The price of the Corridor Coaches was 7s 6d, compared with 6s 6d for the No. 2 Passenger Coach.

The contents of the larger train sets were revised to include these latest coaches; the No. 2 Special Pullman Train Sets were replaced by the No. 2 Special Passenger Train Sets which were named 'The Yorkshireman', 'The Scarborough Flyer', 'The Bristolian', and 'Folkestone Flyer'. The No. 3 Pullman Train Sets for the LMS, LNER and GW were replaced by the No. 3 Passenger Train Sets; but the 'Golden Arrow' remained as a Pullman train. All the revised clockwork sets had one coach and one brake/composite; the corresponding changes were also made to the electric train sets, but these were given two coaches plus the brake/composite.

The practice of giving names to the passenger train sets was also extended to the smaller sets, the No. 1 Special and E120 Special names being 'The Comet', 'Queen of Scots', 'Torbay Express' and 'Bournemouth Belle'. The LMS 'Comet' and GWR 'Torbay Express' were also revised to include No. 1 Passenger Coaches and the Guard's Van instead of the No. 1 Pullman coaches still supplied in the other two sets. The names for the No. 1 Passenger Sets were LMS 'The Pines Express', LNER 'Aberdonian', GW 'Cambrian Coast Express', and SR 'Bournemouth Limited'. Each of these named passenger train sets was identified by a sticker on the outside of the box, and a label inside the lid described

The Princess Elizabeth Locomotive was one of the most important new products of 1937. Most LMS locos of the 1937–38 period had new transfers with block letters instead of serif.

61

the famous train represented by the Hornby train.

The range of No. 0 vans was expanded in 1937 from four to twelve, the eight new types being the LMS, NE, GW and SR No. 0 REFRIGERATOR VANS, the NE and GW MEAT VANS and the LMS and GW FISH VANS. All were new tinprintings, in realistic styles, at the remarkably low price of 1s 6d each.

There were new loads for the High Capacity wagons, BRICKS for the NE version and COAL for the LMS and GW wagons. There were also changes in the load of the Flat Trucks and the Trolley Wagons with Cable Drum, the latest of which were 'Liverpool Cables' instead of 'British Insulated'. The Cement Wagon became 'Blue Circle' Portland Cement, in a striking yellow colour instead of plain red, and with an appropriate 'Blue Circle' transfer on the flap.

Another interesting innovation was the No. 0 STREAMLINE TRAIN SET, a different tinprinting of the No. 0 Silver Jubilee, in two colour schemes; maroon/cream or light green/dark green.

The loco, tender and coaches were also available separately. The Streamlined Train did not represent any prototype livery, and the loco numbers (3917 and 7391) were derived by shuffling the digits 1937. It seems a little odd that the year that saw the realistic 'Eton' and 'Princess' locos should also have produced these toy-like liveries. After all, the 'Silver Jubilee' had been overshadowed as the 'Fastest Train in the Empire' by the 'Coronation' service between King's Cross and Edinburgh, which maintained an average 72 miles per hour. The same streamlined engines were used, but in garter blue livery with red wheels, and coaches in two-tone garter blue and lighter Marlborough blue, with stainless steel lettering. This train was fully described in the 1937 HBT, and it is a mystery that the Streamlined Hornby train was not tinprinted in these colours; perhaps with another in LMS 'Coronation Scot' livery, just for fun!

So far as accessories are concerned, the most striking changes were in the platforms of the Stations, and of the Goods, Island and Passenger Platforms, the design drawings for which were revised from March 1937 to delete the embossing of the sides and allow production in material tinprinted with a speckled brown/buff colour. Although this change was made to the No. 1 and No. 2 Stations, the new platforms were also used for the new-style No. 3, No. 4 and No. 4E STATIONS which were catalogued from 1937. The No. 4 improved designs incorporated a through booking hall entrance, with a casting representing the ticket office barrier. The chimney pots were also changed to a casting instead of pressed tinplate. The tinprinting was in a more modern 'Ferrocement' style, in keeping with modern railway practice; but there was still no attempt to reproduce the all-important canopy, so the improvements were putting the cart before the horse. The No. 3 Station was a simplified type without the fences, ramps, or the through booking hall. The fact that it was said to be 'more strikingly coloured' than the No. 1 scarcely justified the increase of price from 4s 6d to 5s 6d.

The 'Princess Elizabeth' Locomotive was capable

Ripon, 1937. A late No. 2E Station and an Island Platform E, with new-style tinprinted roofs. 'Bramham Moor' is now in the darker green used from 1936 onwards for LNER locos, as is the No. 0 Loco 5508, a revised type with cylinders and piston rods.

Reading, 1937. E320 Loco 'Caerphilly Castle' arrives with a train of the new No. 2 Corridor Coaches, while an E220 Special Tank Loco passes through hauling GW No. 0 Vans from the enlarged range offered in the 1937–38 catalogues. Solid steel rails were available, but in short supply. The No. 3 and No. 4E Stations were also new in 1937–38.

of lurching in ungainly fashion round a 2 ft radius track, but it really required a more satisfactory set of rails, and the SOLID STEEL RAILS were the Hornby answer to the problem. They comprised the EA3 Curved Rails (3 ft radius) and the EB3 Straight Rail, with appropriate curved and straight half rails, straight quarter rails and points. As the name implied, these rails were of solid cross section, and generously supplied with sleepers (by Hornby standards!). The rails were joined by fishplates. Only electric rails were available in the Solid Steel range, and then initially in limited supply; the first 'Princess Elizabeth' instructions were over-printed with a note apologising for the delayed production of the Solid Steel Rails, 'Owing to the present shortage of high quality steel.' This shortage was not entirely unrelated to an urgent re-armament programme swinging slowly into gear in the uneasy political climate of the times.

It was probably a shortage not of materials but of time that delayed the production of the No. 2A BUFFER STOPS. These were included in the 1937 catalogues but were not actually made available until 1938. They were of less expensive design (incorporating a mazac casting all too susceptible to 'fatigue'), and ultimately replaced the No. 2 Hydraulic Buffer Stops.

Deletions from the Hornby range in 1937 were the No. 4 Cutting, the Metal Tunnel, and the Flexible Leads.

1938

'Unpack the box, then lay out the rails . . . and begin to run your own railway! It's the greatest fun in the world!'
(December 1938 MM)

The 1937 catalogues had shown some fresh price cuts, with prices generally at the lowest-ever levels, and representing the best ever value for money. All too soon, however, the changing times brought about increased costs, and a revised prices list took effect in January 1938.

It would not be quite fair to say nothing happened in the Hornby Series of 1938. After all, there was a new private owner PALETHORPE'S SAUSAGE VAN, and also a 'POWER ETHYL' PETROL TANK WAGON No. 1 which replaced the 'Shell-Mex and BP' tanker; even so these required only new sets of transfers. The delayed No. 2A Buffer Stops were issued, and also a version for the Solid Steel Rails, the No. 3A Buffer Stop. The No. 2E Buffer Stops were withdrawn, having been made unnecessary by the introduction of the LIGHTING ACCESSORY FOR BUFFER STOPS, which fitted into slots on the No. 2A and

Margate, 1938. An SR E420 'Eton' Locomotive (available from 1937) with No. 2 Corridor Coaches. The McAlpine Side Tipper and Power Ethyl Petrol Tank wagons were new; the Portland Cement Wagon had been introduced the previous year. The Palethorpes Sausage Van joined the 5 private owners' vans already available in 1938.

3A Buffers, or onto brackets on the latest No. 1 and No. 2 types. Another change in 1938 was the revision and extension of the range of Train Name Boards, a step that probably became necessary with increased demand from owners of the popular No. 2 Corridor Coaches. The obsolete No. 1, 2 and 2E Stations were no longer listed.

The remaining electric M1-type locomotives and sets in both 6 and 20 volts were withdrawn from sale, and the Speed and Reverse Switch was no longer catalogued separately, although it was still sold with the EPM16 Locomotive. Still on the electrical side, the Circuit Breaker was replaced by two separate versions, one for 6 volt and one for 20 volt operation, after the belated realisation that they should 'trip' at

different currents.

The E320 METROPOLITAN LOCO-MOTIVE and TRAIN SET were rather curious late introductions. The Metropolitan had been anomalous among the 1934 types in being available only for 6 volt and not for 20 volt working; the 6 volt mechanism used was unique to this locomotive. The 20 volt version with automatic reverse appeared in 1938–39 for one season only.

The reason for the virtual lack of developments in the Hornby Gauge O system was not that a peak of perfection had been reached, nor was there a scarcity of resources or of ideas. Nor were the gathering storm clouds of the political scene so gloomy as to deter any new departures – far from it.

The works were in fact embarked on nothing less ambitious than a complete new model railway system, the HORNBY DUBLO TRAINS; but they are another story, told by Michael Foster in 'Hornby Dublo Trains' in this series. The tooling and production of these, and of the ever-increasing range of Dinky Toys, had simply not left time to develop the Hornby Series any further.

1939

'Hornby Trains for endless hours of pleasure in the long winter evenings.' (December 1939 MM)

There had been few new introductions in 1938. But there were to be none at all in 1939! The Hornby

Dublo Trains had proved an instant success, and had clearly begun to displace the Gauge O trains in importance to the company's production and profits. While the Dublo range continued to expand, the deletions from the Hornby Series gathered pace, and in 1939 the deletions included all the remaining Control System items, the Points on Solid Base with Ground Disc, all the Metropolitan Trains, the EPM16 Loco, both Switch Rails, the French-type Wagon, Cuttings Nos. 1 to 3, the glass globe No. 1 and No. 2 Lamp Standards, No. 2 and No. 2E Water Tanks, Telegraph Poles, and the No. 1E and No. 2 Buffers. The No. 0 Train Sets also disappeared – but not the separate locos.

Since the explosion of colour in the 1933–34 season, year by year from 1934 there had been a gradual move back to more realistic colours; in 1939 the No. 2 Timber and Lumber Wagons and the Trolley Wagon were finished in grey, with red stanchions, and the No. 1 Timber, No. 1 Lumber and Fibre Wagons were painted black. By 1939 several of the other wagons had started to appear on black bases and bogies, instead of the previous bright colours, and a thin matt varnish was commonly used on bases and bogies, instead of the shiny varnishes characteristic of earlier years. The matt varnish was also used on the latest locomotives and tenders.

The use of white letters on vans and other Hornby wagons had become more general through the late '30s, and by 1939 the gold letters were virtually out of use – except on the Breakdown Van and Crane.

The January 1939 MM announced a revised part exchange scheme, now applying to locomotives only and not to rails; and in October the MM announced that 'The deferred payments scheme for Meccano and Hornby Trains is now discontinued'. The scheme was omitted from the 1939–40 catalogues and lists.

The outbreak of the Second World War caused no immediate changes in the Hornby product range, but the increasing devotion of manufacturing resources to war contracts inevitably restricted production, and Gauge O train production during the war was only on a very limited scale, compared to the many thousands of train sets that were formerly produced each year. The November 1939 MM said that 'Everything will continue as far as possible, as far as Meccano and Hornby Trains are concerned, but the introduction of new lines at present is doubtful.'

Ripon, 1938. An E320 'Flying Scotsman', with LNER Corridor Coaches. Contemporary Dinky Toys enliven the approach road.

1940 to 1944

'Ready to go! Departure time for the Hornby express draws near. . .' (March 1940 MM)

Ready to depart for the duration, at least. Indeed, the war was to sweep away the production of the best of the Hornby Series not just for the duration but for ever. The postwar production never recovered to allow once again the proud claim 'Everything for the complete model railway'.

1940 did see the introduction of a single new product, the 'POOL' Petrol Tank Wagon No. 1, which was advertised in the October 1940 MM; however the relentless pace of withdrawals increased, and not least among the items never to re-appear was the 'Princess Elizabeth' Locomotive.

During 1940 there were repeated price revisions, the first on 1st January; 'Owing to rising costs of production, the prices of Hornby Trains . . . have been unavoidably increased.' The New Zealand agents, not subject to censorship requirements, were able to be more specific: 'Owing to the abnormal increase in the price of raw materials, huge expenses in connection with air raid precautions, compulsory insurance with the Government against war risks, all skilled workers on war work and scarcity of unskilled male labour due to the recruiting requirements, Messrs. Meccano Ltd have been compelled to increase prices . . . Hornby products are subject to

an increase of 10% in price. . .' There were also revised price lists in April and in August, then finally on 21st October 1940, when for the first time the Government imposed a stiff purchase tax on Hornby Trains. No catalogues or illustrated folders were produced for the UK in 1940, but UK price lists noted the many items that were in short supply or not available.

Nonetheless there was some production during 1940; many wagons were made in batches of several thousand, and some accessories including the Dinky Toy figures were also made. The familiar red boxes were replaced towards the end of the year by plain buff cardboard boxes of lower quality, and the shortage of paper and card meant taking extra care to

A No. 2E Goods Platform in 1939, with Matt No. 1 Tank and No. 0 Locos.

Wembley, 1939. A matt-finish No. 3 'Royal Scot' hauls the Merseyside Express, while a humbler No. 0 loco arrives on a suburban service. Many 1939–40 wagons had matt black underframes.

Reading, 1939–40. On the high level, an E320 'Caerphilly Castle' (note the black nameplate) enters Reading General with a train of No. 2 Pullman stock, while Lord Nelson arrives at Reading South with No. 2 Special Pullmans. In the foreground is a matt No. 2 Special Tank, with some goods stock.

From the Liverpool Evening Express, 19 December 1944.

How Meccano Went to War

FROM TOYS TO ARMAMENTS

BEFORE total war swept across the globe, bringing its toy famine, the fascinating products of Meccano Limited went abroad to every land. Books of instructions for assembling toy engineering models were printed in many languages.

Today the toy makers are at war. The engineering shops of Meccano Limited, at Liverpool, are turning out not scale models of railway locomotives or cranes, but integral parts of the engines of war.

Youths who played only a few years ago with Hornby trains and model 'planes are now using weapons and flying war 'planes which depend for their efficiency on products from that same works which produced their toys.

Scores of parts and instruments are being made there—from bomb release units to fuses, from tools for fitting de-icing equipment of aircraft to hypodermic needles.

Little change in the machinery of production was necessary for the changeover from peace to war. The first shots of the war had scarcely been fired before aircraft general stores were being made by Meccano Ltd. Their toys had always been engineering jobs. Their world-famous model engines and trains were the products of precision, and wonderfully accurate models of real engines and trains down to small details. Their workers had the necessary skill to turn their labours to the new type of work.

There came a day when the last toy came from the workshops. But the work of producing war parts had already begun and was well under way.

This is one of the few works in the country where complete fuses can be made, from the first die-casting to the final inspection. Most other workshops have to depend on someone else for some part or other.

Night and day work went on without cessation. Shift-work has been in operation since 1940.

With few exceptions, work went on during air-raids. Today the works enjoys the confidence of many Ministries and Government departments for the quality and prompt execution of its war work.

Targets have been exceeded and many times contracts completed months ahead of schedule. Great importance is attached to the conveyor system and all tasks are viewed from the mass-production angle.

Speed of the conveyor belts is accurately estimated and set against the time necessary to complete a set of operations. If the conveyor travels too slowly, production goes down. If

Women workers busy on automatic spraying.

it is too fast, quality of work suffers. A comfortable speed for the operators has to be ascertained, otherwise they would experience physical and mental strain and, towards the end of the day, mistakes would be liable to occur.

It would be impossible to enumerate all the types of war parts that have been turned out at this works, but they include bulletproof petrol tank details, complete fuses, millions of aircraft screws, electrical testers for aircraft cameras, explosive bullets, and power unit chassis for aircraft wireless.

The works are extremely proud of the fact that they can turn out 90 different types of plugs and sockets for aircraft wiring.

One proud feat was the making of millions of hypodermic needles for the Russian front. It was an urgent job. A typhus epidemic had broken out.

It was found impossible to undertake the task in another part of Britain. The work was sent to Meccano. Needles were turned out at the rate of 40,000 a week. Production beat the schedule.

An interesting time-saving device for summoning any person who is

wanted is in operation in all the departments.

A red light flashes in the centre of the room accompanied by the ringing of a bell. The rings and flashes correspond with a code, indicating the particular person required. The signals continue until that individual has answered the nearest telephone.

Before the war the die-casting shop on account of its hot atmosphere was the domain of men workers exclusively. But during the war, women invaded this sphere.

Meccano Ltd. played an important part in the production of bomb-release units and became main contractors. Several types have been turned out during the war.

The Meccano Magazine, known to all boys, is still produced and reaches 55,000 boys each month, telling them all the news of 'planes, ships and trains.

But the toy-makers will not always be at war. The day will come when they drop the making of war-like things and turn again to satisfying the "toy-starvation" of children the world over.

And the change will be as smooth as was the call to war.

---

conserve supplies by carefully re-labelling surplus boxes. Most of the buff boxes carried no printers' code, so it is difficult to be sure what was produced in 1941. By then production of Hornby Trains was virtually at a standstill, and only a very small number of items were produced.

The July 1941 MM gave even more bad news; the repair service was temporarily discontinued due to pressure of work. Sales of Hornby Trains continued, and price lists were issued in May and November 1941; prices were increased substantially, in some cases to double the prewar levels. Nonetheless stocks had been falling fast by the time the further production of Hornby Trains was prohibited under Government order, as from 1 January, 1942. In point of fact the pressures of war work would have precluded any further toy train manufacture even in the absence of a direct Government order. It is nonetheless interesting that the latest known wartime printers' code is dated January 1942 (for a batch of 750 No. 1 Passenger Coaches) – perhaps a few items were made 'on the quiet'! By May 1942 the number of Meccano Magazines printed had to be reduced because of paper shortages; the size of the magazine had already been cut at the start of 1942, and it was announced that no new orders or subscriptions for the magazine could be accepted.

Even the production of Hornby Railway Company and Meccano Guild badges was affected by the ban on manufacturing, and eventually none were available; the export of all badges had been prohibited earlier. The ban on production of toys was soon extended by the Misc. Goods (Prohibition of Manufacture and Supply) (No. 4) Order (SRO966), which ordered that no metal model or toy goods complete or in parts or castings were to be sold, either new or secondhand after 30 September, 1943.

1945

'We are sorry that we cannot supply these famous toys today, but they will be ready for you again after the war. Look out for the good times coming!' (May 1945 MM)

'VE day has brought nearer the time when we shall be able to supply these famous toys. Our works, which are still on war production, will change over to our own goods as rapidly as conditions permit – soon, we hope!' (July

'Our works, while still engaged on Government contracts, are changing over to the familiar products as rapidly as possible. . .' (November 1945 MM)

The early postwar years in the Meccano factory are interesting, simply because so little information about the period seems to have been recorded.

Even if life could never be expected to go back to the old pattern, there was a general expectation that after the horror and grief of the World War, there would be a quick return to a reasonable standard of living after years of shortages, of 'make do and mend'. There could not be an immediate return to toy-making at Binns Road because of unfinished government work. But the production of toys was no longer prohibited, and the company looked forward optimistically to serving the needs of a new

Reading, 1940. E220 Special Loco 'County of Bedford' on a suburban duty, and a matt E120 Special Loco. The Pool Petrol Tank Wagon was the only new product announced in 1940.

generation of toy-starved lads, with their usual exciting range of products. Gradually came the realisation that the grim and austere conditions of wartime could not be made to vanish overnight, and that postwar recovery was to be a slow and uphill process; indeed by 1947 the public was feeling some hardships and shortages unknown even at the worst moments of the blockade of Britain's supply lines. The key to national recovery lay in a strong export drive, and the goods that industry was gearing up to produce, including the toys from Binns Road, were destined to satisfy the needs of our export market, however desperate the shortages at home.

The first priorities of Meccano Ltd were the manufacture of Meccano, then of Dinky Toys; the latter without the 'fatigue' problems of earlier years, the problem having been finally solved. It is rare to find any sign of fatigue on any of the postwar Hornby or Dinky castings in mazac.

1946

'It will not be long now before the good times are here again.' (January 1946 MM)

'A further limited supply of Hornby Trains will be ready before Christmas.' (November 1946 MM)

'Meccano Outfits and Dinky Toys are once again in the shops along with a few of the smaller Hornby Train Sets. An early visit to your local Meccano dealer is recommended.' (December 1946 MM)

It was not until 1946 that any regular production of Hornby Trains could be undertaken. The Meccano Magazines of the period are understandably vague on availability; in fact the successive advertisements reflect both the hopes and the frustrations of the delays in meeting demand.

So in what state was the works when production re-started? What tools, materials and part-finished

work had been preserved for the day that production resumed? Probably not as much as might be supposed. The production of Hornby Trains had not been stopped suddenly, like turning off a tap, nor could it be restarted with the same ease. With the pressures of munitions work, storage space would have been at a premium. Furthermore the assembly of Meccano Ltd's range of toys required vast numbers of tools and dies, all made in high quality tool steels that were in short supply, and with a high scrap value. In the light of the national scrap drive Meccano Ltd are bound to have looked most carefully at their stocks with a view to clearing out some of the items they could not hope to use in the near future. It is unlikely that all the press tools had survived the war, even if the materials had been ready to hand and the production lines had been idle. In any case many of the old tools had become badly worn. The stockroom may have held the remains of the prewar range (including locomotives with badly 'fatigued' wheels!), but not in sufficient quantities to make it possible to offer them in lists or catalogues.

A fresh start was evidently decided upon, and it was late in 1945 that there began a period of wholesale revision of the production drawings for Hornby Trains of all sorts, including several items destined never actually to re-appear. The thoroughness of the revisions in the early postwar period show that it was not the intention of Meccano Ltd simply to dust off the old tools and to carry on where they left off, but to give considered thought to the design of all the products that were re-appearing. For example, from 1946 the rails in the postwar sets were given sensible all-level sleepers, and the brake rail levers were revised to a more compact shape that made them easier to use, and easier to pack in the set boxes.

At first, the most thorough updating was for the MO and M1 Trains that were to be the mainstay of the postwar range. The first regular production of trains in 1946 included the MO GOODS and PASSENGER SETS, with a choice of red or green locos; the locomotives and rolling stock were all similar to the prewar types, albeit with differences of detail. The M1 GOODS and PASSENGER SETS were again sold with red or with green locos, and were very similar to the prewar sets. The M1 Pullman Coaches were 'Marjorie', 'Aurelia' and 'Viking', only two per set; the earliest postwar M1 Pullmans appear to have had white roofs instead of the prewar cream, but soon both the MO and the M1 coaches adopted the grey roof colour used for the postwar No. 1 Coaches. The rails in the sets were of the usual postwar patterns.

A little later in 1946 than the M series sets came the No. 101 TANK PASSENGER SETS and the No. 201 TANK GOODS SETS. The No. 101 Locomotives were equivalent to the former M3 clockwork locomotives; the same tinprinting was used, there were only minor changes in style and they had the same type of mechanism. The rolling stock in the passenger set comprised two No. 1 Coaches and a Passenger Brake Van, with head and tail lamps provided (similar to the prewar design but without the wire handle). The coaches were similar to the prewar style but with lighter grey roofs. The

An MO Passenger Train set, one of the very first postwar products after the long break in production since 1942. The M Station Set and M Level Crossing were made after the war, but were not catalogued.

An early postwar M1 Passenger Train, with Pullmans 'Aurelia' and 'Viking'.

No. 201 Goods Set included a Timber Wagon, a Tank Wagon and an open Wagon.

The close similarity to the prewar sets has often caused speculation that the 'frozen' stock left over from 1941 may simply have been re-packaged in 1946, or the sets made up from left-over parts; while there may have been a small contribution in this manner, the majority of these sets were of genuine postwar manufacture. One sure sign of postwar assembly is the embossed 'Hornby' trademark in the base of most postwar wagons, which was added to the design drawings in 1946. The 'Hornby Series' designation was rarely used in postwar years, 'Hornby' or 'Hornby Trains' being the preferred style.

The 'Pool' Petrol Tank Wagon in the 201 Sets was virtually the same as the wartime equivalent, but the 'Royal Daylight' Oil Tank Wagon that appeared briefly in 1946–47 was a plain grey instead of the prewar red.

The 101 and 201 Sets were available in LMS, LNER, GW or SR liveries, the latter two being (uncharacteristically) no less common than the others.

1947

'Hornby Trains. Loads of fun.' (December 1947 MM)

'. . . We are doing our utmost to increase production.' (January 1947 MM)

'Every minute spent playing with Hornby Trains is brimful of thrills and enjoyment!' (November 1947 Price List)

The Hornby Train Sets listed in the small March 1947 illustrated price list (the first postwar UK list to include Hornby Trains) were the M0 and M1 Goods and Passenger Train Sets, and the No. 201 Goods Train Set in the four different company liveries. The No. 101 Tank Passenger Set was not listed until the November 1947 illustrated price list, the delay being caused by restricted supply; 1947 was to prove if anything an even more difficult year than 1946. There is, however, clear evidence from the date-stamping of guarantee forms that the No. 101 Passenger Set had actually been made as early as November 1946.

The range of different Hornby Train Sets was abysmally limited, although each of these few sets was made in quite large quantities. There were virtually no accessories or items of rolling stock

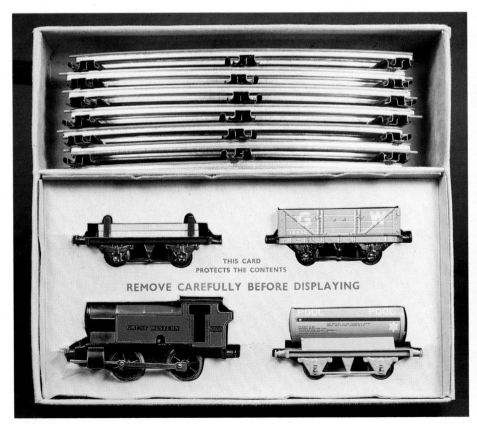

A 201 Tank Goods Set of 1946.

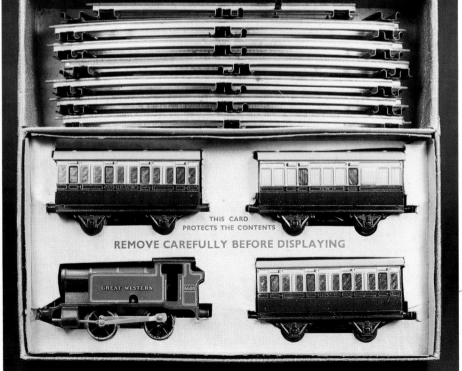

A 101 Tank Passenger Set of 1947. The loco is matt-finished.

available for sale outside the sets. In March 1947 the MM apologised that 'The scarcity of Hornby Railway accessories is as bad as ever, and there is not much likelihood of an improvement in the near future.' It is nonetheless interesting to note that the Gauge O train production took precedence at the time over the production of Hornby Dublo.

From 1946 the sets had been packaged in cheaper (but not altogether unattractive) boxes, and curiously a very large quantity of buff-coloured boxes were made in 1946 for certain items other than boxed sets; the 10,000 boxes for No. 1 wagons, 20,000 for Petrol Tank Wagons and 20,000 for No. 1 Timber Wagons were evidently made for separate sales of the 201 set wagons, and 100,000 boxes for No. 1 Buffers would be a reasonable batch. But why 9,000 boxes for the No. 0 Refrigerator Van? The question is necessarily academic since the plans to use the boxes (evidently produced at the height of post-war optimism!) came to nothing, and most of them were to be used up for items made in 1948. Some blue labels were printed as early as 1945 for buff boxes containing the postwar M Station Set. Similar yellow labels (not dated) were printed, e.g. for early postwar No. 1 Level Crossings and No. 2 Signals. Because of the long delay known to have occurred before the rolling stock boxes were used, it is very difficult to guess the date when these accessories were actually made.

1948

'Hornby Trains are strong-pulling, long-running, tested and guaranteed.' (October 1948 Price List)

Reasonable supplies of Hornby Trains began to re-appear in the shops in the 1948–49 season, although there was little hope of satisfying every demand. These supplies disappeared rapidly to the homes of delighted users; the care and appreciation with which many of these early postwar sets were handled is reflected in the good condition in which many of them have survived.

In October 1948 a new illustrated price list gave welcome news of a reduction in prices, and of an increased range both of Hornby Trains and of Hornby Dublo. The No. 501 PASSENGER

An LMS 101 Tank of 1947, with the wagons from the 201 Tank Goods Set, including the main 1946–48 variations of the Petrol and Oil Tank Wagons.

TRAIN SET and the No. 601 GOODS TRAIN SET were listed; interestingly enough the 501 set was listed as available in GW and SR liveries in addition to LMS and LNER, and the No. 601 Set was listed in SR, LMS and NE. Neither the GW or the SR No. 501 Locomotives were made in large numbers, unlike the No. 101 Tank Locos for which the GW and SR versions were widely available. Most of the GW and SR 501 Sets that were made seem to have been exported.

The No. 501 Locomotive was equivalent to the prewar No. 1 Locomotive, with an enamelled finish and a matt varnish. The same matt varnish was used for a while on the tinprinted No. 101 Locomotives.

Electric versions of these new sets, the E502 PASSENGER SETS and E602 GOODS SETS, were made in reasonably large numbers. These were the only electric 20 volt locomotives available in the Hornby Gauge O range after the war, and they were never catalogued in the UK since they were reserved for export, many to Australia. They were in production until hit by the shortages of materials around 1951, and altogether several thousand sets were produced. Although not a large quantity compared

The 601 Goods and 501 Passenger Train Sets were available on the home market from 1948, and a limited range of wagons became available for separate sale.

to the tens of thousands of clockwork sets sold each year, the high unit price would have made the production viable. Electric rails for these sets were also catalogued abroad until 1952; the EB1 Straight and EA2 Curved Rails, the EPR2 and EPL2 Points (on solid base) and the Terminal Connecting Plate (also supplied in the sets) were available. A full instruction leaflet was included with each set, and the T20 Transformer instructions of the period also showed the method of operating a 20 volt Hornby Train. One change from the prewar practice was that no lamp-holders were fitted to the smokebox doors.

The October 1948 list was the first to list wagons and rails available for separate sale in the UK. Nineteen wagons were listed, including the bogie No. 2 Goods Van (the postwar name for the Luggage Van). Also listed were the No. 1 Coach and Passenger Brake Van. The No. 2 Coach also appeared, but no further details were given except the price of 12s 6d. In fact all four railway companies were represented, and both the 1st–3rd and Brake-3rd versions were available. These postwar coaches were almost identical to the prewar versions except for the lighter grey colour of the roofs, and the gold trademark transfers on the No. 2 Coach which were also used on some other 1948–49 products.

Wagons of 1946–47 production typically had underframes and bases identical to the prewar pattern, except for the embossed trademark. But many 1947–48 wagons, although using the same pressing for the base, lacked axlebox slots (which had been more or less superfluous even in 1930, since so few special order axleboxes were sold).

Other changes from prewar practice were the addition of lamp brackets to the ends of various vans, including the No. 1 and No. 2 Goods, Refrigerator, Cattle, Milk Traffic and Brake Vans. The latter were also fitted with lamp brackets on the sides, which took a special new SIDE LAMP with two aspects; silver facing forward and red to the rear. The lettering on these vans was not in the prewar style; small company letters, tare and wagon number were applied to the lower left-hand corner of the van, in imitation of the standard prototype practice; a change that had been needed for some time. The Milk Traffic van piercing had to be altered to give a flat panel for lettering; and on the standard postwar issues neither the Milk Traffic Van nor the Cattle Truck were pressed with imitation planking on the body or doors.

The colours were also different for the re-issued goods vehicles, with LMS vans in brown with light grey roofs, and NE in bauxite with white roofs. The GW vans were in a rather fetching dark grey, and the SR in dark chocolate brown, each with white roofs. The exceptions to this rule were the Refrigerator Van (issued in white for NE and buff for LMS) and the Milk Traffic Van, issued only in 'Southern' green. The standard colours were also used for the Flat Trucks; the Hopper Wagon was green, with yellow LMS letters.

An interesting feature of the postwar wagon range was that it became standard practice to spray the solebars of many of the wagons in the colours used for the body upper-work; a suggestion to this effect had been rejected as too costly back in the 1930s!

The Petrol Tank Wagon was changed in 1948 from the grey 'Pool' version to a new-style 'Shell' Tank Wagon No. 1, with a red tank and black base (entailing a new method for assembly after spraying). The dark blue lettering was, in common with some other lettering of the period, applied by a rubber stamp. Of the other re-issued wagons the Side Tipping and Rotary Tipping Wagon had virtually unaltered transfers, but were applied to buff-coloured tippers instead of the prewar yellow. The 'Wagon with Tarpaulin Support' was similar to the prewar Open Wagon 'B', but with tinprinted sides and not embossed with planking.

The October 1948 lists also offered a single accessory, the No. 1 Buffer Stops; and there was also a range of rails and points of 1 ft and 2 ft radius, and two crossings. The supply situation for all these items was inadequate, and as late as December 1948 the Meccano Magazine was still apologising that 'Unfortunately, Hornby rolling stock cannot yet be bought separately.'

1949

'Start a Hornby railway today. It's wonderful fun!'
(April 1949 Price List)

'Limited supplies of steel and tinplate continue to control our distribution of many products – Meccano and train goods in particular.' (Trade leaflet, June 1949)

The big news of 1949 should, of course, have been the adoption of British Railways liveries, following the nationalisation of the railways in January 1948. Unfortunately it was to be another five years before Hornby trains caught up with real life!

The new items in the 1949 price lists included several further wagons; the Cement wagon was to be the last of the prewar four-wheeled wagons to reappear in the lists. Some bogie wagons were listed in addition to the No. 2 Goods Van: the Breakdown Van and Crane, No. 2 Cattle Truck, High Capacity Wagon No. 2, Lumber Wagon No. 2 and Trolley Wagon. The bogie No. 2 Coaches were still available.

The postwar four wheel wagons were fitted (from 1949, and in some cases earlier) with a revised base, similar in general form to the previous 1930 design but with different embossed details. The design drawings are ambiguous on the actual date of the change; it appears that the design may have been revised as early as 1946, but not adopted for actual use until much later.

The range of accessories offered in 1949 included the No. 1 Footbridge (finished in grey with green trim), Island Platform, Level Crossing No. 1, Platform Crane, Signal Cabin No. 2 (without the hinged roof of prewar days), No. 2 Double Arm and Single Arm Signals, No. 3 Station, Turntable No. 2, Water Tank No. 1, Goods Platform No. 1, Posters and the Station Hoarding. The rails available for separate sale now included right angle crossings, and MO rails; but the MO rails were not listed again until 1952.

This enlarged range of Hornby Trains was to be the high point of postwar production, although it may not have seemed so at the time because supply could still not keep pace with the unprecedented demand, despite achieving production levels unknown since the 1930s.

A photograph taken of a Meccano Ltd exhibition stand at the British Industries Fair in early 1949 shows the full glory of the postwar range, including some of the bogie wagons, and a range of boxed sets

The 501 Loco in GW livery, 1948.

An E502 Loco in LNER livery, with some unlettered goods stock (probably intended for export). The No. 2 Cattle Truck had only a short postwar run.

An LMS E502 Passenger Set, 1948. Available to export customers only.

An M1 Passenger Set of 1948.

1949 list of gauge O rolling stock.

HORNBY ROLLING STOCK

	each		each
Breakdown Van and Crane	11/6	Hopper Wagon	5/–
Cattle Truck No. 1	4/9	Lumber Wagon No. 1	3/–
Cattle Truck No. 2	8/6	Lumber Wagon No. 2	6/6
Cement Wagon	3/6	Milk Traffic Van No. 1	5/6
Coach No. 1	3/9	Passenger Brake Van	3/9
Coach No. 2	11/3	Petrol Tank Wagon No. 1	3/–
Crane Truck No. 1	5/6	Refrigerator Van No. 1	4/9
Flat Truck	2/9	Rotary Tipping Wagon No. 1	3/9
Flat Truck (with drum)	3/9	Side Tipping Wagon No. 1	3/6
Flat Truck (with container)	4/–	Timber Wagon No. 1	2/3
Gas Cylinder Wagon	2/9	Trolley Wagon	8/6
Goods Van No. 1	4/9	Wagon No. 1	2/6
Goods Van No. 2	8/6	Wagon with tarpaulin	
Goods Brake Van	5/6	support	2/9
High Capacity Wagon No. 2	8/3		

75

A 1949 trade exhibition; note the SR 501 Loco and the BR Compound!

A number of accessories and buildings became available in 1949, including the Station and Footbridge. →
The 'Electric Cables' drum was issued briefly in 1948.

No. 2 Coaches were available in four liveries from 1948 to 1950, and No. 2 Goods Vans were also
available; these were the only bogie vehicles to be sold in any quantity in the UK.

A selection of GW postwar Hornby Trains, form the 1946–51 period.

A similar selection of SR Hornby Trains, from 1946–54. Both GW and SR finishes appeared only sporadically.

including an SR No. 601 set; also some unexpected items, such as a Compound Loco in British Railways black livery, and a Southern 4-4-2 Tank. Although the design drawings for the No. 2 Special and No. 2 Special Tank Locomotives were updated by the drawing office, and it was evidently intended that they would be produced, these plans were regrettably never carried out. Nonetheless the Hornby Railway Company booklets in 1948, 1949 and 1950 editions showed the old products with a note: 'At the time of printing, some of the pieces of equipment shown in the illustrations in this booklet are not available. They will be produced as soon as circumstances permit. . .'

Why did these plans come to nothing? A shortage of materials continued to frustrate expansion, and

demand for the existing products had still not been satisfied. But the most important reason was the phenomenal success of the Hornby Dublo Train. The pattern that became established was that the Gauge O trains were marketed for the younger child, and the playroom railway; in 1949 the clockwork sets were priced from 17s 6d for the MO, to 52s 6d for the No. 501 and No. 601 Sets. The most expensive Gauge O train set was therefore less than half the price of the cheapest Hornby Dublo Electric Tank Goods Set, at 125s! And many more Dublo than Gauge O trains could be made with the same amount of material, netting more cash for Meccano Ltd. The Hornby Dublo system was more suited to meeting the aspirations of the increasingly sophisticated model railway buyers, who were demanding

near-scale models. There was also an undeniable attraction simply because of the smaller size, and there was a certain 'cachet' in owning one of the Dublo sets; Trix Twin Railways had already shown that even a crude OO-Gauge railway could succeed commercially. But Dublo was better suited to providing a realistic model railway, to be operated on railway-like principles, in the preferred Hornby Railway Company style!

The Hornby Gauge O Trains were destined to remain what they had always been; a jolly good toy railway, strong and durable, and sold at a reasonable price. The circumstances of 1949 and 1950 decided that there would be no attempt to bridge the gap to Dublo either by selling 'wind-up' Dublo Locos as before the war, or by providing once again the larger and more realistic electric Gauge O trains.

1950

'You can rely on Hornby Trains.' (November 1950 MM)

'Full of thrills for boys and for Dad.' (June 1950 Meccano Products Folder)

The difficulties of supply that had already bedevilled production became a fraction more obtrusive in 1950. A new price list issued in February 1950 showed Gauge O prices revised sharply upwards, raising the price of the No. 501 set for instance from 52s 6d to 61s 6d. Fewer items were listed than in 1949; the No. 2 Coaches and the bogie rolling stock were no longer listed and never reappeared. Furthermore the range of accessories was temporarily cut, the Goods Platform, Platform Crane, Posters, No. 2 Signal Cabin, and Water Tank being the items affected.

There was little change in those items that stayed on sale; the only noteworthy difference was that the Petrol Tank Wagon was produced in a silver 'Esso' livery, replacing the 'Shell' tanker.

1951

'The supply situation is difficult just now.' (October 1951 MM)

Standard postwar wagons of the 1949–54 period. The Milk Traffic Van was the only Southern item to be made in large numbers.

'Another year, another deadly blow'! The Korean War caused even greater shortages of materials, creating further difficulties in manufacturing over the whole range of Meccano Ltd products. Worst hit were the supplies of nickel, brass – and mazac, leading to the temporary closure of Meccano Ltd's Speke factory.

In late 1951 there were hasty revisions to the O Gauge production drawings to cope with the latest shortages. Many of the castings used for the trains (loco chimneys, crane truck hooks, water tank columns, head and tail lamps, and many others) had been changed from lead to zinc based (mazac) castings between 1946 and 1950. They were changed back again to lead castings in late 1951, and it was not until late 1952 that supplies allowed a full return to mazac.

Another change was in the nickel plated parts, for example the locomotive coupling rods and their pins, the brake and reverse rods, water tank fittings and chains, and 501 mechanism sideplates, among others. The shortage of nickel necessitated a black 'Brunofix' finish, which became characteristic of 1951–53 products; indeed the 'Brunofix' finish was maintained on certain of these parts after there was no longer any need to do so, because the appearance was not unattractive.

Perhaps most importantly, plastic wheels were designed in March 1951 to help with the tinplate shortage; these moulded wheels were a very satisfactory substitute for the tinplate type, and gave smoother, quieter, and longer running because of reduced friction. The typical wagons of the period had plastic wheels and black 'Brunofix' axles. Not surprisingly, the decision was finally made (although not until the middle of 1954) that plastic wheels would continue to be used, rather than going back to tinplate. A letter to Bruce Baxter from the MM Editor dated 9 March, 1953 reads 'I agree with you about the plastic Hornby Train wheels. They were

More wagons of the standard postwar range, 1949–54.

M1 Locos, Pullmans and Wagons; best sellers in the postwar Hornby Train range.

introduced in order to overcome the difficulties that arose when metals were in short supply. No particular mention of this was made in the MM because of the possibility that we should return to the older type when metals again became sufficiently plentiful. Whether we shall do this or not is now something of a problem, as the new wheels are so successful, but the point is not yet settled. As far as possible I will continue to include details of additions and changes, just as was done in the prewar days.'

The September 1951 MM had apologised that 'It may not be possible for many owners of Hornby Trains to build extensive sidings and goods yards at present, owing to the scarcity of equipment.' Apart from detail differences, and these inevitable shortages, there were no major changes in the range; it was difficult enough for Meccano Ltd to keep going, without making changes!

1952

'Manage your own railway! Any boy can boss his own railway if he has Hornby Trains.' (July 1952 MM)

The February 1952 pocket catalogue announced even higher prices, and several accessories were again temporarily unobtainable with 'Supplies expected by the autumn'. Although they reappeared in the September catalogue, it was still a matter of luck whether they could be found in the toy shops. The September catalogue also listed the MO rails, available separately for the first time since 1949.

There was an easier situation with mazac supplies in 1952, and the Dinky Toy figures for Gauge O were advertised in the April 1952 MM. The No. 1 Station Staff Set was similar to the prewar set, but without the Stationmaster. The No. 4 Engineering staff were also reduced to a strength of five men by the loss of the Electrician. Contents of the No. 2 Farmyard Animals, No. 3 Passengers, No. 5 Train and Hotel Staff and No. 6 Shepherd Set were unchanged; but the crude new colour schemes lacked the detail of finish that had made the prewar sets so distinctive.

There were few other introductions. The four MO wagons of prewar days re-appeared at last (MO

Crane Truck, MO Rotary and Side Tipping Wagons, and the MO Petrol Tank Wagon); the colours were unchanged, except for the silver tank of the 'Shell-BP' tanker. Certain sundry items were catalogued separately from 1952, including the locomotive winding Keys, the Head, Tail and Side Lamps, and the Wheels and Axles for Rolling Stock.

Apart from the No. 101 and 201 sets, there had been sporadic attempts to produce batches of wagons in SR and GW livery; one apparent effect of the shortages was that these two company liveries disappeared from the Hornby range, the 'Southern' Milk Traffic Van being the only exception.

There is an interesting advertisement in the July 1952 Model Railway News in which Hattons of Liverpool offered 20 volt and 9 volt transformers and controllers, rails and goods rolling stock, and Hornby 20 volt and clockwork 4–4–0 and 4–4–2 Locos and Train Sets all as clearance offers.

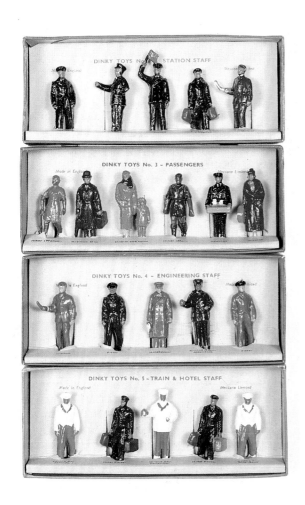

Postwar Dinky Toy Station Staff, Passengers, Engineering Staff and Train and Hotel Staff.

By 1952 the Signals and Island Platforms had shorter, non-latticed posts. ↗

Wembley Station, postwar style. From 1952 the Footbridge had → *solid sides.*

During the 1954–55 season, BR Hornby Trains at last replaced the pre-nationalisation versions. The footbridge was tinprinted instead of enamelled, and 'Trent' Island Platforms replaced the other names. The No. 40 Tank Loco is seen with No. 41 Coaches.

1953

'Every boy dreams of running his own railway – a dream that is realised with Hornby Trains.' (October 1953 Meccano Products Catalogue)

'Clear the line . . . she's waiting. Ready to go whizzing along with a good load, on another round the room trip!' (December 1953 MM)

1952 was probably the last year to feel the postwar pinch; in the Coronation year of 1953 there was a proper climate of optimism. . .

Once again, there were few changes in the range of Hornby Gauge O Trains; perhaps the stagnant pattern from 1949 reflected the fact that, in a sellers' market, there is little incentive to change or to improve. There was one further re-introduction, the No. 2 Junction Signal, in a revised version with shorter posts and without the lattice pattern of the prewar product; the same changes had been made a year or two earlier to the Single Arm and Double Arm Signals, and the Island Platform. There was also another change in the livery of the Tank Wagon No. 1, to 'National Benzole', replacing 'Esso'.

The February 1953 MM announced the Dinky Toys No. 752 Goods Yard Crane, which was a useful accessory in cast metal with hoisting, slewing and jib raising movements. Although it was advertised as suitable for use with the Gauge O Trains, and listed as a Hornby accessory, it was double the price of the tinplate Hornby Platform Crane.

1954

'Load up the goods! What opportunities there are for lasting fun with a goods depot made up of Hornby equipment.' (July 1954 MM)

The fact of railway nationalisation had to be faced sooner or later, and it was in 1954 that the wholesale revision of liveries to British Railways colours was announced in the Meccano Magazine and in the 1954–55 season catalogues.

The first announcement was in the April 1954 MM, and concerned the MO Locomotives, '. . . the first Hornby Gauge O Trains to appear in the attractive British Railways livery. In addition, both Goods and Passenger Sets have been revised, and they are now known as Goods Train Set No. 20, and Passenger Train Set No. 21'. The No. 20 LOCOMOTIVE and tender were in a dark green livery, lined in orange and black, with a cabside number in British Railways style, and the 'Lion and Wheel' emblem on the tender. The No. 20 WAGON was tinprinted in BR standard grey, and the No. 21 COACH was in BR crimson and cream. Curved rails of 1 ft radius were supplied in the sets, and the 9 inch radius MO rails were soon withdrawn from the catalogues. But the sets did contain one special rail – the straight brake rail which could not be bought separately.

The following month, in the May 1954 MM, the announcements concerned the No. 40 TANK GOODS SET and the No. 41 TANK PASSENGER SET, which replaced the 101 and 201 Sets. The tank locomotive was finished in black – 'it is a long time since the Hornby Train system included a black engine' – with lining of the boiler in red, and the tanks and bunker lined in red and grey. The No. 41 COACHES and No. 41 PASSENGER BRAKE VAN were tinprinted in crimson. The No. 1 Wagon supplied in the Goods Set was finished in the BR standard grey, with white lettering on a black panel.

Although the article in May gave details of the No. 50 GOODS TRAIN SET and the No. 51 PASSENGER TRAIN SET, no pictures were yet available; but these sets (which replaced the 501 and 601) were in the catalogues, and showed the black enamelled livery of the No. 50 and the dark green enamel of the No. 51 locomotives. The No. 51 Coaches were issued in two types, 1st Class and 3rd Class, and there was also a Passenger Brake Van in the same tinprinted crimson and cream colours, 'modelled to represent standard corridor stock'; the No. 41 Coaches were in suburban style.

The BR wagons were each issued in only one regional version; BR–E Brake Vans, Flat Trucks, Goods Vans and Refrigerator Vans, BR–S Milk Traffic Vans and BR–B Hopper Wagons and Cattle Vans. The Wagon and Wagon with Sheet Rail were BR–M. The Wagon and Hopper Wagon were BR standard goods grey, with white letters on a black panel. The Goods Van, Cattle Truck, Flat Trucks and Goods Brake Van were bauxite brown, to

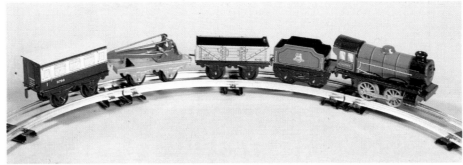

The M0 trains were replaced by the BR No. 20 loco, No. 21 Coaches and No. 20 Wagon.

represent stock fitted with automatic brakes and suitable for fast traffic. The 'XP' designation was incorporated in the transfers for wagons suitable for express passenger traffic. The Refrigerator Van in BR standard white, and the Milk Traffic Van in BR coaching stock crimson, could also be used in passenger trains.

1955

'Young boys find endless delight and satisfaction in all that a Hornby Train has to offer.' (1955–56 Meccano Products Catalogue)

Three new wagons were issued in 1955; two new tankers, Tank Wagon No. 1 'Shell Lubricating Oil' in yellow with red lettering, and 'Manchester Oil Refinery' in green. They replaced the National Benzole tanker. The third new issue was the Flat Truck with Insulated Meat Container, an alternative to the Furniture container which was already available.

Apart from these, the only notable changes were in the tinprinting of the buildings. The roofs of the Signal Cabin, Station No. 3, and Goods Platform were printed with orange tiles instead of green, and the tinprinting of the Signal Cabin and Goods Depot buildings was also changed. The name of the Island

BR locos of 1954; No. 40 Tank, No. 51 in passenger livery, and No. 50 in goods livery.

Many wagon liveries were changed in the BR era, between 1954 and 1957.

A No. 51 Loco with No. 51 Coaches at Trent Station. The tinprintings for many of the buildings were revised around 1955.

Platform was altered to 'Trent', and the roof was also changed to orange in later issues. It was probably in late 1954 that, as part of this series of tinprinting changes, the No. 1 Footbridge appeared with tinprinted finish, making it unnecessary to spray one of the Enamelling Department's bulkiest pieces of work. The savings in cost were probably the reason for the slight fall in the price of the Footbridge, at a time when there was a general price rise for the other goods.

1956

'Main line clear – it started, as most Hornby Railways do, with a Hornby Train set. But half the fun is in adding accessories and planning developments to the system! There are plenty of accessories to choose from – all made in strong metal to withstand the rigours of a hard-working playroom railway.' (December 1956 MM)

After two years of delay, the No. 30 GOODS SET and No. 31 PASSENGER SET that had been designed in 1954 to replace the M1 series were finally issued. They were not (as the No. 20, 40 and 50 trains had been) simply BR finishes applied to the same vehicles, but a radical re-design. The new No. 30 LOCOMOTIVE housing departed from the USA-style M1 Loco single-piece pressing, and had a proper separate cab. The M1 mechanism was used, but special (rather clumsy) mazac castings were used for the rods. The much improved tender was completely re-designed in the No. 50 style, but on a smaller scale; the finish was tinprinted in BR dark green.

The No. 30 Wagon for the goods train was another completely new design, mid-way in size between the No. 20 and the No. 1 Wagon. The No. 30 GOODS VAN used the same base as the wagon, and was tinprinted in brown with appropriate detail. The No. 31 COACHES were in crimson and cream finish, in two versions; 1st/3rd and Brake/3rd. The coach body was longer than that of the old M1 Pullmans, although the same base was used. None of the No. 21, 31, 41 or 51 Coaches had '3' printed on the doors of the 3rd Class sections, so the change to 2nd Class from 3rd Class shown in the

The Goods Platform was also changed to an orange-roofed version. The three wagons were each new in 1955.

September 1956 and later price lists did not necessitate any change in the tinprinting.

The July 1956 price list offered three more sundry items – the No. 1 Cable Drum (why No. 1?) and the No. 1 Insulated Meat and Furniture containers, for separate sale in neat individual boxes. On the debit side, the Dinky Toy figures were withdrawn after only four seasons.

1957

'Hornby Trains are perfect models in O gauge' (1957–58 Meccano Products Catalogue)

By 1957 sales of the Gauge O trains were tailing off, while interest in Dublo was still gaining pace; the last major development in the Hornby Train story, the No. 50 series of goods rolling stock, was a final attempt to develop the Hornby Train on more modern lines. Many of the new series of wagons were tinprinted to take advantage of the pleasing amount of detail that could be incorporated, although printed detail was a poor substitute for the details in the injection-moulded plastic Dublo wagons. The No. 50 Cattle Truck, No. 50 Flat Truck, No. 50 Goods Van and the No. 50 Refrigerator Van were now tinprinted, and the last two vans had realistic hinged double doors. 'Tommy Dodd' wrote in the June 1957 MM that 'in accordance with modern practice there are no side doors to the verandahs' on the No. 50 Brake Van. All the new wagons had been fitted with the new No. 50 base, which was 'given special attention, and a big step forward has been made in providing this with die cast ends, with each buffer beam and its buffers cast in one piece, and attached to the base itself'. There was a dummy brake lever on each side of the wagons, except of course the Brake Van.

The wagons which did not appear in the No. 50 range were the Timber Wagon, Milk Traffic Van, the Wagon with Sheet Rail, and the Cement Wagon. The latter was replaced by a handsome 'Saxa Salt' private owner's wagon, tinprinted in the No. 50 style. The Side and Rotary Tipping Wagons and others in the series were still spray finished; in each case the bases were sprayed in a black with a deep gloss, a contrast to the matt black of the No. 1 type

The No. 30 Loco, No. 31 Coaches, No. 30 Wagon and No. 30 Goods Van replaced the M1 Trains.

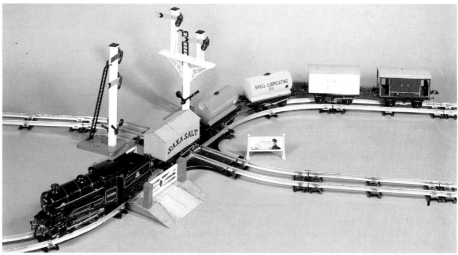

A No. 50 Loco with a train of No. 50 wagons, introduced in 1957.

The No. 50 wagons. (No. 50 Low Sided Wagons were also sold with Furniture Container, and with no load.)

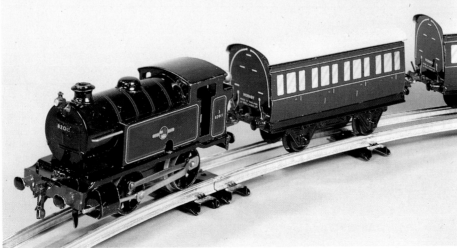

The last version of the No. 40 Tank Loco.

wagons. The same glossy black was also used for the later No. 41 and No. 51 Coaches, and indeed for black-sprayed Meccano parts. The No. 50 Tank Wagons (in a new wide-bodied style) were in the old colours but with shiny bases.

The complete revision and re-tooling of the wagon range – apart from the couplings and wheels there were virtually no common components in the No. 1 and No. 50 series – was a most surprising change to undertake at this eleventh hour of Hornby Train history; it was too late to turn the tide in favour of O Gauge, and the costs must have wiped out much of the profit from the new lines without giving the hoped-for upturn in sales.

There were still large stocks of the No. 1 vehicles at the factory, and the July MM said that 'The goods vehicles that have been standard up to now are still available. . .'; they stayed in the price lists until stocks were exhausted. In some cases this was almost immediately, for others up to two years later. It is interesting to note that the No. 1 Coaches that should have been replaced by the No. 41 and No. 51 Coaches in 1954 had stayed in the price lists up to the end of 1958!

The new wagons were included in two new sets; one was the No. 45 TANK GOODS SET, with the No. 40 Loco, No. 50 Wagon, No. 50 Lumber Wagon, and No. 50 Tank Wagon ('Shell Lubricating Oil' rather than the No. 50 'Manchester Oil Refinery') and the usual rails. The other was the No. 55 GOODS TRAIN SET with the No. 50 Loco and tender, No. 50 Low Sided Wagon, No. 50 Wagon and No. 50 Goods Brake Van. Within a year the No. 40 Tank and the No. 50 Goods Train Sets (which, confusingly, still had the No. 1 type wagons) had been sold out and were no longer listed.

Apart from the deletion of some of the No. 1 wagons as a result of these important No. 50 introductions, there were also some other portentous deletions; the Footbridge, No. 3 Station, Goods Platform, Island Platform, and the No. 2 Signal Cabin. The loss of these buildings from the Hornby range was an admission that (new series of wagons or not) the Hornby Gauge O Trains were on the way out. Although production was to continue for several more years on the existing products, there were to be no further improvements or develop-

ments; just a steady tide of deletions, as for item after item it was no longer worth producing new batches when stocks were exhausted.

THE LATTER YEARS AT BINNS ROAD

The production of Hornby Trains was doomed by falling sales to slow down, and eventually to stop. There are no records to show the exact date of the final manufacture of Gauge O Trains at Binns Road; except in the case of the No. 50 Wagons, for which we can be quite precise. The spin riveting fixtures used to secure the castings were issued from the tool stores, and the record cards show that they were used regularly every year from 1957 until they were returned for the last time in September 1962. The No. 20 Trains are likely to have been the last in actual production, not long after this.

The No. 50 and 51 Locos and Sets were not listed in the June 1961 Hornby Train folder; the No. 40 Tank and the No. 30 Locomotives were sold out in 1966, as were the No. 20 Sets, although the No. 20 Loco remained in the January 1967 price list.

The last Meccano price list to include the Hornby Trains was issued in 1969; there were no locomotives or sets, just the remains of the once-proud range of rolling stock and accessories. Included were most of the rails, several No. 20 and No. 50 Wagons, and some signals and other accessories. The remaining stocks were finally cleared in 1969 by sale to specialist dealers in surplus stock, and Messrs. Hattons of Liverpool advertised these items in the model railway press for some time afterwards.

There was one final, and noteworthy, Gauge O Train sold by Meccano Ltd – although it was not a 'Hornby'. The 'Percy' Play Train issued in 1965 was a totally new set in injection moulded plastic, featuring the Reverend W. Awdrey's 'Percy, the Small Engine'. The green engine was complete with Percy's face on the smokebox door, and there were two goods wagons for him to pull; a yellow Open Goods Truck, and a red Closed Goods Wagon with sliding doors. There were special 1 ft 6 in radius plastic rails, which clicked together and were stepped to make it easy to put Percy on the track. There was a special brake rail. Percy could also be used on

ordinary Gauge O tinplate rails. The novel motor had a free-wheeling mechanism that allowed the train to be pushed safely along the track without damage, even after it had run down. Try that with an M1! So it was suitable even for very young children who had not quite got the knack of winding up. In 1969 a similar set was available, but it was just called the 'Play Train'; not quite so attractive as 'Percy' since it lacked the face and copper trim. These sets were an interesting new departure, and deserved a better commercial success than they actually enjoyed.

The troubled commercial history of Meccano Ltd in these later years is, sadly, now a matter of record and not worth re-telling here since the production of Gauge O Trains was no longer a major interest of the company at the time of the take-over by Lines Brothers in 1964. Although the Hornby and Meccano trade-names live on, the Gauge O enthusiast knows that the days are gone for ever when tinplate toy trains were produced in large numbers and at such reasonable prices; interest in Gauge O for scale models is another story.

It is not just for economic reasons that these tinplate trains are unlikely to be produced again. The

overwhelming network of safety regulations that cocoon buyers in today's climate of 'consumerism' would have prevented the sale of most of the Hornby Trains; not just the obviously dangerous items, like the hedges with protruding nails, or the High Voltage Metropolitan (would any present-day advertiser be able to claim as did the December 1925 MM that there were 'no difficulties or dangers'?). Of course, the amount of lead and lead alloys melted down by Meccano Ltd for castings would have been enough to sink a moderately sized battleship; not counting the lead content of the paints used in liberal quantities by the Enamelling Department. The sale of metal toys without carefully radiused edges and corners is now prohibited, and it is in this respect that most of the old Gauge O Hornby Trains would fail to meet current requirements. Whether the officials who drafted the regulations were traumatised as children by contact with the sharp corners of No. 2 Goods Depots or the like, we shall never know. Happily there are no published records of fatal accidents with Hornby Trains, however often they may have drawn blood!

Collecting? Well, that too is another and a happy story. In 1968 the MM had articles by Peter Randall

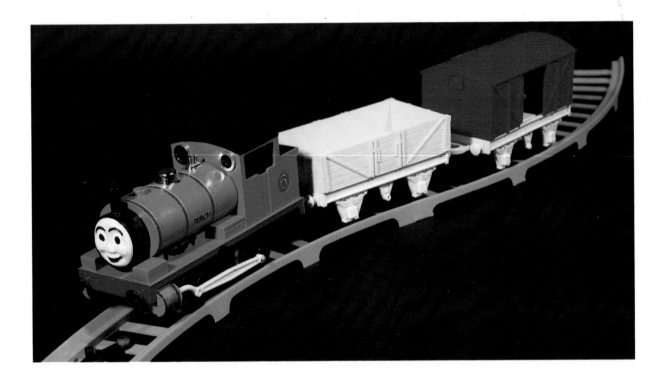

The 'Percy' Play Train.

Lid of the 'Percy' box.

The ultimate collectors' item! Sales brochure for the Binns Road works, 1980.

on the early Hornby Trains; this developed into a series of articles on 'Tinplate Topics' by Peter Gomm and Peter Randall in the Model Railway News, starting in April 1969, and from these sprang the idea of the 'Hornby Railway Collectors' Association.' The H.R.C.A. has gone from strength to strength, and publishes a Journal at regular intervals, full of news and interest for the enthusiast. It is a valuable source of information on Hornby matters, Gauge O and Dublo, contributed from the hundreds of members world-wide. Although not run on strict Hornby Railway Company lines with boy directors and officials, the HRCA is the next best thing!

The range of trains that Frank Hornby created gave pleasure when new to innumerable boys and girls. Now the collector takes as much pleasure in tracking down the same trains at second hand. There are as many reasons for collecting Hornby Trains as there are collectors; the thrill of the chase when buying; the more cerebral delights of puzzling out Hornby variations; sheer pride in the ownership of the finest toy trains, or the hope of a good invest-

ment; the simple pleasures of putting the trains on the rails and running them as a toy train, or even in the prescribed H.R.C. railway-like manner. For others the pleasure is in meeting other collectors. Most collectors combine these reasons, and others, in their individual ways.

Would it matter if Frank Hornby had called it a day in 1919 and decided not to expand his factory – at least not for toy trains? The question is as interesting as it is impossible to answer. It is undeniable that Frank Hornby's inspiration created and sustained thousands of jobs over half a century, without which life in Liverpool would have been poorer. And that his 'million boy friends' would have missed an indefinable part of their childhood, and would have lived lives perhaps a fraction less rewarding. Present-day enthusiasts would have missed the sustained interest (which, rather sadly, must now be all in retrospect) in the toys produced by his factory; a moderately harmless pastime that Frank Hornby would have regarded with incredulous wonder, if not with delight!

Manufacturing and Marketing

Where did the ideas for Hornby Trains come from? One has only to read the 'In Reply' pages of the prewar Meccano Magazines to realise that the boys who bought the Hornby Trains were very quick to write and ask for whatever they thought would be a useful improvement or new product. Some ideas were obviously impractical, but a surprising number were eventually put into production. The unused suggestions included, to take but a few examples, bookstalls, horseboxes, slip coaches, motor trains, mail coaches, gasometers, armoured trains, gunpowder kegs, and every conceivable type of locomotive from humble saddle tanks to 'decapods' and Garratts. Careful records were kept of each request, and the best ideas were printed. If a lot of interest was shown by other readers then production became all the more likely. Most of the new products of the late 1920s and 1930s had been suggested at some time or other by MM readers.

Of course, the catalogues of other toy manufacturers were the source of some of the best Hornby ideas. There was a lot of influence from the German Bing trains in the early 1920s (would the idea of a rotary snow plough have occurred naturally to a Liverpool manufacturer?); and Frank Hornby's denunciations in the MM of his American competitors' unfair and unscrupulous imitations of Meccano Outfits make amusing reading in the light of the Electric Hornby Train's debt to Lionel. But whereas some Hornby Trains may have been similar to competitors' products, none were actually identical.

Of the items that were most closely copied from Bing designs, the Tinprinted Trains are the best-known example. The No. 2 Loco mechanisms (in the first version) were similar to the Bing equivalent, and the Hornby Water Tank was not unlike the Bing version. Apart from rails and the Tinprinted Trains, the greatest similarity in appearance to Bing products was for the No. 2 Hydraulic Buffers, but close

inspection shows that the Bing buffers were of all-soldered construction, whereas the Hornby pattern used lugs in slots. Bing luggage was similar in size and appearance to the Hornby luggage, but again was of different construction as well as different tinprinting. Many wagons in the Hornby range were suggested by their foreign equivalents; Snow-ploughs, Side Tipping Wagons, and Barrel Wagons for example.

Despite many suggestions to the contrary, Meccano made virtually the whole of their range of products themselves, with only a few items contracted to outside suppliers; the few such products included the Ferranti Transformers, light bulbs, accumulators etc. Whereas at one time it was a common view among enthusiasts that such parts as motors, and even perhaps complete trains, might have been bought in from outside the company, there is now a considerable weight of evidence to suggest what should perhaps have been obvious all along; that Meccano Ltd were competent in both design and engineering, and capable of producing their high quality products entirely within the walls of the Binns Road works.

Frank Hornby seems to have had more than his fair share of inspiration, as we have already seen. He was also sufficiently inspired to hire an inventive staff of designers who could turn raw ideas into saleable products. Patents were taken out by Meccano Ltd for the more original inventions, and these are some of the most important:

27,533 26–11–10 Tables Games (Raylo)
250,378 23–3–25 Toy Railways (Control System; Rodding Traverse, and cranks on points; rails with permanently attached traverse)
253,236 23–3–25 Toy Railways (Control System: Control Guide Brackets, and sleepers with integral guide brackets)

356,567 8–11–30 Toy Locomotives (Clockwork mechanisms, with the second gear wheel on a stub axle mounted on the side plate of the motor, thus allowing the spring to expand further. Describes also the construction of sideplates for the M1 and M3 motors)
365,701 18–11–30 Mechanical Toys (Automatic couplings, for four-wheel and bogie vehicles)
366,291 13–2–31 Railways: Toys made in box form (A model tunnel made from corrugated cardboard, that could be used for packing the loco.)
368,975 4–3–31 Improvements in winding keys
389,188 27–11–31 Toys; railways (Revised brake and reverse rail)
397,533 17–2–32 Toy Scenery (Countryside Sections; also hedges, trees and haystacks with rubber suction caps, detachable contoured covers etc.)
429,525 30–1–34 Toy locomotive reversing mechanism; electromagnetic switches (Automatic reversing mechanisms).

There were of course many equivalent patents taken out in other countries. Some parts made by Hornby were also registered designs; for example the nut-and-bolt coaches of 1921.

ITEMS PLANNED BUT NOT PRODUCED

Several items that were planned but never put into production have already been mentioned; for example the South Eastern and Chatham Railway, the Great Eastern and the Etat open wagons which were designed in 1920 but were never catalogued, although the wagon sides were actually made. The MM said in August 1921 that it was hoped that steam trains would be introduced, but nothing further transpired.

An elaborate Automatic Reversing Rail was

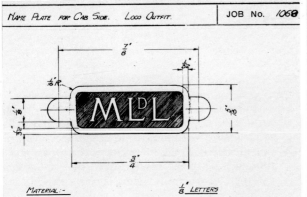

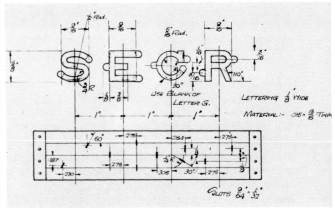

planned in 1921. This had a spring-loaded pivoting trip for the No. 2 Loco reversing mechanism, operated by a trackside lever. In the event it must have been decided that it held no special advantage over the ordinary Brake and Reverse Rail.

Gauge 1 rails were designed in July 1922, but not made, although the December 1922 MM had said that rails for gauge 1 would be introduced shortly.

One of the important omissions from the Hornby range in the early years was any form of suburban bogie coach, only Pullman Cars and Dining Saloons being available. The 5-door coach of 1922 was therefore extremely important, since detailed designs were prepared but apparently not put into production. The style was consistent with the other coaches of the period, with the window surrounds attached as separate frames. The most significant difference was that the compartment doors, five on each side, were hinged; at the time the doors of other Hornby coaches were not made to open, although many were later fitted with similar hinged doors.

The Loading Gauge of 1923 design was first drawn with the round base weighted with the heavy casting used at the base of the Lamp Standards. Production versions of 1924 omitted the weight, and in consequence were prone to toppling over since the centre of gravity was in the wrong place, and the base was too small.

A 'High Power Motor Housing' was designed in 1925, intended for use with Meccano motors, probably running on the high voltage system. It was of 'steeple-cab' design, and built on the right scale for gauge 1, although gauge 0 operation was almost certainly intended. It had hinged cab doors, and at each end Snowplough lamps were fitted. It would have made a diverting toy for the Meccano enthusiast, but it fell between the two systems; not an accurate or interesting enough model to satisfy the Hornby Train enthusiast, and not challenging enough for the Meccano boy, since the parts were pre-assembled by lugs. It was almost certainly the

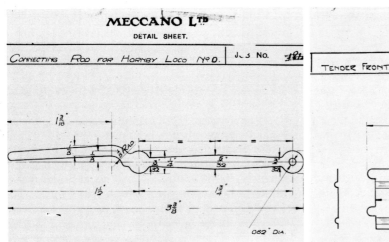

Loco connecting rod, 1922. Not adopted, but similar to M1 rods of 1930.

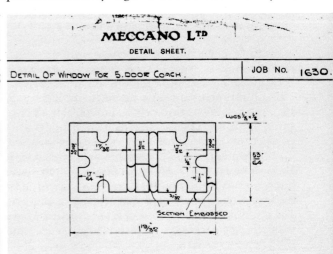

A tender front for the No. 1 Tender, 1922. Not adopted.

5-door coach window surrounds, 1922.

Part of the 'Automatic Reversing Rail', 1921. Not adopted.

A High Power Motor Housing, constructed by Harry Walker in 1982, based on Meccano Ltd drawings dated 1925.

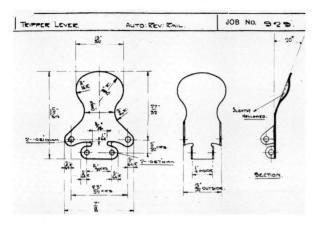

advent of the Hornby Electric Train (the Metropolitan) in the same year that killed hopes of supplying the High Power Motor Housing.

In 1927, the Electric Solid Base Point with Ground Disc, fitted for Hornby Control, was designed. Although the following year the points were actually issued as clockwork-only versions, this electric point design pre-dated them and was clearly considered of too limited appeal, or just too expensive to make. Surprisingly there was no wiring or lampholder inside the ground signal, although it was possible for electric lights to be fitted; why else would celluloid discs have been used, and ventilation holes pressed in the top of the lamphouse? The design of the points was based very much on equivalents in the American Lionel range.

The planned use of permanent magnet motors in No. 1-type electric tender engines in 1931 has already been mentioned, as have the patent corrugated cardboard tunnels of 1931. Double-light Signal Boxes were one electrically lit accessory dropped before production got under way, and the Countryside Section system was never developed as envisaged in the patent. But none of these ideas of the early 1930s could have been an important moneymaker. The most interesting Hornby might-havebeens were planned in 1936, and nothing at all is known about them except for a very few words in the 1936 Trade Bulletin to dealers. They concern No. 2E Electric Silver Jubilee Train Sets: 'This handsome train set will be very popular. It consists of a streamline electric Locomotive (automatic

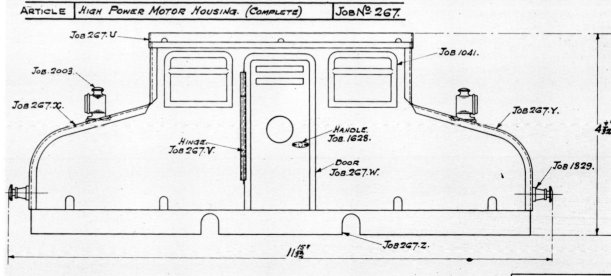

Drawing for High Power Motor Housing, 1925. It was designed to fit a standard Meccano Electric Motor.

91

MECCANO LTD

DETAIL SHEET

| ARTICLE | LOADING GAUGE. (COMPLETE.) | JOB No. 1980 |

JOB.1965.

PRICK-PUNCH TO SECURE FINIAL.

JOB.1983.

JOB.1984.

JOB.1985.

$\frac{1}{16}"$ FLATS TO SECURE BEAM.

JOB.1981.

$\frac{1}{8}"$ DIA. INDENT TO SECURE COLUMN.

JOB.1963.

JOB.1982.

DRAWN BY
TRACED BY
CHECKED BY

MEMO. No.
3450.

Date FEB'Y 7TH 1923.

Scale $\frac{1}{1}$

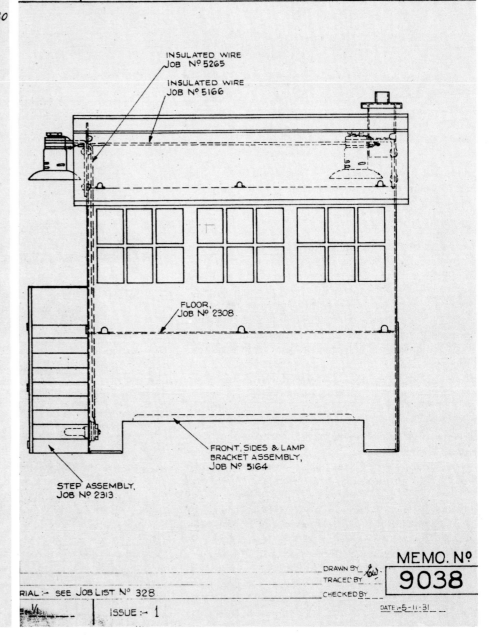

MECCANO LTD

| ARTICLE | No 2 SIGNAL CABIN - ELECTRIC (DOUBLE LAMP) | JOB No. 5160 |

INSULATED WIRE
JOB No 5265

INSULATED WIRE
JOB No 5166

FLOOR,
JOB No 2308.

FRONT, SIDES & LAMP
BRACKET ASSEMBLY,
JOB No 5164

STEP ASSEMBLY,
JOB No 2313.

DRAWN BY
TRACED BY
CHECKED BY

MEMO. No
9038

RIAL :- SEE JOB LIST No 328

DATE :- 5-11-31

ISSUE :- 1

reversing), Tender, pair of articulated Saloon Coaches, and set of Rails . . . The set is beautifully finished in correct shades of silver and grey. Retail price 52/–'. Also listed were the No. 2C Clockwork Silver Jubilee Train Set retailing at 37s 6d, and the No. 0 Silver Jubilee Train Set at a mere 7s 6d. Of the three, the No. 0 was the only one to go into production. The fact that the prices had been decided and the trade announcement made shows that plans must have been very well advanced. To judge from the price, the trains were to have been made in quite a substantial size; perhaps they would have turned out as much the same sort of 4–4–2 as the French 'Etoile Du Nord'? But this must be speculation since no plans, pictures or samples seem to have survived.

Another plan for the 1930s that never came to fruition was the printing of container sides in 13 different varieties, instead of the 4 that were actually made. It is a shame that the series was never completed, since it might have increased their popularity.

After the war there were so many plans to re-introduce the grander prewar items that it would be tedious to mention every one. The No. 2 Special and No. 2 Special Tank locos were perhaps the nearest to actual production, having been actually shown at trade fairs. There were no plans for new products, just revivals of the old prewar ideas. Perhaps the most interesting was the Coal Wagon, which in the 1949 designs was to have had tinprinted sides (without the embossed planking), lettered GW and fitted with embossed coal as on the prewar 'Meccano' and 'Hornby Railway Company' wagons. But unlike the Dublo range there was not a great fund of postwar inventions. One or two liveries are mentioned in the drawings that one would be pleased to see in real life, such as the postwar GW and SR Refrigerator Vans, and the 'Regent' Petrol Tank Wagon livery mentioned on the works drawings of 1949, which would have made a change from the usual 'Esso'.

When the No. 50 Wagons were planned, it was originally envisaged that the base of the wagon would be fitted with an alloy casting on each side, detailed with brake gear and so on in the style of the Dublo wagons. This most interesting plan never took effect, although the shape of the No. 50 wagon

Planned 'Silver Jubilee' trains, from a 1936 trade circular.

New Hornby Train Sets

Four new train sets are being added to the Hornby Train Series this year, as described below. Three of them are modelled and finished on the design and colouring of the latest L.N.E.R. "Silver Jubilee" train, already world-famous, and will be extremely popular with boys of all ages.

No. O "Silver Jubilee" Clockwork Passenger Train Set

This fine new Train Set is composed of a streamline Locomotive, Tender, pair of articulated Saloon Coaches and a set of rails. One of the rails is an MB9 Curved Brake Rail, by means of which the train can be braked from the track. The complete train set is very attractive in appearance, the colour scheme being silver and grey.

Retail price 7/6d.

Hornby E2 "Silver Jubilee" Electric Passenger Train Set (20-volt)

This handsome Train Set will be very popular. It consists of a streamline electric Locomotive (automatic reversing), Tender, pair of articulated Saloon Coaches, and set of Rails. A Terminal Connecting Plate is included for the connection of the power supply (20-volt Transformer) to the track. The set is beautifully finished in correct shades of silver and grey.

Retail price 52/-

Hornby 2C "Silver Jubilee" Clockwork Passenger Train Set

This set is identical with the E2 "Silver Jubilee" Electric Passenger Set, described above, except that the Locomotive is fitted with clockwork mechanism. The electric rails and fittings are replaced by a set of clockwork rails, including a BBR1 Brake and Reverse Rail.

Retail Price 37/6d.

base clearly owes much to the shape of the casting that was to have been fitted. The actual production versions with plain tinplate sides and only a simple brake lever were decidedly tame compared to the original concept.

Apart from the items that were planned but not made, there were of course many items that were made but not planned. There were so many possibilities for mistakes in production that errors were bound to occur from time to time. A common

mistake was to leave off the transfers from a wagon or coach, and sometimes part or the whole of a coach or wagon would be left unvarnished.

Tinprinted coaches were very prone to assembly errors. Many had handed sides, particularly brake coaches, and it is quite common to find coaches with two left-hand or two right-hand sides. Missing or upside-down doors were surprisingly frequent on the larger Pullman-type coaches (and also on goods brake vans). The No. 1 Coaches with opening doors

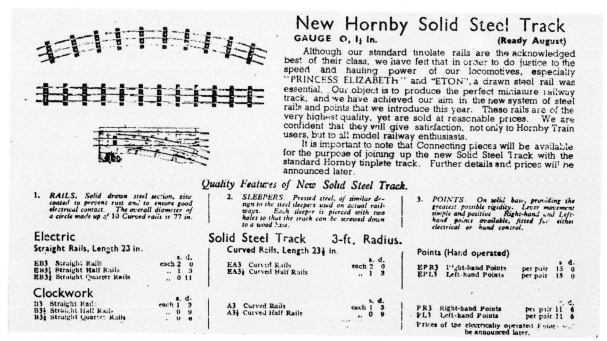

New Hornby Solid Steel Track

GAUGE O, 1¼ in. (Ready August)

Although our standard tinplate rails are the acknowledged best of their class, we have felt that in order to do justice to the speed and hauling power of our locomotives, especially "PRINCESS ELIZABETH" and "ETON", a drawn steel rail was essential. Our object is to produce the perfect miniature railway track, and we have achieved our aim in the new system of steel rails and points that we introduce this year. These rails are of the very highest quality, yet are sold at reasonable prices. We are confident that they will give satisfaction, not only to Hornby Train users, but to all model railway enthusiasts.

It is important to note that Connecting pieces will be available for the purpose of joining up the new Solid Steel Track with the standard Hornby tinplate track. Further details and prices will be announced later.

Quality Features of New Solid Steel Track.

1. RAILS. Solid drawn steel section, zinc coated to prevent rust and to ensure good electrical contact. The overall diameter of a circle made up of 10 Curved rails is 77 in.	2. SLEEPERS. Pressed steel, of similar design to those sleepers used on actual railways. Each sleeper is pierced with two holes so that the track can be screwed down to a wood base.	3. POINTS. On solid base, providing the greatest possible rigidity. Lever movement simple and positive. Right-hand and Left-hand points available, fitted for either electrical or hand control.

Electric
Straight Rails, Length 23 in.

		s. d.
EB3	Straight Rails	each 2 0
EB3½	Straight Half Rails	„ 1 3
EB3¼	Straight Quarter Rails	„ 0 11

Solid Steel Track   3-ft. Radius.
Curved Rails, Length 23½ in.

		s. d.
EA3	Curved Rails	each 2 0
EA3½	Curved Half Rails	„ 1 3

Points (Hand operated)

		s. d.
EPR3	Right-hand Points	per pair 15 0
EPL3	Left-hand Points	per pair 15 0

Clockwork

		s. d.
B3	Straight Rails	each 1 3
B3½	Straight Half Rails	„ 0 9
B3¼	Straight Quarter Rails	„ 0 6

		s. d.
A3	Curved Rails	each 1 3
A3½	Curved Half Rails	„ 0 9

		s. d.
PR3	Right-hand Points	per pair 11 6
PL3	Left-hand Points	per pair 11 6

Prices of the electrically operated Points will be announced later.

Solid Steel Rails, including 2-rail track and electrically operated points which were not produced. From a trade circular, early in 1937.

The Coal Wagon drawing, revised for postwar issue.

A 'Regent' tanker was planned in 1949.

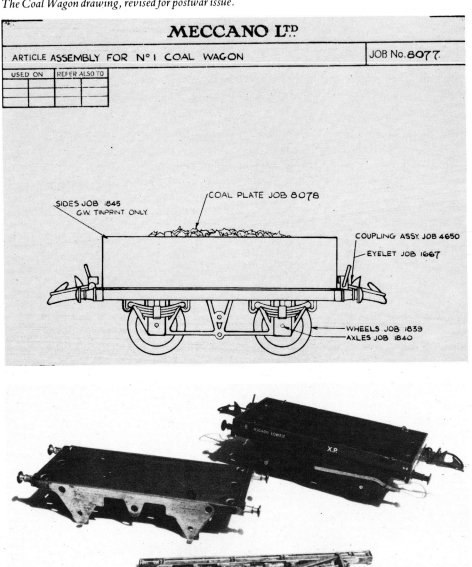

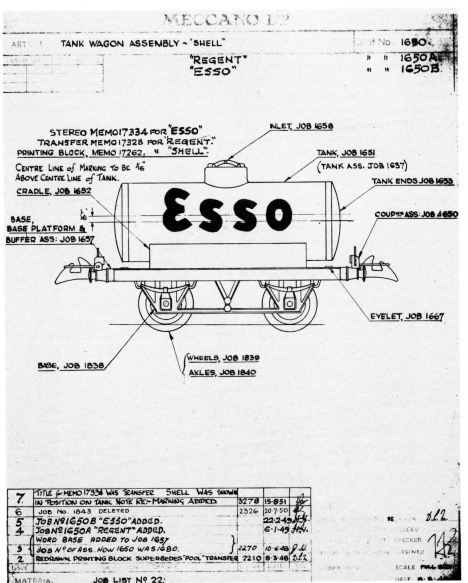

Pre-production No. 50 wagon base, with diecast sides.

were often assembled with 1st class and 3rd class doors fitted on opposite sides of the same compartment! Passenger coach doors on guard's vans and even guard's van doors on passenger coaches have been sighted. Passenger coaches with guard's van duckets are not unusual. American Pullman cars with 'Madison' one side and 'Washington' the other are also known. Perhaps the oddest-looking error was on the No. 1 Pullman Composite 'Ansonia' in the late 1930s, made in a large batch with the guard's van door embossed with the window surrounds of the ordinary coach. Many items were sent out by mistake with no trademark transfers, or using the wrong ones. Some wagon and coach underframes, and also bogies, were stamped inside out (or not stamped at all) from time to time.

Not surprisingly, occasional mistakes were made with the locomotives. Some M3 Tank engines were assembled with the No. 1 Tank rear underframe under the cab, and GW locos with domes were made from time to time, by mistake. It is not surprising that when the change-over from one type of transfer to another was made, mismatches occurred; for example an LMS No. 2 Special Tank loco with sans-serif lettering on one side and serif letters on the other! Accessories were not immune either, for example at least one Island Platform was made with 'Reading' and 'Margate' on opposite sides of the nameboard. There were many examples of the use of the wrong tools, or the wrong finish, but it would be unfair to give the impression that such mistakes occurred on more than a fraction of the total Hornby output.

MATERIALS

It was the proud claim of Meccano Ltd that only the 'finest materials obtainable' were used for their manufactures. The quantity of materials kept in the Raw Material Store was large not just in the sheer tonnage, (although the sight of the hundreds of tons of steel in stock impressed many visitors to the works), but also in the variety of grades and sizes. For instance the Hornby Train designers called for the use of mild steel, bending quality steel, hard steel, tinned steel wire, bright drawn steel, free-cutting mild steel rod, hard rolled steel, steel pinion wire, steel heading wire, half-hard coil steel, soft steel wire, soft forming steel and many others, in a bewildering variety of gauges. Plus of course the all-important spring steel. And stainless steel was used for many locomotive collector shoes – which is why they do not go rusty.

Brass was also used in various forms – for example, hard rolled brass, spring brass, riveting quality brass rod, brass heading wire, drawing brass and half-hard brass. Then add the bronzes such as the

Spot the errors! Some imperfectly-made wagons, and a Pullman which has received neither transfers nor varnish. The locos have unusual numbers.

Production errors of the BR era. The Low Sided Wagon has no transfers or black paint, while the Milk Traffic Van has Cattle Truck body pressings! The M1 Tender couplings are the wrong way round.

The Tool Room at Binns Road, circa 1919.

phosphor bronze used for motor bushes. Then there were the specialised electrical materials; black fibre for insulation, Presspahn for washers, Erinoid, Concordin oxidised-finish resistance wire, tinned copper wires, single and double cotton-covered wires, Herkulaker wires, and soft Swedish iron for motor laminations. Other materials included zinc-based alloys or lead alloys for castings, and vulcanised rubber. All these materials and many, many more had to be kept in stock ready for production, and the staff that carried out the work of stock-keeping and progress planning were every bit as essential to the manufacture of the Hornby Train as the girls on the assembly lines.

This list of materials serves to illustrate the point that although we commonly call the Gauge O products 'tinplate trains', there is much more to it than that imprecise generalisation implies. However the majority of the structural parts of the trains were made from tinplate sheets. The normal thickness was .015 in, but some of the lighter parts (such as the M Series trains, signal posts, buildings and in fact a fair amount of the tinprinted work) were in .012 in sheet, as were the rails (but not the sleepers, which were in .015 in tinplate). Only a few items, such as the No. 2 Special Locomotive frames were in a heavier sheet (e.g. .020 in). The gauge of the material had to be carefully chosen for the needs of the job in hand. Forming steel was sometimes specified instead of tinplate, and some of the earliest drawings specified mild or soft sheet steel as the material. Tinplate printed in black on both sides ('Litho blackplate') was used for the parts of some 'M' series products to avoid the necessity of a black enamelled finish.

Tinplate is simply a sheet of low carbon steel thinly coated with pure tin. It has the strength and formability of steel, but the protective layer of tin resists rust and gives a good surface for enamelling or printing. It resists corrosion because the oxygen in air combines with the tin to form a thin invisible protective film on the surface. The material remains ductile, and can be formed by press tools and dies into complicated three-dimensional shapes, without tearing or becoming too thin in the stressed areas.

The steel used by Meccano Ltd's suppliers of tinplate was commonly made on strip mills in a continuous roll, cold rolled under enormous pressures to the correct gauge, and cleaned by pickling in an acid bath to remove oxides. Before the war the plating was usually by hot-dip tinning; electrolytic plating became increasingly important after its first commercial use in 1937. The strip of steel was first cut up in rectangles (typically 20″ by 28″) for the hot dipping; the sheet was passed into the bath of molten tin, usually with a layer of palm oil floating on the surface. The molten tin wetted the surface of the steel, and as the sheet was drawn out of the bath, the tin drained rapidly leaving an even coating that was bright and lustrous. The thickness of the tin coating could be controlled by drawing the sheet out through pressure rollers, but even so the tin was probably a less uniform and certainly a thicker coating than the electrolytic method is capable of giving; a typical thickness would be between one thousandth and one ten thousandth of an inch. After burnishing the product was ready to use.

Meccano Ltd prided themselves on buying only the best quality Welsh steel tinned plate, but they were a very small customer compared to the food giants using the same tinplate in vast quantities for canning. The mass production of tinplate for cans was an important factor in bringing this basic Hornby raw material to an affordable price.

TOOLMAKING

Once the designers had translated their ideas into drawings (and sometimes before, when the Drawing Office was forced to revise the designs to bring them into line with production!), it was up to the toolmakers to design and produce the necessary press tools and dics. This was one of the best-paid and most highly skilled jobs in the factory, and no wonder, for it was on the accuracy and careful workmanship of these men that the quality of the product depended.

A great deal is known about what Hornby Trains were made, both from a study of the trains and from surviving copies of workshop drawings used to make them. In contrast, little is yet known about how the individual parts were made; the drawings give no details of the tooling used to translate the

designs into the finished product. Clues are given by the few trains that escaped quality inspections and left the factory unfinished or imperfectly made. For example, the underframe of the 1930 wagon base is a single piece. Because we have seen imperfectly made wagons where the details of the springs etc. were not embossed, we can tell that the blanking (cutting the part to shape) was carried out as a separate operation from the embossing. Thus although the imperfectly finished items are no more valuable in collectors' terms (usually worth less!) they can repay study. The wagon base is an example of an item produced in hundreds of thousands, by successive steps rather than in a single automatic operation. Although there were some compound tools that combined the operations of blanking, forming and piercing, the manufacture of Hornby Trains largely depended on

having hundreds of workers carrying out a sequence of arduous, repetitive jobs, at a pace that would bring most modern factories out in an instant fit of striking.

TINPRINTING

Right from the start of production, Meccano Ltd were making trains in the two finishes common for tinplate toys; enamelling and tinprinting. The tinprinting process was generally associated with the cheaper products, but there was a balance of advantage between the two methods. Printing the sheets of tinplate in colour before they were cut up into shape was an expensive process, for the most part carried out in chromo-lithographic printing by outside

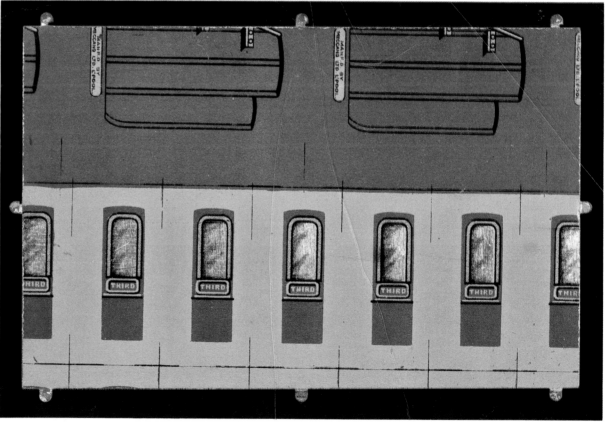

Doors and ends for the opening-door SR No. 1 Coach, found inside a No. 1 Signal Cabin of the late '30s.

Pressure diecasting bogie wheels.

companies. The greater the number of colours, the greater the cost; but the cost also depended on the number of sheets printed, and if used in large quantities it was much cheaper than enamelling after assembly. Thus large quantities of tinprinted sheet were produced and carefully stored for subsequent use, sometimes over several years, being much more valuable in printed form than the raw tinplate. In theory, no tinprinted toy train should be rare, since large numbers of sheets were usually printed.

A few tinprinted items did become obsolete, however, and remaining stocks of tinprinted sheet were used for other purposes (usually on an inside surface where the original printing would not show). Thus collectors carrying out restoration work are confronted with unexpected sights when disassembling inaccessible parts – such as the insides of No. 1 Signal Cabins, inside Lumber Wagon bolsters, and behind door handles. There have even been sightings of B.R. coach sides folded into rails, with the printed side inwards! Sometimes the tinprinted material was used up in this way because it had a useful plain colour on the reverse side. The tin-

printed sheets were usually sprayed or printed on the reverse where both sides would show, for example on the insides of Engine Sheds and No. 2 Signal Boxes. A very small number of tinprinted items had detail printed on both sides of the sheet – including the early Engine Shed doors, and the signal arms. This caused headaches if the front and back were printed out of register, and so the method was avoided where at all possible.

The disadvantages of tinprinting were that it was expensive for small quantities; that care was needed in the Press Shop to line up the press tools with marks printed on the tinplate when blanking; and that the depth of finish was not as good as with enamelling. The lithographic inks gave less protection to the metal surface than an enamel layer, although they did help (tinprinted coaches always seem to rust from the windows first, not from the printed areas). A good varnish would have helped but the varnishing of many tinprinted items was carried out sparingly. Another problem was that some of the inks did not have the covering power of the enamels – a fact that is responsible for the

Pressing parts for No. 1 Special Locos, etc.

Casting Dinky Toy figures, by hand.

Assembly of No. 1 Special Locos, and other items, prior to enamelling.

iridescent 'metallic' finishes on some M Series locos. On all tinprinted products, there was a risk of damage (especially to edges and corners) during the cutting and forming.

As much detail as was required could be incorporated in the tinprinting (even including the trademark), making the process invaluable for buildings and certain other accessories, for which the cost of hand-finishing would have been prohibitive. Windows could be particularly effectively represented, without an expensive pressing operation. But tinprinting was most valuable for the cheaper lines, like the M series and the No. 0 Vans, which could not otherwise have been made at the price.

MAKING THE PARTS

Tinplate components were made in the Press Shop at Binns Road. The biggest power presses (used for the largest pieces of work or the heaviest gauges of material) worked at pressures up to 100 tons. More typical were the presses of 10 to 30 tons, and these were used for most of the toy train parts. Most numerous were the lighter 'fly' or hand presses that were distributed through the factory not just in the Press Shop, but on the assembly lines as well, although these were not usually used for blanking.

Some of the cheaper toy trains made elsewhere used gear wheels stamped out with press tools, but in Binns Road all the gear wheels were accurately cut in the Machine Shop. The design and manufacture of smooth running and powerful clockwork motors was one of the most consistent successes of the Meccano Works, and failures due to faulty gear cutting were by no means common.

Other departments in the Binns Road works involved in making toy train parts included the Woodworking Department (busying themselves with timber & lumber loads, containers, tunnel parts and the like), and the important Electrical Department where the transformers and electric motors were assembled and tested. Another section dealt with castings for locomotive parts and wheels; the early wheels were usually cast by hand, although pressure diecasting was later used, for the mazac wheels.

PRELIMINARY ASSEMBLY

Having made the parts in the press shop, the next step was a preliminary assembly before finishing, presuming that the Progress Stores held sufficient stock of all the parts required. The assembly was mostly carried out on a conveyor-belt system, with a line of girls (almost invariably girls, to judge from the few photos that survive of the works in action) each side of the conveyor, carrying out their alloted task as the parts reached them.

For locomotive bodies, the assembly operations (carried out in stages) involved fixing chimneys, safety valves, weights, buffers and other castings, as well as assembling the tinplate pressings.

ENAMELLING

The enamelling process was much more expensive and laborious than the alternative, tinprinting. The Enamelling Department was among the least pleasant parts of the factory in which to work, although naturally colourful and eye-catching for the casual visitor.

Since the enamelling followed pressing and the preliminary assembly work, the parts to be painted were greasy. First it was necessary to thoroughly clean and de-grease the parts, especially in crevices and corners, either by trichlorethylene baths or by baking to high temperatures. It is a tribute to the care and craftsmanship with which these processes were carried out that problems with paint flaking and adhesion are so rare, although there was a period in the late 1920s when certain items were badly affected by such faults.

After cleaning the parts, the enamel was sprayed, using spray guns driven by compressed air carefully filtered to remove the tiniest particles of dust. Attention to this and to the viscosity of the paint gave the characteristic fine finish.

Two main methods of spraying were used for Hornby Trains. In the first the individual items (such as loco bodies), or groups of items spring-clipped to frames, were manually painted in spray booths. But by the 1930s an automatic method of spraying was also used, which was suitable for the smaller components such as wagon underframes. In these machines the parts to be sprayed were mounted on upright spindles on a rotary conveyer system, on the outer edge of a turntable about 4 feet across. As the turntable moved, the spindles reached the spraying section, where they were rapidly rotated under the jets of three sprays to get an even coverage of paint. The parts were then lifted from the spindles and travelled through a tunnel oven which baked the enamel to a hard and durable finish; similar ovens were used for the hand-sprayed work.

The use of the automatic sprays became more ambitious in later years, and some complete wagons were sprayed on these machines; at first Lumber Wagons and similar light types, but by the end of the 1930s some Petrol Tank Wagons and even some vans were sprayed in this way. Parts to be sprayed had to be pierced with a central hole for the spindle (.172 in or .312 in diameter). This explains the presence of such holes in a number of unexpected places, such as the top of the No. 1 Special Tender.

STENCIL SPRAYING

A few early wagons, such as the LNW Zulu wagons, were lettered by spraying white paint through a stencil mask onto the grey body. The method was also used for the 'brickwork' of the early Lattice Girder Bridges. Simple masks were used when spraying the different colours on the two-tone green and cream Pullmans, and the LNWR No. 1 Coaches.

An unusually severe problem with paint adhesion. Circa 1928.

The slightly diffuse borders of the sprayed areas on these coaches were hidden by the clipped-on window surrounds, but on the later larger Pullmans the border was disguised by a hand-painted gold lining.

Masks were also used for a few interesting 'conversions', like the early No. 0 Mitropa Coaches which were USA Pullman lithographed sides, sprayed in Crawfords red through a mask covering the doors and windows, so that these details were retained while the 'Pullman' livery was obliterated. A similar method was used on some Platelayer's Huts. Certain Dinky toys and figures, for example some black and white Cows, were also sprayed using masks.

FINAL ASSEMBLY and HAND FINISHING

The finished parts or assemblies were taken to a conveyor line in the Train Room for the final assembly; for example, vans would be completed by fitting the couplings and base to the body, then the doors and roof.

The next stage was hand-finishing, to add any necessary details. On the more expensive locomotives this involved hand-painting the steps, steam pipes, cab roof, whistles or safety valve covers, as well as the black on the smokebox and chimney, and red on the buffer beams. The lining of the boiler also had to be added. Retouching was also carried out where parts were scratched in the assembly – often on lugs, such as those on the No. 2 Special Loco running plates. The lugs of tinprinted buildings were often retouched to match the colour of the roof; in later years the lugs were either printed in the correct colours, or the mismatch was ignored.

Another part of the hand finishing operation was the application of transfers, which involved trimming to shape, painting with gold size, fixing the transfer and floating off the paper backing.

The sources of transfers used by Meccano Ltd are uncertain, but the quality was usually fine. These crests were used on MR, LNWR, GN and CR coaches, and on certain LMS, LNER and GW locos. The LBSC transfer provides an interesting puzzle.

VARNISHING

The next step was to apply a coat of varnish. Most of the enamels used for Hornby Trains dried to a semi-flat finish, and it was the varnish that gave the final deep gloss. Varnishing was carried out in the same way as the enamelling, under dust-free conditions; it is unusual to find traces of dust, grit or hairs in the finish.

Many of the items made before 1924 were varnished sparingly, if at all. The varnishes used in the mid 1920s were usually applied in a heavy coat, and they age to give a characteristic yellowed finish that is both appealing and impossible to describe. From the later 1920s the varnish coat was thinner and more uniform, and less subject to yellowing (except when exposed to damp). By the late 1930s a lighter varnish was used, in still thinner coats that hardly affected the colour of wagon bodies at all, while locos and wagon bases were given a thin matt varnish which was extremely attractive when new and unused; but unfortunately it soon picked up slight traces of grease from lubrication, or fingerprints, and lost the matt appearance.

TESTING, PACKAGING and DESPATCH

Each Hornby Train locomotive was thoroughly tested before it was allowed to leave the works. The test tracks were constantly busy with trains set in motion by the testers, who carefully noted the performance. Any deficiencies that could be remedied on the spot (for example wheels rubbing against the housing) were put right immediately; other locomotives that failed the tests were put aside for more thorough investigation. 'Tested' labels were attached to the locomotives that passed the tests. For postwar locomotives these included a count on the number of laps of the circuit, checking the reversing four successive times on the 501 Locos, and the operation of the brake of all locos from the brake rail; there was also a standard climbing test track. Mechanisms were tested before final assembly into the housing, to ensure that they completed a certain number of circuits within a specified period, neither too fast nor too slow.

After testing, the locomotives were packed ready for immediate despatch, or sent to the vast first-floor store room to await the dealers' orders.

SELLING SERVICE

Meccano Ltd chose their retailers with great care. References were required, and the Meccano traveller would have to be satisfied that a reasonable amount of trade would result. Even well-established toy shops could be refused if they were too near an existing Meccano dealer whose trade might be damaged by competition. Large towns could support more than one shop, but most provincial towns had only one recognised Meccano dealer; in all there were over 2,000 UK stockists. There was no question of competition by price-cutting, since retail price maintenance was strictly enforced. Nor could the larger shops demand more favourable trade terms than the smaller shops – often to the frustration of their buyers. There was a 33⅓% trade discount, with a further 2½% discount for prompt payment; carriage was free on orders over 40s.

Not even the largest stockists were expected to hold the full range of Meccano Ltd products, but any item that was in stock at Binns Road could be ordered rapidly using a series of telegraphic codes (first used in 1928) for quick despatch using carriers as instructed by the shopkeeper; goods were even

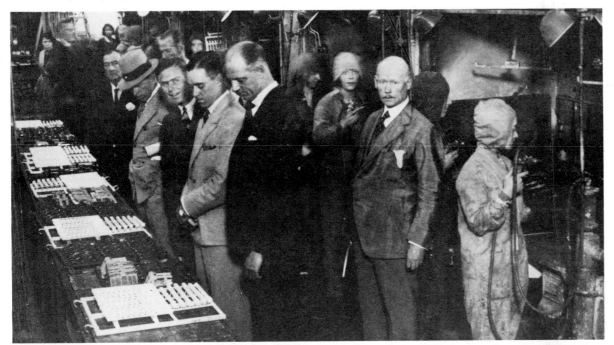

Frank Hornby and a party of visitors inspecting the varnishing shops, circa 1928.

sent by passenger train if necessary, bearing in mind that boys with pocket money to spend were likely to be impatient!

As well as the premises in Marshall Street in London, there were also London offices and a ware-house in Walnut Tree Walk, Kennington Road SE11, for the convenience of traders in the South East.

It was very important for Meccano Ltd to offer support to their retailers, not just by supplying their orders as fully and as speedily as possible, but with a range of other services to help maximise sales. These services were described in a series of printed booklets like the 'Increased Sales and Profits' book of 1920 and the later 'Selling Service' circulars. The services included the provision of display stands and display

Testing No. 2 Trains, circa 1922.

Final assembly of No. 1 Special Tank Locos.

layouts for the Hornby Trains, of various types and sizes; display showcards to promote Hornby Trains, and paper streamers for the windows to catch the customer's eye. Special 'Hornby Train Week' posters were supplied, to support the annual promotion held just before Christmas; the dealer was encouraged to send out special invitation cards printed by Meccano Ltd. These invited favoured clients to special displays of Hornby Trains which the zestful dealer was supposed to organise, to coincide with a national advertising campaign.

The national advertising by Meccano Ltd could be supported by the dealer in his local paper. Meccano Ltd were able either to supply standard advertisements (with the name and address of the dealer added), or to design special advertisements for which they could provide suitable printing blocks from their vast store.

Since gravure and offset lithographic printing are now the norm, it may perhaps be necessary to explain that these 'blocks' were blocks of typographic metal (or 'stereo' matrices) used for printing pictures. They were printed together with the text which was usually typeset in hot metal. Meccano Ltd kept a huge stock of different types and sizes of blocks for use in catalogues and in advertisements. The most expensive blocks were those made to print full-colour work as in the Hornby Books of Trains. Having tied up a lot of money in these and other blocks (they were expensive to produce) Meccano Ltd were understandably reluctant to update them each time there was a change in the product – even

quite noticeable changes of colour or design. Furthermore, the blocks were often prepared from a picture of a pre-production sample which was not exactly like the eventual production models. Thus the advertisements in MMs, catalogues and the press were usually accurate with descriptions and prices (although mistakes were sometimes made) but the pictures cannot be relied upon as correct and up to date. For example, the early postwar catalogues showed some items made obsolete by the 1923 regrouping changes! A certain amount of modification was possible, to save the expense of a complete new set of blocks, if the change was only small.

Other parts of the selling service to the Hornby Train dealer were the provision of coloured price tickets for window displays, and price stickers

A No. 2 Hornby Train Display Board of the late '20s. Despatched to Messrs. R. W. Weekes of Tunbridge Wells on 29 October 1928.

Hornby Train showcard; late prewar or early postwar.

More showcards, circa 1930.

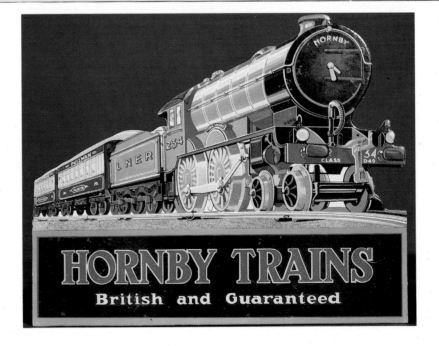

Hornby 'Royal Scot' showcard, circa 1928.

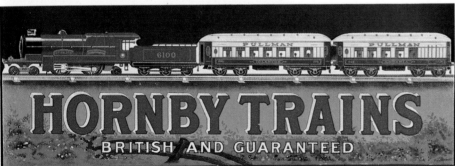

'Yorkshire' showcard, 1930.

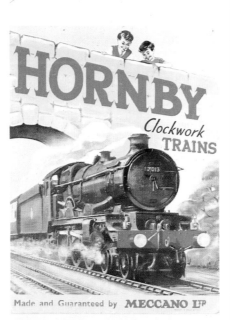

Many shops had their own attractive stickers for Hornby boxes. These are among the largest and most splendid, used by Messrs. Salanson.

Probably the last Hornby O gauge showcard, circa 1960. →

This St Bruno advertisement shows Hornby Trains as they were usually used – on the living room carpet! Father is happily dismantling a non-Hornby coach, but the Royal Scot and other accessories are all Hornby. Probably based on a photograph.

(printed in red) for Hornby boxes. The dealers also operated the Meccano Xmas Club, for which they were issued with club cards; young lads were supposed to pay in part of their pocket money regularly each week until Christmas, when they could cash it in for their desideratum – be it M series or a 'Princess'. The scheme operated until 1939.

Meccano Ltd regularly printed trade circulars, which gave details of the new products for the season, and other news. They also advised the shops of the dates of the annual British Industries' Fair, usually held in the spring, at which Meccano Ltd were regular exhibitors. Hornby Trains were exhibited at the B.I.F. in 1921, and in 1922 a Meccano model of the Forth Bridge was demonstrated with Hornby Trains crossing it. It was, incidentally, reported in the Meccano Magazine in May–June 1922 that an 11 stone Meccano representative stood on the model and it did not collapse; it does not say if he stood on it deliberately! The April 1934 MM showed Ramsay Macdonald visiting the Meccano stand at B.I.F.

PART EXCHANGE SCHEME

Meccano dealers were required to operate the Part Exchange Scheme, by which customers could buy new Hornby locomotives at reduced prices by trading in their old one; no matter what the age or condition of the old locomotive, so long as it was one of the listed types Meccano Ltd allowed up to half the purchase price. The trade leaflet of October 1930 described the scheme, and said that 'We are confident that this new selling plan will result in a substantial increase in Hornby sales. It will revive the interest and enthusiasm of thousands of boys who already own Hornby Locomotives, and will stir in them a desire to re-organise and re-equip their miniature railway systems. The consequent demand for Rolling Stock and Accessories will be considerable – additional business to your ordinary everyday trading.'

Although the dealer gained the extra trade, his profit margin on the sale of the new locomotive was reduced; for example, if he took a locomotive with a part exchange value of 6s against a new locomotive

priced 18s, his profit margin was reduced from the normal 6s to 4s, and out of this he also had to pay carriage for the old locomotive to Binns Road (where it was probably destroyed). The reduced margin was usually more than compensated for by extra business, and the removal of the old locomotives from the second-hand market meant that more new ones were sold. Tenders were not included in the scheme, and the allowance given covered only half the cost of the old loco and not the tender; the curious Hornby habit of selling the locomotives and tenders separately meant that some owners saved money by running new locomotives obtained under the scheme with unsuitable tenders from their old locos! The exchange scheme explains in part why there are now more spare tenders than there are tenderless locomotives.

To avoid interference with the normal Christmas trade, the Part Exchange Scheme was temporarily suspended after Hornby Train week, until the New Year.

The part exchange prices varied with the current list prices, and the boast that 'A Hornby Train is always worth at least half the price you pay for it' began to look a little dubious at times. In the July 1936 MM, the new extension of the Part Exchange Scheme to cover the exchange of clockwork for electric rails was introduced. But from July 1938 both Hornby Part Exchange Schemes were discontinued. A new part-exchange scheme for locos only, with less generous allowances, was re-started in June 1939 only to be suspended again a year later in July 1940.

After the war the part exchanges were not revived until March 1958, when the MM announced them again in a form almost too horrible to contemplate; the part exchange through the dealers of Gauge O locomotives for Hornby Dublo. The only

Meccano Ltd Price Tickets and Stickers. The Meccano cardboard ruler was for free distribution to customers; it carried an advertisement for Hornby Trains.

redeeming feature of the scheme was that only post-war engines could be swapped!

OTHER SERVICES

The travellers who visited the Meccano dealers made sure that they were kept aware of items that could be obtained from Meccano Ltd by special order, although certain of the items mentioned in the Meccano Magazine as special orders could only be obtained direct from the factory.

Another scheme that the dealers were required to administer was the Deferred Payments Scheme, available in Great Britain and N. Ireland from 1937 to 1939.

THE HORNBY RAILWAY COMPANY

The Meccano Guild run by the Meccano Ltd Advertising Department had been an outstanding success, and in view of this the March 1928 MM asked for 'ideas and suggestions regarding the formation of a Hornby guild, to be devoted entirely to the interests of Hornby model railway enthusiasts'; although that was not quite the impression conveyed to those on the other side of the counter in the 1928 trade booklet, which made it clear that the interests of the dealers (and of Meccano Ltd) were not entirely neglected: 'A new organisation to be known as the Hornby Railway Company is now being developed with the object of stimulating interest in Hornby goods and thereby increasing sales!'

A mysteriously worded postcard was enclosed with each train set packed in early 1928, asking the purchasers to send their name and address if they wanted to receive details of 'a fine new scheme' to get the best fun from their miniature railway. No further details were given, but in May 1928 a large number of leaflets were printed, which asked 'Which is the Greatest Railway Company in the world?' to which the reply was 'Why, the Hornby Railway Company of course! Join it now, and get far more fun out of your trains. Learn to organise your system on real railway lines, and how to use a real timetable with your Hornby Trains.'

The formal announcement of the formation of the HRC 'with branches in every town and village' came in the October 1928 MM, and the HRC lapel badge, included in the membership fee of 7d, was shown. (The badge was enamelled in blue, green and red on brass, but after the war a plain blue-enamelled badge was issued.) Details were given of the local branches of the HRC which could be formed, with their own 'boy directors and officials' – General Manager, Engineer, Traffic Superintendant, Stationmaster, Signalman, Drivers and any others considered necessary. Any branch with at least 6 members (later 4), an adult Branch Chairman, and a Branch secretary could apply to Headquarters in Binns Road, where the Chairman (Frank Hornby, then Roland Hornby from 1936) would consider their incorporation into the HRC. Activities of the branches could be reported to HQ on special report forms which were in due course abstracted for publication in the official organ of the HRC – the Meccano Magazine.

As well as the reports of branch activities, the MM also had monthly articles which were the main means by which members were told how to run their home railways more realistically. There were also regular competitions to test railway knowledge. Each member was sent a booklet when he joined, which was full of information on how to run a railway, including the use of correct headcodes, bibliographies for building up a branch library, notes on how to arrange timetable working, and on the care of equipment. Furthermore any member could write to the Company Secretary (the staff of Ellison Hawks and his successors) for advice on any aspect of Hornby Train operation – from designing a layout to deciding which trains to buy.

In the November 1928 MM the 'immediate success' of the HRC was announced, and pictures of the first members were shown. Forms for railway operation were available to members at 5d per pad of 50. They were:

GW1 General Working Timetable
SD4 Stationmaster's Arrivals and Departures
EJ5 Engineman's Job Card
SB6 Signal Box Instructions
SR7 Stationmaster's Report Forms.

COME INSIDE AND SEE OUR SPECIAL DISPLAY OF **HORNBY TRAINS**

Each of these forms was printed on a distinctive coloured paper. They appeared in several editions after the first announcement in November 1929.

The HRC booklet was first shown in the December 1928 MM, and in January 1929 a similar booklet for the HRC Junior Section was being prepared, ready for 1st February. Both Senior and Junior Section booklets were printed in several editions before the war; the age of the applicant determined which booklet he was sent, the Junior Section booklet going to the under-12s, although either booklet could be bought separately. After the war, the Junior Section booklet was printed unaltered in 1946, with everything from the Princess Elizabeth downwards still shown. But soon the old Senior Section booklets were the only ones available, reprinted in revised form in 1948 and in many subsequent editions up to 1957; in the last edition there was much greater emphasis on Hornby Dublo Trains.

The HRC generated a vast amount of printed matter quite apart from these booklets; each member was sent a membership certificate and covering letter along with his badge when he joined up. Then there were HRC Writing Pads, announced in the April 1930 MM, and HRC Envelopes in December 1930.

There were branch affiliation application forms, report forms, and instructions on running branches of the HRC. For those more isolated members who were unable to join or to form a local branch, there was a Hornby Railway Company Correspondence Club, announced in the April 1929 MM. Admission was free, but required a separate application form; these were still being issued after the war.

In addition, millions of HRC official application forms were printed – to judge from the printing codes, during the life of the HRC some 5 million were printed – 2 million before and 3 million after the war. They were packed with each locomotive and train set. Despite the low cost of joining (7d in the UK at first, 6d from late 1928, and 10d after the war until 1961, when it went up to 1s 3d) only a small number of these forms were actually used. The prewar rate of recruitment was about 7000 members per year, but the peak of postwar production saw an increase to about 25,000 new members each year; in the late 1950s and 1960s this tailed off markedly, and by the time the HRC was wound up in 1964 the membership numbers had risen to only 325,000 or so.

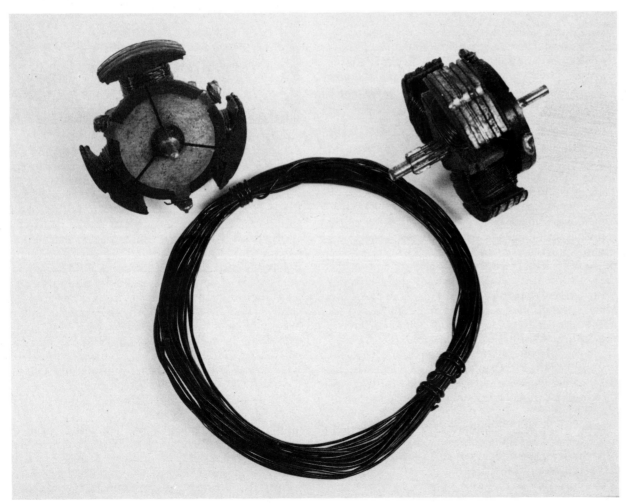

Parts supplied to Meccano agents in Denmark for repairs, but never used.

REPAIR SERVICE and GUARANTEE WORK

Meccano Ltd advertised the Hornby Trains in 1921 with the claim that 'the clockwork mechanism is strongly built, and does not easily get out of order'. Nonetheless, guarantees were an important feature of the sales promotion of Meccano Ltd trains – 'The trains with the guarantee.' The Repair (or Returns) Department was an established part of the factory, and it dealt with guarantee work and other repairs on Hornby Trains. The standard guarantee was for 60 days from the date of purchase. It warranted that the loco was free from defects at the time of purchase, and provided there had been no misuse and the instructions had been carried out, the loco would be repaired or replaced if it failed within the 60 days. Although the guarantee was paid for by the customer, since the price was higher than would have been necessary in the absence of the guarantee, many of the forms were not stamped with the dealer's name and address or dated at the time of purchase – probably only half were correctly filled in. Presumably the other customers resorted to banging on the toyshop counter if they were dissatisfied!

The M Series guarantee was not limited to 60 days, and Meccano Ltd carried out repairs under guarantee even outside this period, without charge – presumably on the generous assumption that the lads would soon be 'hooked' on buying one of the bigger engines. But the penny-pinching change in the mid-'30s of restricting the M3 and No. 0 Loco guarantees to 30 days instead of leaving them unlimited shows that this was considered by the factory to be an important economy.

Over the years, many Hornby Trains returned to the factory for attention; perhaps as many as one in six. If there were weak points in the design of a loco, they showed up in the returns, and this was of course the reason for some of the modifications in design over the years. Apart from the failure of mechanical and electrical parts of mechanisms, a common reason for return was trouble with the wheels. Many fault-free locomotives were sent back to the works under guarantee by 'hypochondriac' owners; these were returned to the customers with a special printed slip to say that the loco was 'not in need of repairs', and giving hints on checking the gauge of rails, free running of wagons, and lubrication, to help cure any remaining problems.

Locomotives were not the only items repaired; coaches, wagons, points and accessories were also sent back when they had suffered accidental damage. If engines were badly damaged, a new housing could be provided. When the London Service and Repair Department was opened in 1929 at 5–6 Marshall Street W1, a most instructive list of repair prices was published; the list included the re-enamelling of housing as an alternative to replacement, at a small saving in cost. Presumably this service was also offered in Liverpool, but no locomotives repainted in this way have yet been positively identified as such.

Locomotives were returned from repair in the original box if it had been sent; otherwise a special 'repair box' was used. These were plain boxes, usually pink or buff, of the appropriate size. Before the war a Service Department label was used. Each box (both before and after the war) bore a sticker corresponding to the invoice number.

The repair service operated after the war in the same way as before. Unfortunately Meccano Ltd would not repair most of the prewar clockwork and electric engines – even those that were perfect except for wheel 'fatigue'. Although it would have taken little enough trouble to cast wheels for this purpose, one can perhaps understand the reasons why Meccano Ltd preferred to sell new locomotives! It is also worth noting that the No. 2 Locos which became obsolete in 1929 could not be repaired even in 1933, because of lack of parts!

The repair service was radically altered in 1962, when Meccano Ltd de-centralised the work by training selected dealers to take on repairs. Servicing leaflets were issued for each of the current locomotives, together with lists of the parts that could be ordered by dealers. The February 1962 MM listed all the 'Accredited Service Specialists', but also advised customers who could not use these dealers that locomotives could still be sent to the Meccano Ltd Service Department, which was then operating at Hanson Road in Aintree rather than at Binns Road.

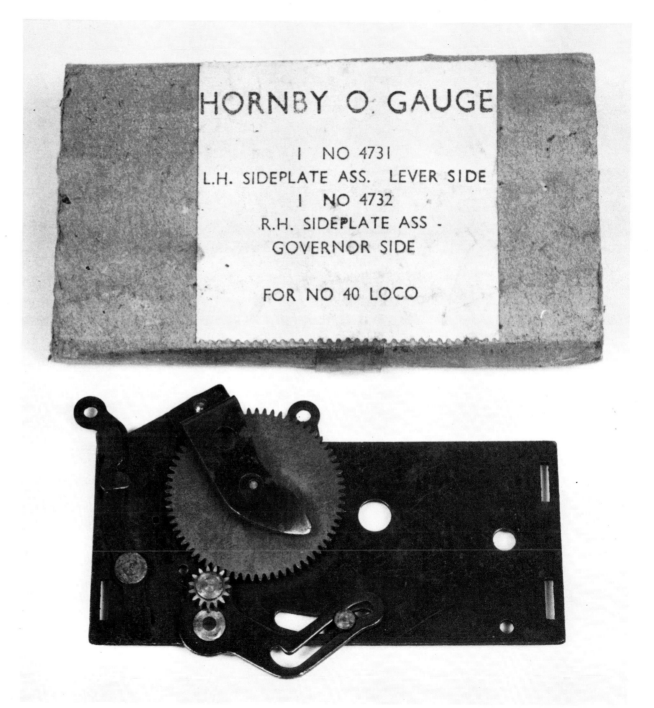

Spare Sideplate Assembly, packed for use by UK repair agents, circa 1962.

Locomotives

LIVERY

The Hornby locos of 1920 were available in three colours to represent GN, LNWR and MR company locomotives, although there were no company initials or crests. CR blue locos were added to the range in 1921. From the middle of 1923, Hornby locos were lettered with the LMS or LNER company initials; locos in CR blue were no longer made, the only colours being LMS red, LMS black, and LNER green. LNER black locos were also available from 1924, giving a choice of goods or passenger livery. From 1926 there were also GW green locos, and from 1928 SR green and SR black locos, making up the total of seven common UK liveries. Goods black engines were catalogued until 1936, when a trade bulletin announced: 'Black locomotives will no longer be included in train sets, nor listed for separate sale; but we shall be able to supply them at the same prices as red or green locomotives when specially ordered.' The availability of black locos was mentioned in the HBTs from 1937 to 1939, and the dealers' order form still had spaces to allow any of the engines (other than M series, No. 2 Special and No. 3 Locos) to be ordered in black finish. After the war LMS red, LNER green, GW green and SR green locos were manufactured, and BR liveries were introduced in 1954.

While it is not unusual to find Hornby Locos where all or part of the housing has been sprayed in one colour on top of another, it is most unusual to find that this has been done over the top of existing transfers or lining.

BOILER BANDS

Between 1923 and 1929, the lining of boilers with painted and later embossed boiler bands was gradually developed. On the LMS and LNER black locos the bands were painted in red, and on the SR black locos in green. GW locos had yellow boiler bands, as did most LMS red locos except the No. 1 Special Tanks from 1929, and the LMS red No. 0, No. 1 and No. 1 Tank locos from 1931 which had gold boiler bands instead of the usual yellow. Nord locos had gold painted bands, and SR green locos had white bands.

The situation was most complicated for the LNER green passenger-livery locos. Boiler bands for these were invariably black up to 1929, but the Special locos usually had white bands from 1929, as did the 1931 series of No. 0, No. 1 and No. 1 Tank Locos. But the exceptions were the No. 2 Special Tanks which had yellow bands, and the 'Flying Scotsman' which continued to have black bands for the whole of its production! None of these styles was strictly accurate, since the bands should really have been white/black/white stripes, a style not adopted by Hornby until lining transfers were made for the boilers for the LNER Type 501 locos in 1948 – when they had already been rendered obsolete by the nationalisation of the railways.

The BR No. 51 Locos had orange/black/orange boiler band transfers, whereas the double red bands on the BR No. 50 Locos were embossed then hand painted.

DOMES AND SMOKEBOXES

In the October 1927 MM two requests from readers were published, one asking for polished brass safety valves on the GW locos, and the other asking for the polished brass domes on other locos to be painted in the same colour as the boiler. In point of fact the change for the GW locos had been started from May 1927, when the No. 3 Loco brass safety valve cover was designed, and was soon adopted for the smaller GW locos in place of the cast GW safety valve. It was probably early in 1928 that the first locos were made with black-painted smokeboxes, although not announced in the MM until June 1928; the domes began to be coloured not long afterwards, and this was announced in August. All the SR locos of 1928 had coloured domes and black smokeboxes. Unfortunately many domes continued to be made in brass rather than in steel, and the paint did not adhere as well as on tinplate. Thus accidental damage and paint flaking sometimes leave them almost devoid of paint, causing confusion among collectors who think the domes were originally polished brass.

TRADEMARK TRANSFERS ON LOCOS AND TENDERS

Between 1920 and 1924, Hornby locos and tenders often had trademark transfers of the types used on Hornby wagons. From 1924, a special 'Hornby' transfer was made for use on smokebox doors, and this continued in use until the war. From 1924 tenders began to carry 'Hornby Series' transfers, and from 1928 'Manf'd by' transfers.

During 1925 and early in 1926 there was a brief period when an attractive 'garter' transfer was used on the boilers of No. 0, No. 1, No. 2 and No. 1 Tank Locos (and probably on No. 2 Tank Locos as well), but its use was soon abandoned.

The No. 2 Tank Locos of 1928–29 had trademark transfers lettered 'Manfd by Meccano Ltd. Liverpool', which were not used on any other loco.

All the No. 1 and No. 2 Special Locos had 'Special' loco transfers reading 'Hornby. Manfd by Meccano Ltd. Liverpool', until 1936 when new versions were made which read 'Hornby. Made in England.

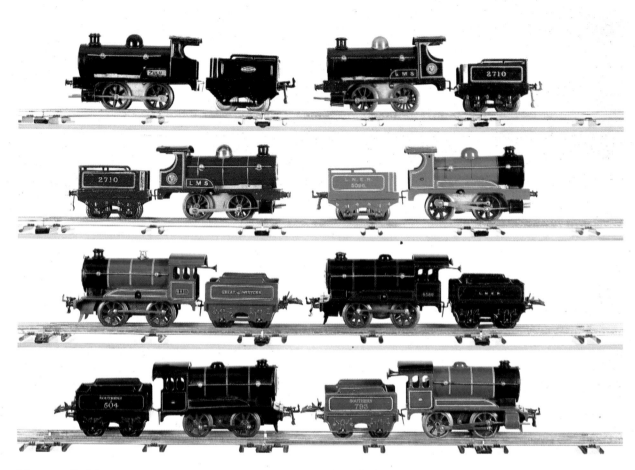

Meccano Ltd.'

Some No. 0/1 tenders and No. 1 Special Tenders had trademark transfers incorporated in the lining transfers. Thus they do not follow the normal pattern for dating purposes; but the No. 2 Special Tenders had normal wagon-type trademark transfers.

LOCO NUMBERS

Up to 1926, no locos had numbers other than 2710 and 2711, except for a few early No. 2 Tank Locos before the '4–4–4' transfers were made. The MM announced in October 1926 that the tank locos would be given 'ordinary serial numbers' as soon as possible, instead of 0–4–0 and 4–4–4; and in January 1927 that 'wheel classification numbers have already been abolished from the sides of locos.' From then onwards the numbers of tank and tender locos were changed from time to time as new batches of transfers were made. Except during the changeover periods, no Hornby loco was sold with a choice of number.

Meccano Ltd chose some loco numbers purely at random, but publicity photographs from the major railway companies, and their published booklets for train spotters, were frequently used to help the choice. An example was the LMS black No. 1 Loco number 2290, taken from the 'Lickey banker' 0–10–0

loco! M series numbers were often derived from the season in which they were first printed, eg '3435'.

The SR re-numbering scheme of 1931 onwards was also reflected in the Hornby range from 1933, when new batches of transfers were made. Different letter prefixes had been used for the three sections of the SR: 'A' (Ashford) for the Eastern Section, 'B' (Brighton) for the Central Section, and 'E' (Eastleigh) for the Western Section. Under the new scheme the prefixes were dropped, and 1000 added to the 'A' loco numbers, and 2000 to the 'B' numbers. Thus E793 became 793, A759 became 1759, and B329 became 2329, for example.

GENERAL

Before embarking on a type-by-type description of the Hornby locos, a few general notes may be necessary. Only the most important changes have been mentioned in the following text; small differences in mechanisms, wheels, control levers and knobs, trademarks and couplings have not been covered, nor have minor differences in the castings for buffers, chimneys, wheels etc.

Where 'shadowed' lettering is mentioned, the standard Hornby style is implied, with the letters in gold, shadowed red to the right, and lined in black.

References to the left or right-hand side of locos are when looking forward from the cab.

There was a minor change in the smokebox door handles of many clockwork locos from 1936, with the shorter handle on the right-hand side (looking forward from the cab) not on the left as earlier.

Investigating wheel types and wheel colours is a particular problem, mainly because of the so-called 'metal fatigue' which affected diecast mazac alloy wheels, and also to a lesser extent certain diecast lead alloy wheels of 1928 onwards. Mazac wheels were fitted to most locos from 1936. Different batches of castings were affected to varying extents; while some were almost perfect, others began to disintegrate (pushed apart by the expansion of the alloy) within months of manufacture, depending on the amount of impurity in the alloy. During the war the problem was thoroughly investigated and the causes eliminated. It is technically incorrect to call the problem 'fatigue', since it has nothing to do with usage; locos kept unused in their boxes suffered just as badly. (After 50 years or so, most of the mazac castings which have survived intact should now be in a stable state, with little risk of serious deterioration.) Because of these problems, and consequent repair work and 'restoration', it is difficult to be sure about the dates of changes of wheel type and colour.

ZULU AND No. 0 LOCOMOTIVES

Zulu Trains were advertised in the May–June 1922 MM as a cheaper alternative to the Hornby Train. There was much in common between the designs; the main differences were that the Zulu loco was non-constructional, (the cab being secured to the base and boiler by eyelets and tabs), and that it was fitted with a non-reversing mechanism similar in shape and size to the 1921-style No. 1 motor. The motor sideplates were at first blued rather than nickel plated. Zulu Locos were finished in black overall even on the brass dome, but red lining was added round the cab windows and side embossing, and the front buffer beam was also finished in red, with the round-headed cast lead buffers hand-finished in black. Rather short handrails were fitted, identical to those of the Tinprinted Train, and similarly finished in gold enamel. 'Zulu' transfer trademarks were applied to the left-hand splasher, and the Meccano Ltd trademark to the other side. 'M Ld L England' was embossed in the cab floor. No details were embossed on the smokebox door, which was in fact identical to the Petrol Tank Wagon end; the boiler also had some tooling in common with the tanker. Although the Zulu Tender was very similar to the Hornby type, the top was secured to the base by eyelets, while cast buffers were used and the axles were thin.

LMS black post-grouping livery was available early in 1924, the loco being virtually identical except that both splashers were lettered 'LMS' and the 'Zulu' trademark was on the smokebox door. Handrails were altered to run the full length of the boiler, with more widely-spaced supports. Presumably by mistake, a front coupling slot appeared although no couplings were (officially) fitted. On some of these locos the chimneys were secured by

eyelets, not cast spigots as on earlier and later versions. The tenders were eyeletted as before, but an unlined '2710' transfer was used (the previous Zulu Locos had no number) and obsolete 1921-type Hornby tender components were used up for some Zulu Tenders.

Later in 1924 remaining stocks of the LMS Zulu loco were updated by overpainting the 'Zulu' transfers and applying a 'Hornby' smokebox door transfer instead. LMS crests were applied to the cabsides. In addition to these 'updated' LMS black locos, LMS red and LNER green or black liveries were also prepared during the 1924–25 season. They had polished brass domes. Mechanism sideplates were now usually nickel plated instead of blued.

A revised No. 0 Loco housing was designed early in 1925, sharing the tools used for the latest non-constructional No. 1 Locos, which were assembled by tabs instead of nuts and bolts. There was no embossed lining on the revised No. 0 cab sides, and a detailed smokebox door was fitted, as on the No. 1 but with no handle attached. Unlike the No. 1, the No. 0 Loco had no fixed lamps and no front coupling; the No. 0-type handrails were unchanged. The bodies continued to be sprayed after assembly, with the polished brass dome fitted after painting. The boilers were unlined (unlike the No. 1), but the cabside transfers, company crests and splasher lettering were in the No. 1 style. Black locos no longer had the windows picked out with red lining. Oval buffers replaced the round type.

From 1925–26 the tenders officially became the same as the No. 1, and were described as No. 0/1, ending what had been a rather artificial distinction since the termination of the constructional system. Some odd tenders continued to be made for No. 0 Locos, however; for example an LNER green tender, with the old plain-back 1920 tender top lettered '2710' and not lined, but with 'Hornby Series' transfers, a red-finished buffer beam and round-headed cast buffers! A convenient way of using up old stock parts. But the standard issue No. 0/1 tenders (of the narrow pattern at first, later in the wider non-constructional pattern) had transfers with the '2710' number and lining.

No. 0 Locos were offered in Great Western Railway livery in 1926, with 'GW' splasher lettering,

cabside company crests, and with '2710' tenders. A diecast safety valve, painted black, replaced the usual Hornby dome. From 1927 the boilers for all liveries were being embossed and painted with three boiler bands. The mechanisms were fitted with coupling rods as well as piston rods. Spraying holes were punched in the floor of the cab, and the 'M Ld L' trademark was no longer embossed. From late in 1927, the GW version was fitted with the No. 3 type brass safety valve cover instead of the black-painted casting used before. By then all the No. 0/1 '2710' tenders had bases the same colour as the tops, whereas before they had always been black.

From early in 1928 all No. 0 Locos had black smokeboxes (and black smokebox doors, which on the No. 0 had previously been the same colour as the boiler), and the domes were sprayed in the same colour as the boiler. Most notable examples of the 1928–29 loco liveries were the SR Locos, which were lettered 'Southern A759' (green) and 'Southern E509' (black) on the tenders. Unlike the others, the base of the SR green tender was black, and the cab roof of the loco was also black.

For 1929–30, revised loco bodies were produced, similar to the previous style but with long splashers over both wheels. Company initials no longer appeared on the splashers, but were moved to the tenders, the '2710' transfers being replaced by more up-to-date styles. The loco numbers 8324 (LMS red), 8327 (LMS black) and 2449 (GW green) were on the cabside of the loco. LNER tenders were lettered 'L.N.E.R. 5096.' (green) and 'L.N.E.R. 5097.' (black). The SR tender transfers remained the same, but the cabside lining transfers were altered, and small imitation number plates appeared on the sides of the SR and LNER engines. Five boiler bands were now embossed and painted on each of the locos – two pairs plus a single band under the dome. Both dome and chimney were of a lower-profile design than the old '2710' style.

The new body was intended for use with a revised motor, fundamentally unaltered but with longer sideplates, and with the rear axle moved backwards to give a longer wheelbase and allow more spring expansion. A few No. 0 Locos used old-type mechanisms with a special extended rear bracket to suit the new bodies. Wheels were nor-

The Zulu Locos of the 1923–24 season were lettered 'LMS' on the splashers.

LNER No. 0 Locos of 1925–26. The green loco has a tender made from obsolete constructional parts, while the black loco still has the 1924–25 narrow pattern tender. The C01 Crossover was first marketed in 1925.

mally painted red, a style used for a few locos made in 1928.

The 1930–31 season No. 0 Locos were unchanged, except that towards the end of the production of this type there was obviously a certain reluctance to order stocks of new transfers for the 1929 style bodies, since the 1931 style revised locos were already being planned. Thus a few odd No. 0 Locos appeared with wrong or incomplete sets of transfers. For example, some GW No. 0 Locos had completely blank cabsides, with no numberplate or lining at all! The LNER green No. 0 appeared with the LMS '8324' number and LMS lining transfers. The LNER black No. 0 also came out with LMS-style cab-lining transfers (although without a cabside number), and with blank splashers. The LMS tenders in later versions were lettered 'LMS' in small shadowed letters, instead of 'L.M.S.' in larger plain gold letters as before. There were doubtless other examples of such oddities.

The 1931 style No. 0 Locomotives were re-designed, with a completely updated housing like that of the No. 1 Loco of the period. They were fitted with a reversing mechanism of a new type, of similar dimensions to the No. 1 type but more cheaply made, with pressed metal sideplates instead of the pillar-type motors used before. This was reversible from the cab but not from the track. Control rods in the cab were now of the normal type with screw-on knobs, instead of the bent-wire loop formerly provided.

Other differences between the 1931-type No. 0 and No. 1 Locos were that the No. 0 Loco had no cylinders, although the wheels were still coupled, and there were no handles on the smokebox door. The No. 0 Loco at first had no firebox inside the cab. The handrail supports were castings instead of turned brass, and the handrails were painted gold. The handrails remain the most reliable way to distinguish these engines from the No. 1 type. Lamp brackets for detachable lamps were fitted. GW No. 0 Locos had taller chimneys than the 'Yorkshire' type fitted to the others.

All the new tenders were lettered with the rail-way company name or initials. Cabside numbers were 500 (LMS red), 600 (LMS black), 5508 (LNER green), 6380 (LNER black) and 2251 (GW green). The SR locos had imitation numberplates on the cabside (nicely lined in red on the black loco) and the tenders were lettered 'Southern A504' (black) or 'Southern E793' (green).

There were no major changes for some time, except for a strengthening ridge added to the left-hand side of the motor in 1932. Minor changes to the transfers were made in the mid 1930s, with the SR tender lettered '793' instead of 'E793', while the GWR tender appeared with a monogram of the GWR initials instead of the 'Great (crest) Western' that had always been used before.

From 1936–37 the No. 0 and EO20 Locos were fitted with cylinders and piston rods as on the No. 1 and E120 Locos, reducing still further the gap between their specifications. It was necessary to alter the cutout of the base to move the mechanism further back, and longer brackets resulted; a No. 1-type firebox was added inside the cab to hide the motor. The colour of the LNER 5508 was changed to a darker green in 1936.

Universal bases common between the No. 0 and No. 1 clockwork and electric engines were fitted from early in 1937; the cutout for the motors was naturally larger. Also from 1937, the number of the LNER green loco changed to 4797, the LMS red to 5551 (in block letters rather than serif), and the GW to 5399.

Apart from the production of matt versions in 1939, the only other change seems to have been that the LMS red loco appeared in a late matt 5600 version, presumably once again the result of a shortage of transfers.

6 volt electric EO6 Locos were catalogued in 1934–35 only, being withdrawn from sale with effect from September 1935 (although almost certainly obtainable by special order). 20 volt EO20 locos were available from 1934 to 1941. These electric engines were exactly like the clockwork in general details of shape and livery, but had the same electric motors as the E120 Locos. In 1934 the price was 22s for the EO6/EO20 against 24s for the E120/E16, compared with 10s 6d for the clockwork No. 0 and 12s 6d for the No. 1. By the end of 1941 the prices had risen to a frightening 27s 6d for the No. 0 and 52s 6d for the EO20.

No. 1 LOCOMOTIVES

It was the policy of Meccano Ltd to update and improve their products continuously, within the constraints of price and production economics. Nowhere is this better illustrated than by the No. 1 Locomotives, which were produced with literally hundreds of production variations.

The earliest series of Hornby locomotives had a simple livery, with the baseplate nickel plated (the standard finish for Meccano parts at that time), but with a bright red enamelled buffer beam, and with boiler, cab, splashers, cylinders, smokebox door, chimney, tender top and tender base all enamel finished – in MR red for the Midland Railway sets, and probably in green for the GN and black for the LNWR sets (although these two have yet to be confirmed in the early 1920 version). The couplings were brass, and distinguished from the later couplings of 1920 by having a large single brass wire loop instead of the three-link steel wire chain used later. Other brass parts included the buffers, the 2710 cabside numberplates, and the characteristic polished and varnished brass dome. (The first catalogue pictures showed riveted domes, as on the Tinprinted Trains, but all production versions seem to have had the dome fixed by lugs.) The handrails were two separate pieces of Meccano-type rod, secured to the handrail knobs by grubscrews, usually at one end only.

The later constructional Hornby engines of 1920 were available in LNWR black, GN green and MR red. The running plates were black, but the green locos had red valances, and the MR red locos had MR red valances. In each case the smokebox door, chimney, cylinders and tender base were black.

Caledonian Railway blue locomotives were made from 1921, and LBSC train sets were mentioned in the MM, although the manufacture of LBSC locos has not been confirmed. Leaf-springs were embossed above the axles on the tender base, and embossed beading was added to the back of the tender top where it had previously been plain. Brass buffers of smaller profile began to be fitted.

Substantial revisions were made to the locomotives for the 1921–22 season, most importantly the change to a larger, more efficient longer-running motor, with flat sideplates connected by pillars instead of the pressed-sheet sideplates of the smaller early mechanism. A more efficient governor was fitted, and the wheels were of larger diameter. The reversing lever was now a rod, instead of the previous 'swan's neck' lever operated through the cab floor. Single-piece handrails folded around the smokebox, made of thinner rod, were friction-held by smaller handrail knobs with smaller grubscrews at first, later with none. Buffers were no longer fitted between the loco and tender, and the new loco/ tender couplings became a standard Hornby fitting. At the front of the loco and the back of the tender large drop-link couplings were provided, instead of brass couplings with wire links; they were secured by eyelets. The transition to the use of the new components was not instantaneous, the old-style parts being used up for some time. Current stocks of loco bases were adapted for the new motors and couplings, and holes for the old couplings and for the 'swan's-neck' reverse lever appeared for some time

1929–30 No. 0 and No. 1 Locos. The cheaper No. 0 Locos can be distinguished by the diecast handrail knobs.

No. 0 SR Loco, circa 1932, with No. 0 Pullmans and No. 0 Cutting.

painted bands, cabsides were finished with lining transfers and with the railway company crest, and company initials were now on both splashers. Brass '2710' cabside numberplates were no longer fitted, although a few locos of the period had old-stock cabs with unused slots for these numberplates. Cab floors began to be marked 'M Ld L England', rather curiously since this was no longer the current embossing for Hornby wagons. 'Hornby' transfers were applied to the smokebox doors, despite the 'Hornby' already embossed! But new smokebox doors with flatter fronts and with embossed hinges, but without the embossed 'Hornby', soon replaced the old type. A fourth choice of livery, LNER goods black, was available from 1924 (but not mentioned in the catalogues, which remained vague on questions of livery). This black loco had splashers lettered 'LNER' rather than the 'L&NER' which still appeared on the green loco.

Constructional tenders for these locos were numbered '2710' each side, with no lining transfers. 'Hornby Series' transfers were used on the tenders from mid 1924. New non-constructional narrow-beam tenders matching the width of the 1924–25 season wagons and clerestory coaches appeared late in 1924; the '2710' transfers for these incorporated lining, and early versions had brass buffers.

Around the middle of 1925, for the 1925–26 season, the No. 1 Loco body was comprehensively revised with non-constructional features. The boiler end and the cab were secured to the boiler by lugs, so the boiler stay was no longer required (allowing further room inside the boiler for spring expansion, giving longer runs), and the smokebox door handle was fixed by a rivet. Lamps were fitted above the

after they became unnecessary.

In 1922 there were no major changes, but the internal spring-clip on the cab front, which had held the reversing lever in gear, was replaced by a coil spring connected between the lever and the cab floor, an unsightly but more practical arrangement. Some intermediate locos had both types of spring. After the advent of Zulu Locos in 1922, some No. 1 Tenders were made with thin-axle constructional bases, but thick axles remained the norm on constructional tenders.

LMS and LNER No. 1 Trains were advertised in the Autumn 1923 catalogues; the first liveries were LMS red, LMS black and LNER green. They were identical to the pre-grouping locomotives, which had no company lettering, except that on the new locos 'LMS' or 'L&NER' lettering was added to the splashers, usually on one side only. Since remaining stocks of pre-grouping locos (some dating back to 1921) appear to have been updated by the addition of these transfers, placing these locos in order of manufacture can be difficult! The 'LMS' splashers were lined in black/white/black (later black/gold/black), and the 'L&NER' splashers in black/white/black. A few No. 1 tenders were lettered 'L&NER', and appear to have been sold with pre-grouping GN green locos. Early in 1924, domes with 4 tabs replaced the 2-tab versions.

A new-style finish was adopted for the 1924–25 season No. 1 Locos. The boilers were lined by 3

front buffer beam. Cab roofs were fixed by lugs, and the cab also clipped to the base by lugs; a semicircular cutout had to be provided in the cab front for access to the mechanism fixing bolt, and there was no longer any embossed beading on the cab side. The same transfers were used, except that the green locos had 'LNER' transfers instead of 'L&NER'. Cast oval buffers replaced the brass fittings on both loco and tender. Five bands were painted on the boiler, in a double/single/double grouping. The chimney was of the non-constructional 'George V' type. In the early part of the season narrow-beam tenders were still supplied, but soon new non-constructional tenders were designed to the standard loco and wagon width.

From late in 1925, the loco bodies were sprayed after assembly of all the parts except the dome and the smokebox door, so the running plates became the same colour as the boiler, whereas before they had always been black. The valance of the LNER green locos was still hand-finished in red.

GW livery was offered from January 1926; the bodies were fitted with the black-painted GW safety valve casting instead of a dome. GW locos were finished only in green; the boilers were lined with two pairs of boiler bands only, the splashers were lettered 'GW', and there was a GWR crest on the cabside. The tender was numbered 2710. Later in 1926, the GW loco and tender transfers were redesigned, with narrower lining.

From late in 1926, LNER green locos no longer had valances hand-finished in red; they were left in green like the running plates. There were few changes until the Spring of 1927, when the mechanisms were substantially revised as a result of the decision to offer No. 1 Locomotives fitted for the Hornby Control System. Two versions of the No. 1 Loco were made, one fitted for Control braking and the other not; both were fitted for reversing from the track, not just from the cab levers as before. More positive engagement of the gears allowed the flat reversing levers fitted with coil springs to be replaced by plain wire control rods like the brake rods. The wheels for the new motors were new castings with shorter crank-pin bosses, and they were fitted with coupling rods. Other changes were that a lead weight was bolted under the cab floor (the cylinders

were always weighted), and the diameter of the boiler handrail was reduced to improve appearance still further. Around this time the 'M Ld L England' embossing in the cab floor was discontinued, and a pair of holes appeared beside the rear coupling, for use while spraying the locos. By this time most tenders were finished with the base in the same colour as the top, instead of always being finished black.

The GW No. 1 locos were fitted with the brass safety-valve covers used for the No. 3 Locos, from late 1927. Red wheels began to be used instead of black, but not without exception. In the early part of 1928, both Control System and normal mechanisms were revised, with extended sideplates, and although the wheelbase remained the same the length of run was improved by changing the positions of the rear bracket and tie-bars. Control mechanisms were now fitted with manual brakes and brake control rods, whereas before none had been provided. Old mechanisms could still be used up in bodies made for these new-style motors, by use of a special long rear bracket.

Black smokeboxes, and domes of the same colour as the boiler, became standard from quite early in 1928, and the new SR passenger green and SR goods black locos of 1928 all had these new features. The

green SR No. 0/1 tenders had black bases, however, and another point of difference was that SR No. 1 cab roofs were finished black. Another difference from the LMS and LNER locos was that the SR locos of 1928–29 had two pairs of boiler bands rather than the usual double/single/double lining. Tenders were lettered 'Southern A759' (green) and 'Southern E509' (black); the first SR cabside transfers did not incorporate dummy numberplates.

Both motor and housing were updated for the 1929–30 season. A thoroughly revised mechanism with longer wheelbase, and with the winding spindle on the left-hand side, gave further improvements in performance; Control System versions were no longer available. The new bodies were easily recognisable by the long splasher over both driving wheels; lower-profile domes and chimneys were fitted, once stocks of the old types were exhausted. Curiously enough, the smokebox doors no longer had a handle riveted on as before. All boilers were embossed and painted with double/single/double boiler bands (with the pairs more closely spaced). Loco transfers were revised in the same way as for the No. 0 (the tenders were of course the same for both, as they had been since 1925). Cabside numbers were 8324 (LMS red), 8327 (LMS black) and 2449 (GW green). LNER tenders were lettered 'L.N.E.R.

5096.' (green) and 'L.N.E.R. 5097.' (black). LMS tenders were usually lettered 'L.M.S.', and GW tenders were lettered 'Great (crest) Western'. SR tender transfers were unchanged; both SR and LNER locos had small dummy cabside number-plates incorporated in the transfers. None of the locos had cabside crests.

It seems unlikely that there were as many transitional liveries for No. 1 Locos in 1930–31 as there were for No. 0 Locos. LMS red No. 1 Locos with the No. 1 Special number 4525 are, however, known. In addition, the number 8324 was used for at least one black LMS No. 1 Loco, but most probably by accident. A GW No. 1 Loco was made with the 2301 No. 1 Special Loco number transfer, and with no transfers on the splashers.

The new No. 1 Locos of 1931 again had completely revised motors giving longer runs and extra power; they incorporated the Hornby patent spur mounting for the No. 2 gear wheel. The housings were different from the previous type in every detail. Smokebox door handles were once again fitted, and lamp brackets were provided – also a packet of black lamps with white bulls.

The numbers 1000 (LMS red), 2290 (LMS black), 6097 (LNER black), 2810 (LNER green) and 4300 (GW green) were all applied to the cabside, but the SR locos had dummy numberplates on the cabside just as on the No. 0, and the tenders were lettered 'Southern E793' (green) and 'Southern A504' (black). The cab roof of the green SR loco was again finished black, unlike the others. All except the GW locos had small 'Yorkshire'-type chimneys, the GW chimney being of the taller 1929–31 No. 1 pattern.

Electric E120 and E16 Locomotives became available in the 1934–35 season, and although the E16 Loco did not re-appear in the 1935–36 lists, the E120 Loco remained available until 1941. These Electric locos were the same as the current clockwork types, except for the different motor cutouts, the bulb holders fitted in the smokebox doors, and of course the absence of keyholes. All post-1934 locos had a hole in the firebox pressing inside the cab, for the electric motor reversing lever.

From 1935 the SR tender transfer was changed to 'Southern 793', and the GW tender had a GWR monogram instead of the former 'Great (crest)

Western' lettering. From 1936 the LNER passenger locos were finished in darker green, and the number of the LMS red locos became 5600 (at first with serif cabside numbers, later sans-serif). From 1937 the GW loco number became 9319. Apart from the fitting of mazac wheels from circa 1936, there were few noticeable production variations, except for the enlargement of the keyhole from November 1936, the revision of the central piercing of the base and alterations to mechanism brackets from April 1937, and the addition of a spot-welded mainspring guard in June 1937. Matt varnishes were used from 1939 until production of the No. 1 Loco ceased in 1941.

After the war, the clockwork version was called the Type 501 Loco, and the electric version Type E502. They were the last locos to come back into production, not being re-catalogued until September 1948. Four liveries were prepared, the LMS red 501 being numbered 5600 (briefly in serif letters, later in block letters), and the LNER green 1842. (It has been suggested that this number may also have been used before the war.) The GW locos were numbered 9319, with a tender lettered 'G (crest) W', and the SR loco had cabside number 793 and a tender lettered 'Southern'. There were no black goods liveries. The wheels were finished black instead of the prewar red, on all except the LNER 501, which had green wheels. The 501 and E502 locos had the

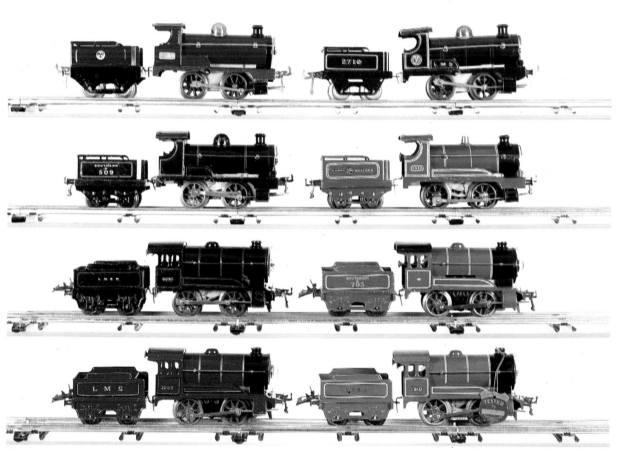

No. 1 and E120 Locos.

tall chimney used before the war for GW locos, except for a few 1948 locos which had the shorter chimney. All had black cab roofs, and no smokebox door transfers were used. They differed in some other details from the prewar designs; a centre lamp bracket was added to the front buffer beam, and lamp brackets were fitted to the back of the tender; trademark transfers were applied underneath the tender, and on the firebox. Boiler lining was by transfers rather than enamelling, and the cabside, splasher and tender transfers were all new, easily recognisable on the GW and LMS locos by the use of yellow instead of gold in the lining. The mock gold used for postwar 501 lettering transfers was of a very inferior quality. Thus there is no difficulty in telling apart prewar No. 1 and postwar Type 501 locos, despite the use of prewar style transfer trademarks on 1948–49 501 locos. Postwar electric locos had no bulbholder in the smokebox door; the hole for the electric mechanism reversing lever continued to appear in the firebox of clockwork locos until production of the electric version stopped. Remaining stocks of LNER prewar and wartime tenders were

re-issued in 1949, with '501' stickers covering the '0/1' description on the boxes.

The SR 501 and E502 Locos seem never to have gone into full-scale production; most GW 501 Locos, and all E502 Locos, were reserved for export, and by 1952 were no longer available.

LMS and LNER 501 Locos continued in production in the early 1950s; Brunofix finish was used for the coupling rods and pins, control levers, and smokebox door handles circa 1951–53. Motor sideplates were also blackened, and remained in this finish. The 501 Locos were replaced in 1954 by two British Railways liveries, the No. 50 Loco in BR goods black (number 60199) and the No. 51 (number 50153) in BR passenger green. Both had numberplate transfers on the smokebox doors. The varnish was shiny, instead of matt as on the Type 501. There were few production variations before they disappeared from the lists in May 1961. The BR 'lion over wheel' emblems on the tender side gave scope for production errors; the lions were supposed to face the front coupling on both sides, but mistakes were common. From 1960 the BR lions should have

faced forwards on the left-hand and backwards on the right-hand side of the tender; but this change was probably not made as it was on Hornby Dublo Trains. The transfers were not even revised to the 1956-style BR 'lion holding wheel' emblem.

No. 1 TANK LOCOMOTIVES

Zulu Tank Locos were introduced in May 1922. Like the Zulu tender engines, they were finished in plain black, over the whole of the body including the dome; the front buffer beam and the cab windows were hand-finished in red. 'Zulu' trademark transfers were applied to the tank sides. Although the loco was not constructional, the cab was secured to the base by four Meccano nuts and bolts (rather than the eyelets used on the Zulu tender engine). Both the cab and the smokebox door were fixed to the boiler by tabs; the smokebox door was identical to the Petrol Tank Wagon end, as on the Zulu loco. The reversing lever was of the coil spring secured type on the majority of the reversing locos. (Indeed the first non-reversing Zulu Tank Locomotives advertised once only in the MM may not actually have been produced.) The 'M Ld L England' trademark was embossed on the cab floor.

Updated versions of the Zulu Tank for the 1923–24 season had 'LMS' letters on the tanksides and 'Zulu' trademarks on the smokebox door. There were no lining transfers, and the colouring stayed the same.

For 1924–25, the loco was officially adopted into the Hornby Series as the Hornby No. 1 Tank Engine, the price being unchanged at 12s 6d. 'Hornby' smokebox door transfers were substituted for the Zulu type, and the tanks were lettered with new transfers 'LMS 0–4–0' and 'LNER 0–4–0', the tanks and bunker sides now being decorated by lining transfers. It is not certain that a choice of goods or passenger livery was available in 1924–25; LMS black and LNER green were the only common liveries, at least in the first part of the season. Apart from the new transfers, distinguishing features of the 1924–25 locos were the continued use of plain smokebox doors, the lack of fixed lamps, and the use of round-headed buffers. The LNER green loco was sprayed overall after assembly, in the same manner as the LMS black loco, but even the chimney, buffer beams and buffers were frequently left green without hand-finishing in black! The only concession was that the polished brass dome was added after spraying, whereas the LMS domes were sprayed black. Late in the season two lamps were fitted above the front buffer beam; by this time the LNER loco buffer beams were red and the chimneys black. The LMS locos had brass domes instead of black, and both front and rear buffer beams were finished in red, with the buffer heads (now oval) in black.

For 1925–26, red LMS and black LNER liveries were offered, as well as the black LMS and green LNER. Detailed smokebox doors (without handles) were fitted. Although the cab was still fixed to the base by nuts and bolts, the cab roof was changed to clip on by lugs, so as to match the latest No. 0 and No. 1 locos. From late in the season, the LMS and LNER black locos no longer had the windows hand-lined in red.

By 1926 GW livery was available; the transfers

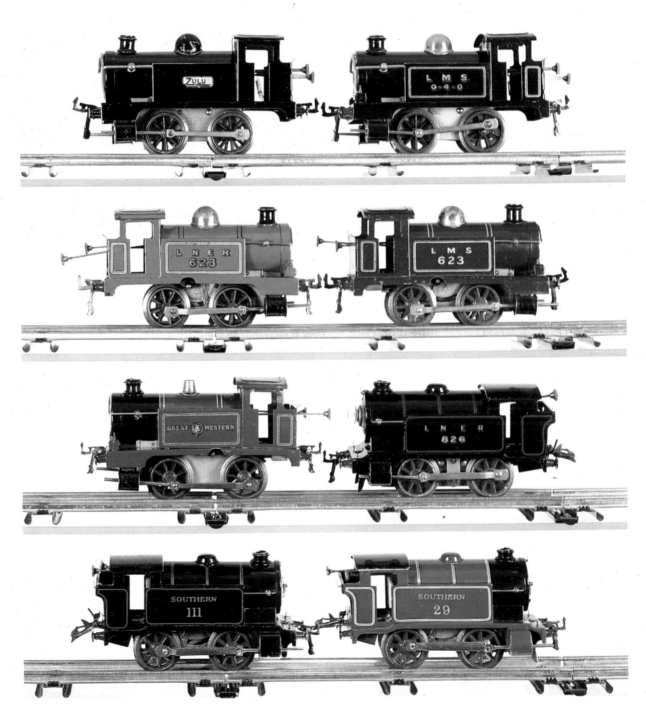

Zulu, No. 1 and E120 Tank Locos.

121

were simply lettered 'Great Western'. Late in 1926, there were revised transfers for all the locos, with all the LMS and LNER locos numbered '623', and the GW transfer altered to 'Great (crest) Western'. There were no railway company crests on the LMS or LNER No. 1 Tank Locos.

From the 1927–28 season, No. 1 Tank Loco boilers had two pairs of painted boiler bands, and the mechanisms were fitted for reversing from the track; Control System versions were also made, at an extra charge of 2s 6d. The boiler handrail was altered to thin wire, as were the two control rods. Wheels were of the latest No. 1 pattern, with coupling rods as well as piston rods. The cab was altered to fixing by tabs instead of by nuts and bolts, and a weight was bolted under the cab. From late in 1927 GW locos were fitted with No. 3-type brass safety valve covers. The mechanism was revised early in 1928, with longer sideplates but still with short wheelbase and right-hand winding. Incidentally, the mechanisms of the No. 1 Tank Locos were always identical to those of the No. 1 tender locos. Red finish became usual for the wheels, and the trademark which had always been embossed on the cab floor disappeared around this time.

In 1928–29, Southern Railway locos were introduced, lettered 'Southern B667' (green) and 'Southern A600' (black). They had black smokeboxes, and domes of the same colour as the boiler, a style that became general. The green SR locos had black cab roofs.

In 1929–30 the left-hand winding long-wheelbase mechanism was adopted, and new lower-profile chimneys and domes were used as soon as stocks of the old types were exhausted. LMS red, LMS black and LNER black locos were by then generally numbered '326'. Indeed some were so numbered in the late part of the previous season. The LNER green locos were numbered '463', and GW No. 1 Tank Locos were still not numbered.

The 1929–30 season also saw the introduction of the No. 1 Electric Tank Loco, with a 6 volt permanent magnet mechanism; early versions usually had the taller chimney but the shorter dome. The first LMS red version was early enough to be numbered 623, although the LNER green PM tank was usually numbered 463. The electric locos used exactly the same transfers as the clockwork locos of the period. Most of the No. 1 Electric Tanks had brass brush-holder caps, although from 1930 some brushcaps had bakelite covers. The stock of the electric tank loco bodies seems to have been sufficient to ensure that, after the clockwork No. 1 Tank was revised in 1931, there was no need to make any more of the old-style bodies; hence the absence of No. 1 Electric Tank Locos with such features as automatic couplings, lamp brackets and bulbholders in the smokebox door. In 1934 the No. 1 Electric Tank was finally replaced by the EPM16 Loco with the same DC mechanism but in the No. 1 Special Tank housing; there were no No. 1 Electric Tanks with the DC motor in the revised 1931-style body.

Towards the end of production of the old-style clockwork No. 1 Tank Loco, different versions of the LMS red, LMS black, LNER green and (probably) LNER black locos were made. The transfers were simply 'LMS' or 'LNER' without any number. The black LMS tank in this series reverted to using the obsolete right-hand wind mechanisms with short wheelbase. The GW loco of the same period had 'Great Western' lettering with no crest, and had LMS lining transfers!

The revised No. 1 Tank Loco of 1931 had the same motor as the No. 1 tender locos, and the housing also had some common tooling, although the boiler diameter was less than that of the No. 1, and a different smokebox door was fitted (similar to that of the M3 Tank but with handles, and with a transfer trademark). 'Yorkshire'-type chimneys and domes were fitted, except on the GW loco, which had a taller chimney of the 1929–31 pattern. Almost without exception, automatic couplings were fitted at the rear, whereas the old-style bodies had the drop-link type. Cranked automatic couplings were used on many No. 1 Tanks in the early 1930s, for no apparent reason since the coupling height was already correct.

The housing was very similar in structure to that of the M3 Tank Loco (introduced at the same time), but was fitted with cylinders, handrail knobs and an underframe beneath the cab floor. The other major difference was that while the M3 Tank sported a litho finish, the No. 1 Tank Loco was enamelled and transferred, with the boiler bands embossed to assist hand painting.

Seven liveries were made for the UK market, with numbers 2115 (LMS red), 7140 (LMS black), 2900 (LNER green), 826 (LNER black), E29 (SR green), E111 (SR black) and 4560 (GW green). None of these numbers were subsequently altered, except that circa 1933 the SR numbers became 29 and 111 without the letter prefixes. There were minor changes in livery, in particular for the GW loco which around 1935 appeared with a black/gold numberplate and 'GWR' monogram, instead of the black/gold/red numberplate and 'Great Western' lettering. From 1936 the LNER passenger loco was a darker green, and for a brief period circa 1937–38 the LMS red tank locos appeared with sans-serif 'LMS' and '2115' characters, but a return was made to the usual serif lettering for later locos. Apart from the matt varnish used from 1939 there were no other livery changes of note.

There were minor changes in the loco body, but none significant from the user's point of view. 'Universal' No. 1 Tank bases were adopted from mid 1937, with an enlarged cutout making the component suitable for clockwork or electric mechanisms, and incidentally giving a handy guide for dating purposes. The base was still different from that of the No. 1 loco, since it was necessary that the mechanism should not protrude too far into the cab area. (There were small clearance holes in the cab floor and at the base of the cab front; fireboxes were not fitted as they were in the No. 1 Loco.) At the same time, a cutout was made in the cab front to clear the spring and allow slightly greater expansion. Resulting weakness of the boiler structure may have been the reason for the fitting of mainspring guards to the No. 1 mechanisms, soon afterwards.

The LST1/20 Electric Tank Locomotive was one of the first 20 volt locos made, in 1932. It had the French-type electric motor, with horizontally arranged brush-holders, and protruding brush-caps which required no special cutouts in the body since they came below the level of the base. A bulbholder was fitted in the smokebox door, but the overall appearance was much as for the clockwork locos, with the same finishes and transfers. In 1934 the LST1/20 was replaced by the E120 Tank Loco and the E16 Tank Loco, both with the revised motor with flat-sided brush-holders. The E16 Tank was withdrawn from sale in 1936, although the E120 and No. 1 Tank Locos were available up to 1941. Production was never resumed.

No. 1 SPECIAL LOCOMOTIVES

The No. 1 Special Locos were available in the usual seven UK liveries on introduction in 1929. The numbers were 4312 (LMS red), 4525 (LMS black), 2301 (GW green), 2694 (LNER green), 2691 (LNER black), A179 (Southern green) and B343 (Southern black). The LNER and SR locos were numbered on the tender, and small but clearly legible number-plates were also included in the cab-side transfers. Each loco had distinctive cabside transfers depicting handrails, an odd feature on a loco that was otherwise a substantial improvement on the '2710'-style locos. The No. 1 Special Locos had up-to-date large boilers, complete with safety-valves and with 'Yorkshire'-type chimneys and domes, and the smokebox doors had much less obtrusive flanges. Lamp brackets were fitted, three above the front buffer beam and a fourth at the top of the smokebox door; the back of the tender was never fitted with lamp brackets. A packet of lamps was supplied. The mechanism was a new design, based in part on that of the No. 2 Locomotive but greatly improved, and more powerful; the gear train was the same as for the No. 2 Special motor. It had a strong edge over even the improved No. 1 mechanisms of 1929–30 in hauling power. The Meccano Magazine reported in January 1930 that a No. 1 Special Locomotive had undergone extensive testing, having run 39,111 yards in 3 days, needing 800 windings, and with the mechanism reversed no less than 4800 times. There was said to be no sign of wear when the loco was dismantled!

All these locos were finished in similar style, but the GW loco had the GW safety-valve casting instead of normal dome and safety valve. It did however have the same low-profile chimney as other No. 1 Specials. SR cab roofs were black.

The earliest 1929 locos did not have the 'Hornby' smokebox door transfer, although all had the Special locomotive transfer on the right-hand side of the boiler. Split pins to retain the mechanism nuts were only used up to late 1929, and from late 1930 the front coupling hole was embossed so that the eyelet was squarely seated. From January 1931 the top lamp bracket design was changed, the lamp bracket being added to the smokebox door as a separate part, after it was realised that the previous lamp bracket (formed by bending upwards the top smokebox door lug) was too fragile. Soon after this, the boiler handrail around the smokebox door was bent to a smaller radius, to give the necessary clearance for lamps to be fitted onto the new brackets. Automatic couplings were fitted to the tender from about the same time.

The 1929–31 wheels had a rounded rim profile, and were in a particularly soft lead alloy that gave much trouble from wear and consequent loose wheels. From 1930 to 1936 the wheels were often plated before painting, but this practice stopped soon after mazac wheels were introduced in 1936. From 1931, the wheels were revised to take larger crank pins, and had a squarer profile. Fluted coupling rods began to be used, as had been planned from the start (as shown by the 1929–30 HBT pictures), but which had not previously been fitted in practice. LMS red, LMS black, LNER black and SR black locos usually had red wheels, and the others green (always LNER green in the early '30s, even on GW and SR locos). From 1934 to 1936 black wheels were usual for the electric locos.

No. 1 Special Locos in the seven principal liveries.

There were few changes of livery during the production of these locos, but an interesting early (1929) version of the LNER green 2694 had a boiler with boiler bands painted in black rather than white; white boiler bands quickly became standard on the LNER green locos. The LNER green 2694 livery was replaced (probably in 1931) by the more usual LNER green loco numbered 1368 on the cabside, with tender lettered 'LNER' only. This number remained standard until 1941.

Tenders for the LMS black 4525 loco were lined red (as were the locos), and had plain gold sans-serif letters at first, then plain gold serif letters from 1930. Tenders for the LMS red 4312 loco were at first in plain and unlined LMS red, with plain gold sans-serif (and later plain gold serif) 'LMS' lettering. They were replaced in 1931 by LMS locos numbered 8712. The tender transfers for these included lining and 'LMS' in shadowed serif letters.

A hole was pierced in the top of the tenders, probably from 1933, for use in automatic spraying equipment.

Electric E120 Special Locomotives were available from 1934 until the war stopped production. The body had to be extensively modified, including a large and ugly cutout from the right-hand side of the boiler, to take the bulky 20 volt automatic reversing mechanism. Nonetheless the performance of the loco was excellent, although not as good as the E120 Special Tank Loco which was heavier and less prone to wheel slip.

In 1935 the GW loco number 2301 was changed to 4700, on a black/gold numberplate instead of the more attractive (but less realistic) gold/black/red of the earlier type. The tender also changed, in the late 1930s, to 'Great (monogram) Western' lettering

instead of the former 'Great (crest) Western'. One batch of GW locos was made with the LMS 8712 number! Circa 1935 the number of the red LMS loco changed to 2700, and around the same time the numbers on the SR loco cabside and tender changed to 1179 instead of A759; transitional SR locos were frequently not properly matched, even in boxed sets. The LNER loco changed to a darker green in 1936.

Neither the clockwork nor the electric tender engines sold as well as might have been expected, mainly because the more popular No. 2 Special Tank Loco was priced only a few pence higher (20s 9d for the No. 1 Special, 21s for the No. 2 Special Tank, in 1934); and the E220 Special Tank was actually cheaper than the E120 Special with tender (32s 6d vs 33s 6d in 1934).

No. 1 SPECIAL TANK LOCOMOTIVES

The No. 1 Special Tank Loco was introduced in 1929, at the same time as the No. 1 Special, and was available in the same seven liveries: LMS red (number 6418), LMS black (16045), LNER green (8123), LNER black (8108), SR green (A950), SR black (A129), and GW green (3580). Each loco was fitted with four lamp brackets in front and four at the rear, even on the earliest versions (shown in the 1929–30 HBT with fixed lamps, although evidently an artist's impression); the usual packet of lamps was supplied. Four pairs of boiler bands were both embossed and painted on, with the exception that some early GW 3580 locos had only seven painted bands, with one missing between the black of the smokebox and the green boiler. GW No. 1 Special Tank Locos had the same low profile chimney as the LMS, NE and SR engines. All cab roofs were black; SR locos also had black tank-tops. SR, GW and late LNER green locos had black running plates at the front.

The changes of detail on tank and tender engines were similar; the earliest 1929 No. 1 Special Tank Locos had no 'Hornby' transfer on the smokebox door, although all had the 'Special' loco transfer on the bunker back. A hole was added over the rear coupling eyelet in March 1930, to allow access to the eyelet, since the cab had a double floor. The front coupling hole was supposed (from November 1930)

to be embossed as on the tender engine, but this was rarely done in practice.

Some early changes in the loco transfers, probably in 1930, produced some new loco numbers: B28 on the SR green version (now with 'Southern' in serif rather than the sans-serif letters of A950), 5500 (GW green, with the number not on a numberplate as it was later), and 2586 (LNER black). Perhaps a little later, the SR black loco number changed to A950; not as one might have expected with the transfers used for the former green A950, but in a new serif-lettered style. The LMS red loco changed to 2120, with the 'LMS' in serif shadowed letters; the cylinders were lined in the full black/gold/red/gold/black style matching the rest of the lining. Later 2120s had 2 pairs of gold bands on the cylinders, and the lining on the tank and bunker was changed to gold and black only, instead of black/gold/red/gold/black. The black LMS loco 16045 changed to serif 'LMS' letters from sans-serif.

The smokebox door was fitted with a separate lamp bracket, at the same time as this change was made on the tender engine, early in 1931, and there was a consequent change in the radius of the handrail

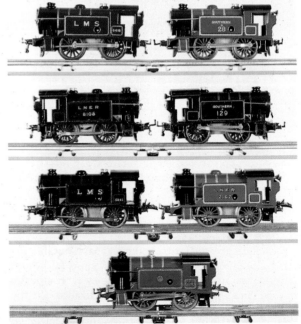

No. 1 Special Tank Locos.

124

An SR EPM16 Loco, circa 1936. The TR6 Transformer/Rectifier and the Speed and Reverse Control Switch were made specifically for use with the DC locos.

An LNER EPM16 Loco, circa 1936.

around the smokebox. The wheels changed to a different casting, at the same time as on the No. 1 Special; the mechanisms and wheels fitted to the tank engines were always equivalent to those of the tender loco, although the control rods were of thinner wire to allow for the difficulty of threading them through the holes in the cab. Fluted coupling rods became the norm, although not invariably fitted the right way up and the right side outwards! Automatic couplings (also early 1931) meant minor alterations to the rear coupling slot.

E120 Special Electric Tank Locos were sold from 1934, and were fitted with the 20 volt automatic reverse mechanism. Electric versions almost always had bulbholders, although a batch of the LNER green 8123 electric loco was made without the bulbholder. Post-1934 clockwork No. 1 Special Tanks can be easily distinguished from earlier types by the very large cutout in the loco base, enlarged from the earlier cutout to make the base suitable for either clockwork or electric loco housings (although many of the upper parts of the bodies were not the same). There was also a hole in the firebox for the electric loco reverse lever. Around this time the LMS red loco number was altered again to 15500. The GW

transfers were changed to a new batch with the number 5500 now on a numberplate, although the tank was still lettered 'Great Western'.

The SR loco number changed to 516 in 1935, and the LNER green to 2162. In 1936, the GW tank loco transfers were altered, with the GWR monogram replacing 'Great Western' on the tankside. The LNER passenger loco came out with unchanged 2162 transfers, but in darker green. In 1936 the LMS red loco number changed yet again, to 70, with 'LMS' in serif letters, amended briefly to sans-serif in 1937–38, after which serif letters were again used. There were no other major changes. Matt varnish was used from 1939.

Apart from the 20 volt version, the EPM16 Special Electric Tank Loco was also available from 1934, with a 6 volt DC motor. This mechanism was the same as had been used for the No. 1 Electric Tank Loco, looking rather extraordinary with its short wheelbase in the large Special Tank body; indeed the mechanism brackets had to be specially extended to fit the housing. The tank side and base had to be cut away to clear the protruding brush caps, which oddly were almost always brass rather than the Bakelite caps of the No. 3E mechanisms of

1930 to 1934. Different batches of EPM16 locos were made, but in each case the transfers were exactly as for the standard issues; for example the LMS 15500 was succeeded by 70 as on the clockwork and 20 volt versions. However, none of the batches were particularly large. The EPM16 was no more of a commercial success than the No. 1 Electric Tank had been, and was withdrawn from sale in 1939. In the same year Meccano Ltd offered the high quality cobalt steel permanent magnets formerly used in the mechanisms, for sale in the MM adverts (for example in November 1939) at 2s 9d, for building motors for Meccano models, or . . . anything!

No. 2 LOCOMOTIVES

The '2711' No. 2 Loco was the first bogie loco made by Meccano Ltd, designed early in 1921 and catalogued from September of that year. It was intended for constructional use, and was assembled using Meccano nuts and bolts. The loco body was in essence an enlarged version of the '2710', with a larger cab and a longer boiler, and fitted with a much larger and more powerful mechanism; to clear the spring, the tie-bar between cab and boiler front had

to be cranked. The single-piece handrail was secured by six handrail supports. The splashers were much longer than on the '2710', and were not solely for decoration as the frame was cut away to allow large 14-spoke wheels to be fitted. Counterbalance weights were detailed in the wheels, which were iron castings turned to the correct profile. The loco was evidently intended to represent an inside-cylinder loco, as (unlike the No. 1) no cylinders were fitted, although the wheels were coupled by rods secured by threaded pins and nuts. The loco was provided with steps at front and rear, and there was a cast LNWR-style safety valve, with fragile lever, mounted in front of the cab. A drop plate was provided between the loco and tender. Brass buffers were fitted at the front of the loco and the back of the tender.

Four liveries were available on introduction, GN green, CR blue, MR red and LNWR black. All had red buffer beams and draw-bar beams, but the GN loco also had a red valance, and the MR loco a valance in MR red. The running plates were black. None of the locos had any transfers or lining of any

sort, except for the trademark transfers on both splashers. The tenders (which had plain black bases, and tops matching the loco colour) were also plain except for the embossed beading on the rear and on both sides, and the trademark transfers each side.

The bogie was mounted on a swivelling bracket, and was weighted with a substantial lead casting to keep it steady. There was also a weight inside the cab, secured by the mechanism fixing bolt.

The first important production variation was embossing added around the edge of the keyhole in the splasher to make it more rigid. In late 1921 the steps were also stiffened by embossed ridges, although the real weakness was in the mounting. A spacer bar was added underneath the back of the cab roof, to strengthen another weak point. The wheels were no longer heavily painted black, but copper plated and then anodised black, wearing to give an attractive coppery finish on the wheel treads.

There were no important revisions for the 1922–23 season, except for the addition of small cutouts in the valance, to give extra clearance for the crank pin

nuts if the mechanism was badly aligned. From later in the same season the lower part of the keyhole in the loco base was embossed in the same way as the upper part in the splasher.

LMS and LNER livery No. 2 Locos were manufactured for the start of the 1923–24 season. The liveries of this season were so varied that it is quite impossible to be certain about what Meccano Ltd's exact intentions were, even if they knew themselves! LMS red locos were exactly like the MR locos, and the LMS black were finished in the same way as LNWR, but in each case with 'LM&S' transfers on both splashers. There was no lining on the splashers, or indeed anywhere on the loco, except for embossed beading. The equivalent green engine for LNER sets (in the same style as the previous GN loco) was not actually lettered L&NER, but had GN crests without lining on each splasher. The next green '2711' had an 'L&NER' transfer (incorporating black/white/black lining) on the left-hand splasher, and the GN crest without lining on the other splasher. Very soon the LMS red locos appeared with 'LMS' on the left-hand splasher, lined in black/gold/red/gold/black, and with the trademark transfer on the other (unlined) splasher. There was probably an equivalent black LMS loco.

The LMS red, LMS black, and LNER green locos also appeared in the same season in more standardised versions, with both splashers lettered 'LMS' or 'L&NER', and lined in the same style as

LMS No. 2 Locos of the 1923–24 season; the loco at the back is later than the two in the foreground.

before. Most of these different locos were sold with tenders in unchanged pre-grouping livery; but some tenders were issued (probably early in 1924) lettered 'LMS' (on red and black tenders) and 'L&NER' (on green), which complemented the locos described, but which may also have been supplied with locos in unchanged pre-grouping livery. Just to confuse matters, all these 1923–24 LMS and LNER locos seem to have reverted to having only the upper part of the keyhole embossed, instead of both parts! Although the boilers were usually unlined, an example is known of a No. 2 Loco (probably produced late in the season) which had three single painted boiler bands, a style more common on the No. 2 Tank Locos.

The new No. 2 Locos for the 1924–25 season, however, had five boiler bands, grouped double/single/double. Cabside transfers were applied, incorporating lining and an LMS and LNER company crest. The 1924–25 locos returned to bases with the strengthened lower keyhole; all but the very first were fitted with 4-lug domes instead of the previous 2-lug type. A pair of lamps were fixed above the buffers at the front of the loco, in the express passenger position – appropriately enough in view of the speed of the loco, which was insufficiently governed! Smokebox doors with flatter fronts and embossed hinges began to be used, and 'Hornby' transfers were applied both to the new doors and to remaining stocks of the old. Since '2711' brass numberplates

were no longer fitted to the cabside, the tenders were numbered '2711' by transfers, but with no lining except for the embossed beading on the sides and rear. Thin axles were fitted to the tenders, but it was to be some time before all the old-style parts were used up, and the thick-axle and thin-axle types coexisted for a while.

A notable landmark in 1924–25 was the production for the first time of locos in LNER goods black livery. These locos had splashers lettered 'LNER', although the green locos continued to be lettered 'L&NER'. (The goods loco required different coloured lining, so the same transfers could not be used on both.) The unlined '2711' tender was soon replaced by a new style, without the embossed beading on the side, and with transfer lining around the '2711' number. The old-style beaded tender back remained in use for a while, but later that too had lining transfers instead of embossing, a change shown on the production drawings in December 1924. Slots for the '2711' plates, and embossed beading, had continued to appear on cabsides with the new style transfers, but in December 1924 the drawings were altered to remove these obsolete features.

Locos manufactured for the start of the 1925–26 season changed little in external appearance, except for the use of oval-headed cast buffers instead of the Meccano-type brass buffers used previously. The crankpin clearance cutouts in the valance were enlarged, and the chimneys were now riveted on,

not bolted. There were minor livery changes; the loco drawbar beam was no longer painted red, and the drop-flaps were frequently left unpainted instead of the previous black finish. 'LNER'-lettered green locos were made, the stocks of 'L&NER' transfers being finally exhausted. Another change was the adoption of a bogie pivoting around a central king-pin, instead of the previous swivelling bracket mounting. The bogie was no longer weighted, since it was pushed down onto the track by a coil spring.

Late in 1925, the method of spraying the locos changed. Previously the base of the loco and other components had been sprayed separately, then assembled. Now the body was assembled, minus the polished brass dome and the smokebox door, before spraying. This change was possible because the constructional aspects of Hornby Train use had long since been abandoned – although the locos were still of the nut-and-bolt style. The result of the change was that the running plate was now the same colour as the boiler whereas it had previously always been black. No doubt LNER green '2711' locos were produced with green running plates but with the valance still hand-finished red, as for the '2710'.

The introduction of GW livery in early 1926 was another advance. The cast GW-type safety-valve was the same as the one fitted to the No. 1 and No. 1 Tank Locos, the ordinary safety valve being omitted. Only two pairs of boiler bands were painted, the single central band being absent. Splashers were

A No. 2 LMS Loco, of mid 1924. The boiler lining is unusual, although similar to that of the No. 2 Tank Loco. The tender is slightly later than the loco; some earlier tenders were lettered 'LMS'.

An LNER black No. 2 Loco, circa 1925.

lettered 'GW', and the cab had the GW crest. The tender was numbered 2711.

For the 1926–27 season the No 2 Locos were available fitted for Hornby Control[1], with special Control mechanisms, at an extra cost of 2s 6d; the ordinary No. 2 was also still available. By this time the valances of LNER passenger locos were being left in green, not overpainted red as before. Early in 1927 the loco bodies were re-designed to eliminate the nut-and-bolt construction, a change made over a year earlier with the No. 1 Locos. Most bodies were now in the new style, but a few nut-and-bolt No. 2 bodies were apparently still being used up in 1928! On the non-constructional locos, the cab was secured to the footplate by lugs, and the boiler was joined to the cab and to the smokebox door (now of the No. 1 riveted handle type) by lugs. The boiler stay was no longer required, nor was the bracing bar under the back of the cab roof, since the tabbed roof was folded down along the back edge to give it the necessary strength. The keyhole was no longer cut into the loco valance, and was now only in the splasher; this made the base much stronger. The lead weight in the cab was riveted into position rather than bolted, being made longer to allow this change, and also shallower to clear the lugs on the boiler. The bogie was still of the kingpin type, but the kingpin was now screwed into a curved threaded plate inside the boiler. The steps were changed to the No. 3 style. Thinner boiler handrails were used on all except the first non-constructional locos.

Early in 1927, the GW loco transfers were revised, with the splashers lettered 'Great (crest) Western', and with '7283' cabside numberplates, although the new tender transfers were still numbered 2711! The style of lining on cabside, splasher and tender changed markedly to a thinner and less widely spaced set of black/gold lines. The safety valve was still of the old cast GW pattern. On the other railway company locos, the safety valves were fitted with shortened but stronger levers.

Around the middle of 1927, GW No. 2 Locos were fitted with the polished brass safety valve cover of the No. 3 Loco, a change shown on the works drawings in May 1927. These locos still had two pairs of boiler bands as on the previous 7283/2711, and the cabside and splasher transfers were

An early GW 2711, circa 1926. The Breakdown Van and Crane is of the same period.

An LMS No. 2 Loco in early 1928 livery. The constructional body style was by then obsolete, and its appearance in this livery is unexpected. The No. 1 Loco is probably slightly later.

unchanged, but now they were sold with tenders having 'Great (crest) Western' transfers (as on the GW No. 3 Tender), so there was no longer a mismatch in the numbers.

At first in the 1927–28 season, liveries were unchanged. It was probably early in 1928 that a new style was adopted, with LMS, LNER and GW loco splashers lined but not lettered. The cabside and tender transfers remained as before. Interestingly, the GW splasher transfer had incorporated both lettering and company crest within the lining, and careful examination of the unlettered splashers will often reveal traces of the old lettering or crest; the transfers were not actually changed, but parts of them were removed when they were applied.

Apart from transfers, the main difference for the passenger locos from 1928 was in the black smokebox, and the change to (usually) three boiler bands only, a pair at the back and a single central band. On all locos domes were sprayed in the same colour as the boiler. The GW loco now had the same three boiler bands as the other passenger locos. Most of these locos have a pair of holes beside the coupling in the cab floor, and later a weight inside the 'bogie anchor' over the front bogie – both changes decided upon in February 1928. The No. 2 Loco wheels were changed from iron to diecast alloy early in 1928, and were (as ever) finished black.

The 1928–29 season saw the introduction of SR liveries, the locos being lined in a new standard style, with three pairs of close-spaced boiler bands, but with no numberplates or company lettering, the tenders alone being lettered 'Southern A760' (green) or 'Southern E510' (black). The cab roof of the SR passenger-livery loco was black. LMS tenders numbered 338 were shown in MM advertisements, but may never have gone into production. Control locos were by now fitted with a manual brake lever in the cab, whereas they had previously had only a reverse lever. The cab weight was increased in August 1928 by deepening the casting (with two semi-circular cutouts to clear the lugs joining boiler and cab), thus identifying locos of this age quite clearly. Since only SR locos are common after this time, it appears that production of No. 2 locos was at a virtual standstill because of the new locos in preparation to replace them – the No. 2 Specials. The last change to the No. 2 designs was the addition to the drawings of embossing for the six boiler bands, early in 1929, but this change may never have gone into production. The No. 2 Locos frequently differed from the current drawings, both because of time lag in altering the tools, and probably because of longish gaps between production batches. An example is that the tenders were re-designed as non-constructional as early as February 1925; this modification apparently never went into production, all tenders for the next four years after the supposed alteration being of the nut-and-bolt type! However most other Hornby products followed the intended designs rather more closely.

Although the '2711' was directly replaced by the No. 2 Special in 1929, the rapid escalation in the price of the No. 2 Special with tender from 28s in 1929–30 to 34s in 1930–31, compared with only 23s 6d for the No. 2 in 1928–29, undoubtably left a gap in the Hornby price range that was never to be properly filled.

ELECTRIC No. 2 LOCOMOTIVES

The 'wonderful force of electricity' (to use Frank Hornby's words) must have suggested itself as an alternative to clockwork propulsion from the earliest days of Hornby Train production. The third rail conversion accessories offered in 1921 were probably intended for use with Meccano models of trains;

but the first complete electric rails, introduced in 1922, were actually made for electric Hornby Trains. The Meccano Magazine for May-June 1922 had said that 'Later this year we intend introducing an electric loco. of 4-volts, similar in type to our No. 2 Hornby Loco.' The October MM was even more definite: 'We are introducing an electric Hornby Train this year.' The loco and mechanism were designed, and the tools prepared for its manufacture. However, it does not appear in any UK catalogue or list that has yet come to light – and only one example of the 1922–23 production is known. This earliest Hornby Electric Train belongs to a collector in Paris, and the French instructions have a picture of a '2711' loco on electric track, together with a rheostat, although the loco shown has a keyhole! These discoveries in France indicate that the export markets were lucky enough to receive supplies, although the loco never went into general production.

The electric loco body differed from the clockwork version in not having a keyhole in the left-hand splasher; but there were staggered holes for the

brush-caps of the motor in the right-hand splasher. The blanks for the sideplates were identical to those of the clockwork No. 2 mechanism. There was a square cut-out in the lower portion of the cab front, to accommodate the motor and wiring. Clockwork No. 2 Locos of 1923 or later were sometimes fitted with these electric loco cabs, the hole presumably serving as an open firebox door! Distinctive features of the mechanism were the roller pick-ups, and the Meccano Motor style of reversing switch bolted into the cab.

Why was this effort unsuccessful? The answer probably lies in weakness in the design of the electric motor, and a failure to develop it to the point where it gave sufficient power with reliability. It was broadly based on the Meccano motors of the period, and difficulty may have been experienced in reducing it to the dimensions of the Hornby loco body. If so, it is a pity that the very intense activity poured into designing and producing an extensive range of electric rails and points in 1922 and 1923 was not diverted to making an efficient electric train to run on

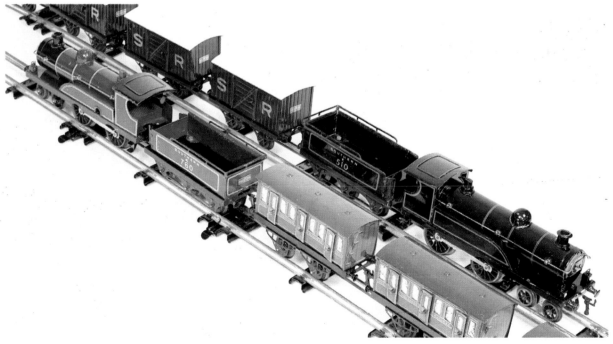

SR No. 2 Locos of 1928.

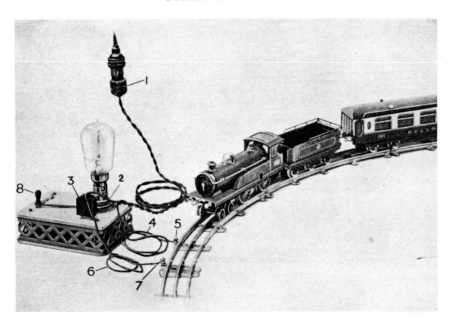

CHEMIN DE FER ELECTRIQUE HORNBY— TRAIN DE LUXE

Il est apporté le plus grand soin à la fabrication du train de Luxe électrique Hornby—Chaque rame est attentivement et rigoureusement essayée avant de quitter les Usines Meccano. Il faut graisser avec de bonne huile à machine les engrenages et autres organes actifs, en prenant des précautions pour que l'huile n'atteigne pas le bobinage, ni l'aimant de champ.

AJUSTAGE DES RAILS.

Bien ajuster les rails et les assujettir avec le dispositif de verrouillage.

VOLTAGE DU MOTEUR.

Le moteur de la locomotive a un bobinage pour courant de 110 volts, continu ou alternatif. Il est relié en série avec une lampe à filament métallique de 110 volts 100 bougies, ou à une lampe carbone de 50 bougies.

ETABLISSEMENT DES CONNEXIONS.

Les connexions s'établissent en insérant la fiche 1 dans la douille de la lampe servant de prise de courant et la fiche 3 dans le rhéostat. On remarquera qu'un fil double est utilisé pour les connexions et que l'un des fils 2 venant de la fiche 1 est relié à la fiche 3 tandis que l'autre fil 4 est relié directement à la borne 5. Un autre fil 6 est relié à la fiche 3 et à la borne 7.

COMMANDE DE VITESSE.

La vitesse se règle en manoeuvrant la poignée mobile 8 située sur le rhéostat.

MECCANO LIMITED   LIVERPOOL

123/1.   Imprimé en Angleterre

'Train de Luxe' instructions, January 1923. 1000 copies were printed.

Showing the mechanism of the No. 2 Electric Loco, its switch gear and the unusual pickups.

them! The rails were sold, however, for use with other makes of train. Another possible reason for the failure of the Electric No. 2 Loco might have been that it could not be made at a realistic price.

The electric No. 2 loco made a brief reappearance for the Empire Exhibition at Wembley in 1924 and 1925. The July 1925 MM shows as one of the 'New Wonders of Wembley' a layout which appears to have used Hornby electric locos, in LMS livery. Three such LMS Locos are known to have survived, and they are probably the ones used at Wembley; certainly the mechanisms are severely worn, apparently from continuous use, as would be expected for locos run at an exhibition. In general style they were similar to the 1922–23 electric loco, but they had up-to-date features such as a lack of embossed beading on the cab side, indicating that they were made in 1924 and were not just old-stock bodies repainted in the latest Hornby colours.

No. 2 TANK LOCOMOTIVES

Just as the No. 2 Loco was a lengthened version of the No. 1, so the 4–4–4 No. 2 Tank Engine was in essence a 'stretched' Zulu Tank. Unlike the No. 2 Loco (and like the Zulu) it was never intended for constructional use, although nuts and bolts were

actually used to assemble the boiler and cab to the frame. The No. 2 boiler stay was fitted, and the boiler was made using the same tools as the No. 2 boiler, with suitable alterations to fit tanks instead of splashers. The handrail was of the same type as that of the No. 2, but was shorter. Steps were fitted to the frame, and the front and rear bogies were mounted on swivelling brackets. Both the upper and lower parts of the keyhole were embossed around the edge for strength. The cab was fitted with nickel-plated handrails; the cab roof was larger than that of the No. 2, and needed a similar beam under the back of the roof for support. The mechanism was the same as for the No. 2 loco, and the wheels were always black-finished.

The No. 2 Tank loco was first sold in 1923, just after the railway regrouping, and before liveries for the new companies had been standardised. The Hornby 4–4–4s seem never to have been sold without company lettering. The earliest known 1923 locos were in LNER green, with red valances. They had small 'L. & N.E.R.' lettering transfers on both tanks, and had lining transfers on the bunker though not on the tanks, also three painted boiler bands. There was an equivalent black loco lettered 'LM&S' in somewhat larger letters on both tanks, again with the bunker lined by transfers although the tanks were not, and with three boiler bands. A similar red 'LM&S' engine was probably made.

The next development (which may have been in the Autumn of 1923) was the production of new transfers for the LNER green loco, for lining the tanks, and adding the number '1534' to the 'L. & N.E.R.' lettering already used. Although this livery

was most satisfactory it was short lived; soon new transfers were prepared for the LMS red, LMS black and LNER green locos. These included full lining, and were lettered 'L&NER 4–4–4' or 'LMS 4–4–4'. Each loco still had three painted boiler bands. It is puzzling that the wheel arrangement should have been used instead of loco numbers, especially since the '1534' livery had already appeared, and a more realistic LMS livery with number '1019' was shown in the October 1923 MM. The '4–4–4' locos appear to have been on sale late in 1923 or very early in 1924.

Further changes were made in the middle of 1924, for the start of the 1924–25 season; two lamps (in the 'express passenger' position) were riveted to the front of the footplate, and five boiler bands (double/single/double as on the No. 2) were painted on. The buffers were still of the brass Meccano type,

A black LM&S No. 2 Tank Loco of 1923.

A Great Western No. 2 Tank Loco of early 1927.

and company crests were not yet applied. 4-lug domes became standard. Detailed smokebox doors were used, as on the No. 2, and all smokebox doors had the 'Hornby' transfer. Curiously, some LMS black locos of the period had the valance overpainted in red, but then overpainted again in black! Some late brass-buffered locos of the period had company crests on the front of the cabside, and black brass-buffered locos with 'LNER 4–4–4' transfers were probably made late in the 1924–25 season.

From the middle of 1925, certain changes were made for the 1925–26 season. The locos were similar to the previous style, but fitted with cast oval-headed buffers, riveted chimneys, and with the front bogie on a kingpin fixing while the rear bogie still had the swivelling-bracket mounting. Unlike the No. 2, the crank-pin clearance holes in the valance were not enlarged. Company crests appeared on the front of the cabside, and 'LNER 4–4–4' transfers (instead of 'L&NER 4–4–4') were used for the green engine. The black LNER 4–4–4 was certainly available.

Late in 1925, the method of finishing the locos was altered, with the bodies assembled before spraying instead of assembling separately sprayed components. Thus the running plates became the same colour as the boiler, whereas they had previously been black. The green LNER locos still had hand-finished red valances.

The introduction of GW No. 2 Tank Locos early in 1926 involved the usual changes to the boiler, omitting the normal safety valve and adding the GW type instead of the dome. The transfers were lettered 'Great Western' and the GW crest appeared on the front of the cabside. The loco was fully lined out with broad gold/black lines, and there were two pairs of boiler bands only, the centre band being omitted.

From the middle of 1926, LMS and LNER 4–4–4 locos had company crests on the bunker side instead of on the front of the cabside. Control system locos became available as an alternative to the normal type.

Late in 1926, new transfers were made incorporating proper loco numbers instead of the '4–4–4' wheel arrangement. These numbers were 460 on the LNER locos and 2052 on the LMS. LNER green locos no longer had valances hand-finished red.

From early in 1927, non-constructional parts began to be used; the cab, boiler and smokebox door were altered to tab fixing, the weight in the cab was riveted, No. 3 steps were fitted, and the keyhole was

SR No. 2 Tank Goods and No. 2 Tank Passenger Trains, 1928.

cut only into the tank and not into the valance. Cab handrails were now painted in the same colour as the body. Thin boiler handrails became the norm; the rear bogie was altered to the kingpin type instead of the swivelling-bracket mounting, and the bogie was no longer weighted. On locos other than GW the safety valves were usually of a new pattern with shorter, stronger levers.

Although a few GW locos were made in the non-constructional style with the old transfers, most now had new transfers lettered 'Great (crest) Western', with narrower tank and bunker lining, and with the number 7202 on the bunker. The GW safety valve casting was still fitted, and there were still only four boiler bands. The existence of non-constructional black locos with 'LNER 4-4-4' transfers argues that the changeover to the 'LNER 460' transfers for the black locos was delayed, compared to the 'LNER 460' transfers for the green locos which were certainly used on nut-and-bolt bodies.

From late in 1927, the GW locos were fitted with the brass safety valve cover instead of the diecast safety valve used before. Further changes were made early in 1928, with black smokeboxes for all the passenger locos, and on all locos domes were painted in the same colour as the boilers, instead of being in polished brass. The GW, LMS and LNER passenger locos now had three boiler bands, one pair at the back and a single band under the dome (or safety valve for the GW). Black locos continued to have five bands as before, except when mistakes were made (as happened on some LMS black 2052 locos which were issued with three bands in the passenger loco style!). The wheels were changed from cast iron to a new diecast alloy type, and the Control System mechanisms were generally fitted with a manual brake, not previously provided.

Soon after this the LMS loco number was changed to 2107, and as on the 4-4-0s of the period the company initials did not appear, although the crest was still on the bunker side. The 2107 transfers were used for both black and red LMS locos. The GW transfer was also changed, with a different number '2243' on the bunker.

The LMS livery changed yet again during 1928, with the adoption of 'LMS' plates on the bunker side

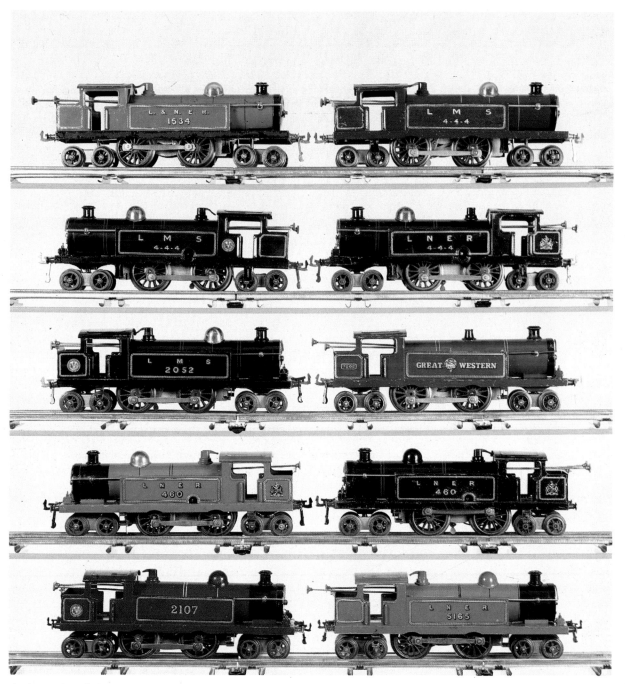

A selection from the large number of No. 2 Tank Loco variations.

instead of company crests, still with the loco number 2107. The LMS loco number changed again quite soon to 2051, and this number was used both for black and for red locos with 'LMS' plates on the bunker side.

SR liveries were available for 1928–29, and these were lettered 'Southern B604' (green) and 'Southern E492' (black). As for the SR No. 2 Loco these had three pairs of close-spaced boiler bands, painted but not embossed. They had the enlarged weight in the cab, and also a weight in the front bogie anchor. The SR green loco had a black cab roof.

During the last months of production of the No. 2 Tank Loco, early 'LMS 2052' transfers were used up (with the crests removed) for the LMS red loco. One of these locos has been seen with lampbrackets, while another has a low-profile No. 1 style dome of the 1929–31 period.

Among the last No. 2 Tanks to be made were LNER green locos numbered 5165 (all the previous examples had still been numbered 460). These were certainly produced during 1929, since they show some very late characteristics; the boiler bands were embossed as well as painted (although oddly there were only five – double/single/double, with the pairs closely spaced). There were still later versions with lamp brackets instead of fixed lamps (and incidentally with embossed single boiler bands) – an extraordinary feature again, since the No. 2 Special Tanks that replaced the 4–4–4 had fixed lamps until late in 1929! These late No. 2 Tank Locomotives remain something of a mystery; the No. 2 Tank Loco was not included in any 1929–30 or later lists, except as old stock.

No. 2 SPECIAL LOCOMOTIVES

Depending on point of view, the No. 2 Special Locomotives may be regarded either as a promising start down the road to scale modelling, or as an aberration from a company more justifiably famous for simple toy trains. What seems quite clear is that Meccano Ltd over-reached themselves considerably in producing what was originally supposed to be simply a replacement for the No. 2 4–4–0 locos. This 'folie de grandeur' produced no less than four complicated new loco bodies, one for each railway com-

pany, all true-to-type representations of real locomotives. Although the parts were not modelled to true scale dimensions, there is no doubt that the Hornby engines caught the atmosphere of the original engines, by suggesting the features of the prototypes rather than by slavishly copying them. Above all, they were designed with a reasonable sense of proportion. But there were constraints of price, and it was most important to build each of the locos to fit the same clockwork motor.

The No. 2 Special clockwork mechanism was a triumph for its designers. It was the largest and most powerful motor to date, but unlike the No. 2 Locos the No. 2 Specials combined power with dignity; although capable of a good turn of speed with a light train, they were not dangerously fast. Considering the power of the spring, it would not have been surprising if the motors had suffered badly from strain and stress; but it is more unusual to find No. 2 Special motors in need of repair than some of the smaller types. And to a large extent the design was right first time; few major changes were made during the long production run of the motor, except in the matter of axles.

Considering the care and attention with which the locos were designed, it was most unfortunate that insufficient attention was paid to the livery. In each case major changes were made within a year. Meccano Ltd were evidently aware of the shortcomings of the SR and GW locos in particular, since they were not shown in the MM advertisements or articles until the locos were revised a few months later.

Each of the No. 2 Special Locos was fitted with four lamp irons at the front, but since the top bracket was formed from the top lug joining the boiler to the smokebox door, it was easily broken off, a problem that was never solved. Each of the locos also had solid and substantial steps to the cab, in each case perhaps rather large but less easily damaged than the No. 3 type. Among the unexpected differences between the classes was that two different bogies were designed, with the same frame but with a shorter wheelbase for the 'Yorkshire'. Needless to say confusion was total, and the fitting of correct bogies seems to have been a matter of chance. Many bogies actually had a wheelbase between the two

extremes. Although the designs for the bogies show that lead weights were going to be fitted, these were not actually put into production.

The No. 2 Special Tenders were very much better value for money than the simple No. 2 type. All four tenders were realistically modelled, with coal chutes, brake levers, filler caps and other details. The LMS tender was flat sided; the SR version was identical to the LMS save for the omission of the air vents and water pickup dome, although the filler was fitted. The GWR tender was based on the 4000 gallon type, and had distinctively flanged edges and ends; there was a large pick-up dome, and air vents at the front, together with a pricker rack and a water gauge. All these tenders had brake columns, but the LNER tender had smaller brake handles mounted on the front end of the tanks, and was fitted with lockers and a rack for fire irons, in addition to the normal features. The sides were flanged outwards along the top edge. None of the tender castings appear to suffer from 'metal fatigue' problems; the material was specified as 'white metal' rather than 'mazac'. The buffer height of the No. 2 Special Locos and Tenders was lower than had been previously used; in 1930 it also became standard for Hornby wagons.

One feature curiously absent from all the locos and tenders was the drop-flap, which had been fitted to the No. 2 Locos. Although this would have been more difficult to arrange than on the No. 2, it seems odd that this feature should be omitted. A weakness in all the first-issue tenders was that the wheels tended to drop out if the tender was roughly handled, so from December 1930 two stays were secured by lugs between the frames at front and rear of the tenders. Other general minor changes to the tenders were the use of a cross-ways spring anchor (the front coupling was sprung, reducing the shock to the train on starting) instead of the earlier lengthways lug mounting. This change was made in May 1936, and a .312″ spray hole was added to the base from November 1937. Matt varnish was used from 1939, and the use of 'Eton'-type buffers on No. 2 Special Tenders (especially export versions) became commonplace.

Hornby boasted about how many separate operations went into the manufacture of these locos, but the cost of making them had been grossly under-

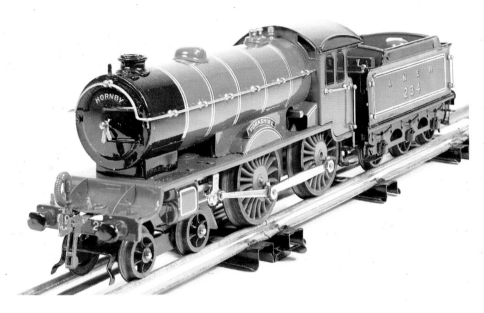

No. 2 Special 'Yorkshire', 1929–30. (The cabside numberplate transfer has been forgotten!)

No. 2 Special LMS Compound, 1929–30.

No. 2 Special SR L1, 1929–30.

No. 2 Special GW 'County of Bedford', 1929–30.

estimated, because of the complexity of the new housings and tenders compared with the simple No. 2 Locos they replaced. When they were introduced in 1929 they offered unparalleled value-for-money, especially when compared to similar products in the Bassett-Lowke catalogues. A dramatic price rise from 28s to 34s (with tender) became necessary in 1930, but despite the increase the locos were still excellent value for the class of model. The E220 Special Locomotives were never cheap, costing 43s 6d (with tender) when introduced in 1934. They were fitted with the new patent automatic reversing 20 volt mechanisms, designed for remote-control operation. Electric versions of the No. 2 Special could not easily have been made before, because of the protruding brush-holder caps of the older-style mechanism.

The one piece castings serving as motor cover, cab front and cab floor were most impressive features of the No. 2 Special series of locos. The floors were ribbed, and the cab front had cast details of steam pipes, gauges, regulator and firebox doors. That these details were practically the same for all except the GW locos, and bore little resemblance to the features of the prototypes, scarcely mattered. At least they were there; although it is a pity that Meccano Ltd did not hand-finish them to accentuate the details! The edges of the cab and cab windows were hand lined in black for each type of loco; the cab floor was not finished black on early locos.

Black No. 2 Special Locos were not usually included on the order forms supplied to dealers; nonetheless they appear to have been available by special order, as was implied by the wording in the HBTs from 1937 to 1939. Export versions were made in black, and black locos were also made with UK liveries, although again mostly for export. The main problem is to tell the 'official' Hornby locos from a plethora of home-made black liveries, with finishes ranging from the product of the tar-and-feather worker to the art of the meticulous forger. Since there are ten fakes for every genuine example, every caution is advisable. The majority of black No. 2 Specials (even those in UK livery) were exported.

Other special order options included No. 2 Specials with 6 volt non-automatic reversing mechan-isms, (already made for the E26 Special Tank Locos), and electric locos with clockwork-type smokebox doors, the latter at no extra charge.

Although many of the works drawings for the clockwork No. 2 Special Locos were revised in 1948–49, no No. 2 Specials (or E220 Specials) appear to have gone on sale after the war, understandably in view of the complications involved in their manufacture. The postwar 'Bramham Moor' loco number was changed by the drawing office to 2736 in January 1948, in light of the LNER re-numbering.

LMS COMPOUND

The LMS Compound was always the most popular of the No. 2 Special Locomotives. The design was based on the latest 1924 series of 3-cylinder compound locos designed by Sir Henry Fowler, which in turn were based on the earlier Midland Railway compound locos of S. W. Johnson and R. M. Deeley. Perhaps the most obvious distinguishing feature was the reverse rod fitted on the left-hand side of the loco, since the LMS locos were driven from the left-hand side, not the right as on the MR. The Hornby loco had a tallish but flat-topped dome, a tall chimney, and Ross Pop safety valves fitted in front of the whistle on the firebox. The cab roof was fitted with a well-modelled ventilator casting.

A handrail was fitted to the smokebox door, above a centrally-placed number '1185' in plain gold letters. The normal 'Hornby' transfer appeared, as on all the No. 2 Specials, in addition to the 'Special' loco transfer which was prominently placed on the left-hand corner of the running plate.

The boiler and firebox (the latter with prominently embossed washout plugs each side) were nicely proportioned, even to the smokebox being pressed out to a slightly larger radius than the boiler. Two boiler bands were embossed between the smokebox and the boiler, and one at the back of the firebox, and they were also lined out in yellow enamel. The smokebox was finished black, as was the centre section of the cab roof, and other details, but on the earliest versions the running plates were left in LMS red.

The splashers and lower cabside were lined out with thick gold bands, and edged black. Small unshadowed gold letters were used for the cabside '1185' number. In addition to the cab steps, the Compound had another pair between the front driving wheels and the bogie. They were solidly mounted to the frame, as were the cylinders; the connecting rod ran behind the steps. The vacuum brake pipe was finished in silver. The tender was in plain unlined maroon, although the top beading was hand-lined black, and the sides were lettered 'LMS' in unshadowed sans-serif letters.

Several changes were made during 1930 to improve the Compound. The only important structural change was that the embossed beading in the cab roof was altered to a wider spacing, to conform to the prototype. Other changes included the adoption of black finish for the running plate and vacuum brake pipe, shadowed '1185' transfers for the cab-side, and white instead of gold numbers for the smokebox door. The gold lining of cab and splashers became much finer, and the 'Special' trademark transfer was moved to the back of the loco. Tender transfers were also updated in 1930, to a fully-lined style, with 'LMS' in shadowed serif letters.

Needless to say, transitional versions were made; for example, the change to the cab roof was decided upon early in 1930, but for some time after this, locos were still made with narrow-spaced embossed beading, but with the black painting of the cab roof extended to the wider spacing, until the new tools could be brought into use. This particular intermediate (with black footplate and shadowed cabside numbers) had only a single front painted boiler band, unlike the earlier and later types which had a pair.

After 1931 Compound wheels were normally black. The E220 Special Electric Compounds of 1934–41 were like the clockwork locos, but for the different mechanism and the bulbholder in the smokebox door which was fitted instead of the handle. Post-1934 Compounds had a third lever hole in the cab front. At some time in the late 1930s (possibly 1936) the left-hand rear splasher of the electric Compound was changed to the full shape, instead of the previous shape cut away to clear the keyway on the clockwork loco. New lining transfers were made for these late electric versions. L1-style domes appear to have been adopted as standard in place of the earlier LMS type – perhaps as early as 1931.

Sans-serif shadowed letters for both the tender and the cabside were used briefly in the 1937–38 period. Matt varnish was used from 1939.

LMS 2P LOCO

Fowler Class 2P 4–4–0 locos were quite similar to the Compound in general appearance, although somewhat shorter, and having inside cylinders only. MM reader D. McIntyre of Bristol suggested that the LMS Class 2P loco could easily be represented simply by omitting the cylinders, slide bars and piston rods from the Compound. In April 1930 the MM replied that 'We have already experimented with this idea and find that it would be quite satisfactory.'

Regrettably the idea was never properly taken up, although it would have cost next to nothing to have provided this as a fifth No. 2 Special Loco, which would probably have proved quite popular. In the February 1933 Meccano Magazine, extensive instructions were given for a home conversion, and a most interesting 2P made by Meccano Ltd themselves was shown. The loco was finished black, and numbered 581 – a useful choice since the Compound '1185' transfers could be cut up and the numbers used in a different order!

A single genuine example of the black E220 Special LMS loco is known to us, dating from about 1937. The loco has been extensively restored, but certain features are clearly original; among them the black boiler with gold lining, the sans-serif 'LMS' transfers on the tender, and the splasher lining. The choice of 700 for the cabside is rather a puzzle (although as representative of the prototype as 581), as is the 1185 number on the smokebox door. The 2P loco was never catalogued, nor offered for sale to special order in the MM or elsewhere.

LNER 'YORKSHIRE'

The LNER 'Yorkshire' was a most attractive representation of the 'Shire' locos introduced in 1927 to work light express services in the North East and in Scotland. The finish was well modelled on the LNER publicity photographs of 'Yorkshire', with the tender lettered 'LNER 234', and a small oval cabside numberplate transfer.

The boiler was embossed with five pairs of boiler bands, which were also enamelled in white. A safety valve unit with a large base was fitted in front of the whistle, the dome being towards the front of the long parallel boiler, and both dome and chimney were low-profile designs that became standard for several smaller Hornby locos.

The boiler sides were extended vertically downwards in front of the front splashers (as well as to form the sides of the firebox at the rear) in order to hide the sides of the motor. Boiler handrails were fitted as a single piece, wrapped around the front of the loco, and held on to the smokebox door by a central handrail support – making it awkward to assemble. The finest feature of the loco was the cab, which was splendidly evocative of the LNER style. The cab handrail knobs were diecastings rather than the turned brass type used for the boiler handrail, and they were finished in gold paint with the rail itself painted silver. 'Yorkshire' nameplates were fitted above the front splashers, the name transfer in gold letters on black. The cylinders were also lined with

No. 2 Special LMS Compound, circa 1938.

transfers, and the loco number appeared on the front buffer beam with the lettering 'No. 234, Class D49'. The trademark transfer was on the left-hand front corner of the running plate; the running plate was left green, while the smokebox, cab roof, steps, and buffer heads were finished black. The smokebox door was fitted with standard riveted-on handles.

In 1930 the livery was altered to conform to the LNER standard practice of the time, with the loco number '234' now on the cabside in large shadowed letters. The colouring was unaltered except for the omission of the cylinder lining transfers, (the cylinder sides now being hand-finished black, although oddly enough the vacuum brake pipe was left in green). The trademark transfer was now at the back of the loco. The tender was lettered 'LNER' only, usually either in small letters (possibly using a portion of the previous No. 2 Special transfer, or the No. 3 transfer), or with unusually large lettering. However some tenders were lettered in the medium-sized 'LNER' lettering which later became standard.

From 1931, the livery changed again, with the running plates and valances, vacuum brake pipe and front underframe all hand-finished in black, but otherwise unaltered. There were no further major livery changes during the production of 'Yorkshire', which was replaced in 1935 by 'Bramham Moor'. E220 Special Electric 'Yorkshire's were sold in 1934–35, fitted with the usual bulbholders in the smokebox door, and with large cutouts in each side of the firebox to clear the motor, which looked painfully obtrusive in such a narrow-bodied loco. The electric 'Yorkshire' usually had black wheels. A third lever hole was added in the motor cover casting.

BRAMHAM MOOR

In July 1932 the MM showed the LNER publicity photos of the latest 'Hunt' Class D49 3-cylinder locos, which were practically identical to the 'Shire' class. The loco shown was the first of the series, number 201 'Bramham Moor'. Inevitably, MM readers wrote to suggest that the Hornby LNER No. 2 Special should be re-named as a 'Hunt', which equally inevitably brought the reply that there would be 'no great advantage' in doing so. In the 1935–36 catalogues the 'Bramham Moor' loco replaced 'Yorkshire'.

The style and finish was exactly the same as for the 'Yorkshire', except that outside steam pipe covers were added between the cylinders and the smokebox, above the level of the running plate. The nameplates were altered to brass plates with raised letters on a black background, surmounted by a running fox (facing forward on each side). These were attached to the sides of the splashers rather than to the top, so the front splashers were no longer lined.

There were no major production variations except for a change of colour to darker green in 1936, and matt varnish from 1939. When the 'Eton' loco came out in 1937 there were some minor alterations to the 'Bramham Moor' (for example a slight change in the position of the smokebox door lugs). There were also some tooling errors such as LNER locos with slots for 'Eton' smoke deflectors, and even the use of an 'Eton'-type smokebox door with side lamp brackets, but with a bulbholder also fitted!

COUNTY OF BEDFORD

The Great Western Railway No. 2 Special Locomotive was 'County of Bedford', one of an elderly class of 4–4–0s, not the later and better-known 'County' class 4–6–0 locos. Rather disobligingly, the GWR had not recently made any suitable 4–4–0 locos as had the other railway groups.

The Hornby Loco was well modelled, with an elegant firebox and a nicely tapered boiler. In front of the cab was mounted the casting which represented the safety-valve on the Compound, but on the County served as the distinctive GWR whistles. The loco was fitted with a Collett-type cast safety valve (the earlier Hornby GWR cast safetyvalve of 1926–27 was more like the Dean-type) hand finished in gold, as were the pipe-covers leading up to it.

The chimney was the largest type ever fitted to Hornby locos, and it was 'copper-capped' by hand-finishing. Embossed details in the smokebox door included hinges as on the other locos, and also a step at the bottom. There were also steps fitted on the

No. 2 Special LNER 'Yorkshire', in the revised 1930–31 livery.

E220 Special SR L1 Class Loco, circa 1934. Later locos were numbered 1759.

LNER E220 Special 'Yorkshire' Loco. (The Modelled Miniature vehicles were briefly part of the Hornby Series.)

curved portion of the running plate just under the smokebox door, and the whole front section (although not the main part of the running plate) was hand-finished black over the green. The boiler hand-rail was a single piece, with a handrail support on the smokebox door as on the 'Yorkshire'.

Inside the cab, the motor-cover casting was better-detailed than the others, with a good representation of the gauges and the regulator handle. Vertical cab handrails were fitted at the back of the cab side; the 'County' was illustrated in the 1929–30 HBT, and it may be as well to point out that this illustration was an artist's impression, with features not found on the production locos. Not least that the tender shown was of the LNER type but in GW livery! Fixed lamps were shown at the front, although they were never actually fitted, and the vacuum brake pipe was shown in the wrong position; the wheels were also decidedly odd. Although the rear cab handrail was shown, there was also a short horizontal handrail on the cabside at the level of the boiler handrail; this feature should really have appeared on the Hornby loco, but it did not.

In the HBT the loco was shown fully lined out with two pairs of lining bands on the firebox, and five pairs of boiler bands on the boiler, the centre pair straddling the pipe-cover. On the actual Hornby locos, the front two pairs of boiler bands and the rear two pairs of bands on the firebox were both embossed and painted yellow. The pipe-cover was finished in gold, not lined. That left two pairs of bands on the boiler which were actually embossed, but not painted! The official GWR publicity photos of the 'County of Bedford' in photographic livery

showed it with all seven pairs of boiler bands as in the HBT.

On the earliest 'County of Bedford's, the trademark transfers were above the cylinder on the left-hand running plate. Cylinders were lined with a square of double gold bands, although examples of this age are known which have two pairs of vertical gold bands, the No. 1 Special transfer having been used, presumably by an inexperienced hand. Name-plates and numberplates were a striking feature of the loco, with the 'County of Bedford' name in red letters shadowed black on a gold background, and the numbers '3821' in gold, black lined, on a red background. The number also appeared on the front buffer beam in stark black letters. The tender was lettered 'Great (crest) Western', and was the only tender transfer not revised in 1930, being a reasonably accurate representation of the GWR style, although purists might argue that the letters should have been shadowed red to the left and black to the right, rather than the Hornby standard red to the right, lined black.

But changes were made to the locomotive in 1930; the trademark was moved to the back of the loco, and the cylinders and running plate were finished black (although the cylinder lining transfer was still used). The pipe-cover to the safety-valve was no longer painted gold, but was left green and lined each side with yellow boiler bands. Most importantly the nameplate and numberplate transfers were changed to show more correct gold letters on black backgrounds. The number on the front buffer beam changed to gold letters. During the changeover period intermediate versions

appeared; and after a while the boiler bands that had been embossed but left unpainted no longer appeared at all.

The E220 Special Electric 'County' was introduced in 1934, once again requiring extensive cutouts from the base of the firebox, and the fitting of bulbholders in the smokebox door, as well as the third lever hole in the cab casting. Circa 1936 the tender transfers were changed to the 'GWR' monogram instead of the 'Great (crest) Western' lettering. Matt-finish 'County of Bedford' locos were made from 1939.

SOUTHERN RAILWAY 'L1'

The Southern Railway No. 2 Special Loco was of an 'L1' Class loco; not a particularly famous class outside a small corner of the South-East, with the result that sales were not as strong as certain others in the series. The expense of producing the loco was reduced by common components and common tooling between the L1 and LMS Compound; the base, front underframe, front splasher, smokebox support and boiler differed hardly at all. The most marked differences were in the cab, which on the SR engine was much longer, and had a wider roof, rather prone to accidental damage. The L1 needed a deeper motor cover casting, adapted from the LMS loco part. The firebox was shorter, and was fitted with the same safety valve and whistles as the Compound; the rear splashers were actually embossed in the side of the firebox. Lining bands were both embossed and painted on firebox and boiler. The dome was shorter than the early Compound type, but the chimney was identical save for the brass-coloured cap painted on.

The L1 was not fitted with the cylinders of the Compound, since it represented an inside cylinder class of loco; neither was the reversing lever fitted, as on the Compound. Curiously, the steam-pipe covers of the Compound were also fitted to the L1.

The L1 was finished in the usual SR passenger green, and differed from the other first-issue No. 2 Special Locos in having the running plates hand-finished in black right from the start (with the valance left in green). The odd thing was that the lower part of the cabside, in addition to having a

No. 2 Special GW 'County of Bedford', circa 1936.

well-executed numberplate, was unnecessarily lined out in white and black. The tender, although correctly lettered 'Southern A759', was devoid of the lining it should have carried. The perpetrators of these mistakes could not plead ignorance as an excuse, since the original SR L1 had been illustrated in the MM in correct colours as early as February 1927!

In 1930 new versions were sold, without the cabside lining and with the tender properly lined. The front underframe and steps were now hand-finished in black, and the trademark moved from the front left-hand corner of the footplate to the rear of the loco. Once again there were transitional variants.

Electric E220 L1 locos were sold from 1934. The cab casting was changed (as on the Compound) both to add a third lever hole and to give clearance for the gear on the rear driving wheel; post-1934 locos have a small triangular raised section on the cab floor to the left of the firebox door, on both L1 and Compound locos.

Around 1936, the number of the loco was changed to 1759 instead of A759, on cabside and tender; the buffer beam transfer was similarly altered, the lettering being in plain gold as before. There were no further significant livery changes except the use of matt varnish from 1939.

WHEELS AND AXLES FOR THE No. 2 SPECIAL MOTOR

The No. 2 Special mechanism was also used for the No. 2 Special Tank Locos and the No. 3 Locos, and the wheel colours followed much the same pattern on these other engines. In 1929 and 1930 LMS red, LMS black, LNER black and SR black locos had red driving wheels, while the LNER green, GW green and SR green locos had LNER green driving wheels. In each case the tyres were most attractively stained black. Perhaps late in 1930, certainly by early in 1931, the wheels were nickel-plated, and they were coloured black, except on the LNER green and SR green clockwork locos, which usually had green wheels matching the loco body. From this time onwards, the bogie wheels (which had previously been black on all locos) were finished in the same colours as the driving wheels. From 1931 it was also decided that thicker axles were necessary, because of problems with loose wheels, and with wheel castings. The new wheels were now locked onto the axle by round nuts which fitted into recesses in the wheel hub, after the style of the No. 3 electric loco wheels but with locating pins in the axle to ensure proper quartering. From 1931 the coupling rods were fluted, as they were planned to be from the start. In

1936 the material for the wheels was changed to mazac, and quite soon the wheels were left unplated. From mid 1937 the wheels were push-fitted onto knurled axles, with colouring generally unchanged.

Electric E220 Special locos, (and the E220 Special Tank and E320 Locos which had the same mechanism), had black wheels at first. (Black wheels had previously been the invariable rule for electric locos.) But from 1935 LNER green and SR green electric locos usually had green wheels, while LMS and GW locos still had black wheels. Mazac was used for electric loco wheels from 1936, and soon the nickel plating of 1934–36 was abandoned. From 1937 press-fit wheels were used for electric as well as clockwork locos.

No. 2 SPECIAL TANK LOCOMOTIVES

Among the many new locos appearing in time for Christmas 1929 was the No. 2 Special Tank Locomotive, which replaced the 4–4–4 No. 2 Tank Loco. It was a remarkable agglomeration of features of other locos, with shortened versions of the No. 3 firebox and boiler, and with the cab and bunker of the No. 2 Tank (although there was no room for front cab windows because of the height of the

firebox and the tanks). The base had much in common with that of the No. 3 Loco, adapted for the No. 2 Special mechanism which was fitted from the start. (There was no Control System version.) No cylinders were fitted, although the No. 3 style cylinders would actually have suited the loco quite well; but presumably the omission helped to keep the price the same as that of the No. 2 Tank, 22s 6d. The 4–4–2 wheel arrangement was the same as for the No. 3, the same 'ashpan' being fitted, but under the cab rather than under the firebox. Fixed lamps were fitted above the front buffer beam.

The usual seven liveries were available, with LMS red loco number 2323 (lettered 'LMS' in sans-serif shadowed gold letters), LMS black 6781 (let-

tered in the same style), LNER green number 6, LNER black 5154, GW green 4703, SR green B329 and SR black E492. The 'passenger' livery GW 4703 was distinguished from the 'goods' by a copper capped chimney, an odd distinction that persisted erratically for a few years although not mentioned in the catalogues of the period. The new-style GW cast safety valve, painted gold, was fitted instead of the normal dome and Compound-type safety valve, although the chimney was normally of the 'Yorkshire' type used for the others. Each loco had a brass whistle.

The SR locos were handsome in their simple liveries, different from the 4–4–4 style; the tanks were lettered 'Southern' in sans-serif plain gold let-

ters, and the loco number was on the bunker side. Hornby always contrived to make the SR locos different, and on the No. 1 and No. 1 Special Locos in passenger livery for example only SR locos had black cab roofs. All the No. 2 Special Tank Locos had black cab roofs except the green Southern!

Early No. 2 Special Tank Locos can be distinguished by the fitting of lead weights inside the bogie anchor above the front bogie. There was no weight in the back of the loco, apart from the weight in the pony truck itself. But the weights were not particularly important since the No. 2 Special mechanism was a more sedate performer than the old No. 2 type. The front weight was abandoned soon after production started in the latter months of 1929. (It is unlikely that production was actually started before September 1929.) In December 1929 it was decided that the No. 2 Special Tank should be fitted with lamp brackets on the smokebox door and on the front buffer beam, the lamp brackets for the outside pair of lamps being designed to fit the same holes that had been used for the fixed lamps.

The typical locos of 1930 thus had four lamp brackets at the front, and at the rear, since the bunker back was also provided with four cracked-up lugs to serve as lamp brackets. Whereas previously the locos had carried both the 'Hornby' smokebox door transfer and the 'Special' loco transfer on the bunker back, the latter was no longer used.

Some of the loco transfers were changed for the 1930–31 season, most notably those of the SR locos, on which unchanged loco numbers (B329 and E492) appeared on the tanks instead of the bunker, underneath the 'Southern' lettering which was now serif lettered in gold. The LMS passenger loco number changed to '2180' instead of '2323', and serif shadowed letters were used, as well as improved lining. (Later versions of the black LMS '6781' also had serif letters.) The GW loco number changed to 2221, with the tanks still lettered 'Great Western' as before. Bogies were now finished black rather than nickel plated.

For the 1930–31 season, the No. 2 Electric Tank Loco was produced. It was an electric version of the No. 2 Special Tank, fitted with the same 6 volt electric mechanism used for the No. 3E Locos. The driving wheels were finished in black only; they

were smaller than the clockwork No. 2 Special type, and there were cutouts in the valance to clear the crankpins. By way of discrimination the electric locos seem consistently to have been weighted inside the front bogie anchor.

From 1931, the buffers on the front buffer beam were set at a lower height, and the link couplings at the front of the loco were now cranked on the electric locos, as they had always been on the clockwork locos. The bunker back was changed to a completely new design, incorporating a deep rear buffer beam and a small frame under the cab floor to which the automatic couplings were fitted. The buffers were set low down on the rear buffer beam as at the front; cranked automatic couplings were fitted to the clockwork locos despite the already lowered coupling position. From about the same time clockwork mechanisms with wheels secured by nuts replaced the type with push-fit wheels; wheel colour changes were as described for the No. 2 Special.

From 1933, bulbholders were fitted in the smokebox door of the 6 volt No. 2 Electric Tank Loco, and also to the LST2/20 Electric Tank Loco which was introduced in that year. The 20 volt motor was of the protruding brush-cap type. By this time the GW loco transfer had been changed, with the number 2221 now on a numberplate, but still with 'Great Western' lettering. The SR loco number was changed to 2329 instead of B329, and the SR black loco number transfer became '492' instead of 'E492'. By then the number of the LNER green loco

had also been changed, to 1784.

In 1934–35, the electric locos were re-named as the E26 and E220 Special Tanks, and updated mechanisms were fitted, with the flat-sided brush-holders that fitted within the confines of the body. The 20 volt loco had automatic reverse. Both the new-style electric mechanisms were fitted with the larger-size driving wheels, but despite this the electric loco bodies remained closer to the ground than the clockwork, mainly because the brackets were arranged to set the mechanism deeper into the body. The clearance cutouts in the valance were still provided, on electric locos only.

Probably in 1935, the SR green loco number was changed again to 2091, and soon the LMS red loco number was changed to 6954. The GW loco transfers were changed yet again, with the 'GWR' monogram being used instead of 'Great Western' lettering, although the loco number 2221 was the same. From 1936 the LNER locos were darker green. Mazac wheels were used from 1936, and push-fit wheels from 1937, as on the No. 2 and E220 Special locos. There were no subsequent major changes of livery, although LMS locos were produced with sans-serif shadowed 'LMS' lettering for a short period in 1937–

38. The later locos were serif-lettered as before. Matt finish versions of the No. 2 and E220 Special tanks appeared from 1939, before production halted during the war.

Around the end of 1948, the designs for the clockwork locos were updated for issue as the Type 1101 Tank Loco, in LMS, LNER, SR and GW liveries. The Type 1101 Loco was certainly shown at a trade show, probably in early 1949, and the failure to get it into production must have been a great disappointment.

RIVIERA 'BLUE TRAIN' LOCOMOTIVES

In 1926 Hornby introduced the 4–4–2 Riviera 'Blue Train' Locos, which were loosely based on the French 'Nord' Pacifics. The frames for the new Hornby locos were of the same length as the 4–4–4 tank, but the buffer beam was deeper and the valance much shallower, which although elegant meant that the front end was quite susceptible to crumpling in the event of accident, a fault also common to the No. 2 Special Tank Locos. The Riviera loco was fitted with a 2-wheel pony truck, a simple bracket

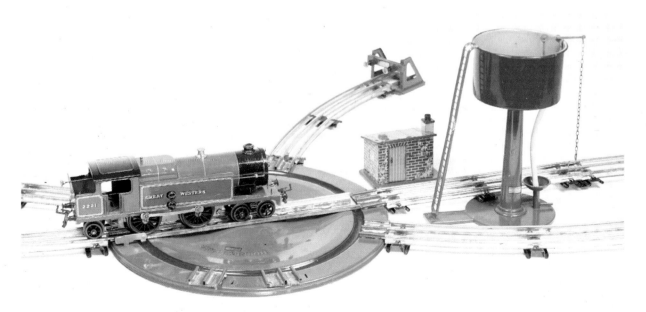

The No. 2 Electric Tank Loco was first sold in 1930. The Electrical Turntable and the Water Tank are of the same period.

arrangement pivoted on the rear mechanism fixing bolt, and weighted to keep it on the track for as long as possible. An 'ashpan' was fitted between the rear driving wheels and the pony truck. The front bogie was kingpin-mounted as on the No. 2 Tank, but the bogie anchor was cut away to allow steps to be fitted under the smokebox; the new-style steps were also fitted under the cab. The outside cylinders were an advance on the simple No. 1 Loco type, being incorporated as an integral part of the body, and fitted with slide-bars to guide the cross-heads that were fitted to the No. 3 piston rods. There was a long flat splasher between the top of the cylinders and the cab. At first, the body was universal, having a keyhole both on the 4 volt No. 1 Riviera 'Blue Train' Loco and on the clockwork No. 2 Riviera 'Blue Train' Loco, these being the titles given to the locos until 1927 when the 'No. 3C' and 'No. 3E' descriptions were first used.

The boiler was of large diameter, and it was joined to a substantial firebox, another 'first' for Hornby. A stove-pipe chimney and two polished brass domes were fitted, and there was a small safety-valve casting on top of the firebox. The cab was short, but with a long roof overhanging the gap to the tender. The tender was another important development, being double-walled to create a water tank, although no filler was fitted. There was a large space for coal, and the tender was mounted on two 4-wheel bogies.

Boiler, cab, splashers and cylinders were painted brown, with two painted gold bands on the firebox and three on the boiler; cylinders were also lined gold. On the first locos the base frame of the loco and the boiler cradle were both black, as were the smokebox door, the funnel and safety valve. The cabside was lined with gold and red lining transfers, with the number '31240'. The tender was brown, on a black base, hand lined in gold and lettered 'Nord 31801'. The discrepancy in the numbers is inexplicable, and it applied not just to the 'Nord' loco but also to the maroon 'PLM' 4–4–2 which was made in Binns Road for sale in France, and which was also numbered 31240 on the cab and 31801 on the tender.

When introduced in 1926, the clockwork loco was available only fitted for Hornby Control. The first mechanisms were identical to the No. 2 type; the No. 2 'Nord' bodies first appeared with keyholes cut centrally in the splasher. Within a short time, certainly by the time the other No. 3 Locos were introduced in 1927, a new Control System No. 3 mechanism had been designed. This had a larger main gear which meant that the winding spindle was set higher in the body, so the keyhole was now in the boiler, clear of the top of the splasher. The electric locos were still fitted with the same body as the clockwork type.

From 1927 the Riviera locos were assembled before spraying (except for the black smokebox door and polished brass domes which were added afterwards), so the base and running plates became brown instead of black; the steps, chimney and safety valve were hand-finished black after assembly (in addition to the usual red and black on the buffer beam). The tender base remained black for this and all subsequent versions. Diecast alloy wheels were fitted to the mechanisms from early in 1928, finished in black as before, and soon the domes were being finished brown along with the rest of the boiler; but unlike the other No. 3 Locos of the period, the smokebox was not coloured black.

In the middle of 1929, there were important changes in the loco body to accommodate the latest motors. Electric locos were now 6 volt, with holes for brush-holder caps cut in the right-hand side of the body, and no longer having the clockwork keyhole. Clockwork locos were no longer fitted for Hornby Control, but were adapted for the No. 2 Special mechanism, with its larger driving wheels most attractively finished in red with black-stained tyres. A new keyhole position was necessary for the new motor, cut partly into the boiler and partly into the splasher. Both clockwork and electric types now had the five lining bands on boiler and firebox

No. 3C Riviera 'Blue Train' Loco, circa 1932; between 1930 and 1936 the smokeboxes were coloured black.

A clockwork Riviera 'Blue Train' Loco of 1926. The motor is the No. 2 Loco type, fitted for Hornby Control. There was also a 4 volt version.

embossed as well as painted. Electric locos were usually weighted inside the bogie anchor and inside the cab.

Later in 1929, new transfers were made for the cabside, with the number '31801', so that loco and tender matched properly for the first time. From 1930 the smokebox was painted black, as on all the other Hornby Trains, and the fixed lamps that had always been fitted were replaced by lamp brackets, three above the front buffer beam and one mounted on the smokebox door. Unlike the other No. 3 locos of the period the clockwork 'Nord' was never fitted with riveted-on door handles. Also from 1930, the front bogie frame was finished black instead of nickel-plated, while electric locos had bakelite-covered brush-caps instead of knurled brass.

In 1931 the tender was altered for automatic couplings, and the front buffers of the loco were mounted lower on the beam. Electric locos were fitted with cranked front couplings, such as had been used on the clockwork locos since 1929 when the mechanism was changed. Post-1931 locos had fluted coupling rods, and clockwork loco wheels were

secured to the axle by round nuts; the spokes were finished black, and the tyres were plated.

E3/20 Riviera 'Blue Train' Locos with 20 volt manual reverse mechanisms were sold as an alterna-

tive to the 6 volt E3/6 Locos from 1933. Both locos had bulbholders in the smokebox door, not previously fitted on the 6 volt version. The mechanisms were identical, except for the windings. The electric

In 1934 the E320 Riviera 'Blue Train' Loco replaced the E3/20. By then smoke deflectors were being fitted.

145

From 1938 the Nord loco number was changed to 3.1290.

locos still had plain black wheels, of the original smaller size.

From 1934 smoke deflectors were fitted, finished black to match the smokebox. The bogie anchor and front weight had to be cropped at the corners to allow the deflector lugs to be clipped to the body. E320 Electric Riviera Locos with the automatic reversing mechanism, and E36 locos with the new-style mechanism with flat brush-holders, replaced the previous electric versions. The wheels of the electric locos were now the same size as those of the clockwork locos, and the wheels were now plated, with the spokes painted black.

By 1936, the 31801 loco was being finished in brown overall, without any black finishing to smokebox, smokebox door, smoke deflectors, chimney, safety valve or steps. The six volt E36 loco was withdrawn from sale in 1936, leaving only the 20 volt and clockwork versions on sale. Mazac wheels were fitted from 1936, and soon were no longer plated.

It was probably in 1937 that the 31801 tender bogies were revised to a new style, fitted with axleboxes, and with a longer wheelbase to allow diecast wagon wheels to be used instead of the smaller bogie wheels fitted before. Both clockwork and electric motors were revised, with splined axles for push-fit wheels. From 1938 new transfers were made for loco and tender, both numbered '3.1290', to represent the number of an actual 'Nord' Pacific loco.

No. 3 LOCOMOTIVES

No. 3 Locomotives were introduced in 1927. The bodies were similar to those of the Riviera 'Blue Train' Loco, but were fitted with a single polished-brass rounded dome (or in the case of the GW loco, a polished-brass safety-valve cover) instead of the two flat-topped Nord domes. They also had two dummy splashers each side, the front ones with nameplate transfers and the rear splashers with lining transfers. The most famous locomotive names of the age were undoubtedly 'Royal Scot' and 'Flying Scotsman', so there was no difficulty in choosing these as the names for the LMS and LNER locos. 'Caerphilly Castle' was chosen for the GW loco name, although perhaps less of a household word. The idea of representing these locos as simple 4–4–2s of rather un-British appearance may strike us today as being a little odd,

and there was much criticism at the time. Indeed it must have been quite severe, since some objections were even mentioned in the MM; in January 1928 a reply in the MM stated that Hornby Trains were designed 'more for long life than as scale models', and in February 1928 'We do not agree with your suggestion that we should either make perfect scale models of these trains or none at all.' It was probably sensitivity to such criticisms that led the designers to the opposite extreme, for the brief but glorious period of true-to-type modelling in 1928 and 1929.

Each No. 3 Loco was finished in the passenger colours of the appropriate railway. There were three painted bands on the boilers, and two on the firebox; the cabsides were lined with transfers which incorporated the company crests of the LMS or LNER, and in the case of the GW loco the number '4073' in shadowed gold letters. The 'Nord' stovepipe chimney was fitted to all the locos, and although the GW loco had the polished brass safety valve it retained the normal safety valve on the firebox as well! The smokeboxes were the same colour as the boiler, but the smokebox doors were finished black. Unlike the first 'Nord' locos, the No. 3 Locos were sprayed after assembly, so the running plate was always the same colour as the boiler.

There were at first two versions of the No. 3, one with a 4 volt electric and the other with a Control System clockwork mechanism.

The tenders were of the simple 6-wheeled No. 2 type, always of nut-and-bolt construction. New transfers were made for each of the tenders; LMS No. 3 tenders were lettered '6100', the LNER

SR No. 3C Loco 'Lord Nelson', 1928. Fitted for Hornby Control.

GW. No. 3E Loco 'Caerphilly Castle', 1927.

✓ A slightly later No. 3C 'Flying Scotsman', with No. 2 Special Tender.

LNER No. 3E 'Flying Scotsman' 6 volt Loco, 1929.

tenders 'LNER 4472', and the GW 'Great (crest) Western'.

Die-cast alloy wheels were fitted to both the No. 3C and the No. 3E locos from early in 1928, in place of the previous type turned from iron castings. For the 1928–29 season, smokeboxes were painted black, and the front boiler band was no longer painted on, reducing the number of lining bands from 5 to 4. Domes were painted in the same colour as the boiler. GW locos retained their brass safety valve, but a brass whistle replaced the cast safety valve on the firebox. Liveries were otherwise unchanged. No. 3 Locos in SR colours were made in the same year, named 'Lord Nelson'. The cabs were lined in the normal style (as on the LNER loco but with no company crest or cabside number) but the SR locos usually had five white boiler bands; a single line between smokebox and boiler, two pairs further behind on the boiler, and none on the firebox. Tenders were lettered 'Southern E850'; and, as on the other locos, the stovepipe chimneys were still fitted. The cab roof was green.

From mid 1929, No. 3 locos were fitted with new motors. The electric locos now had 6 volt mechanisms with protruding brush-caps, and no longer had keyholes since the bodies were now different. Clockwork locos were fitted with No. 2 Special mechanisms and wheels, instead of the Control System No. 3 mechanism which had been fitted before. Although electric loco wheels remained in black, clockwork loco wheels were now coloured – red for the 'Royal Scot' and LNER green for the other three. The 'Yorkshire'-type chimney was fitted to all four versions, replacing the stovepipe, and cranked front couplings were fitted to the clockwork locos. LMS, LNER and GW locos had the three boiler bands and two bands on the firebox embossed as well as painted; SR locos now had three single bands embossed and painted on the boiler, with no bands embossed on the firebox, although two bands were sometimes painted on!

Late in 1929, cabside transfers for the LMS and LNER locos had the loco number in plain gold lettering in place of the company crest. Because the LNER tender transfers had been altered a few months earlier to read 'LNER' only, instead of 'LNER 4472', many Flying Scotsman locos of the interim period had no number on loco or tender. There was no corresponding change to the LMS tender transfers, tenders numbered '6100' were still usually supplied with the loco. SR and GW liveries were unaltered, except that the SR locos now had only the three boiler bands embossed and painted, with none on the firebox. Smokebox door handles were fitted from late in 1929, and electric locos were weighted in the cab and inside the front bogie anchor.

In 1930, the fixed lamps were replaced by lamp brackets above the front buffer beam and on the smokebox door, and front bogies were finished in black rather than nickel plated. Bakelite brush-caps were used instead of knurled brass on the electric versions. However the most important change was that the old style No. 3 tenders were no longer supplied, but were replaced by the No. 2 Special type; the LMS, LNER and GW tenders were suitable without alteration, but now a second SR No. 2 Special Tender was necessary, which at first had the same 'Southern E850' transfer that had been used for

the No. 3 tender. Apart from these SR transfers, the tenders followed the same pattern of variations as described for the No. 2 Special.

From 1931, the loco buffers were moved to a lower position on the beam, and cranked couplings were fitted to electric engines as well as clockwork. Fluting was added to the coupling rods. Post-1931 GW No. 3 Locos usually had the taller chimney that was fitted to GW locos other than the 'Specials'. Clockwork loco wheels were fitted to the axles by round nuts, instead of push-fitted, and the wheel colours changed thereafter as described for the No. 2 Special.

When stocks of the old-style 'Southern E850' transfers were used up, new transfers were made, still lettered 'Southern E850' but with L1-style lining.

For the 1933–34 season, both E3/6 and E3/20 Locos were offered, the 20 volt motors being like the 6 volt mechanism with the protruding brush-holder caps, but differently wound. The wheels were still of smaller diameter than those of the clockwork locos, and were finished in black. Bulbholders were now fitted to all the electric locos.

Between 1932 and 1934, new sets of transfers were made for the LMS, LNER and GW locos. The LMS cabside number was changed to shadowed lettering, and the rear splasher was given a simple outlining in gold instead of the broad gold band (lined black and red) of the previous splasher transfer. On the LNER engine shadowed letters were used for the number, and the rear splasher lining was changed to the outline instead of the former broad gold band lined black and white; and the 'Flying Scotsman' nameplate changed to gold lettering on black instead of gold on red. The GW loco retained the broad gold band for the rear splasher, unlike the others, but the cabside transfer was changed early in 1934 with the number 4073 now on a numberplate. The SR transfers changed only in the outlining of the rear splasher instead of the LNER-type broad gold band used before; the nameplate was still gold on red, as was the 'Royal Scot' nameplate.

In 1934, the E320 automatic reverse and the E36 manual reverse electric locos replaced the E3/20 and E3/6; the main difference was that the flat-sided mechanisms no longer needed the holes for the brush-holder caps, and electric locos were now fitted with wheels of the same size used for the clockwork loco. E320 wheels were coloured as for the E220 Special. During 1934–35 remaining stocks of the old E3/20 locos were sold off at reduced prices of 25s (loco only) compared to 35s for the automatic reverse version.

Smoke deflectors were added to the 'Royal Scot' locos of the LMS following a collision at Leighton Buzzard in 1931, for which reduced visibility caused by smoke was blamed. In May 1932 the MM had said that 'manufacture of these sides sheets has not been considered', and instructions were given for home-made deflectors in cardboard. Although the

An LMS No. 3C 'Royal Scot', circa 1934, passing a Meccano 01P aerodrome.

'Royal Scot' and 'Lord Nelson' locos were not advertised until 1936 as having deflectors, these may well have been fitted earlier, perhaps in 1935, but later than for the Nord locos which had smoke deflectors in 1934. A few Flying Scotsman locos were fitted with 'Royal Scot' deflectors, presumably by mistake.

The SR tender transfer was altered (circa 1934) to 'Southern 850' instead of 'Southern E850'; while LNER No. 3 Locos were painted a darker green from 1936, at which time the GWR No. 2 Special Tender was changed to show the GWR monogram instead of 'Great (crest) Western' lettering. Also in 1936 the 6 volt E36 Locos were withdrawn from sale. The 1937–38 LMS tenders were block lettered instead of serif lettered, but there were few further alterations except for the adoption of splined axles for push-fit driving wheels from 1937, and matt varnish from 1939. Late matt-finish versions of 'Caerphilly Castle' had gold on black nameplates instead of the previous gold on red.

There were special export No. 3 locos, on which the normal splasher lining transfers were applied to all four splashers, and there were no nameplates. Early export No. 3 locos in red livery had no company crest on the cabside, but had tenders numbered '6100' as in the UK. Black No. 3 Locos were made in the later 1930s in both export and UK liveries, mostly for export. The LNER black version was lined out in white, with white boiler bands, and had the normal LNER tender transfer. Both splashers were lined only, there being no nameplate, and the No. 1 Special Loco number transfer '1368' was used on the cabside.

No. 4 'ETON' LOCOMOTIVES

The 'Schools' Class locos of the Southern Railway, the heaviest and most powerful 4–4–0 locos in Britain, were not made until 1930, just too late to be represented in the No. 2 Special Loco range. Although the Hornby 'Eton' Locomotives were not made until 1937, they were one of the most popular of the true-to-type 4–4–0 Hornby locos. They were probably made only because, by coincidence, the SR locos could be represented by making some minimal alterations to the frame and boiler of 'Bramham

An E36 'Flying Scotsman', circa 1935.

An unusual special order E320 Loco in LNER black. Circa 1937.

transfer used; the only trademark was the 'Special' loco transfer at the back of the loco. Lamp irons were fitted at each side of the smokebox door, in addition to the normal four, so that the complicated SR route indicating system could be used. Diecast white-painted SR route indicating discs were supplied instead of normal loco lamps with the 'Eton' loco only, and not with any of the other Hornby SR locos.

Unfortunately, it was decided to sell these locos with standard No. 2 Special SR tenders. Although the 'Eton' tender was suitably lined and lettered to go with the loco, the flat sides looked incongruous since the top section was not turned inwards to match the angled cab sides. Since major structural alterations to the tender would have been necessary, if it were to have been made properly, the decision is comprehensible in economic terms, although many users might have prefered to pay more for a properly made No. 4 tender. Notwithstanding this reservation, the overall effect of the 'Eton' loco, with one of the most accurate representations so far of the colour and lining style of the real railways, was nothing less than magnificent.

It was particularly unfortunate that the 'Schools' Class loco appeared just when the SR were beginning to experiment with liveries. From 1938 the SR locos had begun to appear from the works in a vivid malachite livery, with the tender lettered 'Southern' only, and with the cabside number in large letters instead of on a tiny plate. This development was not effected on the Hornby locos. The only variation in the livery was the production of a few black 'Eton' locos, mainly for the export market.

'PRINCESS ELIZABETH' LOCOMOTIVE

The largest Hornby Gauge O loco was announced in the April 1937 MM: 'On 1st May we introduce a wonderful scale model of the LMSR locomotive "Princess Elizabeth" . . . This notable introduction forms another outstanding landmark in the development of the Hornby Railway System.' It was naturally the most expensive as well, at 105s, which put it well beyond the reach of many. The loco was available only with a 20 volt automatic reverse

Moor', and by adding a completely new cab in the authentic style of the SR engines, with the upper cabside angled to clear the narrow tunnels of the Hastings line. The cab front and motor cover casting was the same as for 'Bramham Moor', the only other important structural change being the addition of smoke deflectors.

The L1 remained on sale as the SR No. 2 Special Locomotive, although it was understandably of more limited appeal than the popular new locos which were sold as the No. 4 and E420 'Eton' Locomotives. 'Eton' Locos were not sold in sets. The price was higher than for the No. 2 Specials, (41s vs 33s 6d for the clockwork and 48s 6d vs 43s 6d for the electric locos with tender), and to help justify the difference the locos were fitted with some extra details. Bright polished brasswork included clack boxes and feed pipes just behind the smokebox, and the steam pipes with a steam turret and projecting horizontal whistle just in front of the cab. Ross Pop safety valves were fitted, which to the credit of the designers were not just the standard LNER casting but were made from brass. The boiler was embossed

with washout plugs, which were also painted black, but the 'snifting' valves on the firebox were not represented on the Hornby locos. The dome and chimney were the same as on the 'Bramham Moor', although the dome was positioned further back on the boiler.

The 'Eton' nameplates were beautifully finished in the distinctive SR style, with raised brass letters on a red background. The transfer applied to the cabside numberplate (embossed as on the L1) was splendidly finished with gold letters on red, lined in black and in white. The front bufferbeam was lettered 'No. 900' in gold. New round-headed buffers with parallel shanks and square bases were used; but unfortunately the heads were finished in black, and not in silver to represent polished steel like those of the 'Princess Elizabeth'.

The smokebox door was slightly altered from the 'Bramham Moor' type by the omission of the top handrail knob, since the handrails ran only along the length of the boiler. Door handles were not fitted on the No. 4 Loco smokebox door, nor the bulbholder on the E420. Nor was the 'Hornby' smokebox door mechanism, and it was not sold in train sets.

Perhaps the most noteworthy difference from the earlier Hornby true-to-type locos, apart from the sheer size, was that no projecting lugs were used anywhere in the housing, all the important joints being soldered. Particularly noticeable was the smokebox front, which did not have the usual overlap over the end of the boiler but (as on the real loco) was fitted inside it.

Both boiler and firebox were tapered, and should have been impressive features. But whereas the 'Eton' loco had been let down by economy on the tender, the 'Princess Elizabeth' was let down by an unforgivable lack of proportion, the firebox being too long in relation to the boiler. In consequence it rose too high, giving the loco a 'hump-backed' appearance.

Four large brass safety valves were mounted on the firebox, along with a distinctive hooter. Two pairs of boiler bands were heavy-handedly embossed.

It was the front end of the loco that had the best features, among them the neatly made parallel smokebox, and details such as the steam pipes, well-made smokebox door handles, chromium-plated handrails (a finish unique in the Hornby range), a coupling with three-link chain, and elliptical-headed buffers, not to mention the detailed valve gear, which included a mazac cross-head all too susceptible to 'fatigue'. Both loco and tender buffers (the latter being of the round-headed 'Eton' type) were painted silver to represent polished steel. The front bogie was well made, but the rear pony truck was probably the least satisfactory part of the ensemble since there was no attempt to represent the outside framing. Detachable lamps were specially painted for this loco, in red with white bulls.

The loco was lined out in gold and black, with the splashers lined in gold only. An LMS maker's

One of the first batch of 'Princess Elizabeth' Locos, with serif lettering. There is no maker's plate on the front splasher.

plate transfer was used on the front splasher of all except the first series, and the centre splasher carried the 'Princess Elizabeth' nameplates, with raised brass letters on a black background. On the cabside was the number '6201' and the '7P' power classification, and the tender was lettered 'LMS'. Although the first Hornby 'Princess Elizabeth' locos had unshadowed serif numbers and shadowed serif 'LMS' letters, the majority of the 1937 and later production were lettered and numbered with shadowed sans-serif transfers.

Both cab and tender front had detailed castings, and unlike the No. 2 Special and 'Eton' locos the

gauges, regulator, reversing screw, and water gauges etc. were carefully picked out in colour. In early locos the inside of the cab was finished in a splendid sand colour, a touch of realism omitted from later versions.

Parts of the motor were similar to those in the normal 20 volt automatic reverse mechanism, but the drive was only to the rear driving wheels, through a single intermediate shaft with reduction gearing, a feature not used since the days of the High Voltage Metropolitan. One anomaly occurred in designing the motor; the driving wheels were unequally spaced, with a shorter wheelbase between

front and centre drivers than between centre and rear drivers, whereas on the original LMS loco it was the other way round. The manual reverse switch was clumsily positioned in the right-hand side of the firebox.

The axleboxes of the tender were mazac castings, the centre boxes allowing more free play vertically to allow for unevenness in the rails, and for tight radii; whereas the 'Princess' was at its best on the new Solid Steel Rails, it would also run on 2 ft radius tinplate lines. Like the tender front casting, the buffers, cross-heads and of course the wheels, the axleboxes were subject to 'fatigue', and it is rare to find a 'Princess Elizabeth' with no trace of disintegration.

Several batches were produced. Apart from the colour of the inside of the cab, the later 'Princess Elizabeth' locos differed in having embossed strengthening ridges around the base of the frame underneath the cabside, and on the rear buffer beam of the loco and the front of the tender. Front steps were braced on the later locos. The final batches were matt varnished.

Black 'Princess Elizabeth' locos were made in small numbers.

The very first presentation cases were red with blue baize lining, with the inside simply lettered 'Meccano Ltd Liverpool' and 'Princess Elizabeth'. But later in 1937 the cases were red with a cream baize lining, and had a printed description of the 'Princess' inside the lid. Later still the cases were blue with green baize lining. It should perhaps be mentioned that the 'Princess Elizabeth' is rarely found 'boxed'. The presentation case was packed inside a cardboard box lined with wood wool, and this outer box is usually missing, although owners were advised to keep it in case the loco had to be returned for repairs. There were (at various times) other wooden and cardboard packing pieces inside the presentation case, which again were usually lost.

METROPOLITAN LOCOMOTIVES

The high voltage Metropolitan of 1925 was called simply the 'Hornby Electric Train', since it was the first to go on general sale. It was also the first Hornby 'true-to-type' representation of an actual loco-

A Meccano Ltd publicity photo.

motive, being based on the engines used by the Metropolitan Railway Co. on the service from Baker Street to Rickmansworth. They were Bo-Bo locos, designed for 600 volt third rail operation, and had been delivered to the Metropolitan Railway by Metropolitan Vickers from 1922 onwards following re-building. They were among the very few electric locomotives in use anywhere in Great Britain at the time.

The actual construction of the Hornby loco-motive was quite simple. The body sides were tin-printed to represent the livery of the Metropolitan locos, with maroon body panels contrasted by black and yellow lining. The valances were coloured bright red, and the sides of the base were extended downwards and embossed with axleboxes and leaf springs, and with piercings to form the collector shoe beams. The body was fitted with brass hand-rails, the handrail supports being tiny compared to the type used on the No. 1 and No. 2 locos of the period; they were later to be used for the No. 2 Special Locos. Another striking feature was that brass window surrounds were fitted behind the body, the brass panels also being visible beneath the ventilator louvres cut in the side of the body at the level of the windows. The roof was secured by four knurled-headed screws; the colour of the roof always seems to have been grey rather than the white that was shown on the early Metropolitan set boxes. The motor was remarkable in comparison with the rather

Cab detail of the 'Princess'. The earlier loco with sand-colour cab interior is to the left. (Neither loco has the original wheels at the rear).

feeble design of the earlier No. 2 loco electric motor. It was well engineered and electrically sound; a reduction gearing was provided on the intermediate shaft between the armature shaft pinion and the driving wheel gears. The wheels were not coupled, and did not have the crank-pin bosses drilled out.

The following year, in 1926, the High Voltage No. 1 Metropolitan Loco was withdrawn temporarily from sale on the home market, and was replaced by the No. 2 Metropolitan 4 volt Loco, intended for use with accumulators instead of the mains supply. The 4 volt motor did not have the reduction gearing used on the high voltage motor. Also new in 1926 was the clockwork No. 3 Metropolitan Loco, available only fitted for Hornby Control. It had the same mechanism as the No. 2 Control Loco, and the wheels were fitted with coupling rods. On the clockwork loco the windows at the rear of the loco were not punched out, but simply had holes for the control rods. They were not fitted with the lampholders or the light switches and connections of the electric locos.

The No. 1 Metropolitan Loco went back on sale on the home market in 1927. From early 1928 both clockwork and electric locos were fitted with diecast alloy wheels instead of the cast iron type, and the clockwork mechanisms were fitted with manual brake levers which were not previously provided. From 1928 the No. 1, No. 2 and No. 3 titles were officially changed to the Metropolitan HV, LV and C Locos. The LV Loco was altered from 4 volt to 6 volt in 1929, and the mechanism with protruding brush-caps was fitted, necessitating a large cutout in the side of the loco. The clockwork locos were no longer advertised as being fitted for Hornby Control, and presumably the change to a non-Control motor was made at this time. By the early 1930s the clockwork Metropolitan was being fitted with the No. 2 Special mechanism, with special deep brackets allowing the mechanism to be sunk into the body so that the large wheels (still fitted with coupling rods on the clockwork locos only) did not obtrude

below the level of the frame. This necessitated the keyhole being moved up into the centre of the panelling.

From 1934, the electric LV Metropolitan (now sold as the E36 Metropolitan Loco) was fitted with a mechanism of the E120 Special type, with flat-sided brush-holders, but wound for 6 volt operation and without the automatic reversing equipment. The No. 1 Special size driving wheels were still fitted to the electric locos, and the bosses were still not drilled out for coupling rods.

In 1938–39 E320 Metropolitan Locos with 20 volt automatic reverse motors were sold as an alternative to the E36 version. The E120 Special motor was used, often fitted with red wheels. The locos had still not been fitted with automatic couplings, a peculiarity which distinguished them from the other Hornby types.

All the Metropolitan trains were withdrawn from sale in 1939. Apart from minor alterations to the body to accommodate different mechanisms,

A No. 1 HV Metropolitan Train, circa 1927.

there was remarkably little change in the appearance of the Metropolitan between the start and the end of production. From July 1933 control of the Metropolitan Railway had passed to the London Passenger Transport Board, but the change of livery to 'London Transport' was never effected by Meccano Ltd, nor was the naming of the original Metropolitan loco in 1927.

SWISS TYPE LOCOMOTIVES

The LEC1 clockwork and LE1/20 electric locos were introduced in the 1932 catalogues, as being 'modelled on the type in use on the Swiss Federal Railways'; they were said to be 'tastefully enamelled in a rich shade of green with a grey roof'. French-type Locos had been designed (for sale in France only) the previous year, in both clockwork and electric versions, although only the electric version was actually made. The bodies of the Swiss-type Locos were virtually the same as those of the French-type locos, with the difference that the Swiss-type loco sides were cut away below the level of the frame, and they

were not fitted with air cylinders under the ends of the cab although slots for fitting the cylinders were often present. No. 3 Loco steps were added under each cab door. The locos had the French-type pantographs that could be raised or lowered. The roof colour was dark grey on the Swiss-type loco, and the transfers were quite different from the French-type. French 'PO' and 'E.31' plates were replaced by one plate with dummy writing and another with the number '10655'. The electric loco had the '20V' lettering used on the French loco but not the 'lightning flash' warning sign transfer. Normal English trademark transfers were applied, usually on the back of the loco; the front end of the electric loco was fitted with a bulbholder, and the bottom of one side was notched to clear the horizontally-arranged brush-caps of the French-type 20V mechanism. Both LEC1 and LE1/20 Locos had round-headed buffers, not oval-headed.

The LEC1 Loco had a specially adapted No. 1 Loco mechanism, with a spring guard fitted to both sideplates (much taller than the post-1937 spring guard for the steam-outline locos). This was necessary to prevent the roof being pushed off as the spring

expanded! The push-fit roof was an unfortunate feature since a great many roofs came adrift and were lost or damaged. The clockwork mechanism was fitted with normal 8-spoke coupled wheels, but the electric motor was in many cases supplied with non-coupled wheels, of the normal 8-spoke pattern but with the crank-pin holes not drilled out.

From 1933 the LE1/20 and LEC1 locos were made with a choice of four new liveries, among the most colourful in the Hornby range; either a blue body with red steps and yellow roof, or a red body with green steps and cream roof, or a cream body with red roof and green steps, or a green body with cream roof and red steps. These liveries continued for all subsequent production.

In 1934 the price of the LEC1 was cut from 15s to 12s 6d, and to 10s 6d in 1935, the last year it was sold. From 1934 the clockwork loco was supplied with 12-spoke M3 type non-coupled wheels; late locos had plain rather than cranked automatic couplings. Again in 1934, the electric loco was renamed 'LE120' instead of 'LE1/20', and was fitted with the latest E120 mechanism. The price was cut from 26s 6d to 25s, and again in 1935 to only 20s. 1935 was the last

A No. 2 Metropolitan Train (LV, circa 1926) and a Metropolitan C (clockwork, circa 1928).

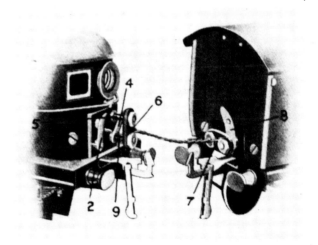

HV coach lighting connectors. The roofs were not made in the form shown for production models.

Four LEC1 Locos, and one LE120, from 1932 to 1936.

year in which the Swiss-type locos were listed in the catalogues, and the price was evidently being cut in order to run down stocks, since the locos were to be withdrawn from sale with effect from September 1936. Their popularity had evidently been limited both on home and export markets, in contrast to the French-type Locos which were best-sellers in France.

LE220 LOCOMOTIVES

The LE2/20 Locomotive was introduced in 1932, and was the largest of the four 20 volt locomotives available at the time. Unusually, it was available only in the electric version and not clockwork-

powered. The 1932–33 colour was dark green with a dark grey roof, and the black base was finished with a red valance. At first the window surrounds were brass. The body was based on that of the Metropolitan loco, but the side plates were cut away below the level of the valance, and steps were fitted under the cab doors. Unlike the Metropolitan Loco, automatic couplings were fitted at each end. The mechanism was of the type used for electric No. 3 Locos, but wound for 20 volts, and the side of the body had cutouts for the brush-holder caps. Pantographs were fitted to the roof. Without outside framing the loco looked incomplete, and in the January 1933 MM the loco was shown with a No. 3 type pony truck at each end, an alteration which

enhanced the appearance considerably, but which was never adopted for production locos.

The transfers for the UK locos were the same as for the Swiss Type, with number 10655. But an interesting export version was also made in Binns Road, using not the Swiss-type but the French-type 'E1.31' transfers, although the 'PO' (Paris–Orleans) section was cut out. This export loco also had the French 'lighting flash' warning sign, but the trademark on the end was the normal English 'Manf'd By' transfer. The valance was not finished red.

From 1933 the LE2/20 was sold in the UK in three new liveries: cream with a Redline-blue roof and baseplate (but still with a red valance), and with

A later LE2/20 Loco in cream, and a red LE220 (automatic reverse) Loco. The No. 3 Footbridge is the final 1933–34 version.

The first version of the LE2/20 Loco.

lighter blue window surrounds; or green with a cream roof; or finally red, also with a cream roof but sporting green window surrounds.

In 1934, automatic reversing versions were sold, called LE220 Locos instead of LE2/20 as before. The price of 33s was unaltered, but the manual reverse LE2/20 loco remained in the 1934–35 Hornby Train Catalogue (though not in any of the other lists) at a reduced price of 25s. Small stocks of the LE2/20 were offered for sale several times in the MM between October 1935 and February 1936, at 25s 9d post free. Although a final attempt was made to stimulate interest in the LE120 and LE220 Locos in the January 1936 MM, it was unavailing, and the locos were withdrawn from sale in September 1936.

Coaches

No. 1 COACHES

Constructional coaches in pre-grouping liveries were sold from 1921, when Hornby Passenger Train Sets were introduced, until 1924 when the clerestory-roof coaches replaced them.

Four liveries were available for the nut-and-bolt coaches; LNWR brown and white, MR red, GN brown, and CR coaches in the GN colours. In each case, the coaches had dark grey roofs, and the bodies were enamelled, having the appropriate company crest transfer on the sides. It is possible that other liveries were planned; the registered design deposition was accompanied by a photograph of an unknown livery, possibly with Great Eastern Railway crests, and this picture was also used in catalogue illustrations.

From early 1922 the coaches were revised to have a shorter wheelbase (although the old holes were still punched in the base, so the coach could be re-assembled by the user with either long or short wheelbase); thick axles of the same diameter as Meccano axle rod were still fitted. Later, probably in late 1922, the detachable axleguards were revised again for thin axles and the roofs were embossed with rain channels.

The Zulu Coaches introduced in May 1922 were identical to the No. 1 Hornby Coaches, except that they had the standard open axleguard base (without detachable axleguards), they were fitted with diecast buffers, and they had no window celluloid. From early 1923, No. 1 Coaches appeared on the same simpler base, and had diecast buffers. Certain later LNWR coaches had tinprinted doors, with the 1st and 3rd class markings printed, rather than having clipped-on brass letters as before.

From 1924 the Zulu Coaches were reduced from 5s to only 4s; at the same time the price of the No. 1 Hornby Coaches fell from 6s 6d to 5s. This latter price reduction was made possible by the introduction of clerestory-roofed non-constructional No. 1 Coach designs. These had three hinged doors each side, and the bodies were tinprinted instead of enamelled, but the roofs were painted dark grey as before. Two liveries were available, LMS red and LNER brown. Matching clerestory-roof Guard's Vans were introduced at the same time, with three opening doors each side, and also with duckets at the rear of each side. The colours were the same, but the company initials did not appear on the Guard's Van sides. In 1925 the prices of No. 1 Coach and Guard's Van fell to only 3s 6d, and the Zulu Coach, which had remained similar to the 1922 design, was no longer listed.

The pregrouping nut-and-bolt coaches: LNWR, CR, GN and MR.

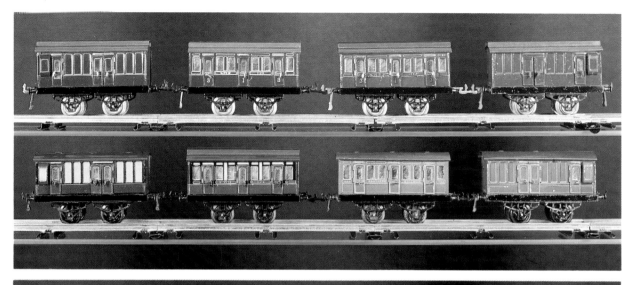

GW Coaches and Guard's Vans in clerestory-roof style, but in appropriate chocolate and cream livery, were sold from 1926. In 1928 SR No. 1 Coaches and Guard's Vans also appeared, but like all the new 1928–29 season No. 1 Coaches the roofs were rounded instead of the clerestory type, and had three embossed ventilators. The price of the coach fell to 2s 6d. Wire door handles with diecast ferrules were fitted from late 1928, then from 1929 each door was hinged on a single long wire instead of two short wires as before, and plain wire door handles were used.

The solebars on the base were crimped from 1931, to reduce the coupling height to the new standard, since automatic couplings were fitted; but the open axleguards and short wheelbase were unchanged. Several tinprinting differences arose as successive batches of coach sides were printed; LMS Coach doors were now marked '1' and '3' only, whereas before they had also been marked 'first' and 'third' in full. From 1932, new printings of the SR coach were numbered 2891 instead of 1728, and SR Guard's Van doors were no longer lettered 'Guard' as before.

In the 1933–34 season, cream roofs were fitted instead of dark grey, and coloured bases began to appear; green on LNER, GW and SR coaches and red on LMS coaches.

As early as November 1931 the MM had hinted that new designs were being considered, and they were completed in 1932. But it was not until 1934 that the new-style No. 1 Coach and Guard's Van went on sale. These were larger than the previous coaches, were not fitted with opening doors, and the sides were printed with 4 compartments. The solebars were folded to form a continuous foot-board, and the base was fitted with a battery box and with axleboxes. Both Coach and Guard's Van had a pair of lamp irons at each end, and lamps were supplied. Four liveries were available, in much the same colours as before except that the LNER coaches were printed to simulate the woodgrain finish of that company's vehicles. In each case the base was black and the close-fitting roof was grey. Because of the width of the Guard's Van the duckets were necessarily thin, and not printed with windows as before, although windows were printed on the front and back of the Guard's Van in addition to the normal details of steps and handrails etc. Apart from slight variations in the tinprinting, there were no further changes except for the matt finish used for post-1939 bases.

After the war, No. 1 Coaches and Passenger Brake Vans (the postwar name for the Guard's Van) were manufactured for the 101 Passenger Train Set from late in 1946. Early postwar coaches are virtually indistinguishable from prewar except for the lighter-grey roofs. Coaches were sold separately from 1948, and from late 1948 the spaces in the axleguards either side of the leafsprings were no longer pierced. No. 1 Coaches and Passenger Brake Vans were still made in all four liveries in 1948, but from 1949 onwards LMS and LNER coaches are the only ones commonly found. The shade of the tinprinting, particularly of the LNER coaches, varied quite noticeably, with some early examples quite pale but most post-1950 examples much darker.

In 1954 BR livery coaches appeared; the No. 41 Coach and Passenger Brake Van, in BR crimson representing suburban stock, and the cream and crimson No. 51 1st Class Coach, 3rd Class Coach and Passenger Brake Van. The LNER No. 1 Coach remained on sale until 1959, and the NE Passenger Brake Van up to 1957. They were cheaper, at 5s 8d against 6s 6d for the BR coaches in 1954. Since a batch of boxes for NE No. 1 Coaches was printed in May 1955, it seems that NE coaches were still being made (at the same time as the BR coaches) rather than just being catalogued until old stocks ran out.

From circa 1957–58, the colour of the bases of both No. 41 and No. 51 Coaches and Passenger Brake Vans was altered to glossy black instead of matt black.

No. 2 PASSENGER COACHES

No. 2 Passenger Coaches were introduced in 1935, and were the first Hornby compartment-stock bogie coaches, discounting the Metropolitan. Two vehicles were produced for each of the four railway companies, one 1st/3rd and the other Brake/3rd. At 7s 6d they were three times the price of the No. 1 Coaches. In shape and style they were more or less a double-length version of the No. 1 Coach, having a longer base, and being mounted on compensating bogies with Mansell wheels. The Brake/3rd coaches were fitted with lookouts for the guard, and windows were printed at the rear end. Lamp brackets were provided at the back and front of both 1st/3rd and Brake/3rd Coaches, and the appropriate tail lamp was provided; aluminium with a dark red bull for LMS and red with a dark red bull for the others. Liveries were generally similar to the No. 1 Coaches, although the GW coaches sported the latest round GWR monogram instead of the 'GWR' lettering of the No. 1 Coaches. All the coach roofs were enamelled grey 'to represent the average condition of a coach roof in actual service'. As on the No. 1 Coaches, ventilators were embossed on the roofs.

All the coaches were lined out to some extent, and there was a minor inconsistency between the Southern Railway 1st/3rd and Brake/3rd liveries, the door windows of the 1st/3rd being lined out in yellow.

There were few intended variations in prewar days, apart from the matt finish bases and riveted couplings used from 1939, and the usual tinprinting shade differences (the LMS and LNER colours being particularly variable); but there were quite a few unintended variations. The common assembly errors on both prewar and postwar No. 2 Brake/3rd Coaches were to fit two left-hand or two right-hand sides, or to fit duckets to ordinary 1st/3rd Coach sides.

After the war, the No. 2 Coaches were catalogued in 1948 and 1949. The full range of four liveries, each in both Brake/3rd and 1st/3rd versions, was produced. The main difference between the prewar and the postwar production was the roof colour, which was a distinctly lighter grey on the postwar coaches. The 1948–49 coaches also had trademark transfers on the bottom of the accumulator boxes, and postwar Mansell wheels were finished all black, without the white rims of prewar days, and happily free of 'fatigue' problems. Couplings were all riveted, and the bases matt, exactly as on the late prewar coaches, and the tinprinting was indistinguishable. Once again, there was a certain variability in shade, for the LNER coaches in particular which varied from pale to moderately dark. The

Prewar LMS, NE and GW No. 2 Passenger Coaches, and postwar SR No. 2 Coaches

price in 1948 was 12s 6d against 4s 3d for the No. 1 Coach. The last listing was in October 1949, but it is unlikely that there was any production apart from a large single batch in 1948. The printer's codes on the boxes (printed June 1948) suggest about 3,300 1st/3rd and 3,300 Brake/3rd No. 2 Coaches may have been made.

No. 2 CORRIDOR COACHES

No. 2 Corridor Coaches were introduced in 1937, in the colours of each of the four railway groups. The body pressings were identical to those of the No. 2 Passenger Coaches except that the ends were cut out, to fit the standard Hornby corridor connections and corridor end plates which were supplied with each coach. Clips for Hornby Train Name Boards were fitted to the white roofs of the LNER, GW and SR coaches; and above the windows on the LMS coaches, which had the same grey roofs as the No. 2 Passenger Coaches. Each coach had lamp brackets, and tail lamps were provided.

There were two versions for each railway company, one being a brake coach. Unlike the No. 2 Passenger Coaches the guard's ducket was not a separate component clipped on.

The LMS and GW 1st/3rd Corridor Coaches represented steel-sided flush-panelled stock. The LNER 1st/3rd Corridor Coaches were in woodgrain finish, with the panelling effectively represented, and interestingly with doors on the compartment side as well as the corridor side, unknown on our present-day railways. The SR Coach was a 3rd-class centre-corridor saloon, not a 1st/3rd side corridor coach like the others, and it was the only Corridor Coach to have identical left-hand and right-hand sides.

LMS, NE and SR Brake/Composites had both 1st and 3rd class compartments, while the GW version was Brake/3rd only. The SR Brake/Composite Corridor Coach was of the side-corridor pattern, and the door window surrounds were finished red, whereas the 3rd Class SR Corridor Coach had door window surrounds in plain green, making the overall appearance quite dull.

The price of the No. 2 Corridor Coaches when introduced was 7s 6d, the No. 2 Passenger Coach price being reduced in the same year to 6s 6d. Although the No. 2 Corridor Coaches were too short to be really satisfactory for use with the better class Hornby Locos, they were good value for money compared to the cheapest alternative corridor stock, the No. 2 Pullmans or Saloon Coaches at 9s 6d. It was unfortunate that the discrepancy in size and finish between Pullmans and No. 2 Corridor Coaches was such as to make them look ridiculous if run in the same train, and perhaps sooner or later a tinprinted Pullman car might have appeared had the war not intervened.

There were few variations during the life of these coaches, although they were made in large numbers in several batches, because of their popularity. Riveted couplings (instead of the earlier fixing by eyelets) and matt bases are signs of 1939 or later production. Some late prewar or wartime SR Corridor Coaches were supplied with grey LMS-type roofs without roof clips. The No. 2 Corridor Coaches were not produced after the war.

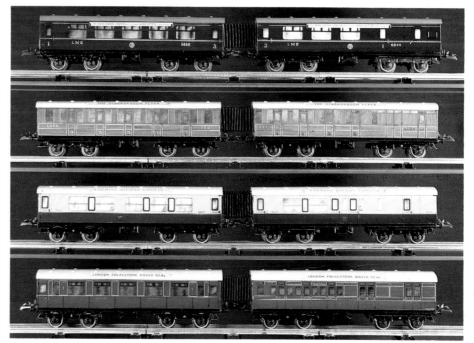

No. 2 Corridor Coaches, from one side . . .   *. . . and the other.*

No. 1 PULLMAN COACHES

Ugliness is hardly an adequate word to describe the No. 1 Pullman Coaches introduced in 1928. They were curiously out of tune with the other noteworthy 1928 introductions, such as the grand new No. 2–3 Pullmans, and their gross lack of proportion and total lack of charm combined to make them the worst three-shillings worth in the HBT.

Opening doors were fitted in the recessed vestibule ends, which were embossed lightly to show where the corridor connections should have been. The windows were pierced, but no celluloids were fitted; the livery was tinprinted, the lower part of the sides in brown with imitation wood panelling, and the upper part in cream. 'Pullman' lettering was printed on the cream fascia boards above the windows. Coaches were named 'Cynthia', 'Corsair' and 'Niobe', and there was a No. 1 Pullman Composite named 'Ansonia' which was fitted with twin opening luggage doors on each side. The No. 1 Pullman Coach and Composite were each priced at

3s when introduced.

From 1929 the door handles were changed, from wire handles with diecast ferrules to plain wire; and from 1930 the colour of the roof was changed from cream to grey. Automatic couplings were fitted from 1931, and 'Aurora' became the usual name for the Composite; 'Corsair', 'Cynthia' and 'Niobe' were still the Coach names.

The 1933–34 No. 1 Pullmans were finished with coloured bases and roofs; 'Niobe' with blue base and roof, 'Corsair' and 'Cynthia' with green base and roof, 'Aurora' and later 'Cynthia' with red bases and roofs. The bases were punched with axlebox slots, rather strangely since no boxes were fitted. Later in the same season, the coaches were made with the same colour roofs but with black bases.

Late in 1934 or early in 1935, the roof colour changed back again to cream, and the designs were simplified, with non-opening doors. In the new style both 'Ansonia' and 'Aurora' composites were available, as well as 'Corsair', 'Cynthia' and 'Niobe'.

There was a small price drop to 2s 9d in the 1935–36 catalogues because of the simplifications. There were few further variations, except that certain post-1936 No. 1 Pullmans were fitted with axleboxes, instead of just the slots. After the war it was obviously felt that Britain had suffered enough without reviving this unsatisfactory monstrosity.

BOGIE PULLMAN COACHES

The first No. 2 Hornby Pullman Train Sets of 1921 contained two bogie coaches, one a Pullman Car and the other a Dining Saloon. Both were finished in green and cream livery, and were constructional. (Incidentally, like many other constructional items the bolts used were usually shorter than the standard Meccano type.) Four different versions of the Dining Saloon were made, one for each of the different train sets (LNWR, MR, CR and GN). They were distinguished by the company crest on the centre of the coach side. The Pullman Car had fine (although perhaps rather large) Pullman Car Company crests each side of the 'Pullman' lettering. The earliest coaches had cream-painted window surrounds matching the upper panel of the coach.

By December 1921 the window surrounds were being enamelled in gold instead of cream, but apart from that there were no major changes until the doors of the coaches were altered from fixed to hinged, probably late in 1923. The opening doors were at first fitted with miniature celluloids clipped behind each door window, as well as having the normal saloon window celluloids. The Dining Saloon was no longer made with the pre-grouping railway company crests, but the 'Pullman' crest was used instead in the same central position between the 'Dining' and 'Saloon' lettering transfers. A minor change was that the steps and gas cylinders were now painted green instead of black.

Soon the hinged doors were altered to omit the punching-out of the window, and the clips for the door window celluloid. The doors were instead tinprinted to give a similar appearance, with a lilac window criss-crossed with a black grid. These coaches (probably dating from early 1924) usually had thin axles, although thick axles were occasionally used later.

In 1925, new transfers were prepared for the

Pullman Car, and the Dining Saloon was no longer made. These new 'Pullman' transfers had a scrolled gold lining around the 'Pullman' name, forming what was in effect a name panel. These transfers were used for a while on the green and cream coaches, but later in 1925 the livery changed to brown and cream. Although some brown and cream coaches had plain brown-enamelled doors, most were fitted with tinprinted doors which had a lilac window panel and circular lining below the window. The window celluloids began to be printed with table lamps (as well as the blinds already printed), in two different versions; on one the lamps had silver stands and plain red shades, and on the other the lamps had red stands and red shades printed with black 'pleating'. The final 1927–28 versions of the brown and cream No. 2 Pullman Coach had door panels tinprinted with very pale windows.

The No. 3 Pullman Train Sets of 1927 were supplied with a new type of Pullman Car, based on the body of the Riviera 'Blue Train' Coach but with important modifications to the windows, which also required the roof supports to be in a different posi-

tion from those of the Riviera Coach. The wide window surrounds were embossed, rather than being clipped on in many sections like those of the No. 2 Pullman, and were hand-finished in gold paint. Corridor connections and brown corridor end plates were provided with each coach. The large size and the flat sides of the new No. 3 Pullman represented the vehicles of the Pullman Car Company much better than the No. 2 type, which had tumblehome. Transfers were the same, and the brown and cream livery was unchanged. Both Pullmans were available concurrently, the No. 3 at 16s 6d and the No. 2 at 12s 6d, although it is probable that production of the No. 2 Pullman was not continued for long.

In 1928 the No. 3 Pullman Coach was substantially re-designed. The old No. 2 Pullmans were no longer listed, and the revised coaches were renamed 'No. 2–3 Pullman Coaches', taking the place of the No. 2 and No. 3 Pullmans in the sets. The new coaches had smaller, better-proportioned windows, with more elegant narrow surrounds, still hand-finished gold; surprisingly the Coach had no kitchen area with 'frosted glass' celluloids as on the Riviera

Blue Train dining cars. Different doors were designed, with oval windows and with wire handles in realistic diecast ferrules (also used for other 1928–29 coaches). Square accumulator boxes under the coach replaced the gas cylinders. Diecast oval-headed buffers were fitted, hand-finished red on the earliest 1928 versions. The tops of the sides were channelled to take the snap-on roof, which was a great advance over the previous design, with embossed detail and tinplate ventilators at the ends. Diecast ventilators were also fitted, finished in blue-grey to contrast with the cream of the roof.

In addition to the No. 2–3 Pullman Coaches, No. 2–3 Pullman Composite Coaches with opening luggage doors were also available. Composites were named 'Arcadia' and the Coaches 'Iolanthe'; the 'Pullman' lettering was above the windows. Compensating bogies were provided, fitted with heavy diecast Mansell wheels. Most surprisingly the prices of the improved No. 2–3 Pullman Coach and Composite were only 11s 6d.

In 1929 there were some minor changes; the buffers were no longer finished red, the wire door handles were fitted without the diecastings, and the diecast roof ventilators were changed to a larger size. The price remained at 11s 6d. Two extra sets of transfers were made, for 'Zenobia' Coaches and 'Alberta' Composites.

For the following 1930–31 season, the No. 3 Pullman Coach of 1927–28 was made again after a two year break, and was re-named the No. 2 Pullman Coach. It sold at 11s 6d. The No. 2–3 Pullmans were re-named the No. 2 Special Pullman Coach and Composite, and prices increased to 15s for the

An interesting transitional version of the No. 2–3 Pullman; the later transfer on an earlier coach body.

Coach and 16s for the Composite.

The No. 2 Pullmans were almost identical to the old No. 3 versions, but had small drop-link couplings and wire door handles, and gold lining bands on the doors. Meccano-type brass buffers were still fitted. The 'Pullman' transfers were exactly as on the old No. 3 Pullmans.

The No. 2 Special Pullman livery was changed early in 1930, with the fascia boards painted brown instead of cream, and the roof colour changed to grey 'as the white roofs of Pullman Cars quickly become discoloured by smoke and appear dark' according to the MM. No extra details, such as lamp brackets, were added. The No. 2 Pullman roofs remained in cream. There were two new names for the No. 2 Special Pullman in addition to the four already available: 'Grosvenor' Coaches and 'Montana' Composites.

From 1931 the ends of the No. 2 and No. 2 Special Pullmans were changed, with diecast round-headed buffers fitted to both, and the steps altered since the fitting of automatic couplings required the non-compensating bogies of the No. 2 and the compensating bogies of the No. 2 Special to be mounted closer to the ends, because of the coupling control wires. Destination board clips were added to the roofs of the No. 2 Special Pullmans, and their Mansell wheels were lightened by hollowing out the back.

On revised transfers for the No. 2 Pullman Coach the Pullman crests were replaced by the smaller No. 2 Special Pullman crests, lettered 'Forward'; in fact the motto of the LNER, although according to the MM '. . . designs were based on particulars furnished to us by the Pullman Car Co. Ltd'. The 'Pullman' name panel on the No. 2 Pullman Coaches was changed to black just before the crests were changed. From about 1936 the name panel was altered again to brown, although the gold border was black-lined.

In 1932–33 the No. 2 Special Composite Coaches were altered so that the cream band along the windows was no longer extended over the luggage section. The 1934–35 HBT showed that 'Iolanthe' had been replaced by 'Loraine', and the following year the 1935–36 catalogues showed 'Verona' replacing 'Arcadia'; the six transfers in use at that time were 'Alberta', 'Montana', 'Verona',

'Zenobia', 'Grosvenor' and 'Loraine'. At no time did the catalogues offer more than 6 of the 8 names. There were no major changes to the No. 2 Special Pullman during later production.

The No. 2 Pullman Coach was fitted with axleboxes and Mansell wheels on the non-compensating bogies for the 1936–37 and subsequent seasons.

SALOON COACHES

When the 1927–28 No. 3 Pullman Coaches were re-introduced in 1930 as the No. 2 Pullman, they were also offered in two non-Pullman liveries, LMS red and LNER brown, representing 1st class end-vestibule centre-corridor Saloon Coaches. No GW or SR versions were offered. Apart from finish, the coach bodies were exactly the same as the No. 2 Pullman and followed the same pattern of changes. Corridor connections and corridor end plates were supplied. As for the No. 2 Pullman, the price of the Saloon Coaches was reduced from the original 11s 6d in 1930 to only 9s 6d in 1934, reflecting the simplicity of their construction.

Both coaches were enamel finished, with grey roofs. The LMS red Saloon Coaches were lettered in gold (shadowed red), and they carried the LMS crest on the side as well as coach number 402. The brown LNER Saloon Coaches were lettered in gold (shadowed dark blue), and were numbered 137. They had no LNER company crest.

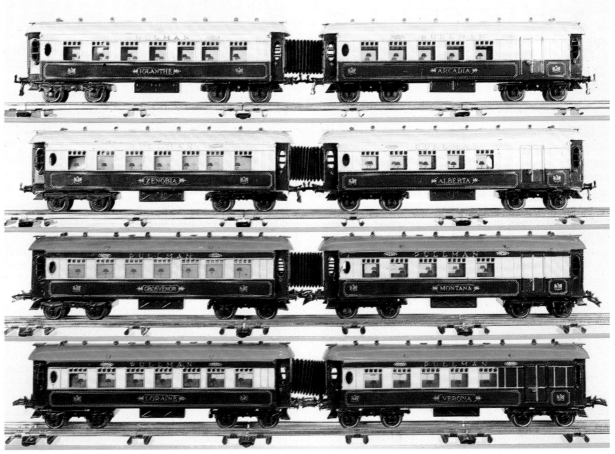

No. 2–3 and No. 2 Special Pullman Coaches and Composites.

164

At first Meccano brass buffers were fitted, but in 1931 the ends were changed as on the No. 2 Pullman, with shorter steps, diecast round-headed buffers, and with automatic couplings, the non-compensating bogies being moved further outwards because of the coupling control wires.

From 1936 the bogies were fitted with axleboxes, and with Mansell wheels instead of the tin wheels used before. Otherwise there were no major changes, although by then the LNER Saloon Coaches had revised transfers with gold letters shadowed red as on the LMS version, but still with no company crest. As on the No. 2 and No. 2 Special Pullmans the trademark transfers were of the same types used for wagons.

RIVIERA BLUE TRAIN COACHES

Riviera 'Blue Train' Coaches were first made in 1926, and were a breakthrough both in their substantial size and in other features; for instance they were the first with corridor connections, later adopted for many other coaches. The corridor end plates for the Riviera 'Blue Train' coaches differed from those of other coaches in being nickel plated instead of enamelled. All the 'Blue Train' Coaches were finished in dark blue, with cream roofs, and had impressively realistic lettering and lining transfers in gold. There were two versions, one a dining car with window celluloids printed with a 'frosted glass' kitchen section and with silver and red table lamps in the dining section; and the other was a sleeping car with plain yellow window celluloids.

Although the livery was never changed, there were a few alterations apart from the usual minor details of trademarks, door handles etc. From 1931, the coaches were fitted with compensating bogies instead of the previous non-compensating type, at the same time as the change to automatic couplings was made. Also, the bogies were moved closer to the coach ends, necessitating shortening the steps under the doors. At the same time the Meccano brass buffers were replaced by round-headed diecast buffers. But these were the only noteworthy changes during the long life of these popular coaches.

MITROPA COACHES

The October 1931 MM mentioned the availability of the No. 3 Mitropa Coaches, which rather unusually had not been included in any of the 1931–32 season catalogues. They were finished in 'Crawford's red' enamel, with a black baseplate and black gas cylinders; the roof was white, and the body was lettered 'Mitropa' in gold. A transfer with the eagle crest of the Mitropa company was applied between the centre windows. There were two different versions of the Mitropa Coach, the 'Speisewagen' (dining car) and the 'Schlafwagen' (sleeping car). The bodies were identical to the Riviera 'Blue Train' Coaches, and the same window celluloids were used. The No. 3 Mitropa Coaches were always fitted with automatic couplings, and compensating bogies with Mansell wheels.

The first versions were hand-finished in black over the red of the ends, although the diecast round-headed buffers were left in red. Corridor connections and end plates were supplied with each coach. Later in the 1930s both sleeping and dining cars were supplied with the ends left in red. A few coaches were without the eagle transfers, probably as a result of a slip up in the factory. There were no further changes; the price fell steadily from 15s 6d when introduced to 10s 6d by 1939. The Mitropa Coaches were never very popular in the UK, possibly because there was no appropriate steam loco to haul them.

No. 0 Mitropa Coaches were also available from 1931; they were finished in red with white roofs as

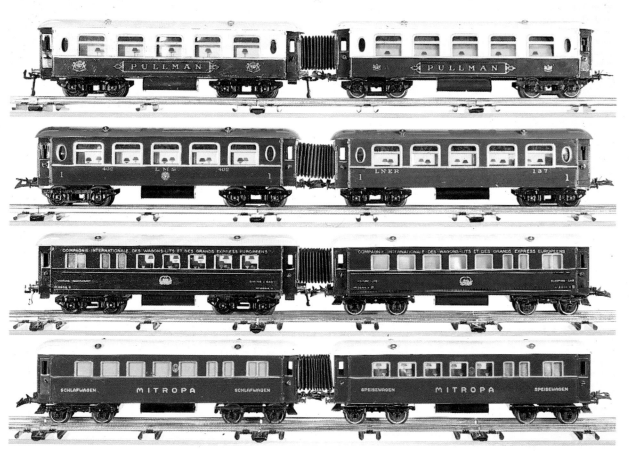

No. 3 Pullman (1927), No. 2 Pullman (1938), LMS Saloon, LNER Saloon (both circa 1935), Riviera Dining Car (1929) and Sleeping Car (1936), and Mitropa Sleeping (1931) and Dining (circa 1935) Cars.

There were two coach names, 'Washington' and 'Madison', each on yellow and on green coaches, making four types in all. Each had a grey roof. Most of these coaches were packed in normal red Hornby boxes, but some were later packed in matt blue M-type boxes, and others in orange-coloured cartons with 'Imported from USA. Product of Meccano Factories' added to the normal wording; this description also appeared in early catalogues. On many early grey-roofed coaches the 'Made in USA' part of the trademark was obliterated in matching paint, though later it was allowed to appear.

Automatic couplings were fitted from 1931, and in 1933 there was a change in the colour of the base and roof; yellow-bodied 'Madison' and 'Washington' had orange bases and orange roofs, while green-bodied 'Madison' and 'Washington' probably had red bases and red roofs. Some transitional versions of 'Madison' and 'Washington' with green bodies had red roofs but black bases, and the yellow-bodied coaches probably had orange roofs but black bases. The tinprinting was unchanged, and the trademarks still read 'Hornby Lines. Made in USA' as before, although there were a few with 'Hornby Series. Made in USA' markings.

By 1936 there were new tinprintings, with green-sided 'Washington' and yellow-sided 'Madison' (the other two combinations may possibly have been made); the roofs were cream and the bases black. By then the tinprinted trademarks, and the descriptions in the catalogues, no longer referred to the coaches as being imported from the USA.

METROPOLITAN COACHES

The Metropolitan Coaches which were sold in the Hornby Electric Train Set in 1925 were based on the No. 2 Pullman Car body, but with alterations to make them much more realistic in style. The sides were lithographed in brown, with a rich wood-grain finish, and were produced in two versions, 1st/3rd and Brake/3rd. Windows were cut out from each compartment, and celluloid strips in plain translucent yellow were inserted behind the windows. One agreeable feature was the provision of well-modelled trussing for the underframe. The roofs were finished in dark grey enamel; but some early HV coaches had roofs sprayed white, with the dark

'Speisewagen' and 'Schlafwagen'. The method of manufacturing the first series was unusual; the coach bodies were of the US type, and the Mitropa livery was obtained by spraying 'Crawford's red' through masks covering the doors and windows of 'Washington' and 'Madison' tinprinted coach sides. Thus the US livery was obliterated while leaving the door and window details still showing. Mitropa gold lettering transfers were then applied on the enamel. The shade of red varied depending on whether the coach was red over green or red over yellow! The price of the No. 0 Mitropa Coach when introduced was 1s 6d, the same as for the US Pullman Car.

In the mid 1930s the coach sides were enamelled overall in red, on plain tinplate, then hand-finished

with gold enamel lining and lettered with the same transfers as before. In the later 1930s the No. 0 Mitropa Coaches were tinprinted, still in both dining car and sleeping car versions.

AMERICAN-TYPE COACHES

The American-type Pullman Cars were included in the 1930 UK Meccano products and Hornby Train catalogues. Early coaches had printed trademarks reading 'Hornby Lines. Made in USA', although it is not clear whether the coaches were actually imported complete and re-packaged, or were made up from imported tinprinted sheets (possibly using the Meccano Inc. press tools); like so much else, the answer seems to have been lost in the mists of time.

Wagons

grey as a second coat on top, suggesting that there were last-minute second thoughts about sending out sets with white roofs as shown on the set box lids.

The first HV Metropolitan Coaches were connected to the loco by large and obtrusive plugs (combined with switches) in each coach end, for the internal lighting, and the same connectors joined the other coaches in the train, each being supplied with a connector and the appropriate light bulbs. HV Coaches were discontinued in 1929.

The LV Coaches introduced in 1926 were usually lighted by a different method; instead of the plug and socket connection from the loco, each coach had a bogie fitted with a spring-loaded roller pickup, unfortunately of such small diameter as to cause a certain embarrassment at points and crossings. The light switches were bulky levers mounted inside the coaches and protruding through slots in the roofs. The clockwork coaches, available from 1926, were not of course fitted with lighting gear.

The appearance of the coaches hardly changed at all during their period of production, particularly since they were never fitted with automatic couplings but retained small drop-links, and some 1938 coaches were still fitted with the nickel-plated wheels abandoned for the rest of the range since 1926! They were also the last vehicles to have Meccano-type brass buffers, since diecast buffers were never fitted. There were one or two small changes, such as the addition of axleboxes to the bogies in 1936, but the tinprinted 'Hornby Series' trademarks on the coach sides were never changed.

When new and shiny, the Metropolitan Coaches were very handsome. Although they were not suitable for use with most of the other Hornby rolling stock, the MM recommended its readers several times to use them to represent the suburban coaches of the LNER. Quite why no different tinprintings in other liveries were made for other railway companies it is difficult to see.

THE AMERICAN-TYPE WAGONS

Three US type Hornby Wagons were introduced in the UK for the 1930–31 season, after the closure of the American Factory, and were advertised as being 'modelled on the types in use on the American railways'. The first Cabooses and Box Cars were marked 'Hornby Lines' and 'Made in USA' (although the latter marking was usually painted out). Since no designs appear to have been drawn up in Liverpool before March 1931, it is possible that tools from the Elizabeth NJ factory were used for the early production, or that tools were produced from the American drawings.

The Caboose featured an open platform at each end, with railings, and what was officially described as a 'monitor' was mounted on top of the roof. The body was tinprinted in green and yellow, and was lettered to represent a New York Central Railroad wagon. The roof was orange.

The Box Car had a yellow and black tinprinted body, 'representing the type in use on the Pennsylvania Railroad'. Sliding doors were mounted on the outside of the body, with runners at top and bottom. The brown roof was fitted with a central cat walk, and a brake wheel was mounted to a shaft running from base to roof.

The Tank Car had a large red tinprinted tank, and represented the cars used by the Union Tank Car Company for bulk oil transport. The tank was fitted with a large red 'manhole cover', and was mounted

Tank Cars, Box Cars and Cabooses. Circa 1930–33 (top row), 1933–36 (second row) and 1936–41 (third row).

on two cradles. The US-type wagon base was common to all the wagons and coaches in the series, with minor tooling differences for the various bodies.

The 1933 colour changes brightened up the wagons; although the tinprinted parts were unchanged, the colour of the base was changed to green for the Tank Car, orange for the Box Car and red for the Caboose. The new roof colours were red (with a green monitor) for the Caboose, and orange (with a green cat walk) for the Box Car. The Tank Car manhole cover was now enamelled in green.

In 1936, the colour of the bases reverted to black, but the other colours were unchanged. Matt black bases were used from 1939. Although these wagons looked out of place in a train with any of the normal Hornby range, they had sold quite well, presumably because they were inexpensive.

BARREL WAGONS

The Barrel Wagon was one of the new types introduced for the 1931–32 season. It was sold as a Continental-type wagon, price 2s 9d; indeed it bore little resemblance to anything that ran on the British railways, although there was a far from coincidental resemblance to a wagon designed by Bing. The long thin wagon base was used, crimped along the sides to reduce the coupling height; automatic couplings were always fitted, and the colour of the base was always red. Four barrels were secured by two chains with a connecting link in the middle, and two protruding nail heads in each barrel clipped onto the wagon base. Following the Bing precedent, the barrels were made of wood rather than of tinplate; they were enamelled in plain blue, with five black lining bands, and there was no attempt to reproduce planking or bungs. The barrels were never available separately.

A central tin clip was designed in November

1931, to enable the chain to be brought down more tightly over the barrels, so that the nails and the short connecting link were no longer needed. The blue barrels were lined in yellow instead of black from 1932, then from 1933 a choice of barrel colours became available; either yellow or green, both black-lined. The choice of colour was not mentioned in the catalogues.

By the middle of 1935, a new type of Barrel Wagon was being made, using the revised No. 1 Coach base, but without the battery box. This '1935 type' Barrel Wagon had wider-spaced supports, with lugs on the side, which seated the barrels more firmly (although not quite firmly enough!) on the base. A single chain replaced the two used previously, and it was secured by a hook at one end, and a spring at the other. The chains on the old version had been awkward to release and re-fit, and were easily broken, with the result that loose barrels rolling around the carpet became a normal operating hazard; on the new type loading and unloading was less troublesome.

Later, paper discs printed with the 'Castrol' trademark were added to the ends of the barrels, to lend verisimilitude to this improbable wagon. These were first shown in the 1937 catalogues, although the discs had been designed as early as October 1935. There was still a choice of yellow or green barrels up to 1941.

Improbable or not, this remained one of the best-selling Hornby wagons, because of the colourful appearance and the attractive removable load. It did not, however, re-appear after the war.

BITUMEN TANK WAGONS

The Colas Bitumen Tank Wagon was a happy idea for extending the use of the tooling prepared for the United Dairies Milk Tank Wagon. It was included in the 1929 catalogues; at first the price was given mistakenly as 2s 6d, although later advertisements showed the correct price of 5s. This was sixpence cheaper than the Milk Tank Wagon, since the ladder, and the special inlet and outlet castings were omitted. The bracing wires were also simpler, with nuts only at the top end. The wagon was enamelled in blue, with two hand-painted black bands on the

A group of Barrel Wagons at a No. 1 Goods Platform of 1939 vintage.

'Colas' Bitumen Tank Wagons.

tank, and red end-stays. The 'Colas' transfers were in bright yellow and black, making the wagon very colourful and attractive.

When the revised wagon base was adopted in 1930, the wagon number transfers were moved from the solebars to the tank ends. From 1931 automatic couplings were fitted. The colour was changed to lighter blue from 1933, and there were some simplifications; the wires were secured to the end-stays by gagging, instead of by circular nuts as before, and when the outlet drain cocks no longer appeared on the UD tanker, the bumps on the Colas tank ends disappeared as well. From 1936, the colour of the tank was changed to red, and the end stays and the base were finished in blue. The catalogues were

reticent on the colour change to the point of complete silence, although references to being 'finished in blue' soon disappeared. An odd feature of the red Colas tanker was that many were made with the filler mounted transversely, instead of lengthways along the tank. 1939 saw the issue of the final version, with the base in black, but still with blue end-stays and a red tank. The Bitumen Tank Wagon was not made after the war.

Had the Bitumen Tank Wagon been finished in the Petrol or Oil Tank Wagon liveries, it would have made a good 'special' series of wagons, less toy-like and more representative of real railway practice; but no plans for such a development were ever made, probably because of high cost and consequent low demand.

BRAKE VANS

The Great Northern and the London and North Western Brake Vans were first advertised in the May–June 1922 MM. They were of course an essential wagon for every Hornby railway, in the days when loose-coupled goods trains were the norm, and the guard used his brakes to help to stop the train, or to hold it in check on downward gradients. A smoky stove was a usual fitting in the van, and although the stove was not reproduced in the Hornby wagon, the chimney in the roof was a standard feature.

Hornby GN Brake Vans were finished in brown, with a black base and a white roof. They were double-ended, with hinged doors and large single windows at each end. The LNW vans were grey, with black base and white roof, and the body was single-ended, with hinged doors at one end and pairs of smaller windows at each end. Curiously, there was no open door in the partition between the ends of the van and the cabin, in either case. Both LNW and GN versions had stencil-sprayed lettering in white. The construction was similar to that of the Luggage Van, assembled by nuts and bolts, although in this case not really intended for constructional use.

The first illustrations showed the Brake Vans on open axleguard bases, but most Brake Vans made in 1922 were fitted with the early wagon base, usually with thin axles. The GN and LNW versions remained on sale in the 1923–24 season, and most of these were on the open axleguard base.

In 1924 the GN and LNW liveries were replaced by LNER and LMS. The LNER van was equivalent to the former GN type but had white 'LNER' transfer letters; the LMS was on the LNW-type body but lettered 'LMS' in large white transfer letters. Both were lettered 'No. 1 Brake Van' on the solebar, which is rather a puzzle since no No. 2 version seems to have been planned. There was, incidentally, a frequently-repeated error in the MMs, with the LNER Brake Van described as 'finished in grey'; it was always brown.

The 'No. 1 Brake Van' transfers were no longer used from 1925. There was an interesting LMS version in 1925 which had the No. 2 Van type close-spaced lettering, instead of the normal spacing of the lettering used for most LMS Brake Vans of the period. White-lettered 'GW' Brake Vans appeared in 1926, still on the nut-and-bolt base; they were finished in grey, and used the same body as the LMS vans.

In 1927, the vans were re-designed for assembly by lugs in slots instead of nut-and-bolt. The GW van was altered to have a single large window at the door end, instead of two smaller windows as on the LMS Brake Vans. White letters were used on one early batch of tabbed bodies, but the white LMS, LNER and GW letters were soon dropped in favour of large gold LMS, NE (not LNER) and GW. The Southern Railway Brake Van, introduced in 1928, was identical to the NE version except for the large gold 'SR' letters.

The revised standard wagon base was adopted for Brake Vans in 1930. There was an odd batch of GW Brake Vans in 1930–31 which had the large window cutout in the van end by mistake. Soon the large gold LMS and GW letters were changed to smaller gold letters.

Automatic couplings were fitted to all Brake Vans from 1931. During the 1931–34 period there were many differences between the lettering styles for the four companies. There were two LMS and two GW versions in 1931 and 1932, first with smaller gold letters, then with white letters. The SR Brake Vans changed late in 1931 from large to smaller gold letters, still on the NE-coloured van. NE Brake Vans were still being made with large gold letters while the others were smaller gold or white, but late in 1932 white NE letters began to appear.

From 1933 LMS and GW vans were in lighter grey, and the SR van in dark brown instead of NE brown; the colour of the NE van was unchanged. Underframes for all four versions were enamelled in green. Whereas all four appeared with white company letters and green underframes, the GW and SR versions (and therefore possibly the other two) also appeared with the smaller gold letters and green underframes! All the 1934 green-underframed versions were white-lettered.

In 1935 the colour of the Brake Van underframe reverted to black on all four versions, the lettering still being white. The colours then remained unchanged to 1939, when matt black underframes were fitted, and the LMS version was produced with white serif letters instead of sans-serif as before.

After the usual wartime break in production, the Goods Brake Van ('Goods' was added to the title to distinguish it from the re-named Passenger Brake Van) re-appeared in the 1948 lists. It was fitted with lamp brackets on the sides and ends, and was lettered in the new standard postwar style, with small letters in the bottom left-hand corner of the van sides. At first the Goods Brake Vans appeared on prewar-type bases without axlebox slots; but from 1949 the standard postwar wagon base was used. The liveries were LMS brown with grey roof, plus NE bauxite, GW dark grey and SR dark brown all with white roofs. Solebars were finished in the same colour as the wagon body, except on the 1948–49 GW Brake Vans.

The GW and SR versions were usually on the standard postwar base, the GW Brake Van being one of the first vehicles to be thus fitted. There appears to have been only one substantial batch of the SR Goods Brake Vans, and they had been overpainted dark brown over a coat of bauxite. British Railways Goods Brake Vans were introduced in 1954, and replaced the LMS and NE types which had remained in production up to then; the BR No. 50 Goods Brake Van in turn replaced the BR No. 1 Goods Brake Van in 1957. The No. 50 remained on sale until 1969.

BREAKDOWN VAN AND CRANE

The Breakdown Van and Crane was first advertised in the May 1923 Rail Formations booklet. The base was similar to that used for the No. 2 Luggage Van, and was fitted with the same bogies. A crane was mounted at one end, and a van body at the other; an open door in the crane end of the van was the only difference from the No. 1 Luggage Van body. The crane and the van were enamelled grey, the roof white, and the base and bogies black. There were Red Cross transfers each side of the van, and the crane was lettered 'to lift 10 tons', rather a limited capacity for breakdown work. There were no company initials.

Later in 1923, two new versions of the crane appeared. Both had white lining round the 'to lift 10 tons' wording, which was now on both sides of the crane instead of one side as before. One version was lettered 'Breakdown Van and Crane' on one side of the base, with a Red Cross on each side of the van; the other had no Red Crosses but was lettered 'Breakdown Van and Crane' on both sides of the base.

In 1924 there were the first versions with company initials; 'LMS' on a van with 'Breakdown Van and Crane' transfers on one side of the base and Red Crosses both sides of the van, and the other 'LNER', with 'Breakdown Van and Crane' both sides of the base and with one Red Cross on the van. These had early un-embossed jibs, and open doors in the crane end of the vans; but later vehicles had hinged doors in the ends of the vans, and the edges of the jib were embossed for strengthening. The next vans were lettered 'Breakdown Van and Crane' one side of the

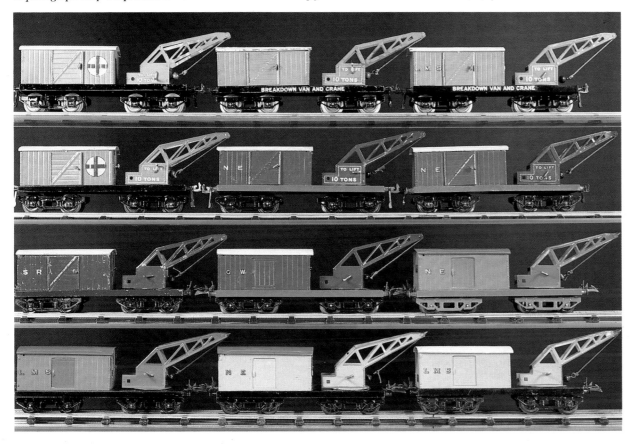

base, had the Red Cross one side of the van and 'LMS' on the other; there was probably an LNER equivalent.

From 1925 the vans were no longer lettered 'Breakdown Van and Crane' on the base, and had a Red Cross on one side and 'LMS' or 'LNER' on the other.

Nut-and-bolt GW Breakdown Vans and Cranes were made in 1926, and it is possible that NE versions in grey may also have appeared. Early in 1927 there was a change of colour, with LMS, NE and GW versions now having blue base, brown van body (now tabbed), brown crane (with 'to lift 10 tons' still white-lettered), and with white roofs. But later in 1927 the 'to lift 10 tons' transfers were re-made in gold lettering, with gold lining. SR Breakdown Vans and Cranes of 1928 were like the others, except that the base was dark brown, not blue; the jib

was also dark brown, and the van body a lighter brown.

From 1931 automatic couplings were fitted, and the cranes no longer had the 'to lift 10 tons' lettering; instead they were lined in red paint. In November 1931 new van bodies were designed with sliding doors instead of hinged; these appeared in the same liveries, with company initials one side and a Red Cross on the other. From March 1932 the Red Cross was no longer used, and the company initials appeared on both sides of the van, instead of one side only as previously. (Some SR vans of 1932 were anomalous, in having 'SR' on both sides of hinged-door bodies.)

In 1933 new liveries were adopted, with green body, green bogies, blue base, blue crane (green-lined), and blue roof; the colours were brighter than those previously used. The SR colours were now the

same as for LMS, NE and GW and remained so. A few Breakdown Vans and Cranes in these colours had the old round jib pulley, but in July 1933 a new jib head was designed, with the string now passing through a hole in the casting.

Late in 1935, the colour of the base and bogies changed to black, and in 1936 the small door was hinged on a single long wire instead of two short ones. Axleboxes were fitted, and Diecast Spoked Wagon Wheels were used instead of tinplate wheels. The 1937 Breakdown Vans and Cranes had light grey bodies, and light grey cranes lined in dark grey. The roofs were blue and the bases and bogies black. Curiously, the LMS transfers changed to gold serif letters at this time, so it seems that the transfers were different from those used for the Hopper Wagons and No. 1 Cattle Trucks. From 1938, the colour of the roof changed to white, and from 1939 matt varnish was used on the base, with bogies and couplings secured by rivets instead of eyelets on the last wartime series. White letters were used for at least one late (GW) version, and possibly for others, although gold letters were more usual.

Breakdown Vans and Cranes were again listed in 1949, but no details are known of any actually produced; the body of the van was to have been fitted with a lamp bracket, in the postwar style.

The Breakdown Van and Crane was a most useful wagon to have on the railway, not just for accidents but for lifting loads; it was a popular present for the Hornby boy. The price fell from 7s when introduced to 5s 11d in 1934, but it remained the most expensive wagon in the range.

No. 1 CATTLE TRUCKS

Cattle Trucks were first shown in the 1923–24 season Meccano Products catalogues. Originally, they were not lettered with any railway company initials, but the bases were lettered 'No. 1 Cattle Truck' on one side. The base was olive green, the sides pale green-grey and the roof white. Although the body was the same size as that of the Luggage Van, the sliding doors were a major structural difference, and the upper parts of the doors, sides and ends were slatted. The price at first was 4s 6d, though it had fallen to 2s 3d by 1937; the Cattle Truck was generally the same price as the Luggage Van, but was more

the doors instead of the left-hand side as before and after. Apparently no thought was given to supplying the Cattle Trucks with appropriate loads of the new Modelled Miniature Cows!

The following season, in 1933–34, LMS, NE and GW wagons were finished in new colours, with grey bodies, green roofs, green doors and green underframes. SR versions also had green roofs, doors and underframe, although the bodies remained dark brown. But in 1934, the underframe colour of LMS, NE and GW (also probably SR) trucks changed to black, while the roof and doors were still green.

Late in 1935, the colour scheme was revised yet again, with the roof in white and the doors in grey (or brown for the SR) to match the body. The underframe was still black. This version lasted until 1939, when a final change was made to white company lettering instead of the shadowed gold letters that had always been used before. LMS trucks now had serif letters, the others sans-serif.

After the war, the No. 1 Cattle Truck was no longer embossed with planking on the doors, sides or ends; lamp brackets were fitted, and the solebars were finished in the same colours as the body. LMS and NE No. 1 Cattle Trucks were first made on the prewar-type base without axlebox slots. Postwar SR and GW Cattle Trucks usually had the later standard postwar wagon base, which was also used for LMS and NE trucks from 1949. The company initials were always in small lettering in the lower left-hand corner. Colours were the same as for the No. 1 Goods Vans.

From 1954, the pre-nationalisation Cattle Trucks were replaced by BR–E No. 1 Cattle Trucks, then in turn these were replaced by the No. 50 Cattle Truck from 1957 to 1965.

No. 2 CATTLE TRUCKS

No. 2 Cattle Trucks were introduced at the same time as the No. 2 Luggage Vans (first appearing in the 1923–24 Meccano Products catalogues), and shared the same type of nut-and-bolt body, but with different embossing and with pierced slatting on the sides and doors. The liveries followed much the same pattern of development.

The first No. 2 Cattle Trucks had olive green bases, grey sides and white roofs; 'No. 2 Cattle Truck' white lettering transfers appeared on one side

popular with the customers, and was made in larger numbers.

LMS and LNER Cattle Trucks were sold in 1924, with the company initials on the side of the body. The roofs were dark grey, in some cases overpainted over the white of the original roof; as with many other wagons of the period it seems likely that stocks of unlettered wagons were updated to LNER and LMS before they left the factory. From 1925, No. 1 Cattle Trucks, were lettered 'LNER' or 'LMS' on both sides of the base instead of on the body, and the 'No. 1 Cattle Truck' lettering no longer appeared; the colours were unchanged. In 1926 GW No. 1 Cattle Trucks were issued in the same colours, still on nut-and-bolt bases, but from 1927 the LMS, NE (shortened from LNER) and GW trucks were on

tabbed bases, and in different colours, with base, roof and doors in blue, and the body in pale blue. Company letters now appeared on the body once again rather than on the base. Dark brown SR Cattle Trucks with black bases and white roofs were available from 1928.

The revised standard wagon base was fitted from 1930 onwards, the colours being unchanged. Automatic couplings were fitted from 1931, then in 1932 the LMS, NE and GW trucks were fitted with red underframes, with the same dark blue roof and doors and pale blue body. The SR colours of dark brown with black underframe and white roof were probably unchanged. Later in the same season a batch of No. 1 Cattle Trucks appeared, identical except that the company initials were on the right-hand side of of the base. White 'LMS' or 'LNER' lettering was added to the sides from 1924, with the roof now coloured dark grey, and from 1925 the 'No. 2 Cattle Truck' lettering disappeared from the base. GW versions were introduced in 1926, and white lettered 'NE' versions replaced 'LNER' at much the same time. In 1927 the colours changed to blue roof, blue base and blue bogies, with pale blue tabbed body. White lettered 'LMS' and 'GW' versions appeared, and probably NE also.

Later in 1927, large gold letters were used instead of white for LMS, NE and GW trucks, and in 1928 SR trucks were introduced, with black bases, black bogies, dark brown bodies and white roofs. From 1930 all had lowered bogies to reduce the buffer height, and the GW truck changed to smaller gold letters. Automatic couplings were fitted from 1931.

In 1933 there was a change to green roof, green base, green bogies, and a light grey body for the LMS, NE and GW No. 2 Cattle Trucks, which retained their gold lettering. On the NE trucks the smaller size lettering was adopted, whilst the LMS trucks appeared with either large or small letters. There was an interesting production error on some of these trucks, which appeared with Luggage Van body planking!

SR versions appeared briefly with green bogies whilst retaining normal black bases, white roofs, and brown bodies with large gold letters; but they soon reverted to black bogies, after which change smaller gold letters were used.

From 1935, the LMS, NE and GW livery changed to grey bodies, grey bases, green bogies and cream roofs. Curiously the LMS version reverted temporarily to the larger gold letter size. But from 1936, all had black bogies (now usually with unused axlebox slots), still with grey bases for the LMS, NE and GW trucks; brown bases appeared on one batch of SR trucks, but most still had black bases. All now had the smaller gold letters.

White-lettered versions of the LMS, NE and GW trucks were made from late in 1938, with black bogies, grey bases, grey bodies and white roofs. Early in 1939 the base was changed to black, but from late in 1939 the bases reverted to grey on each of the three, and riveted couplings and bogies were used. White-lettered SR No. 2 Cattle Trucks were made, probably late in 1939 or early in 1940, although the early 1939 SR trucks still had gold letters.

The No. 2 Cattle Truck was catalogued briefly in 1949, but was made in only small quantities, and mostly for export. The only examples known are in the NE Goods Van colours, but devoid of lettering.

CEMENT WAGONS

The Cement Wagon was one of the group of items that first appeared in the May–June 1922 MM. The price was 4s 6d. It was not a nut-and-bolt design, the body always being clipped to the open-axleguard base by lugs. The body was finished in grey, with the hinged flap in the roof painted black, and large white 'Cement' lettering was stencil-sprayed on both sides of the wagon body. The base was painted black.

From 1923 the painted letters were replaced by gold 'Cement' lettering transfers, again on both sides. Early in 1924 remaining stocks of both the white-lettered and the gold-lettered versions were converted to LMS and LNER liveries by the addition of small gold company initials on one side of the base; the whole wagon was also sprayed in varnish. Later versions were lettered 'Cement' on one side in gold letters, and 'LMS' or 'LNER' in matching gold serif letters on the other side of the body. A grey-bodied GW version was probably made in 1926, but in 1927 the Cement Wagon colour changed to red overall instead of grey and black. In 1928 SR Cement Wagons were offered, coloured red like the others, although both the GW and SR versions had large gold sans-serif letters instead of the serif letters used on the LMS and LNER wagons. The supply of these special LNER and LMS transfers must have been quite large, since they were never changed; and

No. 2 Cattle Trucks.

unlike other wagons the Cement Wagon did not appear with the 'LNER' shortened to 'NE' only.

From 1930 the company initials no longer appeared, although the 'Cement' transfers were still used on one side. The revised standard wagon base was fitted, but otherwise there was no change. A lighter shade of red enamel was used from 1933.

In 1937 the 'Portland Cement Wagon' appeared. This was bright yellow, with a black base and a 'Blue Circle' transfer on the opening door flap. The 'Cement' lettering no longer appeared. Except for a change in 1939 to matt black for the base, there were no further changes up to 1941.

After the war, the re-issued Portland Cement Wagon was similar to the war-time version, although the trademarks and the wagon base were of course different, and the solebars were painted to match the body. The wagon was usually on the standard postwar base, although it is reported also to have appeared on the prewar-type base but without axlebox slots. The Cement Wagon was replaced by the No. 50 'Saxa Salt' Wagon, which was listed from 1957 to 1969.

COAL WAGONS

The Coal Wagon was one of the bright and colourful group of wagons introduced for the first time in the UK in 1931, although it had actually been on sale some time earlier in France; unlike the French version it was not issued in the UK with company initials for the LMS, NE, GW or SR, but was a private owner's wagon with large 'Meccano' lettering transfers. This was of course a pure fiction, as Meccano Ltd did not run any railway wagons, and despite the close proximity of the railway there were no sidings at Binns Road. The price on introduction was 2s 3d, compared to 1s 9d for the No. 1 Wagon. The body of the Coal Wagon was bright red, and the base black. A sheet of tinplate embossed to represent coal was inserted in the body of the wagon, and this too (naturally) was painted black.

The transfers were changed to even more unlikely 'Hornby Railway Company' lettering (in gold on a red wagon) in 1936, and the new wagons were shown in the 1936–37 catalogues. But in 1940 there were new transfers with 'Hornby Railway Company' lettered in white instead of gold, and the

Cement Wagons.

colour of the wagon body was changed to maroon. It is infuriating to note that this tidy sequence of changes was upset by other maroon versions with the 'Meccano' transfer; this may have been because of a shortage of the HRC transfers in the final production run.

Although the Coal Wagon was re-drawn in May 1949 for issue with GW tinprinted sides, nothing resulted, and no postwar versions are known.

CRANE TRUCKS

The Crane Truck was advertised in the May 1923 Rail Formations leaflet, and in the June 1923 MM. It had a crane like that of the Breakdown Van and Crane, but fitted with a lead counterbalance weight. The ratchet wheel for the winding drum was made using the same blanking tools as for the Meccano ¾ inch Sprocket Wheels. String was similar to the Meccano type, and changed several times during the production of the Crane Trucks. The crane was finished in grey, with white 'to lift 10 tons' lettering on one side. It was mounted on a standard open axleguard base, finished black. There was another version later in the same year, with larger white 'to lift 10 tons' lettering now on both sides of the crane, and with white lining not plain as before. This version also appeared later lettered 'LMS' or 'LNER', still with the crane sides unstrengthened.

The 1924 Crane Trucks were lettered 'LMS' or 'LNER' on both sides of the base; rather unusually they were not lettered 'Crane Truck' on the side, perhaps because their function was considered self-evident. The edges of the crane sides were embossed with ridges, to strengthen the jib. The same black and grey livery was used for GW Crane Trucks in 1926; black and grey Crane Trucks were lettered 'NE' instead of 'LNER' in the same year.

From 1927, the base was finished in blue, and the crane in brown with gold-lettered and gold-lined 'to lift 10 tons' transfers. These colours were used for LMS, NE and GW versions, and also for SR from 1928. Some Crane Trucks made in 1930 appeared with no company intials on the open axleguard base, and later in 1930 the new standard wagon base was used, which of course had no room for lettering. The introduction of automatically coupled versions in

1931 was followed quickly by a change to cranes with jibs hand-lined in red enamel, no longer having 'to lift 10 tons' transfers.

There was a change of livery in 1933, to yellow for the base, with a blue crane lined in yellow enamel. Late in 1933, the jib-head changed from a fixed pulley to a new type with the string passing through a hole, and the jib was lined in red instead of yellow.

From 1935, the base colour changed to black, and the blue crane was lined in green; then late in 1936, the blue crane was given red lining instead of green. The price had started at 4s 6d, the same as the goods vans, and followed them down to 2s 3d in 1937;

Red, blue and black Fibre Wagons behind GW No. 1 Loco 9319. Note the bufferless M Fibre Wagon in the foreground.

FLAT TRUCKS

The Flat Truck was introduced in the 1934–35 season catalogues, price 1s 6d. It consisted of the standard wagon base, fitted with low sides which had lipped tops, and two rings on each side for securing the load. The LMS, NE and GW versions were finished in light grey, the SR in brown; all were rather unusual in having the lower part of the base mask-sprayed in black, leaving the solebar in the same colour as the body. White lettering was applied, which was rather prone to wear and tear in normal use. There were no major variations in prewar days, except for a few SR Flat Trucks produced in grey, presumably by accident.

The Flat Truck with Cable Drum was also catalogued in 1934, price 1s 9d. This was the ordinary Flat Truck loaded with a miniature electric cable drum, made from wood (painted or stained on early versions) and covered with paper sides lithographed in colour. The two sides were differently printed, and there was also a covering around the outside of the drum, printed with planking and with straps (thin black lines on early versions, broad bands printed with rivets later). The drums were secured to the wagon by Meccano-type string, which varied in colour from time to time.

The first drums in 1934–35 were BI Cables, with thin black bands and black-stained wood; the 1935–36 drums were of noticeably smaller diameter, and wider. For 1936–37 the BI Cable Drums had the same papers but on green-stained drums. New 'Liverpool Cables' sides were printed for 1937–38, together with new outside wrappers with the broad riveted straps, still on green-stained drums. This version had two Liver birds printed on each side; the 1938–39 printings were the same but for the addition of 'Regd. Trade Mark' printed under the birds. Again the drum was green-stained. The 1939–41 cable drums reverted to 'BI Cables' sides, now with the broad straps with rivets on the outside, and with the wooden drum not stained at all. 'Electric Cables' stencils were designed during the war, for mask-spraying the drums in black with white letters, presumably because stocks of the lithographed paper sides had run out, but they are only known to have appeared in this form in 1948.

there was a jump in price to 2s 9d in 1938, and another colour change, with the crane now in grey with dark grey lining, mounted on a black base which changed to matt finish in 1939.

After the war, the No. 1 Crane Truck reappeared in 1948. Unusually (for wagons not in sets) they first came out on the prewar-type base with axlebox slots, but of course with the postwar embossed trademark. Shortly afterwards the base was changed to the prewar-type without slots, then from 1949 the standard postwar base was fitted. The base was matt black, and the crane red with white 'to lift 10 tons' lettering. The hook colour changed from black to red circa 1950. Apart from small differences in the lettering, there were no further changes of note before the No. 1 Crane Truck was replaced in 1957 by the No. 50 Crane Truck (in similar colours but on a shiny black base), which remained on sale until 1969.

FIBRE WAGONS

Fibre wagons were added to the UK Hornby range in 1931; the standard UK catalogue picture showed an earlier French Hornby PLM version of 1930, (usually with the PLM letters obliterated), which had the open axleguard base, with eight stanchions. The UK production versions however were always on the revised standard wagon base of 1930, fitted with automatic couplings, and with only six stanchions. The fibre load was made up from wood wool, tied up with red cotton thread. The wagon was enamelled in red from 1931 to 1933, when the colour changed to blue. There was a fall in price from 1s 11d to 1s 3d in 1934. These wagons were also made in a version without buffers for the M11 Complete Model Railway. The colour of the wagon changed again to matt black in 1939. Although the drawings were updated in 1946, there was no postwar production.

Flat Trucks with Containers were sold from 1936. The Containers were shaped pieces of wood with lithographed paper sides, fitted with chains and a ring for hoisting. They were not secured to the truck. The four containers available were LMS Furniture, LNER Goods, GW Refrigerated, and SR Ventilated. It had originally been planned to produce thirteen, including Goods, Furniture and Refrigerated Containers for each company, as well as the SR Ventilated.

After the war the Flat Truck re-appeared in the 1948 lists for separate sale, and was also included in the 601 Goods Train Set. The Flat Truck liveries were SR brown, GW dark grey, NE bauxite and LMS brown. The first bases were the prewar-type base, at first with and later without slots for axleboxes. Later in 1948 or early in 1949 the standard postwar base was used.

The Flat Truck with Cable Drum was sold at first with 'Electric Cables' drums, as planned during the war, but with the normal postwar litho wrapper round the outside, printed with the broad straps with rivets, and distinguishable from prewar by the 'Printed in England' marking on one of the planks. The Cable Drums changed quickly to 'Liverpool Cables', with 'LEC' trademarks instead of the prewar Liver birds. Single cords replaced twin cords in August 1949.

Flat Trucks were sold with Containers from 1948. The LMS Furniture, LNER Goods, GW Refrigerated and SR Meat Containers all had 'Made in England' incorporated in the lithography (although sometimes lost by the guillotine!); LMS and NE containers were otherwise unchanged, but the GW Container was in cream with a grey roof instead of the prewar white, and the SR version was in reddish-brown, instead of the prewar silver. (The GW and SR versions may not have appeared until quite late; both were made in large batches early in 1951.)

BR Flat Trucks replaced the pre-nationalisation liveries in 1954; there were two containers, Furniture and (from 1955) Insulated Meat; Cable Drums were unchanged. Both the Containers and the Cable Drums became available again for separate sale in 1956, as they had been before the war, with the difference that the postwar items were individually boxed. There was a change of name to 'Low Sided Wagon' in 1956. No. 50 Low Sided Wagons went on sale from 1957 to the late '60s, again either with or without load; the Insulated Meat and Furniture Containers and the Cable Drums were unaltered, although cable drums were secured to the later No. 50 Flat Trucks by thread rather than string.

FRENCH-TYPE WAGONS

A small range of French-type rolling stock was produced for the British market, mainly for use with the Nord locomotive.

The French-Type Brake Van was introduced for the 1927 season, and was the same as the vans already produced for the French market. Based on the Snowplough body, with sliding doors but with the windows not cut out, the van's most striking feature to English eyes was the quaint guard's lookout on the back, with a set of steps leading up to its hinged door. The first colours were blue for the base and roof, with pale blue sides, and with 'Nord' in small gold letters on the van sides. The catalogues showed an earlier version with white lettering, which may possibly have been made for a short while. The 1930s provoked the usual riot of colour. In 1933 the van appeared with the revised standard wagon underframe finished in dark 'Redline' blue, also used for the doors; the van sides were in lighter blue, and the

French-type Wagons, Covered Wagons, French-type Brake Vans, Single and Double Wine Wagons from the UK Hornby range.

roofs were both red. Later versions circa 1934–35 had a black underframe, dark blue doors, lighter blue body, a white roof on the van, and a red roof on the lookout. However, low demand led to the early withdrawal of this van with effect from September 1936.

The French-type Wagon was introduced in 1927. It was similar to the normal Hornby open wagons, but was fitted with a lookout hut, and lettered 'Nord'. The base was blue and the body was pale blue with white lettering. Soon the transfers were changed to large gold letters. In common with other French-type wagons, the base was not changed immediately to the new style in 1930, so cranked automatic couplings were fitted to the open axleguard base to reduce the coupling height. In 1933 new versions appeared which had the revised standard wagon base, with light blue wagon sides, red underframe and red roofed lookout, at first with large gold letters but later with smaller gold letters. In the late 1930s the final version appeared briefly with a grey body, black underframe and the smaller gold letters, but the wagon was no longer listed in the 1939–40 catalogues.

The French-type Covered Wagon was later on the scene than the other Nord wagons, arriving in 1929 at a price of 2s 6d. It was in different colours to the other two, for no obvious reason; however the 1929 and subsequent Hornby Books of Trains showed it incorrectly in the blue and pale blue colours! No doubt it would have made for a better-looking train had this version been made, but in fact it was finished in grey with a black base, and with large gold 'Nord' letters. It was similar to the ordinary open wagon, but with extra pressings in the body to take the three wire hoops which supported the pale green tarpaulin; the tarpaulin was also tied with strings to the wagon ends. The revised wagon base was adopted in 1930, unlike many other French-type wagons which still appeared on the open axleguard base. In 1933 the colour was changed to a lighter grey, still with the large gold letters and black underframe; circa 1936 smaller gold letters were used instead. At about the same time there was a change in the wagon sides, which now had smaller cracked-up lugs to support the hoops. The last series of French-Type Covered Wagons appeared in 1939; they had white 'Nord' letters. Unlike the other Nord wagons the Covered Wagon was available until 1941, and was in fact one of the last wagons in war-time production. Sales of the Covered Wagon were quite high compared to some of the other French-types, so it had remained in the catalogues; but no French-type wagons were produced after the war.

The Wine Wagon was introduced in 1928, and was similar to the 'Wagon a Foudre' on sale in France. The colour scheme was green for the base and ladder assembly, and red for the twin barrels, which were lettered 'Wine Wagon' in gold. Although scarcely a typical English wagon, it was appealing, and sold well even at 3s 9d. The long thin wagon base was used, and in the early 1930s cranked automatic couplings were used to reduce the coupling to the new standard height; the base could not be crimped along the side because of the ladder fitting. From around 1933, drain cocks and top inlets were no longer fitted, and a lighter green enamel was used for the base. In 1936, the Double Wine Wagon was redesigned, and became the only wagon to be fitted with the French standard wagon base. It is even possible that the parts were imported from the Paris factory. Colours were unchanged, but the final version of 1939, which was available through to 1941, had a black base and ladder assembly instead of green.

Gas Cylinder Wagons.

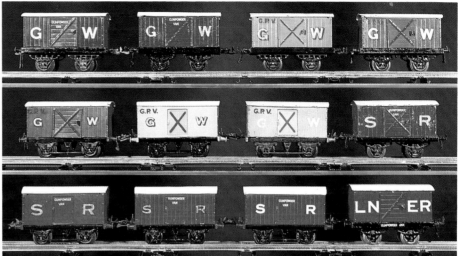

A Single Wine Wagon was listed from 1929, at which time the name of the other changed to 'Double Wine Wagon'. At 3s 9d, it was the same price as the Double Wine Wagon, and it had only a single barrel, mounted on an open axleguard base together with a lookout hut. Cranked automatic couplings were fitted from 1931, still on the open axleguard base, but from 1933 the revised wagon base was fitted, finished in a lighter green. The difficulty of punching slots for the lookout-hut and tank-cradle lugs through the two layers of the new base caused problems in tooling, which probably contributed to the early demise of this wagon. It did not appear in the 1935–36 season or later catalogues.

GAS CYLINDER WAGONS

The Gas Cylinder Wagon was an odd but interesting choice of prototype; although gas cylinder wagons were known on the British railways, they were not by any means common. Their purpose was servicing the gas lighting on passenger coaches, rather than bulk transport. The gas cylinders were filled at the gas-works, then the gas was transported under high pressure to the carriage sidings, where the coach reservoirs were filled as required.

The original design drawings of the wagon were marked 'Paris Works only'; apparently the intention was that it should be manufactured only for the French market. But in the event, it was actually manufactured in Liverpool early in 1923, and was advertised in the June 1923 Meccano Magazine at 4s. Since even the early French-market versions were marked 'Fabrique en Angleterre', the Gas Cylinder Wagons were probably made only in Liverpool during the early 1920s.

On the first versions, the three cylinders were made as separate parts, then clipped together on the cylinder ends; the unit was clipped to the open-axleguard base by two metal straps and by lugs on the cylinder ends. The base was black, the cylinders red, and the two side cylinders were each lettered 'Gas Cylinder' with a gold transfer. 'L&NER' and 'LMS' versions were created early in 1924, by adding the company initials to one side of the base. Later 1924 versions were lettered LNER (and probably LMS) on both sides of the base. From 1925 the LMS and LNER company initials were on one cylinder, rather than on the base, while the cylinder on the opposite side still had a 'Gas Cylinder' transfer. In 1926 a GW version appeared, and the 'LNER' lettering was changed to 'NE' only. The SR version issued in 1928 came with strikingly different green cylinders; it seems to have been one of the earliest SR items to have been produced.

From early 1930, the company initials no longer appeared, although 'Gas Cylinder' lettering was still used on the other cylinder. There was a short-lived version on the open axleguard base which had no company initials, but from later in 1930 the revised standard wagon base was used. The 'Gas Cylinder' transfer was still applied on one side, until 1932 when it too disappeared.

From 1933 the colour of the base was changed to blue, and the construction was simplified, with a single piece forming the sides of all three cylinders, and with the straps embossed rather than being attached as separate parts. The straps were mask-sprayed in the blue colour of the base, until 1937 when they started to be hand-finished in blue. From 1939 the base was finished in black, and the straps on the cylinders were usually finished in black.

The postwar Gas Cylinder Wagon was very similar to the last prewar type, with red cylinders and matt black base, but the straps were not hand-finished in black. At first the prewar-type base without axlebox slots was used, but by 1949 the standard postwar wagon base was being used. The wagon remained a firm favourite, probably because of the low price and the bright colour rather than because of its realism. It survived until 1969 in the No. 50 series, the No. 50 Gas Cylinder Wagon still finished in red but on a shiny black base.

GUNPOWDER VANS

Gunpowder Vans were first offered in the May 1922 MM. They were finished in the same bright red as the Shell tanker, and were lettered 'LNWR' by stencil-spraying in enamel, rather than by the clip-on letters used for the Luggage Van.

Early LNWR Gunpowder Vans were on the early wagon base, but usually with thin axles, and the roofs were normally embossed with rain strips. The doors were lettered 'Gunpowder Van' to identify the dangerous nature of the load, in case the colour was not sufficient warning. These early-base LNWR vans were sometimes assembled using eyelets instead of the usual nuts and bolts, clearly indicating that they were not intended even in the early days for constructional use. When new batches of the van were made late in 1922, the open axleguard nut-and-bolt base was fitted.

The LNWR Gunpowder Vans remained on sale in 1923, but in 1924 the LMS and LNER vans replaced them. These vans were still in red, but lettered with white transfers instead of stencil-sprayed, and on many 1924–25 vans the 'Gunpowder Van' lettering was on the side of the base instead of on the door. Another curiosity was that the red was often sprayed on top of yellow, in fact other van sides prepared for the Colman's Mustard Van, but not required since it had been superseded by the four other private owners' vans of 1924.

For a short period during 1925 the LMS and LNER Gunpowder Vans appeared with no 'Gunpowder Van' transfer at all, but this lettering was soon reinstated on the doors of all Gunpowder Vans. It appeared on the 1926 LNER vans, before they were replaced later in the same year by vans lettered 'NE' only. GW Gunpowder Vans in red with white letters were also available in 1926.

The 1927–28 season LMS, NE and GW Gunpowder Vans were each finished in red, with large gold company initials, but with 'Gunpowder Van' still lettered in white on the doors. These vans were tabbed, not constructional.

In 1928 an SR Gunpowder Van appeared in red with gold letters, and for once it was the Great Western van that was the odd one out. This was now finished in an authentic GW style, in grey with a

No. 2 High Capacity Wagons, with appropriate Hornby loads of Bricks and Coal.

cross both embossed on the doors and painted in red enamel, with 'GPV' lettering in the top left-hand corner instead of 'Gunpowder Van' on the doors, and with large gold company initials. The same doors with embossed cross were used on the normal red bodies of the 1928–29 LMS, NE and SR Gunpowder Vans.

For 1929–30 the GW Gunpowder Van was a darker shade of charcoal grey, but still using the same transfers and the doors with embossed cross. But LMS, NE (and probably SR) vans now had only single embossed straps on the doors, as on the Luggage Vans.

The revised standard wagon base was adopted in 1930. The GW van was still dark charcoal grey, but with smaller gold letters. The other vans were still red with large gold letters. From 1931 automatic couplings were fitted, and later in the same season the vans were fitted with sliding doors instead of hinged. For the GW Gunpowder Van this entailed a change to a red cross transfer since the doors could no longer be embossed. The LMS and SR vans

(possibly also NE) appeared with large gold letters and sliding doors, but in common with the No. 1 Luggage Van, by 1934 the LMS, NE and SR vans all had smaller gold letters as on the GW vans. Post-1933 GW Gunpowder Vans were in the light grey used for Luggage Vans; the transfers were the same, except that on one batch in the late 1930s the 'GPV' transfers seem to have been forgotten.

The final 1939–40 versions of the LMS, NE, GW and SR Gunpowder Vans had white company letters instead of gold, and had matt bases, but were otherwise unchanged. No Gunpowder Vans were made after the war.

HIGH CAPACITY WAGONS

The No. 2 High Capacity Wagons were first offered in the 1936–37 Meccano Products Catalogues, price 3s 9d, and were available in three versions: GW Coal, LMS Coal and NE Brick. The sides were tinprinted; the buffers were the oval-headed type, and the bogies were fitted with axleboxes and with Spoked Wagon Wheels rather than tinplate wheels.

There were no important differences between the various batches, but there were some minor changes; the early versions had plain flat bases, but from 1937 a ring-shaped embossing was added around the bogie eyelets, to reduce friction between the bogie and the base, and to give a slight increase in height. From early in 1939 the base and bogies were finished in matt instead of shiny black, and late in 1939 or early in 1940 the couplings and the bogies were secured by rivets instead of eyelets.

Loads for the No. 2 High Capacity Wagons were first advertised in the 1937 catalogues. The Coal was made from granulated cork, (sieved through a $\frac{5}{8}$ inch square mesh but not passing through a $\frac{1}{8}$ inch square mesh); the pieces of cork were coloured black. The Bricks were cut from beech, and stained brick red. Both loads were provided in long boxes of the same shape as the wagon base, so that the lid could be put inside the wagon as a platform, with the load placed on top. The Coal load weighed $\frac{3}{4}$ ounce, and the Bricks (about 100 per box) 3 ounces.

The No. 2 High Capacity Wagon was listed in the UK in 1949, but it was made only in limited quantities, probably in a single batch around July 1949, and supplies were mainly reserved for export. Although the works drawings showed that an embossed trademark was to have been used, most production versions seem to have had trademark transfers instead. No loads of Bricks or Coal were available.

HOPPER WAGONS

The Hopper Wagon appeared, priced 4s, in the Autumn 1923 Meccano Products catalogue; it was not expensive considering the complexity of the operating doors in the base, and as a result the price did not fall so fast as that of the Luggage Van, for example, and in 1938 the Hopper wagon still cost 3s. The first Hopper Wagons had no company initials, just a plain grey-enamelled body, and a black open axleguard base lettered 'Hopper Wagon' on one solebar. A lever was provided on the other side of the wagon to operate the two hinged doors which dis-

charged the load. What that load consisted of was left to the imagination of the user; the March 1923 MM had mentioned that a 'Slack Wagon' was being prepared, and by this they may have meant the Hopper Wagon. Early in 1924 some of these Hopper Wagons without company initials were varnished.

LMS and LNER company initials in gold were added to the sides of the hoppers from 1924; there was no other change, the wagons still being lettered 'Hopper Wagon' on one solebar up to 1925. Hoppers with 'GW' initials appeared in the same grey and black colours in 1926. From 1927 the colours changed to a dark green overall, the base now being the same colour as the body. LMS, NE (not LNER),

and GW versions appeared in these colours, but the SR Hopper Wagon of 1928 was finished in red with a black base, again with gold company initials on both sides.

The revised standard wagon base was fitted to the Hopper Wagons from 1930, and automatic couplings from 1931, but there was no change of colour until 1933 when the LMS, NE and GW Hopper Wagons were finished in a lighter green, still with gold letters. SR colours were unchanged.

It was not until 1939 that any further change was made; in that year matt black bases were fitted to all the Hopper Wagons; LMS versions appeared with black bases and with gold letters, but the NE and

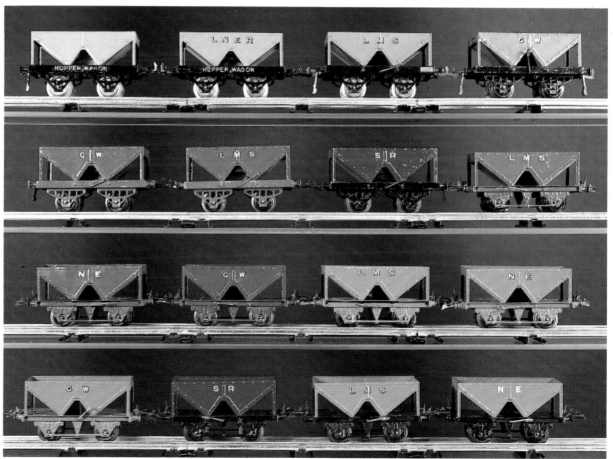

Hopper Wagons.

GW equivalents were usually white-lettered. It is probable that SR white-lettered versions also appeared in 1939 or 1940, and the LMS Hopper may later have been given white serif letters (as on the No. 1 Cattle Truck).

September 1948 price lists advertised the return of the Hopper Wagon; only one version was available, in the prewar livery of green body and black base, but now with yellow 'LMS' lettering. At first the prewar-type base without axlebox slots was fitted, but soon the standard postwar wagon base was used instead. The embossed Hornby trademark could not be used for the Hopper Wagon, because of the cutouts for the discharge doors; standard trademark transfers were used instead.

In 1954 the British Railways No. 1 Hopper Wagons appeared, with grey bodies and black bases, curiously reminiscent of the earliest colours in 1923, although the black lettering panel reflected modern-day practice. The No. 50 Hopper Wagon which replaced the No. 1 in 1957 was finished in similar colours. It was still available in 1969.

No. 1 LUGGAGE VANS

Covered Luggage Vans were added to the Hornby range in May 1921. They were the second type of goods vehicle to be made, and were intended for constructional use, unlike later vans which were still assembled using nuts and bolts but which were not intended for dismantling and re-building. The first Luggage Vans had clip-on white-painted MR letters on the grey van sides, and were fitted with hinged opening doors. The early wagon base was fitted, and at first the roofs had no embossed rain-strips.

From 1922 the MR Van was fitted with the open axleguard base. The body still had clip-on letters, but with the addition of 'Luggage Van' transfers on the doors, and with embossed strips on the roof. In 1923 the name changed to 'No. 1 Luggage Van' when the No. 2 Luggage Van was introduced.

The first LMS and LNER No. 1 Luggage Vans did not appear until 1924, the MR Vans having remained on sale during 1923. The LMS and LNER vans had grey bodies, with large white lettering

transfers instead of the clip-on letters. Some early catalogue pictures showed the 'Luggage Van' transfers on the door, so this style may have been used for a while. More usually, LMS and LNER vans were lettered 'Luggage Van' on the solebar. A few 1924–25 LMS and LNER Luggage Vans appeared on old-stock constructional coach bases with detachable axleguards. The 'Luggage Van' lettering was abandoned from 1925, after which only the company initials were used.

In 1926 the vans were available in grey with large white GW letters, and later 'LNER' lettering was changed to 'NE' only. Both NE and GW vans were made with nut-and-bolt bodies, but from early in 1927 LMS, NE and GW vans were supplied with the body secured to the base by tabs, and with large gold lettering transfers. SR vans in dark brown with large gold letters were added to the range in 1928. From 1930 the revised standard wagon base was used, the van bodies still having hinged doors and gold lettering, although the GW vans now had smaller gold letters.

Automatic couplings were fitted from early 1931, and from later in 1931 or early in 1932 the Luggage Vans were fitted with sliding doors instead of hinged, 'more in accordance with modern practice' according to the MM.

In 1933 the LMS, LNER and GW van body colour changed to a lighter grey, the SR brown being unchanged. The LMS and NE No. 1 Luggage Vans appeared in the lighter colour with large gold letters, but by 1934 smaller gold letters were being used for LMS, NE and SR vans as well as the GW.

By 1937, the price of the vans had fallen to only 2s 3d from the 1921 price of 6s. From late in 1938, the No. 1 Luggage Vans began to be lettered with white transfers instead of gold, for all four versions, with the body colours unchanged.

After the war, there was a sensible change of name to 'No. 1 Goods Van' instead of No. 1 Luggage Van. They were catalogued from 1948. Colours were brown with grey roofs for the LMS, bauxite with white roofs for NE, dark grey with white roofs for GW, and dark brown with white roofs for SR. All four had more realistic lettering than the prewar vans, having small letters on flat panels in the lower left-hand corners of the van sides.

No. 1 Luggage Vans.

ferences between the door handles), with the result that the bracing straps embossed on the doors were inconsistent.

LMS and LNER No. 2 Luggage Vans replaced the unlettered type in 1924; large white company lettering transfers were used on the van sides, and the 'No. 2 Luggage Van' lettering was moved to the side of the base. Roofs became dark grey rather than white. It should be mentioned that existing stocks of early vans were converted to the latest style by adding 'LMS' transfers (LNER transfers could not be used since there was not enough room). Like all the 1924 and later vans they were varnished overall.

From 1925 the 'No. 2 Luggage Van' lettering no longer appeared on the LMS and LNER Vans, and from 1926 GW versions were made, while LNER lettering was shortened to NE only.

Early in 1927 the vans were revised to tabbed instead of nut-and-bolt construction, and the colours changed to pale blue for the body, with blue base, blue bogies and blue roof. White company initials were still used for a while on GW vans, and possibly on LMS and NE also. But later in 1927 large gold letters were used for the LMS, NE and GW vans, and of course on the SR vans from 1928. SR vans were in dark brown with black bases, black bogies and white roofs.

When the revised standard underframes for four-wheel wagons appeared in 1930, there was a corresponding change to the bogies of the No. 2 Vans, lowering them to bring the buffers to the same height as the four-wheel stock. Colours were unchanged, but smaller gold letters began to be used for the GW vans.

The LMS, NE and GW No. 2 Luggage Van colours were changed in 1933, to light grey body, black base, white roof and (usually) black bogies; the SR vans were unchanged. But No. 2 Luggage Vans did not quite escape (as the No. 1 Luggage Vans had done) without any added bright colours; there were GW vans of the 1933–34 period fitted with green bogies, and so presumably there are LMS, NE and possibly SR equivalents. But black bogies were certainly the norm from 1934 onwards, and by 1934 smaller gold letters were used for the LMS, NE and SR Luggage Vans as well as for the GW. By then the price had fallen to 4s 6d. The Luggage Van was

Lamp brackets were fitted, and the solebars were mask-sprayed in the same colour as the bodies, except on 1948–49 SR and GW versions. The first vans were on the prewar-type base without axlebox slots; later standard postwar bases were used for the LMS and NE vans, the SR and GW vans having been discontinued.

The BR No. 1 Goods Vans were designed late in 1953; they were in brown with grey roofs, and had lettering in both corners of the van side. They were replaced from 1957 by the No. 50 Goods Vans, which were a completely new type, with tinprinted livery and twin hinged doors.

No. 2 LUGGAGE VANS

The No. 2 Luggage Van first appeared in the Meccano Products catalogue published in the Autumn of 1923. The first versions had no company initials, just a white-lettered 'No. 2 Luggage Van' transfer on the right-hand side of the grey-enamelled body. The base was olive green, the bogies black and the roof white. No varnish was used for the first batches. It is interesting that whereas some of the 1922–23 season wagons had been tabbed, these somewhat later vehicles were designed for the already outdated nut-and-bolt construction. The reason was that they had first been designed in 1921 as 'High Capacity Vans'. Hinged double doors were fitted, but both doors were made using the same tools (except for dif-

not as popular as the No. 2 Cattle Truck, although it was the same price, and therefore fewer batches were produced. Incidentally, one substantial batch of No. 2 Luggage Vans was made inadvertently with the body pressing of the No. 2 Cattle Truck!

Axlebox slots appeared on the bogies from 1936, although axleboxes were not fitted. The bases of the LMS, NE and GW vans were sprayed the same grey as the body, although black bases were still normal for SR No. 2 Luggage Vans. From late in 1938, white letters began to be used in place of gold, and from 1939 the vans had riveted couplings and bogies.

No. 2 Goods Vans were listed in 1948 and 1949, and were similar to the prewar vans apart from the livery, and the addition of lamp irons and a flat lettering panel on the van side in the postwar style. LMS vans in brown with grey roofs, and NE vans in bauxite with white roofs, were the common finishes, but unlettered versions (possibly for export) are also known.

No. 1 LUMBER WAGONS

The small Lumber Wagon was first manufactured early in 1923. It was a simple wagon, consisting of the open axleguard wagon base fitted with two bolsters with stanchions and chains, also used on the No. 2 Lumber and Trolley Wagons. The No. 1 Lumber Wagon was enamelled olive green, with the bolster finished at first in black but very soon in red. There were no company initials, and no load was provided. Although when it was introduced it was 6d more expensive than the No. 1 Timber Wagon, from 1924 the price dropped to 2s, that of the Timber Wagon, and fell further to 1s 3d by 1937. Consequently they were very popular on account of the low price.

'LMS' or 'L&NER' company initials in small gold letters were added to both sides of the wagon base late in 1923, both on existing wagons still in stock (including some very early wagons with black bolsters) and also on new production. Early in 1924, the more standardised 'LMS' and 'LNER' letters

were applied to one side of the wagon and white 'No. 1 Lumber Wagon' lettering transfers to the other, but from 1925 the 'LMS' and 'LNER' lettering was on both sides and the 'No. 1 Lumber Wagon' transfer no longer appeared. GW-lettered wagons were available from 1926, and 'NE' transfers replaced 'LNER' not long after. Two holes were added in the top of the bolsters early in 1927. Light Brown SR No. 1 Lumber Wagons with blue bolsters were made from 1928 to 1930. Early in 1930 several No. 1 Lumber Wagons were made with the open axleguard base but with no company lettering (both in olive green and in light brown colours), but soon the new standard wagon base was used. The colour was still olive green with red bolsters. Automatic couplings were fitted from 1931.

In 1933 the colour of the No. 1 Lumber Wagon changed to a light green with yellow bolsters, and these colours were unchanged until 1939 when black wagons with red bolsters replaced them.

Early postwar No. 1 Lumber Wagons were in the same colours, on the prewar-type base without

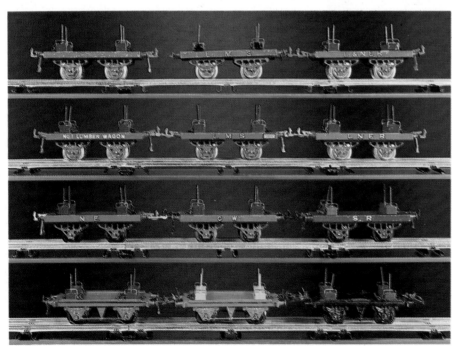

No. 1 Lumber Wagons.

No. 2 Lumber Wagons.

axlebox slots. Later they were on the postwar standard base. These Lumber Wagons were sold from 1948 to 1957, when they were replaced by the No. 50 Lumber Wagon, which was catalogued to 1969, still being in similar colours but of course on a glossy black No. 50 base.

No. 2 LUMBER WAGONS

No. 2 Lumber Wagons were shown in the May 1923 Rail Formations leaflet, together with the No. 1. They too were in olive green, with black bolsters, and with no lettering transfers at all. A load of beech dowel was supplied.

Within a matter of weeks from the first batches, the colour of the bolsters was changed from black to red. In 1924, LMS and LNER versions appeared, with white 'No. 2 Lumber Wagon' lettering on one side, and gold company initials on the other. The colour was still olive green with red bolsters. From 1925 the 'LMS' and 'LNER' initials appeared on both sides of the wagon, and the 'No. 2 Lumber Wagon' lettering was dropped. In 1926 GW versions appeared, and 'NE' lettering replaced 'LNER'. Two holes appeared in the top of each bolster from early in 1927. The first SR No. 2 Lumber Wagons of 1928 were in light brown, with blue bolsters; later they became dark brown, again with blue bolsters.

There may have been 1930 versions with no company lettering, and with lowered bogies, both features which are certainly found on the post-1931 No. 2 Lumber Wagons fitted with automatic couplings. The bogies were also re-positioned nearer the ends of the wagon because of the control wires. From 1933 the colour changed to bright yellow, with light green bolsters and bogies, but by 1935 the bogie colour had changed back to black. Axlebox slots appeared in the bogies in 1936, but axleboxes were not fitted. The late 1939 and 1940 versions of the No. 2 Lumber Wagon were in grey, with matt black bogies and red bolsters. (There was a transitional yellow version with red bolsters.) The final versions had couplings and bogies secured by rivets instead of the eyelets used before.

No. 2 Lumber Wagons were advertised in 1949, but were in fact mostly reserved for export. No details are known, but they were probably similar to

the wartime versions.

Minor variations during the life of the No. 2 Lumber Wagon included the size and shape of the chain links, and the staining of the lumber load, which varied from none at all at first, to light staining later in the 1920s, and to almost complete blackening from the mid 1930s.

MILK TANK WAGONS

In March 1929, the MM reported 'We have definitely decided to produce a model of a glass lined milk tank. This will be coloured in correct accordance with the standard practice of the "United Dairies".' Glass-lined milk tank wagons of 2000 to 3000 gallon capacity had been used since October 1927 by the

GW and LMS Railways, in collaboration with United Dairies, and they were followed by the LNER in December 1928. Previously milk had been carried mainly in churns.

Design of the Hornby Milk Tank Wagon had started in August 1928, although it was not catalogued until 1929. It was a substantial improvement on the Hornby wagons that had preceded it, as it attempted to reproduce many interesting features of the real UD tankers. The large diameter tank was set on cradles, and was fitted with end stays and bracing rods; it also had a ladder to reach the top inlet. The central filler cap was the same as that of the Petrol Tank Wagon, but there was a second inlet and a taller top outlet (complete with tap), which were specially-made castings. Drain cocks were also fitted at each end of the tank.

A typical Hornby design of the period, the Milk Tank Wagon was elaborate and expensive to make, and even at a price of 5s 6d it is doubtful if any profit remained. But whatever the economics, it was a most satisfactory wagon, definitely in the 'special' category. Consequently it looked out of place with the ordinary wagons.

The first issues were on the open axleguard base, painted in blue-grey with a white tank, and with the cast fittings hand-painted in blue-grey. By 1931 the revised standard wagon base had been fitted, with white tank, blue base, and with the fittings now left in white and not hand-finished. The bracing wires were simplified by gagging the lower ends instead of fitting them with the 10 BA circular nuts used previously; the wires were no longer nickel-plated as on the first issues, and consequently tarnished easily. Automatic couplings were fitted.

The colour of the base was changed to a lighter blue in 1933, and from 1934 the ladder was re-designed to allow the central inlet to be fixed directly to it, instead of to a separate inlet dome on the tank. This simplification helped to reduce the price of the United Dairies tanker to 4s 6d. The bracing wires were further simplified by gagging at the top end of the wires as well as the bottom, and another later change was the removal of the drain cocks from the ends.

The 1936 catalogues offered a new line, the Nestle's Milk Tank Wagon, produced concurrently with the United Dairies version. It was finished in green and white, with a blue lettering transfer, which in one version had a special all-blue trademark incorporated. After 1936 the special castings for the inlet and outlet were made in mazac, and often suffered from fatigue problems. The United Dairies Milk Tank Wagon was last advertised in the July 1937 MM, and it did not appear in the 1937–38 catalogues. At some time in 1937 or 1938 the colour of the Nestle's Milk Tank Wagon changed to blue and white, then in 1939 it appeared with a white tank, blue ladder and end stays, and a black base.

Although the design drawings were amended for the embossed trademark in 1946, it is unlikely that any Nestle's tankers were produced after the war.

MILK TRAFFIC VANS

Since the rattle of milk churns was as much a part of life on a country station as the porter's trolley and the station cat, it was not surprising that a Milk Traffic Van was made by Meccano Ltd from late 1923, at the same time as the No. 1 Cattle Truck. The two vans were very similar, being finished in the same colours (olive green base with pale green-grey sides and white roof), and both had sliding doors. But the slatting of the Milk Traffic Van sides extended down to the base, and the ends were not slatted as they were on the Cattle Truck. Construction was of course by Meccano nuts and bolts. One side of the base was lettered 'Milk Traffic Van', and there was a special feature: the base was fitted with four sets of clips to take milk churns, which were supplied with the wagon, and which could be loaded and unloaded by the nimble-fingered, or by those cunning enough to take off the roof! The milk churns were an accessory created specially for this van, and it was

not until the following year that sets of Platform Accessories were catalogued, featuring the same churns plus a trolley.

Only the very first Milk Traffic Vans had the clips for cans, as it was quickly realised that they were impractical; the four milk cans were still supplied, but not clipped to the base. In common with its predecessor, this second version of the van had no railway company lettering. The roof colour was changed to dark grey.

For the 1924–25 season, the vans were lettered 'LMS' or 'LNER' on one side, and 'Milk Traffic Van' on the other, but from 1925 'LMS' or 'LNER' lettering appeared on both sides. GW vans were first made in 1926, still nut-and-bolt bodied and in the same colours as the LMS and LNER.

Early in 1927 the Milk Traffic Vans were made with tabbed bodies instead of nut-and-bolt, and the colours altered. The 'NE' van (changed from 'LNER') had blue sides and roof with the olive green base, and although GW and LMS vans may possibly have been made in these colours, most LMS and GW vans, together with later NE vans, had a brighter green base. In 1928, SR Milk Traffic Vans were made, with cream roofs, green sides and black bases, the green sides representing the passenger train colours.

In 1930 the decision was made to abandon company lettering on the Milk Traffic Van, and a batch without lettering was made on the open-axleguard base. But within a short time the 1930–31 season vans were fitted with the revised standard wagon base; the colours were unchanged, with blue van sides and roof, and green underframe (and also green

Early version with clips for cans.

Nestlé's Milk Tank Wagons.

buffer beams and upper base platforms on a few 1930 wagons). A batch was also made in 1930 in the SR colours, with revised standard wagon underframe in black, green van sides and cream roof, but of course without the railway company lettering.

Automatic couplings were fitted from 1931, and in 1933 there was a spectacular livery of a lighter and brighter blue body, with a red underframe and a cream roof. The underframe colour changed to black around 1935, and (apart from a large batch made unintentionally with no planking embossed) there were no major changes until 1939–40, when Milk Traffic vans were made with blue roofs matching the body, and with matt black underframes.

Only 'Southern' green Milk Traffic Vans were made after the war; planking was no longer embossed, and the slatting was changed to leave a lettering panel in the lower left-hand corner of the van sides. The vans were finished in green with white roofs. Prewar-type bases without axlebox slots were fitted at first, and a few early vans were not overpainted green on the solebar as were the later postwar versions. Standard postwar bases were adopted from 1949.

There was a BR–S maroon version to replace the green 'Southern', and this was available from 1954 to 1957. There was no No. 50 Milk Traffic Van.

OPEN WAGONS

'Open' was never officially part of the description of the Hornby Wagon, although they are almost universally known as 'open wagons' to distinguish them from other types. Open wagons were made in extremely large numbers, and in very many batches, so the variations during their production make them among the most confusing subjects to tackle.

The first constructional Trucks of 1920 had the early wagon base with thick axles, fitted with brass buffers and brass couplings. The sides had embossed planking (strangely enough with no representation of a door), and were enamelled in grey, with clip-on letters 'GN', 'MR', and 'LNWR'. 'LBSC' and 'CR' wagons were added in 1921, by which time nickel-plated drop-link couplings and smaller brass buffers were fitted. There were subtle changes in the shade of grey used during the production of the pre-grouping wagons, and for the 1922–23 season some

wagons were fitted with thin-axle early wagon bases, and others with open-axleguard bases. All still had nickel-plated couplings and brass buffers. Zulu Wagons were available from 1922; they were lettered 'LNW' by stencil spraying, and were usually eyelet-fixed to the early wagon base, with thin axles on some versions but thick axles on others. The buffers were castings, and the couplings were sprayed black with the base.

The 1923–24 season No. 1 and No. 2 Hornby Goods Sets had LMS or LNER wagons, with white lettering by transfers rather than the clip-on letters used before, on wagon sides without holes for clip-on letters. Some had early wagon bases, with cast buffers and black couplings; others had the open

axleguard base with cast buffers and black couplings; but the No. 2 Goods Sets often had wagons on the open axleguard base with brass buffers and nickel-plated couplings.

In 1924 the long, thin wagon base came into use. At first LMS and LNER No. 1 Goods Sets usually had wagons with black couplings and cast buffers, while the No. 2 Goods sets usually had wagons with nickel couplings and brass buffers, all on the long thin base. But the brass-buffered version was in production only for a short time, after which all had the cast buffers and black couplings.

Zulu sets usually had LNW wagons in 1923, but in 1924 they were provided with wagons on old stock early wagon bases, with cast buffers and black couplings, with LMS white lettering transfers on old-stock wagon sides having unused slots for clip-on letters. There was no trademark transfer.

From early in 1925 there began a period in which the old stocks of constructional wagon parts were used up for No. 1 and No. 2 wagons (or No. 0–1–2 Wagons as they became known from later in 1925). These LMS and LNER wagons had either the early wagon base or the open axleguard base, now always with black couplings and cast buffers, and usually had sides slotted for pre-grouping letters. Working out what railway companies these slots correspond to reveals not just the expected combinations (MR, GN, LNWR, CR, LBSC, PLM & NORD) but also GE, SECR and ETAT. Since none of these three are known to have been marketed, these sides present an interesting puzzle; the common factor is the letter 'E', and it seems possible that the tools for making this letter were never completed although those for slotting the sides were.

The long, thin wagons continued on sale at the same time, but designs had been drawn up in April 1925 for an open axleguard wagon with tabbed construction, and these went into production and replaced the other wagons late in 1925.

In 1926, tabbed GW wagons were made, with white lettering transfers like those of the LMS and LNER wagons. White 'NE' lettering replaced 'LNER'. Late white-lettered and subsequent open wagons had single-piece sides, instead of the two-piece sides of the earlier tabbed wagons. The 1927 No. 0–1–2 Wagons were marked 'LMS', 'NE' and 'GW' in large gold letters, and in 1928 SR wagons in dark brown with large gold letters were also made.

In 1929, different No. 0 and No. 1 Wagons were offered instead of the single No. 0–1–2. The No. 0 Wagons were tinprinted in plain grey, with white LMS, NE, GW and SR letters, and cost 1s 6d, whereas the No. 1 Wagons continued to be enamelled, with large gold letters as before, and cost 1s 9d.

From 1930, the No. 0 Wagon sides were printed with detail; the planking and wagon doors were nicely represented in the printing, and planking was no longer embossed. All had the same wagon number, 12530, and it has been ingeniously suggested that this may have been the date on which the designs for the sides were drawn (i.e. 12 May, 1930). The

Some Hornby Wagons of the period 1923 to 1927.

LBSC Hornby Truck. The guarantee slip is dated July 1921.

188

No. 1-type Wagons of 1927 to 1930 (top row), 1930 (second row), 1930 to 1932 (third row) and 1932 to 1941 (bottom row).

No. 0 Wagons of 1929–30 (top row), 1930 (second row), 1930 to 1932 (third row) and 1932 onwards (bottom row). There were many other tinprinting and shade differences.

same wagon number was used on the M Wagons, but unlike the M equivalent, the SR No. 0 Wagon with detailed printing was brown not grey.

Late in 1930, the revised standard wagon base was adopted for both No. 0 and No. 1 Wagons. No. 1 Wagons appeared in quick succession on the new base first with large gold letters and drop link couplings, then with white letters and drop link couplings, and from early in 1931 with white letters and automatic couplings. Late in 1931 the single piece No. 1 Wagon body was revised, with the tabs in a different corner, a modification which also affected other open wagons (e.g. Coal, Open B etc.). The tinprintings of the No. 0 Wagons were revised in mid 1931, with the planking in black and white lines instead of just black lines, and again later in 1931 with rivet heads printed on the corners of the wagon.

Late in 1932 the decision was made that both No. 0 and No. 1 Wagons would be tinprinted, and to justify the extra cost of the No. 1, tinprinted clip-on solebars were added. Planking was no longer embossed on the No. 1. But briefly in 1933–34 a few enamelled No. 1 Wagons were made (for the last time for the home market, although export wagons

were still enamelled) for sale in the No. 2 Mixed Goods Train Set. These wagons had light grey bodies with white lettering transfers (LMS and GW versions are known) and had green underframes to match the rest of the set. However most sets continued to have tinprinted No. 1 Wagons, which always looked out of place with enamelled stock.

The only changes thereafter were minor ones in the tinprinting. At first the LMS, NE and GW colours tended to be greenish-greys; early in 1934 new printings (still greenish-grey) had thicker-lettered '12530' numbers. In the mid 1930s the colours were more neutral greys, and in the late 1930s pinkish or yellowish shades of grey were normal. Matt bases were used from 1939. All the SR wagons were dark chocolate brown.

The first postwar 201 Goods Sets had LMS, NE, GW or SR Wagons with prewar style printing and with clip-on solebars. The prewar-type base with axlebox slots was used, distinguishable by the embossed trademark. Rivet-heads were not usually embossed on postwar Wagons, as they had been on prewar Wagons.

Early in 1948 new printings were used for brown

LMS and grey NE Wagons; both had large letters, and the insides of the wagons were printed black to match the base. The bases were now the prewar-type without axlebox slots. Solebars were fitted for a short period until April 1948 when their use was discontinued. From 1949 the standard postwar wagon base was used, still with the large-lettered LMS and NE tinprinted sides. It was not until 1950 that small-lettered LMS and NE wagons were made, matching the style of the postwar vans.

These wagons continued in production with only minor changes in the shade of the tinprinting, until 1954 when the No. 1 Wagon in BR grey was announced. The BR No. 1 Wagon was catalogued until 1958, and the No. 50 Wagon which superseded it, from 1957 to 1968.

OPEN WAGON B

'Open Wagon B' was the rather curious name adopted for the wagon that was originally to have been sold as the 'Mineral Wagon'. No 'official' explanation was ever given for the 'B' in the title. However, the wagon itself was a perfectly satisfactory vehicle,

189

Shell and BP Tank Wagons.

Open Wagons B, circa 1931 (top row), 1933 (second row) and after 1934 (bottom row).

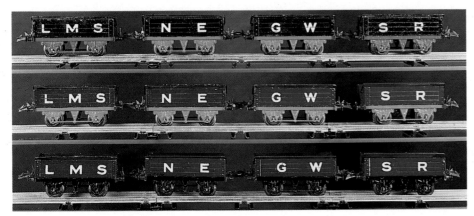

Pratt's, National Benzole, Redline and Redline Glico Tank Wagons. There was also a Redline Glico tanker with diecast filler cap. (The filler is missing from the 1930 Redline tanker).

190

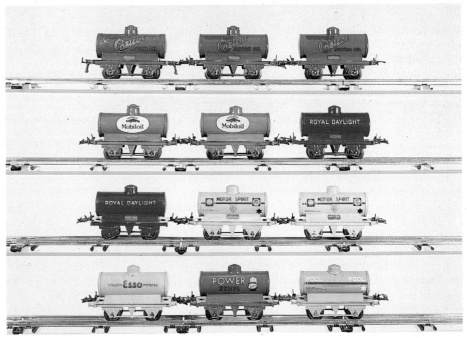

Castrol, Mobiloil, Royal Daylight, ShellMex and BP, Esso, Power Ethyl and Pool Tank Wagons.

based on the No. 1 Wagon but with a sheet rail added. The body was enamelled in black, and the underframe in green; the sides were lettered LMS, NE, GW or SR, always in white letters.

There was a change of colour in 1933, to Redline-blue for the body and lighter green for the underframe. In 1934 the price fell from the original 2s 3d to 2s. The colour of the underframe was changed again to black from late in 1934, and early in 1935 the sheet rail, which had been riveted to the wagon, was bent to clip into plain holes in the wagon ends. Both body and sheet rail were still painted blue, but from 1936 the sheet rail was finished in black. The last versions in 1939 and 1940 all had matt black underframes, while the last LMS version had serif letters instead of the former sans-serif.

There were substantial changes when production resumed in 1948. The name was changed to 'Wagon with Tarpaulin Support', and the sides were now tinprintings identical to the No. 1 Wagon, being brown sides lettered 'LMS' and grey sides lettered 'NE', both in the postwar large-letter style. The first wagons were on the prewar-type base without axlebox slots, and with the postwar embossed trademark; later versions had the standard postwar base.

The wagons produced late in 1950 were called 'Wagon with Sheet Rail', a description used in the catalogues from early 1951. The sides were tin-printed with small LMS and NE letters. The only differences between the No. 1 Wagon and the Wagon with Sheet Rail were the addition of the rail, and of course the extra 3d on the price.

A British Railways version of the Wagon with Sheet Rail was introduced in 1954, but there was no No. 50 version; the Wagon with Sheet Rail disappeared from the lists in 1958.

PETROL AND OIL TANK WAGONS

Petrol Tank Wagons were first made by Hornby in 1922, and the 'Shell' tanker was shown in the May 1922 MM, price 3s 6d. It was finished in bright red overall (whereas most other wagons at the time had black bases), with buffers hand-finished in black, and it had a gold 'Motor SHELL Spirit' transfer. The tank was fitted with the diecast safety valve of the No. 2 Loco, by way of a filler. A few were sold with the lever arm intact, but except on the earliest tank wagons it was cut off in the factory prior to enamelling. At first the thin-axle early wagon base was fitted, but from late in 1922 the open axleguard base was used.

The first batch of National Benzole Petrol Tank Wagons was made in April 1923, in a smart yellow enamel, with black buffers on the open axleguard base. They were lettered in gold, not very suitably because of the lack of contrast with the tank colour.

From 1924, both Shell and National Benzole tankers were altered to take a new filler assembly, secured to the tank by four lugs in the same way as the loco domes. The filler dome was flat-topped, and was fitted with an inlet casting.

Pratt's 'Angloco' Petrol Tank Wagons were added to the range in 1925. They were finished in green, with black buffers. The next addition to the range was the BP Motor Spirit Tank Wagon, introduced in the 1927–28 season catalogues. This was finished in cream, with attractive transfers incorporating a broad red line. The buffers were not finished black, nor were those of the 1927–28 season or later Shell and Pratt's tankers.

Redline Petrol Tank Wagons were included in the range from 1928; they were finished in blue, with a red line as part of the transfer. The early National Benzole tanker was last listed in the 1928–29 catalogues, although it is likely that production had stopped much earlier and that only remaining stocks were available for sale.

The four Petrol Tank Wagons available in 1929–30 were Shell, BP, Pratt's and Redline. In 1930 the tank wagons were redesigned for the revised standard wagon base; all four were re-issued on the new base, together with a fifth tank – the green Castrol Oil Tank Wagon (all the others had been Petrol or Motor Spirit Tank Wagons). The Pratt's tanker was changed to a new style, enamelled in orange instead of green and with 'High Test' transfers instead of 'Angloco'. There were special trademarks incorporated in the 'High Test' transfer, with red lettering, although ordinary trademarks were sometimes used.

Automatic couplings were fitted to all five of these tankers from 1931, and the flanges on the tank ends were reduced in depth, when the tools for the No. 1 Tank Loco smokebox door were revised. The Pratt's High Test transfers were changed to a new style with a circular 'High Test' emblem. Also new was a Mobiloil Oil Tank Wagon, finished in a dull grey, with a distinctive 'gargoyle' transfer. Also from 1931, the Shell Petrol Tank Wagon was made in a version without buffers for the M3 Tank Goods Set.

The 1932–33 range of tankers was unchanged except that the 'Redline' tanker was re-named 'Redline Glico' on new transfers, and the BP transfers changed to a new style with large gold letters, without the red band and detailed lettering of the earlier BP.

Whereas the colours of most Hornby wagons were brightened in 1933, the tankers were hardly affected since they were already a fairly bright crowd, but the Pratt's tanker was changed to a lighter shade of orange. Early in 1934 all six (Shell, BP, Pratt's High Test, Redline Glico, Castrol and Mobiloil) were made with the top of the inlet embossed with the inlet cap instead of having a separate casting attached. From 1935 there was a change of name to 'No. 1 Petrol Tank Wagon' because of the introduction of the MO Petrol Tank Wagon, but there was no alteration in any of the wagons.

There was a change in the range of tankers in the middle of 1936, with three of the longest-standing names, Shell, BP and Pratt's being replaced. The No. 1 ShellMex and BP Petrol Tank Wagon was issued because of the amalgamation of the two companies; it was in cream, and replaced the BP tanker. The Royal Daylight Oil Tank Wagon replaced Shell tankers both for separate sale and in the boxed sets. Esso tankers, in buff, replaced Pratt's. Although the ShellMex and BP tanker lasted for only two years, being replaced from mid 1938 by the green No. 1 Power Ethyl Petrol Tank Wagon, it was made in several different batches, the later versions being in a richer cream colour.

In October 1940 the Meccano Magazine showed the Pool Petrol Tank Wagon, finished in grey but with a red-lined transfer. It does not appear to have replaced all the other tankers, several of which were sold in the same wartime buff coloured boxes; Royal Daylight, Castrol, Redline Glico and probably others. These tankers were among the last items to be made in Binns Road during the war.

The first 201 Tank Goods Sets of 1946 had Pool Petrol Tank Wagons or Royal Daylight Oil Tank Wagons. The Royal Daylight tankers were grey, not red as before and during the war. Both were on the prewar-type base with axlebox slots, but had embossed trademarks. Several batches of Pool tankers were made, including one that was a particularly dark grey, and a later one on the prewar-type base without axlebox slots; this base may also have been used for 'Royal Daylight' tankers. Up to 1948, tank wagons were sold only in sets, not separately.

From the middle of 1948 a new tank wagon was made; a Shell tank wagon, with red tank, lettered 'Motor SHELL Spirit' in dark blue letters applied by a rubber stamp, varying in shade according to the ink used. The colour of the base was changed to black, for this and all subsequent postwar tankers, the tank and base now being sprayed separately. The first Shell tankers were on the prewar-type base without axlebox slots, but by 1949 the standard postwar base was used. The Shell tankers were sold separately, as well as in sets, the buff-coloured boxes having been printed much earlier, in 1946.

Colman's Mustard Van, 1923–24.→

Carr's Biscuit Van, 1924.↘

↙ Seccotine Van, 1924–25.

192

No. 1 Esso Tank Wagons replaced Shell from late 1949 or early 1950; the finish was aluminium on a black base, with plain black lettering. National Benzole replaced Esso in 1953, again with an aluminium tank but with more attractive lettering transfers. It was not until 1955 that the customer was offered a choice, when the No. 1 Shell Lubricating Oil Tank Wagon and the No. 1 Manchester Oil Refinery Tank Wagon replaced National Benzole. Colours were yellow and green respectively.

In 1957 both tankers were replaced by the No. 50 Shell Lubricating Oil Tank Wagon and the No. 50 Manchester Oil Refinery Tank Wagon. The No. 50 series tank wagons were much improved on the old No. 1 style, with larger tanks and more realistic fillers, better representing the contemporary vehicles of British Railways. The No. 50 Manchester Oil tanker was dropped from the lists in 1961, but the Shell Lubricating Oil tanker was still on sale in 1969.

Although the Manchester Oil Refinery Tank Wagons were green, there were two components in the colour. When exposed to bright light the yellow component fades to leave the tank in a pale blue-green; the prewar Shell tank wagons were also liable to fade in bright sunshine, to a pale pink.

PRIVATE OWNERS' VANS

One of the best features of the Hornby Series was that it offered a wide range of rolling stock, and in particular dozens of different vans. Private owners' vans were among the most colourful and were also (as indeed they remain) among the most popular.

The first private owner's van was the Colman's Mustard Van introduced for the 1923–24 season; it was on a standard nut-and-bolt open axleguard base, like the Gunpowder Van, but was coloured yellow and had most attractive transfers on the whole van side. It was short-lived, and did not re-appear in the following year's catalogues; according to the MM it 'did not prove popular'. There were one or two minor variations, such as the varnish used on some 1924 Colman's Van sides. The buff boxes had the Covered Luggage Van label, but were also rubber stamped 'Colmans'.

Crawford's Biscuit Vans, circa 1924, 1928 1932, 1933, 1935 and 1938.

Carr's Biscuit Vans, circa 1925, 1927, 1933 and 1935.

There were no less than four new private owners' vans for 1924–25, a Seccotine Van with a dark blue body and orange roof, and three Biscuit Vans: a blue Carr's Van, a red Crawford's Van and crimson lake Jacob's Van, each with a white roof. The earliest Carr's Biscuit Vans of mid 1924 were in a markedly lighter blue than the later 1924–25 versions. During 1925 several private owners' vans were fitted with the old nut-and-bolt coach bases with detachable axleguards, while a few had the early wagon base, but most were still on the open axleguard base. From mid 1925 the roofs of the Biscuit Vans were finished in the same colours as the bodies. Jacob's Biscuit Vans were only crimson lake on the first issues, from 1925 they were finished in a maroon colour, often

appearing near to brown under the coat of varnish.

From early in 1927 there were new bodies for all the private owners' vans, still on the open axleguard base but tabbed instead of nut-and-bolt. The colours were unchanged, except that the colour of the Carr's Biscuit Van became a duller grey-blue.

The revised standard wagon base was fitted from 1930, and automatic couplings from early 1931. A fifth van was added to the series in 1931, the Fyffes Banana Van. It had been available in France the previous year, but although the French versions were originally made on the open axleguard base all UK models had the more modern base and automatic couplings. Colours were yellow for the body, green for the underframe and cream for the roof.

These first Fyffes vans had hinged doors, in common with the other vans, but later in 1931 the bodies were re-designed with sliding doors. The colour scheme and the transfers of the sliding-door Fyffes van were unchanged. It was quickly discovered that the transfers of the Seccotine, Carr's, Crawford's, and Jacob's Vans were unsuitable for the new sliding-door van bodies, (although sliding-door Crawford's and Carr's Vans and possibly others were briefly made with the existing transfers), and rather than make new transfers, from 1933 these vans were produced once again using the old-style hinged door bodies. The Fyffes vans continued to have sliding doors, and the Cadbury's Chocolate van added to the range in 1932 had transfers designed for

Fyffes Banana Vans, circa 1931, 1932, 1937 and 1939.

194

Jacob's Biscuit Vans, circa 1924, 1929, 1933 and 1935. The final version (not shown) had a brown body with a maroon roof and a matt base.

the sliding door body and did not appear with hinged doors. The Cadbury's Van was blue, with a white roof (although mistakenly advertised as having an orange roof!) and the transfers were a surprisingly good reproduction of the real railway vans owned by Cadbury, except that the lettering should have read 'Cadbury's Bournville' instead of 'Cadbury's Chocolate'.

In 1933 there were some colour changes, with the Carr's and Cadbury's Vans in lighter blue, the latter on a green underframe instead of black. The Fyffes Van became a different shade of yellow, with red underframe and red roof, and the Seccotine Van may also have appeared at this time with a red roof, but still with the dark blue body. The Jacob's Van was unchanged. Fyffes and Cadbury's Vans were still the only ones with sliding doors, but during 1935 new transfers were made for the Biscuit Vans, and the Crawford's and Carr's Vans reverted to the sliding door body, while the Jacob's Vans appeared in this style possibly for the first time. The colour of the Cadbury's Van underframe changed back to black. No new transfers were made for the Seccotine Van, which was dropped from the range in 1935. The Fyffes Van was given revised transfers in a darker blue.

There was little further change until 1938, when the lettering of the Cadbury's Van transfers became block instead of serif, and there was a small amendment to the Crawford's Van transfers which now read 'By Appointment to the late King George V' instead of just 'By Appointment'. Carr's Vans were unchanged except in minor detail.

A new private owner's van was issued in 1938, the Palethorpe's Sausage Van. Made in large numbers, it represented some vehicles recently put into service on the railways, and shown in the February 1937 MM. The body was maroon, and the roof grey.

The only subsequent change was that the Fyffes Van underframe became black instead of red in 1939. No private owners' vans were made after the war.

REFRIGERATOR VANS

It seems very likely that Refrigerator Vans were actually on sale well before they were first advertised

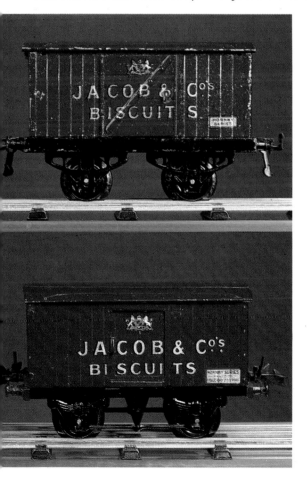

Cadbury's Chocolate Vans, circa 1932, 1933, 1936 and 1938.

195

Palethorpe's Sausage Van.

Refrigerator Vans.

in May 1923; otherwise it is hard to explain why they appeared in so many different Midland Railway versions before they were replaced in 1924 by LMS and LNER vans. The first MR vans were exactly like the Covered Luggage Vans of 1921, having early wagon bases (with thick axles), plain roofs, and early door handles, but being finished in white enamel with black clip-on letters. There was a slightly later version with 'Refrigerator Van' transfers on the door. Unlike the Luggage Van, the Refrigerator Van kept this lettering on all subsequent versions. The next series of MR vans had the open axleguard base, and roofs embossed with rain strips which had in fact been used for some earlier vans.

The LMS and LNER Refrigerator Vans of 1924 had black transfers rather than clip-on letters; the body and roof were still white, and the base black. A few 1924–25 versions had the 'Refrigerator Van' transfer on the solebar, but soon they were lettered on the door again as before. GW Refrigerator Vans went on sale in 1926. From early 1927 the LMS, LNER and GW vans were tabbed instead of nut-and-bolt; later in the same year the 'LNER' lettering was changed to 'NE' only. In 1928 SR Refrigerator Vans appeared, which were enamelled in pink instead of the usual white, and had large gold SR letters as used on the Luggage Vans, rather than specially-made black SR lettering transfers, although these were made for subsequent SR Refrigerator Vans.

From 1930 the Refrigerator Vans were fitted with the revised standard wagon base. Automatic couplings were fitted from 1931, and from late 1931 sliding doors replaced hinged doors. Around this time the 'Refrigerator Van' transfers on the doors, which had been white letters outlined in black, were altered to simple black lettering. Blue underframes and blue roofs were used for the LMS, NE and GW Refrigerator Vans for the 1933–34 season only; no pink and blue SR version has been sighted! The bodies of the LMS, NE and GW vans were still white, but there were new LMS transfers with smaller black letters. In 1934 the colour of the roof was changed back to white, and the underframe to black. New SR transfers with small black letters were used from 1937, and small letter transfers were also used for GW and NE vans from 1939.

After the war, the Refrigerator Van was available

in LMS and NE liveries from 1948; GW and SR versions were mentioned on the production drawings but may never have been made. Lamp brackets were fitted, as on the No. 1 Goods Van.

The LMS Refrigerator Van was buff coloured, with a grey roof, and except on the very first postwar issues solebars were painted in the same colour as the van. The first issue LMS Refrigerator Vans were on the prewar-type base without axlebox slots, and some lacked the usual flat panel for lettering in the bottom left-hand corner of the van, the lettering being applied over the embossed planking. Later the standard postwar base was used, at first (and most commonly) with a flat lettering panel on the left-hand side, but later with flat panels on the right-hand as well. The No. 1 Goods Van had been changed to BR livery a few weeks before the Refrigerator Van, and the last version resulted from using the updated Goods Van tools for Refrigerator Van bodies. In fact, strictly speaking the design drawings indicate that the pre-BR Refrigerator Vans should not have had any flat panels at all, and that the use of Goods Van bodies was incorrect.

NE Refrigerator Vans had white roofs and bodies, and black bases. The solebars were never white-painted. These vans were lettered on the lower left-hand corner of the body, and as on the LMS Refrigerator Van the size and style of the lettering varied, more than for most of the other postwar vehicles. Again there was confusion over the flat lettering panels, and both the first NE version on the prewar-type base without axlebox slots and the later NE vans on the standard postwar base appeared both with and without a flat panel.

The LMS and NE versions were replaced in 1954 by BR No. 1 Refrigerator Vans, in white with grey roofs. These in turn were replaced in 1957 by the tinprinted No. 50 Refrigerator Vans, which remained on sale until 1969.

No. 0 ROTARY TIPPING WAGONS

The No. 0 Rotary Tipping Wagon was introduced in 1934; the first versions had blue-enamelled tippers, and red-enamelled open axleguard bases. They had no buffers, and were fitted with cranked auto-

Rotary Tipping Wagons; No. 0 versions on the bottom row.

matic couplings; the price was only 1s 6d. A 'Meccano' transfer was applied only on one side of the tipper; because of the hinge of the tipper, the letters were much smaller than those of the Coal Wagon. There was no lining on the top of the sides.

From 1935 the No. 0 Rotary Tipping Wagons had plain blue sides without transfers, although mask-sprayed red lining was added on both sides at the top of the tipper. The final versions of 1939–40 had matt black bases, with blue tops now mask-sprayed on each side with Redline-blue lining. Despite a lack of aesthetic appeal, the No. 0 Rotary Tipping Wagons had been popular because of their low price, but they did not re-appear after the war.

No. 1 ROTARY TIPPING WAGONS

The Rotary Tipping Wagon was first shown in the May 1923 Rail Formations leaflet, with a black base, and 'Rotary Tipping Wagon' lettering on the side of the tipper. The price was 3s 6d. On production versions one side of the grey-enamelled top was actually lettered 'Rotary Tipper', and the other was blank. Later in 1923 'Sir Robert McAlpine & Sons, London' transfers were used; there were two versions with black bases, one with McAlpine both sides, and the other with McAlpine one side and 'Rotary Tipper' the other.

Probably late in 1923, the base of the tipper was enamelled in olive green instead of black, and at first there were McAlpine transfers on both sides of the tipper. From 1924 one side was lettered 'Rotary Tipper' and the other McAlpine, then later both sides were again lettered McAlpine. The confusion over the lettering had been remarkable even by Binns Road standards!

The Rotary Tipping Wagon was one of the first to appear in the new colour schemes that were used for most wagons in 1927. In fact it was probably late in 1926 that the colour was changed to orange. Unchanged McAlpine transfers were used on both sides. It is not clear exactly when the transfers were altered to 'Meccano', but it was probably late in 1929 or early in 1930; the 'Meccano' version was first mentioned in the May 1930 MM. The colour was still orange. The revised standard wagon base was fitted from 1930, and automatic couplings from 1931. The colour of the 'Meccano' Rotary Tipping Wagon was changed to blue with a yellow top in the early '30s; interestingly the 1932 Meccano Products catalogue gave the new colours, so once again the Rotary Tipper may have been one of the first to be changed to the new colour schemes.

There was a change of name to No. 1 Rotary Tipping Wagon in 1934, following the introduction of the No. 0. The 'Meccano' No. 1 Rotary Tipping Wagon was superseded by one with 'Trinidad Lake Asphalt' transfers, first shown in the 1936 catalogues. The colours were unchanged, yellow and blue; in 1937 the price was 1s 11d. There was a new 'Trinidad Lake Asphalt' livery in 1939, with a matt black base instead of blue, although the yellow tipper and the transfers were unchanged.

After the war, No. 1 Rotary Tipping Wagons were available from 1948; the first were on the prewar-type base with axlebox slots (but with the postwar trademark), then on the same base without slots, and by 1949 had the standard postwar wagon base. The 'Trinidad Lake Asphalt' transfers were similar to the prewar type, but the body colour was buff, not yellow, though still on a matt black base. The No. 50 Rotary Tipping Wagon of 1957 was in similar colours but on a shiny black base. The No. 1 was available to 1959, and the No. 50 to 1969. The Rotary Tipping Wagons were a popular choice at the toyshop counter, and the many variants make an interesting and colourful collection.

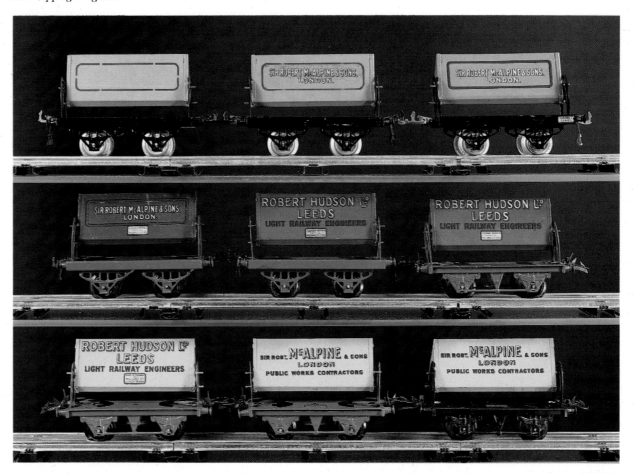

SIDE TIPPING WAGONS

The Side Tipping Wagon was first made early in 1923, and was finished (like the Rotary and Hopper Wagons) in grey, with a black open axleguard base. The first versions were lettered 'Tilting Wagon' on top of the base, whereas the catalogue pictures (for example in the Rail Formations leaflet of May 1923) showed 'Side Tipping Wagon' lettering. The grey tipper section was unlettered, but was stencil-sprayed with rectangular red enamel lining. Later the top of the base was lettered 'Tipping Wagon' instead of 'Tilting Wagon'.

By 1924, the sides of the tipper were lettered 'Sir Robert McAlpine & Sons, London' with the same transfers that were used for the Rotary Tipping Wagon. At first the bases were lettered 'Tipping Wagon' as before, and the red lining was mask-sprayed; later the lining was changed to a transfer, and later still from early in 1925, the 'Tipping Wagon' lettering no longer appeared.

The colours changed early in 1927, with the wagon now finished in blue on both body and base, but with the same transfer lining and McAlpine lettering. In 1929 new transfers were prepared, lettered 'Robert Hudson Ltd. Leeds Light Railway Engineers'; the Robert Hudson Side Tipping Wagon and the McAlpine were both catalogued in 1929, but from 1930 only the Robert Hudson appeared; it is probable that the McAlpine was only being offered until stocks ran out. In 1930 the Robert Hudson wagon was fitted with the revised standard wagon base, and as usual with automatic couplings from 1931.

Early in 1933 the colours changed to yellow for the top and lighter blue for the base, but transfers were unaltered. From 1935 'No. 1' was added to the name because of the introduction of the MO. The lowest price was 1s 9d in 1937.

In 1938 the Robert Hudson No. 1 Side Tipping Wagon was replaced by a new version lettered 'Sir Robt. McAlpine & Sons, London. Public Works Contractors'. These new wagons were shown in the 1938 HBT and Meccano Products catalogues. The colours were yellow and blue as before, but the final prewar versions of 1939 were made with matt black bases instead of blue.

The postwar No. 1 Side Tipping Wagons, available from 1948, were coloured buff with black bases; the first were on the prewar-type base without axlebox slots, then from 1949 the standard postwar base was used. There were minor differences in the transfers; on some the holes in the 'R' of 'SIR' and in other letters were filled in, on others they were not.

There was a change of livery to green for the tipper section circa 1956; the transfers were unchanged. However the No. 50 Side Tipping Wagons of 1957 which replaced the No. 1 had completely different transfers, with 'McAlpine' in yellow instead of gold, and lettered 'Sir Robert McAlpine & Sons Ltd. Civil Engineering Contractors', not Public Works Contractors as on the No. 1. The No. 50 version was still on sale in 1969.

SNOWPLOUGHS

The first Snowploughs were made late in 1923 or early in 1924, too late for the 1923–24 season catalogues; they were not advertised until the following season. They were based on the nut-and-bolt van, on the open axleguard base, but having a rotary plough with headlight mounted on the front, with a rotating fan connected to the front axle by Meccano Spring Cord running on pulleys. Discharge was to the right of the track (facing in direction of travel). The van was enamelled grey, with a red fan, black base and dark grey roof. The doors were grey, with white

'Snowplough' lettering and lining. Black lining was used for the plough section and for the corner uprights of the van; there were no company initials. The price on introduction was 5s 6d, and by 1934 this had fallen to 3s 6d.

Later in 1924, existing stocks of these vans had LMS (and possibly LNER) lettering added to both solebars, and an overall varnish was applied. New batches of Snowploughs now being made had LMS or LNER lettering on both sides, but without the black lining of the uprights, although the plough section was still lined. A few LMS vans were produced without the 'Snowplough' lettering on one or both doors, probably inadvertently. GW Snowploughs were made in 1926, in grey and black with black lining, but later in 1926 the colour of the headlamp and of the lining of the plough changed to red from black on the LMS, LNER and GW versions, which were still of nut-and-bolt construction. Soon dark grey tinprinted doors were fitted instead of enamelled doors.

Colours were changed for the tabbed-body LMS, NE and GW Snowploughs of 1927, which had

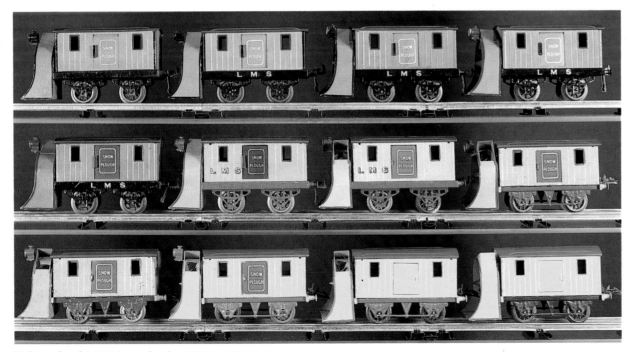

Unlettered and LMS Snowploughs, 1924 to 1940.

An LNER Snowplough, circa 1925.

199

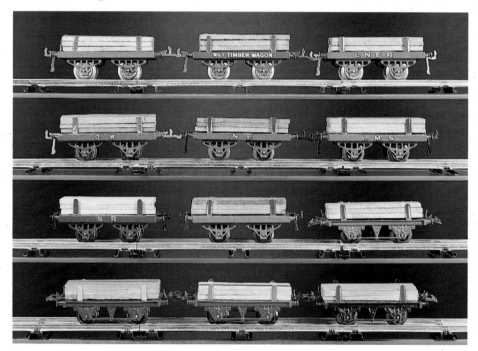

green bases, green roofs, green fans, and pale green-grey sides. Company initials were now on the side of the vans, not on the base as before. At first the doors were in the darker grey, but from 1928 they were tinprinted in green to match the base and roof of the LMS, NE, GW and new SR vans. Late versions of the Snowplough on the open axleguard base had the fan discharge to the left instead of to the right, and from early in 1930 Snowploughs no longer bore company lettering; some were made on the open axleguard base but with no initials. Later in 1930 the revised standard wagon base was adopted, with the plough still mounted in the old position, too low for proper clearance of the track. Soon new versions were made with the plough mounted higher on the van end than before. Automatic couplings were fitted from 1931, and in 1932 the colour of the Snowplough underframe was changed to red, with the other colours unchanged.

In 1933, the Snowplough emerged with a bright yellow body, blue underframe, blue roof, blue fan, green sliding doors (still with 'Snowplough' letter-ing), and blue-lined chute. The headlamp was still fitted, and was coloured blue. But in 1934 the Snow-plough was simplified, with no headlamp, and with sliding doors now replaced by an embossed outline and embossed door handle. Colours were blue and yellow.

From 1936, the underframe was finished in black, and Meccano rubber drive bands replaced the Spring Cord. Bases were matt-varnished from 1939, and the final 1940 version had the discharge chute still placed on the left-hand side but now arranged for throw to the right. Snowploughs were not available after the war.

No. 1 TIMBER WAGONS

The Small Timber Wagon advertised in the November 1922 MM was simply made, being formed from the open axleguard base by pressing upward four stanchions, and loading the wagon with three planks of timber, secured by Meccano-type string (which varied in colour and thickness over the years)

threaded through the coupling eyelets. Finish was olive green enamel; the wood load was usually left with a rough sawn surface and not planed. The earliest No. 1 Timber Wagons had no lettering of any sort, and were priced at a modest 2s (reduced to 1s 3d by 1937), which made them among the cheapest in the range, and consequently most popular. Loading and unloading the wagon (and of course normal accidental damage) revealed weaknesses in the pressed-metal stanchions, which frequently snapped off.

It seems likely that a 1923 version would have been made, with white 'No. 1 Timber Wagon' let-tering transfers on the base but without company initials. The 1924 versions were lettered 'No. 1 Tim-ber Wagon' on one side of the wagon and 'LMS' or 'LNER' on the other, but by 1925 the company initials appeared on both sides of the wagon.

GW lettering was offered from 1926, and from early in 1927 'NE' lettering replaced 'LNER', and the stanchions were painted in red. Soon the form of the stanchions was changed from flat-topped to round-topped. In 1928 SR versions became available, in the lighter-than-usual (for SR) brown also used for the SR Lumber Wagons and Brake Vans of the period. The stanchions were finished red.

Company lettering was omitted from open axle-guard base No. 1 Timber Wagons from early in 1930, and within a short period the revised standard wagon base was being used, in the same colours, olive green base with red stanchions. From early in 1931 automatic couplings were fitted to the olive green wagons, but by the end of the year the colour of the No. 1 Timber Wagon had changed to red, with green stanchions. Bufferless Timber wagons were made from 1931 for the M3 Tank Goods Train Set. Apart from slight changes in shade, the No. 1 Timber Wagon remained the same (except for a reduction in the number of planks from three to two in 1934) until 1939 when black wagons with red stanchions were manufactured. A few red versions with yellow-painted stanchions had been made circa 1933.

Postwar No. 1 Timber Wagons were made from 1946 for sale in the 201 Goods Set. The postwar wagons were in black with red stanchions, at first on the prewar-type wagon base with axlebox slots, but with embossed trademarks. Later postwar versions were on the prewar-type base without slots, and from 1949 on the postwar standard base. No equivalent of the Timber Wagon was included in the range of No. 50 wagons, and it was no longer catalogued once stocks ran out in 1959.

No. 2 TIMBER WAGONS

When the Timber Wagon was added to the range of Hornby Trains in January 1922, it was the first bogie wagon to appear (indeed, it was only the third wagon of any description). It was the same shape as the No. 2 Coach base, with the addition of five very thick U-shaped stanchions riveted to the base, and was non-constructional (except that the bogies and the Meccano-type brass buffers unscrewed). Five planks were tied down to the olive green base by two loops of Meccano-type string (which as on the No. 1 Timber Wagon varied in thickness and colour over the years). As on the No. 2 Coach, the bogies were held on by pivot bolts, and were fitted with thick

axles. Couplings were nickel plated. The early Timber Wagon was the most solid and weighty wagon made by Meccano Ltd, and they recommended its use (as for all subsequent bogie wagons) only on 2 ft radius rails, although it was actually capable of negotiating tighter curves (until bogie stops were fitted in the mid '20s).

Early in 1923, following the introduction of the No. 1 Timber Wagon, the Timber Wagon was re-named No. 2, and it was re-designed in a new form with stanchions pressed out from the base, instead of being attached as separate pieces. The new stanchions were shorter, so the number of planks was cut from five to three. To save weight, two short pieces of timber were added under each end to raise the planks above the level of the base, rather than having a complete fourth plank below. Couplings were

now in olive green, and buffers were diecast, not the Meccano type. The bogies were revised for thin axles, and for attachment by eyelets instead of the pivot bolts. There was still no lettering of any sort. Later in the year white 'No. 2 Timber Wagon' lettering was added on both sides of the base.

The earliest post-grouping wagons, late in 1923 or early in 1924, had 'LMS' or 'L&NER' lettering one side, and 'No. 2 Timber Wagon' the other. There was probably a version with 'LNER' instead of 'L&NER', still with 'No. 2 Timber Wagon' lettering one side; but from 1925, the company initials 'LMS' or 'LNER' appeared on both wagon sides, and the 'No. 2 Timber Wagon' lettering was discontinued. GW versions were sold from 1926, and from 1927 'NE' lettering replaced 'LNER', and the stanchions were finished in red. The SR version of 1928

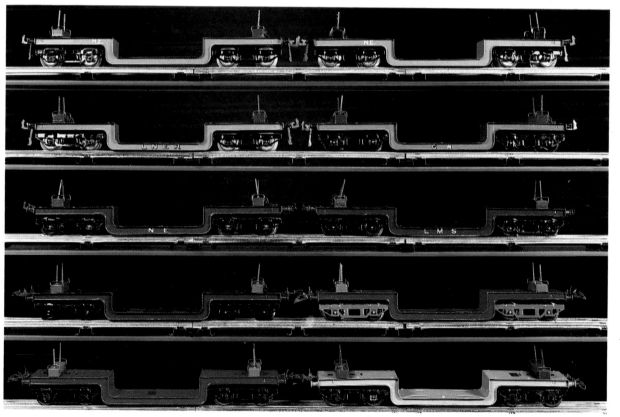

Trolley Wagons.

was finished in light brown, with red stanchions. But in 1930 (or perhaps not until 1931, when automatic couplings were fitted and the bogies moved nearer the end of the wagon) the wagon was re-designed for the lower buffer height by simply pressing the stanchions in the opposite direction and using the base the other way up. (It was unfortunate that this had not been done from the outset in 1923, and the taller No. 2 Lumber wagon bogies fitted to give the correct height.) Company lettering was no longer applied.

In 1933 the colours changed to red, with green uprights and green bogies. By 1934 the price had fallen to 2s 6d, not much more than for a four-wheel van; it was the cheapest bogie wagon, and consequently extremely popular. In 1936 the bogies changed back to black. From late in 1936 axlebox slots appeared, although boxes were not fitted. Late versions of the No. 2 Timber Wagon in 1939 had grey bodies with red stanchions, and from late 1939 riveted couplings and riveted bogies were the norm. The No. 2 Timber Wagon did not re-appear after the war.

TROLLEY WAGONS

The Trolley Wagon was shown in the May 1923 Rail Formations leaflet, and distinguished itself by being the first Hornby Wagon to appear in post-grouping colours, being shown lettered 'NE' (although it is just possible that this may have been North Eastern Railway livery!). The earliest known examples were made in May 1923, and were finished in grey enamel, with black buffers, and with white 'NE' letters above one of the bogies. They were lettered '50 Ton Trolley Wagon' in white on top of the well, whereas the catalogue illustrations had shown them lettered 'Well Wagon' on the side. As with the Lumber Wagons there was some confusion on the colour of the bolsters, black and red versions both appearing in the same month. Red bolsters became standard very quickly.

From 1924, the more standard post-grouping letterings 'LMS' or 'LNER' were used, the gold lettering transfers being applied on the sides of well, and '50 Ton Trolley Wagon' still on the top in white letters. From 1925 the '50 Ton Trolley' transfer was

in gold and from 1926 it was no longer used at all. Also available in 1926 were GW Trolley Wagons, still with black buffers, although all Trolley Wagons from late in 1926 had grey buffers.

The LNER initials were shortened to 'NE' only late in 1926, and in 1927 the colour of the LMS, NE and GW Trolley Wagons changed to brown with blue bolsters. SR Trolley Wagons were sold from 1928, finished in dark brown with blue bolsters.

From 1930, company initials ceased to be used, the colour being the 'normal' brown of the LMS, NE and GW wagons. Cranked automatic couplings were fitted from 1931, and the height of the buffers was changed by deepening the buffer beam. Lowered bogies could not be used, since the well would then have fouled the rail heads, so special cranked couplings had to be used.

The colour changed in 1933 to Shell tanker red, with green bogies and green bolsters, although from 1935 black bogies were used again. By 1936, the price had fallen from an initial 6s 6d to a low point of 3s 9d. Trolley Wagons with Cable Drums were

added to the range in 1936, as an alternative to the ordinary Trolley Wagon; no extra tooling or alterations were required, since the load could be tied to the slots that had always been provided in the base. The cable drums varied in type as on the Flat Truck with Cable Drum, the first versions for the Trolley Wagon being green-stained BI Cable drums. At first there were no axleboxes, but from later in 1936 the Trolley Wagons were fitted with axleboxes and spoked wagon wheels instead of tinplate wheels. From 1939 the colour of the Trolley Wagon changed to pale grey, with matt black bogies and red bolsters; later grey versions had couplings and bogies fixed by rivets instead of eyelets.

There were a few minor variations, for example in the shape of the chain links on the bolsters, and in the string used to fix cable drums. Two small holes were added to the top of each bolster from early in 1927.

Trolley wagons were listed twice only in the UK after the war, in 1949. No details are known of any actual production.

Meat, Fish and No. 0 Milk Traffic Vans of 1931 (top row) and 1933 (second row). Also 1935-series Banana and Meat Vans.

No. O VANS

A new series of Hornby vans for perishables traffic was created in 1931, following several requests from MM readers. These were the No. 0 GW Milk Traffic Van, the NE Fish Van and the LMS Meat Van. All were tinprinted in grey, with black detail and white letters, and the roofs were tinprinted in cream, with square ends not rounded as on the No. 1 Vans. The No. 0 Vans were cheaper than the standard No. 1, at 2s 6d instead of 3s. Sliding doors were fitted to each, as on the latest No. 1 Vans, and automatic couplings were used. It is not clear if the details on these early wagons were based on photographs or on drawings of actual railway company vans as were the later series. The 'No. 0' description was, and is, commonly applied to the Fish Van and Meat Van although there were no No. 1 Vans from which to distinguish them.

Underframes were black until 1933, when the same three vans were made with green underframes, but otherwise unchanged. The price fell to 1s 11d in 1934.

Each of the vans was revised in 1935, in a new style without the sliding doors, and on a black underframe not green. The NE Fish Van was printed in a more attractive bauxite colour, still with black detail and white letters; the new style resembled a van illustrated in a picture in the August 1931 MM. The GW No. 0 Milk Traffic Van was in 'coach brown', with black detail and yellow lettering. LMS Meat Vans were similar in colour to the previous type, although printed with better detail than before. With these changes the price of the vans fell to 1s 9d. A fourth van was added to the range at the same time, the LMS No. 0 Banana Van. It was in LMS standard light grey, with white lettering except for the lettering 'to be returned to Avonmouth' which was black. The box was often printed with a picture of the 'Fyffes' Van!

There were eight more new vans in 1937, bringing the total to twelve; some of the old vans were altered, for example the LMS No. 0 Banana Van was re-issued with 'to be returned to Avonmouth' in white letters instead of black, and the NE Fish and GW Milk Vans were reprinted with slightly different trademarks but otherwise unchanged. The LMS Meat Van was also unchanged.

The twelve No. 0 Vans in the 1937 series.

Four new No. 0 Refrigerator Vans were made; the SR version was in plain buff (the shade varied in subsequent re-printings), with brown lettering and black details. The MM said that it was 'finished in the peculiar buff shade favoured on that line'. The NE No. 0 Refrigerator was in white with black detail, the GW 'Mica B' No. 0 Refrigerator in white with black detail and red letters, and the LMS No. 0 Refrigerator in grey with black detail and white lettering, including a white cross to indicate that it was suitable for express working.

The new LMS No. 0 Fish Vans were in LMS coach red (again indicating that they were suitable for express working) and in addition to the black detail were beautifully lined in yellow, and had yellow lettering; a photograph of the original LMS Fish Van was printed in the August 1931 MM, and it had obviously been faithfully copied for the Hornby van. The GW No. 0 Fish Van was in brown, with black, white and silver detail, and yellow lettering.

There were also two new Meat Vans; NE 'Perishables' in bauxite with black details and white letters, and the GW 'Mica' in greenish grey with black detail and white lettering. Like the GW Mica B it was tinprinted with authentic detail. In common with most of the No. 0 Van series it was based closely on photographs supplied by the railway companies concerned, and represented the latest railway practice better than any other vehicles in the range. In consequence the series was very popular, especially since the price in 1937 was only 1s 6d. Details such as lamp brackets, ventilators, despatch note clips, steps and handrails, rivets etc. were all reproduced where appropriate in the tinprinting.

Although an early batch of the LMS Fish Van was issued with white roofs, later LMS Fish Vans, post-1937 LMS Banana Vans, LMS No. 0 Refrigerator Vans and post-1937 LMS Meat Vans were issued with grey roofs, whereas the NE, GW and SR vans had white roofs.

Accessories

SPRING BUFFER STOPS

After the Lattice Girder Bridge, Spring Buffer Stops were the second Hornby Train accessory to be offered. They were shown in the May 1922 MM. The first versions had the sides and the beam enamelled grey, while the sleepers were left unpainted. The colour was changed early in 1923 from grey to olive green; apart from many changes in the trademark transfer type and position, there were few further changes (save varnishing, which was carried out from the middle of 1924) until 1927, when a single-piece base replaced the two large rectangular sleepers fitted before. The buffers were now sprayed overall in green, and the buffer stocks were finished in red. The new base was lipped at the front edge to join up to the rails by track clips; the previous sleepers had been for the earlier rails with locking wires.

The name was changed to 'No. 1 Buffer Stop (Spring)' in 1928, but there was no change in the product apart from slight variations of shade. In 1929 the No. 1 Buffers were re-designed for a lower buffer height (the beam being simply fixed lower down on the sides); the colour was unchanged. But in 1930 the colour was altered to blue instead of green, with the buffer stocks still in red. There was a new electric version in 1932; the 1E Buffer Stops had a bracket on the rear of the beam, to which a lamp was mounted. Two brass prongs at the base of the lamp provided the plug-and-socket connection. The lamp top had a red celluloid aspect; there was a dummy ventilator in the top, which at first was supposed to be finished black like the rest of the lamp, but which was nickel plated on all but the first 1E Buffers.

A lighter blue was used for No. 1 and 1E Buffers from 1933, and from 1935 the 1E Buffer connection changed to a single screw terminal. A bracket was added to the rear of the No. 1 Buffer beam from 1937, for the planned Lighting Accessory. Although the 1E Buffers were unnecessary after the introduction of this Lighting Accessory in 1938, they continued to be made, and were catalogued until 1939. The colour of the No. 1 Buffer Stops changed to grey in 1939. The front of the beam was now red, and the buffer heads were usually painted red over the nickel plate, except for a late batch in 1940.

Production of No. 1 Buffer Stops was resumed in 1948; wartime and early postwar buffers would be hard to distinguish, were it not for the track being painted grey on all postwar versions, instead of unpainted as before. There were many trademark transfer variations in the 1948–50 period. From 1950 the base was no longer pierced in the centre, but had a solid base, and the clip for the lighting accessory was deleted. (No Lighting Accessories were made after the war.) Apart from a period around 1952 when Brunofix black finish was used for the buffer heads, there were no further changes, the No. 1 Buffers remaining in the lists up to 1966, with the total number produced since 1922 well over the million mark.

HYDRAULIC BUFFER STOPS

Hydraulic Buffer Stops were first made early in 1924. The colour was dark grey, lined out in black on the edges of the base and on the bracing bars, and in silver on the front section of rail; they looked uncannily like the Bing equivalent unless closely inspected. These buffers were sturdily built, and well able to withstand the impact of a speeding train. Much more satisfying to the operator than using a brake rail!

From later in 1924, the No. 2 Buffers were finished with gold lining instead of black, at first unvarnished; later still in 1924 the buffers were varnished, with the result that the colour appeared to change to a very dark green, although in fact the dark grey enamel was still the same.

In 1927 the colour was changed to green, darkening slightly in 1928–29 versions. The name was changed to 'No. 2' in 1928. From late in 1929 or early in 1930, the No. 2 Buffer Stops were finished in blue, with gold lining and silver-painted track as before. The height of the buffers was lowered on the blue versions to suit the latest rolling stock. At first remaining stocks of the old bases for the early track with locking wires were used, but new bases with lips for track clips were soon in production. From 1931, the rails were left in blue and not hand-finished silver, and the bracing bars were no longer finished gold, although the end-plates and the edge of the base were still finished gold. In 1932 No. 2E Buffers became available, with lamp-holders as on the No. 1E Buffers.

Both No. 2 and No. 2E Buffers were made in lighter blue from 1933, and the lighting connections changed from plug-and-socket to a screw terminal in 1935. Brackets for the Lighting Accessory were added to the back of the No. 2 buffer beam from 1937. When the Lighting Accessory appeared in 1938, the No. 2E Buffers were no longer listed. The No. 2 Buffers were deleted from the lists in 1939, having effectively been replaced by the No. 2A Buffers. These were designed in 1937 (although not made until 1938) in a cheaper style, without the elegant bracing bars and hand-lining that had made the No. 2 Buffers such a distinctive and expensive toy to make. The No. 2A Buffers had a much simpler body, with the buffer beams supported by a mazac buffer-beam casting, finished in red while the body and base were blue. Holes were incorporated in the casting to allow the Lighting Accessory to be fitted. The No. 3A Buffer Stops fitted with Solid Steel Rails were similar, but about $\frac{1}{4}$ inch lower in height despite maintaining the same buffer-height above the rail heads, showing just how deep the tinplate track was compared to Solid Steel Rails.

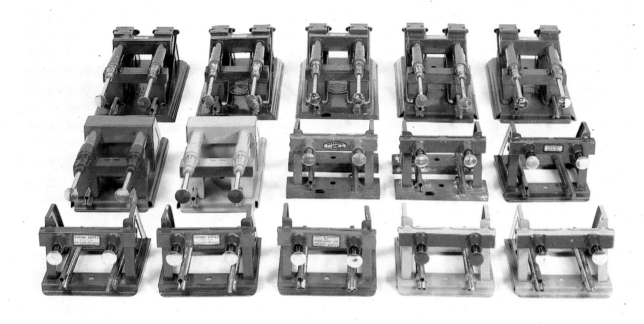

The colour of the No. 2A (and possibly the No. 3A) Buffers changed to grey in 1939, with the front of the buffer beam and the buffer heads in red. 2A and 3A Buffers were catalogued up to 1941, but did not re-appear after the war.

THE HORNBY CONTROL SYSTEM

Purchasers of the first Signal Cabins, in 1924, were probably puzzled by the hinged roof and back, and the hole in the floor of the cabin. The April 1924 MM had mentioned that 'A signal box with lever frame is in the course of preparation', but it was not until 1926, two years after the Signal Cabin was catalogued, that the Lever Frame became available as part of the ambitious Hornby Control System. The April 1926 MM mentioned that Meccano Ltd were 'carrying out a number of experiments in regard to the operation of Hornby Signals from the Signal Boxes and various points in the track,' and from then onwards Meccano booklets and instruction manuals advertised the system.

The Hornby Control System provided six-lever frames which could remotely control the operation of the whole railway. The levers were connected by wire rodding to points and signals specially fitted for Hornby Control, and also to special rails which controlled the reversing or stopping and (for Control Locos only) re-starting of trains, without the need to touch the locos at all, except of course for rewinding!

Aspects of the Hornby Control System were covered by patents 250,378 and 253,236. These showed, as did many of the early catalogue pictures, the Control System fitted to the older style of Hornby rail with narrow sleepers and locking wires – although all the Control System Rails and Points so far discovered have the revised sleepers for connecting plates. The Control Guide Brackets, however, had 3 holes for attachment, one central hole for use on the old type sleepers, and a pair of holes for the revised sleepers.

The patents covered some ideas not put into production – Guide Brackets made as an integral part of the sleeper, and Rodding Traverses made as an integral part of the rail. The patent shows that the need for a Rodding Traverse (to operate accessories

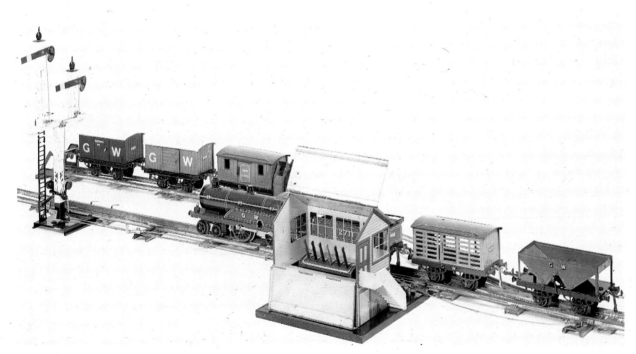

A Hornby Control System Lever Frame, Point, Control Rail and Junction Signal, circa 1926.

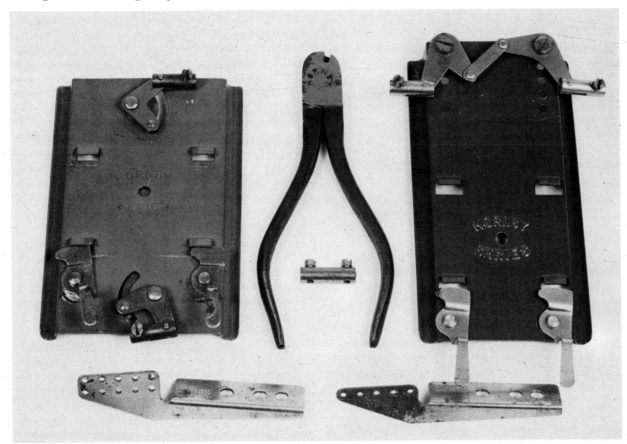

on both sides of the track from a single lever frame) was appreciated, although there was a five year delay before it was made, in a different form.

The locomotives fitted for Control were provided with a special spring-loaded brake, the spring returning the brake to the 'off' position. Thus when the loco ran onto the Control Rail in the 'Brake' position it stopped, but re-started when the control rail was moved by means of the lever frame, releasing the brake trip. The brake was revised to engage on a cone on the governor shaft, so the loco stopped more gradually than the normal type; hence the need for a long Control Rail.

The Control Lever Frame was clamped to the rails at a convenient central position in the layout; the base had four holes so that the Signal Cabin could be fitted on top, with the levers accessible by opening

the hinged roof and back. The Control Signals, Home or Distant, also had a special base secured to the rails by clamps. The Control Signals were fitted with bellcranks on the post, with rigid links to the normal manual lever arm. The Control Junction Signal had bellcranks on each side of the post, one for each signal arm. A hole had to be punched in the ladder to clear one of the control wires. The levers were arranged to point away from the track, to ensure adequate clearance – a nicety ignored on several later versions. The post was usually fitted centrally on the flat part of the base – but again later versions sometimes had the post fixed on the front edge of the base.

The Control Wire, sold in 24 ft coils, was connected from the Lever Frame to the Signals or to the Points. The wire was threaded through the Control

Guide Brackets (securely bolted to the sleepers of the rails at regular intervals by means of Meccano Nuts and Bolts), then cut to the correct length using the Wire Cutters – also sold as part of the system, and naturally enough carrying the 'Hornby' embossed trademark. The Control Coupling was a simple brass collar with two set screws, which could be used to allow fine adjustments of the length of the wire, or to re-join wires cut for previous layouts.

Once the wire was in place, fine adjustments to the length could be made by turning the connecting rods between lever and bellcrank on the Lever Frame. These were cleverly designed with a left-hand thread at one end and right-hand thread at the other; thus turning the rod lengthened or shortened the link. The rod was square in section so that it could be gripped easily. The Lever Frame was fitted with six levers of various colours; green for distant signals, red for Home Signals, black for points and silver for spare levers. The blue lever was intended for the Control Brake and Reverse Rail or the Control Rail. The relative positions of the levers in the frame could be altered by pulling out the pivoting rod passing through their centres, changing the levers then replacing the pivoting rod.

The conventional arrangement was that pushing signal levers forward should set the signal at 'Danger'. The Control System Rodding Compensator reversed the direction of 'pull' for the rodding, so this arrangement could be maintained for Hornby Control Signals whether they were placed on the left-hand or on the right-hand side of the Lever Frame. The Rodding Compensator had 5 alternative positions for the bellcranks, corresponding to the positions of the five holes in the Guide Brackets.

The Hornby Control System was mentioned in the 1926–27 season Meccano Products Catalogues, the Hornby Book of Trains and the Hornby Trains Folder. The only details given were of the Train Sets and Locos fitted for Control, but interested customers were invited to send for 'The Hornby Control System', a special 4-page booklet (the first known printing was in September 1926), forwarded post-free, listing the components of the system and giving instructions on how to set it up.

The Control Train Sets included a Control Rail – but none of the other Control System Accessories.

A Hornby Control System Outfit No. 1, 1927. Boxes within boxes!

To operate the system properly required the additional purchase of a Control Outfit No. 2, offered in the Hornby Control System booklet, price 35s. The contents were not actually listed, but comprised the Lever Frame, left-hand and right-hand Control Points (2ft radius), two Control Signals (one Home and one Distant), two Rodding Compensators, a box of three Control Couplings and 36 Meccano Nuts and Bolts, and 20 Guide Brackets. The Control Rail, coil of Wire and the pair of Wire Cutters completed the outfit. Since the Control Rail was also included in the Control Train Sets, it was easy to end up with two! Neither the Signal Cabin nor the Control Junction Signal were included in the No. 2 Outfit.

Control Outfit No. 1 had very similar contents, but was intended for use with M, No. 0, and No. 1 Locos which were not available fitted for Control. The 2 ft radius points were replaced by points of 1 ft radius, and the Control Rail by the Control Brake and Reverse Rail. This was shown in the Hornby Control System booklet as being similar to the later 1927-style Brake and Reverse Rail, but fitted with a Control bellcrank instead of the lever. It was suitable for all locos not fitted for Control, including the No. 2 and No. 2 Tank; it could not be used to re-start the train after braking.

The Control System Outfits and accessories of the 1920s were packed in green boxes distinguishing them from the red boxes of the rest of the range. The 1926–28 Outfits consisted of a large green box containing a pile of individually boxed items! But in 1928 the Outfits were packed in a new box with the contents better presented, separated by shaped cardboard partitions and not all individually boxed.

The April 1927 MM showed the latest additions to the Control System – No. 1 and No. 1 Tank Locos fitted for Control. There were now two Control Rails, No. 1 (which was 15 in long) and No. 2 (20 in long, equivalent to two full straight rails). The Control Brake and Reverse Rail appears to have been withdrawn from sale, as it was no longer listed – so it became impossible to buy a special Control System rail for locos not actually fitted for Control. The Control Rails varied a great deal during their relatively short production (1926–29). The earliest Control Rails shown in the leaflets had plain bell-

cranks with a swivelling brass coupling for the control wire. Later Control rails had the bellcrank extended to form a lever for manual use (not all the purchasers of Train Sets fitted for Control – especially the No. 3 where there was no choice – would have wanted to buy a Lever Frame). The manual lever prevented the coupling from swivelling, so this version could only be used on the left-hand side of the Lever Frame. Later Control Rails were provided with a double-ended coupling to overcome the difficulty. There were other detail differences apart from the usual changes in the sleepers; the later bellcranks on the Control Rails were painted black, and later still were fixed by a rivet rather than by a nut and bolt.

The May 1927 MM carried articles telling Meccano Boys how to convert ordinary points for Control System working, using Sleepers with Bellcrank and Coupling supplied by Meccano Ltd at 8d each. The sleepers for conversion were also mentioned in the December 1931 and April 1932 MMs.

Other changes in 1927 were that the colour of the Signal and Lever Frame bases changed to the blue that was being adopted as standard for the ordinary signals. Hand brakes began to be fitted to the Control engines, for use when picking up the loco to rewind it, or to stop it other than at a Control Rail. Electric Railways could also use the Control System, and the December 1927 MM said that electric 2ft radius Control Points were 'already available'. The price was 12s pair instead of 10s pair for the normal electric type. For the benefit of those planning ambitious systems, the Guide Brackets were revised to have 10 holes for the wires instead of 5.

Points on Solid Base with Ground Disc and Lamp were the only major addition to the system in 1928 – apart from the availability of SR locos fitted for Control.

The control of Hornby locos from the lever frame had not been an outstanding success, partly because many customers just could not afford the extra cost. It was a tricky business to set up the Control System successfully, especially for the majority of children who could have only temporary layouts; to get the necessary stability it was advantageous to screw down the track and Control accessories firmly. A particular problem was that the lever

end of the points could not be clipped to the rails, so the control wires tended to push the joint apart. The new range of improved locomotives offered in 1929 no longer allowed Hornby Control, and the existing Control Locos, Sets, Control Rails and Control Outfits were not listed in the 1929–30 season catalogues. The Lever Frames, Signals and Points fitted for Control, and other Control accessories, continued to be catalogued and sold. In fact the range of points fitted for Control was increasing – for example the Control Crossover Points were offered at 12s pair in the June 1929 MM (12 months after they were designed). But the Hornby Control System was drifting into the doldrums, and it was two years before a fresh effort was made to revive it.

In January 1931 the MM announced a reduced price of 1s for the Control Wire Cutters. The August 1931 trade circular announced that Meccano Ltd proposed 'to give considerable prominence to the Hornby Control System during the coming season. Its advantages will be strongly emphasised in all our advertising literature, and an attractively printed leaflet, describing the system fully, will be included in all Hornby Clockwork Train Sets from No. 0 upwards'. The March 1931 MM replied to a reader that the Hornby Control System was 'perfectly satisfactory on non-permanent layouts, with proper attention to the use of rail connecting clips and to the secure clamping of Lever Frames and Signals'; but perfection may have meant different things to Meccano Ltd and to their customers! It would certainly be a fiddly business to set up a temporary layout re-using wires cut for a previous layout.

From 1931 the standard colour for the Control System boxes became orange instead of green, since the latter colour had begun to be used for electric items.

The revised range of Control System accessories now included a choice of 2, 4 or 6-Lever Frames at 6s 6d, 9s 6d or 12s 6d respectively. Extra Lever Assemblies, price 1s 6d, could be inserted into the 2-Lever or 4-Lever Frames if required. (Each frame was the same size, and had six slots – they differed only in the number of levers fitted.) They were fitted by removing the pivot wire from the frame, inserting the lever, and screwing the bellcrank to the base. Control Outfits were not re-introduced, but for

Late Control System items seem to have been used →
mainly for electric Hornby railways. Here a Two-Lever
Control Lever Frame controls an electric crossover and
an electrically lit 2E Signal fitted for Control.

Points on Solid Base, for Control System
or manual operation.

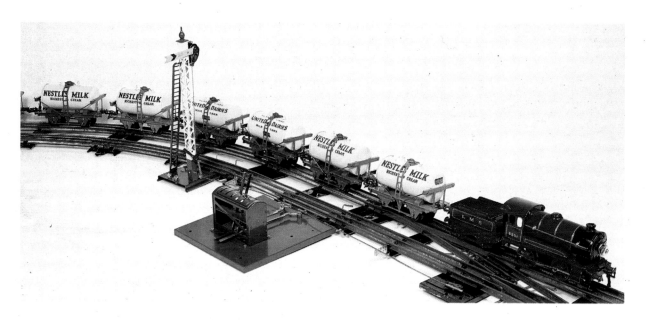

the convenience of customer and dealer specially chosen Assortments A, B and C (for clockwork railways, with 2-, 4- and 6-Lever Frames respectively plus appropriate accessories) could be ordered. Similar assortments of electrical Control accessories could be obtained to order.

When the Control System was introduced, there was a substantial extra charge for accessories fitted for Control. Control Points were 3s 6d instead of 2s 6d, Control Signals 3s 6d not 2s 6d, and the Control Junction Signals 7s 6d not 5s 6d as for the normal type. But from the time of the 1931 revisions, Control System Points and Signals were sold at the same price as the ordinary items. Furthermore, a complete range of points fitted for Hornby Control, both clockwork and electric, was offered – although all except the Control PR1/PL1 and PR2/PL2 were special orders. The Control Signal and Junction Signals were still listed, and Control Double Arm Signals (and from 1932 Electrically-lit Single Arm, Double Arm and Junction Signals) became available by special order.

It is surprising that the large range of special-order items was kept so quiet; these useful accessories were not mentioned in any of the several revised editions of the 'Hornby Control System'

booklet. In fact the booklet gives the standard Control items as 'A complete list'! Even trade circulars do not appear to mention them. Perhaps the special order items were regarded as rather a nuisance, and hence were not encouraged – but if that was the case one wonders why they were supplied at all.

A new Hornby Control System accessory listed in 1931 was the Rodding Traverse, following several requests in the MM to devise a means to control accessories on both sides of the track from a single lever frame. The Traverse clamped to the track in the normal way; two bellcranks and a solid strip under the base transmitted the thrust of the rodding to the other side – but only one rod could be carried across by each Rodding Traverse, and the position of the bellcranks was not adjustable as on the Rodding Compensator. An alternative to the Rodding Traverse was to buy the special order 'reversed switch' Control Points.

It is difficult to know exactly which of the possible special order points were actually ordered by customers, and supplied by Meccano Ltd. Would anyone have ordered Control 1 ft radius Double Symmetrical points, for example? We have not yet seen any special order clockwork Control System points, although they were certainly made. Electric

Points seem to have been made in greater numbers – Control EPR1/EPL1, EPR2/EPL2 (with and without reversed switches), and EPPR2/EPPL2 Parallel and ECOR2/ECOL2 Crossover Points are all known to have been made. Control EPR2/EPL2 Points on Solid Base were also made in the late 1930s. Electric railway owners seem to have paid greater attention to the Hornby Control System – perhaps because they could better afford to pay for it.

Both the catalogued and the special order Control System Signals followed the same general pattern of production variations as the normal products, but the 1933 colour change to a choice of lighter blue or green bases etc. did not apply to the Control System signals. Darker blue shades continued to be used up to the late 1930s – possibly to match the Lever Frames and other Control Accessories – though needless to say a few items in the lighter blue were produced. Green-based Control Signals are (so far) unknown. From 1933 the colour of the lever arms on Control Signals changed to red, as on the 'normal' signals, and in 1934 flat caps replaced finials on the Control non-electric signals. Yellow Distant arms were used from 1936.

There appears to have been no definite public announcement of the end of the Hornby Control

System. The 1937–38 Meccano Products Catalogue was the last to mention it and to invite readers to send for the booklet, the last known edition of which was printed in December 1937 with over-printed price revisions from January 1938. The quantity printed was one thousand, indicating just how limited interest in the system was at that time.

It should perhaps be mentioned that some clockwork Bassett Lowke Locos, both in prewar days and in the 1950s, were fitted for a similar Control System. The tinplate Control Rails, very similar to the Hornby type except for the trademark, may possibly have originated in Binns Road. Ordinary clockwork rails (without trademarks) were certainly made by Meccano Ltd for Bassett Lowke at various times.

COUNTRYSIDE SECTIONS AND SCENERY

It was in 1932 that the Hornby Series began to burst out into greenery, with the Countryside Sections, Trees, Cuttings, Tunnels and Hedges. In fact the first of the wooden tunnels (the M Tunnel, later No. 1 Tunnel) was advertised in December 1931, and the others, Nos. 0, 2, 3, 4, 5 and 6 followed early in 1932, along with Cuttings 0, 1, 2, 3 and 4. Tunnels and Cuttings changed little over the years except in colour and in the trademark labels. There is a slight mystery surrounding the No. 0 Tunnel, the drawings for which showed two types, 'MO' and 'MOW'. The MOW lacked the puckered fabric overlay used on the No. 0. It is not known for what purpose they were planned.

Fencing with Four Trees was advertised in the April 1932 MM; lengths of Paled Fencing each with four Trees were supplied in a box, complete with black-painted tinplate clips to secure the Trees to the Fence. The Trees were of the type used for Countryside Sections, green-dyed loofah mounted on a pointed wooden stick.

The Countryside Sections themselves first appeared in the 1932–33 catalogues and lists. The sections available were:

Hornby Countryside Sections, used for a layout with the Right-Angle Crossing ECR.

Field F (square field)
Fields J1 & J2 (rectangular fields)
Field J3 (half rectangular field)
Fields G1 & G2 (inside curved sections)
Fields K1 & K2 (triangular sections)
Fields L1 & L2 (outside curved sections)
Fields M1 & M2 (outside corner sections)
Road H, and
Support R (for level crossing).

Four each of the F, G1 and G2 sections were needed to fill the space inside a simple 2ft radius circle. All the sections were of thick cardboard covered with printed paper surfaces, even the Support R (which was completely hidden in use underneath the No. 1 Level Crossing) was covered in green. No changes in the Fields themselves are noticeable during their production, nor in the gates and hedges. The first trees supplied with the Countryside sections had three or four small sections of loofah mounted horizontally on the 'trunk', and shaped to the right profile; but from July 1933 the trees were just a single section of shaped loofah mounted vertically.

When the Oak Trees, Poplar Trees and Diecast Stands for Trees were added to the range in 1933 these changes had already been made, so these trees were usually single-piece. Assorted Trees with Stands became available at the same time. Apart from the packaging change in 1936, after which Oak and Poplar as well as the Assorted Trees were sold with stands, there were no significant changes, other than some hue differences in the green stain. The

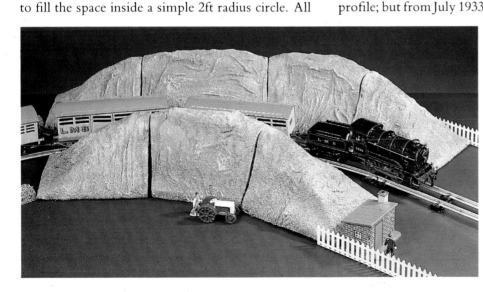

Cuttings No. 1 (two pairs), No. 2 and two No. 3.
The Cattle Trucks are hauled by LMS No. 1 Loco 2290.

The largest Cutting, No. 4. SR E220 Special Loco 2329 pulls a breakdown train.

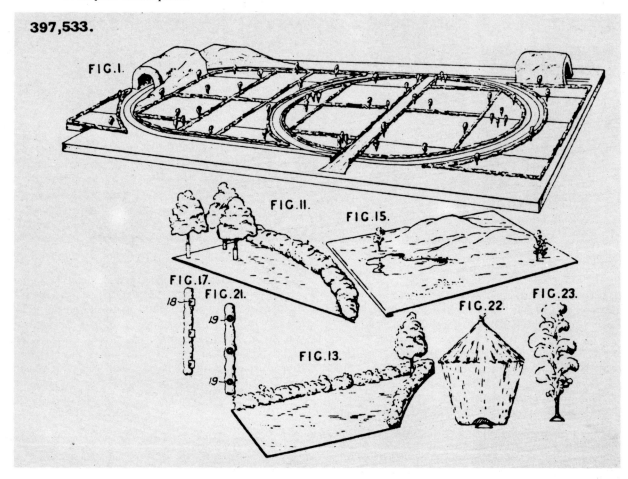

397,533.

FIG.I.
FIG.II.
FIG.15.
FIG.17.
FIG.21.
FIG.13.
FIG.22.
FIG.23.
18
19
19

early trunks were stained either lightly or not at all, but late tree-trunks usually had dark brown staining. The Diecast Stands (which remained on sale despite all the trees being supplied with stands) had the words 'Made in England' added to the trademark in 1938. The colour of the stands changed around the same time, to brown from metallic green. The Fencing with Trees remained popular, despite the lack of any means of standing the fence upright other than screwing or nailing it down, and remained in production even in 1940.

Hedges were advertised in the 1933 catalogues; each piece (they were boxed in dozens, like the trees) was the length of a straight rail. They consisted of green-dyed loofah glued and pinned by nails to a wooden base. Early Hedges had wide bases lightly stained brown, but later the Hedges became less bulky, and the wooden bases were narrower. From the mid '30s the Hedges were generally a more vivid green, and the bases were stained darker brown.

After 1936 the Countryside Sections were no longer available. No trees, hedges, cuttings or tunnels were catalogued after the war.

DINKY TOY FIGURES

The first set of Modelled Miniature figures, the No. 1 Station Staff, were advertised in the November 1931 MM; the set included a Stationmaster, a Guard, a Ticket Collector, an Engine Driver, a Porter with Luggage, and a Porter. All were in dark blue uniforms, (except the Driver who was in light blue) and had detailed eyes, mouths, collars and ties etc. Stationmasters had gold buttons, Guards and Ticket Collectors silver. But the ordinary porters' buttons were left plain blue! Each of these Station Staff had an orange-painted base, rather than yellow-cream which would have matched the platforms.

The No. 2 Farmyard Animals were advertised in 1932; the Horses were available in brown and in white, and Cows in brown representing a Devon Red, and in black and white representing a British Holstein. There were also cream-coloured Sheep and pink Pigs. All were hand-finished with details of eyes, feet etc. Being quadrupeds, they did not need bases like the other Hornby figures.

The No. 3 Passengers were also sold from 1932. They were the Woman and Child, a Business Man, Male and Female Hikers, a Newsboy, and a Woman. All were well-detailed by hand finishing, including a nice contrast between the sun-tanned skin of the hikers and the palid pink of the others. The bases were yellow-cream.

No. 4 Engineering Staff were also available in 1932, and had figures from the No. 1 Station Staff set painted in other colours. The set comprised the Electrician (like the Porter with Luggage), Fitters (Porters) in blue (dark at first, light from 1935) and in brown overalls, Storekeeper (Stationmaster), Greaser (Driver) and Engine Room Attendant (Ticket Inspector). The bases were yellow-cream.

Modelled Miniatures No. 5, Train and Hotel Staff, were also made from 1932. These again had figures from the Station Staff set painted in other colours; a Pullman Car Conductor (Ticket Inspector), and two identical Pullman Car Waiters (Porters), in white and blue uniforms, with two Hotel Porters (Porters with Luggage) in red and in green uniforms, each carrying suitcases whimsically lettered 'FH' in honour of the great man. The bases were painted yellow-cream. This set had only five instead of the usual six figures, which accounts for the lower price (in 1934) of 1s 3d, against 1s 6d for Nos. 1 to 4.

Modelled Miniatures No. 13, the Hall's Distemper Advertisement, was also available from 1932. These were not 'figures' in the same sense as

No. 1 Station Staff.

No. 6 Shepherd Set.

No. 3 Passengers.

No. 2 Farmyard Animals.

No. 4 Engineering Staff.

No. 5 Train and Hotel Staff.

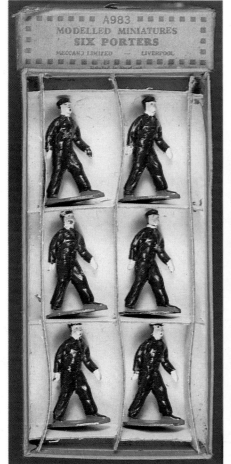

Miscellaneous Hornby figures; three small figures with early-colour bases, an interesting Hotel Porter, and two larger-size figures with revised buttons!

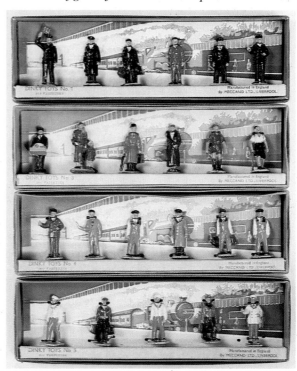

Smaller-size figures of the 1937 to 1939 period.

A No. 1A Engine Shed, circa 1935, with LMS No. 0 Loco 600, and M3 Tank Loco 2270.

Wartime figures, circa 1940, with revised colour schemes.

the others, and were larger and heavier. The printed cardboard sign they carried was intended as a lineside advertisement. The two men were painted with white overalls, and were as usual detailed by hand finishing. In each set one man had a blue paintbrush and the other green. The boxes varied much more than the figures over the years, the usual box colours being red, pink or cream. The Modelled Miniatures No. 21 Train Set, and the Modelled Miniatures No. 22 Motor Vehicles may actually be considered as part of the Hornby Series; they are described in Volume 4 of this series.

The last set of figures to appear was the Dinky Toys No. 6 Shepherd Set. This was advertised in the April 1934 MM, the first occasion on which the other Modelled Miniature figures were referred to under their new name, 'Dinky Toys'. The Shepherd Set included a Shepherd, three cream-coloured Sheep (identical to those in the No. 2 set) and one black Sheep, together with a Sheepdog, painted black and white. Whereas all the other Hornby animals were marked 'Hornby Series' underneath, the Sheepdog was too small to be trademarked; it was quite the smallest of the Hornby figures. There were two prewar versions of the Shepherd; both used the same casting, but one had a brown smock and the other blue.

At some time in the mid 1930s it was realised that

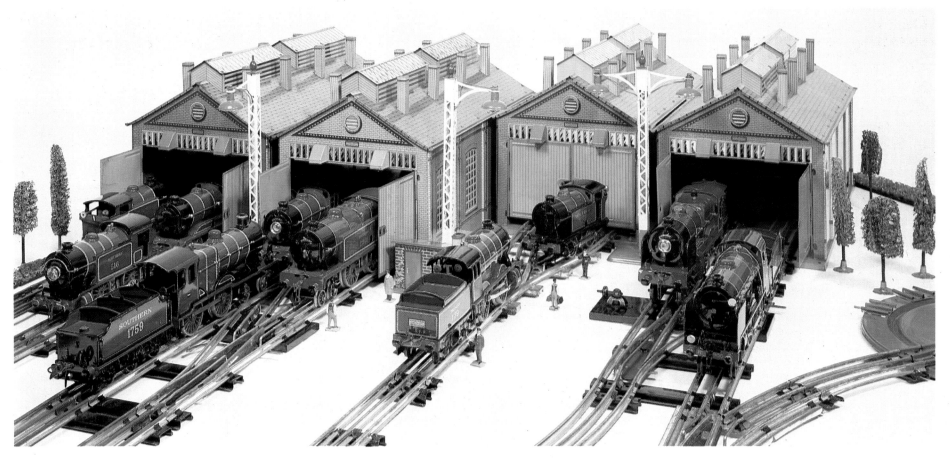

the Porter's buttons were on the wrong side of his jacket. The tools were clumsily altered to correct this error, and also to reduce the size of the base. The change also affected the Pullman Car Waiters and the Fitters. It is fascinating to see that attention was given to such a trivial detail, while 4-4-2 'Royal Scots' were considered quite acceptable!

Between 1937 and 1939, the Station Staff (and hence Train and Hotel Staff and Engineering Staff), and the Passengers, were changed to new-size figures which were smaller and in better scale for gauge 0, as well as being (quite coincidentally) cheaper to make. The Station Staff set was finished very much as before (considering the difficulties of painting such small figures), with details in the faces, but usually with black ties rather than the former red

(except for the Guard). Each figure now had gold or silver buttons, even the Porters. The Engineering Staff and the Train and Hotel Staff were again in very similar colours to the larger-size figures, and had the same sort of detail on the faces and clothing. The Passengers were quite different from the previous style both in shape and in colour; for example the Woman and Child had the Child holding the Woman's left hand, not the right, in the smaller version, and the Newsboy had put on a few years and now sold his papers from a tray rather than dashing about with them. The Male Hiker had lost his walking stick (though not his suntan), and his mate's brown hair had changed to bright yellow. The Businessman had changed his suit for a raincoat, and the Woman wore a long coat instead of a pleated

skirt and a jacket.

In 1938 the colour of the bases for these Dinky Toy figures was changed to pale buff. Since the changeover to smaller figures had already begun, but was not yet completed, there were several 'transitional' figures with bases in different colours from the 'normal' rule that small figures have buff bases, and the larger size yellow-cream (or orange for Station Staff). The most common examples are the small-size Newsboy and Woman with yellow-cream bases. There was also a small-size Guard with orange base, and (going the other way) a large-size Stationmaster with a buff base. There were doubtless many other examples. The Shepherd Set and Farmyard Animals were not affected by the size change.

During 1940, figures were issued in smaller boxes, with the figures for the most part finished in much plainer colours, without the painted details in the clothing but still with face details. Red Hotel Porters carried red and buff suitcases instead of blue and red; green Hotel Porters carried green and buff cases instead of orange and red, and the 'FH' initials were left off. There were also differences in the wartime Passengers; for example the Female Hiker had a blue blouse instead of white. There is no difficulty in telling these war-time figures from the postwar, which were also in a plain style, because the faces were still detailed on the 1940 figures.

After the war, production of the Dinky Toy Nos. 1 to 6 figures did not resume until 1952; they were listed until 1956. The Station Staff set had no Stationmaster, and the Driver was re-named 'Engine Driver'. The Engineering Staff now had no Electrician. The Train and Hotel Staff were unchanged in content although the Pullman Car staff were re-named 'Dining Car Attendant' and 'Dining Car Conductor'. The Passengers were still a set of six, with changes of name to 'Mother and Child' rather than 'Woman and Child'. The Farmyard Animal set was unchanged except in colour, and in the absence of 'Hornby Series' trademarks. The colouring was simpler and less detailed, not just on the animals but as already mentioned, on the other figures too.

Before the war, there were certain other Dinky Toy figures which, although not intended for use with Hornby Trains, were quite suitable, although on the small side; these included the AA men, RAC men, Policemen, and the Postman and Telegraph Messenger. After the war the Cook's Man was the only possibility apart from the postal staff. Throughout, the range of Hornby figures was not particularly wide, and the lack of any seated figures especially unfortunate.

ENGINE SHEDS

Engine Sheds No. 1 and No. 2 were introduced in 1928. They were the largest tinprinted buildings made by Meccano Ltd, and a typical production of that era in Binns Road history; over-ambitious perhaps, but extremely imposing. The sides, ends, roof, doors, chimneys, skylights and ventilators were all tinprinted, only the base being enamelled. Although early bases should have been in the pale blue-grey used for platforms at that time, and indeed that colour is shown in the Hornby Book of Trains, the colour of most early bases was yellow-cream. The No. 2 Engine Shed was the length of two straight rails, adequate for any Hornby Loco at that time, and the No. 1 was simply a shorter version. Double hinged doors were fitted at each end. Little expense seems to have been spared in the creation of the Engine Sheds, their assembly being a complicated job involving the use of special wooden jigs.

Although no electric-track versions of these early Engine Sheds were catalogued in the UK, they were in France, and could also be obtained by special order in the UK.

In 1932 E1E and E2E Engine Sheds were offered, fitted with electric track and for electric lighting, but otherwise like the No. 1 and No. 2. Connections were by plug-and-socket, and there was just one single lamp-holder in each shed.

There was a change of colour in 1933, with the bases of the sheds in green instead of yellow-cream. Two new Engine Sheds, No. 1A and No. 2A, were catalogued in 1934. These were the same size as the No. 1 and No. 2, but simplified. The No. 1A Engine Shed had no skylight, ventilators or chimneys, and had doors at one end only. The No. 2A Engine Shed had only a single skylight in the centre of the roof, and had no ventilators or chimneys, although it did have doors at each end. These simplifications gave a price of 10s 6d for the 1A and 17s 6d for the 2A, compared with 15s for the No. 1 and 22s 6d for the No. 2. In 1934 the No. E1E cost 18s 6d and the E2E 26s, although in 1935 there was a drop in price for both these when the new system of connection by screw terminals instead of by plug-and-socket was introduced. There were also tinprinting changes to the sheds; the doors began to be printed in plain green on the inside, instead of detailed on both sides; and the No. 1A and No. 2A sheds, which had rather dull blue ridge tiles in the first issues, now had yellow ridge tiles. There was also a change in the tinprinting of the skylight sides. No further important changes took place, although the maroon hand-finishing on the corners of the early sheds was not carried out in the later 1930s.

Prices fell sharply in 1939, perhaps to clear stocks for extra space; but all the sheds were still listed in November 1941. They were not made again after the war.

FOOTBRIDGES

THE LATTICE GIRDER BRIDGE

The Lattice Girder Bridge was the first Hornby Train accessory, designed in September and advertised in November 1921. It was the only accessory built on the Meccano principle, the enjoyment of the user being somewhat limited by the single possible way of assembling it. One advantage of the constructional design was that it needed only a small box, since the user could be left to assemble it!

There were many variations during the production of the Lattice Girder Bridge. The first version had white lattice girder and step sections; the 'brickwork' was stencil-sprayed in greenish-brown on top of the reddish-brown wing-walls; posts were the same colour as the 'bricks'. There were 5 rows of 'mortar'. Later versions were sprayed olive green on top of bright red, using the same stencil for the spraying. From 1922, the colour of the bridge and step sections was usually cream instead of white; but in 1923 the bridge colour was changed again to pale green-grey, and soon a revised stencil with 9 rows of mortar (i.e. smaller bricks) was used, still with olive green bricks sprayed over bright red.

Late in 1924, new support sections were used. Whereas before the pillars had been wooden, screwed to the wing walls by woodscrews and with pyramidal brass caps nailed to the tops of the posts, the new designs had metal posts with the wing walls and caps held on by lugs. There was also an improvement at the top of the step sections, so each step section was held on by four nuts and bolts instead of just two.

There was another colour change in 1927, with the bridge now white again, but with hand-lining on the edges and on the post-caps in dark blue; the posts were white. A new colour scheme was also used for the supports: grey bricks and blue mortar. These colours were retained in 1931, when the walls rather surprisingly were changed to tinprinted instead of stencil sprayed finish; they now incorporated a tinprinted trademark. The same tinprinted sides were used for the final version of the Lattice Girder Bridge made in 1933, with a cream bridge and cream posts instead of white, and lined out on edges and post-caps in lighter blue. The Lattice Girder Bridge (or No. 3 Footbridge, as it had been known since 1930) was dropped from the catalogues in 1934.

No. 1, No. 1A AND No. 2 FOOTBRIDGES

The Footbridge No. 1 With Detachable Signals, and the Footbridge No. 2 Without Signals, were first sold in 1924. The prices of 6s and 3s 6d placed them much more in the reach of the average user than the 10s 6d of the Lattice Girder Bridge. The bridge and step sections were formed from a single large sheet of metal, pressed to shape, and with triangular fillets inserted in each of the corners, always the weakest point of the design. Latticework was pierced in the sides. The bridge section was white-enamelled with blue edges, and the bases were pale blue-grey; from 1925 the bases were embossed with a circle and four radiating lines, for extra strength. There was a colour change around 1927, to blue bases instead of pale blue-grey; there was also a reversal of the names in 1928, to 'No. 1 Footbridge Without Signals', and 'No. 2 Footbridge With Detachable Signals', but the products were unchanged apart from subtle variations of shade.

From 1933 there were three new colour schemes for the bridge; all had cream bridge sections, but the bases and the top edges were finished in red, green or blue. The colour was indicated by stickers on the box, but the choice was never mentioned in the catalogues. It appears that from 1939 green and cream was the only colour scheme offered.

After the war, production of No. 1 Footbridges resumed in 1949. The first colours were grey with green lining, the bridge being more or less as before the war, including slots for the Signals, production of which was never resumed. From 1952 the bridge was cream with green lining and green bases, and still embossed with rivet detail although no longer pierced with latticework or slots for signals. The final version appeared late in 1954 or early in 1955, and it had tinprinted sides, rivet-heads no longer being embossed. The details printed included panelling on the buff coloured sides. The Footbridge disappeared from the Hornby range in 1957.

FOOTBRIDGE SIGNALS

Footbridge signals were sold in pairs, priced 2s 9d at first; one had a tall post, and the other short. They clipped to the side of the bridge in slots provided. The first type had white posts, and black-finished bases, levers and finials. They were distant only, but the tall post bore a home arm instead of distant from 1925. From 1927 the black colour changed to blue, and between then and 1933 the blue changed shade as on the 'normal' signals. The distant arm tinprinting changed from plain stripe to chevron in 1928.

In 1933–34 there was a choice of No. 2 Footbridge Signal colour, with cream posts, red, green or blue bases and finials, and red levers.

However, from 1934 the No. 2 Footbridge and Signals were withdrawn from sale. The reason was that the No. 1A Footbridge with Detachable Tinprinted Signals had been introduced in 1930, with exactly the same bridge as the No. 1 and No. 2 but with M-type signals (at first with the criss-cross latticework printing, later with blue and white stripes). There was a rationalisation in 1934, to give a choice of No. 1 and No. 1A only, with No. 1-type

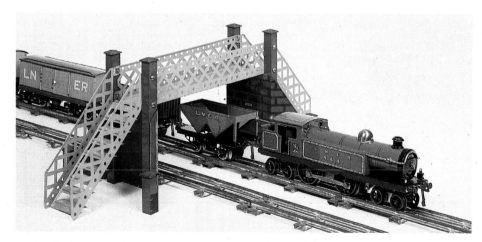

Lattice Girder Bridge with metal posts, circa 1925.

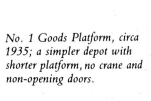

No. 1 Goods Platform, circa 1935; a simpler depot with shorter platform, no crane and non-opening doors.

pyramid-topped signals adopted for the No. 1A as a compromise between the previous two types. The caps were finished in red, green or blue to match the bridge lining, the levers (now with the arms removed) in red, and the posts in cream. Yellow-arm distant signals were provided instead of red-arm from 1936, but there was no other change until 1939, when black-topped signals were the only ones supplied.

GOODS PLATFORMS

The first Hornby Goods Platform was sold in 1926; it had a platform more or less the same shape as that of the Station, but somewhat higher, and with a set of steps cut into one corner and a jib mounted at the step end. A simple canopy with a tinprinted roof was attached to the base by wing nuts on threaded bolts in the columns. The colour of the platform was pale blue-grey, while the crane and crane base were red. There was a substantial improvement in 1928, when a tinprinted building with sliding doors replaced the simple canopy, and the crane was changed to rotate using worm-drive gearing, instead of just being turned by hand. At the same time the colour of the crane base was changed to grey. The platform colour was changed in 1929 to a shade of dark green, with maroon crane base and grey jib, then in 1930 the platform colour changed again to yellow-cream; the crane colour also changed, to blue on a red base.

In 1932, the E Goods Platform was introduced, with the same yellow-cream platform, identical save for the twin lights with plug-and-socket connections to the transformer. In 1933 the platform colour was changed to green, and the colour of the crane also changed to green with a red base. Although for a while the tinprinting of the building was unchanged, from 1934 there were new printings with brighter colours, particularly for the roof. A new simplified Goods Platform also went on sale in 1934, the No. 1 Goods Platform, which had a building similar to the existing Goods Platform (which became 'No. 2', with the electric version as 'No. 2E'). The green platform of the No. 1 was shorter, and not fitted with crane or steps, while the building had no sliding doors. In 1935 the 2E Goods Platform changed to screw terminal connections.

From 1937 the platforms of the Nos. 1, 2 and 2E were changed to the 'speckled' tinprinted pattern, and the platform sides were no longer embossed as before. The last colour change was late in 1938, when the No. 2 and 2E Goods Platforms had grey cranes instead of green, and the No. 2E electric lampshades changed from blue to green. Despite tempting price cuts in 1939, the No. 1 and No. 2E Goods Platforms were still in stock in 1941, the No. 2 having sold out in 1940.

After the war, only the No. 1 Goods Platform came back into production. It was listed from 1949, and was produced in two main versions, at first green-roofed, and from 1955 with an orange roof and with the wording 'Goods Depot' above the doors. The Goods Platform was not listed after 1957.

ISLAND PLATFORMS

The first Hornby Island Platforms of 1926 were finished in pale blue-grey, and had a simple tin-printed canopy like that of the Goods Platform, but usually longer, and lettered 'Windsor' on a central nameboard. The latticework columns were screwed to the base by wing-nuts, and were thus detachable. In fact the canopy could have been sold separately, since the Passenger Platform base was identical to the Island Platform base, both having holes for canopy and fencing. The early catalogue pictures showed simple destination indicators attached to the posts, but the production models did not have this feature. The ramps supplied were finished in matching colours.

There was a change of platform colour to yellow-cream in 1929, and there were also other differences; the posts were by then simply clipped to the base by lugs, and the canopy was of the shorter type used for the old Goods Platforms. Holes for fencing no longer appeared. An electrically lit version, the Island Platform E, was sold from 1932 in the same colours. It was fitted with two electric lights, with plug and socket connection. The following year the colour of the platform was changed to green, and the canopy returned to its original length. Soon after that the colour of the tinprinted canopy changed to a darker blue. In 1935, the electric version changed to screw terminal connection, and early in 1936 other station names began to be used instead of Windsor: Wembley, Bristol, Ripon and (probably) Margate. The Bristol name was changed to Reading by the time that versions with tinprinted platforms appeared in 1937. These no longer had the emboss-ing on the sides of the platform, which had been on one side only, and the white lining was incorporated in the tinprinting on both edges, whereas it had been enamelled on one side only. The tinprinting of the roof changed to green square tiles instead of blue round tiles; some transitional versions had the new roof on the green enamelled base. There were no further changes except that late electrically-lit ver-sions had green lampshades instead of blue.

After the break in production, Island Platforms were sold again from 1949. Tinprintings for both platform and roof were different from the prewar

No. 2 Goods Platform, 1937.

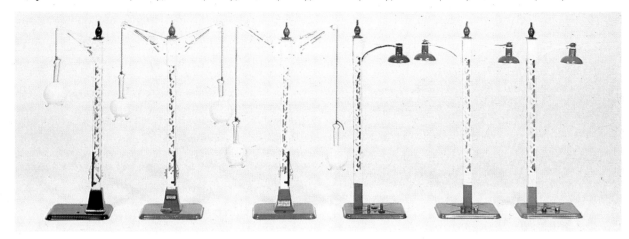

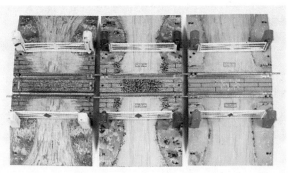

No. 1 Level Crossings circa 1928, 1931 and 1935, showing some of the tinprinting changes.

style, the platform now being a plain buff with brown detail, rather than the prewar 'speckled' buff. The posts were still latticed for the first issues, which had the same names as before: Wembley and Reading, and probably Ripon and Margate. From 1952 the latest types had solid posts instead of latticed, and were named Wembley, Ripon, Reading, Bristol and Margate. There was a change to a single name, 'Trent', in 1954, still with white posts and a green roof. Later 'Trent' Island Platforms had orange posts with a green roof, then finally orange posts with an orange tinprinted roof from late in 1955, not long before the Island Platform was withdrawn from sale in 1957.

LAMP STANDARDS

The Single Lamp Standard and the Double Lamp Standard were introduced into the Hornby range in 1923. Each had a rectangular tinplate base, with substantial lead mounting for the post, necessary to prevent it being overbalanced by the overhanging crane-like supports for the delicate glass globes. A winding drum with ratchet allowed the globe, or both globes on the Double Lamp Standard, to be lowered (presumably to change the carbons in the arc!) then raised. The finial was at first a simple lead fitting plugged into the top of the column; it subsequently changed in the same way as finials on the

Signals. The colours were white for the post, and black for the base, ratchet panel and finial. The inside of the glass globe was sprayed white.

From 1927, the colour changed to blue for the base, ratchet panel and finial. The actual shade of blue varied. It soon became usual for the ratchet panel to be finished in black instead of blue. From 1928 the names changed to 'No. 1 Lamp Standard' and 'No. 2 Lamp Standard'.

The No. 1 and No. 2 Electrical Lamp Standards introduced in 1931 had blue bases, lampholders and finials, and white posts; the large lampholders were on simpler and stronger mountings, and lead-weighted bases were not required. The names changed to 'No. 1E and No. 2E Lamp Standards' the following year.

A lighter blue colour was used for both electrical and glass-globe Lamp Standards from 1933, the latter still with black ratchet panels. There was a change to screw-terminal instead of plug and socket connection for the electrical versions in 1935, with a consequent change in the mounting of the lamps. In 1938, the colouring of the 1E and 2E Lamp Standards changed to green bases, white columns and red finials, with green lampholders. Although it is possible that the glass-globe standards may have been made in similar colours, they were withdrawn from sale not long afterwards, in 1939. The electrical versions continued on sale until 1941, but were not made again after the war.

LEVEL CROSSINGS

The first Level Crossings of 1924 set the pattern for all future Hornby Level Crossings, in being made with a base formed from a tinprinted sheet, pressed with rail sections in the middle, ramped at each end and with tin supports under each side. The hinged gates were mounted on posts clipped to the base. The posts and gates were painted white, with red warning diamonds clipped to the road side of each of the four gates, which were also lettered 'Beware of The Trains'. The length of these first versions was awkward, since it was shorter than a straight rail, and the double track was narrow spaced, unsuitable for use with either the 1 ft or the 2 ft radius Parallel Points.

From 1925 the gates were embossed on the diagonal for strengthening, so different left-handed and right-handed gates became necessary. Slots for Control System wires were added in the supports circa 1926. The early pattern continued in production up to 1928, with many variations in trademarking, and in the lettering style used on the gates.

New Level Crossings were designed in 1928. One was called the No. 1 Level Crossing, and was a single-track version with only two gates (mounted on white posts) of a new pattern with the warning diamond as part of the pressing, mask-sprayed in red on top of the white. The other was the No. 2 Level Crossing, which replaced the old pattern; it too had

the revised gates on white posts, and was made to the length of a full straight rail and to the spacing of double track, whereas the No. 1 was the length of a straight half rail, and was supplied with a half rail to complete the other side of an oval track. The new No. 2 Level Crossing was not illustrated in any 1928 catalogues (indeed the old pattern was still shown in the 1939 HBT), but it was shown in the MM in January 1929, used in conjunction with double track.

The MM in November 1926 had excused the lack of electric Level Crossings by saying that 'in actual practice "live" rails are not laid down on level crossings owing to the great danger . . .'. In fact electrifying the Level Crossing was by no means a simple adaptation, but nonetheless it was successfully achieved, and in 1930 the No. 2 Electrical Level Crossing appeared. By this time the colour of the gateposts on all the Level Crossings was green. In 1931 the No. 1 Electrical Level Crossing appeared; whereas the 1930 No. 2 Electrical version had red insulators, the No. 1 and the later No. 2 Electrical Level Crossings had the more usual black insulators for the third rail. In 1932 the range of Level Crossings expanded to no less than six, with the addition of electrically lit Nos. E1E and E2E Level Crossings. (The ordinary electrical versions were now called E1 and E2 Level Crossings.) These electrically lit versions had two warning lamps, with red aspects each side, mounted on the gates, the left-hand gates in the case of the E2E.

In 1933 there was a change to lighter green for the

gateposts of all six versions, then another change to light brown posts in 1938. All six were still listed in November 1941.

After the war, production of the No. 1 Level Crossing was started around 1948, although they were not listed until 1949. The tinprinting was different, and like many postwar tinprinted accessories they did not recapture the subtle charm of the prewar style. Road supports (which in early days had been brown, then occasionally black in the late '30s), and also the posts, were enamelled in green. The earliest postwar supports were still slotted for Control System wires! Apart from trademarks there was little change in appearance over the many years of postwar production, the No. 1 Level Crossing being listed until 1969.

LOADING GAUGES

The Loading Gauge which first appeared in 1923 was a simple affair, with a plain post fitted with a wire frame from which the bent-wire gauge was suspended by chains. The finial was at first a one-piece casting, and subsequently changed as on the Signals. The round tinplate base, the bottom of the post and the finial were finished black, the post white. Although the trademarks varied, there was little other change until early in 1927, when the round-based gauge appeared in blue and white. But later in 1927 there was a major revision of the design, with the gauge suspended by plain wires from a

support cut from sheet steel. The gauge was also formed from sheet, and hinged flaps were fitted on each side of the gauge. The base was changed to the rectangular type used for signals etc., while the blue and white colours were unchanged.

In 1933 the colour had become a lighter blue, and in 1934 the top of the post was fitted with a plain tinplate cap instead of a finial. There was a colour change to green base, white post and red cap in 1938, and the cap became black in 1939. The Loading Gauge was listed up to 1941, but did not re-appear after the war.

PASSENGER PLATFORMS

Passenger Platforms were available from 1926, either to turn the 'Windsor' Station into a terminus or to lengthen its platforms. The platform was finished in a pale blue-grey to match the Station, with a white line along the platform edge. The front edge and top of the platform were embossed with paving sections. Five holes were punched in the back edge, to allow the length of paled fencing that was supplied to be fitted, using the packet of Meccano Nuts and Bolts provided. The colour of the Paled Fencing was at first white to match that of the Station, but from 1927 the usual colour was green, the most common colour for the lengths of Paled Fencing available separately. Platform Ramps to match the Passenger Platform could also be obtained; these had no fences, but were otherwise the same as the normal Station Ramps, and they

A Loading Gauge of the rectangular base pattern, circa 1927.

were coloured in the standard platform colours. They were supplied boxed in pairs.

By 1929 the colour of the platforms had changed to yellow-cream, and the holes for Island Platform canopies no longer appeared. The fencing was now usually white, and at some time around 1931 the base of the Paled Fencing began to be cut away to allow the fence to be bent. Previously the base had been a solid strip $\frac{1}{4}$ in wide, but now only a thin strip was left, except where the bolt-holes were required, where the original width was retained.

There was a change of colour to light green for Passenger Platform and Ramps in 1933, but whereas the fence was still usually white, a few were painted in the same green as the platforms, though whether for sale with the platforms or separately is not clear. In 1937 there was a change to 'speckled' buff tin-printed platforms, and these were no longer embossed on the sides; the deletion of the embossed marking on the side of the ramps meant that there were no longer right-handed and left-handed versions. The Passenger Platforms and Ramps were usually printed with the 'stonework' sections on both sides, but in 1940 Passenger Platforms were also made with the back in the 'speckled' finish of the top, and with a white line down one edge only instead of two. Whether this was the result of a planned change or a shortage of the usual tinprinted sheets is not clear.

Passenger Platforms, Paled Fencing and Platform Ramps were catalogued up to 1941, but they were not catalogued after the war.

PLATELAYER'S HUTS

The smallest tinprinted building in the Hornby range of 1930 was the new Platelayer's Hut, a nicely-observed model, representing a small brick-built hut, detailed with a window and with climbing plants. It was fitted with a chimney stack, and a planked door which was hinged to open inwards, with a spring to return it to the closed position. The roof was enamelled in a rather unlikely blue, and the base in green. There were two main variants, the inside of the chimney being either red or green. At 2s 6d the Platelayer's Hut was not for every pocket,

but there was a price cut to 2s in 1932, and to only 1s in 1934, the sharp drop being because of simplifications carried out early in that year. The 1934 version had a fixed door instead of hinged, and the chimney pot was replaced by a plunged hole in the top of the stack. The tinprinted sheets used for the sides were not yet changed, the door being mask-sprayed in green enamel over the blank section where the door used to be cut out, and silver-painted door handles added. By 1936 new printings had been made with the planked door incorporated, so it was no longer necessary to do the enamelling. The Platelayer's Hut was listed until 1941 but was never re-issued.

Platelayer's Huts circa 1930, 1934 and 1936.

PLATFORM CRANES

The Platform Cranes introduced in 1928 were based on the crane used for the Goods Platform, but mounted on a special base. They were always fitted with a worm-drive to rotate the jib. An irritating feature was that in prewar days they were crammed into boxes that were a fraction of an inch too small, and consequent damage to the jib was common.

The first colours were red for the jib, and grey for the centre and base. From 1929 the colours changed to grey for the jib, dark red for the centre and dark green for the base, then from 1930 blue for the jib,

Platform Cranes circa 1928, 1929, 1930, 1934, and 1939.

221

red for the centre and yellow-cream for the base. There was another change in 1933 to green for the jib, red for the centre and yellow for the base, with the base lined out with green on the edges, all previous bases having been lined in white. There was a detail change soon after this, with the fixed pulley that had been used at the jib head replaced by a casting (also used for Crane Trucks) which held the string in place. In 1938 the colour of the jib changed to grey, but other colours remained unaltered. The final pre-war version of 1939 had a grey jib, a red centre and a buff base.

In contrast to the frequent colour changes of the pre-war years, the colours chosen for the first post-war Platform Cranes (grey jib, red centre and buff base) lasted right through from the first production late in 1948 to 1969, with only minor detail differences.

POSTERS AND HOARDINGS

HOARDINGS

The introduction of a set of 'field signs' was suggested in the May 1930 MM by a reader, and the idea was promised 'careful consideration'. As a result the Station or Field Hoarding was shown, price 8d, in the 1931 Hornby catalogues. The Hoarding was diecast in lead alloy, finished in the dark blue of the period, and was supplied complete with attached gummed paper posters. One side had a single large advertisement, and the other side two smaller posters side by side. A unique gold 'Hornby Series' transfer trademark was applied to the left-hand post, but soon this extravagance was rendered unnecessary by embossing a 'Hornby Series' trademark in sunken letters. This trademark also was short-lived, and for the rest of the prewar production the 'Hornby Series' lettering was raised rather than sunken. Another minor change was that, instead of the small posters for the Hoardings being cut out in pairs, it became usual to attach two separate small posters. Hoardings were sold to the shops in boxes of six, although intended for separate sale.

Apart from the change of colour to a lighter blue in 1933–34, and a cut in price to 6d in 1934, the only major change was that mazac was used for castings from 1936 onwards, with the unfortunate result that few late prewar hoardings survive, because of 'fa-

tigue'. The price was halved to 3d in 1937.

After the war the title changed to 'Station Hoardings', and they were advertised from October 1949 until 1969, with only a short break (caused by supply difficulties) in 1952. The colour was pale buff instead of blue, and the trademarks were altered.

POSTERS

The first series of Hornby Posters in Miniature were advertised in the December 1931 MM at 6d per packet of 51. There were also Poster Boards at 6d per packet of six: three large and three small. The Poster Boards were rectangles of tin, with two lugs at the top to allow them to be hung from the Paled Fencing. They were finished in various colours, usually dark green or lighter green, but sometimes red or black, and occasionally with different colours on opposite sides. In the early 1930s sample Poster Boards were included in each packet of Posters, bearing printed slips advertising (what else?) the Poster Boards.

The Posters in Miniature were an astonishingly well-prepared series of advertisements, in the style of contemporary posters, covering a wide range of products from soaps to sauces, and from Seccotine to suet. They were printed in full colour to an excellent standard, guillotined to size, then each of the 51 posters was picked out by hand to make up the set, and was packed in the translucent packet. To do this (in quantities of 5,000 or so per year, to judge from the printers' codes on the poster board slips) for a retail price of only 6d, was a remarkable achievement.

The first Posters were sufficiently popular to encourage the preparation of a second set, first advertised in the January 1934 MM. Posters in Miniature Series 2 were in the same size and style as the old series (now known as Series 1) but were more up to date; Kemex, Elektron and Meccano Motor Car and Aeroplane Constructor Posters were included. Brand names for petrol were brought up to date, and other changes were subsequently made both in Series 1 and in Series 2. It is impossible to know which particular Posters should have been included in which set, since the contents were never officially listed, and in any case they varied considerably both between batches and between different

packets in the same batch. Mistakes were also made in making up the sets, with duplicates of some posters (being gummed on the reverse they naturally tended to stick together) and others missed out. The following is a list of Posters known to have been printed before the war. Stars have been used to indicate the Posters from which the Series 2 sets were normally selected.

LARGE POSTERS

* ATORA 'Make it with Hugon's . . . The good beef suet'
  BOVRIL 'Prevents that sinking feeling'
* BOVRIL 'Take . . . and develop strength'
  BP Ethyl 'Banishes Pinking'
  BP Plus 'Gives you more, costs no more'
  CHERRY BLOSSOM Boot Polish
* CHIVERS' Jellies 'Where the rainbow ends'
  CLARK'S Creamed Barley 'A meal in a moment'
  COLAS '. . . makes perfect drives and paths'
* COLAS 'the perfect surface for drives & paths'
* ELEKTRON Electrical Outfits
  ESSO and ESSOLUBE 'When you buy these you buy quality'
* FRY'S Chocolate Cream, 'The famous original'
  FRY'S Milk and Hazel Bars, 'Thick Bars for flavour'
  FRY'S Sandwich 'I said you'd like it'
* HARTLEY'S Table Jelly, 4d only
* HORLICK'S 'Guards against night starvation'
  HORLICK'S 'Brings deep, sound sleep'
* HORNBY SPEED BOATS
  HORNBY TRAINS, 'British and guaranteed'
  JACOB & Co.'s Jabisco Assorted Biscuits
* KEMEX
  LIBBY'S 'The blue and white label'
  LYON'S Coffee and Chicory Extract
* MARMITE with Cook, Butler, Boots 'Good for soups . . . etc'
  MECCANO 'Begin Meccano now. . .'
* MECCANO Aeroplane Constructor
* MECCANO Motor Car Constructor
  ODOL 'The perfect British dentifrice'
  OXO 'Beef in brief'
  PRATTS High Test 'Hi! Test High Test!'
* ROBERTSON'S Golden Shred
  SECCOTINE 'In handy tubes. Sticks Everything'

SECCOTINE in red on yellow, red border 'Sticks everything'

★ SECCOTINE in white on red, yellow border 'Sticks everything'

★ SECCOTINE 'Sticks everything. Sold in handy tubes'

★ SHELL Lubricating Oil 'for reliability'

SHELL 'That's Shell . . . That was'

★ SKIPPERS 'The tastiest meal that ever came out of a tin'

WAKEFIELD CASTROL 'Sir Malcolm Cambell used . . .'

★ WAKEFIELD CASTROL ' . . . patent . . . reduces cylinder wear'

★ WAVERLEY Oats 'Better porridge'

★ YARDLEY Lavender 'the lovable fragrance'

Prewar Hornby Posters, from both series.

223

SMALL POSTERS

ATORA 'The good beef suet', blue background
★ ATORA 'Make it with Hugon's Atora, the good beef suet'
★ BEEFEX 'Best of the beef'
BIRD'S Custard, 'More sold than ever'
★ BIRD'S 'The quality custard. Quality counts!'
★ BIRD'S Custard Creams, 'Something to sing about'
★ BOVRIL '. . . promotes that singing feeling'
BRASSO 'for brightness'
★ CADBURY'S Bourn-Vita 'for sleep and energy'
CAMP Coffee 'is the best'
    ('Don't be misled!!!' is in red on early printings)
CARR'S 'Pioneers of the biscuit industry'
CHIVERS' Jellies 'make a meal a banquet'
CLARK'S Creamed Barley
COLMAN'S Starch 'Nothing to touch it'
★ ELEKTRON Electrical Outfits
FORCE 'Whole wheat in flakes'
★ GLO 'The warming winter drink. Keeps you in tune'
★ GOLDEN SHRED Marmalade, 'Golly it's good'
HARTLEY'S Marmalade
★ HARTLEY'S Strawberry, 'Judge it by its flavour'
HORLICK'S 'for sound sleep'
★ HORNBY SPEED BOATS
HORNBY TRAINS
HP SAUCE 'Mary had a little lamb with lots of . . .'
KARDOMAH Tea 'Makes better tea'
★ KEMEX chemical outfits
★ KLG plugs 'Fit and forget'
LIBBY'S 'a whole sliced pineapple in a can'
LIFEBUOY Soap 'for health', red and blue triangle background
★ LIFEBUOY Soap 'for health', with boy's face
LUX 'If it's safe in water, it's safe in . . .'
★ LUX 'Prolongs the life of all lovely fabrics'
★ LYONS' Tea 'Huge sale tells own tale'
LYONS' Tea 'The best tea value'
MARMITE with Cook, 'is good for soups . . . etc'
★ MARMITE, with Cook, 'I must have Marmite for soups . . . etc'
★ MARMITE with Cook and Butler, 'good for

soups . . . etc.'
MECCANO 'Begin Meccano now . . .'
★ MECCANO Aeroplane Constructor
★ MECCANO Motor Car Constructor
MERIDIAN Underwear, Slumber wear, Bathing wear
NESTLE'S Milk, 'Best for baby'
★ NESTLE'S, 'Thanks to . . .'
★ NESTLE'S, 'Happy Days'
OVALTINE 'Country Health for you'
★ OVALTINE 'for radiant health'
★ OXO 'Beef in Brief'
PEARS Soap 'King of soaps, soap of Kings'
★ PEARS 'Golden Glory soap, 6d per cake'
PERSIL 'Used by over 2,000,000 housewives'
QUAKER Oats 'For health – Quick . . .'
★ SHELL 'You can be sure of . . .', with anchor
SKIPPERS 'are tasty for tea'
★ SKIPPERS, 'A feast of flavour, and no bones about it'
SOUTHERN RAILWAY 'South for Sunshine'
SOUTHERN RAILWAY, 'Sunny South Sam, still at your service'
★ SPRATTS Bonio 'A bone shaped biscuit for all breeds'
SUNLIGHT Soap, 'Don't worry, use . . .'
★ SUNLIGHT Soap 'for extra soapiness use . . .'
★ SWAN Ink 'for all pens'
SWAN Pens 'World Famous'
★ SWAN Pens (no slogan)
★ SWAN VESTAS 'British made by Bryant and May. See there's a swan on your box'
TREX 'for better cooking'
VIM 'Cleanser . . . Polisher'
★ VIM 'The double action cleanser. Loosens the dirt, then absorbs it'
★ WAVERLEY Oats 'Perfect Porridge'
★ WILLS Capstan Cigarettes 'They're good, they're Capstan'
★ WILLS Gold Flake Cigarettes, 'Always fresh'
★ WINCARNIS 'for glorious health, take . . .'
★ Young WOLSEY, 'finest woollen underwear'
★ YARDLEY LAVENDER 'The lovable fragrance'

The posters used for the hoardings were chosen at random from the current range. In the late 1930s the size of the translucent packets used for the posters

was reduced, (although the number of posters was unchanged), and the sample Poster Board was no longer included, although a slip advertising the poster boards was still enclosed.

After the war the Posters were first advertised in the October 1949 Meccano Products Folder, in packets of 12 only. They were advertised again from April 1950 through to the end of production, with a short break in 1952. The postwar posters were usually packed in cellophane packets, and there were two different sets of 12 although this was not mentioned in the catalogues. All were different from the prewar designs, and were printed on glossy paper. The advertisements included:

LARGE POSTERS

SET 1, BEV
SET 2, BIRD'S Custard 'Something to sing about'
SET 1, BRYLCREAM ' . . . your hair and be set for the day'
SET 2, CADBURYS Bournville Cocoa
SET 1, CASTROL 'Give me Castrol every time'
SET 1, HARTLEY'S 'The greatest name in jam making'
SET 1, HP SAUCE 'improves all meals'
SET 2, LIFEBUOY Soap 'for health'
SET 2, RALEIGH 'The all steel bicycle'

SET 1, SMITHS KLG
SET 2, SPRATTS Bonio 'is what we're waiting for'
SET 2, WILLS CAPSTAN Cigarettes; with yachts
and liner

SMALL POSTERS

SET 1, BIRD'S Custard 'something to sing about'
SET 2, BRYLCREAM ' . . . your hair for perfect
control'
SET 1, CADBURYS Bourn-vita
SET 1, CAPSTAN 'Have a Capstan'
SET 2, CASTROL 'The masterpiece in oils'
SET 2, HARTLEY'S 'The greatest name in jam
making'
SET 2, HP SAUCE 'Improves all meals'
SET 1, LIFEBUOY Soap 'for health', yellow on
red background
SET 2, LYONS' Tea 'Always the best – on sale
here'
SET 1, RALEIGH 'Reg rides a Raleigh'
SET 2, SMITHS KLG
SET 1, SPRATTS 'Builds up a dog'

Little is known of the early postwar posters, but it seems that a small remaining stock of prewar posters, the large 'Chivers' Jellies' poster for example, appeared on early postwar hoardings. The large 'Capstan' advertisement was printed in an early

version with fishing boats rather than yachts in the background, which appeared frequently on early postwar Hoardings, but which differed from the other postwar Posters in having a matt surface.

No Poster Boards were made after the war, although a Dinky Toy Road Hoarding was sold from 1959 to 1964, for which two sets of 6 self-adhesive posters (4 large and 2 small) were issued. These were not catalogued for use with the Hornby Trains.

RAILWAY ACCESSORIES

RAILWAY ACCESSORIES NO. 1

Platform Accessories Set No. 1, containing four pieces of Miniature Luggage and a porter's barrow, was first sold in 1924. Sets Nos. 1 to 3 were planned soon after the Windsor Station appeared, and the first pieces were too early to carry the 'Hornby Series' trademark which came into general use later in 1924. The pieces of luggage were all tinprinted, and at first were marked 'Meccano Ltd Liverpool'. They were a plain brown suitcase, a wickerwork hamper (with 'Carlisle' label on the lid), a flat-topped trunk in brown and cream, and a round-topped trunk in black with red bands and brown detail. The barrow was enamelled in green and had no trademark. Its wheels were adapted from the

pressing used for the tops of the Milk Cans.

The printed trademarks were soon altered to 'Hornby Series', and there were minor tinprinting differences, for example the label on the hamper now read 'London'. The next major change came around 1928, by which time Sets 1 to 3 were known as 'Railway Accessories' rather than 'Platform Accessories'. The difference was structural; the bottoms of the cases were not simply folded at the corners as before, but were accurately cut and folded to shape, and assembled by lugs in slots. This method evidently proved too expensive, since by 1932 the bottoms of the cases reverted to being folded as before. The wheels of the barrow were changed to castings, instead of tinplate, and the small brown suitcase was changed to green alligator-skin finish. There were subsequent tinprinting variations, most importantly in 1938 when a new set came out which had a bright orange flat-topped trunk, green and orange bands on the round-topped trunk, and also orange instead of brown printing on the hamper. The alligator-skin green case now had black corners where these had previously been green.

RAILWAY ACCESSORIES NO. 2

The set of miniature Milk Cans and Truck was also available in 1924. It consisted of six Milk Cans

No. 2, Milk Cans & Truck.

No. 3, Platform Machines etc. Contents of an early set on the left, a later set on the right.

No. 1, Luggage & Truck, circa 1924 (front), 1927, 1932, and 1938 (rear).

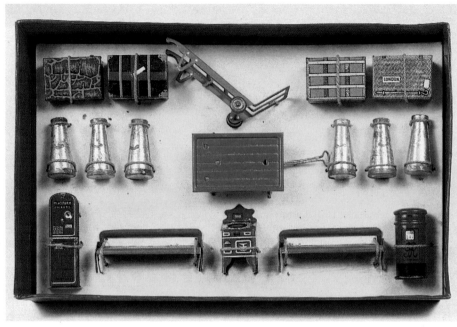

No. 4, a combination of sets 1 to 3.

(already made for the Milk Traffic Van) and a four-wheel Truck. The first colour for the Truck was green, but very soon this was changed to the orange used for the Seccotine Van roof. The wheels were changed to castings instead of tinplate around 1932, then from 1933 the colour of the Truck changed to light blue. There were no noticeable variations in the Milk Cans themselves except minor differences in the pressings. The Milk Cans were available for separate sale by special order until 1932, and subsequently through dealers. They were also sold either in boxes of 12 or singly between 1954 and 1969.

RAILWAY ACCESSORIES NO. 3

The third of the 1924 sets contained miniature Platform Accessories: a post box, two seats, a platform ticket machine, and a nametape machine in brown. All were tinprinted except the seats, which were enamelled in green. At first none of the pieces were

trademarked, although trademarks later appeared on the nametape and platform ticket machines. Around 1932 the colour of the nametape machine was changed to green, and when the diecast Dinky Toy Pillar Box came out in 1935, it replaced the tinplate pillar box in the sets. It is not clear exactly when the next change took place, which was the addition of a fire-hose box; this was based on the Dinky Toy RAC box which first appeared in 1935, but was of course differently tinprinted, in red with a grey enamelled roof. It was probably added to the Railway Accessory Set No. 3 in 1936, certainly by 1937 when it was shown in the catalogues.

RAILWAY ACCESSORIES NO. 4

Platform Accessories No. 4 were sets combining the contents of sets Nos. 1, 2 and 3. The contents varied in the same way as for the individual sets, since only the packaging was different. The name changed to

'Railway Accessories No. 4' in 1928, but there was no further change in the description; contents were given as '17 Pieces', but when the fire-hose box was added in 1936 or 1937, the labels on the boxes were altered to read '18 Pieces', a change not directly mentioned in the catalogues.

RAILWAY ACCESSORIES NO. 5

The Gradient and Mile Posts were an interesting set first catalogued in 1928. The contents were four mileposts ($\frac{1}{4}$, $\frac{1}{2}$, $\frac{3}{4}$ and 1 mile) and eight gradient posts: 1–130/Level, 1–210/1–250, 1–300/1–210, 1–165/1–189, 1–147/1–260, 1–120/Level, Level/1–156 (uphill) and Level/1–156 (downhill). At first the signs were tinprinted in black on white, but within a short time they were altered to have crude and often illegible rubber-stamped lettering on white-enamelled posts. (There were of course still eight different pressings.) The gradient descriptions were unchanged. The later

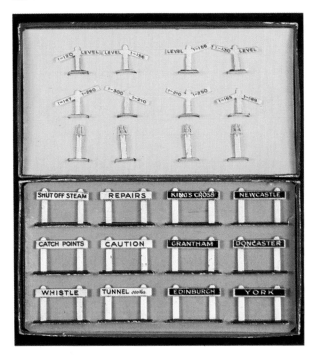

RAILWAY ACCESSORIES NO. 7

The Watchman's Hut, Brazier, Shovel and Poker set was introduced in 1928; it had all the hallmarks of a product of that period, an attention to detail that extended not just to the largest engines and coaches but also down to the smaller lineside accessories. The hut itself was quite a complicated assembly, with base, sides, top and also a seat; on each side there was a cracked–up lug on which hung the poker (simply the bolt from the No. 2 Level Crossing gate, painted black) and the shovel, a well-formed piece of tinplate also enamelled black. The hut was enamelled blue, with a red roof.

The brazier was another piece of clever tinplate design, simple but effective. The fire-effect inside the brazier frame was tinprinted with red coals on a black background. Yellow dots were also added, apparently in enamel paint. There was also a short-lived printing with small black dots on a red background. The Hut itself varied little, except in the trademark transfer and the change to a lighter blue from 1933.

RAILWAY ACCESSORIES NOS. 8 and 9

When the Railway Accessories No. 6 set was withdrawn in 1929, the contents were split into set No. 8 (Notice Boards) and set No. 9 (Station Name Boards). The actual contents of the new boxes were unchanged from those already described, and there was little change for the remainder of production, except for the use of lighter blue for the bases from 1933, and green instead of blue for the last sets of 1939–40. The Railway Accessories Nos. 1, 2, 3, 4, 5, 7, 8 and 9 were all still listed in 1941, but despite their former popularity none re-appeared after the war except the humble Milk Can.

SIGNAL CABINS

No. 2 and 2E SIGNAL CABINS

The first Hornby Signal Cabins went on sale in 1924. They were, from the outset, designed for use with a Hornby Control System Lever Frame, although it was to be another two years before the Control System was introduced. The roof and the upper part of the back wall were hinged for access to the frame, and the feet of the Signal Cabin could be bolted to the Lever Frame base. Hornby Signal Cabins were amongst the most realistic of all the Hornby buildings, with the right proportions and impressive appearance, especially when the Lever Frame was fitted. One certainly gets the impression that the designers had actually gone out to see what a real Signal Cabin looked like.

The first Signal Cabins were named 'Windsor', and had square-tiled roofs and cream steps. Later they had tinprinted trademarks instead of transfers, and a few had light brown steps.

Around 1928 it was decided that the Signal Cabin would no longer be named, so on new tinprintings there was no name panel. Signal Cabins now had holes in the floor to allow Resistance Controllers to be fitted if required, and the floor was strengthened by embossed ridges. Soon the pattern of the tin-

series were much more neatly lettered in black, perhaps by stencil-spraying, onto posts pressed from plain white tinplate. The bases were always in the same finish as the posts, blue in the very earliest sets, white thereafter.

RAILWAY ACCESSORIES NO. 6

Another set of accessories issued in 1928 was No. 6, Station Name Boards and Notice Boards. There were twelve boards in the set, six with station names (King's Cross, Grantham, Doncaster, York, New-castle and Edinburgh) and six Notice Boards (Whistle, Tunnel 200 Yards, Caution, Repairs, Shut Off Steam and Catch Points). The signs were enamelled in white, with bases over-painted blue, and the names were applied as transfers; black lettering for the Notice Boards, and white letters on a black background for the Station Names. This set was catalogued for only one season, being split up the following year into sets Nos. 8 and 9.

No. 7, Watchman's Hut with Brazier, Shovel and Poker.

227

printed roof changed from square-tiled to round-tiled. The walls were printed with white mortar between the bricks, but around 1931 there was a new printing with the brickwork having black mortar, the general style being much the same as before, although dustbins were no longer printed under the steps. There were further new tinprintings around 1932 in brighter colours, with the woodwork window surrounds printed brown and yellow, and the inside walls pink. A blank name panel was added on the front wall, and the roof reverted to a square-tiled printing. The No. 2E Signal Cabin of 1932 was at first in these colours, with a single lamp inside the cabin, connected to the transformer by a plug and socket connection. New printings were again made in 1934, with the window surrounds now in green and yellow. The colour of the steps was soon changed from cream to yellow. The inside walls were changed later in the 1930s to sand-colour, often with confusion of colours since different parts of the box had different coloured inside walls. The final electrically-lit versions had green instead of blue lampshades, but there was little change in the external appearance of either No. 2 or No. 2E Signal Cabins, except for the fitting of light brown steps instead of yellow from 1939.

After the war, the No. 2E Signal Cabins did not reappear. The No. 2 Signal Cabin was however substantially modified, and re-issued with fixed roof and back, not hinged as before, and without the cutouts for the Control System Lever Frame. The first version of 1949 had a green tinprinted roof; in 1955 this was replaced by an orange-roofed version with updated printing, which remained on sale up to 1957.

No. 1 SIGNAL CABINS

The simple No. 1 Signal Cabins were first sold in 1928. The most striking difference from the No. 2 Signal Cabin of that time was the colour of the roof, which on the No. 1 was printed with red tiles. A chimney of the No. 2 type was fitted to the roof, but there was no hinging of roof or back, the windows were printed and not cut out, and no steps were fitted, although they were printed on. A base was fitted inside the box; some of the bases were in fact surplus floors from the No. 2 Cabin, with a central hole for the lever frame, although obviously the Lever Frame could not be fitted to the No. 1.

Around 1931, there was a change of colour, with pale blue roof tiles, and the mortar in the tinprinted brickwork was now black instead of white as before, amongst other changes. There was another tinprinting change around 1934, with bright yellow and green window surrounds, and the colour of the roof was changed to darker blue. The No. 1 Signal Cabin was still in stock in 1941 but did not re-appear after the war.

SIGNALS

PREWAR No. 2 SIGNALS

The Hornby Signal was first shown in the May 1923 Rail Formations leaflet. It had a very tall latticed post mounted on a simple tinplate base, with a ladder reaching up to the signal arm. The colours were black for the base, the lower part of the post, lever, ladder and finial, and white for the post. The arm was tinprinted. Somewhat curiously, the green and red aspects were printed on the arm, then punched out, and a spectacle frame with red and green celluloid aspects clipped over the top. The lever arm was fitted with a balance weight, mounted not on the end of the arm as shown in many early illustrations, but offset from the centre.

There was an early change, probably early in 1924, from the first single-piece cast finial (which was not attached by lugs, but simply plugged into the column) to a tin cap with edges flanged downwards and with a diecast spike attached. Late in 1924 or early in 1925, Signals with Distant arms (with the same printing as the Home arm but fishtailed at the end) were introduced. In order to improve the strength of the Signal, which was vulnerable because of its size, the lever arm was from 1925 embossed with a ridge, the base was embossed with a circle and four radiating lines, and the ladder was altered to a

No. 1 Signal Cabins, circa 1928, 1931 and 1935.

No. 2 Signal Cabins, circa 1924, 1929, 1931, 1932, and 1940.

228

less flimsy pattern, with the edges folded into tubes. A minor change was that the flat-based dummy lamp was changed to hollow-based.

In 1926, because of the introduction of Control System Signals, the lever arm was punched with a total of four holes for wires etc., thus undoing the previous year's good work of strengthening the arm; now they frequently snapped off at the unused and unnecessary extra holes.

In 1927 there was a colour change for the Signal, to blue and white instead of black and white. From 1928, it became known as the 'No. 2 Signal' following the introduction of the No. 1, and the tinprinting of the signal arms was changed, with a white chevron printed on the 'Distant' arm instead of the straight white band of the 'Home' type. Soon the signal arm was simplified by the removal of the brass collar on the pivot wire, and another minor modification was that rounded balance weights replaced flat-fronted weights. The colour became a noticeably deeper blue, the early shade being a greyish blue. Other changes around this time were the attachment of new one-piece cast finials, this time clipped to the posts by long lugs, and the fitting of new dummy lamps recognisible by the collar on the post side of the mounting. Around 1929 there was an alteration to the lever, which now had the arm to the right instead of the left-hand side of the post, and which was fixed directly to the pivot wire without a brass collar as before. The post fixing was also simplified, being attached to a plunged hole in the base instead having the lugs bent over a cap (actually the part used as the base of the Milk Can). By 1930 a large plunged hole also appeared in the centre of the base. Electrically lit No. 2E Signals appeared in 1932, in the same colours: blue for the base, lower part of column, lever arm, ladder and finial, and white for the post. The lighting connection was by plug and socket; the lamp was mounted behind the celluloid aspects, the lampholder itself having a plain celluloid aspect. The rear of the lamp had a small hole, to show the lamp was alight.

In 1933 there was a change of colour, with the customer offered a choice of green or lighter blue. The levers were finished red, the post still in white. Finials were still fitted to all the No. 2 Signals, and painted in green or blue to match the base and ladder.

No. 2 and No. 2E Single Arm Signals, circa 1924, 1925, 1927, 1932, 1933, 1935, 1935, 1936, 1938 and 1939. Available in home or distant from 1925.

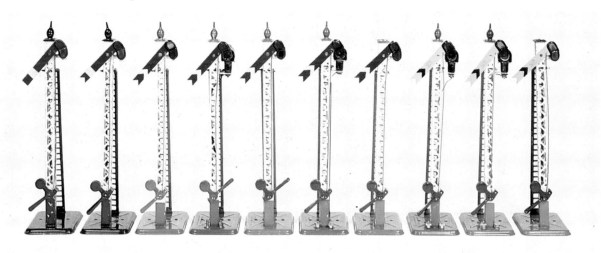

No. 2 and No. 2E Junction Signals. Circa 1924, 1930, 1933, 1935, 1935, 1938 and 1939. Available in home or distant from 1925.

The following year, in 1934, there was a change to flat tin post-caps (flanged downwards at the edges) and a return to lever arms pointing to the left of the post; the colours remained the same. Electrically lit 2E Signals continued to be fitted with finials. In 1935, the 2E Signal wiring was simplified, and the change made to connection by screw terminals.

In 1936, the tinprinting of the 'Distant' signal arm changed to yellow with a black chevron instead of red with a white chevron, and the celluloid aspects became orange and green on the 'Distant' arm; these changes, which had been 'under consideration' since 1928, were long overdue to reflect general practice.

In 1938 the signals were no longer available in a

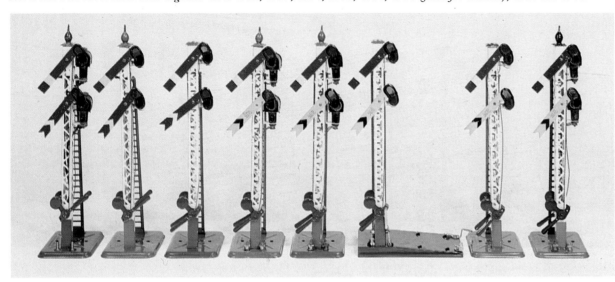

The 'Royal Scot' passing under a No. 2E Signal Gantry of 1938 vintage.

1924. Initially they seem to have been made only in 'Distant' versions, with the lever arms for the two signal posts (tall to the left and short to the right) pointing one to the left and one to the right-hand side of the column. The Junction Signals were finished in the same black and white colours used for the ordinary Signal. Quite soon the Junction Signals were altered to have both levers pointing to the right of the post. 'Home' as well as 'Distant' versions were being made by the time that Hornby Control System Junction Signals became available in 1926. The method of attaching the platform to the main post had also been simplified.

In 1927 the colours were changed to blue and white, again as on the ordinary signals. The following year No. 2 Double Arm Signals and Signal Gantries were introduced. Again the colour scheme was as for the single-arm No. 2 Signal, although the bridge of the Gantry was lined out in blue. The new signals, and the latest 'Distant' Junction Signals, had distant arms with the chevron instead of the plain stripe (except on very early examples). There were minor detail changes broadly as described for the No. 2 Signal.

Electric versions called the Junction Signal E, the No. 2E Double Arm Signal and the Signal Gantry E were sold from 1932, all in the usual colours; blue bases, blue on the lower part of the main posts, blue levers, blue ladders and blue finials, with white posts.

There was a choice of colour from 1933, with the customer offered either green and white, or lighter blue and white, in either case with red lever arms. The Signal Gantries were sold only with blue bases, red levers, blue finials, and with green lining around the bridge!

There were simplifications in 1934 for the Double Arm and Junction Signals, to eliminate the bellcranks that had formerly been used, and to use plain wire working rods instead. The bellcranks could not actually be removed from the Signal Gantry, but the working arrangements were nonetheless simplified. No. 2 Double Arm and No. 2 Junction Signals (the new name since the introduction of the No. 1 in 1934) were fitted with the old No. 1-type flat post caps instead of finials. The No. 2 Gantry Signal however kept its finials, as did the 2E Double Arm, 2E Junction and 2E Gantry

choice of blue or green; only the green signals were offered, and the colour for the cap of the No. 2 and the finial of the No. 2E became red, although one or two 'transitional' blue Signals appeared with red tops!

The colour of the ladder, lever and cap (or finial) changed to black from 1939, with the base and the lower part of the column still coloured green. A few transitional versions had red caps with black levers and ladders.

PREWAR No. 2 JUNCTION, No. 2 DOUBLE ARM, and GANTRY SIGNALS

The first Junction Signals were offered for sale in

Signals.

In 1935, the Signal Gantry was offered in 'Home' and 'Distant' versions, with four arms the same, instead of having two home and two distant arms as before. The electric signals were changed to connection by screw terminals instead of plug and socket. From 1936 all distant signals had yellow arms instead of red.

The choice of colours for the Double Arm and Junction Signals was no longer offered from 1938, all versions now having green bases and ladders, red lever arms and red finials or caps; these colours were also used for the Signal Gantries. There was a further change in 1939 to black ladders, black lever arms and black finials or caps, still with green bases. Signal Gantry bridges were no longer lined in green.

There were of course many detail variations over the years, for example in the spectacle frames, the changes from clinching cups to plunged-hole fixing for the post, finial differences, differences in the latticing, the position of the lugs, trademarks, dummy lamp castings, bellcranks and lever arms etc., quite impossible to list in detail. These variations combine to make Hornby Signals perhaps the most confusing subject apart from Open Wagons!

No. 1 SIGNALS

The first of the simplified No. 1 Signals were marketed in 1928. The differences from the No. 2 Signals were mainly that there was no ladder, the post being mounted centrally on the base, the signal arm had printed aspects, there was no dummy lamp behind the signal arm, and there was a plain post-cap instead of a finial. These Signals were boxed in pairs of Home and Distant No. 1 Signals, or of No. 1 Double Arm Signals. Each was finished in blue and white, and the distant arms had the chevron. At first the lever had a flat weight, and pointed to the left of the column. Later versions had lever arms pointing to the right of the posts, and rounded balance weights.

As with the No. 2 Signals, from 1933 two colours were available, green and white or blue and white. Both had red levers. But there were important structural changes in 1934. Firstly, the bases of the No. 1 Signals and No. 1 Double Arm Signals became round instead of rectangular, and the flat tin caps (now used for No. 2 Signals) were replaced by forming the sides of the post into a pyramid-shape at the top. They were now boxed in trade packs of half a dozen. The working rods of the No. 1 Double Arm Signals were simplified. No. 1 Junction Signals

and No. 1 Signal Gantries were introduced in 1934, both with the round bases now used for the other No. 1 Signals, and both boxed singly. There was no longer a choice of colour, all the No. 1 Signals now having green bases, red levers, white posts (no longer coloured near the base), and the pyramid tops painted green. The lever arms for the single arm No. 1 Signals reverted to left-handed.

From 1935, the No. 1 Gantry Signals were supplied with a choice of Home or Distant arms, instead of combined Home/Distant as before. Yellow distant arms were used from 1936, and from 1938 the tops of the posts were picked out in red instead of green. The last changes came in 1939, when the latest No. 1 Signals had black tops and black levers, and the No. 1 Junction Signals and No. 1 Signal Gantries had the bridge sections painted in white rather than the previous green.

POSTWAR SIGNALS

After the war, No. 2 Signals and No. 2 Double Arm Signals were catalogued in the UK from 1949, although they may possibly have been in production in 1948. The early postwar signals were quite similar to the last prewar types, with somewhat darker

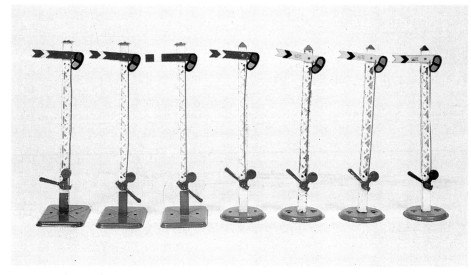

No. 1 Single Arm Signals. Circa 1928, 1933, 1933, 1934, 1936, 1938 and 1939. Available in home or distant versions.

No. 1 Double Arm Signals. Circa 1930, 1933, 1936, 1938 and 1939.

231

green bases, all-white posts, black ladders, black levers and black post-caps. The bases were almost invariably marked by trademark transfers, and (except on some early postwar signals), the signal arms did not have printed trademarks, while embossed trademarkings were not used on the base. These signals were re-designed in 1950 with shortened posts and with the latticework deleted. The No. 2 Junction Signal did not re-appear until 1953, again in a revised form with the latticework missing and with shortened posts. Perhaps it would have been a good idea to have made the prewar No. 1 Signals in this smaller and simpler style; in fact these small postwar signals were more satisfactory in many ways than the prewar No. 2, which were rather overscale.

In 1954, the colour of the dummy lamps behind the signal arms was changed from white to black, and apart from variations in the shade of green used for the base (and of course in trademark transfers) there was little further change. No. 2 Signals, No. 2

Double Arm Signals, and Home and Distant Junction Signals were all still in stock in 1969.

STATIONS

The Railway Station (or 'Windsor' Station as it was sometimes listed) was first made in 1923. A tin-printed station building was mounted on a large platform, enamelled in pale blue-grey, and with a white line along the platform edge. Inside the building was fitted a pair of candleholders, strategically placed under the chimney stacks, although these were more for ornament than for ventilation; the windows were cut out for this purpose.

By 1924, several alterations had taken place; three hinged doors were fitted at the front, whereas before this the doors had only been printed, but the window of the Stationmaster's office, the ladies' waiting room and the telegraph office continued to be cut out; soon however only the telegraph office window remained so. From the middle of 1924 varnish had been used for the platform, on both these versions. From early in 1926, there were further modifications, with candleholders no longer fitted and with none of the windows cut out. Pegs and slots were fitted in the front edge of the platform, to allow termini to be created using the Island Platform and the Passenger Platform.

In 1927 there was also a new tinprinting for the building, hardly altered except that the booking office windows were labelled '1st' and '3rd' instead of '1st' and '2nd', and all the windows were properly printed, with none of the former blanks.

When the Wayside Stations were first manufactured in 1927, however, the buildings still had the early tinprinting, and the platform was the same pale blue-grey as for the Railway Station. This Wayside Station differed from the Railway Station in having no fence, no chimneys, no ramps and no opening doors. The names changed to No. 1 and No. 2 Railway Stations in 1928, by which time the No. 1 Station had the same revised printing as the No. 2 Station.

From late in 1928 or early in 1929, the platforms were enamelled in yellow-cream. Soon the ramps each had a peg and a slot, to connect to a peg and a slot on the station end, whereas before this the ramp had had two pegs, and the station end two slots.

Sometime in 1930 or 1931, the tinprinting of the building was again altered; this was a more substantial revision, bringing the passengers' clothing fashions and motor cars up to date. The right-hand car on the back of the station gives a convenient way of recognising the different printings; the number of side windows changed from two on the first and second printings, to three on the third printing, and to one on the fourth printing. No. 1, No. 2 and No. 2E Stations were each produced using the third printing. (The 2E Station, introduced in 1932, was similar to the No. 2, but fitted with a pair of electric lamps, outside rather than inside the building.)

The fourth printing appeared briefly on the yellow-cream platform, certainly in the No. 1 version, but from 1933 the colour of the platform became light green. Early stations with the green platform still had pale blue roofs, but by 1934 a more colourful dark blue roof was fitted. Screw terminal connections were used for the 2E Station from 1935. Early in 1936, a choice of No. 2 and No. 2E Station names was offered for the first time; 'Wembley', 'Ripon', 'Bristol' or 'Margate' instead of 'Windsor' only. Although 'Brighton' was mentioned in the 1936–37 Meccano Products catalogue (instead of 'Margate'), there is nothing to suggest this was other than a mistake. Late in 1936 it was decided that 'Reading' would replace 'Bristol'.

In 1937 new tinprintings of the roof and the building were prepared. Platforms also began to be tinprinted, and the sides were no longer embossed. The new No. 3 Station used these new tinprintings, but was otherwise unchanged from the No. 1. The No. 4 Station differed somewhat more from the

No. 2 Station 'Windsor', circa 1934.

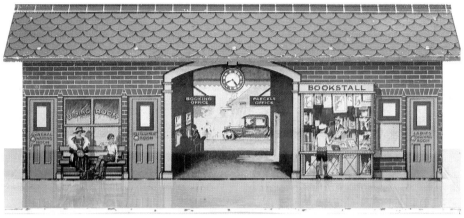

No. 1 Station, circa 1931.

No. 1 Station, circa 1934.

No. 3 Station, circa 1937.

No. 3 Station, circa 1939.

No. 2; it had no opening doors, but was modified to be cut away in the centre for a walk-through booking hall, complete with a mazac ticket office barrier. The chimneys had cast chimney pots instead of tinplate as on the No. 2 type. Perhaps the most striking difference was in the colour of the new stations; the roofs were green instead of blue, the buildings were buff instead of red brick, and the platforms were in a 'speckled' buff pattern instead of green. There was a No. 4E Station, fitted with lights in the same way as the No. 2E. The names of the No. 4 Station were the same as for the No. 2.

Although the Nos. 3, 4 and 4E Stations eventually replaced Nos. 1, 2 and 2E, there was a period when the Nos. 1, 2 and 2E were still being made, using some of the No. 4-type tinprintings. Common examples are the No. 1 Station with the old building and roof on the tinprinted platform, and also the old-style No. 2 platform and building with the new No. 4 roof. The old style stations were listed along with the new in the 1937–38 Meccano Products Catalogue, but were not included in the January 1938 revised price list although mentioned in

the February 1938 MM.

There were revised tinprintings for the Nos. 3, 4 and 4E Station buildings in 1939, which among other differences had a square arch printed over the booking hall instead of a round arch as before. The lampshades on the electrically lit version were green instead of blue as previously.

After the war, only the No. 3 Station was produced. It was catalogued from 1949, and was tinprinted in a style quite similar to the late prewar No. 3, and a pair of ramps was supplied, but as usual the postwar building lacked the spark of life. The green-roofed version was produced until the orange-roofed version of 1955 replaced it. The No. 3 Station was withdrawn from sale in 1957.

TELEGRAPH POLES

Heavy cast iron bases, square and somewhat smaller than the usual accessory bases, were used for the first Hornby Telegraph Poles introduced in 1923. The tall post was fitted with a post cap, and three tinplate bars were rivetted in place, each fitted with four ceramic

insulators. The colours were grey for the post and crossbars, and black for the base. Soon the cast iron base was changed to the standard rectangular tinplate type used for Signals etc. On the iron base, the post had screwed directly into a threaded hole in the base, and on the first tinplate based versions the same threaded post was used, but fixed to the base by a hexagonal nut. Later in 1923 there was a change in the spacing of three bars: $\frac{7}{8}''$ apart instead of $\frac{5}{8}''$ as before, and on these wide-spaced three-bar versions the post was riveted to the base. Early in 1924 it was decided to delete one of the crossbars and have only two wide-spaced bars, and the 1924 catalogue pictures were touched up to show this change.

From 1925, the base was strengthened by embossing a circle and four radiating ridges, as on the Signals.

In 1927 the Telegraph Poles were enamelled in blue-grey, with white posts and blue-grey crossbars, still with the insulators attached by wires as separate pieces. The Telegraph Poles were now boxed and sold in pairs rather than singly.

From 1928, the colour changed to an overall blue, with simplifications to the crossbars which were now lead alloy castings incorporating the insulators. Two of these crossbars were fitted, at the same $\frac{7}{8}''$ spacing as before. The top of the post and the insulators were hand-painted in white to contrast

A late No. 1 Station, circa 1937. No ramps were supplied, but they could be bought separately.

with the blue. A light blue colour was used from 1933, still with white details, and otherwise unchanged. A smaller number of Telegraph Poles were made in light green with white details.

Telegraph Poles were not included in the 1940 or 1941 price lists, since stocks had presumably been exhausted. This is not surprising since the 1939 lists had cut the price to only 1s each compared to 3s each in 1923.

TRAIN NAME BOARDS

In 1931, the No. 2 Special Pullman Coaches began to be fitted with clips on the roof to take Train Name Boards, which were simple strips of tinplate with train names or destinations for many routes on each of the four railway groups' main lines. The boards were tinprinted with gold lettering on a blue background, and there were sixteen varieties:

A selection of Hornby Train Name Boards.

No. 1, THE FLYING SCOTSMAN
No. 2, THE SCARBOROUGH FLIER
No. 3, THE ROYAL SCOT
No. 4, THE MERSEYSIDE EXPRESS
No. 5, THE GOLDEN ARROW
No. 6, BOURNEMOUTH BELLE
No. 7, CORNISH RIVIERA EXPRESS
No. 8, TORBAY LIMITED EXPRESS
No. 9, KING'S CROSS, YORK & EDINBURGH
No. 10, KING'S CROSS, EDINBURGH & ABERDEEN
No. 11, LONDON (EUSTON) & LIVERPOOL (LIME STREET)
No. 12, LONDON (EUSTON) & GLASGOW (CENTRAL)
No. 13, VICTORIA AND DOVER
No. 14, WATERLOO, SALISBURY & EXETER
No. 15, PADDINGTON, EXETER & PLYMOUTH
No. 16, PADDINGTON & BRISTOL

The price per packet of four was 4d when they were first announced in the January 1932 MM, having been too late for inclusion in the 1931–32 catalogues. Also offered in the January 1932 MM were packets of Roof Clips for No. 2 Pullmans (also suitable for Metropolitan and Saloon Coaches), and for old No. 2 Special Pullmans without clips. These were sold in packets of 12 (enough for 6 coaches) at 1s per packet, rather than in fours as the Train Name Boards. Although the range of boards was described as 'only a beginning . . .' demand evidently did not prove sufficient to add extra boards for other well-known expresses, as had been hoped. The first printings in some cases were sufficient for several years' supply, but around 1935 or 1936 a new series was printed, using exactly the same names but now with gold letters on surplus blue fibreboard material. This cardboard had been used in 1934–35 for Meccano Flexible Plates (which were now made from tinplate), and the cardboard Train Name Boards had the Meccano pattern of diagonal gold bands printed on the back! We have not seen nos. 5, 6, 8, or 10 to 14 yet in this style, but it is probable that most if not all of the series were reprinted in this form.

Following the introduction of the No. 2 Corridor Coaches, which also had clips for Train Name Boards, there was a revival of demand which led to the printing of a new series in 1938. These were printed with black letters on white boards (in the case of the GW boards, serif lettered in the authentic GWR style) and the range of boards was expanded to 19:

No. 1, THE FLYING SCOTSMAN
No. 2, THE SCARBOROUGH FLYER
No. 3, THE ROYAL SCOT
No. 4, THE MERSEYSIDE EXPRESS – LONDON (EUSTON) AND LIVERPOOL (LIME STREET)
No. 5, THE GOLDEN ARROW
No. 6, THE BOURNEMOUTH BELLE
No. 7, CORNISH RIVIERA LIMITED
No. 8, TORBAY EXPRESS
No. 9, THE YORKSHIREMAN – LONDON (ST PANCRAS) AND BRADFORD (EXCHANGE)
No. 10, KING'S CROSS, EDINBURGH & ABERDEEN
No. 11, LONDON (EUSTON) & LIVERPOOL (LIME STREET)
No. 12, THE MANCUNIAN – LONDON (EUSTON) AND MANCHESTER (LONDON ROAD)
No. 13, THE QUEEN OF SCOTS
No. 14, WATERLOO, SALISBURY & EXETER
No. 15, THE YORKSHIRE PULLMAN
No. 16, THE BRISTOLIAN
No. 17, CHELTENHAM SPA EXPRESS
No. 18, LONDON, FOLKESTONE, DOVER, DEAL
No. 19, OCEAN LINER EXPRESS

All these were printed in the black and white style, just possibly excepting numbers 11 and 14. The Train Name Boards remained in the lists until 1941, but after the war there were no coaches to carry them, so they never reappeared.

METAL TUNNELS

Tunnels were first catalogued in 1924. The Tunnel was made entirely from tinplate, with a single centre

section modelled to represent a hillside, and two portals representing the tunnel mouth and wing walls. There was a plain lining wall inside the tunnel (black towards the track, sometimes brown on the reverse), secured to the outside by two metal stays. Both sides and ends were tinprinted. There was little change in appearance, apart from minor trademark differences, until sometime around 1931, when a batch was made with the centre section enamelled instead of tinprinted; it may have been made this way because of a shortage of tinprinted sheets. Not long afterwards, new tinprinted tunnel sides were prepared, which were completely different in style, being printed to represent a mountainous scene complete with mountain streams, cottages and hikers, among other unlikely-looking features. This tinprinting was prepared in at least two different printings with detail differences. Some of these late Tunnels had the inside tunnel wall in brown instead of the usual black. The last versions of the metal tunnel had the same scene with hikers, but the ends were enamelled grey, and stencil sprayed with 'brick-work' and smoke effects, not tinprinted as before. The Tunnel (Metal), as it had been described since

the introduction of Tunnels 0 to 6 in 1932, was not listed in the 1937–38 or later catalogues.

Pairs of Tunnel Ends were catalogued from 1930 to 1941. The tinprinting was identical to that used for the Tunnel (Metal), but they were made with different tooling to allow them to be fitted to Meccano framework, made to the size required, and covered as appropriate. Predictably, since these were unsuitable for temporary layouts, demand was not high and consequently they sold in smaller numbers than the complete Tunnel. No variations are known, except that of each pair only one usually carried the trademark transfer. The boxes were blue, as for the No. 0 to No. 6 Tunnels (which were originally envisaged as M-Series Tunnels); the Tunnel (Metal) had a normal red Hornby box.

TURNTABLES

The trademark transfers of the first Turntables, sold in 1923, were splendid and distinctive features that set the Turntables apart from other accessories. They were marked 'Meccano' in large letters radiused to match the curve of the Turntable, which was a large

and heavy piece of sheet tinplate, stamped to shape in one of the largest presses in the works. The pivoting rail section was also pressed from sheet, as were the eight shorter outer rail sections joining the table to the rest of the layout. A locking lever on the pivoting rail section locked into slots in each of the eight positions. Colours were olive green, with red lining in the embossed circular trough at the edge of the table.

In 1924, the same 'Meccano' transfer was used (with the turntables now varnished), and from 1925 there were new large-lettered 'Hornby Series' transfers, and the rail sections began to be aluminium-finished instead of plain tinplate. In 1927 there was a change to a brighter green, still red lined, both for the Large Turntable and for the new Small Turntable introduced that year 'for No. 0 or No. 1 Locos', according to the October 1927 MM, although in fact neither would fit on! The green colour was darkened slightly in 1928, by which time the names had been changed to 'No. 1 and No. 2 Turntables' instead of 'Small' and 'Large'. Around 1929 the central rail section began to be pivoted on eyelets instead of on a special nut and bolt with a spring washer as before.

A No. 2 Turntable (Electrical) was marketed from 1930; this was like the No. 2, but the wiring arrangements and the insulation of the centre rails made it a very complex job, justifying the price of 8s 6d against 4s 6d for the No. 2. The No. 1, No. 2 and No. 2 Electrical Turntables were all finished in dark blue, with red lining. The earliest electrical versions are recognisable by the use of red material for the insulators; black insulators were used later.

From 1933, the customer was offered a choice of turntables in red with green lining, in light green with red lining, or in light blue with red lining. There was a major simplification in 1935 of the E2 Turntable pivoting, from a complex brass collar arrangement to a simple large plunged hole in the rail section, turned over at the edges as if it were a large eyelet.

After the war only the No. 2 Turntable was catalogued, from 1949 to 1969. The colour was black, with the rail sections aluminium-finish, and usually with the outside edge of the table speckled green.

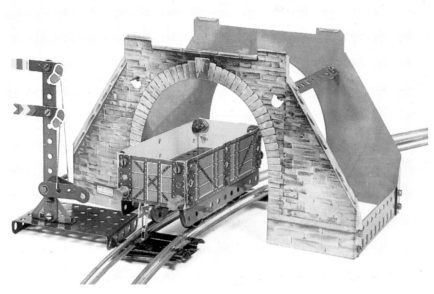

Tunnel Ends, sold to allow home-made tunnels to be built up on Meccano frames. (The cardboard parts are from the Meccano 000 Outfit.)

Tunnel, circa 1931, with enamelled centre section and tinprinted ends.

Tunnel (Metal), in the later versions with tinprinted centre sections. The Tunnel on the left has enamelled ends.

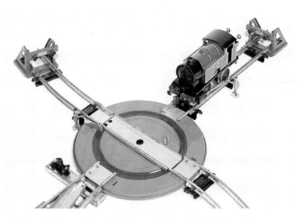

A No. 1 Turntable of the late '30s; suitable for tank engines!

237

VIADUCTS

The Hornby Viaduct was first listed in the 1924–25 catalogues; it consisted of the bridge section with a tinprinted base, and enamelled side girders which were the best feature of a somewhat uninspired accessory, based on similar German products. Two approach ramps were supplied, but the following year in 1925 the Centre Section became available separately. The Electrical Viaduct was also marketed from 1925, either with or without ramps.

Apart from the tinprinting colours (which brightened up in the 1930s) and the shade of green enamel used for the girders (dark grey-green from 1924, dark green from 1927 and lighter green from 1933; usually with the rivet heads nicely hand-painted in gold) there was little variation, except in trademarks. No Viaducts were made after the war.

WATER TANKS

When the Hornby Water Tank was first catalogued in 1924, it was described as being in 'red, yellow and black'. Nonetheless the usual colour was olive green,

with red outside the tank and blue-grey inside. The tank was actually capable of holding water, and discharging it through the India-rubber hosepipe when the valve chain was pulled. A hose drain was fitted, and the lower end of the hose had a brass tube inserted to locate it in the drain. It was a well-executed piece of tinplate craftsmanship, with a well-engineered column, better in many ways than the German products on which the design was based.

From 1925, the ladder was strengthened by folding the sides into tubes. There was the usual change of colour in 1927, from olive green to green, and around 1929 the column support was clipped to the base by tabs, not simply soldered as before. A different colour scheme was used circa 1930, with a blue base, column and ladder, and with the tank red outside and blue-grey inside as before. But whereas before the inside of the hose drain had been blue-grey, now it was green.

Around 1932, new brighter colours were used for the tank; it became yellow outside and red inside. The column, ladder and base were still blue, and the inside of the hose drain was left in blue. The Water

Tank E, with an electric lamp bracket and plug-and-socket connections to the transformer, was in the same colours. The following year, however, the base, ladder and column were finished in light green instead of blue, the tank still being yellow outside and red inside. The only later modifications were the omission of the hose drain and the brass insert in the hose, and the provision of a hose clip on the column, on post-1934 versions, and also the change to screw terminals for the 2E Water Tank from 1935.

The smaller No. 1 Water Tank had been introduced in 1934, causing the change of name to No. 2 and No. 2E for the larger tanks. The No. 1 Water Tanks were smaller and simpler, although still functional. They relied on washers to make the joint between tank and column watertight, rather than soldering as on the No. 2, the diecast post being screwed to base and tank by a steel rod insert threaded for Meccano Nuts at each end. The column and ladder were enamelled yellow, the tank red, and the base light green. The pipe clip was fitted in a 'bulge' in the column, which was enlarged in 1935 by thickening the casting at that point. Early in 1939, the colour of the ladder was changed from yellow to black, and late in 1939 the column was changed to light brown instead of yellow. Unlike the No. 2 and No. 2E Water Tanks, which were not catalogued in 1939, the No. 1 Water Tank was still listed in 1941.

The No. 1 Water Tank came back into production by 1949, and was in much the same form as before the war, except that the base was a darker green and the column and ladder were both black. The tank was still red. In 1950 the hose was lengthened from 3 in to 4 in, and the hose clip was no longer fitted. Black 'Brunofix' finish was used for the valve chain and lever assembly between 1951 and 1953, instead of the usual nickel plate. There was a final change in 1961, eliminating the Meccano Nuts fixing the base and tank by redesigning the column without the central steel rod, the column being fixed instead by spin riveting.

SUNDRIES

LUBRICATION

Meccano Lubricating Oil went on sale in 1928. At first it was sold in round bottles with blue labels;

Clockwork and Electric Viaducts. Extra centre sections could be bought separately.

from 1935 the bottles were shown in the catalogues as being flat rather than rounded, and the labels were yellow. The price remained at 6d. It is interesting that some (unopened) bottles of Meccano Oil have a rich golden colour, whilst others are completely colourless.

Oil Cans were offered as Meccano Accessories very early on, but the first cans to reach the Hornby Catalogues were the Oil Can No. 1 and the No. 2 'K' Type Oil Can, both in the 1928 HBT. The latter was an expensive-looking copper can made for Meccano Ltd by Messrs Joseph Kaye and Sons of Leeds,

who supplied full-sized oil cans to the 'real' railway companies. At 3s 6d, the Hornby item was not merely a toy, but an efficient way of lubricating the trains. The No. 1 Oil Can was still effective, however, at only 6d. The first No. 1 Oil Can with a rectangular body was replaced by an improved

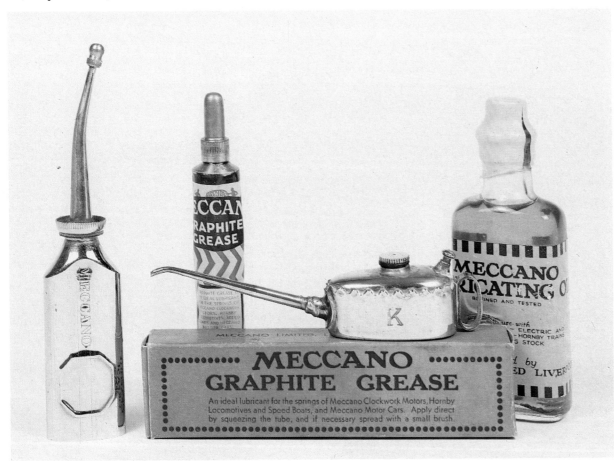

obtained separately, and were offered in the July 1930 MM at 1s doz. These Lamps were lead alloy castings with wire-loop handles, painted black with white glasses. These Lamps, and Detachable Tail Lamps were catalogued from 1935 at 1s dozen. The tail lamps were in two varieties; red with dark red bulls for LNER, GW and SR trains, and aluminium with dark red bulls for LMS. There were also black lamps with dark red bulls, sold in the late 1930s for use as loco tail lamps. The 'Eton' route indicator discs were not catalogued for separate sale; nor were the special red/white 'Princess Elizabeth' lamps. In 1937 there was a change for the lamp casting, to a somewhat smaller size, still fitted with the wire loop. It was probably in 1938 that the colour for the bulls of the black and aluminium rear lamps changed to red instead of dark red.

After the war, the Head Lamps for Locomotives and Tail Lamps for Locomotives were without the wire loops, but still in the same size. The colours were black with silver bulls for the Head Lamps, and aluminium with red bulls for LMS Tail Lamps, and red with a dark red bull for other Tail Lamps. In 1949 the shape was revised, making the lamps somewhat taller. There was a special Side Lamp for Brake Vans after the war, which was in black with a silver bull at the front and a red bull at the back.

KEYS

Winding keys for Hornby locomotives are a somewhat esoteric study; only the more important variations will be mentioned here, but there is great scope for the dedicated variation hunter. Good luck with it!

The first Hornby Locomotive keys were embossed 'M Ld L' to distinguish them from ordinary clock keys; very soon, by January 1921 in fact, they were replaced in the No. 1 Hornby Train Sets by a familiar-looking key, with a flat top forming a built-in 'gauge for rails', enabling the owner to adjust his rails to the optimum gauge should he have the misfortune to tread on them. The new pattern key appeared in a late and short-lived version, with the end of the shaft squared on the outside, not a plain tubular shaft as before. The tops of the next No. 1-type keys were radiused in a concave shape to

design with a round body (at the same price, 6d) early in 1932.

Tubes of Graphite Grease were advertised from 1933 to 1941, for use on the springs of clockwork motors. The price was 6d, for a tube which was large enough to last for several lifetimes. Meccano Graphite Grease was also sold in the 1960s.

WHEELS AND AXLES

Diecast Spoked Wagon Wheels were catalogued from 1932 to 1941, and Mansell Wheels from 1928 to 1941. They were packed in boxes of one dozen pairs of wheels on axles, for sale through the dealers. Axles for these wheels were also sold separately,

being offered in the April 1929 MM for 3d per dozen. Axleboxes for Hornby Wagons were offered on several occasions in the MM at 6d per dozen, through dealers or direct. Plastic Wheels and Axles for Rolling Stock were catalogued after the war, from January 1952 to 1968. Diecast Spoked Wheels and Mansell Wheels appeared again after the war, probably in 1952 after production of bogie vehicles had ceased. It seems they were never catalogued.

LOCO LAMPS

Detachable Head Lamps for Locomotives were supplied as standard with the Hornby engines fitted with brackets, starting in 1929. They could also be

Postwar sundries.

enable electric as well as clockwork rails to be gauged; the shaft was a tube, pressed flat to join it to the upper part of the key, and was not riveted on as before. The last design of key for the M1, M3, No. 0 and No. 1 Locos was folded from a single sheet of steel; it was a thoroughly unsatisfactory design, which caused much unnecessary damage to winding shafts and loco housings by its awkward shape and sharp corners.

There were larger keys for the bigger Hornby Locos, generally scaled-up versions of the 1921-type keys. Late versions had squared ends on the outside of the shaft, earlier types had plain tubular shafts. In 1935, the winding keys were catalogued for separate sale; and in 1937 the keys were described as four different types: 'A' Keys (small simple keys pressed in a single piece), for the MO, Silver Link and Streamlined Locos; 'L' Keys for the M1, M3, No. 0 and No. 1 Locos; 'H' Keys for the No. 1 Specials (large keys, but for smaller winding shafts than on the No. 2 Specials); and 'J' Keys for the No. 2 Special, No. 3 and Metropolitan Locos.

After the war, 'H' keys were sold for the M1, 101

Some Hornby and Meccano keys. The two top rows are prewar.

241

and 501 locos and their successors; 'S' Keys were supplied for the MO Locos (although early postwar MO sets still had the 'A' key). The 'H' keys were at first very like the pre-war type, and were nickel plated; the S keys were a new two-piece design, in essence a scaled down 'H' key. From late in 1951 both keys were made in black 'Brunofix' finish. By the time the British Railways locos were made, the keys were being diecast from mazac. Late versions of the 'S' key for the Meccano Magic Motor were lettered 'Meccano' instead of 'Hornby', and late 'H' keys were finished in black paint, while after 1964 'Gauge for Rails' and 'Hornby' lettering was removed by crude alterations to the dies, since they were now supplied mainly for use with the larger Meccano Motors.

Electric locos were at first supplied with a simple rail gauge made from the top part of a clockwork key; the Combined Rail Gauge, Screwdriver and Spanner was standard issue from 1930, and was also available for separate sale. The 'screwdriver' end was cut in the centre to allow it to be used for tightening wheel nuts.

MECCANO PARTS

Several Meccano parts were related to the Hornby Train System. These included part No. 120 Buffers (brass buffers in the two Hornby Train styles), and Part 120A Spring Buffers (never fitted as original to Hornby Trains, but frequently used as replacements). Meccano Train Couplings were sold in several styles; large brass hooks, then small brass hooks, then large drop-link couplings from 1925 and finally small drop-links by the 1930s. There were also Meccano Home (158A) and Distant (158B) Signal Arms, similar to the Hornby arms but with Meccano bosses and without the printed trademark, and also generally in thicker metal. Meccano Rail Adaptors (173) were available for connecting Hornby rails to Meccano strips.

ODDS and ENDS

Many miscellaneous items were mentioned in the 'In Reply' pages of the MM as being obtainable from Meccano Ltd, or in some cases from dealers. It is probable that virtually any Hornby Train part could be obtained on making a request to Binns Road (with the exception that they refused to supply transfers); so these items mentioned in the MM may be regarded just as examples of what could be obtained.

Automatic Couplings were mentioned in the October 1931 MM as available from Meccano Ltd, price 3d each plus postage. They were also included in 1966 and 1967 Hornby Price Lists. Bogies and Pony Trucks for converting locos to different wheel arrangements were advertised in the January 1933 and July 1932 MMs, at 1s 7d and 11d respectively. Corridor Connections (1s plus 2d post) and Corridor End Plates (1s 4d doz plus 2d post) were offered in March 1932. Extra spans for Lattice Girder Bridges (for that extra wide layout!) were offered in August 1932, price 2s 3d plus 3d post. Logs for the No. 2 Lumber Wagon were offered in April 1929, at 4d per set. Mechanisms were also offered: 'Any kind of Hornby mechanism may be obtained from this office. Prices and particulars may be had on application', according to the March 1929 MM, and a similar offer was made in August 1931. Rail pins were mentioned in November 1930 at 3d per dozen, 1d per dozen in November 1934, and 2½d per dozen

Meccano Parts for use in conjunction with the Hornby Series.

Ferranti Transformer, circa 1931. Earlier versions had a deeper 3-part casing.

Rheostats, T20A and T6A Transformers (front row); T20, T22M, T20M, T6 and T6M Transformers (back row).

post free in November 1935. Their availability was also mentioned in October 1936 and November 1937. Signal Arms (of the Hornby type, rather than the more expensive Meccano type) were offered in March 1927 and September 1929, at 3d each. The Shovel and Poker of the Watchman's Hut were offered in October 1930, at 1d each, through dealers. Timber Loads for the No. 1 and No. 2 wagons were available at 1d or 2d per set, according to the April 1929 MM, and Vacuum Brake Pipes were obtainable at 2s 3d per dozen, plus 3d postage, in February 1933.

ELECTRICAL ITEMS

RHEOSTATS and RESISTANCE CONTROLLERS

The Rheostats supplied with the 1925 Metropolitan Train Sets plugged directly into the electric light supply. The voltage was switched through three resistances formed as cotton-bound flat wire grids. The case was, most interestingly, based on the case from a mindless toy planned by Meccano Ltd in 1923 but never made. This was a Sand Elevator; two buckets on a chain raised sand from a box, lifting it to the top of a chute whence it slid back into the box again. Although this was a popular German-made toy of the time, it was obviously felt not to be the sort of thing to offer the intelligent Meccano boy. The base of the early Rheostat has two tiny holes in the bottom, which correspond to the position where the sand chute was to have been mounted. The sides of the Rheostat case were, however, embossed and perforated with a decorative pattern. The top of the box was a sheet of asbestos-like material painted black. On this was mounted the lamp (in series with the train and the resistances), and the 5-stud control switch.

The revised Rheostats of the 1927–29 period can be easily recognised by the cases being enamelled red instead of grey, and by the way they had been rendered somewhat safer, by covering up the exposed studs of the resistance switch with an extra casing. The inside of the Rheostat had also been made safer by winding the three resistances on large ceramic cores, and the material for the top had been changed to Paxolin (also used for some grey-cased versions).

The Resistance Controllers for the 4-volt trains were of the familiar pattern, enamelled in maroon, with white-lettered 'off' and 'max' transfers. The six volt Resistance Controllers were similar but gold-lettered. The Speed and Reverse Control Switches for the DC trains were similar, but of course with an extra lever.

In 1933 the colour of the Resistance Controller and the Speed and Reverse Switch was changed from maroon to red. The first 20 volt Resistance Controllers in 1934 were identical except for the winding and for the blue colour. Later in 1934, the 20 volt versions were re-designed for OFF-MAX-MIN switching instead of OFF-MIN-MAX as before, to make them suitable for automatic reversing engines; new transfers were made for these re-designed controllers. There were no further significant changes, although details of insulator colours etc. varied, and some 20 volt Controllers for auto reverse had the levers on the left (as on the 6 volt Controllers) not the right as usual. Incidentally, the cores of the 20 volt version were wound with no less than 54 in of 26 swg 'Constantin' resistance wire.

TRANSFORMERS

The first Transformer for the low voltage trains was advertised in a Meccano leaflet in September 1927. This was manufactured for Meccano Ltd by Ferranti, and was a standard type used in many radio sets of the period. The windings were fully encased for safety, and the transfers on the case bore both the Ferranti and the Meccano names. Apart from the change in voltage to 10 volts (for operation of 6 volt locomotives) in 1929, there was no change up to 1931, when a second Ferranti-type Transformer was offered; this was at the lower price of 22s 6d instead of 30s, and was available for all standard voltages, and all frequencies from 50 cycles upwards. The old type remained on sale, with the difference being that it could be wound for frequencies below 50 cycles. Some of these Ferranti transformers have a two-piece case, while others have a three-piece case with an extra central section. Incidentally, Messrs. Ferranti advertised their own transformers in the Meccano Magazine and elsewhere for use with toy trains in general and Hornby Trains in particular, and this must have been instrumental in deciding Meccano Ltd to make their own units.

In 1932 the 20 volt T20 and T20A Transformers went on sale. These were manufactured in Binns Road; they were available for most common mains supplies. The standard voltages were 100/110, 200/225 and 225/250 volts at 50 cycles, but transformers could be specially wound for other supplies at no extra cost. The T20 was suitable for any of the new 20 volt Hornby Locos, and the T20A added a 17 volt lighting circuit for accessories, and a 20 volt output for Meccano Motors; both had 5 stud speed controllers, and had a most attractive scrolled plate on the lid embossed with details of operating voltage etc.

In 1933, the scrolled-plate labels were replaced by

Resistance controllers; 4 volt, 6 volt (1929), 6 volt (1933) and 20 volt, with Circuit Breaker and TCP6 Terminal Connecting Plate.

plain rectangular labels, and the colour of the 20 volt transformers became lighter blue instead of dark blue; the voltage of the lighting circuit on the 20 volt transformers was changed from 17 to 3.5 volts. In addition to the T20 and T20A, there was now a T20M Transformer with no speed controller, for use with Resistance Controllers yet to appear. The T20M had a red case. There were new 6 volt T6, T6A and T6M Transformers (the actual output was 9 volts), corresponding to the 20 volt types; they replaced the Ferranti Transformers (which had confusingly been referred to in some catalogues as the T6 and T6a Transformers). The cases of the T6 and T6A Transformers were enamelled green, the T6M red. Like all the Meccano Transformers they were 'scientifically designed and perfectly constructed' and were said to 'comply fully with the requirements of the British Engineering Standards Association'. The insulation of every transformer was 'tested to a pressure of 2,000 volts'.

In 1934 the TR6 Transformer-Rectifier was introduced, for use with the EPM16 Loco. The case, enamelled red, was the same size as for the T20A,

but was slotted above the rectifier for ventilation.

In 1935 T22M (blue case) and T26M (red case) Transformers were offered, with 50 VA windings to allow two trains to be run at once. They were sold by special order only (mentioned in the December 1935 MM) until 1936, when they began to be catalogued.

The T20A and T6A Transformers had always been supplied with fuse plugs for the lighting circuits; from 1935 they were also supplied with an earthing clip and a coil of wire for the new lighting system. Around 1937 it became usual for the Transformers to be supplied without plugs, and for the labels to be silver-coloured instead of brass. Previously transformers had been fitted with plugs for electric light sockets; now it was left to the purchaser to fit an appropriate plug. These later Transformers had a three-core lead including an earth (labelled by a printed tag); previously the lead had been two-core only, and an earthing screw had been provided on the back of the Transformer case. There was also some variation over the years in the colour of the labels; for example the T20A label went from blue on brass, to green on brass, then green on silver or red on silver.

A limited supply of transformers was available in 1943, by special arrangement, and these were listed in the MM. After the war the T20 Transformer (now with a black-enamelled case) was sold from 1949 to 1953. The T20M was sold from 1952 to 1956, but not of course for use with Hornby Trains.

ACCUMULATORS

Accumulators suitable for use with the low voltage Hornby Trains were advertised in the 1926 Meccano Products catalogue (they had previously been available for Meccano Motors). There were two versions; 4 volt 8 amperes (17s 6d) and 4 volt 20 amperes (25s). The 8 and 20 ampere figures referred not to the current but to the capacity in ampere-hours; both would allow several hours of play before they needed re-charging. 6 volt 20 ampere accumulators (shown as manufactured by Seco rather than Block as before) were catalogued from 1929, and customers were assured 'This accumulator has been specially designed for running 6 volt electric locomotives. It is of very substantial construction, and the celluloid container is guaranteed not to leak if given reasonable treatment. Provided that this accumulator is re-charged at regular intervals it will give perfect satisfaction for years.' The price was 28s 6d. The following year, a 2 volt 20 ampere accumulator was listed, to allow 4 volt accumulators to be used for 6 volt trains. The rapid spread of the 'electric light' and the ready availability of transformers, and of cheaper accumulators from elsewhere, led to the withdrawal of Accumulators with effect from September 1935, except for unsold stocks.

OTHER ELECTRICAL ITEMS

Many other electrical items were offered. Spare Bulbs had been available to order for the High Voltage and Low Voltage Metropolitan Train Sets. It was not until April 1933 that there was any specific reference to Bulbs for Hornby Trains; they were offered in the MM at 1s 3d (20 volt) or 1s (10 volt), plus 2d postage. These loco lamps usually had white glasses. From 1934 Meccano Light Bulbs were catalogued; these were 184a (2.5V), 184b (3.5V),

184c (6V), 184d (10V) and 184e (20V). The glasses were no longer painted white, and the 20 volt bulbs now usually had flat fronts. Many of these bulbs (though not all) were marked 'Meccano'.

Three sorts of Fuse Wire were available: 41 swg Tinned Copper for 6 volt trains, 24 swg Lead for 3.5 volt lighting circuits, and 32 swg Lead for 20 volt trains. The 32 swg Lead Fuse Wire was also sold after the war, for use with the E502 Locomotives, and Meccano Motors; it was packed in the same way, wound on a circular yellow card. Circuit Breakers were advertised from 1936; they were made from Bakelite (as were some of the transformer parts). Bakelite was by the 1930s a common material, its use having become widespread since its first commercial use for Rolls Royce gear lever knobs in 1916. From 1938 different versions were offered for 20 volt and 6 volt trains, since they needed to 'trip' at different currents.

Distribution boxes and 9 in, 18 in and 36 in Flexible Leads, for the plug-and-socket system of electrically lighting accessories, were sold from 1932. The leads had two separate blue cotton-covered leads, one of which was threaded with white so as to enable 'live' and 'neutral' to be distinguished. Similar leads were supplied with early transformers, and in the case of 6v transformers these leads were green not blue. From 1935, coils of Connecting Wire (thin single leads, covered in green plastic) and Earthing or Bonding Clips were sold for the simplified lighting system.

Plugs and Sockets could also be bought separately. These were as used for the Flexible Leads; they were made of brass (later nickel-plated) with red Erinoid caps.

Terminal Connecting Plates were available for High Voltage and Low Voltage trains from 1926. These had screw terminal connections; later 20 volt Terminal Connecting Plates were arranged for connection by plugs into the transformer and by sockets onto the Terminal Connecting Plate. Postwar Terminal Connecting Plates were supplied in the E502 sets. All the Terminal Connecting Plates incorporated screw terminals for connecting the appropriate fuse wire. From 1937, Terminals TSR for Solid Steel Rails were listed.

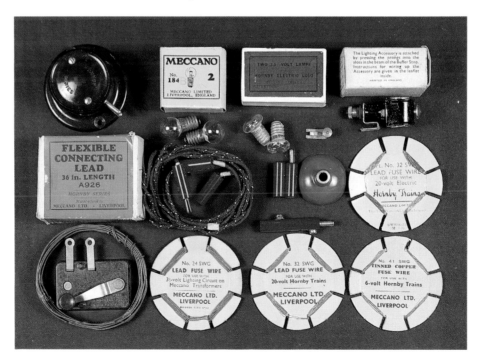

Electrical sundries, including Distribution Box, Bulbs, Lighting Accessory, Flexible Lead, Plug and Socket, Earthing Clip, Elektron Lampholder, Fusewire, Fuseholder (supplied with transformers) and an Elektron Switch.

The M Series

It was in 1926 that the term 'M SERIES' was first used to describe the smallest and cheapest range of Hornby Trains. Quite what the 'M' stood for was never revealed; in the USA the Hornby Trains were described as 'mechanical' rather than clockwork, and in France 'mechanique', which may give a clue. M Series Trains still had the full Meccano Ltd guarantee, despite the budget prices, and although they were not as well engineered as the larger Hornby Trains, they were better than the run-of-the-mill trains sold in toy shops – even though they came

nowhere near to matching the cheapest prices. First of the Hornby M Series in 1926–27 were the Series M No. 1 and No. 2 Passenger Trains, and the Series M No. 3 Goods Train. The titles were later abbreviated to M1, M2 and M3 etc.

MO TRAINS

MO Trains were introduced in the 1930–31 season, being the smallest M series trains in the Hornby range. Although of the same gauge, they were built

on a different scale to the normal Hornby items, and could not be used satisfactorily with them, particularly as the MO couplings were not the normal type but were part of the pressing of the tender and rolling stock bases. The style of the MO locos was clearly based on the US Hornby locomotive, and the smokebox door and position of the dome were very reminiscent of the US loco.

The first MO Locomotives were tinprinted in two liveries, one in green with a tender numbered '4472' (although the loco was not named 'Flying Scotsman'), and a red version numbered '6100' on the tender, again with no nameplate or railway company lettering. On the earliest MO locos the cab windows were cut out rather than printed. Apart from the spring anchorage and the spur-mounted second gear wheel, the MO motor was similar to that of the old-style M1 loco, but had a pressed metal brake lever in the cab instead of a wire control rod, and had the sideplates blued rather than painted black. The key was fixed permanently to the winding shaft. Special 10-spoke wheels without crankpin bosses were cast for the MO Loco; these wheels were not painted, and look most attractively bright and shiny on well-preserved examples.

For the 1932–33 season, possibly earlier, there were new MO Locos with cab windows printed instead of being cut out. The new tender printings were numbered '2595' for the green and '6161' for the red MO. A minor change was that from early 1932 two small holes were punched in the fixed winding keys to make them easier to grip.

Coloured baseplates were fitted to the locos for the 1933–34 season, giving four colour combinations – red or green boilers on red or green enamelled bases. The green loco was tinprinted in a bluer shade than before. The tenders kept the same numbers, but their bases were never printed in red or green to match the bases of the locos.

The range of MO Trains announced in 1930 included Goods and Passenger Train Sets, M Rails and Points, and the M Station Set.

From 1931 the M Level Crossing, M2 Telegraph Poles and M Loading Gauge became available. The 1936–37 season MO Locos had cylinders.

Several revisions were made to the design of the loco late in 1935, for production in 1936. These changes included the provision of a cab front, tin-printed with firebox, gauges and controls. M1 style cylinders were fitted (the base of the loco was the same width as that of the M1, so the same cylinders were used) and simple rods were added. Wheels were usually cast in mazac, in much the same shape as before but with bosses for crankpins on the rear wheels; the wheels were still unpainted, but were no longer shiny as before. The colour of the loco base and cylinders was now black, and only red/black and green/black locos were available. Instead of fixing a key to the winding shaft small removable keys were provided. The dome was moved to a more central position on the boiler to line up with the central printed boiler band, and a revised chimney with a flat base was fitted, instead of the ring-shaped chimney with no base.

In 1937 two lugs were deleted from the sides of the cylinders, for no readily apparent reason, and lead weights were added inside the housing over the rear wheels for extra adhesion on the 9 in radius rails. Performance on normal Hornby rails was excellent for the size of the loco, but it was unstable on the 9 in radius MO rails, particularly when they were new and springy. The weights helped to counteract the tendency of the loco to 'climb' the inside edge of the rail and fall off.

By 1935, an M Footbridge and a new range of MO Wagons were on sale. Colours were changed in the mid '30s.

247

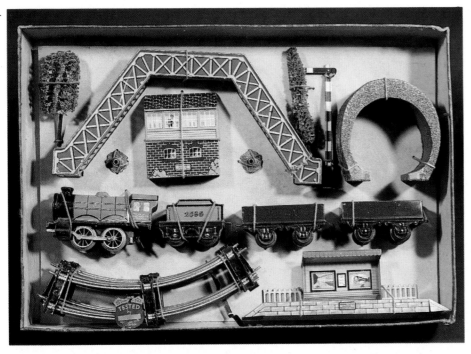

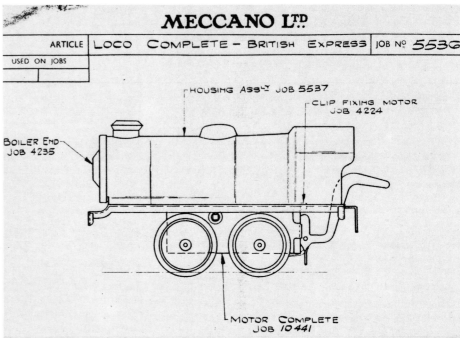

Not long after these changes, revised tinprintings were produced for both the red and the green MO locos. The most conspicuous difference was that instead of a single splasher, two separate rounded splashers were printed. Two widely-spaced cab windows were printed instead of two small windows close together as before.

After the war, the MO was the first Hornby Train to get back into production. The tinprinting appeared identical to the late prewar style, including the 'Hornby Series' trademark on the cabside, but the mechanism was stamped 'Made in England' on early postwar locos. Thicker axles were used than before the war, and revised bosses for the front wheels allowed them to be fitted more easily.

Soon revised tinprintings were made, with 'Hornby' in black on both sides of the cab. The cab front was lettered 'Type MO' and 'Made in England by Meccano Ltd', and the tender trademark was altered to 'Hornby' not 'Hornby Series', although the 2595 and 6161 numbers were unchanged. Only minor alterations were made over the next few years

production – a cutout keyway was added in January 1947, and a ballast weight fitted inside the front cylinder from September 1947. In October 1950 an improved smokebox door was designed, with hinges and door handles among the new features. 'Brunofix' finish was used for the rods and pins between 1951 and 1953.

The 1954 British Railways No. 20 Loco (number 60985), which replaced the MO, was identical to it except for the tinprinting in BR green livery. Apart from tinprinting shade differences there were no important production variations.

MO ROLLING STOCK

MO Pullman Coaches 'Joan' and 'Zena' were supplied in the MO Passenger Sets. They changed remarkably little over the years except for the roof colour, which was brown from 1930 to 1933, but changed to red and green (Joan and Zena having different coloured roofs) in 1933–34. Not long after-

wards the colour of the name panels was changed from brown to red. During the 1935–36 season cream roofs began to be used for Joan and Zena, and the first postwar MO Pullmans also had cream roofs. But the roof colour was soon changed to grey, and 'Hornby' trademarks replaced 'Hornby Series'. New tinprinted coach sides in BR crimson and cream instead of Pullman livery were made for the 1954 No. 21 Coaches, which were otherwise identical to the MO Pullmans they replaced.

The MO Wagons of 1930 were tinprinted in red with black detail, and there were no major changes during the prewar production. Most postwar MO Wagons were tinprinted in green, but there were also some in red; they can usually be recognised by the postwar style of the trademark, although early postwar MO wagons had the same trademark as before the war. The 1954 BR No. 20 wagon was like the MO Wagon but tinprinted in grey BR livery.

The other MO goods wagons were catalogued in the 1935–36 season, but had been designed earlier, in November 1934. The first versions had black enamelled bases, rather in contrast to the bright colour combinations still used for much of the standard Hornby range. MO Crane Trucks had a blue crane on a black base, the MO Rotary Tipping Wagon was green on a black base, and the MO Petrol Tank Wagon had a lithographed cream Shell-Mex and BP tank also on a black base. The MO Side Tipping Wagon probably appeared at the same time with a yellow tipper on a black base.

The 1935–36 Book of Hornby Trains and Meccano Products shows the MO wagons in what became their normal colours, with red bases for the MO Petrol Tank Wagon and the MO Rotary Tipping Wagon, and green bases for the MO Crane Truck and the MO Side Tipping Wagon. An embossed trademark was added from May 1935; before this transfer trademarks were used, except for the tanker which had tinprinted trademarks on both tank ends.

A later colour variant was the MO Rotary Tipping Wagon in blue on a red base, the colours used for the contemporary No. 0 Rotary Tipping Wagon; but the colours soon changed back to green and red, although there were also a few transitional three-colour versions! There were also permanent changes in the tinprinting of the tanker, which was lettered 'Shell' on one side and 'BP' on the other on the revised versions. One end (the ends were incorporated in the clever one-piece design of the tank) still had a printed trademark but the wagon number '731' no longer appeared. Extra lettering was added, including the words 'For repairs, advise Shell-Mex and BP Ltd. . .' – at least one youthful owner did just that when his MO coupling broke, and the MM related how the wagon was forwarded from Shell to Meccano Ltd for the necessary repairs!

After the war these four wagons were not catalogued until 1952; until then only the MO Wagon was available for MO goods trains. The first postwar issues in the middle of 1952 each had the prewar embossed trademark, but on all subsequent batches the embossing was altered to read 'Hornby' instead of 'Hornby Series'. Colours were similar to those of the prewar wagons, except for the tanker, which in postwar issues was tinprinted silver instead of cream, lettered very much as before but without the tinprinted trademark. From 1954, the wagons were

renamed No. 20 instead of MO; the No. 20 Crane Truck was given a much lighter green base than had previously been used for the MO stock, but otherwise the wagons were identical.

The bases of the MO wagons often had .172 in (occasionally .312 in) holes, for automatic spraying, from April 1935. These spraying holes also appeared on most postwar MO Wagons, MO Coaches, and MO Tenders, although they were optional if litho blackplate was to be used instead of enamel finish. Other minor changes include the adoption of plastic wheels circa 1951, which made the fabrication of special small-size tinplate wheels for MO trains unnecessary. On prewar MO wagons the ends of the axles were supposed to be secured by 'gagging', but this was frequently forgotten, and was not considered necessary for postwar wagons.

'BRITISH EXPRESS' TRAINS

Apart from the Raylo set, the 'British Express' is probably the least well-known of the Meccano Ltd trains. They were made from 1932, for sale in chain stores and shops other than the normal franchised Hornby dealers, at the same time that 'British Model Builder' constructional outfits were made by Meccano Ltd for distribution in the same way.

The British Express locos, tenders, wagons, coaches and accessories were identical to the MO series except for the tinprinted finishes, which were quite different. In order to avoid the wrath of the

regular dealers, who would not have been pleased to see them sold as Hornby Trains at lower prices than the standard range, no trademarks of any sort appeared. Nor did the sets offer any guarantee.

The British Express locomotive was red, and in contrast to the MO had one instead of two printed cab windows, different boiler bands and handrails, and a cab roof printed in black. British Express tenders were printed in the same style as the MO 6161 tender but were numbered 3233 (derived from the season in which they first appeared). There were differences of detail from the 6161 tender, for example there were printed handrails, and the lining was differently arranged.

British Express coaches were quite different from the MO coach, and probably more effective as a model. They were printed in red with yellow lining, unusually with white windows, as three-compartment 1st class coaches rather than as Pullmans. Details of the British Express wagon are not known.

The trains were sold only in sets, which included M-style accessories as well as the British Express trains. British Express accessories were exactly the same as the contents of the M Station Set, but with different tinprinting. The Station was tinprinted as a wooden building instead of brick-built, and the only person on the platform was a seated businessman, instead of the boy and porter on the M Station. The platform was printed in a plain light buff colour, not speckled with black as was the Hornby version.

'British Express' items. The M Stations are from late Hornby M Station Sets, and are mixtures of Hornby and British Express parts.

Flower gardens were printed onto and in front of the fences. There was of course no trademark.

The hut of the British Express Wayside Station was red rather than the green of the Hornby hut, and the adverts for 'Scarborough' and 'Meccanoland' on the latter were changed to more ambiguous unlettered adverts. The British Express Signal Box can be recognised by the different colour, absence of trademarks, and the open window from which the signalman looks out. The Hornby M signal is known in a version with no tinprinted trademark on the arm, perhaps for use in these sets; Hornby M Telegraph Poles had never carried any trademark.

The labels used for the very first postwar MO Train Sets appear to have been printed for the 'British Express'. They were lettered only 'Manufactured in England' and 'Printed in England' with no indication of the maker, although for the postwar Hornby sets a circular 'Product of Meccano Ltd' sticker was applied. It covered a yellow circle printed 'No. 2. PRICE', with a space for the shopkeeper to write in the price, which was presumably not subject to retail price maintenance. The 'No. 2' implies that at least two different British Express sets were offered – perhaps one goods and one passenger. The full-colour picture on the box showed an LMS loco 5999, cheered on enthusiastically by two young lads – very much in the style of the HBT covers of the 1930s.

Lid from an early postwar MO set; probably surplus labels from the prewar 'British Express' range.

The first M1 Passenger Train, 1926.

No printed matter concerning the British Express is known, although there were leaflets and instruction manuals for the 'British Model Builder'. Thus no certain date for final production is known. In September 1936, following the addition of cylinders and cab front to the MO, the British Express drawings were re-traced in the old style without these additions (although the dome was moved, as on the MO); these omissions presumably helped to keep the cost down. Since British Express locos are known to have been made with (fatiguing) mazac wheels, they must be of 1936 or later origin. But the use of British Express tinprintings for Hornby M Station Sets in the late 1930s indicates that the British Express must have been withdrawn from sale soon after 1937.

M1 TRAINS

The Hornby Series M No. 1 Loco of 1926 was copied from a Bing design, but there were enough differences of construction to make the Binns Road origin quite clear; the shape of the cab windows and the provision of wire handrails were the most obvious. The new mechanism was very compact, and non-reversing; the brake lever control knob (like a round lead shot) was apparently cast in-situ on the wire, which made removal of the mechanism for repair difficult. The brake lever passed vertically through the cab floor, so it was rather awkward in use. The sides of the mechanism were actually painted black, rather than blued.

A green livery was used for the M1/2 loco, which was not lettered for any particular railway company but was lined black and white very much in the LNER style. The smokebox was tinprinted black. There was a large cut-out keyway in the footplate – unnecessary, since the key was fixed to the winding shaft. Special heavy lead-alloy 10-spoke wheels with a curiously rounded profile were designed, since despite weights in the cab and under the front buffer beam, the loco would have been too light without the extra weight of the wheels. The wheels were left unpainted.

Tenders were in the narrow-beam style of the 1924–25 No. 1 Tenders, but the coal rails were not cut out, no buffers were fitted, and the finish was tinprinted to match the loco. The first series locos and tenders were numbered 2526, then in 1928 the second series were numbered 2728. Later 2728 locos had black winding keys, instead of the earlier nickel plate, and tall pressed-tinplate chimneys replaced the cast chimneys fitted previously. The 2930 printings of 1929–30 were virtually identical to 2728 except for the number. Because the numbers were on both loco and tender, mismatches were frequent. After the new style M1 locos were made in 1930, the old M locos remained on sale until 1933 with the title 'M2930 Loco and Tender', at an attractive price of 2s 6d.

From 1930, M1 and M2 sets were supplied with a different engine, similar in style to the 1927 USA Hornby Loco, with a single-piece pressing forming boiler and cab. The mechanism was a new reversing type, incorporating the latest patent ideas for longer runs. Various patent numbers were marked underneath, the markings changing as British and foreign patents were granted, and later expired. The wheels were a new type, smaller and more finely cast; they were finished in red. The smokebox door was the same as on the old M1.

There was a choice of colour for the new locos – red or green, each with tinprinted black and white lining and with some details nicely printed to represent a metallic brass finish. The tenders were similar to the 2930 tenders but tinprinted in colours to match the locos; although inexplicably with black and gold rather than black and white lining, an error perpetuated through many reprintings before and after the war. Only the tenders were printed with the loco number, 3031. At first the cab windows were punched out, and there was no cab front.

For the 1931–32 season, a dark red livery was offered as an alternative; there were also revised tinprintings of the red and green locos, because the windows were tinprinted instead of cut out on all three versions. Plain black cab fronts were fitted, and another change was that the latest tenders were numbered 3132.

On the 1933–34 season M1/2 Locos, the colour of the footplate and cylinders was changed from black to green, giving three colour combinations; green/green, red/green and dark red/green. Tender bases were also green; red and dark red tenders were still numbered 3132, but supplies of green 3132 printings soon became exhausted, and a new tinprinted green

3133 tender was issued, also on a green base.

1934–35 saw the introduction of the electric EM120 and EM16 Locos, with special cheaply-made 20 volt and 6 volt electric mechanisms, with a single pickup made from thin brass strip. The electric locos had a single heavy weight at the back, moulded at the sides to form steps to the cab. Electric M locos were sold until 1938.

Liveries were revised late in 1934. Dark red M1 Locos were no longer offered, but two alternative colours were used for the base of the loco and the cylinders; colour combinations for the boiler/base were green/green, red/green and red/red. Green/red M1 Locos may also have appeared. Tenders were

numbered 3435, and the tender base was red or green to match the loco.

In late 1935 the production drawings were altered to show the cab front as tinprinted rather than plain black; associated with this change was the reversion to black enamel for the bases of both red and green locos, instead of the previous coloured bases. Chimneys with flat bases were fitted, as on the MO Loco. There were no significant changes to the loco from then until the war, but there were minor changes to the cylinders; a slot was added in May 1935 to avoid having to crop the back of the coupling, and cylinder end lugs were deleted in May 1937.

In 1932 dark red locos were offered, as alternatives to red or green. The No. 1A Footbridge has tinprinted signals.

From 1933 the M1 trains were more colourfully finished.

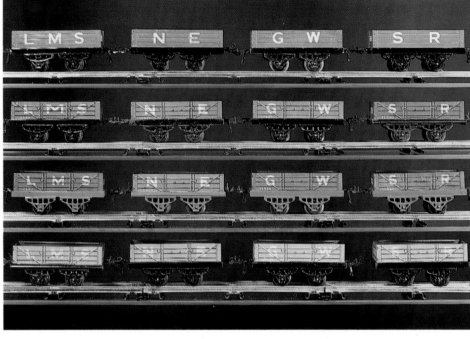

After the war the M1 locos were among the first back in production. The tinprinting was different from the prewar style, with 'Hornby' on both cabsides in tiny gold letters. The mechanism was re-designed, with bigger axles; early postwar mechanisms were stamped 'Made in England' as on the MO.

From 1947 lead weights were added inside the cylinders, and the spring anchorage point was altered from the back to the front of the motor. By 1948 M1 locos had 'Hornby' on the cabside in black letters, and the cab front was also trademarked. Tenders were still numbered 3435 on both red and green versions, and also had revised postwar trademarks; from 1948 there was a cross-piece at the front of the tender, strengthening it at its weakest point. A mainspring guard was added from 1949. The only other noticeable change was the 'Brunofix' black finish used for the rods and pins between 1951 and 1953.

The BR green No. 30 Loco (number 45746),

The M1 Loco colour schemes were changed again in 1934, and black bases became the norm for M1 Pullmans and Wagons.

Electric EM120 and EM16 Locos were first catalogued in 1934. This EM120 is circa 1937.

designed in 1954, was not sold until 1956 since Meccano Ltd found it 'impractical' to introduce it earlier; perhaps because of large remaining stocks of the M1, which remained in the price lists until January 1958.

M1 ROLLING STOCK

The only items of rolling stock made for use with M1 locos were an M1 Wagon and an M1/2 Pullman Coach. Like the M1 Tender, they were fitted with link couplings, although they could also be used in conjunction with auto-coupled stock.

Unlike the previous M3 Wagon, which had been grey enamelled and gold-lettered LMS or GW, the 1929 M Wagon was tinprinted with LMS, NE, GW or SR in white letters on a plain grey body. (The SR version was not the brown that might have been expected.) Planking was embossed. As a rule there were no buffers, although a few mistakes were made. The NE wagon also appeared in an odd grey-enamelled version with white 'NE' transfers.

For the new-style 1930 sets, the M1 Wagons (a

change of title due to the introduction of the MO) were tinprinted with details of planking, wagon number etc. and were no longer embossed with planking. The sides were still based on dark grey. Later post-1931 printings can be distinguished by the printed rivet heads in the corners of the wagon.

The 1933–34 season M1 Wagons were identical in tinprinting, but had green enamelled bases. The 1934–35 season saw a reversion to black bases, and the colours used for the tinprinting generally became lighter 'greys'; although there were several variations in the actual shade in subsequent re-printings, as for the No. 0 Wagons. Axles were supposed to be gagged to prevent their falling off in the hands of younger children, but this operation was frequently forgotten; after the war the practice was not resumed.

The early postwar M1 Wagons were similar in style, but the tinprinting was different; there were no SR or GW versions, just buff-sided 'LMS' and buff-sided 'LNE' wagons. (There were also brown-sided LNE wagons of the same era.) Later versions had dark brown sides for LMS and grey for LNE, still on the 1924-style long thin base. But a revised M wagon base was used from 1949, which had a longer wheelbase, and axleguards like those on the standard Hornby wagons of the period. The No. 30 Wagon which replaced the M1 in 1956 was of completely new design, as was the No. 30 Goods Van which accompanied it in the train sets.

M1 PULLMAN COACHES

The Series M No. 1/2 Pullman Coach appeared in the 1926–27 catalogues. In the HBT the cream roof was shown secured by a pair of knurled-headed screws, as used on the No. 2 Pullman Cars, but all production models seem to have had dark grey roofs, secured by tabs. No names were given to the earliest cars, which were lettered 'Pullman' where the name panel appeared on later coaches.

From 1927 the colour of the roof changed to a pleasant brown, and from 1928 the tinprinting was altered to give three different name panels, 'Marjorie', 'Aurelia' and 'Viking'; the 'Pullman' lettering was moved to a position above the windows.

The No. 0 Pullman Coach introduced in 1931 was exactly the same as the M1 Pullman, except for being fitted with automatic couplings; about this time, the base of the coach was elongated – possibly to give the effect of a buffer beam, although buffers were never fitted. Nor were the coaches ever given corridor connections, despite the open gangways cut in the ends of the coaches!

Colours of the roofs and bases for the 1933–34 season were changed to yellow for 'Aurelia', yellow and later red for 'Marjorie', and green for 'Viking'. By that time the door windows were being printed in red instead of the earlier lilac. From 1934–35 the colour of the base reverted to black while the roofs were still coloured yellow on 'Aurelia', red on 'Marjorie' and green on 'Viking'. Naturally, some different colour combinations occurred from time to time, usually by accident.

1935–36 season Pullmans began to sport the cream roofs which continued in use until 1941. In 1946 a few of these cars were produced with the prewar tinprinted trademarks, but the majority were new printings of 'Marjorie', 'Aurelia' or 'Viking', each with postwar trademarks. The earliest postwar

roof colour was white, then grey from 1947. Viking had a very short postwar run. Improved bases for the M1 Pullmans were designed in 1947, and were actually fitted from 1949 onwards. No. 0 Pullmans were also re-designed in 1947, although they were never in fact destined to re-appear.

The M1 Pullman was replaced in 1956 by the No. 31 Coaches, tinprinted in BR crimson and cream, in two versions – one 1st/3rd and the other Brake/3rd. They used the same base as the M1 Pullman, but were made longer by the use of bowed ends.

TINPRINTED, GEORGE V, No. 00 and M3 TRAINS

Tinprinted Train Sets were introduced at the same time as the first Hornby Trains, in fact there are signs that they may have been manufactured shortly before the Hornby Trains in 1920. The locomotive was clearly copied from a Bing design, but there were many differences of detail and of finish.

Three liveries were available, the most colourful and attractive locomotive being in Great Northern Railway green. The green boiler was lined with black bands edged in white, and the cab, splashers and cylinders were also lined black and white. Cabsides were lettered with the loco number '1452', and there was a maker's plate printed on the splasher. The smokebox was black, on a cradle printed with rivets and edged in red. Running plates were tinprinted black, but the whole of the valance was printed red, with the loco number on the front buffer beam. 'GNR' lettering appeared on the sides of the tender, which was also lined out in black and white.

The black LNWR loco was lined in red and white

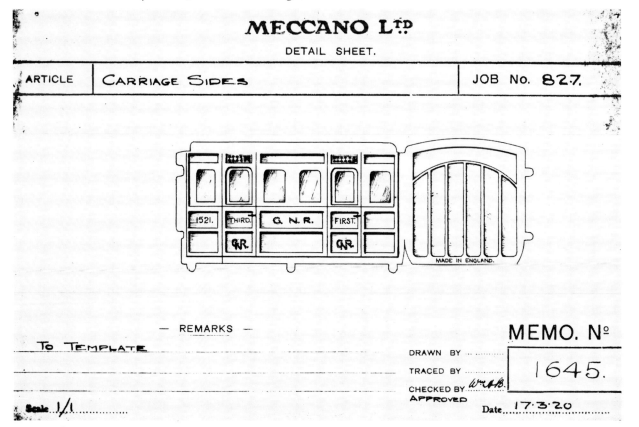

Tinprinted Train carriage sides, 1920 works drawing.

on the cab, cab roof, splashers, valance and cylinders. 'George The Fifth' nameplates were printed on the splashers, and the cabside number was 2663. The boiler was lined in red with a row of white rivet heads marking the edge of the smokebox. The tender was lettered 'L.N.W.R.', and the red and white lining style matched the loco.

Midland Railway red livery also suited the tin-printed loco very well. Here the boiler was lined in black edged yellow, a style also used for the cabsides, splashers, cylinders, and valance. Again the smokebox was printed black. There was no MR lettering as such on the loco, but the crest on the cabside was clearly lettered 'Midland'. The tender had a maroon base (on the GN tender it was black) and the number '483' appeared on the black and yellow lined sides.

The well-chosen tinprinted liveries of these locos were the best feature of the train set, and were not matched for style by the enamelled locos for many years. A shame to waste the quality of finish on such an unsatisfactory design! Although the locomotive was small in size, and far too narrow – a defect accentuated by the extraordinary width of the cylinders – the appearance could have been

improved by a more appropriate tender. It was much too low for the loco, and the flat platform at the front emphasised the length of the couplings, which on this set accounted for a quarter of the length of the train! A saving grace was that an embossed representation of coal was fitted, an odd but consistent omission from all the Hornby engines.

On the early locomotives the handrails were of the cast type later used for the Zulu Locos, and the cast chimney became a standard pattern for non-constructional Hornby locos. The dome, however, was a flat-topped type secured by a rivet between the top of the dome and the boiler underneath. This unsatisfactory arrangement was later changed, and the tabbed dome used on Hornby locos was adopted. Embossed trademarks were 'M Ld L' on the smokebox door, and 'M Ld L England' on the base of the tender. All three locos were marked 'Made in England' on the outside of the cab front. All parts of the loco were different in detail from the Bing equivalent, but it was the base of the tender that was most different. An interesting feature was a tabbed cross-brace fitted between the axles at the bottom of the tender, frequently omitted (or perhaps lost!) on later versions.

The earliest Tinprinted Train mechanism differed from the earliest known Hornby type, in having a much narrower spring; there were no strengthening pillars across the mechanism, and the winding spindle protruded through a plunged hole in the sideplate rather than a plain hole as on later types. The gear train was similarly arranged and spaced, but many details differed. The motor was embossed 'M Ld L', unlike later Hornby types, and the sideplates were 'blued' not plated in all except the earliest motors. The wheel castings were different in profile from the Hornby type although similar in size. Despite its small dimensions the motor would not quite fit in the housing, necessitating two small slits and a fold in the bottom of the cab front to clear the gears.

Improvements were made to the loco over the years. The original mechanism had a 'swan's-neck' reversing lever through a hole in the cab floor. According to the catalogues, the Tinprinted Train (or 'George V Train' as it became known from 1923) remained as a reversing type until 1924. It is therefore probable that the 1921-style reversing mechanisms were fitted (but not necessarily as early as 1921 if there were still stocks of the old type). Certainly some bodies were fitted with a cracked-up lug for the spring on the reversing lever.

From 1924 the George V loco was advertised as non-reversing, and the Zulu-type mechanism was fitted. The larger mechanisms had necessitated a bigger cut-out in the frames, projecting into the cab, as well as requiring cut-outs both in the cylinders and in the lead weights fixed inside them.

In 1925 the set was re-named the No. 00 Train Set (no relation to Dublo!) and the rails were changed to 1ft radius. Some people have assumed, because the early edition of the 1925–26 HBT showed these trains on pages headed 'No. 00 Clockwork Trains' instead of 'Hornby Trains. British and Guaranteed' (as on all the other pages) that these trains were not British. The correct inference is that they were not Hornby Trains, (although made by Meccano Ltd in Binns Road), and that they were not guaranteed. The saving on the cost of the guarantee repairs was one of the ways in which Meccano Ltd were able to offer the complete OO Train Set at 10s 6d; the same price as the No. 0 Loco alone without a tender!

The 1926 Hornby M3 Locomotives were identical to the previous non-reversing OO type; the price rise from 6s 6d to 8s 6d for the loco was largely accounted for by the fact that the loco was now guaranteed. The tenders were now in the M1 style; the GN green loco had a green '2526' tender (not '1452' as shown in the catalogues) which differed from the M1 tenders in having a cut-out coal rail, and in being fitted with round-headed buffers. Later versions of this green 2526 tender had oval buffers, and subsequently none at all. The red M3 Loco was given a specially printed M3-style tender, in black with yellow-lined red panels numbered '2527'. The cut-out coal rails were printed red, and the trademark on the back of the tender was in black and yellow. The colour scheme would have been very suitable for the CPR! 'George The Fifth' locos were given a similar specially printed '2527' tender with cut out coal rails, finished in black and lined red and white. The 'Hornby Series' trademark was tinprinted on a red panel at the back.

From 1927 the locos were fitted with coupling rods as well as piston rods. Front couplings had been unnecessary since 1924 when the loco became non-reversing, and the couplings and slots began to disappear circa 1927. The late 1927/early 1928 versions showed that supplies of tinprinted material were running out, and were not being replaced. Enamelled parts began to be used; for example the LNWR cab front, and the whole of the boiler of the MR red loco (hand-finished with a black smokebox and three yellow-enamelled boiler bands). All three locos were given enamelled cylinders with no lining. The 'Made in England' printed trademark on the MR loco was obliterated by careful mask-spraying, which left the lined cab windows untouched. 'M Ld L' was no longer embossed on the smokebox door, and instead a barely legible 'Meccano England' trademark was embossed in a corner of the cab. This was later replaced by use of a 'Manf'd by' transfer in the same place. In 1928 the green '2728' tender came out in the M3 style with a cut-out coal rail but no buffers.

Soon supplies of the special tinprinted 2527 tenders began to give out, so tenders for the red and the black M3 Locos were enamelled, and were given '2710' transfers and lining. Cut-out coal rails were still featured, and there were no buffers. These tenders can easily be distinguished from the 1924–25 No. 1 Tenders by the 'Manf'd By' transfers on the back.

In the Summer of 1928 it was decided that the 'Tinprinted' style of engine would no longer be made. But M3 Goods Sets were still sold, with different M3 Locos. The bodies were based on the No. 0, but modified to the extent of having no front buffers! Except for this and the finish they were identical to the No. 0, and were excellent value at 8s 6d when the No. 0 price was 10s 6d. The red and green M3 Loco boilers were plain, with no black smokebox and no boiler bands; but the black engines had boiler bands embossed. There was no company marking or number on the loco, but the cabside and splashers had simple lining transfers. The chimney was finished black, and the handrails gold. For the black locos (and probably for the red) the tenders were of the standard No. 0/1 pattern, instead of the narrow type, but they had no buffers. They were priced 9d, instead of 2s 6d for the No. 0/1 Tender!

LMS M3 Trains, 1926–27. Both have tenders numbered 2527, while the green equivalent had an M3 2526 tender.

1927–28 M3 Locos had coupling rods, and enamelled 2710 tenders were supplied with red and black locos. Green locos had tinprinted 2728 tenders.

The green M3 was supplied with the tinprinted 2728 M3 Tender, since this could still be made from sheets tinprinted for the M1 Tenders.

These 1928–29 locos were exceptionally good value for money, and it was perhaps not surprising that they disappeared from the catalogues in 1929.

M3 ROLLING STOCK

Tinprinted Train Coaches were very short, having only two 'compartments', and were almost as tall as they were long – hardly ideal proportions. Simple Tinprinted Train couplings were fitted, and the base was lettered 'M Ld L England'. Only one set of tools was used for the coaches, so there was no Guard's Van as had been produced by Bing. The three liveries were brown (lettered 'GNR'), red (lettered 'Midland') and brown and grey lined yellow and red (unlettered, but intended for the LNWR set). The Midland Coaches were 1st class only, but the others had 1st and 3rd class compartments, although the sides were not 'handed', so the compartments were differently marked on opposite sides! Each coach was printed 'Made in England' above the couplings. The only major changes in the coaches were that whereas the early roofs were lithographed (certainly on the LNWR coaches which had cream roofs) later versions had roofs enamelled in dark grey. Early wheels were black, probably tinprinted, but later nickel-plated wheels were fitted. The holes in the coupling also changed from T-shaped to circular. There must have been a surplus of coaches when production ended, since they were used as chairs on Meccano shop-window display models of a funfair ride, built at Binns Road in 1926.

The M3 Goods Train Set of 1926 contained the long thin style of open wagon that had previously been abandoned for No. 0/1/2 Wagons. The M3 set wagons were grey-enamelled, with white company letters; 'GW' with the green locos and 'LMS' with the red or black locos, never 'NE' or 'SR'. These 1926–27 M3 Wagons had buffers, and the 'Hornby Series' transfer was on the end of the wagon. The 1927 and later M3 Wagons had 'LMS' or 'GW' gold letters on the same wagon bodies, but they were not fitted with buffers. Since these were M series wagons, the ends of the axles were gagged whenever the assembly workers remembered.

M SERIES ACCESSORIES

At the same time as the new ranges of MO and M1 trains were issued in 1930, an M Station Set appeared, comprising an M Station, an M Wayside Station, an M Signal Box, two M Telegraph Poles and two M Signals; a bargain at 3s 6d for the seven pieces, which were also available separately if required.

There were three principal versions of the M Station, most easily recognisible from the colour of the short canopy extending from the roof; brown on the earliest type, red from about 1933, and green in the late 1930s. Other details such as the colour and shape of the printed roof tiles were also changed. On the earliest type the roof clipped to an internal extension of the front wall of the building (which was originally intended to be the roof, and was actually printed with tiles); later the roof was clipped directly to the side walls. When the British Express range was withdrawn in the late 1930s, remaining tinprintings for these stations were used to make Hornby M Stations, often in combinations with the standard Hornby roof, building or platform. When the British Express platforms were used, transfer trademarks were often applied since there was no printed trademark.

The final series of M3 Locos had No. 0-type bodies in simple enamelled liveries. (The red loco has the wrong tender.)

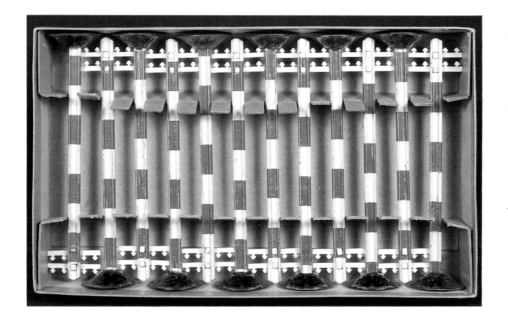

M1 Telegraph Poles;
boxed in dozens.

Apart from minor changes in shade, there were few variations in the M Wayside Station; the earliest 1930 printings can be distinguished by the gold background to the printed trademark, which was yellow on later printings. In the late 1930s British Express tinprintings were also used for the Hornby M Wayside Station, with either the red hut on the Hornby platform or the green Hornby hut on the British Express platform.

The M Signal Box was revised in the second series of printings with the woodwork surrounding the windows in a paler brown colour – almost orange.

The neat rail-section posts of the M Signals and M Telegraph poles were at first printed with a diagonal latticework pattern, but after two or three years new printings were made with blue and white horizontal stripes. In the late 1930s the stripes changed to red and white. M Signal arms were printed with a trademark, but versions with plain signal arms are also known – presumably printed for the British Express sets. M Telegraph Poles had no trademark even in the Hornby version.

More M accessories were catalogued in 1931, including an M No. 2 Telegraph Pole, the same as

the No. 1 but taller and with a simple tinplate cap, and priced at 6d instead of 3d. Only the latticed and the blue and white striped versions are known to have been manufactured.

Also new in 1931 was the M Level Crossing, the length of a normal half rail, but much more simply made than the No. 1 Level Crossing. The gates were not hinged, but were removable, and plugged into holes in the base with the road either open or closed to traffic as required. The gates were at first tinprinted, in white with black posts, then enamelled in white with either yellow or green posts from 1933. The base printing also changed in the late 1930s from a buff to a grey colour for the road section.

M Loading Gauges were introduced in 1931. The post and cross piece were blanked from an unusually thick steel sheet, and were set into a substantial lead-alloy base. The first types were white with a blue base, a Hornby Series trademark being embossed in both base and post. Later the trademark was incorporated in the base as part of the casting, and the post was not marked. From 1933 a lighter blue was used, and in 1938 the base colour changed to green. The top of the post was always picked out in the same colour as the base. Although the M Loading

Gauges were intended for sale singly, they were supplied to the dealer boxed in pairs. M Stations and most of the other M accessories were supplied to the dealer packed in half-dozens or dozens.

Almost the last of the new M Accessories was the M Footbridge, first catalogued for the 1933–34 season. It changed little except for the shade of blue, which varied from pale to dark in different printings, and in the colour of the steps, which were blue in a few cases instead of the usual yellow.

The M8 set contained a tiny solid-wood tunnel which was not sold separately from the set.

After the war, box labels were printed for the M Station Set in October 1945, although there may well have been some delay before the contents of the boxes were made. Apart from the plain white tin-printed posts of the M Signals and M Telegraph Poles, the contents of the set were indistinguishable from the sets of the late 1930s. The M Level Crossing also re-appeared in boxes printed in August 1946. The gateposts were green. None of these postwar M accessories were catalogued, and their production was short-lived.

M3 TANK LOCOMOTIVE

The M3 Tank Loco, added to the Hornby range in 1931, was one of the most popular in the series. It looked much the same as the No. 1 Tank, but the M3 Tank price of 7s 6d compared most favourably with 13s 6d for the No. 1 Tank.

Few parts were actually interchangeable between the two locos, although there was a great deal of common tooling for the housings. The most obvious difference was in the livery, which on the M3 Tank Loco was lithographed instead of being enamelled like the No. 1 Tank. Further economies were made by omitting cylinders from the front underframe, and leaving off the rear underframe, the handrail knobs, the smokebox door handles, and the transfer trademark (the trademark being printed on the bunker back). Boiler bands were not embossed on the M3 Tank Loco, and to make a tiny saving the couplings were secured by tin eyelets instead of the solid metal eyelets used on more expensive locos! As a further small economy, the M3 driving wheels were not coupled. The mechanism was significantly different for the M3, so the keyhole position and the base cutouts were changed. The M3 did not need the small cutouts at the base of the No. 1 Tank Loco cab front, since the motor did not protrude into the cab. The M3/No. 0 mechanism was of cheaper construction and was reversible only by manual control rods in the cab, not from the track. It had folded metal sideplates. The performance of these motors was quite satisfactory, giving good long runs with reasonable loads; their worst vice was a tendency to jump out of gear unexpectedly when they became worn by hours of play, and their brakes were seldom efficient.

There were only four tinprinted M3 Tank liveries, instead of the usual seven; all were passenger colours, SR green (loco number E126), LNER green (460), GW green (6600) and LMS red (2270). They varied remarkably little in appearance during their production. GW locos were usually fitted with a taller chimney, and also had cast safety-valves instead of the usual dome. Automatic couplings were fitted to all these locos from introduction. Both the front and rear of the loco were fitted with lamp brackets.

The first season's eight-spoke wheels were specially cast for the M3, with no boss for the crank-pins – making the economics of leaving off the coupling rods rather shaky! These wheels were replaced in 1932 by 12-spoke wheels, again specially cast without the boss. Some minor improvements were also made to the mechanism, principally pressing a heavy ridge (for strengthening or stiffening) along the length of the motor, just above the axles on the left-hand side.

The LSTM3/20 Electric Tank Locomotive introduced in 1932 was one of the pioneer 20 volt locomotives. It was fitted with the French-type motor, with horizontally-arranged brush holders, as used for the LST1/20 Tank Loco introduced at the same time. There was a bulbholder in the smokebox door, and the price of 22s 6d against 25s for the LST1/20 was a fair reflection of the actual difference in manufacturing costs. The dramatic drop to 16s 6d vs. 24s in 1934 owed little to changes in specification or to production cost, but was evidently intended to improve the differential between the M series and the E120 prices. The latest E120-type mechanisms without protruding brush caps were fitted, and there were no differences between the EM320 and E120 Tank electric motors, as there were between the motors of the clockwork equivalents. EM36 Tank Locos with 6 volt motors became available from 1934 onwards.

In late 1936, the M3 body was substantially revised, and fitted with cylinders for the first time – at no extra charge, making the loco even better value for money. The changes involved moving the mechanism backwards to clear the cylinders, extending the cutout in the base, swapping the front and rear brackets of the mechanism, making a very large cutout in the cab front to clear not just the spring but the whole back of the mechanism as well, and re-positioning the keyhole. Normal eight-spoke wheels with coupling and piston rods were fitted, but it is not unusual to find earlier M3 Tank Locos with eight-spoke wheels and coupling rods; this was most frequently the result of a repair, when the No. 0-type motor assembly was fitted.

In April 1937 the cutout in the base was enlarged

An early GW M3 Tank Loco.

A slightly later SR M3 Tank Loco.

to make it suitable for both clockwork and electric motors. Soon after this the clockwork mechanisms were fitted with an enlarged rear bracket for more stable fixing. The only other alteration of note before the war was that M3 Tank Locos were finished with matt varnish from 1939.

After the war, the M3 re-emerged as the Type 101 Locomotive, the same four liveries being produced. There were different printings, however, and the printed trademark on the bunker back changed several times. The first was marked in the prewar style 'Hornby. Manf'd by Meccano Ltd. Liverpool' (up to 1948), the second style was 'Hornby. Made in England by Meccano Ltd', without the rectangular border (up to 1949). The third type was marked 'Hornby. Type 101. Made in England by Meccano Ltd.', and was used on LMS and LNER 101 Tank Locomotives from 1949 to 1954.

Bunker backs are actually one of the main sources of interest to the variation hunter on the M3 and 101, and for some reason pressings with the trademark upside-down are not uncommon. Furthermore, when stocks of tinprinted bunker backs ran out, enamelled ones with transfer trademarks were substituted; even, on one postwar 101 Tank Loco, with Dublo-type transfers!

Distinguishing features of the postwar 101 Tanks included the colour of the wheels; usually green for SR and LNER and black for GW and LMS, instead of the prewar red. Postwar locos were fitted with central lamp brackets on the front buffer beam, with tall chimneys on all four railway companies' locomotives, and with slots instead of square holes for the control levers. A dead matt finish was used for many of the 101 Tank Locos between 1947 and 1949. Solid-metal eyelets were usual in the early postwar years, until 1950 when the couplings were fitted with round-headed copper semi-tubular rivets. As usual, Brunofix black finish was used for control rods, coupling and piston rods and pins between 1951 and 1953. Control rods continued to have the black finish long after this date, however. The postwar 101 mechanism was improved from the M3 type, and had efficient brakes.

The 101 Tank Locomotives were withdrawn when they were replaced by the BR Type 40 Locomotive in 1954. This loco was in just one livery, an

appropriate goods black, and it carried the number 82011. It still had redundant holes under the cab, which had been used in prewar days for fixing the rear underframe on No. 1 Tank Locos! A redesigned smokebox door was made, with more clearly-defined handles, and with a raised portion for a smart black-and-white numberplate transfer. Post-1960 printings of the Type 40 body had the latest style 'lion holding wheel' BR emblem, with the whole enclosed by a gold border, instead of the earlier 'lion over wheel' emblem with a lion straddling a wheel. It was last listed in 1964.

M3 WAGONS

M3 Tank Goods Train Sets were provided with special wagons, which were not available for sale separately; they were an M3 Wagon, an M3 Petrol Tank Wagon, and an M3 Timber Wagon. Like the M3 Tank Loco they appear always to have been fitted with automatic couplings.

The M3 wagon was mounted on a crimped version of the long thin wagon base, similar to that used for the No. 1 Coaches of the period but not fitted with buffers; the crimping was necessary to bring the couplings to the right height. From 1933 the bases were green, then from 1934 they became black again. The tinprinted wagon sides changed exactly as on the M1 Wagon.

The M3 Tank Wagon was like the ordinary Shell tanker, except that it too had no buffers. The cast filler cap was replaced by a simple pressed top in 1934, and Royal Daylight transfers were used from 1936.

The M3 Timber Wagon was usually red with

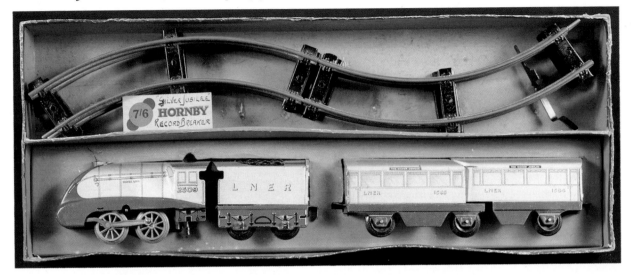

green stanchions, but a late version with black base and red stanchions was made in 1939–40. Once again the difference from the standard No. 1 Timber Wagon was that no buffers were fitted. The number of planks was reduced from three to two from 1934.

M3-style Fibre Wagons with no buffers were available from 1934, but only in the M11 Complete Model Railway Outfit. The colour was usually blue, although black versions were made in the 1939–40 period.

No. O 'SILVER LINK' & STREAMLINE LOCOS

The 'Silver Link' Locomotive of 1936, with its accompanying articulated coach set, was the only streamline train in the Hornby range, and it must have taken Meccano Ltd rather by surprise that it did not prove more popular than was actually the case. It was not 'officially' part of the M series, although clearly it should have been, since it was on a par with the MO Locomotive although a fraction more realistic. But some might have considered it an affront to Sir Nigel Gresley to represent one of his magnificent A4 Pacific locomotives as an 0–4–0!

The initial price of 4s 6d was above that of the MO loco, and the same price applied to the No. 0 Streamline Loco (later called 'Streamlined') when it was introduced in 1937. Two colour schemes were offered; one was two-tone light and dark green, and the other maroon and cream. Both were tinprinted, like the No. 0 'Silver Link' Loco, although one difference was that neither the cab front nor the tender front were printed with details in the fashion of the 'Silver Link'. The coaches were tinprinted to match, and the trains were short but colourful. Why did they not sell better? It is hard to say, particularly since in 1939 the price of the No. 0 'Silver Link' and Streamlined Locos fell to only 3s 3d with tender, less than the MO! This almost certainly signalled that stocks were to be run down prior to withdrawal from the Hornby range, as would have happened if the war had not intervened.

After the war the Streamlined Train was to make a brief but interesting appearance in the MS Passenger Train Set for the Canadian market, being enamelled in CPR colours.

No. 0 Streamlined Train Sets.

Hornby Trains in France

France was one of the most important export markets for Meccano Ltd in the early years after the Great War. Before the war Hornby had opened a small office at 17 Rue Bleue in Paris; then moved to larger premises at Rue Ambroise Thomas, and although these quickly became cramped they had to serve until hostilities ceased. After the war a purpose-built 9000 square foot office and warehouse was erected at 78/80 Rue Rebeval, Paris. The building was designed in an odd but interesting style, and was probably the only building put up by Meccano Ltd which had any pretentions to architectural merit. The registered offices of Meccano (France) Ltd were moved from Binns Road to Rue Rebeval, and shortly afterwards in 1921 the first French Meccano factory was opened at Boissy; however at least in the early years the French Hornby Trains were to be made at Binns Road.

THE EARLY 1920s

The first trains to be built specially for the French market were the wagons designed late in 1920. Only the wagons in the Hornby Train Set were made with French railway company lettering – the locos were identical to the unlettered British types.

The Covered Luggage Van was the next item to be made available in French livery. This 1921 style vehicle did not have clip-on letters like the English MR van, but had stencil-sprayed 'Etat' letters. No constructional No. 1 Coaches, or 'green and cream' No. 2 Coaches, are known to have been specially made for France; although crests for the Etat, Nord or PLM companies may possibly have been produced, only coaches with the English company transfers are reported to have been sold in France. The 1923–24 No. 1 Passenger Sets were apparently supplied with a French-livery loco and English pre-grouping coaches!

Meccano Ltd premises at Rue Rebeval.

The grouping of the British railway companies in 1923, and the decision to adopt LMS and LNER liveries for the English Hornby locos probably gave the incentive to produce the first French loco liveries. The three colours were Nord (green), Etat (black) and PLM (red), with transfers and finish similar in style to the contemporary British locos; all were made and finished at Binns Road.

The range of items of rolling stock with French liveries was more or less equivalent to the range in the UK. The accessories were also the same as the UK versions except in detail of transfers and trademarks, and in the fact that the early Stations and Signal Cabins were lettered 'Arras' instead of 'Windsor'. The tinprinting of the station buildings was identical, so the French children were left to puzzle over the advertisements and lettering in English!

THE LATE 1920s

The importance of the French market to Meccano Ltd can be judged from the introduction of the Riviera 'Blue Train' in 1926, the largest and best Hornby Train to date – in France it replaced the No. 2 '2711' Locomotives and Sets. The Riviera 'Blue Train' Coaches were not the only new types for the French market, since the No. 2 Pullman Coach (the smaller-size 1921 type Pullman, but in brown and cream) was made available in 'Fleche D'Or' livery, giving the French a choice of two No. 2 Passenger Sets. Soon the Riviera 'Blue Train' was offered in France with either a brown Nord engine or a red PLM engine, although the 'Fleche D'Or' was sold only with the Nord engine.

The French No. 1 Coaches of the later 1920s were of the clerestory type, identical in style to the UK coaches but with no company lettering. There were two colours, a red 1st Class Coach no. 2605, and green 2nd Class Coach no. 2650; the doors were lettered with distinctive Roman numerals. There was no clerestory Guard's Van.

Although the '2711' loco was no longer listed, the 4–4–4 No. 2 Tank Loco in French liveries was still sold until replaced by the 4–4–2 tank loco.

The 1927 and 1928 lists were among the last in which the French and the English Hornby ranges

The M1 Train in French livery. Made in England.

developed in parallel; the range in France was always more limited. There was not the same emphasis there on the Hornby Control System, and although many of the French-type wagons developed in the late 1920s were sold in both France and the UK, some of the special wagons (Refrigerator Vans, No. 2 Cattle Trucks and No. 2 Luggage Vans and Milk Traffic Vans all with lookouts) were only sold in France. The Disc Signals and Checkerboard Signals were also sold only in France. Engine Sheds were catalogued in France in electric-rail versions (without lighting), available in the UK only by special order.

Special versions of the M1 Locomotive and M Pullman Coach were made, identical to those in the UK except for being tinprinted in Riviera 'Blue Train' colours, with the engine in brown with yel-low lining, and the M1 Pullmans in blue with red panels and lettered 'Pullman' rather than 'Wagons-Lits'. Interestingly enough the brown No. 2526 tender carried 'Hornby Series' rather than 'Serie Hornby' printed trademarks; this mistake was put right when the next printings (numbered 2528) were produced – although the 2528 engine was marked 'Meccano Ltd Liverpool' to indicate the country of origin.

The major changes to the range of locos which took place in the UK in 1929 did not take effect in France. Even the change to 6 volt operation was not made (the 4 volt Riviera being the only electric train, apart from the Metropolitan – which incidentally seems to have been offered only in the HV version in France). The No. 1 Special, No. 1 Special Tank and No. 2 Special Locos were never sold in France (although shown in one or two illustrations, adapted from English blocks by changing the lettering!); nor were the permanent magnet locos. The No. 2 Special Tank loco, when it replaced the 4–4–4 tank, was given the same 'No. 2 Loco-Tender' designation. (It should be explained that in the first French catalogues the Hornby tank engines were described as 'Locomotive Reservoir', but this was later changed to the highly confusing but more correct 'Locomotive-Tender' still meaning 'tank engine'.) Early French-market 4–4–2 Tanks still had the '4–4–4'

transfers, and this was also true of early UK-made No. 2 Special Tanks for the Argentine.

The change to long-splasher No. 0 and No. 1 locomotives was also delayed, compared to the UK change in 1929.

THE EARLY 1930s

It was becoming increasingly obvious that as the French toy train market expanded – and of course this covered the French colonies like Algeria, Tunisia and Morrocco as well as France itself – it made sense to continue the establishment of Meccano (France) Ltd as independent manufacturers, if only to take some of the pressure off Binns Road.

One reason for the French to expand their factories was a very proper national pride, and a consequent sales resistance to goods not made in France. There were customs regulations that required each imported item to be labelled with the country of origin; this meant that 'Serie Hornby' trains imported from England had to be emblazoned with 'Fabrique en Angleterre' ('Made in England') transfers to identify them as foreign goods.

During the 1920s the French Meccano factories had been entrusted with an increasing amount of work on the 'Serie Hornby', and most of the products previously made in the UK were by the late 1920s at least finished and packed, if not all actually made, in France; although certain of the larger items such as the Riviera Blue Train and the larger accessories were still made only in the UK. It would be an overstatement to claim that the quality of finish of the early French goods was equal to that of the Binns Road products; neither the enamelling nor the varnishing was carried out with the same success, and the quality of the French transfers (especially in gold) was markedly inferior.

The key factor in the establishment of an independent product range was the completion of the new Bobigny factory in the early 1930s, with a workforce of skilled and competent craftsmen who were able to tailor their range of products exactly to the requirements of the French market. By the end of the 1930s the number of imported Hornby Trains had been reduced to a very low level, and quality had been improved substantially. The tinprinted products in particular were every bit as good as the UK made Hornby Trains – as well as being exciting and original designs.

Although the French did not follow the English in the matter of improved locomotives, in 1930 they were the first to offer the Fyffes Banana Van ('Bananes' on the transfers), Fibre Wagon, Coal Wagon, Barrel Wagon and Open Wagon B. Of these only the Barrel Wagon was specifically a French-type wagon; all these were offered in the UK a year

later, but not on the open-axleguard base used for these first French issues. The Coal Wagon was sold in France with company letters instead of the 'Meccano' transfer. In common with the other 1930 wagons it was available with a fourth choice of company lettering, the extra one being 'Est'. The locomotives were also available from 1930 in brown livery with 'Est' letters. There was no choice of goods or passenger livery in France as there was on our home market. The only exception to the normal colour rules was that the Nord 4–4–2 tender loco was brown instead of the green used for all the other 'Nord' locos.

Private owners' vans were not well represented in France, the Huntley and Palmers Biscuit Van and the Union Refrigerator Van being the only choices apart from 'Fyffes'. Nor was there a good choice of petrol tank wagons; at first there was only the red 'Wagon Citerne' (the early versions having company lettering), then an 'Eco' Petrol. The latter was replaced by 'Standard' in 1932 and the former by 'Esso' in 1938. Incidentally cans, and later bottles, of 'Standard' oil were sold for lubrication rather than 'Meccano' oil. As in the UK, the number of wagons with company lettering declined in the 1930s, with the Snowploughs, Milk Traffic Wagons and others coming out unlettered.

A splendid set of whistles was offered in the French 1930 catalogues, four different types – one for each of the railway companies. These must have

been popular with children, perhaps a little less so with their parents. What a shame that there was never a No. 1 'Acme Thunderer' issued from Binns Road!

One of the earliest examples of the independent line the French were to take was the introduction of Modelled Miniature figures. Binns Road had never seriously contemplated manufacturing lead cast figures, probably because the 'Britain's' figures were so cheap and successful. But the French Modelled Miniatures were advertised from the start of 1931, and this development probably prompted the introduction of similar figures (and ultimately, the Dinky Toys) in the UK a few months later.

The French range of figures was also (it must be said!) much the more varied and interesting. Not for them the idea of including the same figure with different painting in several sets. There was a wide variety of both staff and passengers, and none were identical to the UK versions.

The first set of railway staff included a Station-master, two Porters (in indolent posture with hands in pockets, and probably whistling), a Guard, a Policeman and a Ticket Collector. The Series 2 Passengers issued late in 1931 included a Normandy Countryman, a Countrywoman (later known as 'Becassine'), a Young Lady, A Boy Scout, and seated Girl and Boy, together with a seat. The Farmyard Animal set (Series 3) issued from mid-1931 was similar in content to the later UK version, but all the

The No. 3 Loco was sold in France in Nord brown or PLM red livery. It was made in England.

The first French Stations were named 'Arras'. Clerestory coaches were similar to the UK versions, except for the door lettering.

Some wagons such as the Open B and the Coal Wagon were fitted with the open-axleguard base in France, but not in the UK. The No. 1 Loco is from the 1931–33 series, and was made in France.

263

castings were different; for example the Cows had larger horns. This French set was frequently seen in the UK catalogues, presumably since the French versions could be used rather than making special pre-production models.

The next set (Series 4) of railway staff included a Chef, Driver, Fireman, Ganger, a Level-crossing Keeper and a Porter with Baggage. These were issued in 1932, followed by a Shepherd Set in 1934 and finally a second set of Passengers (Series 5) late in 1935, including a Woman and child, Gentleman traveller, Lady Tourist, Cleric, Newsboy and Sportsman. There was also a combined set (Series 10) including sets 1, 2 and 4.

The lithographed French 'M' open wagon mentioned in the 1930 catalogues was one of the first distinctly French-made items of rolling stock, and was included with a new-style French 'M' loco (which replaced the British-based brown 'M' loco)

The first set of lead figures; genesis of the 'Dinky Toy' range.

The first version of the 20 volt electric PO loco, 1931.

in the new M3 goods set. The loco was also included in the MO, M1 and M2 Passenger Sets, with new French-style 'M' Pullman Coaches.

Also for the M Series, an 'M' Station Set was introduced in 1931 that was similar in style to the UK set but with distinctive tinprinting, and with French-style Semaphore signals. The new M4 Passenger set included the 'M' Station Set with an 'M' Passenger train set as a complete outfit.

The most notable advance of 1931 was the adoption of 20 volts as the standard voltage, a year before the UK and without having adopted the compromise 6 volt system. The 'Metropolitan' Set was dropped from the catalogues, effectively replaced by the new French-type PO-Midi electric outline locomotive. This loco was based very loosely on the types used on the Paris–Orleans lines, and was to be produced in a prodigious number of colours and varieties. It was of English design.

A 20 volt version of the Riviera 'Blue Train' replaced the previous 4 volt type in 1931. One other electric locomotive was introduced at the same time, a steam outline No. 1 tank engine fitted with the same 20 volt mechanism used for the PO loco. This necessitated special cutouts and a raised section in the footplate to accommodate the horizontally-arranged brush-holders. The revised No. 1 and No. 1 Tank Locos introduced in the UK in 1931 were never sold in France; this electric tank (like the PM tank at home) was in the early style. It looks odd to British eyes because (unlike the PM Tank) it had a bulbholder in the smoke-box door. No equivalent

No. 1 electric tender engine was made.

The clockwork No. 1 and No. 1 Tank Locos of the 1931–33 period also look odd, because they were adapted for a new-style mechanism designed and made for Bobigny-produced locos only. It was similar to the UK M1 mechanism, but was more powerful and was fitted for reversing from the track. The high position of the winding spindle necessitated cutting keyholes in the splashers (or tanks), which look strange on the early-style locos. The mechanism was a very tight fit in the housings, and the strain often pushed the boiler apart from the cab! The transformers offered in 1931 were also different from the later UK types. The Bobigny works was very strong in electrical skills, and over the years produced fine transformers at reasonable prices. A difference from the UK market was that transformers or rheostats were usually included in the electric train sets.

Another significant new 1931 product was the No. 1 Special Coach. The 1-S was a four-wheel saloon vehicle, with opening doors in the recessed ends. The 1931 sets including these and other new items were all fitted with the latest automatic couplings, soon adopted for the rest of the range.

The English-style No. 1 and No. 2 Electrical Level Crossings were introduced briefly in France in 1931–32, as were the English-style No. 1 and No. 2 Electric Lamp Standards. But the French works produced a number of most interesting new accessories for the 1932–33 season to replace previous British-made types. One was a Continental-style Level Crossing in two parts, one clipped each side of the track; one side had a level crossing keeper's hut. This new type was suitable for clockwork or electric single or double tracks, and replaced the four British types. A neatly-cast Water Crane was produced, replacing the British Water Tank; it would have been a useful item in the British catalogues. The 'Arras' station was replaced by a No. 2 French type with a completely different tinprinted building and canopy; (with notices in French!) and fences, but on a platform similar to the old type, but without ramps. A No. 1 Station was also available, in a simpler style without the fencing. Both stations could be fitted with clip-on station names on the buildings the names offered were Dijon, Lille, Lyon, Nantes

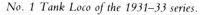

No. 1 Tank Loco of the 1931–33 series.

and later Nancy; the nameplates could be bought separately. There was also a French-style No. 3 Goods Platform with a different building.

Tunnels and Cuttings similar to the English types were also manufactured, and soon replaced the tinplate Tunnel. Hedges (straight or 2 ft radius curved) and trees also became available in the early 1930s.

There were two new transformers in 1932, No. 1 with 1 amp output for the No. 1 locos, and No. 2 with 2 amp output for the No. 2 locos or for extra lighting. Also available for the first time were 60 volt high voltage versions of the No. 1 Locos (both steam and PO types) for use with the HV Rheostat.

1933 was the year in which new-look No. 1 steam-outline engines first appeared, two years after the equivalent change in Britain. The tender engine was designated No. 1 (sometimes called No. 1 Special), and there was also a No. 1 Tank Loco. Both were of distinctly Continental appearance, with twin domes and high running plates; the cylinders were castings. Automatic couplings were fitted at the front. Locos were available in the usual four colours

– Nord green, Etat black, PLM red and Est brown. The No. 0 Locomotive continued to be offered in the old '2710' style, although now without cylinders; the tender was still fitted with a coal plate at the front which distinguished it from the UK-made type.

In 1933 the 'M' series was expanded by the addition of 'Trains Express Hornby' Nos. 1 to 3, roughly equivalent to our MO Passenger Trains. In 1934 there was a new 20 volt 'ME' loco; like the clockwork 'M' Loco but fitted with smoke deflectors (soon to be fitted to the clockwork type as well, but without the distinctive electric 'lightning' warning signs). The electric ME Loco was sold in two sets ME1 and ME2, which were 'complete model railway' sets, the ME2 in a smart carrying case. There was also a clockwork M5 complete set which contained the full range of M accessories, which by then included Telegraph Poles, a Continental-type 'M' Level Crossing, 'M' Footbridge, and an 'M' Tunnel similar to the British No. 0. The 'M' Semaphore Signal was also joined by an 'M' Checkerboard Signal. The electric outfits did not have the full range of accessories, but contained an 'M' Transformer

which was built into two M signal cabins placed back to back, and incorporated a two speed controller.

In 1934 automatic reversing was offered on all the 20 volt electric locomotives except the ME Loco, and remaining stocks of the old 1ET Loco; manual versions were still available for all except the 4–4–2s. The high voltage No. 1 types were described as for 'tous courants' rather than 60 volt, to avoid confusion; they could actually be used on any of the common power supplies by using the correct lamp in the rheostat. The 20 volt transformers could be used only with 110 volt or 220 volt alternating current supplies.

Some of the larger of the English-made accessories were removed from the French catalogues and not replaced; the Lattice Girder Bridge, Engine Sheds, and others already mentioned; and later the Telegraph Pole. The Junction Signal (which presumably looked as odd to French eyes as their checkerboards and discs do to us) was also withdrawn; our Double Arm and Gantry Signals appear never to have gone on sale in France.

None of the British-made electrically lit acces-

A high voltage No. 1E Special Loco.

French Railway Accessories.

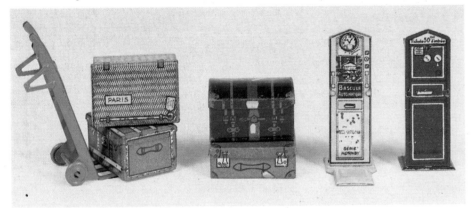

A French Hornby No. 1S Loco.

A French Level Crossing, with No. 1S Tank Loco.

sories were sold in France, except the Lamp Standards which had been replaced in 1933 by the first of an independent French-made range of electrically lit accessories, a single Lamp Standard; there was also a French glass-globe single Lamp Standard in a similar new style. In 1934 electrically lit Buffers were introduced, and there were also three different clip-on Lighting Accessories for converting non-electric items; No. 1 for Signals, No. 2 for Stations, and No. 3 for Buffers and Level Crossings – an idea that later caught on in England, but not with the same versatility. These lights could be connected to the transformer via flexible leads and a distribution block – using a simplified form of the 'plug and socket' method of connection.

Other accessories new in 1934 included Checkerboard Signals, now offered either on the rectangular base with a ladder or on a round base with no ladder. The Checkerboard Signal was roughly equivalent to our 'Home' signal, with the Disc Signal used as an advance warning.

An interesting French addition to the range of railway accessories was the electric Truck, Trailer and three Mailbags which formed set No. 8. On the subject of these accessories, there were the usual differences between French and British manufacture, not least of which was that the milk churns were castings instead of tinplate!

THE LATE 1930s

The 'Fleche D'Or' set was from 1932 illustrated with two Pullman Coaches of the No. 2 Special type (but with 'Golden Arrow' transfers); no Composite Coach was shown. From 1935 the Composite Coach Models of the 200 kph record-breaking Bugatti Railcars run by the Etat and PLM companies were introduced in 1935. These cars were the first serious attempt in French Hornby to model an actual prototype, and were sold in single-car units, both clockwork and 20 volt (manual reverse) versions; the electric sets were provided with a 'Panneau de Decoration' folding out from the lid to give a background behind the layout. The tinprinted finish was blue and cream for PLM or red and cream for Etat. By 1938 there were also 2-car and 3-car clockwork and 20 volt sets.

was sold separately, not in 'Fleche D'Or' livery but lettered PLM, Nord, Est or Etat.

In 1935 the French also built a most successful series of tinprinted perishables-traffic vans, similar in shape to the 1–S Coach, but fitted with sliding doors. They were the No. 1–S Cattle, 1–S Refrigerator, No. 1–S Milk Van (with churns), No. 1–S Milk Van with lookout, and 1–S 'Primeurs'; also included in the series were the 1–S Postal Van and the 1–S Goods Van.

Many other wagons were re-designed in 1935 for a new standard wagon base, longer than the old type but not quite so wide. The revised open Wagons also had a new top, with ribbed sides and round-topped ends. No. 1 Timber, No. 1 Lumber and Fibre wagons were redesigned on the new base, and became identical wagons but carrying different loads.

Greater attention was given to 'M' rolling stock in the late 1930s. In 1935 an 'M' Side Tipping Wagon, 'M' Esso Tank Wagon and 'M' Crane Truck were sold, both separately and in the M6 mixed goods train sets.

A series of wooden stations – oddly called 'Gares Plastiques' – was offered in the late 1930s. These

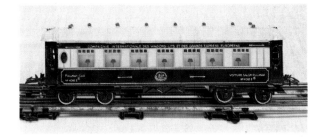

were No. 10 Nice, No. 11 Biarritz, No. 12 Amiens, the short-lived No. 13 Reims, the largest No. 14 Lyon, and the smallest No. 15 Limoges. They were said to be 'superb scale reproductions of real country stations painted and hand-finished with the greatest skill'; letter boxes, indicator boards, clocks and timetables were among the painted details. They were actually executed in the bad taste that is forgivable – and enjoyable – only in retrospect. They should not be confused with the postwar range of collapsible buildings.

In 1935 there was a new 4-light Colour Light Signal, fitted for electric lighting but mechanically

Hornby Trains of the mid '30s; all made at Bobigny.

switched, and electrically lit Checkerboard and Disc Signals. It was partly to cope with the extra demands of the increased range of lit accessories that the transformers were once again improved in 1935, to give a higher output; 50 watts instead of 40 for the No. 2 and 30 watts instead of 20 for the No. 1. The extra capacity was also useful for running a second train from a single transformer. The Resistance Controller was of the standard British type, but the nicely named 'Antiparasite "M"' and 'Antiparasite No. 1' were uniquely French, being suppressors for radio interference.

The No. 3TE Loco listed in 1936 was an electric version of the 4–4–2 tank, which unaccountably had previously only been available in clockwork. Like the No. 3 'Riviera' and 'Fleche D'Or' it was available only with the 20 volt auto reverse motor. The 1E steam-outline and 2–E Type PO Locos were still available fitted with either 20 volt manual or 20 volt auto reverse motors, or 'tous courants' HV.

The next important Hornby streamlined train model was the type AD 'Train Aerodynamique'. This was an 'M' series loco in style and size, but grander than the 'Silver Jubilee'. Although an 0–4–0 and not an Atlantic like the PLM train on which it was modelled, the low streamlined body all but hid the shortage of wheels. The finish was tinprinted, with the loco in blue and the coaches light and dark blue with cream roofs. Connections between the 4-wheel coaches were successfully designed to allow any number of cars to be added without gaps, unlike the 'Jubilee' set. Both clockwork and 20 volt manual reverse AD Trains were available. By 1938 the 20 volt trains in the M series, the autorails and the new AD trains could be operated from the new 'M' and O Transformers. These were conventional designs that replaced the old-style 'M' Transformer built into the 'M' Signal Cabins.

Following the French railway nationalisation in 1938, Hornby Trains were made available in SNCF livery. It should be mentioned that the change-over was not immediate for all items, and the old railway company letters continued to appear for some time, right into the 1960s on the 1S Luggage Van!

Simplified versions of the No. 1 Locos were offered in the 1938 catalogues. The 1–TE Tank Loco became available with a simpler and less expensive 20 volt mechanism; this new SNCF OT–E Tank Loco was finished in black.

There was also a new O–E version of the PO loco, with the cheaper mechanism and simple bent wire non-folding pantographs, coloured SNCF black or aluminium. The more expensive 2–E Type PO loco was still available, in two unspecified (presumably SNCF) colours. For the first time, there was a clockwork Type PO loco, called the No. 0 and replacing (at last!) the '2710' steam outline No. 0 loco. The colour was SNCF chestnut brown; it was not available after the war.

After nationalisation the bogie Composite Coach came out in SNCF-lettered chestnut brown or crimson. These late coaches were interesting in that, although of the 'special' type, they were fitted with non-compensating bogies secured by large eyelets. The No. 1–S Coaches were altered in the late 1930s from two types with opening doors (brown 1st class, green 2nd class), to three types with fixed doors (green 3rd class, yellow 2nd class and red 1st class). Clerestory-roofed No. 1 Coaches were still sold (even in 1939–40), although for some time the axle-guards had been crimped to reduce the coupling height.

In 1938 there were further additions to the range of M wagons; 'M' Cattle, 'M' Double Wine (with wooden tanks!), 'M' Primeurs, 'M' Barrel Wagon (with only 3 barrels) and an 'M' Covered Wagon. Like the others in the range, most were tinprinted finishes, and were larger than the British MO wagons. All were fitted with automatic couplings.

By 1938 the range of standard wagons had been reduced by withdrawal of a number of goods vehicles on the 1930–35 base: Bananas, No. 1 Cattle, Coal, No. 1 Luggage, Brake Van, all Refrigerators except 'Union', Open B, both Milk Traffic vans, and Gunpowder. Some of these had effectively been replaced by the 1–S series of vans. Accessories deleted included the No. 1 and No. 2 Signal Cabins, Loading Gauge, and Cuttings. Because of declining interest in clockwork trains, the double track curves and straights were no longer listed.

The third, last and best of the French Hornby streamlined trains was not announced until 1939, and it is not certain that production was actually started before the war; the majority of these trains were of postwar origin, not that the quality of the postwar goods was in any way inferior. The new passenger train set was called No. 4–1E 'Etoile du Nord'; the loco was a 4–4–2 of similar size to the No. 3 locos but with the smaller No. 2E mechanism and small driving wheels. The special streamlined coaches in the set had some distinctive features, notably the oval windows, and the opening doors which were provided only at two diagonally opposite corners (the other two doors being only tinprinted!). The loco was finished in SNCF green at first, later and more usually brown, and the coaches were in SNCF green. It is not clear why it was decided to model the Nord streamlined loco with the Etat company streamlined 'sausage' coaches, as the streamlined Etat loco would have made an equally spectacular and probably no more expensive model.

There was the usual Hornby discrepancy between the number of driving wheels of the prototype and of the model, but the result was no less magnificent. The headlamp in the front of the locomotive was, incidentally, also used to provide a red glow from the chimney. A 4–4E goods set was also listed in 1939–40, as were the 4–2E 'Fleche D'Or' and 4–3E Riviera 'Blue Train' sets which replaced the No. 3 equivalents.

OE tender engines with the cheaper 20 volt mechanism were also listed in 1939–40, as an alternative to the 1E loco. There were few other changes, except that the No. 2 Timber Wagon was shown in a revised form, with only 3 sets of French-type stanchions. The amazing 1939–40 No. 2 Tunnel (and the new No. 4 curved tunnel) were shown modelled in three dimensions with tiny houses, mountain streams etc.!

Meccano (France) Ltd were of course seriously affected by the war; a May 1940 trade leaflet said that 'Most of our technicians, foremen and salesmen have been called up, and cannot be replaced . . . the lack of materials will be felt more and more, and the same for packing materials . . . equally the needs of the country require us to contribute to the national effort.' It recommended shops to place end-of-year orders immediately. Because of successive rises in the cost of raw materials, no guarantees could be made on stock or on prices; goods would be invoiced at the price ruling at the time of delivery. With some

The 4–4–2 Locos continued to be made in England for sale in France.

PLM 'Train Aerodynamique'.

A PLM 4–4–2 Tank Loco, with French No. 1 Station.

'Train Express', equivalent to the English MO trains.

Three of the No. 1S Vans, equivalent to the UK No. 0 Vans.

2-car SNCF Autorail. Also showing the versatile Lighting Accessory.

optimism supplies of the 4–1E 'Etoile du Nord' and 4–4E Goods Set were promised for October 1940. The notice also advised that the Part Exchange Scheme (which had operated in France as in the UK) was suspended.

The fall of France and the subsequent occupation meant changes in plans for the Meccano factory. The remaining toy production was mainly devoted to producing Meccano parts, some of which are reputed to have been sold under the Marklin label. It is a curious fact that PO type locos exist with no Hornby trademark but with Marklin transfers, and they may belong to this unfortunate period.

It is nonetheless a surprise that whereas in Britain all production of toys ceased under Government order, in France there were (for example) Meccano Aeroplane Constructor sets packed as late as April 1944! The only difference from the prewar outfits was a printed note apologising for the lack of nickelled parts. Presumably only civilian versions were offered; a military plane daubed with swastikas might not have been received very kindly.

POST-WAR FRENCH HORNBY

A trade bulletin of May 1946 listed the items that were to be produced 'As soon as conditions permit' – they included the 'Trains Express' 1, 2 and 3, 'M' sets M0 to M4, and the single-unit Autorails. The 0–1E goods and 0–2E passenger sets contained the simplified Type PO Loco, 20 volt with manual reverse. The more expensive 2E–PO Loco was contained in the 2–VE set, still offered with 20 volt automatic reverse mechanism and larger wheels. The 4–1E 'Etoile du Nord' passenger set was listed, but the 4–4E goods set was not. In each case the contents of the sets were the same as before the war. Indeed the distinction between prewar and postwar products was very much less clear than in Britain, since the complications of nationalisation had already been faced, and also because the 'Serie Hornby' trademarks were used for a long time after the war.

The first proper catalogue of French Meccano products, including the Hornby Trains, was issued in 1949. The 0E steam-outline tender engine and sets had been added to the range listed in 1946, but the single-car Autorails were not listed.

Although no bogie goods vehicles were listed in

1949, almost the full range of postwar four-wheeled wagons was available: 'Saint Freres' Covered Wagon, 1–S Goods Van, Crane Truck, Double Wine Wagon, Side Tipping Wagon, open Wagon with vigie and 'Esso' Petrol; only the 'Primagaz' tanker and the 'Stef' van were not yet sold. The 1949 and 1950 lists also included a Barrel Wagon. The Timber Wagon and open Wagon without lookout were not available except in the goods sets, but the 'M' Coach, 1–S Coach and No. 4 Coach from the passenger sets were each catalogued separately. The postwar 1–S Coaches were as prewar except that the green coach became 1st class not 3rd.

Regrettably neither the metal nor the 'plastique' stations reappeared after the war, but they were replaced by a splendid and constantly changing range of 'demontable' (collapsible) accessories. The first of these was the No. 14 'Chalons' station (this in the 1949 catalogue, although in most cases alternative names were offered). The buildings were in wood and hardboard, usually with 'plexiglass' windows and canopies; they were supplied packed flat in boxes. Other collapsible accessories at the time were the Island Platform, Signal Cabin, and Tunnel.

Conventional accessories in 1949–50 included platform Fencing (but not the platform or ramps), Trees and Hedges, and Railway Accessories No. 8 (truck, trailer and mailbags). These accessories were short-lived, and may in fact have been old stock re-released but not produced postwar; they were all out of the range by 1950.

Other accessories offered in 1949 included No. 1

Buffers, 4–light Signal, No. 1 and 'M' Level Crossings, Checkerboard Signals, M1 Station Sets, and the Railway Accessories No. 1 (Luggage). Also listed in 1949–50 were six-figure sets 1 to 5 of the 'Sujets en Miniature' (no No. 6 shepherd set!). These sets were identical to the prewar range but moulded in unbreakable plastic. In 1950 the contents of sets 1, 2, 4 and 5 were revised to give only five of the unbreakable plastic figures in each set. (Set No. 3, Farmyard Animals, was withdrawn.) The countryman, 'Becassine', chef and sportsman were the ones removed from the lists. Accessories added in 1950 included the No. 15 Station, the electric Lamp Standard, and the No. 2 Footbridge – still made in tinplate and fitted with 'M'-type semaphore signals.

The OT–E Tank Loco was listed in 1950, but this was short-lived, and by 1953 it was no longer available.

By 1953 the Autorails were back in full production, but now only in two-car SNCF sets, clockwork or 20 volt electric. The more expensive 2–E Type PO Locos were no longer on sale.

The rolling stock in 1953 included the 'Primagaz' Tank Wagon, distinctively finished in white. The Barrel Wagon had by then disappeared, but the No. 2 Cattle Truck and the Breakdown Van and Crane were once again available. By 1953 the collapsible stations on offer were No. 17 'Lille' and No. 18 'Chalons'. The 'demontable' Viaduct was a new item, but the Island Platform was no longer made as such, nor were the electric Lamp Standards available. There was a short-lived Disc Signal with electric lighting, not really necessary since the three clip-on Lighting Accessories had been available from 1949. By 1953 the No. 1 Transformer had been replaced by No. 2, which had an automatic thermal cutout to prevent difficulties with short circuits.

The 1954 season saw the final replacement of the Type PO Loco and the 1–S Coaches. The 'type BB' were the first major postwar trains that were not a straightforward re-introduction of prewar types. The loco, BB–8051, was a short but reasonably true-to-life representation of the SNCF engines that were winning such an enviable reputation in the world for the electrified French railways. The usual 4-wheeled 20 volt motor was mounted in the centre of the loco, but the impression of 4-wheeled bogies was given by adding a pony truck at each end which (thanks to the deep side frames) gave the right appearance, at least while the engine was stationary.

A new pair of bogie coaches, of squat and compact design, was made to go with the novel engine. The new brake coach was fitted with sliding luggage doors. Different tinprintings appeared, with the coach as either 3rd or 2nd class, and the composite as either 2nd or 1st class. These new coaches were sold with the BB loco in passenger set OE–BV which with goods set OE–BM replaced the PO sets. There were also new sets with these coaches and the steam-outline OE Engine. Each of the new goods sets included the new 1–S type 'Stef' Refrigerator Van and the 1–S Goods Van.

In 1954 the ever-changing range of collapsible stations included No. 18 (shown as 'Cannes' instead of 'Chalons') and No. 19 'Marseilles'; No. 17 was

no longer listed. Sets of figures 1, 2, 4 and 5 were replaced by two completely new sets of plastic figures, Nos. 10 and 11.

In 1955 there were two new bogie coaches, a Pullman Coach and a 'Wagons-Lits' Restaurant Car. These coaches were of course fitted with the revised automatic couplings, adopted in the mid 1950s, which had a more compact design.

THE LATE 1950s

By 1956 the magnificent 4–1E 'Etoile du Nord' set was no longer available; it had understandably limited appeal, particularly in view of the 'modern image' sets of 1954 available at close to half the price.

In the late 1950s a new range of superior bogie vehicles was made; in 1956 there was an 'Arbel' Hopper Wagon, a bogie Low-Sided Wagon, and a bogie Lumber Wagon, and in 1957 an 'Azur' Tank Wagon and a tinprinted bogie Goods Van. Last of the series was the 1958 'Saint Frercs' public works bogie Covered Wagon, which had an injection-moulded plastic body. By 1961 the older style Cattle Truck and Breakdown Van were no longer listed.

The 1956 BB–M Locomotive was a smaller 0–4–0 version of the 0–BB electric type, fitted with a clockwork M series motor. It was sold in sets M5, M6 and M7 which had similar contents to the sets M1, M2 and M3 that they replaced. But the MO set which had lapsed in the early 50s was revived, so the steam-outline 'M' clockwork loco stayed available for a while – although by 1961 it was no longer listed. The coaches in the M5 and M7 passenger sets were tinprinted in SNCF instead of Pullman car colours.

Postwar rolling stock of the 1950s.

OBB Loco with SNCF bogie coaches.

The 1956 list of accessories no longer included collapsible Viaducts, but there was a large new collapsible Goods Depot with crane. In 1957 Stations 18 and 19 were replaced by Nos. 20 and 21. Plastic Poplar or Pine Trees, and straight or curved plastic Hedges, were also offered. The 4-light Signal and the electrically lit Disc Signal had been withdrawn by 1956, but from 1956 there was a new Automatic Colour Light Signal which automatically controlled the departure of trains when the lights were changed.

A 20 volt DC TNB Loco, with late bogie coaches.

From an M4 train set, 1954.

This was one of the series of modern-practice products which had no counterpart in the English Hornby range.

The 1957 catalogues saw the next stage in these developments, with the introduction of the first trains with 20 volt DC motors. The 'Serie ST "Securite Totale" Trains Hornby Telecommandes' combined all the best features of 20 volt working, the high power and low-loss power distribution, with the convenience of remote-control DC reversing. The new ST Transformer had a 40 watt output suitable for running a train and electric lighting; a second train could also be run from the same transformer through a matching speed controller available from 1958. The new transformer was similar in appearance to the Hornby Dublo transformers of the period, complete with the same thermal cutout switch.

The TBB Locomotive was very similar to the OBB Loco from the outside, except for the improved pantographs; the older OBB Loco had retained the 2–E PO Loco pantographs. It was finished in an altogether more attractive two-tone tinprinted colour scheme of green and grey instead of overall dark green. Naturally the catalogues gave full coverage to these important new lines, with full colour illustrations of both the TB–BV passenger set

(with Pullman and Restaurant Cars) and the TB–BM goods set with Low-Sided and Lumber wagons. The text boasted that the new loco could pull a train of no less than twenty bogie wagons.

Both the OBB and TBB Locos were fitted with electric lamps, and the 1957 catalogues also showed new light fittings for coaches which could be clipped into the bogies. A single standard Lighting Accessory replaced the separate Nos. 1, 2 and 3 Lighting Accessories.

The 'Aiguilles Talonables' (which had been available from 1955 as an improvement on the ordinary electric points) were sold in the late 1950s in remotely-controlled versions, and the electric solenoids and switches could be bought separately for the conversion of existing points to remote operation on either the AC or the DC system. The frogs of these late electric points were in plastic, and were designed for the new cast wheels fitted to all rolling stock. They were unsuitable for the deep flanges of tin wheels.

By 1961 two important new locomotives had been introduced, mounted on two 4-wheeled bogies, one of which was fitted with a 20 volt DC motor. The TZB Locomotive of 1958 was a 'steeple cab' type, and the TNB Locomotive a more conventional BB engine with cabs at each end. The bodies

were well-detailed metal castings, instead of the traditional tinplate. The 20 volt DC TBB Loco was still available, although the TB–BV and TB–BM sets were replaced by TNBV 'Le Basque' passenger and TZBM 'Le Lorrain' goods sets, with the new locos and similar rolling stock. The OBB electric and OVA steam-outline 20 volt AC engines were still available, as was the clockwork BB–M Loco; but the Autorails and the clockwork steam-outline 'M' loco were no longer on sale.

Between 1958 and 1961 a new range of all-plastic accessories was developed. The 1961 range no longer included the metal Footbridge, the plastic figures, the Disc Signal or the 'M' Level Crossing. The 'demontable' buildings (Stations 20 and 21, Goods Platform and Signal Cabin) were all withdrawn, and the new plastic No. 22 Station and Passenger Platform were issued. These were well-detailed models with features such as drainpipes, loudspeakers, seats, steps and so on carefully incorporated; there was also a still more impressive No. 22A extension to the already imposing No. 22 Station, with clock tower and booking hall. The Tunnel had been replaced in 1958 by a new plastic type, and a revised Level Crossing was also made in plastic. However, the old No. 1 Level Crossing remained, as the only traditional large tinplate accessory in the catalogue.

In 1962–63 and 1963–64 the range of 'Trains Hornby' was more or less unchanged; the latter was the last occasion on which the Gauge O Trains were catalogued. The Hornby Acho trains introduced in 1960 had sounded the death knell of the Gauge O range – whatever had been the intentions of Meccano Ltd about keeping the old items in production. The greater opportunities for true scale modelling in 'Acho' were among the qualities that made the 'Acho' range a success, as the 'Dublo' trains had been in Britain. It should be said that Meccano (France) Ltd did not have such a high market share in France as Meccano Ltd did in the UK, because of strong competition from other manufacturers.

It has often been argued that it was the advent of the Dublo train that held back the further development of the Hornby Series in England, so the comparison with Meccano (France) Ltd is all the more interesting because they made no HO trains before 1960. Although there was a choice of bogie vehicles

The magnificent 'Etoile Du Nord' was the largest and best train in the postwar range.

and coaches in the French Gauge O range of the 1950s, and the OBB, TBB, TNB and TZB locomotives were important developments, neither locos nor rolling stock were really satisfactory as models; there were no large and imposing products on the scale of, let us say, the 'Princess Elizabeth' Locomotive. Indeed the largest sets, the 'Etoile du Nord', did not survive for more than a few years in the 1950s. The developments in the use of injection-moulded plastics were promising, but expensive in materials – eight times as much as for the HO equivalent. It was the sheer size and expense of modelling in Gauge O, and the consequent high price and limited sales, that doomed Gauge O production.

After the War Meccano (France) Ltd had offered a cheap clockwork 'M' series for 1 ft radius, and a more expensive range of all-electric sets for 2 ft radius lines, while making a range of rolling stock perhaps narrower than in the UK but eventually with a much better choice of bogie vehicles. This mixture provided a most satisfactory choice for the French enthusiast.

A TZB Loco at a splendid all-plastic No. 22 Station, with 22A extension and No. 23 Island Platform.

Hornby Trains for Export

The list of foreign agencies on Meccano Ltd's headed notepaper showed just how wide an area of the world was covered by their marketing, in dozens of countries within and without the Empire. Meccano sets were universal, and needed only different labels and instructions to make them suitable for anywhere in the world. But since Hornby Trains were mostly finished in British railway company liveries, the situation was not so simple for them.

Hornby Trains in special liveries were prepared for only a few countries, and not always those with the largest Hornby Train sales. Often only a few hundred were made in each batch.

South America, and in particular Argentina, was the earliest and most important export market after France. South Africa, New Zealand and Canada, then Holland, Denmark, Switzerland and Sweden were all offered trains in special liveries. Others were made, such as 'ESR', but no written records appear to have survived. There were countries (such as Australia and Belgium) that had established agencies with good sales, but for which no special liveries were created. The agencies had special responsibilities as local distributors of Meccano products; apart from publicity, they were also required to provide a repair service for Hornby locos, and they were

supplied with the necessary spare parts to allow this to be done properly.

With the exception of a few Canadian Pacific Streamlined Trains, no locos or rolling stock with foreign markings were produced after the war. There was an interesting series of standard Hornby vans in 1948–49 which were issued without company lettering or other transfers; they may well have been intended for export. The only difference between the UK and export postwar catalogue ranges was the inclusion of the Electric E502 and E602 sets and rails, not available at home.

The lettering found on prewar export Hornby Trains included:

ARGENTINA:	FCO, FCS, FCBAP, FCCA
CANADA:	Canadian Pacific
DENMARK:	DSB
FRANCE:	ETAT, EST, NORD, PLM (SNCF trains all made in France)
HOLLAND:	(not known)
NEW ZEALAND:	NZR
SOUTH AFRICA:	SAR/SAS
SWEDISH:	SJ
SWISS:	SBB/CFF

A large number of Hornby tenders in export livery (mostly those made in the late 1930s) were still in stock in England when the war broke out. For this reason, the export tenders are found in the UK much more often than the locos.

On the whole, the range of Hornby Trains available, and the colours for goods rolling stock and accessories, were subject to the same variations as in the UK. However, the transfers for export items were not used up as quickly, because of the lower turnover, and so were not always in the most up-to-date lettering style.

No tinprinted trains or accessories were made specially for export, but certain tinprinted coaches were turned into export versions by overpainting the British lettering with enamel, and putting a different sticker on the box! This was most usually done on LNER coaches, but sometimes LMS.

The locos in export liveries often had the same loco numbers as the UK types – except where the number was an integral part of the railway company lettering transfer. Some tender locos were identical to the English types except for the label on the box, and only the tender lettering was different. Special export versions of the No. 3 Locomotives were made without nameplates (although named versions were also exported) because the name would be inappropriate with foreign lettering on the tender. The splashers of the export versions had plain lining transfers.

ARGENTINA

Argentina was the principal export market in South America for Hornby Trains, and was important enough to have warranted special railway company liveries as early as 1922. The first wagons were for the Ferrocarril Buenos Aires al Pacifico (FCBAP), the Ferrocarril Oeste (FCO) and the Ferrocarril Sud

'ESR' Hornby locos. No records appear to exist as to the meaning of the initials; 'Egyptian State Railways' is one suggestion.

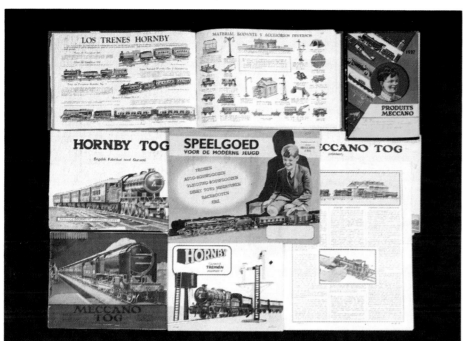

A selection of Hornby literature printed in England for export to Argentina, Belgium, Denmark, Holland and Sweden.

An early FCBAP wagon; the only one known with these letters.

(FCS). Very soon FCCA (Central Argentina) lettering was used instead of FCBAP, giving a choice of three – although by 1939–40 only FCO and FCS were mentioned in the catalogues.

Enamelled Hornby engines with these letterings were sold with a choice of goods or passenger livery (not true of all other countries); even the No. 2 Special, No. 3, 'Eton' and 'Princess Elizabeth' locos were available in goods or passenger livery, each sold either with nameplates or without! The 'Nord' trains were available, but only in the normal colours. About half the trains sold in Argentina were lettered for the UK, so the confusion of liveries was understandably frequent! In the late 1930s black goods engines appear to have been no less common than the passenger types, unlike the situation in the UK.

Catalogues for Argentina were published annually, in Spanish, and priced in Pesos. Special Meccano Manuals and other leaflets were also printed, as for all the other agencies. Printing blocks almost invariably showed the UK trains, and until the late

No. 2 Special Loco with FCS tender, 1929–30.

FC0, FCS and FCCA were the three common Hornby letterings for Argentina. The TT20M Transformer was not advertised in the UK.

A mishap at the crossover.

1930s the availability of special liveries was not usually mentioned.

In the catalogues of the late 1930s there appeared two transformers of more than usual interest; the TT20M made in the French 'M' style, with two M Signal Cabins back to back enclosing the transformer, and the TT20A (catalogued as being made in Argentina) inside a No. 1 Signal Cabin, and provided with a built-in resistance controller.

The Buenos Aires equivalent of Hamley's was the Burlando Hermanas toy shop, the major stockists of Hornby Trains and Meccano Products. Each year in the 1930's they mounted an exhibition of Hornby Trains, the most spectacular of these layouts incorporating long elevated tracks and railway stations built from Meccano; these were layouts that can have had few contemporary equals anywhere in the world.

A layout in Burlando Hermanas toyshop in Buenos Aires, 1935. Looking towards the shop window.

The same layout looking into the shop. LE120 and LE220 Locos are in evidence, along with many Dinky Toys etc. These magnificent layouts were arranged by Sr. Pedro Lloret.

276

NEW ZEALAND

Hornby Trains with UK lettering had already been exported to New Zealand for some time, before special NZR liveries were offered in the 1930 NZ catalogues. The July 1930 catalogue said that 'Hornby Locos and Rolling Stock, with the exception of No. 2 Special and No. 3 Locos and Tenders (available with English lettering only) will be supplied in NZR lettering unless English lettering (LMS, LNER, GW or SR) is specified. This applies to enamelled goods only, and not to tinprinted goods.' The most common colours for NZR-lettered locos were LMS red, LNER green and goods black. Tender engine numbers were usually the same as in the UK, but most NZR tank locos were not numbered. Plain gold 'NZR' letters were the norm on tank locos and on tenders, except in the late 1930s when wagon-type letters were used since loco transfers had run out. NZR No. 2 Special and No. 3 Locos were made available soon after 1930, and the

Shop window display, 1936. Using Meccano, Dinky Toys and Hornby Trains.

E220 Special Tank and No. 1 NZR Locos of the 1930s.

277

SAR/SAS Hornby Trains, for South Africa. The export E320 Loco lacks nameplate and number.

No. 3 Loco could be obtained either with nameplates or in the export version without. No. 2 Special Locos were identical to the UK types, except for the tender lettering.

NZR goods wagons were available (for a short period only) on the open axleguard base, but most NZR wagons were on the lower 1930-type underframe. The small 'NZR' letters were almost invariably in gold, (shadowed red and lined black), and placed in a corner of the wagon side.

SOUTH AFRICA

Hornby Trains in SAR/SAS livery were made between 1927 and 1940. Usual colours for the locos were LMS red, LNER green and goods black (although GW and SR coloured locos in SAR/SAS lettering are occasionally found), each lettered 'SAR' on the left-hand and 'SAS' on the right-hand side of the tanks or the tender; one set of initials in English, and the other Afrikaans. The loco instructions were sometimes bilingual. The green SAR/SAS locos

An early SAR/SAS No. 1 Special Tank, and a later No. 2 Special Tank.

CPR Streamlined Loco and Coaches, circa 1949.

278

usually had gold/red/black lining instead of the black/white used for LNER engines. There was a special loco number transfer, about ½ in diameter, lettered 'Hornby Series' around the number 6027, which was used for early No. 0 and No. 1 Locos with fixed lamps, and for the No. 2 Tank; a similar transfer with the number 6270 was used on the green No. 2 Locos. The fixed-lamp No. 1 Tank Loco was numbered 7206 in ordinary lettering (not the round numberplate) on the tankside; note that the 6027, 6270, and 7206 transfers all used the same digits in different orders! When the No. 1 Special Tank Loco first appeared in SAR/SAS livery in 1929, it had no loco number.

In the 1930s, the No. 1 Special Tank Locos usually had the same numbers as in the UK (e.g. 2120). The No. 1 Tank and No. 2 Special Tank usually had no numbers, just the SAR/SAS lettering, while tender locos had the same numbers as in the UK but with SAR/SAS tenders.

Wagons were also lettered with 'SAR' on one side and 'SAS' on the other.

CANADA

The Canadian market was fascinating in several respects; some unique products were offered there, although the volume of trade was not particularly high. Canadian Pacific No. 3 Trains, sold in 1930, have already been mentioned, as have the US Hornby Locos sold there. It is odd that the normal range of Hornby Trains was never made with CPR lettering for sale in Canada!

The postwar CPR Streamlined Train Set was a unique product; the Streamlined Train was catalogued in no other country after the war. It was finished in green, with a black front end, valance and tender base. It appears to have been enamelled rather than tinprinted (a rational choice in view of the small number produced), with silver CPR letters on both loco and tender. Black/white lining bands at the level of the cab windows ran the length of loco and tender; they appear to have been LNER 501 Loco boiler lining transfers! Both loco and tender had the postwar (grey background) transfer trademarks. The coaches were brown, with five silver windows plus two oval door windows; there were no numbers on

HORNBY TRAINS

Hornby Trains are manufactured by Meccano Limited and are made from the finest materials obtainable. All Hornby Locomotives are splendidly built with strong and reliable mechanism, and are beautifully enamelled in correct railway colours. They are thoroughly tested before leaving the factory and are fully guaranteed.
Every hour spent in playing with a Hornby railway is brimful of thrills and enjoyment! The fun and fascination are never-ending.

Hornby Mechanical Passenger Train Set CM 1

This Train Set is a realistic model consisting of Locomotive, Tender, two Passenger Cars, and track. The Locomotive is strongly built and is made of pressed steel with a one piece boiler and cab. Colours: Locomotive, red and black. Passenger Cars, green and gold.

Hornby Mechanical Passenger Train Set CM 2

The contents of the CM 2 Train Set are similar to those of the CM 1 but differently coloured. Locomotive, green and black, with gold trimming. Passenger Cars, yellow and black.

Hornby Mechanical Freight Train Set CM

This fine freight Train Set consists of Locomotive, Tender, Box Cab, Tank Car, Caboose, and track. Colours: Locomotive, red and black. Box Car, yellow. Tank Car, red. Caboose, green. Packed in attractive cardboard box.

Canadian Pacific Hornby Electric Passenger Train Set (15 volts)

This new Electric Train Set is distinctive in design and beautifully enamelled in colours. It consists of Locomotive, Tender, two Passenger Cars and Electrical Track. The powerful electric motor in the locomotive is operated from the electric light main (alternating current only) through a transformer capable of supplying 1 ampere at 15 volts. The Locomotive is fitted with reverse gear, controlled by a lever in the cab.

loco, tender or coach. The coaches were apparently of the MO type rather than articulated.

The set was catalogued in the Canadian edition of the 'Meccano. World Famous Toys' booklet of October 1949, as the 'HORNBY MS PASSENGER TRAIN SET – Similar to the MO Passenger Train Set but lettered CPR', at $5.50 compared with $4.50 for the MO set.

EUROPE AND SCANDINAVIA

By and large, the Hornby trains sold in Europe and Scandinavia were the same as in the UK, except that from 1931 special liveries were prepared for certain countries. The only product that actually required different tooling was the Continental semaphore M Signal, for Belgium and Holland (the signal arm of which was enamelled, not tinprinted, the post being

of the standard UK type); most of the special continental trains differed only in the painting and transfers.

Belgium did not have special loco or rolling stock transfers, the trains being the same as in England, except that catalogues of the early 1930s showed unlettered French-type brake vans in certain goods sets.

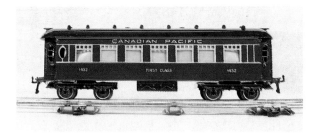

Hornby 'Canadian Pacific' Coach.

279

DSB goods wagons, with No. 2 Special Tank and No. 1 Tank Locos.

Swiss Hornby locos were usually finished in GW green (although with the normal dome rather than the cast safety valve); Swiss locos and wagons were lettered SBB/CFF. Danish tank locos were produced in green, red or black; each used a DSB transfer similar to those used on coaches and wagons, together with LMS-type loco lining transfers. Swedish locos were also in green, red or black, and the rolling stock was lettered with an 'SJ' monogram. Some export tender locos had special transfers on the cabside (e.g. 'Nr 955 R' on an export L1), with lined but unlettered tender sides. Banana Vans for Denmark, Sweden and Switzerland had special transfers.

Train Sets for these countries were much the same as in the UK, except that on the Continent in the 1930s Swiss-type locos were sold in sets with No. 0 American-type Coaches. No Hornby Trains with German railway markings were made, apart from the Mitropa Coaches; competition on Marklin's home ground would have been unprofitable.

No. 2 Continental Coaches were made by spraying the No. 2 Pullman body in Castrol green, lettering with special transfers (although sometimes they were left unlettered), and lining out in gold. The Swiss version was particularly attractively finished, as a second class saloon for smokers. The No. 2 Special coach bodies were also finished in the Continental Coach colours. The American-type Pullman Car was mask-sprayed in Castrol green for sale as the M1 Continental Pullman Coach and as the No. 0 Continental Coach. Incredibly, the Caboose (with the tinprinted name panel obliterated by mask-spraying in plain green) was sold with Danish, Swedish or Swiss transfers as the No. 1 Continental Coach!

UNITED STATES OF AMERICA

The Meccano Company Inc. was formed in the US in September 1913. In 1922 the Meccano factory in Elizabeth, New Jersey (12 miles from New York City) was finished. It was managed by J. P. Porteus, with H. Hudson Dobson as Sales Manager – Dobson was later to become President of Meccano Inc., and

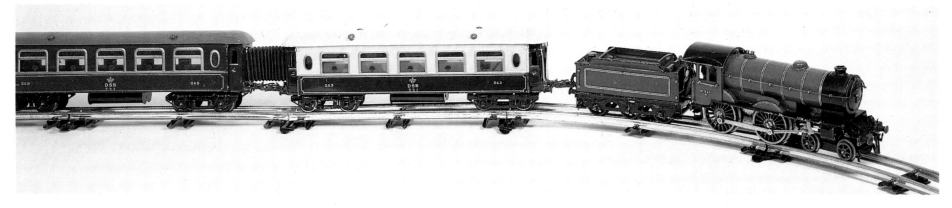

A No. 2 Special 'Yorkshire' Locomotive with normal LNER colouring and lining, but with export cabside number and blank nameplates. The LNER-style tender has, inexplicably, been finished in GW green with GW lining transfers. The coaches are in No. 2 Pullman and LMS Saloon colours, in each case with DSB 2nd/3rd transfers.

after the factory closed he continued to act as importer of Binns Road toys (other than Meccano), an arrangement maintained after the Second World War.

The August 1927 Meccano Magazine (the American editions were independently produced, much smaller and less attractive magazines than in Britain) announced the new trains made in Elizabeth: 'We announce with great pleasure that the famous Hornby Trains are now being made in America, and in a very short time they will be on display in the stores. As some of our readers may know, Mr Hornby, the inventor of Meccano, is the largest manufacturer of mechanical trains in Europe, and throughout most of the world the name Hornby Trains is as well known to boys as Meccano. As would be expected, Hornby Trains are in a class by themselves and they would more correctly be styled "model" trains than toys. The new Hornby Trains that are now being made in Elizabeth are reproductions of the most up-to-date American railroads,

An unusual No. 2 Special Loco, possibly for Holland or Denmark. The cabside number Nr 955 R is applied on top of the L1 numberplate! The unlettered tender has inappropriate LMS lining.

Hornby Luggage Van and No. 0/1 Tender for Switzerland.

Hornby Luggage Van and No. 1 Special Tender for Sweden.

A mixture. An M Signal for Belgium and Holland, DSB wagons, and an export tender. The loco is for the UK, but has two interesting production errors.

even including coloured locomotives, such as have been introduced on a few leading railroads only this year.'

'The locomotives are of pressed steel, with a one-piece boiler and cab, and are operated by a most powerful speedy motor. No pains have been spared in their construction, and careful attention to such details as the headlight, brass bell and boiler rail on the locomotive has produced a most realistic effect. The Pullman Cars are accurately proportioned and are made of steel throughout. They are beautifully lithographed in colours and bear the names of the Presidents Washington and Jefferson. The effect of these cars, in conjunction with the handsome locomotive is very striking, and will give you an entirely new idea of the fun of model railroading. Watch for Hornby Trains. Ask your dealer when his stock will be in, so that you may be one of the first to see them. A set of locomotive, tender, two Pullman Cars, ten sections of track and the necessary track connections will sell for three dollars, seventy five.'

The first 2527 locos were shown with 10-spoke wheels, but 8-spoke wheels were more usual. The key was attached to the winding spindle by a screw thread, and the motor was not identical to any British type. The couplings were like a cross between the early Tinprinted Train type and the much later No. 30 couplings! US Hornby trains were evidently designed and built quite independently by the Elizabeth works; they had an important influence on the design of the later M series trains both in the UK and in France – the similarity of French and US type M tenders being particularly striking.

Hornby could scarcely have chosen a less propitious moment than 1927 for the introduction of the 'Hornby Lines' gauge O trains. Only a year later, A. C. Gilbert (one of Meccano's US rivals, famous for their 'Erector' brand constructional sets) took over Meccano Inc. with sole rights to use the Meccano name and patents in the USA. The American Hornby Trains were last advertised in the US Meccano Manuals in 1929, and the following year remaining stocks were sold in Canada.

In 1927 the US locomotive was offered in two sets, the M–1 Mechanical Train with a red and black loco with green and gold Pullmans, and the M–2

Mechanical Train, with a green and black loco with yellow and black Pullmans. Although 'Jefferson' was shown in the early illustrations, it may have only been a pre-production version; 'Washington' and 'Madison' were the more usual names, and these were shown in later publications. In 1928 the new

M–3 Mechanical Train became available; it was a goods set with the red and black loco, a yellow Box Car, a red Tank Car, and a 'brown' Caboose; the 1930 Canadian Meccano instruction manual gave the colour as green, so it seems that a change had been made in the tinprinting.

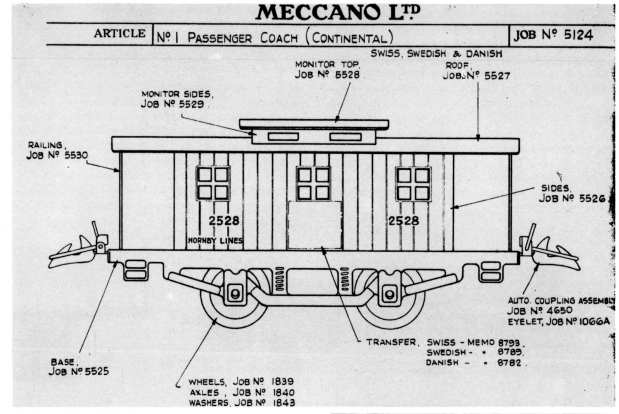

Continental Coach No. 1.

Meccano Ltd's US factory.

Hornby Lines Loco, made in the USA.

Hornby and Meccano Publications

The printed ephemera issued by Meccano Ltd falls into two categories – the products of the Advertising Department, and the instructional leaflets that accompanied the trains.

The Advertising Department kept up a truly prolific rate of production of catalogues, folders and price lists, of different sizes and forms varying from full colour booklets with stupendously long printing runs (over half a million copies in some cases) down to quantities of only a few hundred for specialised items and for exports.

The staff of the Advertising Department were past masters of the art of hard selling. They created such a forceful publicity machine for Meccano Ltd that even after fifty years their material still instils the magic and the excitement – and the craving to buy – that it was designed to produce. How many present day enthusiasts are still held in thrall by the enduring power of this advertising, even though the products have long vanished from the shops?

The work of the Advertising Department was carried out in many languages, with special printings required for all the principal export markets. There were special 'no price' (NP) editions of some catalogues and Hornby Books of Trains; others were fully priced in the appropriate foreign currency. So many different versions of the catalogues and price lists were made and exported that it is impossible to make a full list of them all, after such a lapse of time and often at distances of thousands of miles. Those which are known show a variety of different styles that make for interesting comparisons with the UK literature – about which much more is known. The following section is mainly confined to the printed matter produced for the United Kingdom.

THE MECCANO MAGAZINE

The 'Meccano Magazine' was one of the key items in the Advertising Department's list of creations. It grew step by step from a simple 4-page paper in 1916, until it had built up into a glorious monthly treat for Meccano Boys.

The main aim of the magazine was to boost sales, as is shown by the July 1920 'Increased Sales and Profits' booklet: 'It has now been decided to enlarge the Meccano Magazine. For the present it will be issued bi-monthly, but we hope that in due course the situation in regard to paper will become easier and that we shall be able to issue it more frequently.

The dealer who values his Meccano trade will take the Meccano Magazine very seriously. It is one of the best trade-makers he can have . . . it should be on every dealer's counter.'

Ellison Hawks (who, incidentally, had a home in Liverpool's Penny Lane) was the driving force behind the Advertising Department from 1921, when he joined as Advertising Manager, until 1935 when he left Meccano Ltd and became general editor of Amalgamated Press. He was already an

Meccano Products Catalogue cover, dated 1925 but showing much earlier Hornby Trains.

283

SALANSON LTD.

Opticians & Photographic Dealers

20, HIGH STREET   4, HIGH STREET
BRISTOL   CARDIFF

established author of children's books, but his output of these and also technical books continued at an astonishing rate after he joined Meccano Ltd, and indeed until he died in 1971. The stamp of his personality on the Meccano Magazine is evident from its dynamic growth – first the change to the use of better quality paper, then to monthly publication from September 1922, and coloured covers from 1923. Full-colour covers were to become a standard feature, and the size of the magazine grew regularly until the 1930s (always with a special large December issue) by which time the price had climbed to 6d. In 1929 the circulation had reached 70,000 copies, and it had become 'the finest boys' paper ever published'.

The number of copies printed went down to 50,000 in 1938 and 1939, and the number of pages fell; wartime shortage of paper caused a cut to half the original page size from the January 1942 issue, and the size remained the same (although with more pages as the shortage eased) through the '40s and '50s.

The magazine gave regular news to the Hornby Train enthusiast about the latest developments of both the 'real' railways and the Hornby trains. Articles on Hornby Trains became increasingly frequent during the 1920s, and in the 1930s there were usually two at least in each issue – one aimed for Senior section HRC members and one for the Juniors.

There were usually pages of Hornby Train advertisements as well, and the Christmas editions in particular showed spectacular double page spreads of the range of clockwork and electric train sets, and pages of rolling stock and accessories. These showed the most recent products from the new season's catalogues; curiously though the MM was frequently reticent about making a special feature of the latest introductions as soon as they appeared.

After the war, the Hornby Train articles reflected the declining fortunes of the Gauge O system, and its reduction to 'nursery' status. There was for the first time a full-colour Hornby advertisement in the November 1956 MM, but advertisements for the Hornby Trains became rarer until in the later years they just faded from the pages; although interestingly there were one or two articles showing an awareness of the former glories of the Hornby Series, prompted by the interest of buyers (or inheritors) of second-hand trains.

THE HORNBY BOOK OF TRAINS

'The finest catalogue in the world', the Hornby Book of Trains, was first published in September 1925 to coincide with the centenary celebrations of the Stockton and Darlington Railway. It was an astonishing production with 44 pages (including the full colour cover). There were 20 pages of catalogue pictures of Hornby Trains, again in full colour, and the rest was packed with interesting articles on the

real railways and their development.

Such was the demand for this beautiful catalogue, at the very modest price of 3d, that the first edition was soon sold out, and another edition was made ready in March 1926. This corrected some minor errors in the first printing; the best distinguishing feature (neither carried a printing code) was the 'No. OO Train' page, which was headed 'Hornby Trains' in the later editions.

It was decided to continue publication of the HBT each season, and the latest editions were advertised each autumn in the Meccano Magazine. There were, right from 1925, special overseas editions but these were printed in quantities of only a few thousand; the total number of copies of the UK editions each year was about 100,000. In some years (certainly in 1925, 1926, 1927, 1929 and 1930) there was more than one printing for the UK.

The 1935–36 season production was the Book of Hornby Trains and Meccano Products (reproduced in full in Volume 1 of this series). This replaced the usual mixture with a full colour catalogue of the whole range of Meccano Ltd products, including the Hornby Trains, but without the varied and informative articles on the real railways. The price increase from 3d to 9d was fully justified by the extra costs, but proved too much for the average customer; the reduced print run of 65,000 copies still was not sold out at the end of the season, and Messrs. Halfords acquired much of the remaining stock to distribute to their customers in 1936–37 at a special reduced price of 6d. No HBT of any sort was issued for the 1936–37 season.

The Hornby Trains had been reduced to a mere 31 pages in the BHT&MP, compared to the best-ever 46 pages in 1934–35. When the HBT reappeared in 1937–38, however, there were 39 pages of Hornby in a new and exciting graphic style with many (but by no means all) of the pictures brought up to date in a series of expensive changes. The 1938–39 HBT (again reproduced in full in Volume 1 of this series) was very similar, but the 1939–40 HBT although similar had only 32 pages of Gauge O trains, both because of deletions and to make way for 7 pages of Hornby Dublo Trains. No HBT could be published in 1940, and there was no postwar equivalent for Gauge O.

HORNBY TRAIN FOLDERS, CATALOGUES and ILLUSTRATED PRICE LISTS

Folders, catalogues and illustrated price lists show-ing the whole or part of the range of Hornby Trains were supplied to dealers for distribution to their customers. Although the dealer usually had to pay a nominal charge, they were for the most part intended for free distribution. A small cover charge was sometimes printed on the late postwar issues, but Meccano Ltd made it clear that (in this case only) retail price maintenance would not be enforced.

The prewar editions were titled 'Hornby Trains'; they were probably issued each season from 1923–24 to 1939–40, except the 1936–37 edition which may not have been produced for reasons of economy. The 1923–24 and 1925–26 editions have not come to light in our researches, but in January 1924 MM readers were urged to 'write for the illustrated leaflet of Hornby Clockwork trains and complete range of accessories'. There was a similar advertisement in December 1925, so it seems likely that both these 'missing' editions were published.

Up to 1928, these Hornby Train catalogues were single-sheet folders, increasing in size as the range of

Hornby Trains expanded. But they were becoming unmanageably large, so in 1928 a stapled pocket-size booklet of 16 pages was produced. The 1929 cata-logue was similar, and in 1930 there was a booklet of 20 pages in horizontal instead of vertical format. The 1931 editions were also booklets, but in 1932 and 1933 the format reverted to a large single sheet folder. In 1934 there were two separate folders, one for clockwork and one for electric trains; both also listed the full range of rolling stock and accessories, and were consequently very large.

In 1935–36 a single booklet was once again pro-duced, this time of 24 pages. The electric train sets were distinguished from clockwork by the use of red ink instead of black. For 1937–38, 1938–39 and 1939–40 folders were issued, but these were smaller in size than the previous editions and did not cover the whole range – just a representative selection. Because there was not the same pressure on space to cram in every item, they had more room for art-work, and were as a result most attractive lists.

After the war, the 'Hornby Clockwork Trains' catalogue came out in new editions every season from 1953–54 to 1962–63. Each was a folder, but the size and the expense of production varied – the 1955–

56 edition was the first in full colour, and the 1956–57, 1957–58 and 1958–59 editions were also in full colour. But 1959–60 saw a return to black and white (although with a background colour) and the 1960–61, 1961–62 and 1962–63 folders were all in this cheaper style.

Each of these Hornby Train booklets and folders can be recognised by their titles or their contents (no other Meccano Ltd products are included). They were printed in large numbers, upwards of half a million in the mid 1930s and up to a quarter of a million after the war, and are thus more commonly found than the Hornby Books of Trains.

MECCANO PRODUCTS CATALOGUES

Hornby Trains are also found in the general Mec-cano Product Catalogues, folders and illustrated price lists that were issued yearly from 1920 to 1939. These were again supplied to the dealer for distribu-tion to customers either free of charge or at a nominal price of 1d or so, at the dealer's discretion. They were the most important and the most widely dis-tributed products of the advertising department. From 1925 a blank panel on the coloured cover could

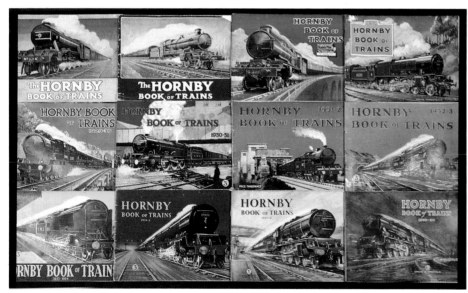

Hornby Books of Trains.

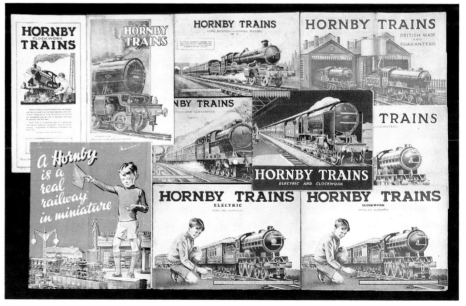

Hornby Train catalogues and folders.

be overprinted with the name and address of the shopkeeper – as part of the Meccano Ltd selling service. Each season the dealer was also offered a choice of several different coloured covers – although the catalogue contents were identical. Halfords, who were among Meccano Ltd's biggest customers, had special 'Halfords' coloured covers printed for each year's Meccano Products Catalogue from the late 1920s through to 1939–40. There were also special covers for Hamley's.

The 1920–21 catalogue consisted of twenty pages, plus the rather plain grey cover. Both the Hornby Train and the Tinprinted Train Sets were included. In 1921–22 the first coloured cover was used, and the complete range of trains, including the new No. 2 sets, was shown. Each year thereafter the full range of Hornby Trains was squeezed in, together with illustrations. The August 1925 edition of the 1925–26 season catalogue was the last in the early 7 in wide by 9 in tall twenty-page format; a pocket size 5 in wide by 7 in tall catalogue was issued later in the same season (probably in early 1926). In the new format the number of pages grew steadily until 1936–37 when the range of Meccano products filled 72 pages! The print run reached its highest point of 1,300,000 copies in 1936–37 – probably because neither the Hornby Book of Trains nor the Hornby Trains folder was issued. In 1937–38 there was a change in size, to 8½ in wide by 5½ in tall, still with 72 pages. The size remained the same for 1938–39 and 1939–40.

In addition to these booklets, there were also special 'Meccano and Hornby Train' folders in 1931 that showed Meccano Sets and a small selection from the range of Hornby Trains.

After the war, there was no possibility of going back to the regular, stapled catalogues – there would have been little point since the range of products was so limited. The first leaflets were printed in 1946, and Hornby Trains were not mentioned. The March 1947 single sheet Meccano products illustrated price list was the first to show any Hornby Trains. There was a 4-page folder in November 1947, then there were several printings each year; at least 3 in 1948, 2 in 1949, 3 in 1950 and 3 in 1951. The size increased with the range of goods, until they ended up as rather unwieldy 8 page affairs.

A stapled, large format 8-page booklet was printed for the UK in 1949 only. Titled 'Meccano, World-Famous Toys', it was more ambitious than any of its predecessors, and was not repeated in subsequent years. It was printed in different editions for the overseas markets, some earlier than the UK edition.

In 1952, the Meccano Products Catalogues resumed in the form of an illustrated pocket-size 16 page booklet, which appeared in 3 editions in 1952 and 2 in 1953. The October 1953 Meccano Products Catalogue however had 20 pages, and once again the dealer was offered a choice of several coloured covers overprinted with his name and address. In all over one million copies were printed. Thereafter the normal pattern of one printing per year resumed; the 1954 catalogue was similar, but only one coloured picture was printed for the cover (so the shopkeeper no longer had a choice), and there were now 24 pages. The 1955–56 catalogue again had a single coloured cover (boys looking into a Meccano shop window) and had 28 pages. The 1955–56 and 1956–57 catalogues were magnificent full colour catalogues – not just coloured covers but coloured catalogue pages as well. In 1957 there was also a full-colour Meccano Products folder, but it showed only part of the Hornby Train range.

The 1958 Meccano Products Catalogue was a 20 page booklet, again in full colour. Although there were fewer pages, they were much larger, and still showed all the Hornby Gauge O Trains. It was however the last such catalogue until 1963, when a smaller pocket-size 20 page full colour catalogue was issued. In 1964 the last such booklet, with 20 larger pages, appeared. As a precaution against obsolescence none of the 1956 to 1964 full colour catalogues were printed with prices, but each was issued with a separately printed price list folded or stapled inside. The 1957 colour folder did, however, quote prices.

A selection of postwar publications.

PRICE LISTS

In addition to the illustrated price lists already mentioned with the Meccano Products Catalogues, and certain Hornby Leaflets, Meccano Ltd also produced numerous other price lists.

Before 1938 most of the non-illustrated price lists had been short lists of revised prices issued as corrigenda to update existing stocks of catalogues or booklets when prices – or the range of products – changed. Usually the items that changed were the only ones listed. But in 1938 there was a major revision of prices across the whole range of Meccano products, and a full list of prices applying from 1 January, 1938 was produced in a number of printings, which were widely distributed with the season's remaining stock of catalogues etc. The many wartime lists – January, April, August and October 1940, May and November 1941, all listed the complete range available at the time of printing together with the latest revised prices. They were the only source of up-to-date information since no 1940 catalogues or folders were printed for the UK.

Before 1953, all the postwar price lists appear to have been illustrated, and are dealt with elsewhere; but from October 1953 onwards a very large number of full price lists, without illustrations, were printed. Over sixty such lists appeared in the period up to 1969, the 1969 edition appearing to be the last to include any Hornby Trains. These price lists are a valuable source of information on the dates of availability for postwar items. As already mentioned, certain of these lists (generally those printed in the largest numbers) were intended for use in conjunction with the full colour catalogues with no printed prices. Others were issued to correct old prices printed in existing catalogues or folders. Although they were not usually printed with the names and addresses of individual dealers, several editions were specially printed for Hamley's of Regent Street, London.

MISCELLANEOUS MECCANO PUBLICATIONS

A number of the booklets issued by Meccano Ltd during the 1920s have a page of Hornby Train advertisements – for example 'Jackie Coogan Visits a Meccano Factory', 'Adventures in Meccanoland', 'The New Meccano', and others.

The 1921 Meccano Instruction Book No. 3 had an inserted sheet (usually glued in) showing the No. 1 and No. 2 Hornby Train Sets. There were two versions of the insert – one in monochrome, and the other with full colour pictures exactly as in the 1921 Hornby Train leaflet.

Most Meccano Instruction Manuals printed between 1922 and 1930 had two or three pages of Hornby Trains at the back. These manuals often gave customers the first sight of the trains for the new season, since they tended to be printed in the early part of the year, and there was less delay between printing and despatch than with some of the catalogues. Certain of these manuals were packed within a month of the date of the printing code, whereas the HBTs were not available until two or

three months after the date of the printing code.

The 1937 to 1941 series of manuals almost invariably had an advertisement for Hornby Trains in general, and the 'Princess Elizabeth' in particular, on the outside back cover.

HORNBY BOOKLETS

In addition to the catalogues, a number of booklets were printed for the information and enlightenment of customers. The longest-lasting of these were the Rail Formations booklets first printed in 1922, and last in the 1960s.

The 'Rail Formations' booklets of the early 1920s had 8 pages. The front cover listed the Hornby rails for clockwork trains (electric rails were given on a separate list only available on request to Meccano Ltd) and the back page showed a selection of rolling stock and accessories. Inside were a series of neatly-drawn diagrams showing possible track arrangements. Although geometrically appealing, for the most part they were unrailwaylike. These booklets were included with each Hornby and Zulu Train set, or were available separately price 3d.

The 1925 Rail Formations booklet gave instructions on the front page on 'How to Get More Fun With Your Train Set' and gave hints on the care of rails. The back page listed both clockwork and electric rails, but no rolling stock or accessories now appeared.

There was a gap in the availability of the Rail Formations booklet when it was effectively replaced by the 'Hornby Train System' booklet printed in September 1926. This was based on the series of articles in the Meccano Magazine on 'How to Run a Hornby Railway System'. It was a more useful and informative booklet than 'Rail Formations' as its 8 pages were crammed with interesting text, as well as 10 photographs of actual layouts, some very extensive, showing the trains in use with accessories, stations and goods yards. The back page continued to show a selection of rails.

The following year came its successor, 'How to Get More Fun Out Of Hornby Trains'. This was a 12 page booklet, still 3d (and free with the larger Hornby Train Sets) printed on much the same lines

but with still more information on real railway practice and with a few extra layout diagrams. It was reprinted with amendments in 1928, and in 1929 was issued with yet another title, 'How to Plan Your Hornby Railway'. The old layout pictures were replaced by more modern photographs (mostly from the MM) of current Hornby products. Revisions and updating took place regularly with each new edition up to 1939. It was available for separate sale at 3d, although still included free of charge in the larger Hornby train sets.

In 1934 the 'Rail Formations' booklet was revived under the title 'Hornby Layouts – 100 Suggestions for Clockwork and Electric Railways'. This booklet was included in both the clockwork and the electric sets from 1934, (all except the M series), and it was printed in several subsequent revised and updated editions. The last printing in January 1940 was reduced to 8 instead of 12 pages; hence the change in title to 'Hornby Gauge O Layouts – 60 Suggestions for Clockwork and Electric Railways' (Gauge O had been added to the title in 1938).

The electric railway owner was catered for by the printing in 1932 of 'How to Plan Your Hornby Electric Railway'. It was only a 4-page leaflet, and rather expensive at 2d, but again it was usually included free in the electric train sets. A 12-page booklet 'How to Choose and Use a Hornby Electric Railway' was printed late in 1934, price 3d, and dealt with the subject much more satisfactorily, although strangely enough it appears to have been printed in smaller numbers.

The Hornby Control System leaflets produced between 1926 and 1937 in over a dozen different UK printings gave details on operating the Control System. The post-1929 editions were revised and updated to delete references to the Control Rails and the control of locomotives.

There was also a two-page leaflet of the same size as all these booklets (roughly A4), called 'How to Develop Your Hornby Model Railway'; it seems to have been an economy edition for inclusion with the cheaper train sets, or with locomotives.

After the war, the 8-page 'Layouts for Clockwork Track' booklet was published until 1952, when the smaller 4-page 'Layout Suggestions for Clockwork Track' became the standard issue. These layout booklets were included with all Hornby Train Sets including the M series, hence the printing of 100,000 copies each year on average (compared with 35,000 copies per year of the prewar '100 Suggestions', not included in the M series sets). The layout booklets could also be bought from dealers.

MISCELLANEOUS HORNBY LEAFLETS

Before 1925 when the pattern of HBTs, Meccano Products Catalogues and Hornby Train Folders became established, a number of leaflets and lists of Hornby Trains were printed – especially during 1922 and 1923 when the range of Hornby train was growing rapidly. Boys were invited to send to the works for the latest list, and by no means all of these have yet been re-discovered.

In 1920 three editions of a 2-page Hornby Train Leaflet were issued, which showed Tinprinted Trains, Hornby Trains and the latest Meccano Products. Similar leaflets in 1921 showed the No. 1 Passenger and No. 2 Goods and Passenger Train Sets as well. There were two 1921 editions; one in black and white, and the other with the trains printed in full colour, both of the same approx. A4 size. These leaflets were primarily for inclusion in Meccano Outfits, to persuade the Meccano Boy that he should set his sights a little higher than just the next braced girder, trunnion or the like.

The 1923 'Hornby Presentation Sets' leaflet, printed one side only on a single sheet 7 in wide and 13 in tall, was inserted in Meccano Products Catalogues, or was available on request. It was the only list to catalogue these sets and list their contents.

An insert was prepared for the 1925 Hornby Book of Trains, titled 'The Hornby Electric Train'. It was a 4-page leaflet, featuring a spectacular double-page spread of the Metropolitan Train Set, which had appeared too late for inclusion in the HBT. There was a smaller black and white insert in the 1927–28 Hornby Book of Trains, showing the No. 3 Trains, which also just missed inclusion in the HBT itself.

Small leaflets (designed as 'throw-aways' for insertion in Meccano Sets, or for the dealer's counter) were produced regularly. In 1925 a single sheet 'Run Your Own Railway' leaflet appeared, which listed Hornby sets; in 1927, 'Hornby Trains', a small leaflet showing the Riviera 'Blue Train' Set. In 1931 there was another such insert 'Hornby Trains, Longer Runs with Heavier Loads', which listed train sets. There was a similar single sheet 'Hornby Trains' printed in 1932, with a short price list of sets and rolling stock. In 1933 and 1934 larger single-sheet inserts were printed, which mentioned all the different ranges of Meccano Products, with the Hornby Trains just mentioned in one corner.

Apart from these leaflets, there were leaflets describing the Part Exchange Scheme, from 1930 to 1939; there were also single-sheet 'Countryside Section' descriptive leaflets, first printed in 1932. After the war the only such leaflets of any note were the splendid 'Percy The Small Engine', and 'Meet Percy in Person' leaflets both in full colour and in brown, black and white; then finally in 1969 a full-colour folder with 'The Play Train by Meccano'.

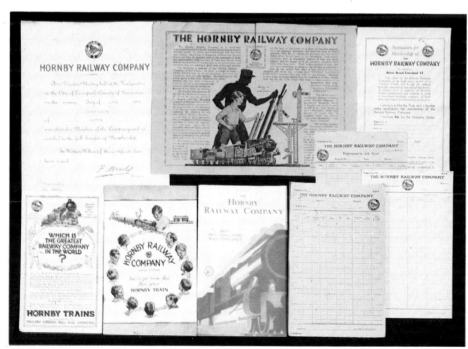

Hornby Railway Company publications.

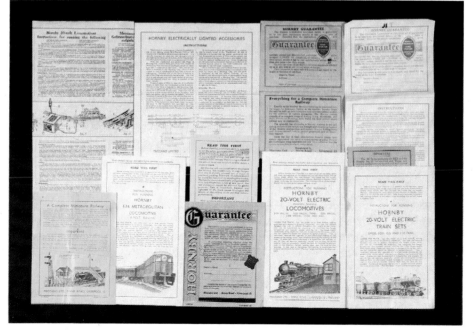

Guarantees and Instructions.

GUARANTEES AND INSTRUCTIONS

The instructions for the first Hornby Train sets were pasted inside the lid of the box, and covered both the operation of the trains and the assembly of the locomotive. All the parts were listed, together with the prices. The 1921 No. 1 and No. 2 Train Set instructions (each in three languages) naturally covered the coaches as well as the locos, tenders and wagons. For repairs, the owner was instructed to remove the motor and send it back to the factory – not the locomotive housing.

Separate instruction sheets were printed for the No. 1 and No. 2 Locomotives of 1921, mainly for the locomotives not sold in sets. But from 1922 the instructions for the No. 1, No. 2 and Zulu locos were printed on the back of the pale blue tear-off Guarantee forms stuck inside the lids of the boxes. By then the instructions were that the whole loco should be sent back if repairs were necessary.

From 1924 the train sets no longer had instructions inside the lid for constructional use, and just had the standard guarantee form with instructions on the reverse. The design of the guarantee form and instructions for clockwork locomotives remained the same until 1929; in that year the form was printed as a single-sided sheet, with the 'instructions' section pasted to the lid (often making them frustratingly difficult to read) and with the guarantee form as a separate tear-off section.

The electric train instructions were somewhat differently arranged, in that separate instruction leaflets were printed. Except for the smaller locos, these were single sheets printed both sides and folded to 4 pages. The guarantee forms were different from the clockwork versions, but were of a similar tear-off type, still pasted to the lid of the box. Often the stub section was printed with exhortations to buy, reminding the owner that he could obtain 'everything for the complete model railway'.

The clockwork train instructions from 1925 to 1932 were often augmented by a small sticker announcing as 'IMPORTANT' the minimum radii required for each of the Hornby Trains. In 1933 this developed into a small 'Read This First' printed slip which gave warnings on the need for proper lubrica-tion as well as the notes on radii. But by 1935 (earlier for the M series) a new type of instruction leaflet was designed. This was a separate sheet, no longer stuck to the lid of the box, and it combined the instruc-tions, the 'important' notes, 'read this first' and 'everything for the complete model railway' for good measure. Together with a separate sheet printed as the guarantee form, they replaced the messy and awkward pasted-in versions.

After 1935 the electric set guarantee forms were also printed as separate sheets, again no longer stuck to the box lids. The instruction leaflets for the electric locomotives continued in the same form throughout, but with different ink and paper col-ours. Apart from the M series, Metropolitan and EPM16 Locos, there were also separate versions for the automatic reversing locos, the smaller 20 volt locos, the small 6 volt engines, and the larger No. 2 Electric Tank and the No. 3E Locomotives. These different series of leaflets each appeared in many different prewar printings.

Apart from these instructions and guarantees for locomotives, each transformer and circuit breaker also had its own instruction leaflet. Electrically lit accessories also had printed instruction leaflets, but they were common to the whole range.

POST-WAR INSTRUCTIONS

After the war, the clockwork train instructions quickly became standardised. They were a small sheet printed on one side with 'Hints on Running Your Railway', and on the other with instructions on laying the track. There were two separate ver-sions, one for the MO Sets and Locos and another for M1 and larger Sets and Locos. Both appeared in many different printings, but the contents varied very little. Sets up to the end of 1946 appear to have used up stocks of prewar guarantee forms (rubber stamped with postwar dates), but soon specially printed general-purpose Meccano Guarantee slips were used. Instructions were also printed for E502/E602 Electric Trains. These were similar in content and style to the prewar editions, but suitably updated. At least two separate printings were made, one in 1948 and one in 1950.

The printers' codes on Hornby Train instruc-tions provide a certain interest, since they are virtu-ally the only guide to the numbers of Hornby loco-motives produced. Although the printers' codes on boxes are interesting, they were only printed after 1937, and in any case were seldom used on set boxes except in the early postwar years; many more locos were sold in train sets than were sold separately, particularly after the war. It is probable that over 1.5 million instruction leaflets were printed after the war for the M1 and larger trains; over 100,000 for each year of manufacture on average, and that not count-ing the MO sets. In the 1930s the No. 1 and larger trains appear to have been made at a rate of about 30,000 to 40,000 per year on average, while the MO and M1 trains together were about 70,000 per year on average; production stepped up markedly during the 1930s. The M3 and No. 0 trains averaged about 25,000 per year (all quantities approximate).

A production of 100,000 sets a year may not sound particularly impressive, unless one works out statistics for warehouse space required, total weight, total value, or the number of sets to be made and tested each minute of each working day. The collec-tor certainly finds no difficulty in obtaining any of the regular sets of the postwar period. In this book we have made no attempt to grade the rarity or otherwise of specific items, but can give an opinion on general guidelines. If an item was made in quanti-ties of less than 200, it could reasonably be described as 'rare'; in quantities of 200 to 2,000, the item could be 'hard to find'. If 2,000 to 20,000 it should be 'easy to find', and over 20,000 'common'. The natural presumption that the rarest items are those that take the longest to find can certainly be misleading! While on the subject of rarity, the number made is not the only factor to be considered; a higher proportion of some items survived. The more expensive trains, like the 'Princess Elizabeth', are easy to find in good condition, because they were more expensive and therefore generally better looked after. The cheaper trains were disposed of more often, for several reasons; they were cheaper, more prone to accidental damage because they generally had younger users, and they were more likely to be part-exchanged.

Hornby Train Packaging

Part of the joy of buying a Hornby Train was that they were packaged in distinctive boxes, all except for the few items supplied to the shopkeeper in trade packs of dozens or half-dozens, and the very few (like half and quarter rails prior to 1930) that were not boxed at all.

The 1921 Hornby Trucks were packed in plain buff-coloured cardboard boxes, like miniature shoe-boxes with shallow lids. The lids were sealed by a circle of gummed parcel tape around the middle of the box; inside the lid there was an individual guarantee slip (with a rubber-stamped code to identify the product, the month of packing, and other details) showing that the wagon had been tested. A white label printed with details of the contents was stuck on the end, and there was often a smaller sticker noting the railway company lettering.

From 1922 the boxes were similar, but more expensive; the card was covered on the outside with buff paper, and the lid was the full depth of the box. Furthermore the labels were printed in three languages, English French and Spanish. Sometimes if the details on printed stickers were not sufficient rubber stamps were used to add information; for example 'National Yellow' stamped on a box with the Petrol Tank Wagon label in 1923. The guarantee slips were no longer used from about June 1923 – except for Locomotives. The No. 1 and No. 2 Locomotives of the period often had more expensive boxes, with embossed 'Hornby Clockwork Train' lids on stout boxes, sometimes covered in leather-paper.

From late 1923 a flimsier style of box in thin cardboard (still covered in buff) was used for most rolling stock. There was no lid, the box being sealed at each end by tucking in the flaps and sticking a label across them. Parcel tape was no longer required. Only the heavier or larger items were packed in the boxes with lids.

In the 1924–25 season 'Hornby Series' pink labels were used instead of the old white labels; apart from the colour, the printed details were also different in that they now included a picture and were printed only in English.

The 1925 Hornby Trains came in the famous red boxes, printed with a dotted border and 'Hornby Series' lettering on three sides; at first the bottom was plain red but it was later printed in the same style. The end flaps were sealed by red labels instead of pink. Larger items were packed in specially printed versions of the red box.

After a couple of years, the flaps on the ends of the boxes were altered to eliminate the sticky labels, and the boxes were specially printed on red-covered card (now rather glossier than before) for each type of item. The basic form of the box then remained unchanged for 35 years; only the shapes of the inside

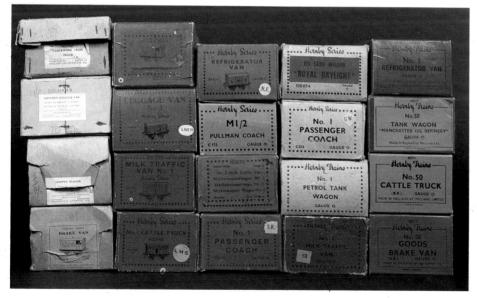

A small selection of Hornby boxes for locos and accessories.

A selection of Hornby rolling stock boxes, from 1921 to the 1960s.

1920–21 set box lid.

Metropolitan Train Set box lid.

No. 3 Train Set box, 1927. Best of the 'Flying Scotsman' pictures.

1921 to 1925 box lid. Another version showed goods wagons instead of coaches.

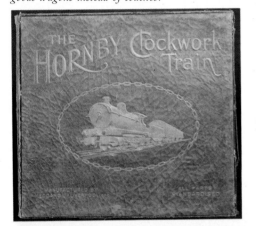

1925–26 standard set box picture.

'Caerphilly Castle' on the 1929 No. 2 Special Train Set box.

'Royal Scot' on the 1929 No. 1 Special Train Set box.

Zulu set box lid. 1922.

1926–31 standard picture.

HORNBY TRAIN

'Royal Scot' on a later No. 3 Train Set box.

A later 'Royal Scot' with deflectors.

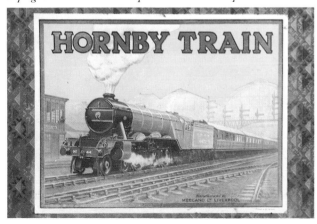

'Flying Scotsman' on a Complete Model Railway Set box.

'Flying Scotsman' in a revised version. Both versions were widely used on sets before and after the war.

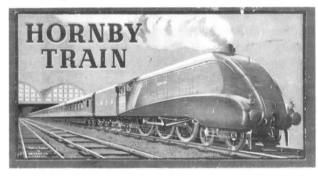

The 'Silver Jubilee' label.

Postwar 'Royal Scot' label, used for M sets.

flaps changed significantly.

In 1930 Hornby code numbers began to be printed on the boxes. Apart from changes in lettering and typography the next major change was the adoption from 1935 of a matt red finish instead of the glossy red. There was a short period when these boxes were printed only on one or both of the ends, but from 1936 printing was resumed on two sides as well as on both ends.

By 1938 the pictures which had almost invariably appeared on the boxes – and which were almost as invariably outdated or inaccurate – were left off.

In the 1930s electric locos, rails and accessories were usually packed in green boxes, similar in style to the red equivalents. The colour adopted for the M Series and a few miscellaneous items was blue, matt even in the early 1930s. Countryside sections came in creamy buff boxes, printed in green, and again matt. There was also an odd series of boxes in the 1938–39 period which were in glossy card with a crocodile skin pattern, in red green or blue as appropriate. They were used for locomotives and a few accessories.

The buff boxes characteristic of the wartime and early postwar period lasted from 1940 to 1948, when a return was made to the traditional style of red box; still with the dotted border, but lettered 'Hornby Trains' rather than 'Hornby Series'. Much of the card was of a lower grade than before the war.

The following year in 1949 the red boxes returned to the normal shiny card; the style of printing was changed, with the characteristic dotted borders replaced by thin lining. Usually one end of the box was printed in English and the other in four other languages. The style of the box was then unaltered to the mid 1950s, when a lighter orange-red was used. The No. 50 wagons were packed at first in green boxes, or in red boxes with green labels, but later were usually packed in the orange-red boxes.

In prewar days tissue paper was usually used to wrap the trains inside the boxes; the colour of the tissue varied. For example, in the mid 1920s it was a pale cream-yellow with a printed pattern of white bars, then from the late '20s blue with white stars. The late '30s saw the use of a plain pale yellow tissue paper.

STICKERS

The stickers which were put on the Hornby boxes for further identification of the contents in the shops (unfortunately not always accurately!) were mainly used for rolling stock, to distinguish LMS, NE, GW and SR; and for a few wagons in 1954–55, BR. Other types were used; colours of the 1933–38 signals were marked on the boxes with blue or green stickers, and similar coloured stickers were used for barrel wagons, the Swiss type locos, and the M series locos among others. Signals also had labels for 'Home' or 'Distant', and boxes for stations had stickers with the station name. Another commonly used sticker was 'Control', on boxes of the fitted items.

There are a few other less frequently encountered types; 'AC' stickers were used on old wagon boxes in 1931 to indicate the new Automatic Couplings. There was no special sticker for boxes printed with the AC (circa 1931–34) but actually containing stock with the link coupling; instead a rubber stamp was used to obliterate the printed AC!

A few loco boxes in 1939 had printed N9 stickers to denote 1939 manufacture. In the early 1950s a few items with the stop-gap 'Brunofix' finishes were identified by a green circle overprinted with the edges of two squares. Later, in the mid 1950s, there were 'LF' stickers thought to note that lead free finishes had been used for the contents, at a time when regulations concerning lead content were being reviewed.

There were also innumerable stickers and labels (usually for small batches) to change the use of a box, either because it was not worth making a special printing, or to use a surplus of boxes, or during the war simply because of shortage of supply. Thus there are 'Electric' stickers on red boxes actually used for electric items, and 'Non-electric' stickers on a few green boxes. The size of the labels varied; some covered the whole ends of the box.

BOX PRINTERS' CODES

Most Hornby boxes from late 1937 to 1941 (and again from 1945 to 1956) carried printers' codes, a useful source of information on the number and sizes of batches of Hornby Trains produced – although they need to be interpreted with caution, not just because of occasional errors in the codes themselves, but also because the number of boxes would not necessarily correspond to a single batch of toy train production. Furthermore the dates of printing and of packing could be months apart.

Codes were generally of the form:

MW–1234   5M   140

or BW1234   5M   1–40

These examples indicate a batch of 5000 boxes ('5M') printed in January 1940 ('140'). Quantities were sometimes printed directly, e.g. '5,000'. Fractions of a thousand were indicated by '.5M' for 500 boxes. The meanings of the BW and MW numbers are not known, but they are believed to refer to the box manufacturer and the order number. There were consistent differences in the 'punctuation' of the BW and MW numbers.

The position of the printing code on the boxes varied. In 1937 they were usually printed on the inside flaps, and in early 1938 they were printed on the outside ends of some boxes. From later in 1938 they were usually printed on the sides, until 1949 when they were once again printed on the ends.

Boxes having a printed label covering the whole end of the box often carried codes of the form:

535/1

which would indicate a quantity of 1000 printed in May 1935. (But probably for only 500 items, since the boxes usually had a label each end!) Only a very small proportion of Hornby items carried this type of code, although they can be of interest as they are often earlier dates than are generally found on boxes. Small packets of items such as Roof Clips and Poster Boards carried similar printers' codes.

THE HORNBY CODE-NUMBER SYSTEM

The printers' code numbers found on Hornby boxes should not be confused with the Hornby Code Number System also printed on the boxes. In 1930 Meccano Ltd introduced this code number system for the majority of their products, mainly for identification in export catalogues. The code numbers were printed on the boxes or packets of most items, as well as in these catalogues. Meccano Motors, Transformers and Circuit Breakers were numbered from M201 upwards, Train Sets from TS401, Locos from L452, Tenders from TE501, Coaches from C551, Open Wagons from W601, other Rolling Stock from RS651. Accessories (including Modelled Miniatures and Dinky Toys when they came out) were numbered from A801 upwards, and in a later series from A2001. Rails were not included in this code-number system, probably because they already carried the codes A1, A2, B1, EA1, etc. which had first appeared in the March–April 1922 Meccano Magazine.

The initial code number series was for the most part in alphabetic order, based on the range in 1930. Later additions were appended to the same series, in chronological order, except that 20 volt locos and sets from 1934 carried the code of the corresponding clockwork item with a 2xxx prefix. 6 volt locos and sets had a '6' suffix. Thus the codes for the M3 Tank were L475 (clockwork), L2475 (20 volt) and L4756 (6 volt).

There are numerous inexplicable gaps in the lists, particularly for the accessories between the A800 series and the A2000 series. The Modelled Miniature items seem to have been re-numbered when they became known as Dinky Toys, and the No. 1 Signals were also re-numbered when the design changed in 1934. Dublo items were coded with a similar system, with Dxxx numbers.

In some cases the code number was printed on a sticker, rather than on the box itself; and some items (such as signals, and No. 2 Special Tenders) appeared with different code numbers on the boxes and on the stickers!

The very first boxes and labels printed after the war, for example the M Station Set labels of 1945, used the prewar code number system. From 1946 to 1949, boxes usually had no code number; the first postwar code number system started in 1949, and numbers were allocated even for items which were very short-lived. This code number system used Rxxx and Axxx numbers for rolling stock and accessories; locos and sets were not coded. These codes were used on boxes dated up to the spring of 1951,

Packets used for some of the smaller items.

then replaced by the second postwar code series. These were 40xxx numbers for sets, 41xxx for locos, 42xxx for M series and tenders, 421xx for rolling stock, 423xx for accessories; later codes were added for the rails (430xx) and for sundries (439xx).

The No. 20, 30, and 50 series, and other additions to the range in the mid 1950s, were allocated numbers between the existing codes in the series. Originally this series was in strict alphabetical order, with numbers going up in fives (with some gaps, for items discontinued after a short run or not produced at all). The code numbers were printed in the 1956–57 UK Meccano Products catalogue, after which they appeared regularly in the lists as well as on the boxes.

PACKING DETAILS

The Hornby boxes also sometimes carried a rubber-stamped marking to indicate packing details, and these may be another useful dating guide, if they remain decipherable, which is by no means always the case. It must also be added that several rubber stamped markings seem to hold no clue as to date.

A typical example of the stamping of the guarantee slips already mentioned for early Hornby wagons would be '1730 – 1 23 95' as found on an early LNWR Brake Van box. The only useful information that can be deduced from this is the January 1923 date; some locomotive labels are dated even more clearly, as for example

'1750 96 2 Oct 1923' for a Zulu Tank Loco.

There are also rubber-stamped marks on the outside of many boxes, but no-one has yet cracked the code. The only identification marks that can be understood (if present) are the N9, N0, N1 and so on used between 1929 and 1940 to denote the year in which the item was packed. For example N9 would be 1929 or 1939, N0 would be 1930 or 1940, N1 1931 and so on. These can be an invaluable tool for dating items packed between 1929 and 1940, where the box

is known to be original – by no means always a safe assumption. Mistakes were also sometimes made in these codes. The purpose of the marks was stock control, and they were often used on items which had been recently revised in colour or style – for example N9 on the new 1929 No. 2 Buffer Stops, N0 on wagons with the new 1930 underframe, N3 on items with the new 1933 colours, and so on; except for the 1939 N9 stamp which was used almost universally.

The early postwar items often had a circular rubber stamped code, the meanings of which are not known.

Later postwar items were sometimes more clearly dated by a rubber stamped mark on an inside flap – e.g. 'TF 356' on a Goods Brake Van packed in March 1956. (This on a 1255 box, illustrating the gap between printing the boxes and using them.) This dating can be useful from 1956 when the printed codes no longer appeared; but as with all these marks, they should be taken as a guide only.

TRAIN SET BOXES

The earliest Hornby Train set cardboard boxes were covered on the outside only in red paper, and had a coloured label showing a Great Northern locomotive – the same picture as shown on the lid of the 'Raylo' set box. Many of the early Hornby set boxes were stamped with a 'Tested' date, before the packing slips were replaced by guarantee forms. A stamp reading 'TESTED 1220' (for example) would appear on a set tested in December 1920.

The revised and improved 1921-type boxes were covered in brown leather-paper on the outside, and lined inside with a glossy crimson paper. The lids were embossed with a most attractive picture of a No. 1 Goods Train Set (although with two wagons!) or of a No. 1 Passenger set, and the embossing was enhanced with gold. The 2711 sets also had the same pictures. Some of the earliest of these boxes had specially shaped cardboard supports for the loco, and slots to grip the tender buffers, but soon these methods were abandoned in favour of simple compartments. Ribbons threaded between the layers of the base secured the loco in transit – similar ribbons appeared in early loco boxes.

The difficulties of representing real Hornby trains on the lids of the boxes became apparent in 1924, when the clerestory coaches and the new loco liveries outdated the pictures. Nonetheless these embossed-lid boxes continued to be used until 1925 for the No. 1 and No. 2 Train Sets.

The Zulu Goods Sets of 1922 to 1924 were usually packed in boxes of the old 1920 Hornby Train type, which were probably left-overs resulting from the change-over. However like the Zulu Passenger sets they bore a superb and not totally inappropriate full-colour label showing an LNWR 4-6-0 locomotive departing from a terminus.

The 1925 boxes were in an entirely different style, made in corrugated cardboard with both lid and base formed from single pieces of card, folded and stapled at the corners. They were lined over the whole of the lid with a full-colour printed sheet, and the bottom of the box was covered on both sides with a plain orange-pink paper, lined at the edges with gummed tape of the same colour. There were usually no fixed partitions, the loco (and tender, if any) being wrapped up in a roll of corrugated cardboard lined on one side only in a matching colour. Other dividers were made from rigid corrugated card matching the rest of the box, not fixed in position but strategically placed to stop the contents moving around during transit. Unfortunately these partitions were soon lost or damaged, as few boys noted the correct way of re-packing in the excitement of using their sets.

The picture used on this style of box was usually of a red LMS '2711' loco with a pair of bogie coaches of indeterminate type; but the 1926-30 set boxes had a new version of the same picture in which two brown and cream No. 2 Pullman Cars were clearly seen. In each case the picture was printed in a circle on the top of the lid, the whole of the surrounding area being in a grey mottled pattern. The sight of this picture on the lids of the smaller set boxes must have raised the hopes of many a youthful recipient, only to be dashed on lifting the lid! The same picture was used for the No. 2 Tank and No. 2 Sets, and for the first Riviera Blue Train Sets, but the Metropolitan Train Sets had a special picture.

The No. 3 Pullman Train Set boxes of 1927 were in the same style, but used a striking picture of a

'Flying Scotsman' – not the Hornby version but an LNER loco. The box was in the same 'mottled edge' style. The 'Special' sets of 1929 required new printings; the picture for the No. 1 Special Sets was 'Royal Scot' emerging from a tunnel, somewhere by the sea. The picture covered the whole top of the box, and had a brown and black squared border. The No. 2 Special Set boxes used the largest picture to date, again covering the whole top of the box, which showed 'Caerphilly Castle' crossing a long trellised viaduct over an estuary.

From 1931 the corrugated cardboard boxes were supplanted by rigid boxes of the traditional type, with fixed compartments; indeed these had continued in use in the late 1920s for the M series trains. The 1926 M sets had used the first of what was to become the most common Hornby box label, which appeared in many different printings. It showed 'Flying Scotsman' passing the 'North Box' at King's Cross.

The rigid card boxes were covered in different coloured papers according to the contents. To generalise, most of the M series set boxes were red at first, then dark blue-purple from 1930. The M series often differed from the other sets in having the rolling stock set into cut-outs in a raised platform in the box; a style used frequently for larger sets after the war. Post-1931 No. 0 set boxes were often red; dark green with a yellow border was used for the No. 1 and No. 1 Special types, and brown for the No. 2 Special and No. 3. In the later 1930s yellow boxes with a green border replaced the dark green, and the new No. 2 Special and No. 3 sets with corridor coaches had orange-red boxes lined inside with pink. The late No. 2 Special Tank Passenger and Goods sets usually had dark blue boxes. Complete Model Railway sets used special mottled multi-colour papers, based on pink.

Most of the smaller sets had the 'Flying Scotsman' label. The early No. 2 Special and No. 3 sets frequently used the old 'Royal Scot' and 'Caerphilly Castle' pictures intended for the corrugated boxes – with the borders removed. Later they used a different picture of 'Royal Scot', showing it steaming out of a terminus looking remarkably like King's Cross! Like the Hornby Loco, the Royal Scot on the box lid was provided with smoke deflectors in revised later printings. The 'Flying Scotsman' pic-

ture was also updated, with a more modern tender amongst other alterations. Towards the end of the 1930s old stock 'Royal Scot' and 'Flying Scotsman' labels were sometimes used for the larger sets.

The Streamlined Train Sets had a marvellous picture of 'Silver Link' leaving King's Cross; the boxes were in two different styles, with blue or pink covering, both lined inside with pale blue.

A nice touch in many of the later Hornby Train set boxes was the 'Hornby Series' label placed as a seal across the rail compartment.

POSTWAR SET BOXES

After the war, the first set boxes were in the prewar style, with corners glued and reinforced. The labels on the lids of the earliest 101 and 201 set boxes used the earlier of the King's Cross 'Flying Scotsman' pictures, but printed with a very yellow sky. Except for the very earliest MO sets which used old stock 'British Express' labels, the M sets usually had another yellow-looking view of 'Royal Scot' (without smoke deflectors) storming through a cutting.

Early in 1947 new 'Flying Scotsman' labels were printed, going back to the prewar quality, and returning to the 'updated' picture. Some time later the 'Royal Scot' picture was also printed in more natural colours. From 1947 the card used was softer and less rigid, and both lid and base were folded in single pieces with the corners and edges secured by staples. Compartments were also created in the same style. The tops were in dark blue covered card, and the bases remained plain buff. Later an embossed 'alligator skin' finish was used for the buff bases, but from 1949 all the bases were commonly finished in the same dark blue as the lid. The compartments inside were usually lined pale blue, or cream for the M series.

The 1954 British Railways No. 20, No. 40 and No. 50 sets were still in the same blue boxes, but the new labels showed a 'Brittania' class loco. Blue boxes were used until circa 1956–57, when orange-red boxes replaced them. The final series of train set boxes in the 1960s had no labels as such, but were printed with a full-colour picture of a 'King' class locomotive. These later boxes also incorporated the instructions, printed inside the lid.

Rails

Four patterns of early clockwork rail; early 1920, later 1920, 1921 and 1922.

Early clockwork Points; 9 in. radius (1920), 9 in. radius (1922), 1 ft. radius and 2 ft. radius.

The first rails made by Meccano Ltd were flimsy affairs, each train set having four curved rails of about 9 in radius (one fitted with a brake trip) plus two straight rails to form the oval. Each rail had three sleepers, with the rails mounted on flat portions of the sleeper. The sleepers had a sloping section between the rails, and had no trademarks. These rails were sold in the Tinprinted Train Set and may possibly have been included in some early Hornby Train Sets.

Most Hornby Train Sets of 1920 and early 1921 had a different pattern of rail, still with four curved rails forming a circle of 9 in radius (one with a brake lever). These rails had plain sloping sleepers, with the flaps of tinplate which held the rail in place now formed in a different way, with the holes in the sleeper under the rails and not to the side. There were no locking pins; each rail had three sleepers. Although straight and curved half and quarter rails were advertised in the January 1921 MM (only), the left-hand and right-hand points which were also made around the same time were never advertised. They were made in the same pattern, with 9 in radius curved rails and without locking pins, but the curved section was not exactly equivalent to a curved half rail.

By May 1921, new rails had been designed; 1 ft radius for the No. 1 Train Set and 2 ft radius for the No. 2 Train Sets. Rails of 9 in radius were no longer made. These new rails were stronger and better-made than the flimsy early pattern. The rails were of larger section, and with bigger rail pins; the new rails could not be used with those of the previous season. The sleepers were similar in shape, but were fitted at one end with a locking wire and had a corresponding slot at the other. This was a satisfactory system for simple layouts, but useless where there were reverse curves. Straight rails had four sleepers, and curved rails five sleepers. The rails that became available in

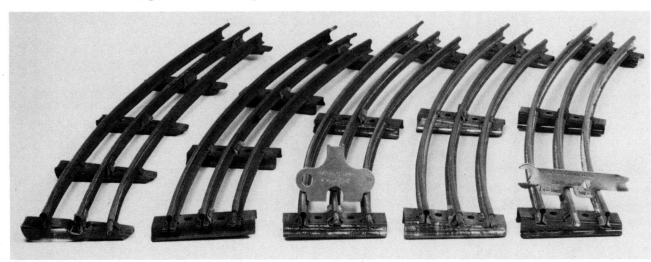

Straight Brake Rail BB1 (1925), and Brake and Reverse Rails BBR1 (circa 1929 and circa 1938).

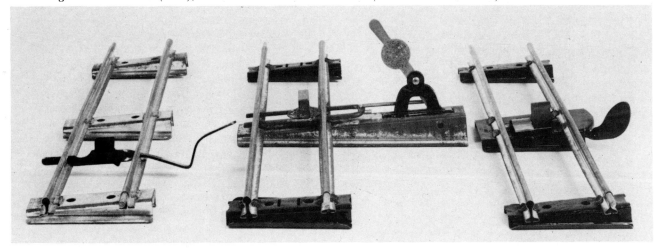

the new style during 1921 were full Straight Rails, 1 ft and 2 ft radius Curved Rails, 1 ft radius Brake Rails, 2 ft radius Brake and Reverse Rails, 1 ft and 2 ft radius left and right-handed points, and also Acute Angle and Right Angle Crossings.

There was yet another revision to the rails within a few months, towards the end of 1921, when it was decided to put the locking pins where holes had been, and holes where the locking pins had been, ensuring yet more problems with compatibility. In November 1921 (only) parts for centre-rail conversion were offered, which gave a raised centre rail.

In 1922, a very large number of new rails were offered, both in clockwork and electric; new clockwork rails included half and quarter rails in straight, 1 ft radius and 2 ft radius versions; 9 in radius curved rails and points, 1 ft and 2 ft radius Double Symmetrical Points, and 1 ft radius Parallel Points. The range of electric rails was the same as that of clockwork, except that Terminal Rails EAT1 and EAT2 replaced the Brake Rails, there were no 9 in radius electric rails, and it was not until the following year that 1 ft radius Electric Parallel Points were offered. The code-number system for Hornby rails was first used in the March-April 1922 MM.

From 1924, clockwork 2 ft radius Parallel Points PPR2/PPL2 were offered; these were the first points to be fitted with a new type of flat sleeper for the turnout ends, whereas ordinary sleepers had been used before. These sleepers soon came into general use for points and crossings only. Electric Parallel Points of 1 ft radius were no longer catalogued.

In 1925 double-track left-hand Crossovers of 1 ft and 2 ft radius were offered. Neither had a standardised spacing for the tracks. Electric Points EPL1/EPR1 and EDSL1/EDSR1 of 1 ft radius were no longer catalogued, but 2 ft radius Electric Parallel Points were added to the lists.

There is some debate as to when rails with the new-style sleepers for track clips came on the market, and the point has not yet been satisfactorily decided. The evidence of catalogues and literature points to dates of 1926 for both clockwork and electric rails; on the other hand, the virtual absence of the earlier rails with 'Hornby Series' trademarks, and the early-style boxes used for some rails with the later sleepers, suggest early 1925 as a more likely date. The first item shown in the new style was an electric Crossing, in the 1925 HBT. It is most likely that the changeover to the new style was well underway in 1925, and even early Metropolitan Train Sets (supplied in 1925) appear to have the modern sleepers for track clips. The new sleepers for electric rails were not cambered. One batch of 1925 EA2 rails had four sleepers, instead of the three that quickly became normal for full straight and curved rails. The clockwork rails of the period had sleepers for track clips, but cambered as on the early clockwork and early electric rails with locking wires. New pattern Crossings with Lionel-type solid bases began to appear; an odd feature of the early electric Crossings was that they lacked the central insulator fitted on later versions.

In 1926, CA1 and CR1 Crossings, intended for 1 ft radius layouts, became available in clockwork versions only. Rail Connecting Plates could be obtained separately, and the electric Terminal Rails were no longer listed following the introduction of Terminal Connecting Plates. Late in 1926, there was a change to black-enamelled sleepers for the ordinary rails; the sleepers for the electric rails had been changed not long before from flat to sloping sleepers, and these too were now painted.

The straight BBR1 Brake and Reverse Rail was introduced in 1927. This had the magnificent but highly vulnerable tall lever also used for switching the points, and had a very effective sliding block arrangement for the trip. In the same year 9 in radius rails were deleted from the lists.

In 1928, the old left-handed CO1 and CO2 Crossovers were replaced by the new COR2/COL2 crossovers. These were new designs, which, like the DS1 Double Track Straight Rails and the DC2 Double Track Curved Rails, were standardised at the spacing of the 2 ft radius Parallel Points. (1 ft radius Parallel Points were no longer offered.) An odd feature of the early Double Track Rails was that the sleepers were not painted black, like ordinary sleepers, and this seems to have been the case until 1930. Electric EDS1 and EDC2 Double Track Rails were catalogued from 1929. Because of the difficulty of arranging turnouts with these rails, 'Reversed Switch' Points became available to special order. These had the lever on the turnout side, and usually lacked the embossed lettering on the switch sleeper.

The tall levers of Hornby Points had always been a weak feature of the design, making the points easy to break and difficult to pack. The problem was tackled in 1930 by the adoption of new shorter point levers, fitted with lead balance weights, which were cunningly arranged to operate effectively and yet be compact. Although not perfect, the new design certainly cut the breakage rate substantially. Another change to the points at about that time was that the switch rails began to be pivoted on larger eyelets.

New introductions in 1930 included Centre Rail Conversion Accessories, and also new MO Rails; 9 in radius Curved Rails M9, BM Straight Rails, MR9/ML9 Points and MB9 Curved Brake Rails. All had the new M sleepers. The following year, ECOL2/ECOR2 Electric Crossover Points were offered.

There was a new design for the BBR1 Brake and Reverse Rail in 1931, on a patent system with a cam operating two diecast pivoted flaps. It was as expensive to make as the previous type, so the new rail was offered (the April 1932 MM was the first mention) at the unaltered price of 1s 6d.

The 1934 catalogues offered M series electric engines, and as a result new 1 ft Radius EPL1/EPR1 Points, and EDSL1/EDSR1 Double Symmetrical Points were offered, for the first time since 1925. Switch Rails EMC6 and EMC20 were also introduced. In 1935 came the less than popular SPSR2/SPSL2 Points on Solid Base. These were followed the following year by the ESPSR2/ESPSL2 Electric Points on Solid Base, which became popular only because the EPR2/EPL2 Points were no longer sold! The Centre Rail Conversion Accessories were no longer listed from 1936, and the sleepers of the ordinary rails ceased to be slotted to allow the conversion.

A great advance in Hornby Rails came with the announcement in 1937 of the Solid Steel Rails. These rails were of 3 ft radius, and there were ten curves to a circle. This number had been chosen mainly because, by happy coincidence, Solid Steel Points made with a curve equivalent to a half curved rail gave the right spacing for standard Hornby double track when used together to form a crossover. Thus the standard Hornby Accessories (such as the No. 2 Level Crossing) could be used, if connected by diecast Adapting Pieces, obtainable at 1s for six. The

Centre rail conversion accessories; centre rails, clips and insulators, available from 1930 to 1935.

Electric points Fitted for Hornby Control. The one at the back has a reversed switch.

Rail Connecting Plates.

Solid Steel Rails were EB3, EB3½ and EB3¼ Straight Rails, EA3 and EA3½ Curved Rails, and EPL3/EPR3 Points. A galvanised finish was used on the rails to protect them from rust as far as possible. Fishplates were supplied with the rails, but were also available separately.

In later production, there were some changes in the Solid Steel Rails, most noticeably in the smaller profile of the rails. The points appeared with a fascinating variety of trademark and detail differences; some even appeared unpainted, whereas most had black bases.

Point Connecting Clips PCC were a belated but welcome addition to the lists in 1938. There had previously been no means of clipping the switch end of the points to other rails, since the switch sleepers did not take track clips. The Point Connecting Clip was a simple piece of wire bent to do this job; the packets were printed with instructions for fitting the clip.

Most of the Hornby rails were still listed in 1941, except the Switch Rails, which were not available from 1939.

Postwar rails were more limited in range than the prewar series, but were carefully re-thought and re-designed to make them a rather better product. The sleepers were changed to level instead of sloping, which was a great improvement. According to a letter sent by Meccano Ltd to an enquirer, 'tapered sleepers were necessary when engines were liable to run too fast; by governing down the mechanisms we could introduce the parallel sleepers'. The rails were distinguishable from the prewar type by a vertical ribbing on the sides; shorter rail pins were used. There was a useful change to the levers of the Brake and the Brake and Reverse Rails; the ends of these levers were made smaller, and curled over to form a handle; this made them more manageable in use, and easier to pack in the boxes.

The Points PL2/PR2 were substantially re-designed to include a solid centre sleeper. This cured a long-standing problem of weakness at the 'V' joint of the diverging tracks.

Electric Hornby Trains of the 1948–51 period had electric rails with level sleepers. The Points (according to the production drawings) were of the prewar type with solid base.

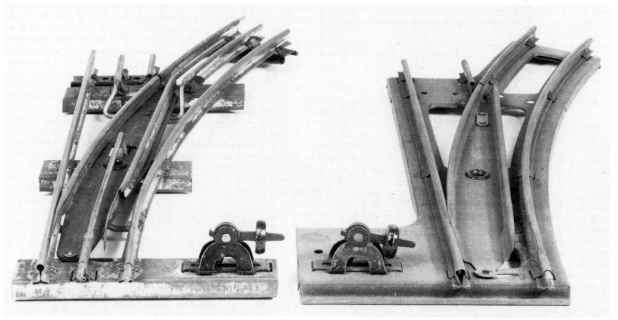

The early postwar MO sets were the only ones which had curved brake rails; in 1949 the MO Brake Rail was redesigned as a straight rail. The postwar BB1 Brake Rail and the BBR2 Brake and Reverse Rail were both straight rails, with one and two levers respectively. The BBR2 Brake and Reverse Rail was re-named BBR in 1951; there was also a change in design, with only a single lever, which slid from side to side, and was held in any position (brake, reverse or normal) by a spring clip. The new BBR Rail replaced the BBR2 and (except in certain sets) the BB1.

The MO Rails were available only up to 1954; the No. 20 Train Sets had 1 ft radius rails. Most of the other postwar rails remained in stock up to 1968 or 1969.

Postwar Brake Rail BB1 (1947), also Brake and Reverse Rails BBR2 (1948) and BBR (1951).

Appendices

APPENDIX I

CATALOGUE DATES
FOR AVAILABILITY OF HORNBY TRAINS

Comparing Hornby Trains with catalogue pictures is not a good way to estimate the date of production; for reasons already discussed the printing blocks were often several years out of date. But catalogues do give a reasonable guide to the dates when the items in question were first sold, and when they were withdrawn from sale. This list gives the date of the first reference to each item in the Hornby literature, the source, and an end date. The end date given is a month before the printing date for a catalogue which does not list the item. In each case dates are taken from the printers' code, if any.

As a general rule items were planned in time to be shown at the trade fairs around February, then included in the catalogues printed during the summer, then made available to the customer from the autumn – certainly in good time for Christmas. The date when the goods went on sale in the shops was often three or four months after the first printed reference – although if production was well advanced some items were released in advance of the start of the new season. As a rule the Meccano

Magazine only advertised items that were already available in the shops; indeed the first MM advertisements were frequently months after the items went on sale, presumably so as not to over-stimulate demand before good stocks were in hand. (Please note that dates given as May 27 (MP) could be three months too early; there may be a misprint in the code 527/300, which could perhaps have been meant to read 827/300.)

These dates apply to the UK market, and export items have not been listed; export literature was occasionally printed with details of new items a month or two in advance of the dates given, presumably to allow for the longer delays in transit.

The individual components of train sets have generally been given the same introduction dates and references as the train sets, whether the reference lists the items as available for separate sale or not. A general end date of December 1941 has been assumed for items still listed in the November 1941 price list. A few items listed in November 1941 had been omitted from one or two of the earlier wartime price lists.

Major changes in the 'official' description of items have also been listed. Asterisks mark each new introduction, and any following lines without asterisks denote changes of description only.

SOURCES:

BHT	Book of Hornby Trains and Meccano Products
BI	By inference
CL	Hornby Control System Leaflet
GS	Guarantee Slip
HBT	Hornby Book of Trains
HL	Hornby Leaflet
HT	Hornby Train catalogue, folder or illustrated price list
HTG	'How to Get More Fun From Your Hornby Train'
HTP	'How to Plan Your Hornby Railway'
HTPE	'How to Plan Your Hornby Electric Railway'
JC	'Jackie Coogan Visits a Meccano Factory'
MI	Meccano instruction manual
MM	Meccano Magazine
MP	Meccano Products catalogue, folder or illustrated price list
PL	Price list
RF	Rail formations booklet
SO	Special order item

CLOCKWORK TRAIN SETS

★ MO Goods Train Set:	Mar 30 (MI) to Dec 41
★ MO Mixed Goods Train Set:	Jul 36 (MP) to Dec 41
★ M8 Complete Model Railway:	Aug 34 (MP) to Dec 41
★ M9 Complete Model Railway:	Aug 34 (MP) to Dec 41
★ M10 Complete Model Railway:	Jun 33 (MP) to Dec 41
★ MO Passenger Train Set:	Mar 30 (MI) to Dec 41
★ MO Passenger Train Set:	Mar 29 (MI) to Feb 30
★ Series M No. 1 Passenger Train Set:	Jun 26 (MI) to Feb 30
★ M1 Passenger Train Set:	Mar 30 (MI) to Dec 41
★ Series M No. 2 Passenger Train Set:	Jun 26 (MI) to Feb 30
★ M2 Passenger Train Set:	Mar 30 (MI) to Dec 41
★ M Goods Train Set:	Mar 29 (MI) to Feb 30
★ M1 Goods Train Set:	Mar 30 (MI) to Dec 41
★ Tinprinted Train:	Jun 20 (HL) to Sep 23
George V Train:	Oct 23 (MP) to Jul 25
No. 00 Train:	Aug 25 (MP) to May 26
★ Series M No. 3 Goods Train Set:	Jun 26 (MI) to Feb 29
★ No. 0 'Silver Jubilee' Train Set:	Jul 36 (MP) to Apr 41
★ No. 0 Streamlined Train Set:	Jul 37 (MP) to Jul 40
★ M11 Complete Model Railway:	Aug 34 (MP) to Dec 41
★ M3 Tank Goods Train Set:	Jul 31 (MP) to Dec 41
★ M3 Tank Passenger Train Set:	Jun 35 (MP) to Dec 41
★ Zulu Goods Train Set:	May 22 (MM) to Jun 25
No. 0 Goods Train Set:	Jul 25 (MI) to Jun 39

★ Zulu Passenger Train Set:	May 22 (MM) to Jun 25
No. 0 Passenger Train Set:	Jul 25 (MI) to Sep 39
★ No. 1 Tank Goods Train Set:	Jul 25 (MI) to Dec 41
★ Hornby Train:	Jun 20 (HL) to Apr 21
No. 1 Hornby Train Set:	May 21 (MM) to Aug 21
No. 1 Hornby Goods Train Set:	Sep 21 (HL) to Dec 41
★ No. 1 Hornby Passenger Train Set:	Sep 21 (HL) to Dec 41
★ No. 1 Special Tank Goods Train Set:	Jun 35 (MP) to Dec 41
★ No. 1 Special Goods Train Set:	Mar 29 (MI) to May 35
★ No. 1 Special Passenger Train Set:	Mar 29 (MI) to Dec 41
★ No. 2 Tank Goods Train Set:	Jul 25 (MI) to Feb 29
★ No. 2 Tank Passenger Train Set:	Jul 25 (MI) to Feb 29
★ No. 2 Hornby Goods Train Set:	Sep 21 (HL) to Feb 29
★ No. 2 Hornby Pullman Train Set:	Sep 21 (HL) to Feb 29
★ No. 2 Special Goods Train Set:	Mar 29 (MI) to Feb 30
★ No. 2 Mixed Goods Train Set:	Mar 29 (MI) to Dec 41
★ No. 2 Special Tank Passenger Train Set:	Jun 35 (MP) to Dec 41
★ No. 2 Special Pullman Train Set:	Mar 29 (MI) to Jun 37
★ No. 2 Special Passenger Train Set:	Jul 37 (MP) to Dec 41
★ No. 3C Pullman Train Set, Control:	May 27 (MP) to Feb 29
★ No. 3C Pullman Train Set:	Mar 29 (MI) to Dec 41
★ No. 3C Passenger Train Set:	Jul 37 (MP) to Dec 41
★ No. 2 Riviera 'Blue Train' Set, Control:	Jun 26 (MI) to Apr 27
No. 3C Riviera 'Blue Train', Control:	May 27 (MP) to Feb 29
★ No. 3C Riviera 'Blue Train':	Mar 29 (MI) to Dec 41
★ Metropolitan Train Set No. 3, Control:	Jun 26 (MI) to Apr 27
Metropolitan Train Set C, Control:	May 27 (MP) to Feb 29
★ Metropolitan Train Set C (or 3C):	Mar 29 (MI) to May 39
★ Presentation Set A:	1923 (HL) to 1924
★ Presentation Set B:	1923 (HL) to 1924

CLOCKWORK LOCOMOTIVES

★ MO Locomotive:	Mar 30 (MI) to Dec 41
★ Series M No. 1 or No. 2 Locomotive:	Jun 26 (MI) to Jun 29
M Locomotive:	Jul 29 (HT) to Jul 30
M2930 Locomotive and Tender:	Aug 30 (HBT) to Jul 32
★ M1/2 Locomotive:	Mar 30 (MI) to Dec 41
★ M3 Tank Locomotive:	Jul 31 (MP) to Dec 41
★ Engine for Tinprinted Train Set:	Jun 20 (HL) to Sep 23
George V Locomotive:	Oct 23 (MP) to Jul 25
No. 00 Locomotive and Tender:	Aug 25 (MP) to May 26
Series M No. 3 Locomotive:	Jun 26 (MI) to Mar 27
No. M3 Locomotive:	Apr 27 (MI) to Jun 29
★ No. 0 'Silver Link' Locomotive and Tender:	Jul 36 (MP) to Apr 41
★ No. 0 Streamlined Locomotive and Tender:	Jul 37 (MP) to Jul 40
★ Zulu Locomotive:	May 22 (MM) to Jun 25
No. 0 Locomotive:	Jul 25 (MI) to Dec 41
★ Zulu Tank Locomotive:	May 22 (MM) to Apr 24
No. 1 Tank Locomotive:	May 24 (MM) to Dec 41

★ Hornby Locomotive:	Jun 20 (HL) to Aug 21
★ No. 1 Locomotive:	Sep 21 (HL) to Dec 41
★ No. 1 Special Tank Locomotive:	Mar 29 (MI) to Dec 41
★ No. 1 Special Locomotive:	Mar 29 (MI) to Dec 41
★ Hornby Tank Locomotive:	Oct 23 (MP) to Apr 24
No. 2 Tank Locomotive:	May 24 (MM) to Feb 29
★ No. 2 Locomotive:	Sep 21 (HL) to Feb 29
★ No. 2 Special Tank Locomotive:	Mar 29 (MI) to Dec 41
★ No. 2 Special Locomotive:	Mar 29 (MI) to Dec 41
★ No. 2 Riviera Blue Train Locomotive, Control:	Jun 26 (MI) to Apr 27
No. 3C Riviera Blue Train Locomotive, Control:	May 27 (MP) to Feb 29
★ No. 3C Riviera Blue Train Locomotive:	Mar 29 (MI) to Dec 41
★ No. 3C Locomotive, Control:	May 27 (MP) to Feb 29
★ No. 3C Locomotive:	Mar 29 (MI) to Dec 41
★ No. 4C 'Eton' Locomotive:	Jul 37 (MP) to Dec 41
★ LEC1 Locomotive:	Aug 32 (HT) to Jun 36
★ Metropolitan Locomotive No. 3, Control:	Jun 26 (MI) to Apr 27
Metropolitan Locomotive C, Control:	May 27 (MP) to Feb 29
★ Metropolitan Locomotive C:	Mar 29 (HT) to May 39

HORNBY CONTROL SYSTEM TRAIN SETS

★ No. 1 Tank Goods Train Set, Control:	Apr 27 (MM) to Feb 29
★ No. 1 Goods Train Set, Control:	Apr 27 (MM) to Feb 29
★ No. 1 Passenger Train Set, Control:	May 28 (MI) to Feb 29
★ No. 2 Tank Goods Train Set, Control:	Apr 27 (MM) to Feb 29
★ No. 2 Tank Passenger Train Set, Control:	Jun 26 (MI) to Feb 29
★ No. 2 Goods Train Set, Control:	Apr 27 (MM) to Feb 29
★ No. 2 Hornby Pullman Train Set, Control:	Jun 26 (MI) to Feb 29
★ No. 3C Pullman Train Set, Control:	May 27 (MP) to Feb 29
★ No. 2 Riviera 'Blue Train' Set, Control:	Jun 26 (MI) to Apr 27
No. 3C Riviera 'Blue Train', Control:	May 27 (MP) to Feb 29
★ Metropolitan Train Set No. 3, Control:	Jun 26 (MI) to Apr 27
Metropolitan Train Set C, Control:	May 27 (MP) to Feb 29

HORNBY CONTROL SYSTEM LOCOMOTIVES

★ No. 1 Tank Locomotive, Control:	Apr 27 (MM) to Feb 29
★ No. 1 Locomotive, Control:	Apr 27 (MM) to Feb 29
★ No. 2 Tank Locomotive, Control:	Jun 26 (MI) to Feb 29
★ No. 2 Locomotive, Control:	Jun 26 (MI) to Feb 29
★ No. 3C Riviera Blue Train Locomotive, Control:	May 27 (MP) to Feb 29
★ No. 3C Locomotive, Control:	May 27 (MP) to Feb 29
★ Metropolitan Locomotive No. 3, Control:	Jun 26 (MI) to Apr 27
Metropolitan Locomotive C, Control:	May 27 (MP) to Feb 29

HIGH VOLTAGE TRAIN SETS

★ Hornby Electric Train Set:	Jul 25 (MI) to May 26
Metropolitan Train Set, HV:	Apr 27 (MI) to Feb 29

HIGH VOLTAGE LOCOMOTIVES

★ Hornby Electric Locomotive:	Jul 25 (MI) to May 26
Metropolitan Locomotive, HV:	Apr 27 (MI) to Feb 29

20 VOLT TRAIN SETS

★ EM120 Passenger Train Set:	Aug 34 (MP) to May 38
★ EM220 Passenger Train Set:	Aug 34 (MP) to May 35
★ EM120 Goods Train Set:	Aug 34 (MP) to May 38
★ EM320 Tank Goods Train Set:	Aug 34 (MP) to Dec 41
★ EO20 Goods Train Set:	Aug 34 (MP) to May 35
★ EO20 Passenger Train Set:	Aug 34 (MP) to Sep 39
★ LST1/20 Tank Goods Train Set:	Jun 33 (MP) to Jul 34
E120 Tank Goods Train Set:	Aug 34 (MP) to Dec 41
★ E120 Hornby Goods Train Set:	Aug 34 (MP) to Dec 41
★ E120 Passenger Train Set:	Aug 34 (MP) to May 35
★ E120 Special Tank Goods Train Set:	Jun 35 (MP) to Dec 41
★ E120 Special Goods Train Set:	Aug 34 (MP) to May 35
★ E120 Special Passenger Train Set:	Aug 34 (MP) to Dec 41
★ LST2/20 Mixed Goods Train Set:	Jun 33 (MP) to Jul 34
E220 Mixed Goods Train Set:	Aug 34 (MP) to Dec 41
★ E220 Special Tank Passenger Train Set:	Jun 35 (MP) to Dec 41
★ E220 Special Pullman Train Set:	Aug 34 (MP) to Jun 37
★ E220 Special Passenger Train Set:	Jul 37 (MP) to Dec 41
★ E320 Pullman Train Set:	Aug 34 (MP) to Dec 41
(From July 1937 only as SR Golden Arrow)	
★ E320 Passenger Train Set:	Jul 37 (MP) to Dec 41
★ E320 Riviera 'Blue Train' Set:	Aug 34 (MP) to Sep 40
★ E320 Metropolitan Train Set:	Jun 38 (MP) to May 39

20 VOLT LOCOMOTIVES

★ EM120 Locomotive:	Aug 34 (MP) to May 38
★ LSTM3/20 Tank Locomotive:	Aug 32 (HT) to Jul 34
EM320 Tank Locomotive:	Aug 34 (MP) to Dec 41
★ EO20 Locomotive:	Aug 34 (MP) to Dec 41
★ LST1/20 Tank Locomotive:	Aug 32 (HT) to Jul 34
E120 Tank Locomotive:	Aug 34 (MP) to Dec 41
★ E120 Locomotive:	Aug 34 (MP) to Dec 41
★ E120 Special Tank Locomotive:	Aug 34 (MP) to Dec 41
★ E120 Special Locomotive:	Aug 34 (MP) to Dec 41
★ LST2/20 Tank Locomotive:	Jun 33 (MP) to Aug 34
★ E220 Special Tank Locomotive, auto. rev.:	Aug 34 (MP) to Dec 41
★ E220 Special Locomotive, 20 volt auto. rev.:	Aug 34 (MP) to Dec 41
★ E3/20 Riviera 'Blue Train' Locomotive:	Jun 33 (MP) to Aug 34
E320 Riviera 'Blue Train' Loco, auto. rev.:	Aug 34 (MP) to Sep 40
★ E3/20 Locomotive:	Jun 33 (MP) to Aug 34
★ E320 Locomotive, automatic reverse:	Aug 34 (MP) to Dec 41
★ E420 'Eton' Locomotive:	Jul 37 (MP) to Dec 41
★ LE1/20 Locomotive:	Aug 32 (HT) to Jul 34
LE120 Locomotive:	Aug 34 (MP) to Jun 36
★ LE2/20 Locomotive:	Aug 32 (HT) to Aug 34
LE220 Locomotive, auto. rev.:	Aug 34 (MP) to Jun 36
★ E320 Metropolitan Locomotive, auto. rev.:	Jun 38 (MP) to May 39
★ 'Princess Elizabeth' Locomotive:	May 37 (MM) to Sep 40

LOW VOLTAGE TRAIN SETS

★ EM16 Passenger Train Set, 6 volt:	Aug 34 (MP) to May 35
★ EM26 Passenger Train Set, 6 volt:	Aug 34 (MP) to May 35
★ EM16 Goods Train Set, 6 volt:	Aug 34 (MP) to May 38
★ EM36 Tank Goods Train Set, 6 volt:	Aug 34 (MP) to Dec 41
★ EO6 Goods Train Set, 6 volt:	Aug 34 (MP) to May 35
★ EO6 Passenger Train Set, 6 volt:	Aug 34 (MP) to May 35
★ E16 Tank Goods Train Set, 6 volt:	Aug 34 (MP) to Jun 36
★ E16 Hornby Goods Train Set, 6 volt:	Aug 34 (MP) to May 35
★ E16 Passenger Train Set, 6 volt:	Aug 34 (MP) to May 35
★ E26 Mixed Goods Train Set, 6 volt:	Aug 34 (MP) to May 35
★ No. 3E Pullman Train Set, 4 volt:	May 27 (MP) to Feb 29
★ No. 3E Pullman Train Set, 6 volt:	Mar 29 (MI) to Jul 34
E36 Pullman Train Set, 6 volt:	Aug 34 (MP) to Jun 36
★ No. 1 Riviera 'Blue Train' Set, 4 volt:	Jun 26 (MI) to Apr 27
★ No. 3E Riviera 'Blue Train' Set, 4 volt:	May 27 (MP) to Feb 29
★ No. 3E Riviera 'Blue Train' Set, 6 volt:	Mar 29 (MI) to Jul 34
E36 Riviera 'Blue Train' Set, 6 volt:	Aug 34 (MP) to Jun 36
★ Metropolitan Train Set No. 2, LV (4 volt):	Jun 26 (MI) to Apr 27
Metropolitan Train Set LV (4 volt):	May 27 (MP) to Feb 29
★ Metropolitan Train Set LV (6 volt):	Mar 29 (MI) to Jul 34
E36 Metropolitan Train Set, 6 volt:	Aug 34 (MP) to May 39

LOW VOLTAGE LOCOMOTIVES

★ EM16 Locomotive, 6 volt:	Aug 34 (MP) to May 38
★ EM36 Tank Locomotive, 6 volt:	Aug 34 (MP) to Dec 41
★ EO6 Locomotive, 6 volt:	Aug 34 (MP) to May 35
★ No. 1 Tank Locomotive, 6 volt DC:	Jul 29 (HT) to Jul 34
★ E16 Tank Locomotive, 6 volt:	Aug 34 (MP) to Jun 36
★ E16 Locomotive, 6 volt:	Aug 34 (MP) to May 35
★ EPM16 Special Tank Locomotive, 6 volt DC:	Aug 34 (MP) to May 39
★ No. 2 Tank Locomotive, 6 volt:	Aug 30 (MP) to Jul 34
★ E26 Special Tank Locomotive, 6 volt:	Aug 34 (MP) to Dec 41
★ No. 1 Riviera Blue Train Locomotive, 4 volt:	Jun 26 (MI) to Apr 27
No. 3E Riviera Blue Train Locomotive, 4 volt:	May 27 (MP) to Feb 29
★ No. 3E Riviera Blue Train Locomotive, 6 volt:	Mar 29 (MI) to Jul 34
E36 Riviera 'Blue Train' Locomotive, 6 volt:	Aug 34 (MP) to Jun 36
★ No. 3E Locomotive, 4 volt:	May 27 (MP) to Feb 29
★ No. 3E Locomotive, 6 volt:	Mar 29 (MI) to Jul 34
E36 Locomotive, 6 volt:	Aug 34 (MP) to Jun 36
★ Metropolitan Locomotive No. 2, 4 volt:	Jun 26 (MI) to Apr 27
Metropolitan Locomotive LV, 4 volt:	May 27 (MP) to Feb 29
★ Metropolitan Locomotive LV, 6 volt:	Mar 29 (MI) to Jul 34
E36 Metropolitan Locomotive, 6 volt:	Aug 34 (MP) to May 39

COACHES

★ Corridor Coach No. 2, 1st/3rd:	Jul 37 (MP) to Dec 41
★ Corridor Coach No. 2, Brake/Composite:	Jul 37 (MP) to Dec 41
★ Metropolitan Coach:	Jul 25 (MI) to May 26

Metropolitan Coach HV:	Apr 27 (MI) to Jun 29
★ Metropolitan Coach No. 2:	Jun 26 (MI) to Apr 27
Metropolitan Coach LV:	May 27 (MP) to Jul 34
Metropolitan Coach E:	Aug 34 (MP) to May 39
★ Metropolitan Coach No. 3:	Jun 26 (MI) to Apr 27
Metropolitan Coach C:	May 27 (MP) to May 39
★ Mitropa Coach No. 0:	Aug 31 (HT) to Dec 41
★ Mitropa Coach No. 3:	Oct 31 (MM) to Dec 41
★ Zulu Passenger Coach:	May 22 (MM) to Jun 25
★ Passenger Coach No. 1:	Sep 21 (HL) to Dec 41
★ Guard's Van:	Jul 24 (MI) to Dec 41
★ Passenger Coach No. 2, 1st/3rd:	Jun 35 (MP) to Dec 41
★ Passenger Coach No. 2, Brake/3rd:	Jun 35 (MP) to Dec 41
★ MO Pullman Coach:	Mar 30 (MI) to Dec 41
★ M Pullman Coach:	Jun 26 (MI) to Feb 30
M1 Pullman Coach:	Mar 30 (MI) to Dec 41
★ Pullman Coach No. 0:	Aug 31 (HT) to Dec 41
★ Pullman Car, American Type:	Aug 30 (MP) to Dec 41
★ Pullman Coach No. 1:	Aug 28 (HBT) to Dec 41
★ Pullman Coach, No. 1 Composite:	Aug 28 (HBT) to Dec 41
★ Pullman Car:	Sep 21 (HL) to Jul 28
★ Dining Car:	Sep 21 (HL) to 1924
★ Pullman Coach for No. 3 trains:	May 27 (MP) to Jul 28
Pullman Coach No. 2:	Aug 30 (MP) to Dec 41
★ Pullman Coach No. 2–3:	Aug 28 (HBT) to Feb 30
Pullman Coach No. 2 Special:	Mar 30 (MM) to Dec 41
★ Pullman Coach No. 2–3, Composite:	Aug 28 (HBT) to Feb 30
Pullman Coach No. 2 Special, Composite:	Mar 30 (MM) to Dec 41
★ Riviera 'Blue Train' Coach:	Jun 26 (MI) to Dec 41
★ Saloon Coach:	Aug 30 (MM) to Dec 41
★ No. 0 'Silver Jubilee' Saloon Coach:	Jul 36 (MP) to Dec 41
★ No. 0 Streamlined Coach:	Jul 37 (MP) to Jul 40
★ Tinprinted Train Carriage:	Jun 20 (HL) to Sep 23
George V Train Carriage:	Oct 23 (MP) to Aug 25
No. 00 Train Carriage:	Sep 25 (PL) to May 26

WAGONS

★ Banana Van No. 0:	Jun 35 (MP) to Oct 41
★ Banana Van, Fyffes:	Jul 31 (MP) to May 35
Banana Van No. 1, Fyffes:	Jun 35 (MP) to Dec 41
★ Barrel Wagon:	Aug 31 (HT) to Dec 41
★ Biscuit Van, Carr's:	Jul 24 (MI) to Dec 41
★ Biscuit Van, Crawford's:	Jul 24 (MI) to Dec 41
★ Biscuit Van, Jacob's:	Jul 24 (MI) to Dec 41
★ Bitumen Tank Wagon, Colas:	Jul 29 (HT) to Oct 41
★ Box Car, American Type:	Aug 30 (MP) to Dec 41
★ Brake Van:	May 22 (MM) to Dec 41
★ Brake Van, French Type:	May 27 (MP) to Jun 36
★ Breakdown Van and Crane:	May 23 (RF) to Dec 41

★ Caboose:	Aug 30 (MP) to Dec 41
★ Cadbury's Chocolate Van:	Apr 32 (MM) to Dec 41
★ Cattle Truck No. 1:	Oct 23 (MP) to Dec 41
★ Cattle Truck No. 2:	Oct 23 (MP) to Dec 41
★ Cement Wagon:	May 22 (MM) to Dec 41
★ Coal Wagon:	Aug 31 (HT) to Dec 41
★ Colman's Mustard Van:	Sep 23 (MM) to Sep 24
★ Covered Wagon (French Type):	Jul 29 (HT) to Oct 41
★ Crane Truck:	May 23 (RF) to May 35
Crane Truck No. 1:	Jun 35 (MP) to Dec 41
★ Fibre Wagon:	Aug 31 (HT) to Dec 41
★ Fish Van:	Aug 31 (HT) to Dec 41
★ Flat Truck:	Aug 34 (MP) to Dec 41
★ Flat Truck with Container:	Jul 36 (MP) to Dec 41
★ Flat Truck with Cable Drum:	Aug 34 (MP) to Dec 41
★ Gas Cylinder Wagon:	May 23 (RF) to Dec 41
★ Gunpowder Van:	May 22 (MM) to Dec 41
★ High Capacity Wagon No. 2:	Jul 36 (MP) to Dec 41
★ Hopper Wagon:	Oct 23 (MP) to Dec 41
★ Covered Luggage Van:	May 21 (MM) to Apr 23
Luggage Van No. 1:	May 23 (RF) to Dec 41
★ Luggage Van No. 2:	Oct 23 (MP) to Dec 41
★ Lumber Wagon No. 1:	May 23 (RF) to Dec 41
★ Lumber Wagon No. 2:	May 23 (RF) to Dec 41
★ Meat Van:	Aug 31 (HT) to Dec 41
★ Milk Tank Wagon:	Jul 29 (HT) to Oct 41
★ Milk Traffic Van No. 0:	Aug 31 (HT) to Dec 41
★ Milk Traffic Van:	Oct 23 (MP) to Jun 31
Milk Traffic Van No. 1:	Jul 31 (MP) to Dec 41
★ MO Crane Truck:	Jun 35 (MP) to Dec 41
★ MO Petrol Tank Wagon:	Jun 35 (MP) to Dec 41
★ MO Rotary Tipping Wagon:	Jun 35 (MP) to Dec 41
★ MO Side Tipping Wagon:	Jun 35 (MP) to Dec 41
★ MO Wagon:	Mar 30 (MI) to Dec 41
★ Open Wagon B:	Aug 31 (HT) to Dec 41
★ Truck, or Wagon:	Jun 20 (HL) to Apr 22
★ Zulu Wagon:	May 22 (MM) to Jun 25
★ Hornby Wagon No. 1 or No. 2:	May 22 (MM) to Jun 25
Hornby Wagon: (No. 0, 1, 2)	Jul 25 (MI) to Jun 29
Hornby Wagon No. 1:	Jul 29 (HT) to Jul 35
Wagon No. 1:	Aug 35 (BHT) to Dec 41
★ Hornby Wagon No. 0:	Jul 29 (HT) to Jul 35
Wagon No. 0:	Aug 35 (BHT) to Dec 41
★ Series M No. 3 Wagon:	Jun 26 (MI) to Aug 28
M Wagon:	Sep 28 (MP) to Feb 30
M1 Wagon:	Mar 30 (MI) to Dec 41
★ Wagon for M3 Tank Goods Train Sets:	Jul 31 (MP) to Dec 41
★ Petrol Tank Wagon, BP:	May 27 (MP) to May 35
Petrol Tank Wagon No. 1, BP:	Jun 35 (MP) to Jun 36

★ Oil Tank Wagon, Castrol:	Aug 30 (MP) to Dec 41
★ Petrol Tank Wagon No. 1, Esso:	Jul 36 (MP) to Dec 41
★ Oil Tank Wagon, Mobiloil:	Aug 31 (HT) to Dec 41
★ Petrol Tank Wagon, National Benzole:	Apr 23 (GS) to Jun 29
★ Petrol Tank Wagon No. 1, Pool:	Aug 40 (MM) to Dec 41
★ Petrol Tank Wagon No. 1, Power Ethyl:	Jun 38 (MP) to Dec 41
★ Petrol Tank Wagon, Pratts:	Aug 25 (MM) to May 35
Petrol Tank Wagon No. 1, Pratts:	Jun 35 (MP) to Jun 36
★ Petrol Tank Wagon, Redline:	Aug 28 (HBT) to Jul 32
★ Petrol Tank Wagon, Redline Glico:	Aug 32 (MP) to May 35
Petrol Tank Wagon No. 1, Redline Glico:	Jun 35 (MP) to Dec 41
★ Oil Tank Wagon, Royal Daylight:	Jul 36 (MP) to Dec 41
★ Petrol Tank Wagon, Shell:	May 22 (MM) to May 35
Petrol Tank Wagon No. 1, Shell:	Jun 35 (MP) to Jun 36
★ Petrol Tank Wagon No. 1, ShellMex & BP:	Jul 36 (MP) to May 38
★ Refrigerator Van No. 0:	Jul 37 (MP) to Dec 41
★ Refrigerator Van:	May 23 (RF) to Jun 37
Refrigerator Van No. 1:	Jul 37 (MP) to Dec 41
★ Rotary Tipping Wagon No. 0:	Aug 34 (MP) to Dec 41
★ Rotary Tipping Wagon:	May 23 (RF) to Jul 34
Rotary Tipping Wagon No. 1:	Aug 34 (MP) to Dec 41
★ Sausage Van, Palethorpe's:	Jun 38 (MP) to Dec 41
★ Seccotine Van:	Jul 24 (MI) to Jul 34
★ Side Tipping Wagon:	May 23 (RF) to May 35
Side Tipping Wagon No. 1:	Jun 35 (MP) to Dec 41
★ Snowplough:	Jul 24 (MI) to Dec 41
★ Tank Car, American Type:	Aug 30 (MP) to Dec 41
★ Timber Wagon No. 1:	Nov 22 (MM) to Dec 41
★ Timber Wagon:	Jan 22 (MM) to Dec 22
Timber Wagon No. 2:	Jan 23 (MM) to Dec 41
★ Trolley Wagon:	May 23 (RF) to Dec 41
★ Trolley Wagon with Cable Drums:	Jul 36 (MP) to Dec 41
★ Wine Wagon:	Aug 28 (HBT) to Jun 29
Double Wine Wagon:	Jul 29 (HT) to Dec 41
★ Single Wine Wagon:	Jul 29 (HT) to May 35
★ Wagon, French Type:	May 27 (MP) to May 39

ACCESSORIES

★ Bricks for High Capacity Wagon:	Jul 37 (MP) to Dec 41
★ Spring Buffer Stop:	May 22 (MM) to Mar 28
Buffer Stop No. 1 (Spring):	Apr 28 (MM) to Dec 41
★ Buffer Stop No. 1E:	May 32 (MM) to May 39
★ Hydraulic Buffer Stop:	Oct 24 (MP) to Mar 28
Buffer Stop No. 2 (Hydraulic):	Apr 28 (MM) to Dec 39
★ Buffer Stop No. 2E:	May 32 (MM) to May 38
★ Buffer Stop No. 2A:	Jul 37 (MP) to Dec 41
★ Buffer stop No. 3A:	Jun 38 (MP) to Dec 41
★ Cable Drum:	Aug 34 (MP) to Jul 40
★ Coal for High Capacity Wagons:	Jul 37 (MP) to Dec 41

★ Container:	Jul 36 (MP) to Dec 41
★ Countryside Sections:	Aug 32 (HT) to 1935
(limited supply to Sep 1936)	
★ Cutting No. 0:	Aug 32 (HT) to Jul 40
★ Cutting No. 1, End Section:	Mar 32 (MM) to May 39
★ Cutting No. 2, Centre Section, straight:	Mar 32 (MM) to May 39
★ Cutting No. 3, Centre Section, curved:	Mar 32 (MM) to May 39
★ Cutting No. 4:	Mar 32 (MM) to Jun 37
★ Modelled Miniatures No. 1, Station Staff:	Nov 31 (MM) to Mar 34
Dinky Toys No. 1, Station Staff:	Apr 34 (MM) to Dec 41
★ Modelled Miniatures No. 2, Farmyard Animals:	Jul 32 (HTP) to Mar 34
Dinky Toys No. 2, Farmyard Animals:	Apr 34 (MM) to Dec 41
★ Modelled Miniatures No. 3, Passengers:	Jul 32 (HTP) to Mar 34
Dinky Toys No. 3, Passengers:	Apr 34 (MM) to Dec 41
★ Modelled Miniatures No. 4, Engineering Staff:	May 32 (MM) to Mar 34
Dinky Toys No. 4, Engineering Staff:	Apr 34 (MM) to Dec 41
★ Modelled Min. No. 5, Train and Hotel Staff:	May 32 (MM) to Mar 34
Dinky Toys No. 5, Train and Hotel Staff:	Apr 34 (MM) to Dec 41
★ Dinky Toys No. 6, Shepherd Set:	Apr 34 (MM) to Oct 41
★ Mod. Min. No. 13, Hall's Distemper Advert:	Apr 32 (MM) to Mar 34
Dinky Toys No. 13, Hall's Distemper Advert:	Apr 34 (MM) to Dec 41
★ Engine Shed No. 1:	May 28 (MI) to Dec 41
★ Engine Shed No. 1A:	Aug 34 (MP) to Dec 41
★ Engine Shed No. E1E:	May 32 (MM) to Dec 41
★ Engine Shed No. 2:	May 28 (MI) to Dec 41
★ Engine Shed No. 2A:	Aug 34 (MP) to Dec 41
★ Engine Shed No. E2E:	May 32 (MM) to Dec 41
★ Fencing with Four Trees:	Apr 32 (MM) to Dec 41
★ Footbridge No. 2, without signals:	Jul 24 (MI) to Mar 28
Footbridge No. 1, without signals:	Apr 28 (MM) to Dec 41
★ Footbridge No. 1A, with det. tinprinted signals:	Aug 30 (MP) to Jul 34
★ Footbridge No. 1A, with detachable signals:	Aug 34 (MP) to Dec 41
★ Footbridge No. 1, with detachable signals:	Jul 24 (MI) to Mar 28
Footbridge No. 2, with detachable signals:	Apr 28 (MM) to Jul 34
★ Lattice Girder Bridge:	Nov 21 (MM) to Mar 30
Footbridge No. 3:	Apr 30 (MM) to Jul 34
★ Goods Platform No. 1:	Aug 34 (MP) to Dec 41
★ Goods Platform:	Aug 26 (HT) to Jul 34
Goods Platform No. 2:	Aug 34 (MP) to Sep 40
★ Goods Platform E:	May 32 (MM) to Jul 34
Goods Platform No. 2E:	Aug 34 (MP) to Sep 40
★ Hedging:	Jun 33 (MP) to Dec 41
★ Island Platform:	Jun 26 (MI) to Dec 41
Island Platform E:	May 32 (MM) to Dec 41
★ Lamp Standard No. 1 (Electrical):	Aug 31 (HT) to Jul 32
Lamp Standard No. 1E:	Aug 32 (HBT) to Dec 41
★ Lamp Standard No. 2 (Electrical):	Aug 31 (HT) to Jul 32
Lamp Standard No. 2E:	Aug 32 (HBT) to Dec 41
★ Single Lamp Standard:	Oct 23 (MP) to Mar 28

Lamp Standard No. 1:	Apr 28 (MM) to May 39
★ Double Lamp Standard:	Oct 23 (MP) to Mar 28
Lamp Standard No. 2:	Apr 28 (MM) to May 39
★ Level Crossing No. 1:	May 28 (MI) to Dec 41
★ Level Crossing No. 1, Electrical:	Aug 31 (HT) to Jul 32
Level Crossing No. E1:	Aug 32 (HBT) to Dec 41
★ Level Crossing No. E1E:	May 32 (MM) to Dec 41
★ Level Crossing:	May 24 (MM) to Mar 28
Level Crossing No. 2:	Apr 28 (MM) to Dec 41
★ Level Crossing No. 2, Electrical:	Aug 30 (MP) to Jul 32
Level Crossing No. E2:	Aug 32 (HBT) to Dec 41
★ Level Crossing No. E2E:	May 32 (MM) to Dec 41
★ Loading Gauge:	May 23 (RF) to Dec 41
★ M Footbridge:	Jun 33 (MP) to Dec 41
★ M Level Crossing:	Jul 31 (MP) to Dec 41
★ M Loading Gauge:	Aug 31 (HT) to Dec 41
★ M Signal Box:	Aug 30 (MP) to Dec 41
★ M Signals:	Aug 30 (MP) to Dec 41
★ M Station:	Aug 30 (MP) to Dec 41
★ M Wayside Station:	Aug 30 (MP) to Dec 41
★ M Station Set:	Aug 30 (MP) to Dec 41
★ M Telegraph Pole:	Aug 30 (MP) to Jul 31
M Telegraph Pole No. 1:	Aug 31 (HT) to Dec 41
★ M Telegraph Pole No. 2:	Aug 31 (HT) to Dec 41
★ Paled Fencing:	Aug 26 (HT) to Dec 41
★ Passenger Platform:	Aug 26 (HT) to Dec 41
★ Platelayer's Hut:	Aug 30 (MP) to Dec 41
★ Platform Crane:	Aug 28 (HBT) to Dec 41
★ Platform Ramps:	Aug 26 (HT) to Dec 41
★ Poster Boards:	Dec 31 (MM) to Dec 41
★ Posters in Miniature:	Dec 31 (MM) to Dec 33
Posters in Miniature, Series 1:	Jan 34 (MM) to Dec 41
★ Posters in Miniature, Series 2:	Jan 34 (MM) to Dec 41
★ Platform Accessories No. 1, Luggage & Truck:	Jul 24 (MI) to Jul 28
Railway Accessories No. 1, Luggage & Truck:	Aug 28 (HBT) to Dec 41
★ Platform Accessories No. 2, Milk Cans & Truck:	Jul 24 (MI) to Jul 28
Railway Accessories No. 2, Milk Cans & Truck:	Aug 28 (HBT) to Dec 41
★ Milk Cans: special order, then	Aug 32 (HT) to Dec 41
★ Platform Acc. No. 3, Platform Machines etc:	Jul 24 (MI) to Jul 28
Railway Acc. No. 3, Platform Machines etc:	Aug 28 (HBT) to Dec 41
★ Platform Accessories No. 4:	May 27 (MP) to Jul 28
Railway Accessories No. 4, comb. sets 1 to 3:	Aug 28 (HBT) to Dec 41
★ Railway Acc. no. 5, Gradient and Mile Posts:	Aug 28 (HBT) to Dec 41
★ Railway Accessories No. 6:	Aug 28 (HBT) to Jun 29
★ Railway Accessories No. 7, Watchman's Hut:	Aug 28 (HBT) to Dec 41
★ Railway Accessories No. 8, Notice Boards:	Jul 29 (HT) to Dec 41
★ Railway Accessories No. 9, Station Name Boards:	Jul 29 (HT) to Dec 41
★ Roof Clips for Train Name Boards No. 2:	Jan 32 (MM) to Dec 41
★ Roof Clips for Train Name Boards No. 2S:	Jan 32 (MM) to Dec 41

★ Shunter's Pole:	Aug 28 (HBT) to Sep 40
★ Signal Cabin No. 1:	Aug 28 (HBT) to Dec 41
★ Signal Cabin:	Jul 24 (MI) to Mar 28
Signal Cabin No. 2:	Apr 28 (MM) to Dec 41
★ Signal Cabin No. 2E:	May 32 (MM) to Dec 41
★ Signal Gantry No. 1:	Aug 34 (MP) to Dec 41
★ Signal Gantry:	Aug 28 (HBT) to Jul 34
Signal Gantry No. 2:	Aug 34 (MP) to Dec 41
★ Signal Gantry No. 2E:	May 32 (MM) to Dec 41
★ Signal No. 1:	Aug 28 (HBT) to Dec 41
★ Signal:	May 23 (RF) to Mar 28
Signal No. 2:	Apr 28 (MM) to Dec 41
★ Signal No. 2E:	May 32 (MM) to Dec 41
★ Signal, No. 1 Double Arm:	May 28 (MI) to Dec 41
★ Signal, No. 2 Double Arm:	May 28 (MI) to Dec 41
★ Signal, No. 2E Double Arm:	May 32 (MM) to Dec 41
★ Signal, No. 1 Junction:	Aug 34 (MP) to Dec 41
★ Junction Signal:	Jul 24 (MI) to Jul 34
Junction Signal No. 2:	Aug 34 (MP) to Dec 41
★ Junction Signal No. 2E:	May 32 (MM) to Dec 41
★ Signals for Footbridge:	Jul 24 (MI) to Jul 34
★ Diecast Stands for Trees:	Jun 33 (MP) to Dec 41
★ Wayside Station:	May 27 (MP) to Mar 28
Wayside Station No. 1:	Apr 28 (MM) to Jul 28
Railway Station No. 1:	Aug 28 (HBT) to Mar 30
Station No. 1:	Apr 30 (MM) to Dec 37
★ Railway Station:	May 23 (RF) to Mar 28
Railway Station No. 2:	Apr 28 (MM) to Dec 37
★ Station No. 2E:	May 32 (MM) to Dec 37
★ Station No. 3:	Jul 37 (MP) to Dec 41
★ Station No. 4:	Jul 37 (MP) to Dec 41
★ Station No. 4E:	Jul 37 (MP) to Dec 41
★ Station or Field Hoardings:	Aug 31 (HT) to Dec 41
★ Tarpaulin Sheets:	Aug 28 (HBT) to Dec 41
★ Telegraph Pole:	Oct 23 (MP) to Dec 39
★ Train name Boards:	Jan 32 (MM) to Dec 41
★ Oak Trees:	Jun 33 (MP) to Jun 36
★ Poplar Trees:	Jun 33 (MP) to Jun 36
★ Trees with Stands, Assorted:	Jun 33 (MP) to Oct 41
★ Oak Trees with Stands:	Jul 36 (MP) to Dec 41
★ Poplar Trees with Stands:	Jul 36 (MP) to Oct 41
★ Tunnel:	Jul 24 (MI) to Jan 32
Tunnel, (Metal):	Feb 32 (MM) to Jun 37
★ Tunnel Ends:	Aug 30 (MP) to Dec 41
★ Tunnel No. 0:	Apr 32 (MM) to Jul 40
★ M Tunnel:	Dec 31 (MM) only
Tunnel No. 1:	Jan 32 (MM) to Jul 40
★ Tunnel No. 2, Straight:	Feb 32 (MM) to Oct 41
★ Tunnel No. 3, Curved:	Feb 32 (MM) to Dec 41

★ Tunnel No. 4, Curved:	Feb 32 (MM) to Dec 41
★ Tunnel No. 5, Left-hand, Curved:	Apr 32 (MM) to Jun 36
★ Tunnel No. 6, Right-hand, Curved:	Apr 32 (MM) to Jun 36
★ Turntable, Small Size:	May 27 (MP) to Mar 28
Turntable No. 1:	Apr 28 (MM) to Dec 41
★ Turntable:	May 23 (RF) to Apr 27
Turntable, Large Size:	May 27 (MP) to Mar 28
Turntable No. 2:	Apr 28 (MM) to Dec 41
★ Turntable No. 2, Electrical:	Aug 30 (MP) to Jul 32
Turntable No. E2:	Aug 32 (HT) to Dec 41
★ Viaduct:	Oct 24 (MP) to Dec 41
★ Viaduct, Centre Section:	Aug 25 (MP) to Oct 41
★ Viaduct, Electrical:	Aug 25 (MP) to Dec 41
★ Viaduct, Electrical, Centre Section:	Aug 25 (MP) to Dec 41
★ Water Tank No. 1:	Aug 34 (MP) to Dec 41
★ Water Tank:	Jul 24 (MI) to Jul 34
Water Tank No. 2:	Aug 34 (MP) to May 39
★ Water Tank E:	May 32 (MM) to Jul 34
Water Tank No. 2E:	Aug 34 (MP) to May 39

HORNBY CONTROL SYSTEM ACCESSORIES

★ Control Outfit No. 1:	Sep 26 (CL) to Jun 29
★ Control Outfit No. 2:	Sep 26 (CL) to Jun 29
★ Control Rail No. 1:	May 27 (MP) to Jun 29
★ Control Rail:	Sep 26 (CL) to Apr 27
★ Control Rail No. 2:	May 27 (MP) to Jun 29
★ Control Brake and Reverse Rail (PU):	Sep 26 (CL) to Apr 27
★ Coupling for Control Wire:	Sep 26 (CL) to 1939
★ Guide Brackets:	Sep 26 (CL) to 1939
★ Lever Assembly:	Aug 31 (CL) to 1939
★ Lever Frame:	Sep 26 (CL) to Jul 31
Lever Frame, 6-Lever:	Aug 31 (CL) to 1939
★ Lever Frame, 2-Lever:	Aug 31 (CL) to 1939
★ Lever Frame, 4-Lever:	Aug 31 (CL) to 1939
★ Points fitted for Hornby Control:	Sep 26 (CL) to 1939
★ Points on Solid Base, PSR2/PSL2:	Jun 28 (HTG) to May 39
★ Rodding Compensator:	Sep 26 (CL) to 1939
★ Rodding Traverse:	Aug 31 (CL) to 1939
★ Signal, Single Arm, fitted for Control	Sep 26 (CL) to 1939
★ E Signal, Single Arm, fitted for Control:	SO, not catalogued
★ Signal, Double Arm, fitted for Control	SO, not catalogued
★ E Signal, Double Arm, fitted for Control	SO, not catalogued
★ Junction Signal, fitted for Control	Sep 26 (CL) to 1939
★ E Junction Signal, fitted for Control	SO, not catalogued
★ Sleeper and Bellcrank: for converting points	SO, May 27 (MM) and later
★ Wire:	Sep 26 (CL) to 1939
★ Wire Cutters:	Sep 26 (CL) to 1939

ELECTRICAL SUNDRIES

★ Accumulator, 4 volt 8 ampere:	Jun 26 (MI) to Jun 29
★ Accumulator, 4 volt 20 ampere:	Jun 26 (MI) to Jun 29
★ Accumulator, 2 volt 20 ampere:	Jul 30 (MI) to Sep 35
★ Accumulator, 6 volt 20 ampere:	Jul 29 (HT) to Sep 35
★ Bulb Holders for glass globe Lamp Standards:	SO, Nov 31 (MM)
★ Bulbs:	1933 to Dec 41
★ Circuit Breaker, 6 or 20 volt:	Apr 36 (MM) to May 38
★ Circuit Breaker, 6 volt:	Jun 38 (MP) to Dec 41
★ Circuit Breaker, 20 volt:	Jun 38 (MP) to Dec 41
★ Connecting Wire for electric accessories:	Jun 35 (HT) to Dec 41
★ Distribution Box:	May 32 (MM) to Jun 36
★ Earthing Clip:	Jun 35 (MP) to Jun 36
Bonding Clip:	Jul 36 (MP) to Dec 41
★ Flexible Leads:	May 32 (MM) to Jun 37
★ Fuse Wire, 41 SWG tinned copper:	Nov 34 (HTP) to Dec 41
★ Fuse Wire, 24 SWG lead:	Jun 35 (MP) to Dec 41
★ Fuse Wire, 32 SWG lead:	Nov 34 (HTP) to Dec 41
★ Lighting Accessory for Buffer Stops:	Jun 38 (MP) to Dec 41
★ Plugs for Transformer sockets:	Jun 35 (MP) to Jul 40
★ Rheostat (for HV train):	Jul 25 (MI) to May 26
	+Apr 27 (MI) to Jun 29
★ Resistance Controller, 4 volt:	Jun 26 (MI) to Feb 29
★ Resistance Controller, 6 volt:	Mar 29 (MI) to Dec 41
★ Resistance Controller, 20 volt:	Aug 34 (MP) to Dec 41
★ Sockets:	Jun 35 (MP) to Jul 40
★ Speed and Reverse Control Switch:	Jul 29 (HT) to May 39
★ Terminal Connecting Plate (high voltage):	Jul 25 (MI) to May 26
Terminal Connecting Plate TCPH (high voltage):	Apr 27 (MI) to Jun 29
★ Terminal Connecting Plate (low voltage):	Jun 26 (MI) to Jul 32
Terminal Connecting Plate TCP6 (6 volt):	Aug 32 (MP) to Dec 41
★ Terminal Connecting Plate TCP20 (20 volt):	Aug 32 (MP) to Dec 41
★ Terminal TSR (or TRS) for Solid Steel Rails:	Jul 37 (MP) to Dec 41
★ Transformer:	Sep 27 (MP) to Mar 32
★ Transformer T6a:	Apr 32 (MM) to May 33
★ Transformer T6:	Nov 31 (MM) to Dec 41
★ Transformer T6A:	May 33 (HTPE) to Dec 41
★ Transformer T6M:	May 33 (HTPE) to Dec 41
★ Transformer T26M: Dec 35 MM as SO	Jul 36 (MP) to Dec 41
★ Transformer T20:	Jun 32 (HTPE) to Dec 41
★ Transformer T20A:	Jun 32 (HTPE) to Dec 41
★ Transformer T20M:	May 33 (HTPE) to Dec 41
★ Transformer T22M: Dec 35 MM as SO	Jul 36 (MP) to Dec 41
★ Transformer/Rectifier TR6:	Aug 34 (MP) to Dec 41

SUNDRIES (DATES FOR SEPARATE SALE)
SO dates are for the first MM ref only

★ Automatic Couplings:	SO, Oct 31 (MM)
★ Axleboxes:	SO, Oct 30 (MM)

★ Axles for Spoked Wheels: special order	SO, Apr 29 (MM)	
★ Bogies for Nord Tender	SO, Jan 33 (MM)	
★ Combined Rail Gauge, Screwdriver and Spanner:	Aug 30 (HBT) to Dec 41	
★ Corridor Connections:	SO, Mar 32 (MM)	
★ Corridor End Plates:	SO, Mar 32 (MM)	
★ Diecast Spoked Wheels:	Aug 32 (MP) to Dec 41	
★ Graphite Grease:	Jun 33 (MP) to Dec 41	
★ Keys:	Jun 35 (MP) to Dec 39	
★ Detachable Head Lamp for Locomotives:	SO Jul 30 (MM)	
	+Jun 35 (MP) to Dec 41	
★ Detachable Tail Lamps for Coaches:	Jun 35 (MP) to Dec 41	
★ Lattice Girder Bridge, extra spans:	SO, Aug 32 (MM)	
★ Logs for No. 2 Lumber Wagon:	SO, Apr 29 (MM)	
★ Lubricating Oil:	Apr 28 (GS) to Dec 41	
★ Mansell Wheels:	Aug 28 (HBT) to Dec 41	
★ Meccano Buffers, part 120:	Feb 20 (MI) to Dec 41	
★ Meccano Spring Buffers, part 120A:	Sep 22 (MM) to Dec 41	
★ Meccano Rail Adaptor, part 173:	Aug 30 (MI) to Dec 41	
★ Meccano Train Coupling, part 121:	Feb 20 (MI) to Dec 41	
★ Meccano Signal Arm, Home, part 158A:	Nov 27 (MM) to Dec 41	
★ Meccano Signal Arm, Distant, part 158B:	Nov 27 (MM) to Dec 41	
★ Meccano Train parts: available concurrently with constructional sets		
★ Mechanisms:	SO, Mar 29 (MM)	
★ Oil can No. 1:	Aug 28 (HBT) to Dec 41	
★ Oil can No. 2, 'K' Type:	Jun 28 (MM) to Dec 41	
★ Pony Truck	SO, Jul 32 (MM)	
★ Rail Pins	SO, Nov 30 (MM)	
★ Shovel and Poker	SO, Oct 30 (MM)	
★ Signal Arms, Home or Distant	SO, Mar 27 (MM)	
★ Timber for No. 1 and 2 Wagons	SO, Apr 29 (MM)	
★ Vacuum Brake Pipes	SO, Feb 33 (MM)	

RAILS FOR CLOCKWORK TRAINS

★ Straight Rails B1:	Jun 20 (HL) to Dec 41
★ Straight Half Rails B ½:	Jan 21 (MM) to Apr 21
	+Sep 22 (RF) to Dec 41
★ Straight Quarter Rails B ¼:	Jan 21 (MM) to Apr 21
	+Sep 22 (RF) to Dec 41
★ Straight Rails, Double Track DS1:	Jun 28 (HTG) to Dec 41
★ Straight Rails for MO Trains, BM:	Apr 30 (HTP) to Dec 41
★ Straight Half Rails for MO Trains, BM ½:	Jul 31 (BI) to Dec 41
★ Curved Rails 2 ft radius A2:	Sep 21 (HL) to Dec 41
★ Curved Half Rails 2 ft radius A2 ½:	Sep 22 (RF) to Dec 41
★ Curved Quarter Rails, 2 ft radius A2 ¼:	Sep 22 (RF) to Dec 41
★ Curved Rails, 1 ft radius A1:	May 21 (MM) to Dec 41
★ Curved Half Rails 1 ft radius A1 ½:	Sep 22 (RF) to Dec 41
★ Curved Quarter Rails 1 ft radius A1 ¼:	Sep 22 (RF) to Dec 41
★ Curved Rails, 9 in radius:	Jun 20 (HL) to Apr 21

★ Curved Half Rails, 9 in radius:	Jan 21 (MM) to Apr 21
★ Curved Quarter Rails, 9 in radius:	Jan 21 (MM) to Apr 21
★ Curved Rails 9 in radius A9:	Sep 22 (RF) to Apr 27
★ Curved Rails 9 in radius M9:	Mar 30 (MI) to Dec 41
★ Curved Rails, Double Track DC2:	Jun 28 (HTG) to Dec 41
★ Points, 2 ft radius, PL2/PR2:	Sep 21 (MM) to Dec 41
★ Points on Solid Base SPSR2/SPSL2, 2 ft radius:	Jun 35 (MP) to Oct 41
★ Points 2 ft radius Double Symmetrical DSR2/DSL2:	May 22 (MM) to Dec 41
★ Points 2 ft radius Parallel, PPR2/PPL2:	Oct 24 (HT) to Dec 41
★ Points, 1 ft radius, PR1/PL1:	Sep 21 (MM) to Dec 41
★ Points, 1 ft radius Double Symmetrical DSR1/DSL1:	May 22 (MM) to Dec 41
★ Points, 1 ft radius Parallel PPR/PPL, PPR1/PPL1:	Jul 22 (MM) to May 28
★ Points, 9 in radius: circa Jan 21 to Apr 21,	not catalogued
★ Points, 9 in radius, PR9/PL9:	Sep 22 (RF) to Apr 27
★ Points, 9 in radius, MR9/ML9:	Apr 30 (HTP) to Dec 41
★ Points, 2 ft radius Crossover CO2:	Aug 25 (MP) to Aug 28
★ Points, 2 ft radius Crossover COR2/COL2:	Sep 28 (MP) to Dec 41
★ Points, 1 ft radius Crossover, CO1:	Aug 25 (MP) to May 28
★ Acute Angle Crossing, 2 ft radius, CA or CA2:	Sep 21 (MM) to Dec 41
★ Acute Angle Crossing, 1 ft radius, CA1:	Aug 26 (HT) to Dec 41
★ Right Angle Crossing, 2 ft radius, CR or CR2:	Sep 21 (MM) to Dec 41
★ Right Angle Crossing, 1 ft radius, CR1:	Aug 26 (HT) to Dec 41
★ Brake Rail, straight BB1:	Oct 24 (HT) to Dec 41
★ Brake and Reverse Rail BBR1, straight:	May 27 (MP) to Dec 41
★ Brake Rail MB9, curved 9 in:	Mar 30 (MI) to Dec 41
★ Brake Rail, curved 9 ft:	Jun 20 (HL) to Apr 21
★ Brake Rail, curved 1 ft, AB1:	May 21 (MM) to Dec 41
★ Brake and Reverse Rail, curved 2 ft, AB2:	Sep 21 (HL) to Dec 41
★ Rail Connecting Plates CP or RCP:	Aug 26 (HT) to Dec 41
★ MCC Rail Connecting Clips for MO Rails:	Jun 38 (MP) to Dec 41
★ PCC Point Connecting Clips:	Aug 38 (HBT) to Dec 41
★ Centre rail conversion accessories:	Nov 21 (MM)
★ Centre rail conversion accessories:	Mar 30 (MM) to Jun 36

RAILS FOR ELECTRIC TRAINS

★ Straight Rails EB1, electric:	Mar 22 (MM) to Dec 41
★ Straight Half Rail EB ½, electric:	Oct 22 (MM) to Dec 41
★ Straight Quarter Rails EB ¼, electric:	Oct 22 (MM) to Dec 41
★ Straight Rails, Double track EDS1, electric:	Jul 29 (HT) to Dec 41
★ Curved Rails, 1 ft electric, EA1:	Mar 22 (MM) to Dec 41
★ Curved Half Rail, 1 ft electric EA1 ½:	Oct 22 (MM) to Dec 41
★ Curved Quarter Rails, 1 ft electric, EA1 ¼:	Oct 22 (MM) to Dec 41
★ Curved Rails, 2 ft electric EA2:	Mar 22 (MM) to Dec 41
★ Curved Half Rails, 2 ft electric EA2 ½:	Oct 22 (MM) to Dec 41
★ Curved Quarter Rails, 2 ft electric, EA2 ¼:	Oct 22 (MM) to Dec 41
★ Curved Rails, Double Track electric EDC2:	Jul 29 (HT) to Dec 41
★ Points, 2 ft electric EPL2/EPR2:	Oct 22 (MP) to Jun 36
★ Points on Solid Base, ESPSR2/ESPSL2, EPR2/EPL2:	Jan 36 (MM) to Dec 41

★ Points, 1 ft EPL1/EPR1:	Oct 22 (MP) to Jul 25
	+Aug 34 (MP) to Dec 41
★ Parallel Points, 1 ft electric EPPL/EPPR:	Oct 23 (MP) to Sep 24
★ Parallel Points, 2 ft electric EPPL2/EPPR2:	Aug 25 (MP) to Dec 41
★ Double Symmetrical 1 ft EDSL1/EDSR1:	Oct 22 (MP) to Jul 25
★ Double Symmetrical 1 ft EDSL1/EDSR1:	Aug 34 (MP) to Dec 41
★ Double Symmetrical 2 ft electric EDSL2/EDSR2:	Oct 22 (MP) to Dec 41
★ Crossover Points electric ECOL2/ECOR2:	May 31 (HTP) to Dec 41
★ Acute Angle Crossing, 2 ft electric ECA:	Oct 22 (MP) to Dec 41
★ Right Angle Crossing, 2 ft electric ECR:	Oct 22 (MP) to Dec 41
★ Curved Rail with Terminal 1 ft EAT1:	Oct 22 (MM) to Jul 26
★ Curved Rail with Terminal 2 ft EAT2:	Oct 22 (MM) to Jul 26
★ Switch Rail, 6 volt EMC6:	Aug 34 (MP) to May 39
★ Switch Rail, 20 volt EMC20:	Aug 34 (MP) to May 39
★ Straight Rails, Solid Steel, EB3:	Jul 37 (MP) to Dec 41
★ Straight Half Rails, Solid Steel, EB3½:	Jul 37 (MP) to Dec 41
★ Straight Quarter Rails, Solid Steel, EB3¼:	Jul 37 (MP) to Dec 41
★ Curved Rails, Solid Steel, 3 ft radius EA3:	Jul 37 (MP) to Dec 41
★ Curved Half Rails, Solid Steel, EA3½:	Jul 37 (MP) to Dec 41
★ Points, Solid Steel, EPL3/EPR3:	Jul 37 (MP) to Dec 41
★ Adapting Pieces for Solid Steel Rails:	Jul 37 (MP) to Dec 41
★ Fishplates for Solid Steel Rails:	Jul 37 (MP) to Dec 41

POSTWAR TRAIN SETS

★ MO Goods Train Set:	Mar 47 (MP) to May 54
★ No. 20 Goods Train Set:	Apr 54 (MM) to Dec 66
★ MO Passenger Train Set:	Mar 47 (MP) to May 54
★ No. 21 Passenger Train Set:	Apr 54 (MM) to Dec 66
★ M1 Passenger Train Set:	Mar 47 (MP) to Jun 57
★ No. 31 Passenger Train Set:	Apr 56 (PL) to May 65
★ M1 Goods Train Set:	Mar 47 (MP) to Jun 57
★ No. 30 Goods Train Set:	Apr 56 (PL) to May 65
★ 201 Tank Goods Train Set:	Mar 47 (MP) to Apr 54
★ No. 40 Tank Goods Train Set:	May 54 (MM) to Apr 58
★ No. 45 Tank Goods Train Set:	Apr 57 (MP) to May 65
★ 101 Tank Passenger Train Set:	Nov 47 (MP) to Apr 54
★ No. 41 Tank Passenger Train Set:	May 54 (MM) to May 65
★ No. 601 Goods Train Set:	Sep 48 (MP) to May 54
★ No. 50 Goods Train Set:	Jun 54 (MP) to Nov 58
★ No. 55 Goods Train Set:	Apr 57 (MP) to May 61
★ No. 501 Passenger Train Set:	Sep 48 (MP) to May 54
★ No. 51 Passenger Train Set:	Jun 54 (MP) to May 61

POSTWAR LOCOMOTIVES

★ MO Locomotive:	Mar 47 (MP) to May 54
★ No. 20 Locomotive:	Apr 54 (MM) to Dec 68
★ M1 Locomotive:	Mar 47 (MP) to Apr 58
★ No. 30 Locomotive:	Apr 56 (PL) to May 65
★ 101 Tank Locomotive:	Mar 47 (MP) to Apr 54

★ No. 40 Tank Locomotive:	May 54 (MM) to May 65
★ 501 Locomotive:	Sep 48 (MP) to May 54
★ No. 50 Locomotive:	Jun 54 (MP) to May 61
★ No. 51 Locomotive:	Jun 54 (MP) to May 61

POSTWAR COACHES

★ No. 21 Coach:	Apr 54 (MM) to 1969
★ No. 31 Coach, 1st/3rd:	Apr 56 (PL) to Aug 56
No. 31 Coach, 1st/2nd:	Sep 56 (PL) to Dec 68
★ No. 31 Coach, Brake/3rd:	Apr 56 (PL) to Aug 56
No. 31 Coach, Brake/2nd:	Sep 56 (PL) to May 65
★ No. 1 Coach:	Nov 47 (MP) to Mar 59
★ No. 41 Coach, 1st/3rd:	May 54 (MM) to Aug 56
No. 41 Coach, 1st/2nd:	Sep 56 (PL) to 1969
★ No. 51 Coach, 1st class:	Jun 54 (MP) to May 61
★ No. 51 Coach, 3rd class:	Jun 54 (MP) to Aug 56
No. 51 Coach, 2nd class:	Sep 56 (PL) to May 61
★ Passenger Brake Van:	Nov 47 (MP) to Oct 57
★ Passenger Brake Van no. 41:	May 54 (MM) to 1969
★ Passenger Brake Van No. 51:	Jun 54 (MP) to May 61
★ No. 2 Coach:	Sep 48 (MP) to Jan 50
★ No. 2 Coach, Brake/3rd:	Sep 48 (MP) to Jan 50
★ MO Pullman Coach:	Mar 47 (MP) to May 54
★ M1 Pullman Coach:	Mar 47 (MP) to Jun 57

POSTWAR SUNDRIES (DATES FOR SEPARATE SALE)

★ Automatic Couplings:	Jul 66 (PL) to Dec 68
★ Fuse Wire, 32 SWG lead:	Oct 50 (MP) to Aug 53
★ Transformer T20:	Apr 49 (MP) to Mar 53
★ Transformer T20M:	Apr 52 (MP) to Dec 56
★ Graphite Grease:	
★ Keys:	Jan 52 (MP) to 1969
★ Head Lamp for Locomotive:	Jan 52 (MP) to Jun 66
★ Tail Lamp for Locomotive:	Jan 52 (MP) to Jun 66
★ Side Lamp for Brake Van:	Jan 52 (MP) to Jun 66
★ Wheels and Axles for Rolling Stock:	Jan 52 (MP) to Dec 68
★ Mansell Wheels	not catalogued
★ Spoked Wheels	not catalogued

POSTWAR RAILS

★ Straight Rails B1:	Mar 47 (MP) to Dec 68
★ Straight Half Rails B½:	Sep 48 (MP) to Dec 68
★ Straight Quarter Rails B¼:	Sep 48 (MP) to Dec 68
★ Straight Rails for MO Trains, BM:	Apr 49 (MP) to Dec 54
★ Curved Rails 2 ft radius A2:	Mar 47 (MP) to 1969
★ Curved Half Rails 2 ft radius A2½:	Sep 48 (MP) to 1969
★ Curved Rails, 1 ft radius A1:	Mar 47 (MP) to 1969
★ Curved Half Rails, 1 ft radius A1½:	Sep 48 (MP) to 1969
★ Curved rails 9 in radius M9:	Mar 47 (MP) to Dec 54

★ Points, 2 ft radius, PL2/PR2:	Sep 48 (MP) to 1969
★ Points, 1 ft radius, PR1/PL1:	Sep 48 (MP) to 1969
★ Acute Angle Crossing, 2 ft radius, CA2:	Sep 48 (MP) to 1969
★ Acute Angle Crossing, 1 ft radius, CA1:	Sep 48 (MP) to 1969
★ Right Angle Crossing, 2 ft radius, CR2:	Apr 49 (MP) to 1969
★ Right Angle Crossing, 1 ft radius, CR1:	Apr 49 (MP) to 1969
★ Brake Rail, Straight BB1:	Mar 47 (MP) to May 51
★ Brake and Reverse Rail BBR2, straight:	Sep 48 (MP) to Jan 51
★ Brake and Reverse Rail BBR, straight:	Feb 51 (MP) to 1969
★ Brake Rail BBM, Straight, for MO trains:	Apr 50 to Dec 54
★ Brake Rail MB9, curved 9 in:	Mar 47 (MP) to Mar 50
★ Rail Connecting Plates RCP:	Mar 47 (MP) to 1969
★ MCC Rail Connecting Clips for MO Rails:	Mar 47 (MP) to Dec 54
★ PCC Points Connecting Clips:	Apr 49 (MP) to 1969

POSTWAR WAGONS

★ Goods Brake Van:	Sep 48 (MP) to Dec 57
★ Goods Brake Van No. 50:	Apr 57 (PL) to 1969
★ Breakdown Van and Crane:	Apr 49 (MP) to Jan 50
★ Cattle Truck No. 1:	Sep 48 (MP) to Jun 57
★ Cattle Truck No. 50:	Jul 57 (MP) to May 65
★ Cattle Truck No. 2:	Apr 49 (MP) to Jan 50
★ Cement Wagon:	Apr 49 (MP) to Jun 57
★ Crane Truck No. 1:	Sep 48 (MP) to Jun 57
★ Crane Truck No. 50:	Apr 57 (PL) to 1969
★ Flat Truck:	Sep 48 (MP) to Mar 56
Low Sided Wagon:	Apr 56 (PL) to Mar 59
★ Low Sided Wagon No. 50:	Apr 57 (PL) to Jun 66
★ Flat Truck with Container:	Sep 48 (MP) to Mar 56
Low Sided Wagon with Container:	Apr 56 (PL) to Mar 59
★ Low Sided Wagon No. 50 with Container:	Jul 57 (HT) to 1969
★ Flat Truck with Cable Drum:	Sep 48 (MP) to Mar 56
Low Sided Wagon with Cable Drum:	Apr 56 (PL) to Mar 59
★ Low Sided Wagon No. 50 with Cable Drum:	Jul 57 (HT) to 1969
★ Gas Cylinder Wagon:	Sep 48 (MP) to Jun 57
★ Gas Cylinder Wagon No. 50:	Jul 57 (HT) to 1969
★ Goods Van No. 30:	Apr 56 (PL) to 1969
★ Goods Van No. 1:	Sep 48 (MP) to Dec 57
★ Goods Van No. 50:	Jul 57 (HT) to 1969
★ Goods Van No. 2:	Sep 48 (MP) to Jan 50
★ High Capacity Wagon No. 2:	Apr 49 (MP) to Jan 50
★ Hopper Wagon:	Sep 48 (MP) to Jun 57
★ Hopper Wagon No. 50:	Jul 57 (HT) to 1969
★ Lumber Wagon No. 1:	Sep 48 (MP) to Jun 57
★ Lumber Wagon No. 50:	Apr 57 (MP) to 1969
★ Lumber Wagon No. 2:	Apr 49 (MP) to Jan 50
★ Milk Traffic Van No. 1:	Sep 48 (MP) to Dec 57
★ MO Crane Truck:	Aug 52 (MP) to May 54
Crane Truck No. 20:	Jun 54 (MP) to 1969

★ MO Petrol Tank Wagon:	Aug 52 (MP) to May 54
Tank Wagon No. 20:	Jun 54 (MP) to Oct 59
★ MO Rotary Tipping Wagon:	Aug 52 (MP) to May 54
Rotary Tipping Wagon No. 20:	Jun 54 (MP) to May 65
★ MO Side Tipping Wagon:	Aug 52 (MP) to May 54
Side Tipping Wagon No. 20:	Jun 54 (MP) to Dec 66
★ MO Wagon:	Mar 47 (MP) to May 54
Wagon No. 20:	Apr 54 (MM) to Jun 66
★ M1 Wagon:	Mar 47 (MP) to Jun 57
★ No. 30 Wagon:	Apr 56 (PL) to Dec 68
★ Petrol Tank Wagon No. 1, Esso:	Apr 50 (MP) to Aug 53
★ No. 1 Tank Wagon, Manchester Oil Refinery:	Jun 55 (MP) to Dec 57
★ No. 50 Tank Wagon, Manchester Oil Refinery:	Jul 57 (HT) to Jan 61
★ Tank Wagon No. 1, National Benzole:	Sep 53 (MP) to May 55
★ Petrol Tank Wagon or Oil Tank Wagon (Pool or Royal Daylight, but not specified as such in lists)	Mar 47 (MP) to 1948
★ Tank Wagon No. 1, Shell:	1948 to 1950
★ No. 1 Tank Wagon, Shell Lubricating Oil:	Jun 55 (MP) to Jun 57
★ No. 50 Tank Wagon, Shell Lubricating Oil:	Apr 57 (MP) to 1969
★ Refrigerator Van No. 1:	Sep 48 (MP) to Jun 57
★ No. 50 Refrigerator Van:	Jul 57 (HT) to 1969
★ Rotary Tipping Wagon No. 1:	Sep 48 (MP) to Mar 59
★ Rotary Tipping Wagon No. 50:	Apr 57 (PL) to 1969
★ Saxa Salt Wagon No. 50:	Apr 57 (PL) to 1969
★ Side Tipping Wagon No. 1:	Sep 48 (MP) to Dec 57
★ Side Tipping Wagon No. 50:	Apr 57 (PL) to 1969
★ Timber Wagon No. 1:	Mar 47 (MP) to Mar 59
★ Trolley Wagon:	Apr 49 (MP) to Jan 50
★ Wagon with Tarpaulin Support:	Sep 48 (MP) to Jan 51
Wagon with Sheet Rail:	Feb 51 (MP) to Aug 58
★ Wagon No. 1:	Mar 47 (MP) to Aug 58
★ Wagon No. 50:	Apr 57 (MP) to Dec 68

POSTWAR ACCESSORIES

★ Buffer Stop No. 1:	Sep 48 (MP) to Jun 66
★ Cable Drum No. 1:	Jun 56 (PL) to 1969
★ Insulated Meat Container No. 1:	Jun 56 (PL) to Dec 62
★ Furniture Container No. 1:	Jun 56 (PL) to 1969
★ Dinky Toys No. 1, Station Staff:	Apr 52 (MM) to Dec 56
★ Dinky Toys No. 2, Farmyard Animals:	Apr 52 (MM) to Dec 56
★ Dinky Toys No. 3, Passengers:	Apr 52 (MM) to Dec 56
★ Dinky Toys No. 4, Engineering Staff:	Apr 52 (MM) to Dec 56
★ Dinky Toys No. 5, Train and Hotel Staff:	Apr 52 (MM) to Dec 56
★ Dinky Toys No. 6, Shepherd Set:	Apr 52 (MM) to Dec 56
★ Footbridge No. 1:	Apr 49 (MP) to Jun 57
★ Goods Platform No. 1:	Oct 49 (MP) to Jan 50
	+Apr 50 (MP) to Dec 51
	+Aug 52 (MP) to Dec 57
★ Goods Yard Crane, Dinky Toys No. 752:	Feb 53 (MM) to Jun 60

★ Island Platform:	Apr 49 (MP) to Dec 51
	+Aug 52 (MP) to Dec 57
★ Level Crossing No. 1:	Apr 49 (MP) to 1969
★ M Level Crossing:	not catalogued
★ M Station Set:	not catalogued
★ Milk Cans:	Jun 54 (MP) to 1969
★ Platform Crane:	Apr 49 (MP) to Jan 50
	+Oct 50 (MP) to 1969
★ Posters:	Oct 49 (MP) to Jan 50
	+Apr 50 (MP) to Dec 51
	+Aug 52 (MP) to 1969
★ Signal Cabin No. 2:	Apr 49 (MP) to Jan 50
	+Apr 50 (MP) to Dec 57
★ Signal No. 2:	Apr 49 (MP) to 1969
★ Signal, No. 2 Double Arm:	Apr 49 (MP) to 1969
★ Junction Signal No. 2:	Sep 53 (MP) to 1969
★ Station No. 3:	Apr 49 (MP) to Dec 51
	+Aug 52 (MP) to Jun 57
★ Station Hoardings:	Oct 49 (MP) to Dec 51
	+Aug 52 (MP) to 1969
★ Turntable No. 2:	Apr 49 (MP) to Dec 51
	+Aug 52 (MP) to 1969
★ Water Tank No. 1:	Apr 49 (MP) to Jan 50
	+Oct 50 (MP) to Dec 68

APPENDIX II

SUMMARY OF UK LITERATURE

The following list of catalogues, leaflets, folders, manuals and other literature published for the UK market by Meccano Ltd (but only those items mentioning Hornby Trains) has been compiled in consultation with experts in the field, notably Ian Button, Jack Steer, Bruce Baxter and Michael Foster. Information has also come from dozens of other contributors, but despite this much remains to be discovered in some sections.

Where colours are given as 'black/white' (for example) the item is printed in black ink on white paper. 'Black/blue/white' would normally mean black text on white paper, with a blue background colour. Colour descriptions are a particular problem (one man's pale blue is another's pale green!), and items listed as being on 'white' paper can be on a range of shades from pure white to cream. Printers' codes are given for each known printing for the UK market. Literature intended for overseas has not been included.

HORNBY BOOKS of TRAINS:

All with full colour cover and full colour catalogue section.

No code	1925 HBT, 44 pp inc. cover, LNER 1471
926/50	1926 HBT, 48 pp inc. cover, GWR 4079
1226/25	do.
927/75	1927/28 HBT, 48 pp inc. cover, GWR 4082
1127/15	do.
828/100	1928/29 HBT, 44 pp & cover, LMS 6100
3/929/100	1929/30 HBT, 44 pp & cover, LMS 5986
3/1029/130	do.
16/830/75	1930/31 HBT, 44 pp & cover, LMS 6100
16/831/120	1931/32 HBT, 44 pp & cover, LMS 5957
16/832/105	1932/33 HBT, 48 pp & cover, LMS 6110
16/833/100	1933/34 HBT, 48 pp & cover, LMS 6100
16/934/100	1934/35 HBT, 64 pp & cover, LMS 6200
7/835/65	1935/36 BHT&MP, 56 pp & cover
7/837/100	1937/38 HBT, 56 pp & cover, LMS 6201
7/837/117	1938/39 HBT, 56 pp & cover, GWR 6005
7/739/100	1939/40 HBT, 56 pp & cover, LMS 6231

'HORNBY TRAIN' CATALOGUES and FOLDERS:

1024/150	(no date) black/white folder
826/100	(no date) black/white folder
1126/25	do.
927/250	(no date) black/white folder
1128/150	(no date) blue/white 16 pp booklet
3/729/300	(no date) blue/white 16 pp booklet
3/1029/100(3)	as above but brown/white
3/1129/50(4)	as above but brown/white
3/1229/20(5)	as above but brown/white
5/830/500	1930/31, brown/white 20pp booklet
5/1130/50(1R)	do.
2/831/450	1931/32, brown/white 20pp booklet
2/1131/100	do.
13/832/500(1P)	(no date) green/white folder
13/1132/50(2P)	do.
13/833/550	(no date) blue/white folder
13/1133/50(2P)	do.
15/834/500(1P)	(no date) blue/white Electric folder
15/834/500(1P)	(no date) brown/white Clockwork folder
13/634/610(1P)	1935/36, red/white 24 pp booklet
13/837/80	(no date) black/green/white folder
8/938/200	(no date) black/blue/white folder
2/739/160(1P)	(no date) black/blue/white folder
13/1053/100	1953 sepia/white folder
16/754/100	1954/5 black/blue/white folder

20/855/200	1955/6 full colour folder	
11/756/250	1956/7 full colour folder	
11/757/250	(no date) full colour folder	
11/858/250	1958 full colour folder	
8/10/59/175	(no date) black/green/white folder	
16/860/175	(no date) black/yellow/white folder	
9/661/175	(no date) black/orange/white folder	
12/4/62/150	(no date) black/yellow/white folder	

MECCANO PRODUCTS FOLDERS, CATALOGUES and ILLUSTRATED PRICE LISTS which include Hornby Trains:

No code	1920/21 catalogue, 20 pp, 7 in by 9 in	
No code	1921/22 catalogue, 20 pp, 7 in by 9 in	
No code	1922/23 catalogue, 20 pp, 7 in by 9 in	
No code	1923/24 catalogue, 20 pp, 7 in by 9 in	
No code	1924/25 catalogue, 20 pp, 7 in by 9 in	
825/50	1925/26 catalogue, 20 pp, 7 in by 9 in	
No code	1925/26 catalogue, 20 pp, 5 in by 7 in	
No code	1926/27 catalogue, 24 pp, 5 in by 7 in	
527/300	1927/28 catalogue, 24 pp, 5 in by 7 in	
928/400	1928/29 catalogue, 24 pp, 5 in by 7 in	
4/829/400	1929/30 catalogue, 28 pp, 5 in by 7 in	
2/830/500	1930/31 catalogue, 32 pp, 5 in by 7 in	
7/731/500	Meccano/Hornby folder	
13/831/500	1931/32 catalogue, 32 pp, 5 in by 7 in	
2/1231/25	Meccano/Hornby folder	
13/832/500	1932/33 catalogue, 36 pp, 5 in by 7 in	
13/633/750(1P)	1933/34 catalogue, 40 pp, 5 in by 7 in	
13/834/900	1934/35 catalogue, 64 pp, 5 in by 7 in	
13/635/938.5	1935/36 catalogue, 64 pp, 5 in by 7 in	
13/736/1302	1936/37 catalogue, 72 pp, 5 in by 7 in	
13/737/1,150	1937/38 catalogue, 72 pp, 8½ in by 5½ in	
13/638/1150	1938/39 catalogue, 72 pp, 8½ in by 5½ in	
13/639/1,1500	1939/40 catalogue, 72 pp, 8½ in by 5½ in	
16/347/50	March 1947,	black/white 2pp
No code	November 1947	4 pp
16/248/10	1948,	blue/white
16/448/30	1st May 1948,	pale green/white 4 pp
16/948/200	October 1948,	violet/white 4 pp
16/449/100	April-May 1949,	light brown/white 6pp folder
16/1049/100	October 1949,	violet/white folder
13/1049/150		black/buff/white 8pp booklet
16/250/100	1st February 1950,	brown/white 6 pp folder
16/450/150	June 1950,	black/blue/white 8 pp folder
16/1050/160	October 1950,	blue/white 8 pp folder

16/251/33	March 1951,	brown/white 8 pp folder
16/651/75	March 1951,	blue/white 8 pp folder
16/1051/25	October 1951,	purple/white 8 pp folder
16/1151/10	do.	
16/152/50	February 1952,	brown/white 16 pp booklet
16/452/50	April 1952,	blue/white 16 pp booklet
16/852/500	September 1952,	brown/white 16 pp booklet
16/153/50	1st February 1953,	blue/white booklet
16/453/50	15th April 1953,	violet/white 16 pp booklet
13/953/678	1st October 1953,	20 pp booklet
13/1053/350 2P	do.	
13/654/995	1954–5,	24 pp booklet, colour cover
13/655/797	1955/6,	28 pp booklet, colour cover
13/756/525	(No date),	32 pp full colour booklet
7/457/150	1957,	full colour folder
13/757/500	1957,	32 pp full colour booklet
13/758/450	1958,	20 pp full colour booklet
7/263/400	(No date),	20 pp full colour booklet
9/464/150 1stP	(No date),	8 pp full colour booklet
9/464/150 2ndP	(No date),	8 pp full colour booklet

PRICE LISTS, MECCANO PRODUCTS and HORNBY:

Illustrated price lists have been included with catalogues and folders.

222/10	1st March 1922, revised prices
No code	19th February 1923, revised prices
No code	1st September 1925, revised prices
6/930/6	Revised prices for Hornby rails
1/1035/31.5	1935–36 revised prices
1/836/13	Season 1936–37 revised prices
1/138/50(2P)	1st January 1938
1/138/50(3P)	do.
1/238/10 (4P)	do.
1/338/25 (5P)	do.
1/538/10 (6P)	do.
1/638/10 (7P)	do.
1/140/50	1st January 1940
1/440/100	April 1940
16/840/50	August 1940
16/1040/100	21st October 1940
16/641/25	May 1941
16/1141/20	1st November 1941
16/1053/150	1st October 1953
16/354/50	1st April 1954
16/454/50	1st May 1954
16/754/20	(no date). Hamleys.

16/954/50	(no date)
16/155/100	February 1955
16/255/100	February 1955
16/355/50	March 1955 (PU)
16/355/100	March 1955
16/555/100	May 1955
16/1055/500	27th October 1955
16/156/100M 1st P	1st February 1956
16/456/100M 2ndP	April 1956
13/656/525	July 1956
16/956/200	September 1956
16/157/100M	1st February 1957
16/457/100M 2ndP	April 1957
16/757/100 3rdP	August 1957
16/857/500	September 1957
16/1057/100 4thP	October 1957
16/158/100 1stP	1st February 1958
16/558/50 2ndP	1st May 1958
16/658/30 3rdP	1st July 1958
16/658/70 3rdP	1st July 1958
10/758/450	1958
16/858/58 4thP	1st August 1958
16/958/50 5thP	1st November 1958
16/1258/70 6thP	December 1958
16/459/100 1stP	1st May 1959
16/859/75	1959. Hamleys
16/959/100 2ndP	1st September 1959
16/1059/145 3rdP	1st October 1959
16/1259/145 4thP	December 1959
8/760/70	1960. Hamleys
8/760/125 1stP	August 1960
16/1060/100 2ndP	August 1960
16/261/100 1stP	1st February 1961
16/561/50 2ndP	1st May 1961
16/761/60	1961. Hamleys
16/861/60	1961
16/861/100 3rdP	1st September 1961
16/1161/100 4thP	1st November 1961
16/1261/100 1stP	February 1962
16/462/170m 3rdP	April 1962
16/662/100m 4thP	June 1962
16/962/150m 5thP	September 1962
16/163/50m 1stP	January 1963
7/463/400	(no date)
16/563/60	1963 (PU)
16/963/125 2ndP	September 1963
16/164/100	1964
9/464/150 1st P	1964
9/664/150 2ndP	1964

16/964/60	1964 (PU)
16/1264/150 1stP	1965
16/665/50	September 1965, Hamleys
1/766/150	July 1966
No code	January 1967
No code	1969

MISC. HORNBY and MECCANO PRODUCT LEAFLETS etc.
which include Hornby advertisements

620/45	Black/white 2pp
820/250	do.
1220/100	do.
921/350	do.
No code	Full colour, similar to 921/350
122/10	Lattice Girder Bridge and Timber Wagon, 2pp
No code	'Hornby Presentation Sets'
No code	'Birthday Gifts. . .', entry form
No code	'The Hornby Electric Train', 4 pp colour
725/400	'Run your own Railway'
426/10	'Jackie Coogan Visits a Meccano Factory', booklet
826/205	'The New Meccano', folder, colour cover
1026/50	'Jackie Coogan Visits a Meccano Factory', booklet
1026/100	'The New Meccano', folder, colour cover
527/175	'Hornby Trains', blue/cream single sheet
727/80	'Adventures in Meccanoland', booklet
No code	'Three new Hornby Trains', (No. 3 Trains)
528/275	'Which is the Greatest Railway Company in the World?'
928/25	'Adventures in Meccanoland', booklet
1/430/280	'Right Away for Happy Days'
2/1030/50	'Boys! Here is a plan. . .', part exchange leaflet
1/731/375	'Longer Runs, Heavier Loads'
?	'Longer Runs with Heavier Loads' (similar to 1/832/200)
1/832/200(1P)	'Boys, Start a Railway of your Own'
1/932/5	'Boys! Here is a plan . . .', part exchange leaflet
1/1232/25	Hornby Countryside Sections
1/233/100	Meccano Products and Hornby, 2pp
1/633/250	Meccano products and Hornby, 2pp
1/534/240	Meccano products and Hornby, 2pp
1/1134/150	Meccano products and Hornby, 2pp
1/539/5	June 1939, Exchange scheme leaflet
16/865/35	'Percy the Small Engine', full colour
No code	'Meet Percy in Person!', black/brown/white
No code	'Meet Percy in Person!', full colour
No code	'The Play Train by Meccano', full colour 4pp

MECCANO INSTRUCTION MANUALS
with HORNBY ADVERTISEMENTS:
  All 'English Edition'

921/15	Book No. 3, full colour or black/white 2pp insert
622/50	No. 22A, pages 59–62
922/10	No. 22.0, page 17
1022/85	No. 22A, pages 59–62
1222/5	No. 22, pages 203–206
1223/2.5	No. 23, pages 203–206
724/25	No. 24A, pages 59 to 62
725/100	No. 25A, pages 59–62
626/50	No. 26.0, page 17
626/75	No. 26A, pages 59–62
626/10.5	No. 26, pages 205–208
No code	1926 'Standard Mechanisms' manual
127/10	1927 'Standard Mechanisms' manual
127(F)30	No. 27.0, page 17
127(F)5	No. 27, pages 205–208
127(F)30	No. 27A, pages 59–62
427/75	No. 27A, pages 59–62
427/10	No. 27, pages 205–208
1027/5	No. 27, pages 205–208
528/15	No. 28, pages 136–138
628/75	No. 28.0, pages 27–28
628/100	No. 28A, pages 108–110
1028/50	No. 28A, pages 108–110
1028/5	No. 28, pages 136–138
1128/15	No. 28.0, pages 27–28
1128/3	'Standard Mechanisms' Manual
329/50	No. 29.0, pages 42–44
629/3(2)	No. 29, pages 137–138
2/130/15(1)	No. 30A, pages 132–134
2/330/75(2)	No. 30A, pages 131–134
2/730/100(2)	No. 30A, pages 131–134

Various 1937–41 Manuals advertised Hornby Trains
on the back cover.

'HORNBY CONTROL SYSTEM' LEAFLET: 4pp

926/12	13/532/15	1/1236/1
1126/20	1/433/40	1/237/2
627/35	1/935/7.5	1/937/1
728/20	1/1235/2.5	1/1237/1
2/831/45	1/436/15	

'HOW TO PLAN YOUR HORNBY RAILWAY'
        and similar leaflets:

926/35	'The Hornby Train System', 8 pp
1127/25	'How to Get More Fun out of Hornby Trains', 12pp
628/80	'How to Get More Fun out of Hornby Trains', 12pp
2/929/10	'How to Plan Your Hornby Railway', 12pp
16/430/50	'How to Plan Your Hornby Railway', 12pp
2/531/40	'How to Plan Your Hornby Railway', 12pp
2/632/2.5	'How to Plan Your Hornby Electric Railway', 4pp
13/732/15	'How to Plan Your Hornby Railway', 12pp
2/433/35	'How to Plan Your Hornby Railway', 12pp
1/533/4	'How to Plan Your Hornby Electric Railway', 4pp
2/1134/10	'How to Plan Your Hornby Railway'
7/1134/20	'How to Plan Your Hornby Electric Railway', 4pp
15/1134/10	'How to Choose and Use a Hornby Electric Railway'
2/1035/15(2P)	'How to Plan Your Hornby Railway', 12pp
2/336/16(1P)	'How to Plan Your Hornby Railway', 12pp
2/636/5(2P)	'How to Plan Your Hornby Railway, 12pp
1/636/50	'How to Develop Your Hornby Model Railway', 2pp
1/1036/6	'How to Plan Your Hornby Electric Railway', 4pp
7/737/14(1P)	'How to Plan Your Hornby Railway', 12pp
1/937/3.5	'How to Plan Your Hornby Electric Railway', 4pp
1/438/10	'How to Plan Your Hornby Electric Railway', 4pp
1/938/3	'How to Plan Your Hornby Electric Railway', 4pp
1/1238/20	'How to Develop Your Hornby Clockwork Railway'
7/1039/10	'How to Plan your Hornby Railway', 12 pp

RAIL FORMATION LEAFLETS:

922/20	'Rail Formations', 8 pp
1122/10	do.
123/10	do.
523/35	do.
525/40	do.
1/1034/30	'Hornby Layouts. 100 Suggestions', 12 pp
1/735/40	do.
1/1235/5	do.
1/136/50	do.
1/737/55	do.
1/737/10	do. (1938 edition)
1/1238/25	do.
1/140/30	'Hornby Layouts. 60 Suggestions', 8 pp
15/849/25	'Layouts for Clockwork Track', 8 pp
15/949/50	do.
15/1149/150	do.
15/151/150	do.
16/152/100	'Layouts for Clockwork Track', 4 pp
16/1052/50	'Layout Suggestions for Clockwork Track', 4pp
16/1253/200	do.
16/1154/100	do.
16/1055/100	do.
15/157/100	do.
10/259/75	do.
10/260/100	do.

10/261/120	do.		
10/1261/100	do.		

HORNBY RAILWAY COMPANY
SENIOR SECTION BOOKLET:

24 page booklets titled 'The Hornby Railway Company'

1028/9–10	Horizontal format
13/1132/5	Vertical format
13/434/5(2P)	do.
13/137/5(3R)	do.
13/140/2	do.
13/241/2	do.
13/1148/20	do.
13/1149/20	do.
13/350/20	do.
13/1250/12	do.
13/1252/30	do.
13/1055/12	do.
13/256/10	do.
13/1058/20	do.

HORNBY RAILWAY COMPANY
JUNIOR SECTION BOOKLET:

24 page booklets titled 'How to Get More Fun from Your Hornby Train'

2/331/5
2/332/5
2/335/5
2/137/5
2/239/5
2/1140/5
2/946/1

HRC FORMS:

Pads of fifty forms: no code, 1/1130/200 pds, 1/232/250 pds

GW1 General Working Timetable, black/yellow
SD4 Stationmaster's Arrivals and Departures, black/cream
EJ5 Engineman's Job Card, black/buff
SB6 Signal Box instructions, black/pink
SR7 Stationmaster's Report Form

HRC MEMBERSHIP APPLICATION FORMS:

1128/50	4 pp	1/1130/95	do.
1228/50	do.	1/431/160	do.
429/175	do.	1/232/160	do.
1/430/100	2pp	1/433/125	do.

1/234/250	do.	5/649/200	do.
No code	do.	5/350/200	do.
1/236/200	do.	5/1250/250	do.
1/636/100	do.	5/1051/100	do.
1/537/150	do.	5/352/100	do.
1/138 200	do.	5/752/100	do.
1/238/200	do.	17/354/200	do.
1/638/15	do.	17/1154/250	do.
1/738/200	do.	17/1255/250	do.
1/139/210	do.	17/157/250	do.
2/440/75	do.	17/1258/250	do.
16/946/50	2pp	10/860/250	do.
5/448/150	do.	10/961/250	do.
5/1048/150	do.		

HRC CORRESPONDENCE CLUB APPLICATION FORM:

only one known,

17/749/2	Post-card

GUARANTEES and INSTRUCTIONS,
CLOCKWORK LOCOS AND SETS:

No code	Instructions, Hornby Train Set (1920, Loco and Truck only)
No code	Instructions, Hornby No. 1 Train Set (1921, with coaches)
No code	Instructions, Hornby No. 2 Train Set
921/5	Instructions, Hornby Loco
1121/25	Instructions, Hornby No. 1 Loco
No code	60 day Guarantee, Instructions on back Several versions known, with different borders
625/25	60 day Guarantee, Instructions on back
No code	'Important', note on radii for No. 0, 1, 2 Trains.
227/75	60 day Guarantee, Instructions on back
1227/50	60 day Guarantee, Instructions on back
No code	'Important', note on radii for No. 0, 1, 2, Metropolitan and Riviera Blue
428/25	60 day Guarantee, Instructions on back
428/75	Unlimited Guarantee, Instructions on back (for M Series)
429/50	60 day Guarantee & Instructions
No code	'Important'; note on radii for M, 0, 1, 2, 3 and Met
6/1129/50	60 day Guarantee & Instructions
1/430/50	60 day Guarantee & Instructions
1/830/60	Unlimited Guarantee & Instructions
1/1230/20	60 day Guarantee & Instructions
1/431/75	'Important'; note on radii
1/431/120 M	Unlimited Guarantee & Instructions
1/531/120 M	Unlimited Guarantee & Instructions
1/531/60 C	60 day Guarantee & Instructions

1/132/15	Unlimited Guarantee & Instructions
1/132/55	'Important'; note on radii
1/232/5	(for MO).
1/232/16	M3 Guarantee & Instruction
1/232/2	M3 30 day Guarantee & Instructions
1/232/20	No. 1 up sets, Guarantee & Instructions
1/232/30	No. 1 up loco, Guarantee & Instructions
1/233/75	M1/2 up 'Read this first', re oiling/radii
1/333/15	M3 30 day Guarantee and Instructions
1/333/20	No. 1 up 60 day Guarantee & Instructions
1/1233/20	M1/2 up 'Read this first', re oiling/radii
1/134/75	MO 'Read this first', re oiling
1/134/200	M1/2 up 'Read this first', re oiling/radii
1/134/15	MO instructions
1/234/30	M1/2 Instructions
1/135/15	MO Instructions
1/235/25	No. 1 up 60 day Guarantee & Instructions
1/335/60	M1/2 up 'Read this first', re oiling/radii
1/335/15	M3 & No. 0 Guarantee & Instructions
1/1035/10	No. 1 up Guarantee & Instructions
1/136/35	M3 & No. 0 instructions
1/136/35	M3 and No. 0 30 day Guarantee
1/336/82.5	MO Instructions
1/336/62.5	M1/2 Instructions
1/336/27.5	M3 and No. 0 Instructions
1/336/9.7	M3 and No. 0 30 day Guarantee
1/336/40	No. 1 up 60 day Guarantee
1/436/40	No. 1 up Instructions
1/936/7.5	No. 1 up Guarantee
1/1136/2.5	MO and No. 0 Silver Jubilee Instructions
1/437/60	M1/2 Instructions
1/437/55	M3 up Instructions
1/537/100	MO Instructions
1/537/40	No. 1 up 60 day Guarantee
1/1037/10	M3 up Instructions
1/338/75	M1/2 Instructions
1/338/50	M3 & No. 0 30 day Guarantee
1/438/75	M1/2 Instructions
1/439/35	M1/2 up Instructions
1/1139/100	MO Instructions
1/1239/30	M3 & No. 0 Guarantee

Postwar 'Hints on Running Your Hornby Railway'

16/646/100	M1 up
17/647/100	M1 up
16/248/75	M1 up
17/348/40	MO
16/449/100	M1 up
16/1049/30	M1 up

16/150/125	M1 up
17/1050/125	M1 up
17/751/110	M1 up
17/1151/150	M1 up
7/1151/2501	Oiling instructions, multilingual
17/253/80	M1 up
17/254/150	30 up
17/1154/75	30 up
17/155/110	30 up
10/1255/75	No. 20/21
10/1255/110	30 up
10/1256/75	No. 20/21
10/1256/75	30 up
10/658/25	30 up
10/758/50	No. 20/21
10/359/50	No. 20/21
10/559/25	30 up
10/161/10	30 up
10/1161/15	30 up

INSTRUCTIONS, ELECTRIC LOCOMOTIVES and SETS:

1126/5	Metropolitan No. 2 and other 4V trains 4pp
No Code	No. 3E Train Sets, 4 volt 4pp
527/1.5	Metropolitan No. 1 HV 4pp
228/1	Metropolitan HV 4 pp
629/5	No. 1 Electric Tank Loco (6V DC) 2pp
629/3.5	No. 3E (6 volt) Train Sets
6/331/.5	Metropolitan LV (6 Volt)
6/331/5	No. 3E (6 volt) Train Sets
1/632/2	LSTM3/20, LE1/20, LST1/20, LE2/20 Instructions 2pp
2/1134/1	EPM16 Special Tank 2pp
2/1134/2.5	E26 Special Tank and E36 4pp
2/1134/.5	Metropolitan E36 4pp
2/1134/5	EM36, E06, E16, E16 Tank 4pp
2/1134/10	EM320, E020, E120, E120 Tank 4pp
2/1134/7.5	20 volt Auto Reverse locos 4pp
2/235/10	20 volt Auto Reverse locos 4pp
1/335/1	EM16 Loco 2pp
1/336/12.5	20 volt Auto Reverse locos 4pp
1/536/2.5	EM320, E020, E120, E120 Tank 4pp
1/936/.25	Metropolitan E36, 4pp
1/1236/1	E26 Special Tank, 4pp
1/1236/1.5	EM320, E020, E120, E120 Tank 4pp
No code	EM320, E020, E120, E120 Tank 4pp
1/137/1.5	EM120 Loco 2pp
1/537/2.5	'Princess Elizabeth' Loco 4pp
1/637/2.5	EM320, E020, E120, E120 Tank 4pp
1/637/15	20 Volt Auto Reverse 4pp
No code	Addenda for Eton E420 Locomotive

1/737/.35	Metropolitan E36
1/338/15	20 Volt Auto Reverse 4pp
1/939/5	20 Volt Auto Reverse 4pp
1/1139/1	E26 Special Tank 4pp
No code	EM320, E020, E120, E120 Tank 4pp
No code	20 volt Auto Reverse 4pp

(All auto reverse instructions covered the E120 Special, E120 Special Tank, E220 Special, E220 Special Tank, and the E320. This last version also included the E420.)

16/948/5	E502 and E602 Train Sets 4pp
16/850/2.5	do.

GUARANTEES, ELECTRIC LOCOMOTIVES and SETS:

428/5	60 day
6/331/5 E	do.
1/531/6 E	do.
1/132/4	do.
1/1232/5	do.
1/1233/5	do. (also version overstamped '30 days')
1/1134/6	30 day, for locos up to E120/E16
1/135/4.5	60 day, for E120 Special up
1/136/10	do.
1/537/15	do.
1/1237/2.5	do.
1/338/22.5	do.

INSTRUCTIONS FOR TRANSFORMERS:

6/432/2	Ferranti Transformer
6/632/1	T20A
1/732/1	T20
1/833/1.5?	T20A
No code	T20A
1/834/1.7	T6A
1/834/2.2	T20
1/135/12.5	T20
1/135/2.5	T20M
1/135/8	T20A
1/335/.3	TR6
1/735/12.5	T20A
1/337/3	T20A
1/537/.5	T6A
1/537/.25	T22M
1/537/.6	T22M
1/637/1.	T20M
1/737/4	T20A
1/338/2.7	T22M
1/438/.3	T6M
1/438/7.5	T20

1/538/6	T20A
1/1039/.25	T6
1/1039/.25	T26M
1/1039/7.5	T20
16/848/5	T20
16/949/20	T20
16/351/25	T20M

INSTRUCTIONS FOR DISTRIBUTION BOX:

1/832/1	1/1232/5
1/932/5	1/1233/5

INSTRUCTIONS FOR ELECTRICALLY LIGHTED ACCESSORIES:

1/735/10	1/1136/20
1/835/4(2P)	1/537/40
1/136/17.5	1/539/20
1/936/3.5	1/739/5.2
1/1036/2	

INSTRUCTIONS FOR CIRCUIT BREAKERS:

1/835/5	
1/336/5	
1/836/5	
1/1136/10.5	
1/437/20	
1/239/5.25	20V
1/439/1.25	20V
1/739/.25	6V
1/640/6.	20V

EGRY LTD., LONDON, W.3. Autographic Recorder Systems. 6-37

Patent No: 196291

MECCANO LTD.

BINNS ROAD, LIVERPOOL, 13.

ADVICE

E

Name

Town

Specification of HORNBY TRAIN SETS included in

Invoice dated 193

SETS (Clockwork)	Qty.	PRICE Retail	PRICE Trade	£	s.	d.
MO GOODS (Red Loco)		4/11	3/3⅓			
MO GOODS (Green Loco.		4/11	3/3⅓			
MO PASS. (Red Loco.)		5/6	3/8			
MO PASS. (Green Loco.		5/6	3/8			
MO Mixed Goods (Red Loco.)		6/11	4/7⅓			
MO Mixed Goods (Green Loco.)		6/11	4/7⅓			
M1 PASS. (Red Loco.)		8/11	5/11⅓			
M1 PASS. (Green Loco.)		8/11	5/11⅓			
M1 GOODS LMS Red		8/11	5/11⅓			
LNE Green		8/11	5/11⅓			
GW Green		8/11	5/11⅓			
S Green		8/11	5/11⅓			
M2 PASS. (Red Loco)		10/6	7/-			
M2 PASS. (Green Loco.)		10/6	7/-			
M8 MODEL RAILWAY (Red Loco.)		8/11	5/11⅓			
M8 MODEL RAILWAY (Green Loco)		8/11	5/11⅓			
M9 MODEL RAILWAY (Red Loco.)		11/6	7/8			
M9 MODEL RAILWAY (Green Loco)		11/6	7/8			
M10 MODEL RAILWAY (Red Loco.)		18/9	12/6			
M10 MODEL RAILWAY (Green Loco.)		18/9	12/6			
3c METROPOLITAN		40/-	26/8			
O STREAMLINE		7/6	5/-			
O SILVER JUBILEE		7/6	5/-			
SETS (Elec. 20 volt.)						
EM120 PASS. (Red Loco.)		15/-	10/-			
EM120 PASS. (Green Loco.)		15/-	10/-			
EM120 GOODS LMS Red		15/-	10/-			
LNE Green		15/-	10/-			
GW Green		15/-	10/-			
S Green		15/-	10/-			
SETS (Elec. 6 volt.)						
EM16 GOODS LMS Red		15/-	10/-			
LNE Green		15/-	10/-			
GW Green		15/-	10/-			
S Green		15/-	10/-			
E36 METROPOLITAN		57/6	38/4			
Carried forward						

SETS (Clockwork)	COLOURS LMS Black	LMS Red	LNE Black	LNE Green	GW Green	S Black	S Green	Riv.	PRICE Retail	PRICE Trade	£	s.	d.
Brought forward													
M11 MODEL RAILWAY	—		—			—		—	25/-	16/8			
M3 TANK GOODS	—		—			—		—	15/-	10/-			
M3 TANK PASS.	—		—			—		—	13/9	9/2			
O GOODS								—	15/9	10/6			
O PASSENGER								—	15/9	10/6			
1 GOODS								—	21/-	14/-			
1 TANK GOODS								—	21/-	14/-			
1 PASSENGER								—	23/6	15/8			
1 SPEC. TANK GOODS								—	26/-	17/4			
1 SPECIAL PASS.								—	31/-	20/8			
2 MIXED GOODS								—	32/6	21/8			
2 TANK PASSENGER								—	37/6	25/-			
2 SPECIAL PASS.	—		—			—		—	52/-	34/8			
3c PASSENGER	—		—			—	—	—	47/6	31/8			
3c PULLMAN	—	—	—	—	—	—		—	58/6	39/-			
3c RIVIERA "BLUE"	—	—	—	—	—	—	—		52/6	35/-			
SETS (Elec. 20 volt.)													
EM320 TANK GOODS	—		—			—		—	24/-	16/-			
EO20 PASSENGER								—	27/-	18/-			
E120 GOODS								—	32/-	21/4			
E120 TANK GOODS								—	32/-	21/4			
E120 SPL. TK. GOODS								—	40/-	26/8			
E120 SPECIAL PASS.								—	45/-	30/-			
E220 MIXED GOODS								—	45/-	30/-			
E220 TANK PASS.								—	50/-	33/4			
E220 SPECIAL PASS.	—		—			—		—	72/-	48/-			
E320 PASSENGER	—		—			—	—	—	67/6	45/-			
E320 PULLMAN	—	—	—	—	—	—		—	70/-	46/8			
E320 RIVIERA "BLUE"	—	—	—	—	—	—	—		65/-	43/4			
SETS (Elec. 6 volt.)													
EM36 TANK GOODS	—		—			—		—	24/-	16/-			

When a column contains a — the colour named at its head is not available

£

EGRY LTD., LONDON, W.3. Autographic Recorder Systems. 6-37

Patent No 196291

MECCANO LTD.

BINNS ROAD, LIVERPOOL, 13.

ADVICE

F

Name ______________________ Specification of **LOCOS & TENDERS** included in

Town ______________________ Invoice ____________ dated ____________ 193__

LOCOS. (Clockwork)	Qty.	PRICE Retail	PRICE Trade	£	s.	d.
MO Red		2/9	1/10			
MO Green		2/9	1/10			
M1/2 Red		4/6	3/-			
M1/2 Green		4/6	3/-			
O STREAMLINE		3/6	2/4			
O "SILVER LINK"		3/6	2/4			
METRO 3C		21/-	14/-			
LOCOS. (Elec. 20 volt.)						
EM 120 Red		8/6	5/8			
EM 120 Green		8/6	5/8			
Resistance Controller 20v.		3/9	2/6			
LOCOS. (Elec. 6 volt.)						
EM 16 Red		8/6	5/8			
EM 16 Green		8/6	5/8			
METRO E36		30/-	20/-			
Resistance Controller 6v.		3/9	2/6			
Speed and Reverse Control Switch		5/3	3/6			
TENDERS						
MO Red		-/6	-/4			
MO Green		-/6	-/4			
M1/2 Red		-/9	-/6			
M1/2 Green		-/9	-/6			
O STREAMLINE		1/-	-/8			
O "SILVER LINK"		1/-	-/8			
Carried forward						

LOCOS (Clockwork)	LMS Black	LMS Red	LNE Black	LNE Green	GW Green	S Black	S Green	Riv.	PRICE Retail	PRICE Trade	£	s.	d.
						Bought forward							
M3 TANK	—		—			—		—	7/6	5/-			
O								—	8/11	5/11½			
1								—	11/6	7/8			
1 TANK								—	11/6	7/8			
1 SPECIAL								—	15/9	10/6			
1 SPECIAL TANK								—	15/9	10/6			
2 SPECIAL	—		—			—		—	27/6	18/4			
2 SPECIAL TANK								—	19/6	13/-			
3C	—		—			—			22/6	15/-			
4C "ETON"	—	—	—	—	—	—		—	35/-	23/4			
LOCOS. (Elec. 20 volt.)													
EM320 TANK	—		—			—		—	16/6	11/-			
EO20								—	19/-	12/8			
E120								—	20/-	13/4			
E120 TANK								—	20/-	13/4			
E120 SPECIAL								—	27/6	18/4			
E120 SPECIAL TANK								—	27/6	18/4			
E220 SPECIAL	—		—			—		—	37/6	25/-			
E220 SPECIAL TANK								—	30/-	20/-			
E320	—		—			—			32/6	21/8			
E420 "ETON"	—	—	—	—	—	—		—	42/6	28/4			
"PRINCESS ELIZABETH" { Loco and Tender	—		—	—	—	—	—	—	105/-	70/-			
LOCOS. (Elec. 6 volt.)													
EM36 TANK	—		—			—		—	16/6	11/-			
EPM16 SPECIAL TANK (perm. mag. complete)								—	33/6	22/4			
E26 SPECIAL TANK								—	27/6	18/4			
TENDERS													
O/1								—	2/-	1/4			
1 SPECIAL						SOUTHERN 1759	850	— 900	3/3	2/2			
2 SPECIAL	—		—						6/-	4/-			
3 RIVIERA	—	—	—	—	—	—	—		4/6	3/-			
When a column contains a — the colour named at its head is not available.									£				

Egry Ltd., London, W.3. Autographic Recorder Systems. 6/37.

MECCANO LTD.
BINNS ROAD, LIVERPOOL, 13.

ADVICE

G1
Patent No 196291

Specification of ROLLING STOCK included in

Invoice .... dated 193

Name ....

Town ....

Table 1

Rolling Stock	Qty	Retail	Trade	£ s. d.
Banana Vans No. O		1/6	1/-	
" " No. 1		2/3	1/6	
Barrel Wagons		2/6	1/8	
Biscuit Vans, Carr's		2/3	1/6	
" Crawford's		2/3	1/6	
" Jacob's		2/3	1/6	
Bitumen Tk. Wgns, Colas		3/6	2/4	
Box Cars, U.S.A. Type		2/3	1/6	
Brake Vans LMS		2/9	1/10	
" LNE		2/9	1/10	
" GW		2/9	1/10	
" S		2/9	1/10	
Breakdown Van & Crane LMS		5/11	3/11¾	
" LNE		5/11	3/11¾	
" GW		5/11	3/11¾	
" S		5/11	3/11¾	
Cabooses, U.S.A. Type		2/-	1/4	
Cattle Trucks No.1 LMS		2/3	1/6	
" LNE		2/3	1/6	
" GW		2/3	1/6	
" S		2/3	1/6	
" No.2 LMS		4/6	3/-	
" LNE		4/6	3/-	
" GW		4/6	3/-	
" S		4/6	3/-	
Cement Wagons		1/11	1/3¾	
Chocolate Vans, Cadbury's		2/3	1/6	
COACHES				
MO Pullman		-/9	-/6	
M1/2 "		1/-	-/8	
No. O "		1/3	-/10	
No. O Streamline		1/9	1/2	
No. O Silver Jubilee		1/9	1/2	

Carried forward

Table 2

Rolling Stock continued	Qty	Retail	Trade	£ s. d.
Brought forward				
COACHES (Continued)				
No. 1 Passenger LMS		2/6	1/8	
" LNE		2/6	1/8	
" GW		2/6	1/8	
" S		2/6	1/8	
No. 1 Pullman		2/6	1/8	
No. 1 " Composite		2/6	1/8	
No. 2 Pass. 1st LMS		6/6	4/4	
" 3rd LNE		6/6	4/4	
" GW		6/6	4/4	
" S		6/6	4/4	
No. 2 Cor'dor 1st/3rd LMS		6/6	4/4	
Brake/ 3rd LMS		7/6	5/-	
" LNE		7/6	5/-	
" GW		7/6	5/-	
" S		7/6	5/-	
Brake/Comp LMS		7/6	5/-	
" LNE		7/6	5/-	
" GW		7/6	5/-	
" S		7/6	5/-	
No. 2 Pullman		9/6	6/4	
No. 2 Saloon LMS		9/6	6/4	
No. 2 Saloon LNE		9/6	6/4	
No. 2 Special Pullman		13/6	8/8	
No. 2 Composite		13/6	8/8	
No. 3 Riviera, Dining		10/6	7/-	
No. 3 " Sleeping		10/6	7/-	
Pullman, U.S.A. Type		1/6	1/-	
No. O Mitropa, Dining		1/6	1/-	
No. O " Sleeping		1/6	1/-	
No. 3 Mitropa, Dining		10/6	7/-	
No. 3 " Sleeping		10/6	7/-	
Metropolitan C		7/6	5/-	
Metropolitan E		11/6	7/8	

Carried forward

Table 3

Rolling Stock continued	Qty	Retail	Trade	£ s. d.
Brought forward				
Coal Wagons		2/3	1/6	
Crane Trucks MO		1/-	-/8	
" No. 1		2/3	1/6	
Fibre Wagons		1/3	-/10	
Fish Vans No. O LMS		1/6	1/-	
" LNE		1/6	1/-	
" GW		1/6	1/-	
Flat Trucks LMS		1/6	1/-	
" LNE		1/6	1/-	
" GW		1/6	1/-	
" S		1/6	1/-	
" with Cable Drum LMS		1/9	1/2	
" LNE		1/9	1/2	
" GW		1/9	1/2	
" S		1/9	1/2	
" with Container LMS		2/-	1/4	
" LNE		2/-	1/4	
" GW		2/-	1/4	
" S		2/-	1/4	
Gas Cylinder Wagons		1/6	1/-	
Guards Vans LMS		2/6	1/8	
" LNE		2/6	1/8	
" GW		2/6	1/8	
" S		2/6	1/8	
Hopper Wagons LMS		2/9	1/10	
" LNE		2/9	1/10	
" GW		2/9	1/10	
" S		2/9	1/10	
Gunpowder Vans LMS		2/3	1/6	
" LNE		2/3	1/6	
" GW		2/3	1/6	
" S		2/3	1/6	
Luggage Vans No. 1 LMS		2/3	1/6	
" LNE		2/3	1/6	
" GW		2/3	1/6	
" S		2/3	1/6	
" No. 2 LMS		4/6	3/-	
" LNE		4/6	3/-	
" GW		4/6	3/-	
" S		4/6	3/-	

Carried forward £

MECCANO L™.
BINNS ROAD, LIVERPOOL, 13.
ADVICE

G2

Esry Ltd., London, W.3. Autographic Recorder Systems. 6-37   Patent No 18491

Name

Town

Specification of ROLLING STOCK & SUNDRIES included in
Invoice   dated   193

Rolling Stock *continued*	Qty.	PRICE Retail	Trade	£	s.	d.
Lumber Wagons No. 1		1/3	-/10			
" No. 2		2/11	1/11½			
Meat Vans No.O LMS		1/6	1/-			
" LNE		1/6	1/-			
" GW		1/6	1/-			
Milk Vans No.O		1/6	1/-			
" No. 1		2/3	1/6			
Milk Tk. Wns, Nestles		4/6	3/-			
Oil Tk. Wgns., Castrol		1/11	1/3¾			
" Mobiloil		1/11	1/3¾			
" Royal Daylight		1/11	1/3¾			
Petrol Tk. Wgns., MO		1/-	-/8			
" No. 1 Esso		1/11	1/3¾			
" Redline—Glico		1/11	1/3¾			
" Shell—B.P.		1/11	1/3¾			
Refrig. Vns No.O LMS		1/6	1/-			
" LNE		1/6	1/-			
" GW		1/6	1/-			
" S		1/6	1/-			
" No. 1 LMS		2/3	1/6			
" LNE		2/3	1/6			
" GW		2/3	1/6			
" S		2/3	1/6			
Rotary Tipping Wagons MO		1/-	-/8			
" No. O		1/6	1/-			
" No. 1		1/11	1/3¾			
Side Tip'g Wgns. MO		1/-	-/8			
" No. 1		1/9	1/2			
Snow Ploughs		3/6	2/4			
Tank Cars, U.S.A. Type		1/9	1/2			
Timber Wagons, No. 1		1/3	-/10			
" No. 2		2/6	1/8			
Trolley Wagons		3/9	2/6			
" with 2 cable drums		4/3	2/10			
Wine Wagons Double Barrel		4/6	3/-			
Carried forward				£		

Rolling Stock *continued*	Qty.	PRICE Retail	Trade	£	s.	d.
Brought forward						
WAGONS						
MO without Lettering		-/6	-/4			
M 1 LMS		-/10	-/6⅜			
" LNE		-/10	-/6⅜			
" GW		-/10	-/6⅜			
" S		-/10	-/6⅜			
No. O LMS		1/3	-/10			
" LNE		1/3	-/10			
" GW		1/3	-/10			
" S		1/3	-/10			
No. 1 LMS		1/6	1/-			
" LNE		1/6	1/-			
" GW		1/6	1/-			
" S		1/6	1/-			
with lookout NORD		3/3	2/2			
Covered NORD		2/6	1/8			
Open "B" LMS		2/-	1/4			
" LNE		2/-	1/4			
" GW		2/-	1/4			
" S		2/-	1/4			
No. 2 High Capacity LMS		3/9	2/6			
" LNE		3/9	2/6			
" GW		3/9	2/6			

	Qty.	PRICE Retail	Trade	£	s.	d.
Meccano Sundries						
				£		
Mechanical Sundries						
KEYS						
B.9/4865	3					
3/4373	5					
M.E 3/4173	3					
Advertising Matter						
				£		

321

EGRY LTD., LONDON, W.3. Autographic Recorder Systems. 5/35.

Patent No. 198291

MECCANO L^TD.

BINNS ROAD, LIVERPOOL 13.

ADVICE

H

Name ______________________

Specifications of **TRAIN ACCESSORIES** included in

Town ______________________ Invoice ______________ dated ______________ 193__

Accessories	Qty.	PRICE Retail	PRICE Trade	£	s.	d.
Buffer Stops No. 1		1/-	-/8			
,, ,, No. 1E★		1/6	1/-			
,, ,, No. 2		5/6	3/8			
,, ,, No. 2E★		6/-	4/-			
C'tryside Sect's F..... box		6/6	4/4			
,, ,, G 1 } box ,, ,, G 2 } box		7/6	5/-			
,, ,, } box ,, ,,						
,, ,, } box ,, ,,						
Cuttings ..... No. O		1/9				
,, No. 1prs.		3/-				
,, No. 2		2/-				
,, No. 3		2/-				
,, No. 4		6/-	4/-			
Engine Sheds No. 1a		10/6	7/-			
,, ,, No. 1		15/-	10/-			
,, ,, No. E1E★		15/6	10/4			
,, ,, No. 2a		17/6	11/8			
,, ,, No. 2		22/6	15/-			
,, ,, No. E2E★		23/-	15/4			
Fences with 4 trees, prs.		2/6	1/8			
Footbridges No. 1		2/11	1/11⅓			
,, No. 1a		4/6	3/-			
Hedges, on bases, box		3/-	2/-			
Hoardings, Station		-/6	-/4			
Lamp Stand'ds No. 1		3/3	2/2			
,, ,, No. 1E★		2/11	1/11⅓			
,, ,, No. 2		3/9	2/6			
,, ,, No. 2E★		3/3	2/2			
Level Crss'gs No. 1		2/11	1/11⅓			
,, ,, No. E1		4/-	2/8			
,, ,, No. E1E★		5/3	3/6			
,, ,, No. 2		5/6	3/8			
,, ,, No. E2		7/6	5/-			
,, ,, No. E2E★		9/-	6/-			
Loading Gauges		2/3	1/6			
M Footbridge		1/3	-/10			
M Level Crossings		1/6	1/-			
M Loading Gauges		1/-	-/8			
M Signals		-/4	-/2⅔			
Carried forward						

Accessories *continued*	Qty.	PRICE Retail	PRICE Trade	£	s.	d.
Brought forward						
M Signal Boxes		-/4	-/2⅔			
M Station Sets		3/-	2/-			
M Stations		1/-	-/8			
M Tele. Poles No. 1		-/3	-/2			
M ,, No. 2		-/4	-/2⅔			
M Wayside Stations		-/9	-/6			
Platelayers' Huts		1/-	-/8			
Platforms, Goods No. 1		7/6	5/-			
,, Goods No. 2		10/6	7/-			
,, No. 2 E★		11/6	7/8			
,, Island		5/6	3/8			
,, ,, E★		6/3	4/2			
,, Pass.		2/-	1/4			
Platform Cranes		3/11	2/7⅓			
,, Fencing l'gths		-/6	-/4			
,, Ramps, prs.		1/9	1/2			
Posters No. 1 Ser. Pkts.		-/6	-/4			
,, No. 2 ,, ,,		-/6	-/4			
Poster Boards Pkts.		-/4	-/2⅔			
Railway Access. No. 1		1/-	-/8			
,, ,, No. 2		1/3	-/10			
,, ,, No. 3		1/6	1/-			
,, ,, No. 4		3/9	2/6			
,, ,, No. 5		2/-	1/4			
,, ,, No. 7		-/10	-/6⅔			
,, ,, No. 8		1/9	1/2			
,, ,, No. 9		1/9	1/2			
Shunters Poles		-/2	-/1⅓			
Signal Cabins No. 1		2/6	1/8			
,, ,, No. 2		3/9	2/6			
,, ,, No. 2E★		4/3	2/10			
Signal Gantries No. 1 Home		4/11	3/3⅓			
,, No. 1 Dist.		4/11	3/3⅓			
,, No. 2 Home		10/-	6/8			
,, No. 2 Dist.		10/-	6/8			
,, No. 2E★Home		12/9	8/6			
,, No. 2E★Dist.		12/9	8/6			
Signals No. 1		1/-	-/8			
,, No. 2 Home		2/-	1/4			
,, No. 2 Dist.		2/-	1/4			
,, No. 2E★Home		2/9	1/10			
Carried forward						

Accessories *continued*	Qty.	PRICE Retail	PRICE Trade	£	s.	d.
Brought forward						
Signals No. 2E★Dist.		2/9	1/10			
,, Double No. 1		1/6	1/-			
,, ,, No. 2		2/6	1/8			
,, DoubleNo. 2E★		3/11	2/7⅓			
,, Jctn. No. 1		2/9	1/10			
,, ,, No. 2 Home		4/9	3/2			
,, ,, No. 2 Dist.		4/9	3/2			
,, ,, No.2E★Home		6/-	4/-			
,, ,, No.2E★Dist.		6/-	4/-			
Stations No. 1		4/6	3/-			
,, No. 2		8/-	5/4			
,, No. 2E★		9/3	6/2			
Telegraph Poles, prs.		3/6	2/4			
Trees, with stands, box		3/-	2/-			
,, Oak, box of 12		2/6	1/8			
,, Poplar ,, ,,		2/-	1/4			
Stands, ,, ,,		1/-	-/8			
Tunnels, No. O		1/3				
,, No. 1		1/9				
,, No. 2		3/6				
,, No. 3		4/-				
,, No. 4		4/9				
,, (l.h.) No. 5		6/9	4/6			
,, (r.h.) No. 6		6/9	4/6			
,, Metal		3/11	2/7⅓			
Tunnel Ends, pair		1/6	1/-			
Turntables No. 1		2/6	1/8			
,, No. 2		3/9	2/6			
,, No. E2		5/6	3/8			
Viaducts		6/6	4/4			
,, Centre Sections		4/-	2/8			
,, Elec.		7/6	5/-			
,, ,, Centre Sect.		4/6	3/-			
Water Tanks, No. 1		3/-	2/-			
,, ,, No. 2		5/9	3/10			
,, ,, No. 2E★		6/6	4/4			
				£		

★ ACCESSORIES MARKED THUS ARE WIRED FOR ELECTRIC LIGHTING.

MECCANO LTD.

TITLE:- TESTING DATA FOR HORNBY CLOCKWORK TRAINS.

MEMO No. 17107:

USED ON	REFER ALSO TO

TEST TRACK "A". 1'-6" DIA WITH TWO STRAIGHTS: 6'-6" PER LAP.

       "   "B". 2'-0" DIA.   "   "   "   8'-0"   "

       "   "C". 4'-0" DIA   "   "   "   14'-8"   "

TYPE OF TRAIN.	M.O.	M.I.	101/201.	501/601.
TYPE OF TRACK.	A.	B.	C.	C.
MIN. No OF LAPS. (LOCO ONLY).	10	12	8½	8½
MIN. No OF LAPS. (STANDARD LOAD).	8	10	7½	7½
MECHANISM SPEED. (BEFORE ASSY).	5 LAPS. 12-14. SECS	5 LAPS. 14-16. SECS	3 LAPS. 12-15. SECS	3 LAPS. 12-15. SECS

501/601 TRAINS TO REVERSE 4 SUCCESSIVE TIMES ON APPLICATION OF TRACK REVERSING MECHANISM:

ALL LOCO'S TO CLIMB STANDARD TEST TRACK:

ALL TRAINS TO STOP ON APPLICATION OF TRACK BRAKE:

STANDARD LOAD AS PACKED — 1951:

   M.O. - TENDER, TWO WAGONS, OR COACHES

   M.I. -   "   "   "   "   "   "

   101/201: - NO TENDER, THREE WAGONS, OR COACHES

   501/601: - TENDER,   "   "   "   "

2:	REDRAWN & REVISED:		3166	5/7/51	
ISSUE	DESCRIPTION OF CHANGE		C.O. No	DATE	SIG

MATERIAL.

LIMITS ON DIMENSIONS   DRAWN

FRACTIONS ±   TRACED

DECIMALS ±   CHECKED

SIZES & LIMITS AS SHOWN   APPROVED

                    DISTRIBUTION   SCALE

DATE 13·7·46

323

APPENDIX IV

SUMMARY OF LOCOMOTIVE NUMBERS

Loco numbers are a useful guide to the period during which a Hornby engine was manufactured, and the following list presents known Hornby Train loco numbers together with an estimate of the dates, and a note of the railway company livery and the colour. For tender engines they are given in the form NUMBER/NUMBER, the first number being that which appeared on the loco and the second that on the tender. If the loco is un-numbered on the cabside but has a number on the tender it is given as –/NUMBER, or –/– if there is no number on either loco or tender. Asterisks denote the use of a very small cabside number plate, frequently barely legible (especially the No. 0 and No. 1 numbers 208 and 232, which can be interpreted differently); 'imit' denotes use of a small numberplate with imitation writing. PU denote items that were probably made but the existence of which is unconfirmed.

Although the usual pairings of locos and tenders are given (and of course the loco number did not always match that on the tender) the locos and tenders were sold separately in the shops, so other combinations are possible and equally correct in the overlap periods. Arguments about which loco should go with which tender are hardly worth pursuing since no firm conclusions can be drawn.

Electric locomotives always had the same numbers as the clockwork versions of the same period.

The end dates for locomotives in black goods livery have been given as 1941, since they were available from 1936 by special order although not included in the catalogues.

In addition to the 250 or so loco numbers listed, there were several mistakes in the factory when wrong transfers were used. These have not been listed, but it may be worth quoting by way of example 2329 and 2091 on different sides of a Southern No. 2 Special Tank Loco, 2810 on an LNER green No. 0 Loco, and LMS number 8712 found on several GW No. 1 Special Locos. 006 on an Eton cabside was the result of applying the transfer upside down! Certain 'transitional' liveries of 1930–31 are not listed.

A number of locos illustrated in the Hornby catalogues were pre-production models with numbers different from the actual production engines. Loco numbers shown in the catalogues but not confirmed by actual observations include:

M3 Loco	1452/1452	1926 HT
101 Tank	7602	LNER. 1949 MP
No. 0/1	– /E825	SR. 1931 HT
No. 0/1	– /A160	SR. 1931 HT
No. 1 Spl. T	7200	LMS. 1929 HT
No. 2 Tank	1019	LM&S. October 1923 MM
No. 2 Tank	2143	LNER. 1928 HBT
No. 2 Tank	4202	GW. 1927 HBT
No. 2	4073/2711	GW. 1926 HBT
No. 2	338	LMS. 1928 HT
No. 2 Spl. T	2145	LMS. November 1929 MM

HORNBY LOCO NUMBERS:

MO AND No. 20

1930–32	– /4472	green
1930–32	– /6100	red
1932–41, 46–54	– /2595	green
1932–41, 46–54	– /6161	red
1932–37	– /3233	British Express, red
1954–68	60985/ –	BR green

M1 AND No. 30

Non-reversing:

1926–28	2526/2526	green
1928–29	2728/2728	green
1929–33	2930/2930	green

Reversing:

1930–31	– /3031	green/black base
1930–31	– /3031	red/black base
1931–33	– /3132	green/black base
1931–33	– /3132	red/black base
1931–33	– /3132	dark red/black base
1933–34	– /3133	green/green base
1933–34	– /3132	red/green base
1933–34	– /3132	dark red/green base
1934–36	– /3435	green/green base
1934–36	– /3435	green/red base (PU)
1934–36	– /3435	red/red base
1934–36	– /3435	red/green base
1936–41, 46–58	– /3435	green/black base
1936–41, 46–58	– /3435	red/black base
1956–65	45746/ –	BR green No. 30

TINPRINTED TRAIN, GEORGE V, No. 00, M3 LOCOS

Tinprinted train style locos and tenders:

1920–26	2663/ –	black (LNWR sets)
1920–26	– /483	red (MR sets)
1920–26	1452/ –	green (GN sets)

Tinprinted train style locos with 'M1' style tenders:

1926–28	2663/2527	black (LMS sets)
1928	2663/2710	black (LMS sets)
1926–28	– /2527	red (LMS sets)
1928	– /2710	red (LMS sets)
1926–28	1452/2526	green (GW sets)
1928	1452/2728	green (GW sets)

'No. O' style locos:

1928–29	– /2710	black (LMS sets)
1928–29	– /2710	red (LMS sets); tender (PU)
1928–29	– /2728	green (GW sets)

SILVER LINK AND STREAMLINED LOCOS

1936–41	2509/ –	LNER Silver Link
1937–38	7391/7391	light green and dark green
1937–38	3917/3917	maroon and cream

M3, 101 AND No. 40 TANK LOCOS

1931–41, 46–54	2270	LMS red
1931–41, 46–54	460	LNER green
1931–41, 46–49	6600	GW green
1931–41, 46–49	E126	SR green
1954–65	82011	BR Black No. 40

ZULU AND No. O LOCOS

1922 style housing:

1922–23	– / –	black (LNW sets)
1923–29	– /2710	LMS black
1924–29	– /2710	LMS red
1924–29	– /2710	LNER black
1924–29	– /2710	LNER green
1926–29	– /2710	GW green
1928–29	– /E509	SR black (PU)
1928–29	– /A759	SR green

1929 style long-splasher housing

1929–31	8327/ –	LMS black
1929–31	8324/-	LMS red
1929–31	232★/5097	LNER black
1929–31	208★/5096	LNER green
1929–31	2449/ –	GW green
1929–31	232★/E509	SR black
1929–31	208★/A759	SR green

1931 style housing:

1931–41	600/ –	LMS black
1931–37	500/ –	LMS red
1937–39	5551/ –	LMS red
1939–41	5600/ –	LMS red
1931–41	6380/ –	LNER black
1931–37	5508/ –	LNER green
1937–41	4797/ –	LNER green
1931–37	2251/ –	GW green
1937–41	5399/ –	GW green
1931–41	imit/A504	SR black
1931–35	imit/E793	SR green
1935–41	imit/793	SR green

ZULU AND No. 1 TANK LOCOS

1922 style housing:

1922–24	–	black
1924	–	LMS black
1924–26	0–4–0	LMS black
1926–29	623	LMS black
1929–31	326	LMS black
1931	–	LMS black
1925–26	0–4–0	LMS red
1926–29	623	LMS red
1929–31	326	LMS red
1931	–	LMS red
1925–26	0–4–0	LNER black
1926–29	623	LNER black
1929–31	326	LNER black
1931	–	LNER black (PU)
1924–26	0–4–0	LNER green
1926–29	623	LNER green
1929–31	463	LNER green
1931	–	LNER green
1926–31	–	GW green
1928–31	A600	SR black
1928–31	B667	SR green

1931 style housing:

1931–41	7140	LMS black
1931–41	2115	LMS red
1931–41	826	LNER black
1931–41	2900	LNER green
1931–41	4560	GW green
1931–33	E111	SR black
1933–41	111	SR black
1931–33	E29	SR green
1933–41	29	SR green

No. 1, 501, 50 AND 51 LOCOS

1920 style housing:

1920–23	2710/ –	GN green
1920–23	2710/ –	MR red
1920–23	2710/ –	LNWR black
1921–23	2710/ –	CR blue
1923–24	2710/(– or 2710)	LMS black
1923–24	2710/(– or 2710)	LMS red
1923–24	2710/(– or 2710)	LNER green
1924–29	– /2710	LMS black
1924–29	– /2710	LMS red
1924–29	– /2710	LNER black
1924–29	–/2710	LNER green
1926–29	– /2710	GW green
1928–29	– /E509	SR black
1928–29	– /A759	SR green

1929 style long-splasher housing:

1929–31	8327/ –	LMS black
1929 30	8324/ –	LMS red
1930–31	4525/ –	LMS red
1929–31	232★/5097	LNER black
1929–31	208★/5096	LNER green
1929–31	2449/ –	GW green
1929–31	232★/E509	SR black
1929–31	208★/A759	SR green

1931 style housing:

1931–41	2290/ –	LMS black
1931–37	1000/ –	LMS red
1937–41, 48-54	5600/ –	LMS red
1931–41	6097/ –	LNER black
1931–41	2810/ –	LNER green
1948–54	1842/ –	LNER green
1931–37	4300/ –	GW green
1937–41, 48–49	9319/ –	GW green
1931–41	imit/A504	SR black
1931–35	imit/E793	SR green
1935–41	imit/793	SR green
1948–49	793/ –	SR green (PU)
1954–61	60199	BR black No. 50
1954–61	50153	BR green No. 51

No. 1 SPECIAL TANK LOCO

1929–41	16045	LMS black
1929–30	6418	LMS red
1930–34	2120	LMS red
1934–36	15500	LMS red
1936–41	70	LMS red
1929–30	8108	LNER black
1930–41	2586	LNER black
1929–35	8123	LNER green
1935–41	2162	LNER green
1929–30	3580	GW green
1930–41	5500	GW green
1929–31	A129	SR black
1931–41	A950	SR black
1929–30	A950	SR green
1930–35	B28	SR green
1935–41	516	SR green

No. 1 SPECIAL LOCOS

1929–41	4525/ –	LMS black
1929–31	4312/ –	LMS red
1931–35	8712/ –	LMS red
1935–41	2700/ –	LMS red
1929–41	2691★/2691	LNER black

1929–31	2694★/2694	LNER green
1931–41	1368/ –	LNER green
1929–35?	2301/ –	GW green
1935?–41	4700/ –	GW green
1929–41	B343★/B343	SR black
1929–35	A179★/A179	SR green
1935–41	1179★/1179	SR green

No. 2 TANK LOCOS

1923–24	–	LMS black
1924–26	4-4-4	LMS black
1926–28	2052	LMS black
1928	2107	LMS black
1928–29	2051	LMS black
1923–24	– or 1019	LMS red (PU)
1924–26	4-4-4	LMS red
1926–28	2052	LMS red
1928	2107	LMS red
1928–29	2051	LMS red
1924–26	4-4-4	LNER black
1926–29	460	LNER black
1923	–	LNER green
1923–24	1534	LNER green
1924–26	4-4-4	LNER green
1926–28	460	LNER green
1928–29	5165	LNER green
1926–27	–	GW green
1927–28	7202	GW green
1928–29	2243	GW green
1928–29	E492	SR black
1928–29	B604	SR green

No. 2 LOCOMOTIVES

1921–23	2711/ –	GN green
1921–23	2711/ –	MR red
1921–23	2711/ –	LNWR black
1921–23	2711/ –	CR blue
1923–24	2711/(– or 2711)	LMS black
1923–24	2711/(– or 2711)	LMS red
1923–24	2711/(– or 2711)	LNER green
1924–29	– /2711	LMS black
1924–29	– /2711	LMS red
1924–29	– /2711	LNER black
1924–29	– /2711	LNER green
1926–27	– /2711	GW green

1927	7283/2711	GW green
1927–29	7283/ –	GW green
1928–29	– /E510	SR black
1928–29	– /A760	SR green

No. 2 SPECIAL TANK LOCOS

1929–41	6781	LMS black
1929–30	2323	LMS red
1930–36	2180	LMS red
1936–41	6954	LMS red
1929–41	5154	LNER black
1929–32	6	LNER green
1932–41	1784	LNER green
1929–30	4703	GW green
1930–41	2221	GW green
1929–33	E492	SR black
1933–41	492	SR black
1929–33	B329	SR green
1933–35	2329	SR green
1935–41	2091	SR green

No. 2 SPECIAL LOCOS

1929–41	1185	LMS Compound
1929–30	234★/234	LNER Yorkshire
1930–35	234/–	LNER Yorkshire
1935–41	201/–	LNER Bramham Moor
1929–41	3821/–	GW County of Bedford
1929–35	A759★/A759	SR L1
1935–41	1759★/1759	SR L1

No. 3 LOCOMOTIVES

1926–29	31240/31801	Nord brown
1929–38	31801/31801	Nord brown
1938–41	3.1290/3.1290	Nord brown
1927–29	– /6100	LMS red Royal Scot
1929–30	6100/6100	LMS red Royal Scot
1930–41	6100/ –	LMS red Royal Scot
1927–29	– /(4472 or –)	LNER green Flying Scotsman
1929–41	4472/ –	LNER green Flying Scotsman
SO	1368/ –	LNER black No. 3 Loco

1927–41	4073/ –	GW green Caerphilly Castle
1928–34	– /E850	SR green Lord Nelson
1934–41	– /850	SR green Lord Nelson

No. 4 LOCOMOTIVE

1937–41	900★/900	SR green Eton

PRINCESS ELIZABETH

1937–41	6201/–	LMS red Princess Elizabeth

LEC1 LOCOMOTIVE

1932–33	10655	dark green/grey roof
1933–36	10655	green/cream roof
1933–36	10655	red/cream roof
1933–36	10655	cream/red roof
1933–36	10655	blue/yellow roof

LE220 LOCOMOTIVE

1932–33	10655	dark green/grey roof
1933–36	10655 (PU)	green/cream roof
1933–36	10655	red/cream roof
1933–36	10655	cream/blue roof

METROPOLITAN LOCOMOTIVE

1925–39	2	Metropolitan

APPENDIX V

DATING GUIDE FOR HORNBY WAGONS

Specific changes of livery, such as the style of railway company lettering and the colours of wagons, have already been discussed. There are other general changes of detail that can give an idea of the age of a piece of rolling stock; the best guides to age are the couplings (if original), and the trademark if it is one of the standard transfers. These two taken together can often pin down the date to within a year or two.

TRANSFER TRADEMARKS

Very few enamelled Hornby wagons were made without either a transfer or an embossed trademark to identify the manufacturer. But when using transfers for dating it is important to remember that some Hornby wagons – including many private owners' vans and tank wagons, especially prior to 1938 – had special trademarks incorporated in larger transfers for the whole wagon side. Because stocks took longer to run out, these transfers were not updated at the same time as the ordinary trademark transfers. Thus they were not always exactly the same as the standard transfers of the same period, for example gold borders were used on transfers for red tank wagons.

Standard Hornby transfer trademarks included:

1920–22 'M Ld L England'. Circular transfer; red letters, lined black, on gold background. Used on some wagons with the early wagon base, up to 1922.

1922–23 'Meccano Ltd Liverpool'. Oval transfer; red letters, lined black, on gold background with red border edged black. Used on only a few wagons.

1923–24 'Meccano Ltd'. Long thin transfer; gold letters, lined black. Rarely used on wagons.

1924–27 'Hornby Series'. Black letters, on gold background with red border edged black.

1927–32 'Hornby Series. Manf'd by Meccano Ltd L'pool'. Black letters, on gold background with red border edged black. It is probable that this came into use late in 1927.

1932 'Made in England Meccano Ltd Liverpool Hornby Series'. Black letters, on gold background with red border edged black.

1932–49 'Made in England by Meccano Ltd. Hornby Series'. Black letters, on gold background with red border edged black. There were three versions with this wording:

   1932–36 Line under 'Meccano'

1936–38 No line under 'Meccano'

1938–41 Line under 'Meccano'. Lower quality gold used for transfer. The same transfer was used for a few wagons, locomotives etc. circa 1948–49.

1949–69 'Hornby. Made in England by Meccano Ltd'. Black letters, grey background with black border. Used for only a few wagons (eg. Hopper Wagons), since the embossed trademark was standard.

Other transfers were occasionally used, either by accident or when stocks ran out. 'Serie Hornby'

transfers were occasionally used by mistake on English trains in the 1920s, and the transfers from the

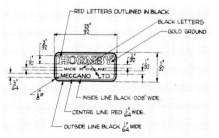

327

Special locomotives are sometimes found on wagons. After the war Dublo-size 'Hornby Made in England Meccano Ltd' transfers (in the prewar black/gold/red style) are found on some accessories, and from 1949 to the late 50s the Dublo-size transfers with grey backgrounds are also found occasionally – again on accessories rather than on wagons.

Export versions other than those for France had the standard English transfer trademarks, often with the addition of an oval 'Fabrique en Angleterre' transfer.

EMBOSSED TRADEMARKS

Embossed trademarks on wagons are a much less reliable guide to dates than transfers, because of delays between making the base and finishing the wagon. The first embossed trademarks were 'M Ld L England', used from 1920 to 1922 (although stocks were still being used up in 1925!). From 1922 onwards new trademarks with the words 'Meccano Ltd Liverpool' embossed in an oval were used (in three readily identifiable styles). After 1925 embossed trademarks were no longer considered necessary, because of the universal adoption of 'Hornby Series' transfers from 1924.

No more embossed trademarks were used on wagons until 1946, when the familiar postwar 'Hornby' embossed trademark was adopted. (The line under the 'td' of Ltd was omitted from new tools made circa 1951, but this is not reliable for dating purposes because of wear in tools prior to that date.) There are a few postwar wagons on which the embossed trademark does not appear, but all the wagons that do have it are of postwar origin. The No. 50 series of wagons had trademarks incorporated in the buffer beam casting.

WAGON COUPLINGS

1930–69   MO COUPLINGS – not separate parts, but an integral part of the pressing of the wagon base.

1920–26   TINPRINTED TRAIN COUPLINGS. Not actually used for wagons. These were simple pressings from strip tinplate, two different versions (one a hook, and the other with a pressed hole) at different ends of the vehicle. A T-shaped hole was used for the first coaches, but later a simple circular hole was provided. Either could be coupled to normal Hornby wagons – after a fashion.

1956–69   No. 30 COUPLINGS. This was one of the best couplings from an operational point of view, but was used only for the No. 30 stock. It was not unlike the Tinprinted Train coupling, but combined hook and hole in a single piece. It locked securely and was unobtrusive in size and shape, and could be used with automatic coupling stock.

1920–21   BRASS COUPLINGS. The first Meccano train couplings (with large flat-sided hooks) do not seem to have been standard issue for Hornby trains, which were fitted with the more compact second type. These had a smaller two-piece brass hook, secured to the buffer beam by Meccano nuts. One end only of the wagon had a three-link steel wire chain (except the very first issues, which had a single brass loop) attached to the coupling; the other hook had no chain, nor the hole for fitting the chain.

Later, the three-link chains were fitted at each end of the wagon, so that it could be coupled either way round.

1921–28   LARGE DROP-LINK COUPLING. In 1921 the brass couplings were replaced by a new pattern, made from strip steel in two parts, one a hook and the other a rigid connecting link. They were attached to the wagons by eyelets. Unlike the old type these couplings were equally satisfactory for forward or reverse operation. They were similar to a type that had been used by Bing, although the drop link was provided at each end of the wagon instead of one end only as was usual for Bing at that period. V-shaped projections in the front edge of the Hornby coupling were supposed to lock the link rigidly in position when the train was reversed.

On the first constructional Hornby Trains these

couplings were nickel plated, but from 1922 wagon bases were usually enamelled after the couplings had been fitted. The enamel finish was unsuitable for such hard-working parts and it is rare to find such wagons with couplings in good condition.

From early in 1925, nickel plated couplings again became the norm for all wagons. When the electro-plating department was cut in size, early in 1927, as a result of the adoption of colours for the 'New Meccano', Hornby couplings were finished in black enamel. They were sprayed before attachment to the wagons, and on tank wagons were also sprayed after assembly, on top of the black!

Any gauge of metal could be used with the tools, so the thickness of the couplings varied. In general they were made in lighter gauges of metal up to 1924, when more substantial metal sheet began to be used. In 1928 thinner metal was again used for a few large drop link couplings.

Operationally these were the most successful of the Hornby Train couplings, being reliable and sturdy enough to withstand all but the worst misuse.

1928–1958   DROP-LINK COUPLINGS. 'Improved' couplings were fitted to Hornby Train from the middle of 1928, following experiments mentioned in the March 1928 MM. They were smaller in all dimensions, including the thickness. Although of improved appearance in keeping with the aim of improving realism, they were less suitable for hard-working toys, and often became unusable because of breakage, or loss of the links which tended to work loose. If bent downwards even slightly, or if they were loose on the eyelets, these links were quite likely to uncouple accidentally. Although less unsightly than the earlier couplings, they were awkward and inconvenient, especially as they were less easily compatible with the automatic couplings which replaced them.

Black enamel finish was usual, but in 1930–31 some wagons were sprayed after the couplings were fitted, so they acquired the same colour as the body of the wagon. Meccano Train Couplings from 1928 to 1941 were also made in the smaller pattern, but were nickel plated; most Hornby wagons with nickel couplings of this size will be found to have been fitted with replacements.

After the adoption of the automatic coupling in

1931, the small link coupling remained in use (although usually in thicker metal) for the M1 Wagons, for the front couplings of locomotives, and for Metropolitan trains. There was a special version of this coupling for M1 Locos, designed for attachment by a small rivet. A section was cropped from the back of these special couplings until 1935 when a clearance hole was cut in the cylinder.

From 1929 onwards the front (and rear) couplings of many locomotives were secured by solid metal eyelets rather than thin tinplate eyelets. These solid metal eyelets were occasionally used for wagons. After May 1950 the solid-metal eyelets on locos were replaced by round-headed copper semi-tubular rivets.

AUTOMATIC COUPLINGS. The use of automatic couplings had been suggested by readers in the August 1929 MM, with the reply that they would '. . . add interest, but would be complicated and expensive'. On 17th November 1930 Meccano Ltd applied for a patent, and submitted the final designs in June 1931, by which time the couplings were already in full production.

There were several different versions of the automatic coupling, for different types of vehicle, but by far the most important was the ordinary type used for four-wheeled wagons. They were made in two parts, a hook, and a link in a special wire of rounded triangular section.

The first automatic coupling had a large solid base and was attached to the wagon by an eyelet. The slots in the wagon base were reduced in size to restrict the was some delay before the movement of the coupling, but it was soon discovered that there was insufficient sideways movement, and existing couplings were adapted by making a second attachment hole just behind the first, and cutting two slots in the hook to allow extra movement in the buffer beam slot. The movement of the coupling was now so free that it was a matter of luck whether or not they coupled automatically on impact! Uncoupling was of course manual, and an extension of the wire link was always provided above the pivot holes for lifting the loops. The two-hole early auto coupling was usually assembled with the eyelet head downwards (the opposite way to normal), for more secure fixing.

Very soon a revised coupling was produced with only a single hole and with a properly shaped neck. This pattern remained in use until early in 1937 when the base of the coupling was made larger, with a larger area behind the eyelet hole, to stabilise the coupling and prevent it drooping if the eyelet worked loose.

Patent numbers were embossed in the couplings as follows: (Away or towards refer to the marking on the coupling top, and to whether the writing faces towards the wagon body or away from it.)

		Side:	Top:
1/	Early	Blank	Prov. Pat. 34652/30 (away or towards)
2/	Early 2 hole	Blank	Prov. Pat. 34652/30 (away)
3/	Small base	Blank	Prov. Pat. 34652/30 (away)
4/	Small base	DRGM 1179362	Prov. Pat. 34652/30 (away)
5/	Small base	Prov. Pat. 34652/30	DRGM 1179362 (away)
6/	Small base	Pat. No. 365701	DRGM 1179362 (away)
7/	Small base	Pat. No. 365701 + 157977	DRGM 1179362 (away)
8/	Small base	Pat. No. 365701 +157977	DRGM 1179362 (towards)
9/	Large base	Pat. No. 365701 +157977	DRGM 1179362 (towards)
10/	Large base	Pat. No. 365701	Blank
11/	Large base	Blank	Blank

There were also minor differences in the punctuation of the DRGM, and in the punches used for types 8 and 9.

Although the full patent was granted on 28th January 1932 (retrospective to 17th November 1930) there was some delay before it was stamped on the couplings. The stamping of the German DRGM patent number on the couplings raised doubts in the minds of some customers as to whether the parts were made in Germany. In the February 1932 MM an assurance was published: 'All Meccano and Hornby Train goods are manufactured in our Liverpool Factory. The French stamping "Fabrique en Angleterre" is necessary to fulfil an obligation

imposed by the French customs authorities . . . the German stamping "DRGM" indicates that the parts so marked are protected against any infringement of design. The copyright law in Germany demands that all parts protected in this manner shall be clearly marked "DRGM"'. The Swiss patent number (marked as '+157977') and the DRGM number should have been deleted in November 1936, when these patents lapsed, and the English patent number when it expired in November 1937; but again there was some delay before the couplings were updated. There was also a Dutch patent 'Ned. OCTR001.31601' which was shown on the production drawings from January 1934 to December 1935, but no couplings were actually made with this marking.

The early postwar automatic couplings were the same shape as before, and were without markings. From February 1950 the corner by the wire pivot was cropped at 45 degrees instead of being rounded – a useful dating feature. Otherwise production continued unaltered to the 1960s, although the No. 50 wagon couplings were secured by copper semi-tubular rivets instead of brass eyelets.

Other types of automatic coupling included the cranked (or stepped) automatic coupling used for No. 1 Pullman Coaches and certain wagons, to reduce the coupling height. Much longer automatic couplings were designed for bogie vehicles, to allow them to pivot nearer the bogie centre; a guide wire was incorporated to control the coupling on curves so as to improve the chances of successful coupling – another patented feature of the system. A different shape of wire loop with squared corners was fitted for the same reason. There were three bogie-type couplings; one stepped for use on the Trolley Wagon, one bent to allow for the recessed eyelet hole on the crane end of the Breakdown Van, and also the normal type. Sometimes unusual adaptations of the bogie-type couplings were made (most probably by mistake) and used for four-wheel vehicles.

None of these special automatic couplings followed exactly the same series of markings as the normal couplings, and although they were similarly marked, there were generally fewer variations over the years. From March 1939 the bogie couplings were altered for fixing by solid steel rivets instead of the eyelets still in use for four-wheeled vehicles. Bogie-type couplings were also made after the war, and the Breakdown Van and Crane and Trolley Wagon coupling drawings were marked 'Production 17-5-49', and also remarkably enough 'Production 3-5-51'.

WAGON BASES

The different standard underframes used for Hornby wagons were as follows:

EARLY WAGON BASE, 1920–25

The first Hornby Trucks had a simple one-piece base, with deep solebars, and plain trunnions for axleguards.

From mid 1921 extra slots were added for the drop-link couplings, but the holes for the old brass coupling were not deleted for some time. The base was revised for thin axles early in 1922, and cast buffers were used instead of brass, except on some open wagons sold in the constructional sets. Remaining stocks of obsolete bases were still being used up as late as 1925, most frequently on open wagons.

EARLY COACH BASE, 1921–25

Constructional coaches had a special base with detachable axleguards, and an embossed 'Registered Design' number. There were three versions – the first with a long wheelbase, and with the holes for the thick axles embossed outwards.

The second type of base had extra holes to allow the axleguards to be fitted with a shorter wheelbase, more suitable for 1 ft radius curves – an extra notch was cut in the top of the axleguards to clear one of the body fixing nuts and bolts. The holes for the thick axles were now embossed inwards.

The third type was the same but with smaller holes in the axleguards, for thin axles. The first two types are found on coaches but not usually on wagons, but around 1924–25 remaining stocks of the third type were used up for various Hornby vans.

OPEN AXLEGUARD BASE, 1922–41

A simplified version of the 1921 coach base was designed in January 1922, and became the standard wagon base. Axleguards were pierced (hence the 'open axleguard' description) and embossed with details of springs etc. but they were not detachable as on the early coach base. Apart from the embossed trademark (and of course tooling differences to suit the different wagon bodies) there were no major production variations. After 1930 they were no longer the standard base, and were used for very few goods vehicles; mainly for French-type wagons (and later for the No. 0 Rotary Tipping Wagons), which were fitted with cranked auto couplings.

Cast buffers were nearly always fitted, except for the wagons of 1922–24 No. 1 and No. 2 Goods Train Sets which had brass buffers, and the No. 0 Rotary Tipping Wagon which had no buffers.

LONG THIN WAGON BASE, 1924–49

Mercifully, the long thin wagon base was not widely adopted as a standard for Hornby wagons. Apart from the 1924–25 open wagons and the 1924–31 No. 1 Coaches, they were fitted only to the Double Wine Wagon and to the M series open wagons of 1926–49.

CRIMPED LONG THIN BASE, 1931–41

When automatic couplings were introduced, a revised long thin base was produced, in which the coupling height was reduced to the standard height of the 1930 revised standard wagon base by a fold along the solebar of each side of the wagon. The crimped base was used for the Barrel Wagon (1931 to 1935), the No. 1 Coaches (1931–34), and the M3 Wagon (1931–41).

No. 1 COACH BASE, 1934–41

From 1935 the Barrel Wagon was fitted with the new-style No. 1 Coach base, in a special version without the battery box and not fitted with axleboxes. It was the only wagon to appear on this coach base.

STANDARD WAGON BASES, 1930–57

1930–47: From 1930 most of the Hornby rolling stock was fitted with a revised standard wagon base, which had a lower buffer height matching the new 'Special' locos. There were two parts; an upper base platform and an underframe. Axlebox slots were punched in the axleguards, but the boxes were not fitted.

Spray holes in the lower part of the base changed from .312 in to .375 in in April 1937; the spray holes in the base platform above depended only on the requirement for spraying the work. Usually the upper holes (if present) were .172 in or .312 in. For wagons that were not finished on the rotary sprays the hole size did not matter.

The base was also used after the war, in 1946 and 1947. It is described in the text as the 'prewar-type base with axlebox slots'; but these bases were usually of postwar manufacture and carried embossed trademarks. A small number of 1948 wagons (e.g. Crane Trucks and Rotary Tipping Wagons) appeared briefly with axlebox slots.

1947–48: Described in the text as the 'prewar-type base without axlebox slots', but again this does not imply prewar manufacture. The base was identical to the previous type except that no axlebox slots were punched out. Remaining stocks were used up in 1948–49.

1948–57: This was the postwar standard base from late in 1948 (possibly early 1949) to 1957. It was similar to the previous type, but with different embossed detail on the axleguards.

No. 50 WAGON BASE, 1957–69

All No. 50 wagons used the new standard No. 50 base, although the No. 50 Brake Van lacked the brake levers fitted to the others.

US BASE, 1930–41

The US base was used for the US Pullman Cars, Mitropa Coaches, and the Caboose, Box Car and Tank Wagon. There were differences of tooling, consequently unused 'extra' holes are frequently seen.

The Tank Car was shown in the production

drawings as secured to the base by eyelets, but in fact it was usually secured by Meccano nuts and bolts – the last 'constructional' wagon!

FRENCH BASES

Up to 1930 the French Hornby wagons had the same bases as in the UK. But the revised standard base of 1930 was not adopted in France. Instead, the French made a more economical decision to adapt the existing base and thus save a great deal of the expense of re-tooling.

The trunnions of the open-axleguard base were no longer pierced, and the depth of the trunnions was reduced by crimping – not along the solebar as on some UK wagons, but at the top of the trunnion itself. This reduced the buffer height without requiring any other alterations in tooling. As in the UK, the change in buffer height came a year before the adoption of automatic couplings.

The French long, thin coach base was similarly treated, with a fold in the axleguard not in the solebar, and with the axleguard no longer pierced. This affected the French-market clerestory coaches and Double Wine Wagon.

A new French standard wagon base was designed in 1935, for all types except vans. It was longer than the former standard base, and narrower (hence its unsuitability for vans) but not as narrow as the old coach base. The shape of the trunnions was the same as the lower part of the open-axleguard base, but of course there were no crimps at the top. It was used for post-1936 Double Wine Wagons sold in the UK; although not advertised as such it is likely that they were made in France, and imported complete except for transfers. In France the base was used almost universally, for Cranes, Barrel, Timber, Lumber, Fibre, and open wagons among others.

Stock of the old-style vans sold out gradually in the late 1930s (when Gunpowder, No. 1 Cattle, Milk Traffic, Refrigerator and Luggage Vans, etc. disappeared). The No. 1 Special series of vans (first issued in 1935) replaced the old type, although the range was different. A different standard wagon base was used for these new vans. There was a third standard wagon base for the French M series wagons.

WHEELS AND AXLES

Tinplate Hornby wagon wheels were made in two pieces; a back, and a front shaped with the tyre profile. The first Hornby wheels were nickel plated overall, and the back was dished in a convex shape. Axles were of the same diameter as Meccano axle rod, again nickel plated, and the wheels were spaced by split pins in holes drilled through the axles.

From 1921 the wheels were retained at the correct gauge by gagging the axle instead of fitting split pins, although old stock axles were used up on later stock. Later versions of the thick axle (from 1922 onwards) often had square ends instead of rounded ends. Wheels for thick axles remained in use for old stock bogies or bases until 1925, although production had stopped earlier.

The same nickel-plated wheels with convex nickel plated backs, but fitted with thin axles instead of thick, became standard (for new products) from March 1922.

The next change was the use of a flat tinplate back, instead of the nickel-plated dished backs, from 1923. Late in 1923 a circular ridge of $\frac{1}{4}$ in diameter was added to the wheel back (presumably for strengthening or stiffening). During 1925 many wheels were stamped with a 'Meccano Fabrique en Angleterre' trademark.

Late in 1925 a few wheels were made with a new back with concave embossing, but still with nickel-plated front and tinplate back. From January 1926 the wheels were of tinplate, and were finished in black overall. To reduce wear and help keep the correct gauge, washers were fitted behind each wheel (so long as the assembly workers remembered!), but by 1950 they had been deemed unnecessary.

Plastic wheels were designed in March 1951, and were used for the rest of the wagon production. Identification numbers were cast in the wheel backs (to trace any faults with the moulds) and all serious collectors try to obtain a complete set of these wheel numbers.

One suggestion from MM readers in the late 1920s was that wheels should be weighted for extra stability. There are examples of tinplate wheels which have been assembled with a lead weight

between the two sections, and although there is no conclusive proof of Binns Road origin it seems likely that they were produced as a short-lived experiment, before the diecast Spoked Wagon Wheels were marketed.

HANDLES FOR HINGED DOORS

The first 1921 series Covered Luggage vans had cast door handles, secured by a bent metal pin which acted as the catch. Although they looked good, they tended to work loose and drop out, which was probably the reason for their replacement in 1922 (although as usual old stocks were still being used up in 1923) by pressed tinplate handles, which turned out to be equally vulnerable. Some were unpainted tinplate, but others were nickel plated. From 1927 they were sprayed black. Although they were made obsolete by changes between 1928 and 1930, a small number were still in use in the 1930s.

In April 1928 the Meccano Magazine said that 'We do not agree that door handles made from bent wire would be stronger than our present type.' Nonetheless the improved No. 2–3 Pullmans, No. 1 Pullmans and No. 1 Coaches of 1928–29 were fitted with splendid bent wire door handles in diecast ferrules, fitting the same holes that had been used for tinplate handles. Although the wire was quite secure in the ferrule, the fixing to the door was less so and the complete unit was prone to loss. The wire was bent to form a realistic handle on the outside; the idea was copied from Bing trains of the period.

From 1929, the die-cast ferrule was no longer fitted, the shape of the wire being altered to give a larger handle. The pressings for the tinplate doors were altered to incorporate a circular embossing round a much smaller hole for the wire. There was little to prevent the wire working loose and falling out.

From March 1931 larger holes in the doors allowed double-ended wire handles to be fitted, an idea which finally succeeded (after a mere 10 years!) in solving the problem of missing handles. Although there were minor changes of shape the handle was basically unchanged even after the war, until the advent of the double-doored No. 50 vans.

VAN BODY STAYS

There were variations in the body stays between the opposite sides of hinged-door vans. On constructional vans there were usually two, one below and one above the door – although early versions with no stay and late versions with one stay are also known. Non-constructional vans usually had a single stay above the door, although again there were versions with no stay.

Round about 1930 a new style stay was designed, suitable for both sliding-door and hinged-door vans. It was cleverly designed to clip to the roof channel while remaining invisible from outside the van.

VAN ROOFS

Rounded-end roofs were shown on production drawings of April 1930, but they are not a reliable dating feature. Some square-ended roofs were used after this, particularly on the No. 0 vans but occasionally on others.

Slots in the sides of vans, at the ends of the roof channel, were made smaller from late 1936 so they were less visible when the roof was fitted.

BUFFERS

Thick brass buffers fixed by Meccano nuts were used until mid-1921, when a type of more conventional profile (also turned in brass) were introduced. The older style remained on sale for some time as Meccano parts, but were no longer used on wagons. Meccano Spring Buffers were never 'officially' fitted to Hornby Trains.

Cast buffers were used for most wagons from 1922 onwards. There were variations in shape impossible to describe but which can apparently be discerned by the keen-eyed expert. More confusing were the various forms of tool used to fix the buffers to the beam – in order of appearance, waffle-patterned, annular and raised-cross patterns (with inevitable sub-variants). In the late 1920s a sunken cross pattern became standard, although the older parts and tools were used up for some time. Study of these details is usually unrewarding!

The postwar buffers of the 1950s were secured by spin-riveting, until the advent of the No. 50 series which incorporated the buffers as part of the buffer beam casting.

SUMMARY OF WAGON DATING GUIDES

These dates apply to 'normal' standard series enamelled wagons only. In many cases the usual caveats re. using up of old parts apply. Items marked '★' should be interpreted with caution. E = early, M = Mid, L = Late.

COUPLINGS:

Brass 3-link	1920–1921
Large drop-link,	
wagon-base colour	1922–E1925
nickel-plated	E1925–E1927
(and 1921–1924 on constructional set items)	
black	E1927–M1928
Small drop-link	M1928–E1931
Automatic couplings	E1931–1969

Automatic coupling sub-variants were:

Early one-hole	E1931
Early two-hole	M1931
Small, blank side	M1931
Small, DRGM on side	M/L1931
Small, Prov Pat on side	L1931
Small, one pat no. on side	L1932
Small, two pat nos on side; DRGM away from body	E1933
Small, two pat nos. on side, DRGM towards body	M1934?
Large, two pat nos. on side	E1937
Large, single pat. no.	M/L1937
Large, blank side	E1938
Large, blank side, 45 degree crop	E1950

TRADEMARK TRANSFERS:
(abbreviated descriptions; see text for details)

M Ld L	1920–E1922
Oval 'Meccano Ltd Liverpool'	E1922–M1923
Long thin 'Meccano Ltd'	M1923–M1924
'Hornby Series', on solebar	M1924–E1926
on body of wagon	E1926–L1927
'Manfd. By'	L1927–E1932
'Liverpool'	E1932–M1932
'Made', underlined	M1932–L1936
not underlined	L1936–M1938
underlined	M1938–1949
Postwar (only on certain wagons)	1949–1957

EMBOSSED TRADEMARKS

M Ld L	1920–1925★
Oval 'Meccano Ltd Liverpool'	L1922–1926★
No embossing	1925–M1946★
Postwar	M1946–1957

HANDLES FOR SINGLE HINGED DOORS

Cast	1921–1923
Unpainted tinplate	1922–1927
Black painted tinplate	1927–1933
Wire in cast ferrule (unusual for wagons)	1928–1929
Single-ended wire handles	1929–1931
Double-ended wire handles	1931–1957

MISC. FEATURES:

Varnished body	from 1924
Non-constructional vans	from E1927
Round-ended roofs	M1930★–1957
Sliding doors for Luggage Vans etc.	from L1931
Bogies with axlebox slots	L1936–1949
Smaller roof-fixing slots in van sides	L1936–1957
Larger spray hole in wagon underframe	M1937–1957
Riveted bogies and couplings on bogie stock	M1939–1949
Matt varnish for base	1939–1957

WHEELS:

Nickel front & convex back, thick axles	1920–1925★
Nickel front & convex back, thin axles	1922–1925★
Nickel, flat tinplate back, thin axles	1923–1925★
Nickel, ridged tinplate back, thin axles	1923–E1926★
Nickel, concave tinplate back, thin axles	L1925–E1926★
Black, concave back	E1926–1951★
Plastic	M1951–1969★

BIBLIOGRAPHY

The Products of Binns Road by Peter Randall (Hornby Companion Series Vol. 1, New Cavendish Books 1977) ISBN 0 904568 06 7; gives a useful perspective on Hornby Trains as just one of the wide range of toys made in the Binns Road works.

Hornby Dublo Trains by Michael Foster (Hornby Companion Series Vol. 3, New Cavendish Books 1980) ISBN 0 904568 18 0; covers the other major range of toy trains made by Meccano Ltd.

Cent Ans De Trains Jouets En France by Clive Lamming (La Vie du Rail, 1981) ISBN 2–902 808–09–07; has a lot of useful information on French Hornby trains, with many colour plates.

Recent Locomotives by P. Randall (Nelson, 1970) SBN 17 213209 6

Older Locomotives by Peter Gomm (Nelson, 1970) SBN 17 213208 8; two small volumes of interest to the Hornby collector.

Along Hornby Lines by Bernard Huntingdon (Oxford Publishing Co., 1976) SBN 902888 69 2; excellent general coverage of the Hornby range, with some imaginative insights into life at the Meccano works.

A Century of Model Trains by Allen Levy (New Cavendish Books, 1974) ISBN 0 904568 00 8; covers the upper crust end of the toy train market, but also goes slumming with memorable pictures of the Hornby trains in the Royston Carss collection.

Hornby Book of Trains 1927–32, R. Gorham (Oxford Publishing Co., 1973) ISBN 0 902888 20X; reprints in black and white the catalogue pages from five HBTs.

Life Story of Meccano, M. Nichols & P. Smith (New Cavendish Books, 1976) ISBN 0 904568 03 2; reproduces an interesting series of Meccano Magazine articles from the early 1930s describing the manufacturing and marketing of Meccano Ltd toys. The Cranbourn Press have also published a useful series of booklets reproducing pages from the Meccano Magazine.

Articles on 'Tinplate Topics' by Peter Gomm and others have been published occasionally, from April 1969 to August 1971 in Model Railway News, and from September 1973 to date in Model Railways. The Hornby Railway Collectors' Association journal, the Hornby Railway Collector, first published in 1969, is another indispensible reference for information on gauge O Hornby.

A FOOT NOTE TO HISTORY

Children in the South of England used to be thrilled by their Nannies' fanciful tales of raw Lancashire life. The gist of the stories was that the Lancashire folks' idea of fun in a wet 'Wakes Week' was to forgather at some bleak industrial wasteland, or similar local beauty spot, to enjoy a good clog fight. For the benefit of effete Southerners, the rules of clog fighting were very simple; the participants faced each other and kicked each other's shins until one or other of the combatants felt disinclined to retain a vertical stance, at which point the proceedings sometimes stopped.

How very different from the life of our own dear Home Counties! But had these tales been true, no doubt the workers on the roughest jobs in the Meccano works would have been subject to such frailties, and the Meccano works-issue clogs with which they were provided would have been renowned as giving some advantage to the wearer in such affrays.

It is pleasant to look back at the actual records of clogs issued to Meccano workers (which by a turn of fate are in our collection), and to imagine the days when strapping no-nonsense Lancashire lads and lasses made the works ring to the sound of their wooden soles on the steel tiles of the machine shop floor.

By coincidence we also have the footware issue records for the year the factory closed. We find that no clogs were issued; instead we note, for example, that one lad was padding round the plant in a pair of works-issue size $6\frac{1}{2}$ Chukka Boots.

A trivial point? Perhaps, but none the less revealing. It is impossible to escape the conclusion that somewhere, between clogs and Chukka Boots, lies the whole history of Binns Road; and perhaps of the British Empire.

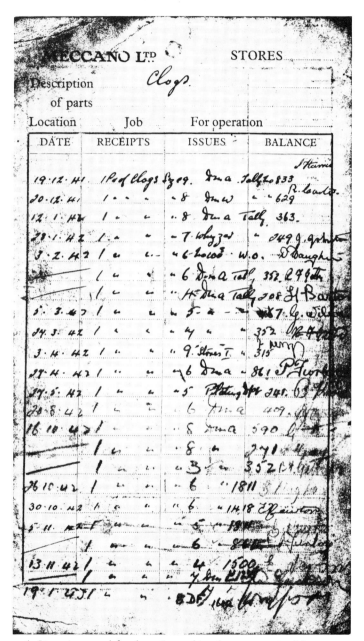

A Stores issue card for clogs. Lancashire clogs were not solid wood like Dutch clogs, but had wooden soles and leather uppers.

Index

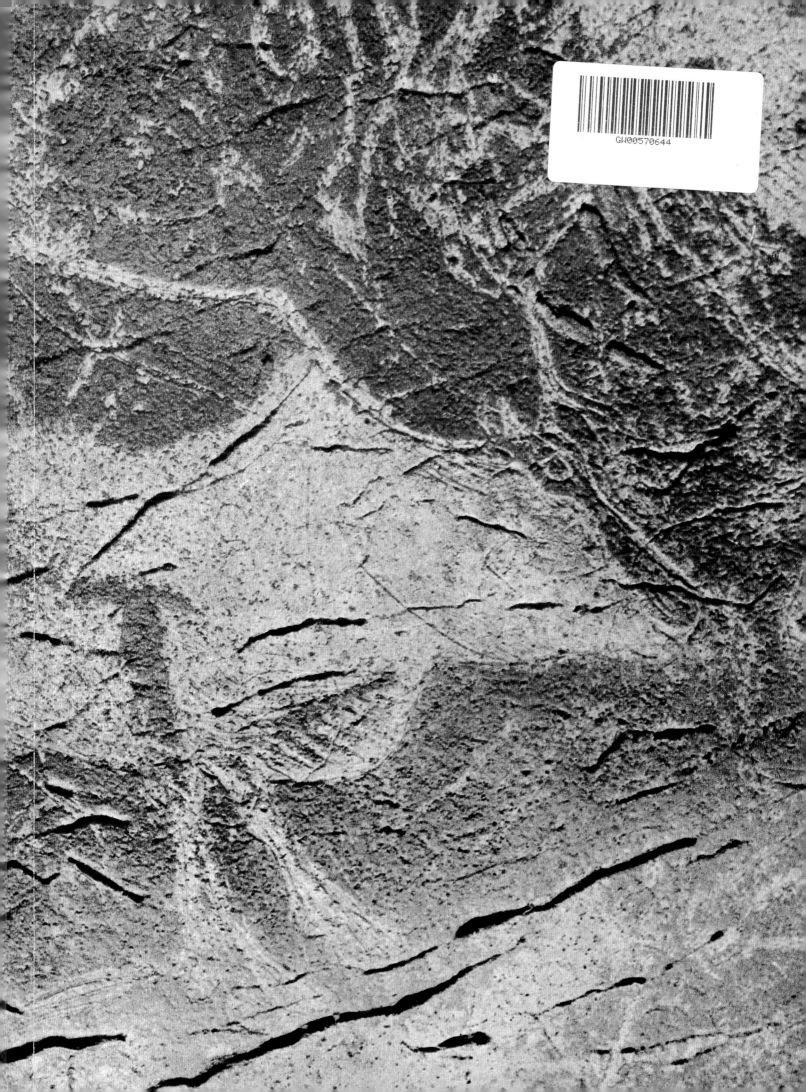

AN/S   £10 - 00

IMAGES OF SCIENCE
A History of Scientific Illustration

Feb 1993

IMAGES OF SCIENCE
A History of Scientific Illustration

Parasite
17. Pig

Aphis
pierced by
Ichneumon
Fly.

E.W

For
Binocular
40 .243 .30

Wing of
White-Plumed
Moth.

40 243 65
Pterophorus
Pentadactylus
F.G.E.

Embryo
Oyster

C. COLLIN
Optician
17. Gt. TITCHFIEL
LONDON. W.

IMAGES *of* SCIENCE

A HISTORY OF SCIENTIFIC ILLUSTRATION

BRIAN J. FORD

THE BRITISH LIBRARY

Front endpapers illustration: Reindeer, from the Cave at Les Trois Frères, Ariège. Photograph by Jean Vertut.

Rear endpapers illustration: Polarized-light photomicrograph (detail) showing xylem from the rhizome of *Osmunda regalis*, the royal fern. The longitudinal section was hand-cut by the author using an open razor of the type beloved of the Victorian microscopist.

Frontispiece: Preparations in the late Victorian era became works of art in themselves. The techniques for preparing whole mounts of insects and injected preparations of mammalian tissues reached very high standards.

First published 1992 by
The British Library
Great Russell Street
London WC1B 3DG

Cataloguing in Publication Data
is available from The British Library

ISBN 0 7123 0267 0

Designed by John Mitchell
Typeset in Lasercomp Garamond Simoncini
by August Filmsetting, Haydock, St Helens
Printed in England by Jolly and Barber Ltd, Rugby

Contents

Cedrus magna sive   *Libani conifera . I.B .*

Preface

Published plates are often damaged by the passing of time, or marked by careless usage over the years. The illustrations in this book have been chosen from the clearest that survive. Some, including the illustration opposite, have never before been reproduced. The bulk are from the British Library collections, and I am grateful to Kathleen Houghton and to Anne Young for their help in retrieving plates from the volumes I chose to illuminate the text. Many others are from private collections, including those of the author, and I should record my thanks to Irene Williams for acting as courier during their preparation, and to David Stone for his valuable technical assistance in the photographic studio.

Many copies of works have been examined and the staff of many libraries are warmly thanked for their cooperation and assistance in the research extending over many years that culminated in this book. Among these are the National Library at Canberra and the University of Queensland Library at Brisbane, Australia; the Library at the University of Hobart, Tasmania; the State University Library at Ghent and the Catholic University of Louvain, Belgium; the Library of the Charles University, Prague, Czechoslovakia; the Royal Danish Academy at Copenhagen, Denmark; the Claude Bernard University at Lyon, the National Library of France, the Sorbonne University, the Centre Beaubourg and the Conservatoire des Arts et Métiers, Paris, France; the former East German State Library, Unter den Linden, Berlin, and the Deutsche Bücherei at Leipzig in the former German Democratic Republic; the Deutsche Bibliothek at Frankfurt, and the Deutsches Museum at Munich, Federal Republic of Germany; Trinity College Dublin, Eire; the Library of the State University at Leiden, the Utrecht University Museum, and the Library of the Royal Netherlands Academy at Amsterdam, Holland; the Autonomous University of Barcelona, Spain; the Royal Library at Stockholm and the University Library at Uppsala, Sweden; the library at the University of Geneva, Switzerland; and the University of Moscow, Russia.

In the United States I have studied the collections of the Smithsonian Institution and the Library of Congress, Washington, District of Columbia; the Library of the National Institutes of Health at Bethesda, Maryland; the Los Angeles Public Library, the San Francisco Public Library, the University of California Libraries at Berkeley, Davis, Irvine and UCLA; Yale University Library, Connecticut; Harvard University Library, Cambridge, Massachusetts; the Illinois Institute of Technology, the Northwestern University Library and the University of Chicago, the Museum of Science and Industry and the State Microscopical Society of Illinois at Chicago; Johns Hopkins University, Baltimore, Maryland; the Free Library of Philadelphia, Pennsylvania; Princeton University, New Jersey; and the University of Wisconsin, Milwaukee. At New York I have been assisted in my studies at the libraries of the City University, Cornell University, and at the New York Public Library.

CEDAR OF LEBANON
Some of the original drawings by Jacob van Huysum survive in the archives of the Royal Society. They show him to have been a good observational botanist, and some of the images portray plant species in a particularly life-like manner. His study of *Cedrus libani*, the cedar of Lebanon, here uses deft selection of brush strokes to lift the tufts of leaves from the page, darker and ligher greens adding depth to the picture. Highlighting of the cones gives them a most satisfyingly rounded and realistic appearance.

Royal Society Manuscripts – van Huysum MS.109.51

In the United Kingdom I have received the willing help of staff at the Royal Society, the Natural History Museum and the Science Museum, South Kensington, the British Library, the Linnean Society, and the Wellcome Institute for the History of Medicine, London; the Public Library, Birmingham; the Cardiff Central Library, and the Library of the National Museum of Wales at Cardiff; the Bodleian Library and other college libraries in the University of Oxford; and University Libraries at Aberdeen, Bath, Exeter, Kent at Canterbury, East Anglia at Norwich, Reading, Stirling, Southampton and the University of Surrey at Guildford. At Cambridge I have been fortunate to have the advice and assistance of the staff of the University Library and many college libraries, together with the Scientific Periodicals Library and the Library of the Whipple Museum for the History of Science.

A host of friends and greatly admired colleagues have offered assistance and advice as the manuscript was prepared. Among those I offer especial thanks to Rupert Hall, William LeFanu, Walter McCrone, Joseph Needham, and William Stearn whose learning has been greatly valued. My daughter Sarah assisted by sub-editing the draft manuscript.

To the many people whose insights have broadened my knowledge and understanding I offer thanks, tempered only with the knowledge that my ability to comprehend cannot match theirs to enlighten.

BRIAN J. FORD
Cambridge, September 1992

Introduction

THE THOUSAND WORDS that a picture is supposed to tell are a small part of the tale. There are hidden influences and cultural pressures underlying what people choose to illustrate, and fashionable constraints on how they make their representation. When a new science is in its nascent phase, the enthusiasms shine through in the drawing. And on the downward slope, when current interest has passed to something new, the lack of interest may equally be reflected in the artwork of the time.

Scientific illustration has many functions. It adds dignity to a text. It can conceal a truth behind a welter of high-flown symbols. But essentially there are two main purposes – a didactic function, but also a separate and secondary purpose: the recording of the state of human understanding. The first time that the Moon's craters were drawn was an historic moment. So too was the drawing of a cell, and the sketches that documented the nucleus. Some classical pictures became trophies. For example, many of the existing copies of *Micrographia* (the first major science book in history, first published in 1665) lack the half-metre pull-out plate of the flea. It was carefully cut from the book and framed, an object of wonder and interest. Clearly, there is an element of celebration in the spectacle of art applied to the machinations of science.

Among the earliest of images bequeathed to the present day are cave paintings. They assuredly had a didactic function, tucked away in the recesses of caves where probably only a select few were admitted. Some boast arrows, stylized like those in a modern textbook, to indicate where a blow might be aimed. Then, from the ancient civilisations of Egypt, Assyria and Greece there survive the painstaking records of the technology then in vogue, illustrated in a variety of media. At Pompeii highly realistic tableaux served as identification 'visual aids' of the species abounding in the sea.

When the knowledge of the ancients was nurtured during the Middle Ages by the Arab philosophers, many of the visual representations were lost; the Prophet had decreed that images of the human form should not be drawn. We find geometrical and highly stylized records of science as a result. And as the Renaissance began, woodcuts and manuscript drawings show how perceptions of the nature of the Universe altered with the growth of scientific understanding, until 'reality' (as now construed) began to raise its head.

In each of the sections of this survey, I have taken some of the earliest surviving examples of illustration, and moved through time until the reality we recognize today had emerged. This freedom from a fixed chronological barrier allows us to let the science shape its own story. Fine studies of plant life were done in the early fourteenth century, for example, whilst the image in microscopy took five centuries more to mature. The erratic, exciting progress of scientific investigation is clearly mirrored by the art which captures it.

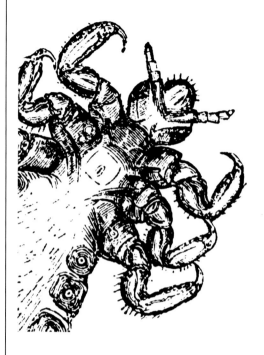

THE HEAD-LOUSE (THE NINETEENTH-CENTURY IMAGE)
Victorian illustrators took pains to ensure the observational accuracy of their subjects. This fine study of the head-louse *Pediculus capitis* (identified in the original as *P. Vulgaris*) is an enlarged detail of a woodcut published in Hogg, J., *The Microscope, Its History, Construction and Application*, Fig. 416, p.626 (1898). Nineteenth-century text-books are a rich source of detailed images based on meticulous observation. Some – for example, studies of the rotifera – have not since been equalled.

THE HEAD-LOUSE (COMPUTER-PROCESSED)

The modern view of *Pediculus* is exemplified by a visually attractive micrograph taken with polarized light. The phase plate used in this technique throws the optically active structures of the louse exoskeleton against a vivid background. False colour is frequently added to monochromatic micrographs by computer processing, and in many such modern images the information content becomes secondary to the vividness of the result.

Preparation and micrograph by the author.

Plagiarism has been rife in science since the discipline emerged. As we shall see, some shrill campaigners against the plagiarists of their work have happily misappropriated others' ideas when the opportunity arose. When a discovery is announced in words, there is every chance for others to claim it as their own. When the discovery emerges as an illustration of a new phenomenon, then plagiarism becomes a spectator sport. The image may simply, be copied – as it is, line for line, detail for detail. Hooke's study of the flea, like Dürer's of the rhinoceros, spawned many generations of derivations. Many of them have protestations of originality printed on the fly-leaf (often a hint that what lies within is anything but original). Or an illustration may be utilized as a 'reference'. This is a vague and all-embracing term beloved of illustrators. A reference is more than an *aide-mémoire*, though less than something plainly to copy. Illustrators need to have a picture of an object before they can compose their art. Perhaps they are faced with an original, new specimen; more likely, they have before them a picture from an earlier publication and wish to borrow its visual information for a piece of artwork of their own. In the same way that texts are paraphrased, thereby avoiding actions for copyright infringement, a redrawn illustration is a way of using someone else's perspective and ingenuity, whilst ensuring that the lines alone are new.

Each generation of copying takes one further from reality. A living specimen, well portrayed, becomes wooden and stiff as it is copied and re-copied. Scientific realities mutate: six-pointed snow-flakes become eight-pointed, just as carefully delineated bacteria transpose themselves into species that seem to exist only in text-books. We shall discover that there are 'icons' that stand out in scientific literature: illustrations to attract respect for learning, but which cannot be intended to represent reality. Scientific illustration may be scientific in nature, but it may be far from scientific in application.

Humans have observed their world and the heavens above since before recorded time. When the first stirrings of philosophy were evident, in Ionia and Persia, it was in the framework of superstition and mythology half a millennium B C. Imagine how striking was the prediction by the Phoenecian Thales of the solar eclipse of 585 B C! By 500 B C Pythagoras had laid the foundations of geometry, and the Greek philosopher Democritus was speaking of atoms by 400 B C. In the same era Hippocrates developed inductive reasoning, and Socrates and Plato defined the notion of ethics. Aristotle's teachings in the biological sciences around 300 B C launched natural history, even taxonomy, knowledge that was extended and developed in the Alexandrian era by Crateuas about 80 B C. By the time of Ptolemy, in the second century A D, the sum of knowledge was great.

The medieval era in the West was counterbalanced by the rise of Islam. Arab philosophers nurtured the teachings of the ancient world. Much of the later knowledge of the ancient philosophers of Greece and Rome has come down to us through translations from the Arabic, in which tongue they had survived. Yet the names of these great Arabic and Persian philosophers are unfamiliar to many. Rhazes (865–923/32) the Persian physician for instance, was one of the greatest medical men of all time; Avicenna (980–1037) likewise compiled a huge and widely-read work on medicine; whilst Al-hazen (965–1038) of Basra founded the optical sciences.

And where was illustration all this while? It languished in corners. Illustrations were infrequent in the Islamic world because of the strictures of the religion; and few survived from the earlier eras. The dawn of the Renaissance broke on a world of philosophy that was still primarily vocal, or literary at best. Pictures were there to decorate, to leaven the load of the words. As teaching aids they were no more developed than the decorations of a millennium before. There were few images of nature as realistic as those of ancient Rome for more than a thousand years. In the cave paintings of the Basque country, dating back to the Stone Age, there was considerably more didactic art.

But this was set to change. The arrival of printing from the East, the development of the wood-cut, the new thirst for knowledge, all gave impetus to new ways of communicating the realities of science. The decorative manuscripts of the medieval era were no longer enough: and the demand for books brought the technology that in turn drove the interest in scientific illustration.

In this volume we glimpse how it happened. We will see how science formed with the aid of its illustrators, and how their art mirrored the value systems of science itself. This introduction has sketched out where science came from – the book will try to illustrate where it went. The recurring themes of influence, of kindly and malicious 'borrowing' of the image that anticipated later developments in the laboratory, are all facets of the tale.

The resonances of these findings fill the world of today. This is no esoteric topic, for we are concerned with how we see ourselves as much as with how science views the world. As I completed these pages I went to the shelf to find an aerosol can standing there, just waiting to catch the eye. It was decorated with hexagonal shapes … not real snow crystals, just something rather like them; these images were old icons of how snow was portrayed. These 'cartoons', distorted shapes that for the artist removed the uncomfortable pressure to stand in the snow and observe its actual construction, had been generated in 1660. They were copied again in 1663, once more in 1681, and turned up a few years ago in a book on microscopes written for the young. And then, there they were again. The entire span of scientific illustration and its peculiar foibles were sitting on the shelf. Let nobody imagine this fascinating tale is – even slightly! – remote from how we live today.

1

The Beginnings

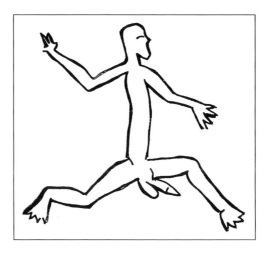

IMAGES OF SCIENCE

A PREGNANT MARE FROM LASCAUX
Dramatically portrayed in charcoal black and ochre, a mare is caught in the act of fleeing by a painter of the Stone Age. This magnificent Upper Palaeolithic image, from the caves at Lascaux, France, was painted more than 20,000 years ago. There may be an instructional purpose in this wall painting. Like many such cave paintings, the image is not in a place likely to have been frequented by the Cro-Magnon peoples in their daily lives, but is tucked away in a corner. The arrow above the shoulder provides the clue: perhaps this was a training aid, for the instruction of the young initiates as they came of age.

Photograph by Jean Vertut

SCIENTIFIC ILLUSTRATION has its roots in the earliest endeavours of *Homo sapiens*. The great cave paintings made by our predecessors, and seen again only in recent years, have attracted attention for the beauty of their line and the balanced composition of the image. They are seen as the beginnings of Art. Yet their artistic nature is a retrospective convenience for those already tutored in the unravelling of representational and interpretative painting. To the painters of Altamira and Lascaux there was no artistic tradition with which the aesthetics of their work might meld. These images were not art, but science.

Many of the earliest images portrayed muscle structure in animals pursued by hunters. There are hunting scenes, diagrams that indicate desired patterns of attack, and anatomical paintings to educate the tyro on how animals are constructed. These images were the work of Cro-Magnon man, a cave-dweller named from the local dialect term for 'great grotto' in the old Dordogne language. Cro-Magnon man was revealed in 1868, when contractors widened a road at Les Eyzies. Whilst excavating a cutting they burst into a cave rich in human remains. The people whose skeletons had lain undisturbed for perhaps 20,000 years were tall, with large brains and wide faces. The number of sites of Cro-Magnon cave art in France alone is now approaching 80. They range in age from 10,000 to 20,000 years.

An early image from the upper Palaeolithic era from the cave of Les Trois Frères in France shows a bear, wounded in the hunt, and bleeding profusely from nose and mouth. At Font-de-Gaume a mammoth is portrayed, caught in a man-made trap. Diagrams of bison in the caves at Niaux show arrows that seem to indicate 'vital points' or targets for young hunters to learn.

Were these merely wall-paintings for decorative purposes? This is an untenable explanation. As has been pointed out by the Abbé Henri Breuil and Johannes Maringer, many of the images are in deep caves, often in inaccessible locations. They were not for public display, but must have been revealed to *cognoscenti* by the elders of a tribal community. It is entirely sensible to construe them as teaching aids, and as diagrams of instruction on the current understanding of the animal world.

The main concentration of these haunting images lies in the region of the Pyrenees, creating the impression that this corner of south-western France and north-eastern Spain was a cradle of European civilisation. It is an extraordinary coincidence that the area contains the home of the Basques, an ancient people today denied a separate identity for their culture. It is the Basque language which provides the link. An ancient tongue, Basque bears no relationship to any of the great swathe of Indo-European languages that other Europeans speak today. Just one of their words may have entered English: 'By Jingo!' may have derived from the Basque word for god: *jinkoa*. But most intriguing of all is the family

of terms for knife, axe, blade; these Basque words derive from the root *aitz*. And aitz is the Basque for 'stone'.

Here we may have the descendants of Europe's earliest culture. A stone-age tongue still exists alongside the carefully delineated images of human understanding that have survived for almost 30,000 years.

The change from Palaeolithic to Neolithic culture marked the change from a hunting life to one rooted firmly in settlement and agricultural development. Weaving, pottery, and finely-produced tools became the objects of attention, and images of prey gave way to decorative art. Abstract and geometrical designs were used for decoration, and it is possible some of these represented early attempts to mark the passage of time.

Five thousand years ago the civilisations of Minoan Crete began to create representational illustrations of sea-creatures and terrestrial creatures. These may in their turn have fulfilled a diagnostic or taxonomic rôle, for great pains were taken to ensure accuracy. Ancient Egypt featured similar images. Accurate paintings of birds were incorporated into a mural for the tomb of Chnemhotep *circa* 1900 BC. Plant life is portrayed too; the preoccupation with hunting as a means of survival had diverted attention from botanical subjects in the palaeolithic paintings. The development of the ancient Greek civilisations began to mirror itself in a growing range

THE STONE-AGE VIEW OF SURFACE ANATOMY
The vivid images of bison in the caves of Altamira, Spain, were drawn at the time of the Upper Palaeolithic by Cro-Magnon artists. The zones of musculature are recorded, and some seem marked as though indicating preferred target areas for the hunters' spears. Each of these energetic drawings was made with charcoal, often of olive wood, directly onto the limestone surface. Their exact purpose is unknown, but they may have served a ritualistic, or didactic, function.

Photograph by Jean Vertut

Figurines made from clay are a common find in
excavations in Mesopotamia. These examples
show the stylized conventions adopted by 5000
B C. The purpose of the models is unknown,
though they may clearly have had uses as charms
or symbols. Some awareness of the principles of
human anatomy may be inferred from the care
with which the figurines were modelled.

British Museum, Department of Western Antiquities 1 17938,
122872, 122873

of artefacts portraying living creatures and plant life. In time, the
representations became stylized and artificial. A form of symbolic
art, in which reality was distorted by current conventions, soon
arose. Its repercussions remain with us today.

Prehistoric images remain in northern Africa, where they are
found at ground level, rather than secreted in subterranean
caverns. The evidence for their pre-Neolithic origins came first
from the portrayal of species that depend for their existence on
conditions far more verdant than those existing during recent millennia. Ostriches and giraffes occur in relief murals discovered in
the Atlas, for example, from which area they have long retreated.
Bubalus antiquus, the giant buffalo, is also featured; it is known to

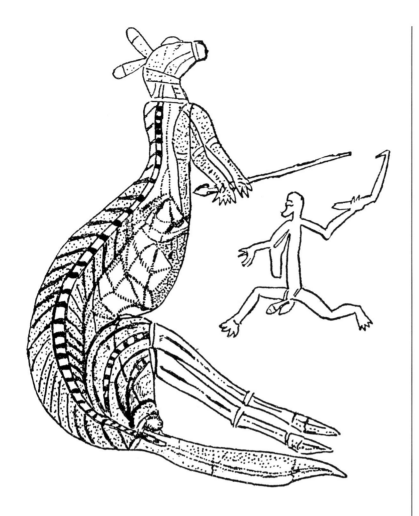

Images that reveal some hint of the internal structure of animals are found in many parts of the world. This example of an 'x-ray' drawing shows the spinal column and pelvis of a kangaroo. Some of the other internal organs are more vaguely portrayed. Here we see the hunter after discharging his spear from a throwing-stick. The drawing, scratched on bark, was made by the Kakadu tribesmen of the Northern Territories, Australia.

The baobab tree produces mystical nuts which are often carried by Aborigines in Australia. They are frequently engraved with drawings of the creatures with whom they share their environment. Fish and mammals are typical subjects. But in this case the king-crab of the Xiphosura has been included. These arthropods, of which *Limulus* is the only genus, have a quasi-religious significance to many tribes.

THE BIRD HUNTER OF ANCIENT EGYPT
This beautifully observed wall painting from
1400 BC is preserved at the British Museum.
The scene shows a government official from
Thebes, named Nebamun, hunting birds in
marshland. He stands on a punt made from
reeds, accompanied by his wife and daughter,
and has a cat trained to retrieve the quarry. The
act of hunting is vividly recorded, and the
vegetation – like the birds he pursues – is
painted with great care.

British Museum, Department of Egyptian Antiquities 37977

have become extinct before the Neolithic. In the Sahara, paintings
rather than carvings, predominate. Many of them are in poly-
chrome and show cattle and human forms in association with each
other. Figurative paintings made by bushmen used a range of
pigments. Red and brown were *haematite* or bole; yellow was iron
ochre; white, zinc oxide; black was carbon from soot or charcoal.
The viscous medium used to render the pigment suitable for painting seems to have been animal fat. It produces a consistency not
unlike that of oil-paint.

It is noteworthy that artistic conventions comparable with the
early cave paintings exist to this day amongst the aboriginal peoples
of Australia. As in Neolithic and Palaeolithic cultures, verbal folklore and instruction is supplemented by representational diagrams.
Rock-face images are commonly carved in relief, and predate
today's aborigines, and it has been argued that painting arrived

MODELS OF INTERNAL ORGANS FROM ANCIENT ROME

Terracotta models of organs have been found among the ruins of ancient Rome. Here we see examples in the form of an eye, an ear, and the intestines. The images are stylized, and may represent charms used to ward off diseases of these organs.

British Museum, Department of Greek and Roman Antiquities
1865 11–18 129; 1865 11–15; 1839–2–14 52

with European colonization. Many of the images are made on bark (northern Australia) or on baobab seeds (in the west). It is of scientific interest that images from the Northern Territory are often diagrams which show internal structures. They have become known as 'x-ray drawings' for this reason.

A related form of anatomical representation is found on the other side of the Pacific. The Eskimo art of Alaska features diagrams that show skeletal structures, and a wall painting of the Kwakiutl Indians of British Columbia depicts vertebrae and some highly stylized internal organs.

Dating some of these images can be difficult, as in cases such as the rock-face images of Abansk, in the Minusinsk district of Siberia. These show hunters with bows and arrows and may well be instructional 'icons'. What is of interest is the portrayal of the hunters as naked. For several millennia, the inhabitants of that area are believed to have worn thick outer garments. The last warm period dates back some 5,000 years and it may be that this indicates the images are of a comparable antiquity.

The earliest image of prehistoric date to be discovered in India takes the form of a rhinoceros surrounded by six male hunters. It was discovered near Mirzapur by A. Carlleyle and J. Cockburn in 1880 and was first published in the *Journal of the Asiatic Society of*

A MESOPOTAMIAN SNAKE PAINTING
This lively image of a snake was painted between 5000–5500 BC, in the Halaf period. Portrayals of creatures of such antiquity are hard to assign to a specific purpose. They may have acted as worship symbols or as a teaching aid.

British Museum, Department of Western Asiatic Antiquities 127617

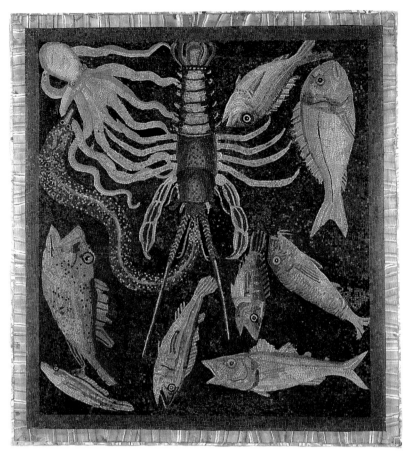

TYPE SPECIMENS OF FISH FROM A ROMAN MOSAIC

Here we see ancient representational illustration at its best. The spiny *Palinurus vulgaris* and octopus are immediately recognizable. On the right are *Dentex dentex*, top; the red mullet *Mullus surmuletus* (middle) and the common bass *Morone labrax*. On the left are comber, *Serranus cabrilla*, the scorpion-fish *Cottus scorpius* with a moray eel, and (below) the rainbow wrasse *Coris julis*. A green wrasse *Thalassoma* is in the middle. These fish are clearly studies from life. The mosaic is from Populonia, Rome, dated A D 100.

British Museum, Department of Greek and Roman Antiquities 1989 3–22

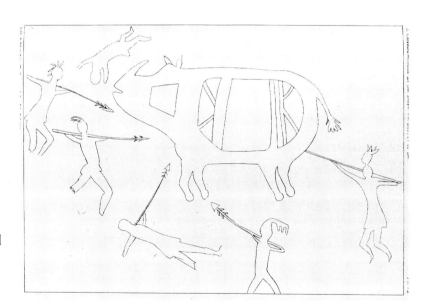

TECHNIQUES OF HUNTING FROM THE BENGALESE

Hunting scenes are found in many cultures. In this illustrated account of a hunt, six Bengalese are seen in the act of slaughtering a rhinoceros at the end of a chase. The image was first published by A. Carleylle and J. Cockburn in the *Journal of the Asiatic Society of Bengal* (1883).

British Library O.I.O.C.

Bengal dated 1883. More recent finds have included stylized studies of humans, birds and farm animals painted in vivid colours. There are geometrical designs associated with some of these images, suggestive of ceremonial or perhaps of a chronological significance.

Japanese images are rare. There are some stone-age relics which

TECHNOLOGY FROM ANCIENT GREECE: WOMEN WEAVING

A loom of Circe is shown in use, in a study from the Temple of Kabeiroi at Thebes. This small illustration, dating from 430 BC, is one of a range of early portrayals of technology. The women weaving are shown with Odysseus, in this scene from a Boetian vase.

British Museum, Department of Greek and Roman Antiquities 1893 3–3 1

A BALANCE FROM ANCIENT EGYPT

The Egyptians did not prepare illustrations of their technology in isolation, though they are a feature of ritual paintings, prepared for other purposes. In this example, jackal-headed Anubis is weighing the heart of a priestess. Considerable refinement in the depiction of the scales is evident.

British Museum, Department of Egyptian Antiquities 9901/3

chiefly show female human forms with grossly exaggerated sexual features. The earliest inhabitants of Japan were not oriental, but were people like the Ainu (some of whom still inhabit the northern Japanese island of Hokkaido). Some claim they were descended from an essentially Caucasian people that crossed from Siberia. They were displaced northwards by Mongolian invaders from the second and first centuries BC.

China offers a similar paucity of graphic images. The earliest artefacts from the Shang Dynasty (*circa* 1500–1000) BC are

A VOLUPTUOUS GODDESS FROM ANCIENT
PERSIA
Feminine attributes have often been exaggerated
in figurines. This example is from the Toprak
Kale site in Northern Iran, on the shore of Lake
Van. The prominent breasts and dynamic
construction of this effigy show a full
appreciation of the feminine form as an object of
worship.

British Museum, Department of Western Asiatic Antiquities
119447

MATHEMATICAL TALLIES AS A RECORD
FOR POSTERITY
The Egyptians used wall paintings as a way of
recording tallies of possessions. The sky goddess
Nut is often shown arching over the scene. Nut
was reputed to swallow the sun each night and to
give birth to it again at dawn with the start of the
new day. This tally is from the Stela of Tjetji,
Thebes, dated 2100 BC.

British Museum, Department of Egyptian Antiquities 614

stylized creatures carved from jade or cast in bronze. In the surviving reliefs from the Han Dynasty (*circa* 200 BC–200 AD) are more representational portrayals of animals. As a step forward in art, birds are seen flying above above trees which are unmistakably growing in the ground.

In AD 105 paper was first produced in China and the stage was set for the development of graphic art. The efforts of the Chinese were directed towards the perfection of artistic nature. The stylized and graceful horses, deer, birds and fish are magnificent and of the highest aesthetic sensitivity. We will learn little of the origins of a scientific tradition, however, through a perusal of these oriental sources.

Around the Mediterranean, accurate images of living creatures were a feature of house decoration at the same period of time as the Han Dynasty in China. The greatest selection has been bequeathed to us by the cloud of poisonous gas and fine volcanic ash that descended from Vesuvius in AD 79. Since 1748 the buried city of Pompeii has been methodically excavated and the resulting site is rich with a haunting evocation of a lost culture. Closer to the coastline, and the natural neighbour to Pompeii, lie the remains of Herculaneum. This resort town (also buried in the eruption of AD 79) was discovered in 1719 and has been excavated over the last two centuries. Both settlements are rich in wall paintings, some of them of an erotic nature. There are many fine mosaics, as well preserved today as they must have been when first constructed, which portray vivid images of terrestrial creatures and marine life. Though of an unmistakably decorative nature, these may well have fulfilled an educative function. The accuracy of portrayal is significant, for it implies careful drawing from the specimen.

We may discern the origins of scientific philosophy in the teachings of the Greek teachers since Socrates, born *circa* 469 BC. Socrates wrote nothing, his philosophies being taken down by followers. A leading student in the group was Plato, aged 30 at the date of his mentor's death, and he founded a school in the garden of Academus in or about 385 BC. Plato's interests embraced mathematics and astronomy as well as social philosophy, and he grasped the concept that physical objects must obey the constraints imposed by fundamental laws of matter. From Stagirus in Macedonia came the 17-year-old Aristotle to join the Academy founded by Plato. Aristotle went on to attempt classifications of plants and animals, and to develop experimental rationales by which to assess his understanding of scientific principles. However, there seems little evidence of interest in the recording of structures through drawn images throughout this period of the birth of scientific thought.

Whilst the Greek traditions were nurtured in Mesopotamia, innovative science had established itself during the Ptolemaic period in Egypt. Following the fragmentation of the Macedonian empire after Alexander the Great died in 323 BC, Ptolemy – one of Alexander's generals – seized power in Egypt and established a dynasty that endured for three centuries. By 200 BC, the library at Alexandria was the centre of the scientific world and scholars were brought there to study with the aid of funding support from the

Ptolemaic government. Among its curators were Eratosthenes (*circa* 276–194 BC) and Appollonius (who flourished around 220 BC) who had studied at the school of Euclid, and wrote a mathematical treatise on conical sections.

Erastosthenes carried out an intriguing experiment to demonstrate the circumference of the Earth. He considered three propositions:

(a)   At Syene (modern Aswan) the midsummer noon-day sun casts no shadow from an upright post;
(b)   Syene is 5,000 stadia from Alexandria;
(c)   Syene is due south of Alexandria.

The measured angle that the Sun's rays subtend with the post at Syene is equal to the angle subtended by 5,000 stadia at the Earth's surface. The *stadium* was equal to approximately one-tenth of a mile, and Eratosthenes calculated the circumference of the Earth at 250,000 stadia (approximately 25,000 miles). The actual measurement of the Earth's equatorial circumference is 24,900 miles. Objections have been raised to the methods Eratosthenes

WATER-FOWL AND FISH FROM NEBAMUN'S TOMB
Stylized ornamental fish are shown in a lotus pool with wild fowl, in this diagrammatic plan of the garden of Nebamun. Fruit trees are planted around the ornamental pond, with figs and dates prominently displayed. The painting dates from 1400 BC.

British Museum, Department of Egyptian Antiquities 37983

employed, and the accuracy of his measurements. But it would be churlish to allow overmuch pedantry to deny an achievement which, in the event, may be considered remarkable.

Astronomy was founded as a science by Hipparchus of Nicaea (*circa* 190–120 BC) who worked at Rhodes. He calculated the interrelated movements of the Sun and Moon, which established the principles for the calculation of eclipses. His theory of the precession of equinoxes was based on accurate observations of constellations in which he demonstrated that heavenly bodies had undergone shifts in position compared with observations recorded one and a half centuries earlier. His star maps set down assignments to constellations and his principles remain the basis of modern astronomy.

The first scientific observations of plants also date from the

Alexandrian period, when Crateuas (flourishing about 80 BC) figured a number of plants of medicinal significance. In his drawings he set out accurately to portray plant structures as an aid to identification. Copies of many of them survive (*see* p.23). These are the earliest examples of scientific illustration, as we would now understand the term, to have come down to present generations.

So many of the earlier workers, in whose heritage such observations were incorporated, left no drawings of their endeavours. Hippocrates of Cos (*circa* 460–377 BC) was born an Asclepiad, that is to say of a medical family stretching back many generations. He travelled widely and his teachings as conveyed to the modern world span too great a time (and cover such a variety of styles) as to be more accurately seen as the compilations of *rapporteurs* rather than the product of one hand. None the less, there is in some of this work a clear vein of progressive understanding of human nature and of the processes of disease. His descriptions of malaria, mumps, tuberculosis and pneumonia are accurate to a degree. His methods came to dominate medicine until the 18th century, and the Hippocratic Oath – which was established many centuries after his death – has remained part of the folklore of medical practice to this day.

As Hippocrates of Cos was the first great authority in medicine to have come down to us, his namesake, Hippocrates of Chios (flourished *circa* 430 BC), was the first to write an *Elements of*

The Mayan peoples used monumental characters
as well as a written script. This carved lintel
bears records from about 681 AD. It was
discovered among the Mayan religious buildings
at Yaxchilan (Menche) in Guatemala. Mayan
mathematicians knew the meaning of zero, and
used a form of binary which enabled them to
calculate time up to five million years.
Genealogy, prophecies and traditional science
were recorded by the Mayan priests in this way.

British Museum, Museum of Mankind

Geometry. It is believed he started his adult life as a trader, and
came to philosophy through meeting mathematicians during a visit
to Athens. Among his geometrical treatises was a method of
attempting to 'square the circle', and it was in this tradition that the
later luminaries – Anaxagoras, Empedocles, Pythagoras –
developed and extended the science of mathematics.

The ascendancy of the Latin scientists may be exemplified by
Lucretius (*circa* 95–55 BC) whose 'ladder of nature'– which is in
some ways derived from the teachings of Aristotle – anticipated
evolutionary theory, and Pliny the Elder, who was born at Como in
AD 23. His great work was to bring together earlier bodies of
scientific knowledge, most notably in his 37-volume *Naturalis
Historia*. This involved summarizing some 2,000 works, many since
lost, by 146 Roman and 326 Greek authorities. Pliny was filled with
a sense of wonder at the majestic confusions of nature, and his
philosophy was to view creation as it might be applied to solving
mankind's practical problems. His curiosity about natural
phenomena eventually led to his death. Driven by a desire to
witness the ravages of Vesuvius in eruption he made an incautious
exploration of Pompeii and was overcome by the poisonous gases
that rolled down upon the city. Thus the volcanic process that has

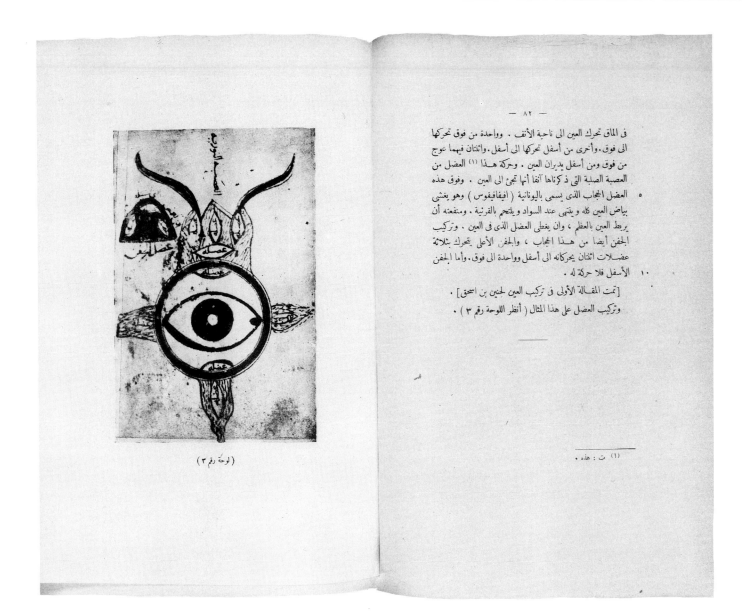

bequeathed to us a unique record of images from the time of Christ, claimed the life of one of the first encyclopaedists in the history of science.

It is to Baghdad that we should turn to find the salvation of the newly emergent concepts of scientific philosophy. The Caliph Ma'mun ruled that city from A D 813 to 833. It is said that he was a devout follower of Islam and was troubled by the conflict between faith and the principles of analytical thought. But in a dream, Aristotle appeared before him with an assurance that there was no conflict between the following of religion and the intellectual use of reason. Given this guarantee, the Caliph constructed a 'House of Wisdom'. It became a repository for the much-neglected wisdom of the ancient Greeks. In this 'university' setting, the most important works of Archimedes, Dioscorides, Euclid, Galen, Hippocrates, Plato, Ptolemy and others were rendered into Arabic.

PERSIAN PHILOSOPHERS AND THE QUEST FOR TRUTH

The debt owed by the West to the scribes and philosophers of the Arabian peninsula is very great. Much of the teaching of the Greeks and Romans was lost to the West during the centuries of barbarism which followed. Arab libraries however maintained these works, through generations of transcriptions. This example is from Hunayn ibn Ishaq, Hira, Persia.

British Library, O.I.O.C. 14535937

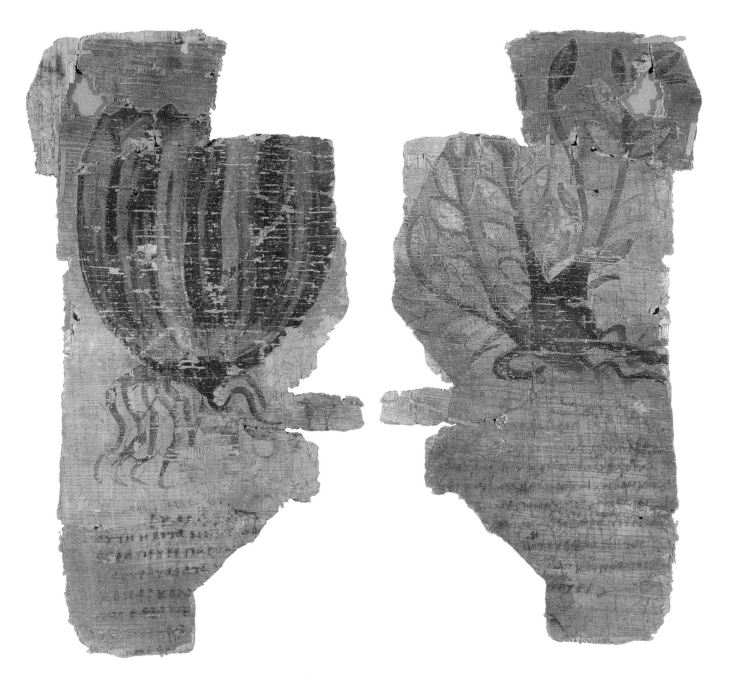

THE GREEK TRADITION OF BOTANY
This fragment of a page of an illustrated herbal on papyrus is the earliest to survive, dating from about AD 400. It shows 'phlommos' (perhaps mullein), *left*, and simphyton (probably comfrey) on the other side, *right*. The artist was highly skilled, but possibly worked from a previous exemplar rather than the living plant. The legible fragments of Greek script indicate that the text consisted of a description of the plant and of its medical uses.

Wellcome Institute for the History of Medicine, London: Johnson Papyrus.

Alongside this growing library of knowledge came translations from India and Persia. We may infer the value placed on scholarship from the fact that the chief of the House of Wisdom, Hunayn ibn Ishaq from Hira in Persia, was paid in gold weighing as much as the works he translated into Arabic. Hunayn was not only an interpreter of the works of others, for he wrote the first textbook on ophthalmology and several other medical texts of his own.

The heritage bequeathed to us from that era is considerable, as just a few examples of borrowed words suggest: *al-kuhl*, alcohol; *al-jabr,* algebra; *al-qili*, alkali; *al-malgham*, amalgam; *buraq*, borax. In this manner, European science inspired the intellectual endeavours of the Arab empire.

REFERENCES

[p.7] A useful summary of the Basque tongue is published in:
Stevenson, Victor (editor), *Words – an illustrated history of western languages*, pp 30–33, Macdonald, 1983.

[p.7] Main European sites of Palaeolithic art include the following:

Dordogne

Font-de-Gaume contains some 200 animal studies, most painted but some carved in relief. The cave, discovered in 1901, is a highpoint of palaeolithic art and includes studies of reindeer, together with extinct animals of the region, notably mammoth and bison.
Lascaux features a cave complex discovered by schoolboys in 1940. The magnificent images of bison, horses and wild cattle from 25,000 years ago have suffered damage since the caves were open to public view, and they were closed in 1963. Conservation is currently under way.
Les Combarelles is noted for its collections of relief carvings. There are 116 panels, some containing several different animals.
Pech-Merle paintings are predominantly descriptive portrayals of mammoths and cattle, often drawn as black line drawings showing the outline only.

Pyrenees

Le Portel is rich with paintings and carvings of animals of the Aurignacian style, which has its origins up to 40,000 years ago. There are about 100 images remaining.
Les Trois Frères includes carvings that are probably of a religious ceremonial kind. Nearby is found:
Le Tuc d'Audoubert a related cave noted for its carvings.
Montespan is a flooded cave which requires scuba equipment for full inspection. An engraving of a hunt round-up is of an instructional or commemorative nature.
Niaux contains fine outline diagrams from 10,000 years ago. Hunting drawings are frequent, with arrows indicating desired target areas during the hunt.

Northern Spain

Altamira shares, with Lascaux, the widest reputation for magnificent wall paintings. The fifteen studies of bison are painted in colour and have become widely recognized as the product of a civilized culture.
Pasiega features Aurignacian-Périgordian paintings dating back some 30,000 years. Most are drawn as red outline diagrams.
Pindal also features red outline drawings, and includes an unusual example for the Palaeolithic of a fish, and also a stylized elephant.

[p.11] Original sources on Egyptian and African murals include:
Winkler, Hans A. 'Rock Drawings of South Upper Egypt', *Archaeological Survey of Egypt*, Sir Robert Mond Desert Expedition, 1938.
Moszeik, O. *Die Malereien der Buschmänner*, Berlin, 1910.
von Luschan, Felix. 'Buschmann-Einritzungen auf Strausseneiern', *Zeitschrift für Ethnologie*, 55: 31 ff, 1923.

[p.11] Art is not a necessary concomitant of civilization or speech, however. Attention has been drawn to the Yoruba, who have a highly-developed plastic art, and the Nupe, with no art tradition. It has been pointed out by Adam, L., (in) *Primitive Art*, Penguin Books, 1940, that both races share a common linguistic stock, and comparable levels of cultural development. See also Nadel, S. F. 'Experiments on Culture Psychology', *Africa*, 10: 424, 1937.

[p.11] An admirable and pioneering publication was the catalogue:
Sweeney, J. J. *African Negro Art*, Museum of Modern Art, New York, 1935.
Munro, N. G. *Prehistoric Japan*, Yokohama and Edinburgh, 1911.
Matsumoto, H. 'Notes on the Stone Age People of Japan', *American Anthropologist*, 23: 50–76, 1911.
An unusual neolithic figure from Japan appeared in:
Singer, K. 'Cowrie and Baubo in Early Japan', (in) *Man*, London, 1940.

[p.17] General works on this period include:
Rostovtzeff, M. *Greece*, Oxford, 1963.
Haywood, R. M. *Ancient Greece and the Near East*, New York, 1964.
Payne, R. *Ancient Greece*, New York, 1964.
A summary of scientific philosophy in ancient Greece may be derived from:
Cohen, M. R. and Drabkin, I. E. *A Source Book in Greek Science*, Harvard and Oxford, 1959; and Taylor, H. O. *Greek Biology and Medicine*, New York, 1963.

[p.21] Jones, W. H. S., and Withington, E. T. *Hippocrates* (4 vols), 1923–1931.
Munro, H. A. J. (ed), *Titus Lucreti Cari de rerum natura libri sex*, (3 vols), 1886, 1928.
Pliny, G. *Natural History* (10 vols), Loeb Classical Library, 1938–1963.

[p.22] The unravelling of middle eastern relationships is expounded in:
Singer, C. *A Short History of Science to the Nineteenth Century*, Oxford, 1941.
See also (for medical and bioscience disciplines):
Nordenskiöld, E. *The History of Biology, a Survey*, New York, 1928, (first published as *Biologins Historia* (3 vols), Stockholm, 1920–1924).

The hidden nature of mankind

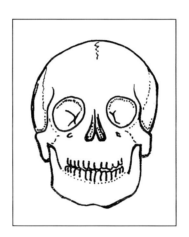

IMAGES OF SCIENCE

SURGERY AND CAUTERY IN EARLY
ENGLISH MEDICINE
The practice of cautery was becoming refined by
the time this 11th-century English miniature
was painted. At left the treatment of a gouty
patient is shown to involve both cutting and
burning of the foot. At right an operation to
remove haemorrhoids is depicted.

British Library, Harley 1585 f9

Tantalizing glimpses of our historic forebears are provided through the media of clay and paint. Some, like the footprints captured in relief in the clay floor of caves in Italy and France, may have been created accidentally. Others, including the outstretched hand seen in the cave of Pech-Merle in the Dordogne, are clearly deliberate. These stencilled outlines are amongst the oldest deliberately recorded images of all, and are to this day part of the aboriginal traditions of Australia. At Gargas in the French Pyrenees survive some outlines of mutilated hands, the fingers being shortened as though phalanges had been removed.

The earliest attempts at portrayal of the human form are the prehistoric carvings in stone or ivory, and surviving models in clay. That great era now known as the Upper Palaeolithic is divided into several zones, of which the earliest is the Aurignacian, named after the cave in Aurignac, Haute Garonne, France. Many exquisite carvings have been found in the French caves, including eight ivory statuettes at Brassempouy, Landes, and six soapstone carvings (together with one of bone) in the Grimaldi cave at Menton. Perhaps the most exquisite is the 147 mm-long statue found in the Grotte des Rideaux, Haute Garonne, by Count Saint Périer in 1922.

We may infer something of the development of society from these relics. Thus the Venus of Willendorf, on the Danube, excavated in 1908 by Professor Obermaier is marked with bangles on the arms and clearly-styled hair. Similarly decorated carvings have been found in the Nilgiri Hills in Southern India and (as we have seen) in Japan. Yet these are not representational portrayals. Rather, they accord with a distorted view of the female form in which sexual features are exaggerated: fattened thighs, enlarged breasts and rotund bodies. As such they are to be regarded as worship symbols associated with tribal ritual. However, there remains a possibility that they also had an instructional rôle to fulfil. In Maori traditions we find the *hei-tiki*, personal carvings in bone, which seem to represent the human embryo. And there remain the attempts of primitive art to show internal features of the body in the so-called 'x-ray drawings' of Northern Australia and British Columbian traditions, which represent mankind's most unrefined attempts at an allusion to what went on inside.

Further insights need a sound philosophical tradition, and the inspiration arose from a subtle fusion of the teachings of Aristotle, Plato, and — above all others — Hippocrates. It fell to Galen to translate this synthesis into the first great work on the structure and function of the human body. Born in Pergamum, Asia Minor in AD 129 of Greek parents, Galen set in train insights into human structure that underpinned medical thought for more than a thousand years. His father, Nicon, was an architect who foresaw a medical career for his son in a dream. The young Galen was initiated into the profession as a result of this supposed 'divine inter-

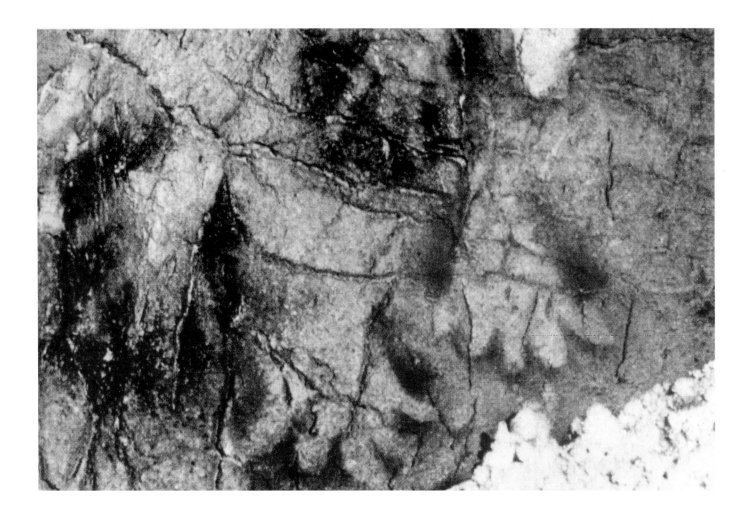

vention'. In Pergamum he studied under Epicureans, Platonists and Stoics and became familiar with the writings of Theophrastus and Aristotle. He studied at Corinth and then Alexandria, returning home in A D 158 where he took on the position of physician at the Temple of Aesculapius for a period of six years. He then moved to Rome and established himself as an innovator. Indeed the jealous response of the establishment led him to flee that city for a time, until summoned to return by the Emperor Marcus Aurelius. He acted as personal physician to the Emperor's family and from this position he continued his investigations. Though he Latinized his name to Claudius Galenus he continued to write in Greek, and is also known as Galenos; estimates of his date of death vary from A D 199 to 210. Galen wrote that he published 256 treatises, 131 of them medical in nature. Of these latter writings over 80 are known to survive.

Earlier workers tended to philosophize on the relationship between mankind and the animal world, but Galen set himself the study of the organs of the human body and saw through this the supremacy of a Creator. He did not dissect the human body, as he records in his writings, but sought insights from animal dissection, notably of apes, which he saw as exemplars of human anatomy. His

A MUTILATED HAND FROM THE STONE AGE
Some of the cave paintings in the Pyrenees contain evidence of the earliest surgical operations. These outlines feature mutilated outstretched hands. Parts of the fingers are missing, as though removed by a knife. We may speculate that these portrayals record the punishment or ritual disfigurement of cave dwellers. From the caves at Gargas, France.

Photograph by Jean Vertut

A DOCTOR EXAMINING A CHILD IN
ANCIENT ROME
Here we see the examination of a child's
abdomen by a (?Greek) physician of the second
century A D. It is a scene which embodies as
much evidence of care and professionalism as we
might wish to see today. This low relief was
carved in marble.

British Museum, Department of Greek and Roman Antiquities

work involved living animal specimens as well as *post-mortem* examinations. His great treatise on the human hand, for instance, is masterly in its detail but is clearly founded on the anatomy of the ape. He moved on to describe the structure of the heart, lungs and blood-vessels, the details of the central nervous system and the peripheral nerves; and he carried out experiments in which he severed different regions of the spinal chord and related these to effects on the corresponding parts of the animal's body.

The insights of his work are impressive. For example, he saw that digestion in the stomach was due to a transformational power, rather than (as Aristotle taught) the effect of cooking. Galen said that the products of digestion went to the liver, where they were transmuted into blood; he knew that the purpose of the kidneys was to remove excess water from the bloodstream; and he dispelled the ancient notion that the left half of the heart contained air. His

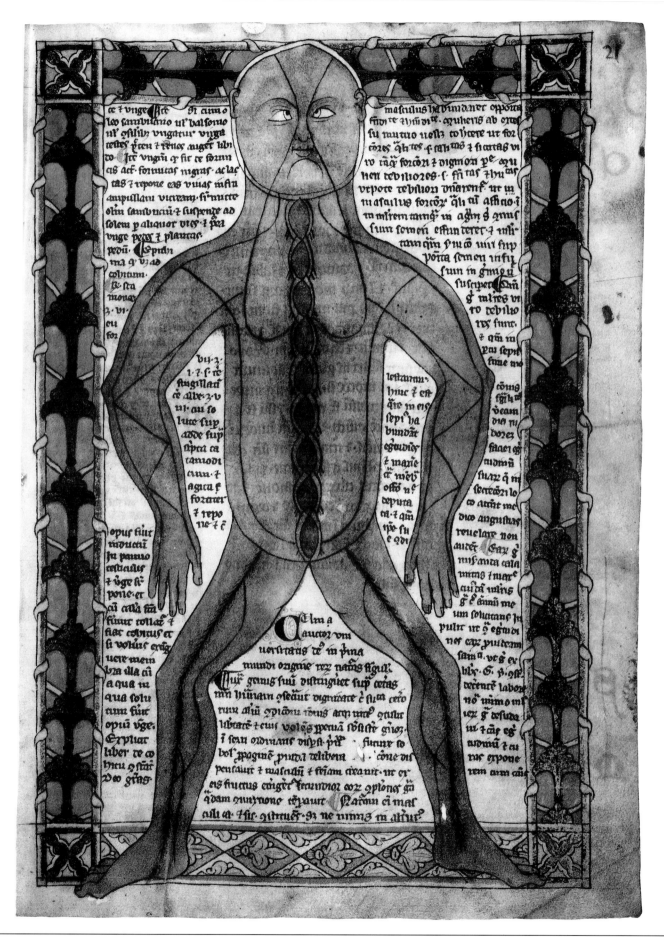

THE ISLAMIC VIEW OF THE VISUAL SYSTEM

Rufus of Ephesus wrote on the structure of the eye around A D 50. Many of the terms he introduced are the basis for today's terminology. This view was recorded by an Arabic scholar, *circa* A D 1000. It shows the optic chiasma, but in highly diagrammatic form. This may be an example of cultural constraint, for the teachings of Islam forbade the drawing of images of the human form.

THE NERVOUS SYSTEM

The nervous system was understood in the most rudimentary way during the earliest years of medicine. This crude depiction from a thirteenth-century English manuscript bears little resemblance to life. It has much in common with the 'x-ray diagrams' drawn by the untutored aboriginal artists of the Australian Northern Territories (*see* above, p.10).

Bodleian Library, Ashmole 399 f21

comments on the 'pneuma' of the blood point the way to the discovery of oxygen, for he saw *pneuma* as part-air, part-fire, part life-principle; and he wrote that he looked forward to the day when the nature of the *pneuma* in the air might be discovered. In other respects he was clearly wrong – noting the spleen as the organ which converted excess food to 'black bile', for example, and claiming that the vertical septum of the heart was porous in order to allow circulation to proceed.

It is noteworthy that Galen's great strides forward were not greatly appreciated by his contemporaries. He wrote of the ingratitude of his colleagues and complained that few understood the importance of his work, a view repeated at intervals throughout the history of science. Leeuwenhoek (*see* p.182) recorded identical complaints and in similar words, for instance; and it is clear that, whereas to innovate slightly can confer acclaim and approval, to innovate profoundly may lead to bafflement and non-acceptance by contemporary authorities. The seed needs nurtured ground if it is to germinate and flourish; ideas that amount to a paradigm shift may well be met by rejection.

Dois que a
plaise de dieu
nauons trait
tie des choses
qui parsont
et gardent la nature des
hommes ✶ Cest main
tenant adiux des choses
qui lui aduiencnt contre
nature et qui les destruu
sent et corrompent · ꟷ
Troys choses sont qui blef
chent la nature de lomme
Cest a scauoir Cause de
maladie maladie Et
accidene suruans mala
die · ꟷ Cause de ma
ladie est ce dont vient ꟷ
maulaise et inmaturele
disposition ou corps come
est mauluaise complexion

Trop grande expletion
ou inanition defection de
vertus Alteration de qua
litez et dissolution de con
tinuite · Toutes ces cho
ses sont cause et occasio
des maladies · maladie
selon Iehan / est la chose
de laquele aduient nui
sement a lopposition de la
lesion du corps · comme
fieure apostene et plu
sieurs aultres teles ma
ladies ꟷ Accidene est
la chose suiuans a ceste
introduitte passion ou
corps soit contraire a ꟷ
nature comme douleur
de chief en la cephalicque
ou non contraire comme
en piplesino / Cest vnguet

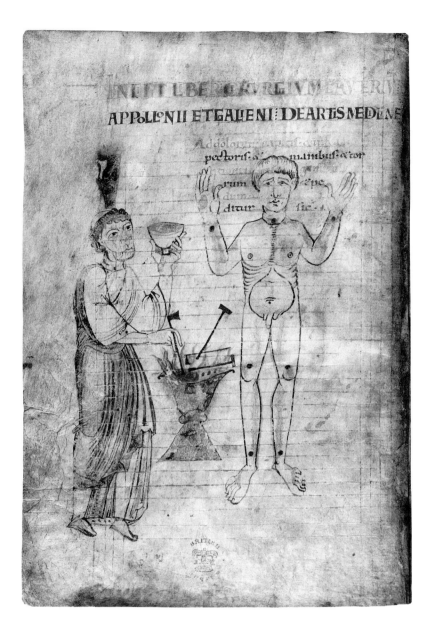

The caption for this diagram reads: *Here begins
Apollonius's Book of Surgery and Galen's Art of
Medicine. For an aching head and flatulence of the
breast and hands, and pains of the knees and feet,
burn thus*. Little wonder the patient bears such
an uneasy countenance. The manuscript is
English, and dates from the late eleventh
century. It is one of the first to show cautery in
use. The cap held up by the physician may
symbolize a pain-killing drink that will shortly be
administered.

British Library, Sloane 2839 flv

AN OUT-PATIENT CLINIC IN
FIFTEENTH-CENTURY FRANCE
In this interesting miniature painting we see a
physician giving consultation to a number of
patients, who are queueing to see him. It has
fittingly been described as an early out-patient
clinic. The manuscript was made for King
Edward IV at Bruges, Belgium, in 1482.

British Library, Royal 15 E II f165

The insights of Galen lay fallow after his death until they were
revived by Avicenna, the philosopher/scientist. He was born Abu
'Ali al-Husain ibn Abdallah ibn Sina at Afshana, near Bakhara (his
Latinized name derives from a mis-pronounciation of Abu Sina –
Avicenna) of Persian parents in the year A D 980, and died at
Hamadan in 1037. Persia at that time existed as many separate
states, each ruled by a prince and in a continual cycle of internicine
border warfare. The intellectual was not unlike his Renaissance
counterpart, versed in mathematics and medicine, astronomy and
art, poetry and prose.

The great work on medicine by Avicenna was the *Qanun*
(= canon) and ran to a million words. Yet it was only a small
portion of his prodigious output. His anatomical descriptions were
those of Galen, for the Arabs were unwilling to dissect the human
body *post mortem* and indeed were expressly prohibited from

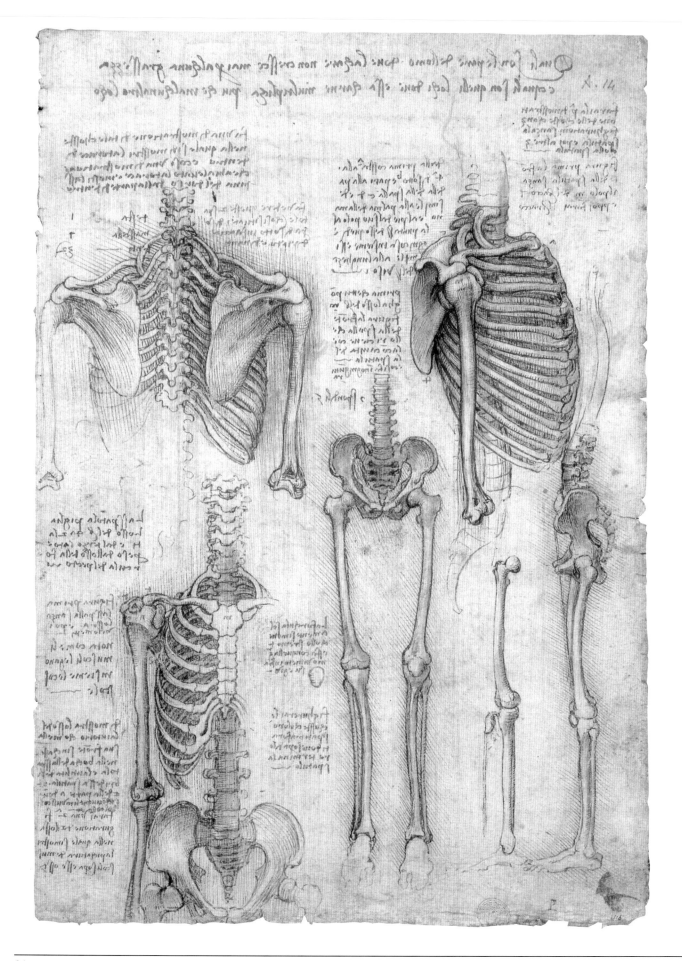

A SCIENTIFIC APPROACH TO ANAL FISTULA

Anal fistula was regarded as an incurable condition. The risk of infection was too great. John of Arderne became famed for his intricate surgical approach to the problem. In the fourteenth century he evolved complex procedures for the management of the condition. He developed spoons to protect the rectal wall and scalpels to make incisions, with probes and dilators to explore, and later close, the wound. His fees were always high: never less than £5 and sometimes – for a wealthy client – more than £40.

British Library, Sloane 56 f44

LEONARDO PROBES THE NATURE OF MANKIND

Leonardo da Vinci made many detailed studies of human anatomy, and recorded his findings in pencil drawings of the highest quality. Much of his work was carried out through dissection of human cadavers. He dissected more than 30 bodies, until Pope Leo X banned him from entering the mortuary in Rome. Leonardo's studies of plant life and natural phenomena were equally detailed and painstaking.

Windsor Castle, Royal Library. © Her Majesty The Queen

doing so in the Qur'an. But he seems to have been the first to realize that light (a corpuscular medium, according to the *Qanun*) travels to an object from the eye.

Perhaps the greatest of the Byzantine medical writers was Paulus of Aegina, whose surgical texts were famed in both Europe and Arabia, but with the fall of the Byzantine Empire in 1453 much of this teaching was lost. The Arabic documents were preserved, studied and translated in the security of the great monastic establishments. And in this way the ancient teachings became available to the earliest universities through the diligence of monastic endeavour. Religion became the saving grace of science.

The few illustrations to the early Arabic texts were crude, and

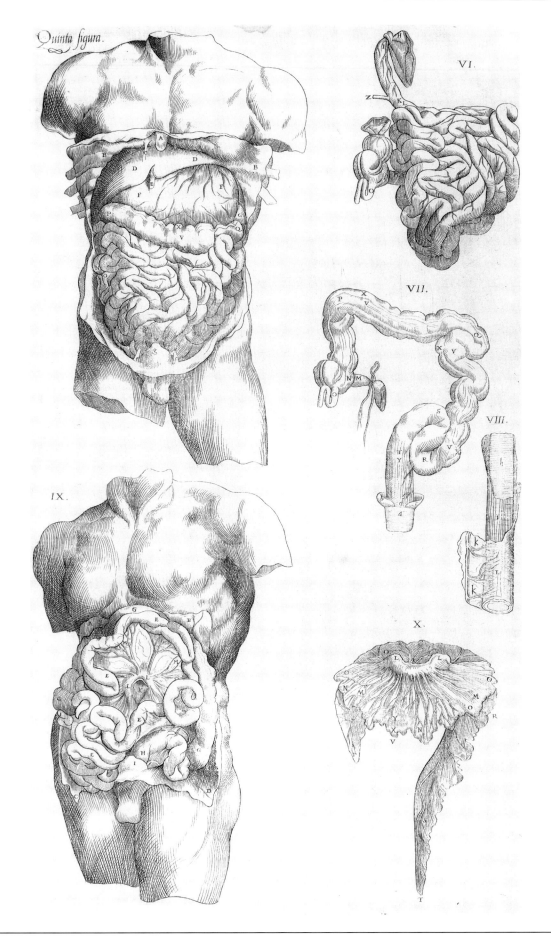

many of the surviving portrayals are copies that were made as much as 1,000 years after the original. Some, however, have origins that are closer to home. An early sixth-century manuscript of Dioscorides is believed to be a copy made in Constantinople of the Alexandrian original. It was prepared for Juliana Anicia, daughter of Flavius Anicius Olybrius (one of the last Roman emperors) in AD 512. It shows physicians and medical botanists with the mandrake, *Mandragora*, and a range of other medicinal plants. The manuscript is preserved in Vienna (and is described below, p.86).

An early example of medical apparatus in use may be found in the writings of the Arabic physician Al Jazari in 1315. It shows a mechanical system of floats and pulleys used to measure the blood. And a pioneering study of human anatomy may be dated even earlier, the so-called 'autopsy miniature' from the thirteenth century. In this graphic portrayal, the deceased lies with the abdomen open via a long median incision, the operator standing nearby with a divided object in his hand. Whether it is a mandrake, inserted to bring on an abortion, or the victim's (lobed) liver, removed for examination, is not apparent from the image. Internal organs are shown around the body, though it is possible they may have been added later to the picture.

Some increase in understanding is revealed by the early sixteenth century, when, in *circa* 1510, Henricus Kullmaurer and Albert Meher produced a medical picture-book which includes portrayals of a pregnant woman with an open abdomen, sketches of skeletons, medicinal herbs, and studies of the uterus. However, a single figure stands out as the Scholastic period gave way to the revival of learning of the Renaissance. As older and inaccurate traditions of scientific drawings persisted in many learned publications, Leonardo da Vinci established a lone pathway towards representational scientific illustration which remained without peer.

The illegitimate son of Ser Piero da Vinci (who became notary to the Signoria di Firenze) and Caterina, a girl from a neighbouring village, Leonardo was born in Vinci, near Florence, on 15 April 1452. He was trained by the painter Andrea del Verrocchio of Florence (1435–1488) and about 1483 he moved to live in Milan. He made his first anatomical drawings aged about 35, though most were made later, during his period as adviser on the Lombard canal system between 1506–1513. Leonardo's great anatomical notebooks are now in the Royal Library at Windsor Castle, and they show how his earlier interests in anatomy – as a fine artist – were supplanted by scientific and medical studies based on dissection of the human body. (Michelangelo, by comparison, also made fine studies of human anatomy as an artist, but was not drawn to further investigations in such detail.) Yet Leonardo suffered indifference from his unappreciative acquaintances, and it is said he was censured by the Pope for his anatomical investigations.

THE ANATOMICAL REVELATIONS OF VESALIUS, 1543
Andreas Vesalius cast a new light on the teachings of Galen. In his *De Humani Corporis Fabrica* he updated the traditional teachings of an earlier era. His studies, illustrated by the Flemish artist Jan Stefan, are firmly rooted in observation. In the same year he published a popular version of the book, entitled *Epitome*, intended for those not versed in medicine. In consequence, his findings were to have far-reaching effects for several centuries.

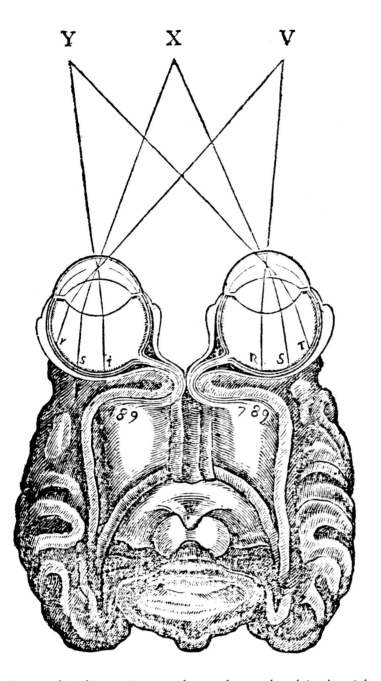

Among his discoveries was the moderator band in the right
ventricle, which is concerned with regulation of ventricular con-
traction. This was re-discovered in 1669 by Lower, and again in
1837 by King, Leonardo's work having been lost to succeeding
anatomists following his death at Amboise in France on 2 May
1519. He recognized the heart as a muscular organ, and has been
described as making studies of the heart that were 'ahead of his
time'. Though this view is frequently expounded, it is important to
note that his understanding of heart function was derived from
Galen's teaching. Thus, he believed the atria filled from contrac-
tions of the ventricles, and he went so far as to draw the non-
existent perforations in the inter-ventricular septum which had
been surmised to exist by Galen.

William Harvey's work on the human circulation was undertaken as part of a wide-ranging medical career. For 40 years he was Lumleian lecturer at the Royal College of Physicians in London, and lectured on every aspect of anatomy. These studies of the veins of the forearm are based on those published by Fabricius in 1603; Harvey's appeared in a slim volume, *De Mortu Cordis*, published in Frankfurt in 1628. His famous lecture explaining the circulation theory had been given in 1616. *De Mortu Cordis* was the first book on the topic.

Leonardo related that he personally dissected more than 30 cadavers, and his ability to utilize his gifts in the conduct of his anatomical investigations remain without parallel. His natural successor was Andreas Vesalius (1514–1564), son of the physician to Emperor Charles V, who was educated at the University of Louvain. His first great teacher was himself a follower of Galen, Jacobus Sylvius (1478–1555), but he studied later under Johann Guinter (1505–1574). The first drawings made by Vesalius were clearly under the influence of his Galenist training, but dissection and study convinced him of the fallibility of this earlier school of thought; and by the time his book *De humani corporis fabrica* appeared in 1543 he claimed to have corrected over 200 of the errors in the Galenist interpretation of the body. Nevertheless, he preserves many other traditional errors, including the view that the *upper* jaw moves in the crocodile – an interpretation still current in the 1680s – and his drawings reveal a multiplicity of sources. His figures of the kidney and the hyoid are clearly taken from studies of the dog, and it is a dog's placenta to which his figure of a human foetus is attached. His figures were plagiarized for 200 years, a

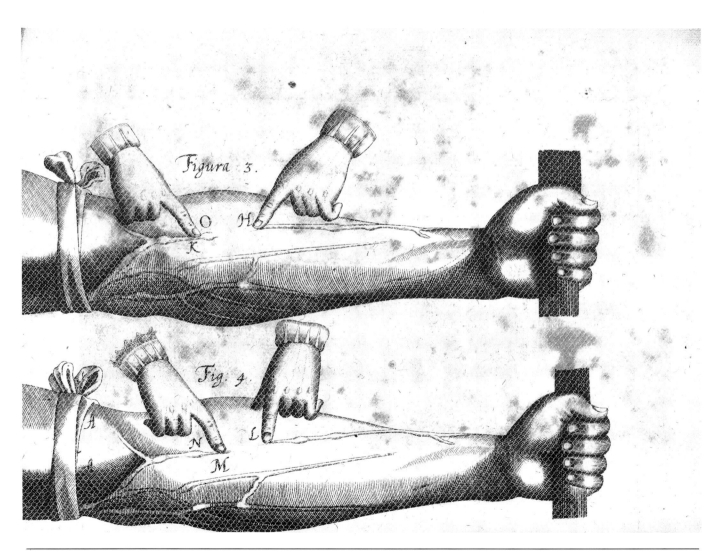

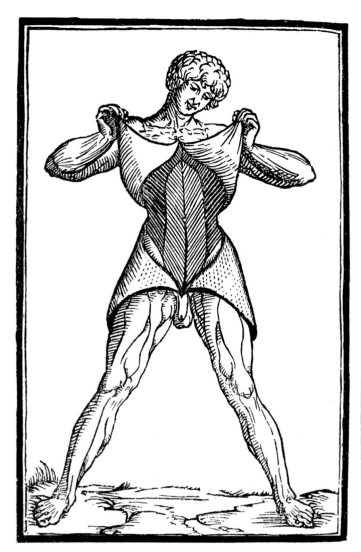 

testimony to the grandeur of his images and the overall accuracy of his dissection studies.

William Harvey (1578–1657) is known for his work on the circulation of the blood, for he used dissection and experimental methods – ligature of blood vessels, for example – to demonstrate the phenomenon. Capillaries were unknown at the time (they were clearly documented by Leeuwenhoek, *see* p.182) and – although it had been invented – Harvey did not have recourse to a microscope though he speaks of using a hand lens to obtain magnified images. He also investigated the circulation in other forms of life, from oysters and earthworms to reptiles and birds. The literature he cites includes 97 references to 21 authors – and of the references, 56 are to Galen and Aristotle. It is a tribute to his clear-sightedness that he continued the trend towards revision and reform of earlier workers, and knew when his findings should supplant previously published hypotheses.

As the scientific discipline began to develop, artists were brought in to illustrate the findings of the researchers. John Hunter

MATCHING VIEWS OF MAN
These two figures illuminate the descriptions in Berengario da Carpi's *Commentaria super Anatomia Mundini . . .* (Benedictis, Bologna, 1521). At first sight they appear to be progressive dissections of the human form. But closer inspection shows that the dissected regions and the lower limbs show identical features. The apparent difference between them is emphasized by the direction in which the block cutter was indicating shading. In one, the layers are indicated by upright chevrons, whilst in the other the chevrons are inverted. From the sternum downwards, these are almost identical illustrations, yet the artist's craft has been used to create the impression that the reader has two iconographic images, rather than one.

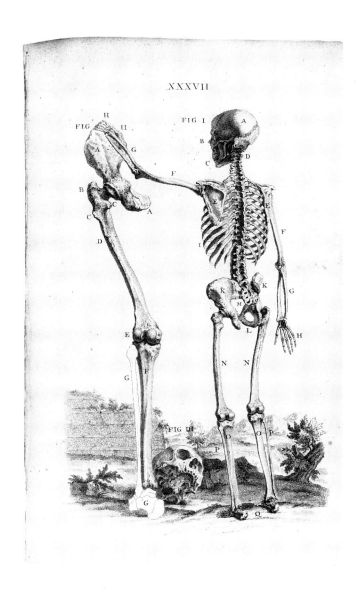

ARTISTIC LICENCE IN THE REALM OF
OSTEOLOGY

One of the most dramatically stylized illustrations
from William Cheselden's *Osteographia* (London,
1733) compared the stature of two men. The
caption explains that the skeleton (right) is from
a man measuring $5\frac{1}{2}$ ft, the limb bones (left)
being from a man 'near eight feet high'. Some of
Cheselden's fine illustrations re-emerged a
hundred years later, when Sir Charles Bell
plagiarized them to illustrate his own work.

(1728–1793), the Scottish surgeon and anatomist, produced a
stream of work with the aid of professional illustrators. William
Bell, whom he employed as a live-in artist in 1775, also took on the
duties of supervisor of Hunter's museum. And what a collection he
had! He carried out endless dissections and collected a great range
of specimens. He borrowed five guineas on one occasion to purchase a dying tiger, for example, and had an agreement with the
Menagerie at the Tower of London which enabled him to dissect
the bodies of deceased exotic animals. A bull given him by Queen
Charlotte once felled him; on another occasion he was said to have
overpowered two young leopards.

He married Anne Home, only sister of Everard Home who was
to become a noted surgeon. Indeed, Hunter took on Home as a
pupil. Anne was a poet with an active social circle. Their friends
included Elizabeth Carter and Franz Josef Haydn, who set some of
her poems to music. John Hunter had many celebrated arguments
with his brother William, known also as an anatomist, some of
them over the question of priority in research. William (1718–

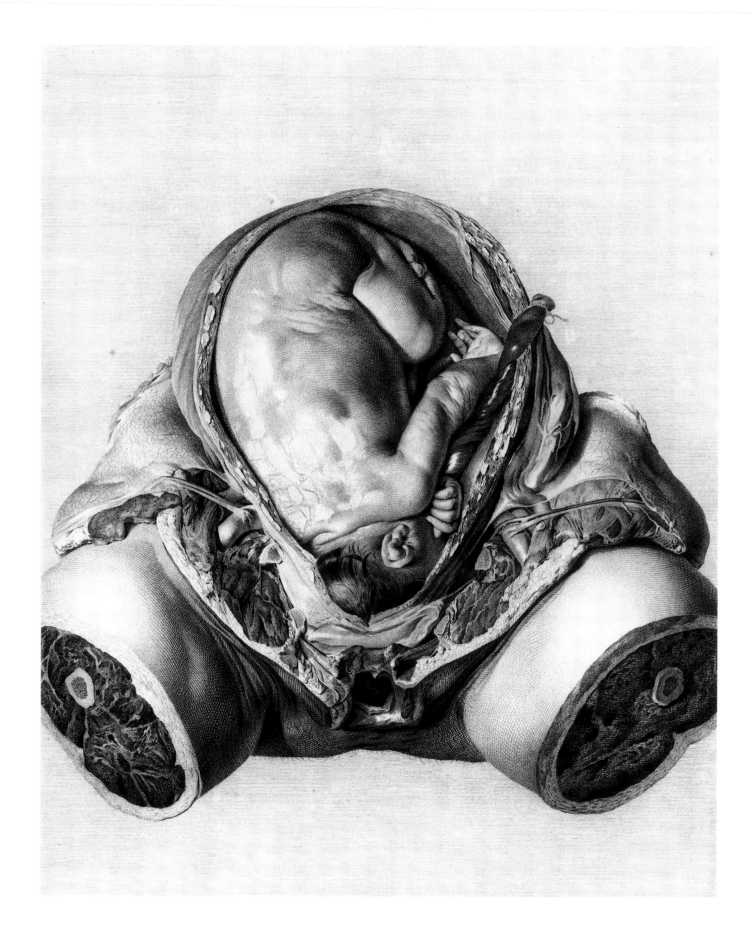

1783), ten years John's senior, had actually trained his younger brother in medical skills, for John had begun life as a cabinet maker. As a prolific investigator, John Hunter deserves his greater reputation. He was clearly a man to reckon with: when the Irish 'giant' O'Byrne died, measuring seven feet seven inches (2.3 m) in height, his will stipulated he should be buried in a lead coffin out at sea off the Thames estuary – a move to defeat Hunter, who had boasted of his wish to own the skeleton. In the event, Hunter prevailed. A bribe of £500 to the undertaker meant that the coffin went down empty, whilst Hunter took the corpse – seated like a living passenger in a horse-drawn carriage – to his home and systematically had the body boiled down and the bones extracted.

Following John Hunter's death, Sir Everard Home was given charge of the voluminous notes and papers, but proceeded to publish them under his own name. Great pressure was put on Home to relinquish the documents and pass them over to the College of Surgeons, but in the end he set fire to them rather than reveal the source of many of his own publications on human anatomy.

Everard Home made many contributions which have been overshadowed by his persistent plagiarism. He also provides a further example of the use of the professional illustrator by the scientific research worker. He employed Franz (Francis) Bauer, brother of the equally celebrated artist Ferdinand; and it was as a result of Bauer's diligence that many of Home's publications became appreciated. The use of line and shade, an unsurpassable accuracy of observation, and even – in the originals – the delicately crafted employment of colour, make Bauer's anatomical studies admirable examples of scientific illustration.

By the mid-eighteenth century, the scientific illustration of the human body was well-established as a discrete discipline. The use of the microscope was considered a normal part of the observer's equipment. In this regard it is noteworthy that Home is the last person to have possessed the Royal Society's collection of Leeuwenhoek microscopes, and the quality of the original Bauer artwork encourages me to conclude that the Leeuwenhoek lenses were used by Bauer to make many of his microscopical observations. (We shall return to the question of microscopy in Chapter Eight.)

Henry Gray (1827–1861) brings the illustration of the human body up to date. Some of the original illustrations from the first edition of the *Anatomy* are still published in the 1990s. His father, who had served as messenger to both George IV and King William IV, sent the precocious youngster to study medicine at St George's Hospital, London, and when aged just 21 he won the prestigious Triennial Prize of the Royal College of Surgeons for an essay entitled: 'The Origin, Connexions and Distribution of the Nerves to the Human Eye and its Appendages, Illustrated by Comparative

THE STUDY OF OBSTETRICS
William Hunter, born in Scotland in 1718, established obstetrics as a medical discipline. He made many detailed studies of the gravid uterus. His younger brother John, born 1728, had not studied medicine but nevertheless went to London to work with his brother. His collection of preserved surgical specimens eventually led to the formation of a museum at the Royal College of Surgeons.

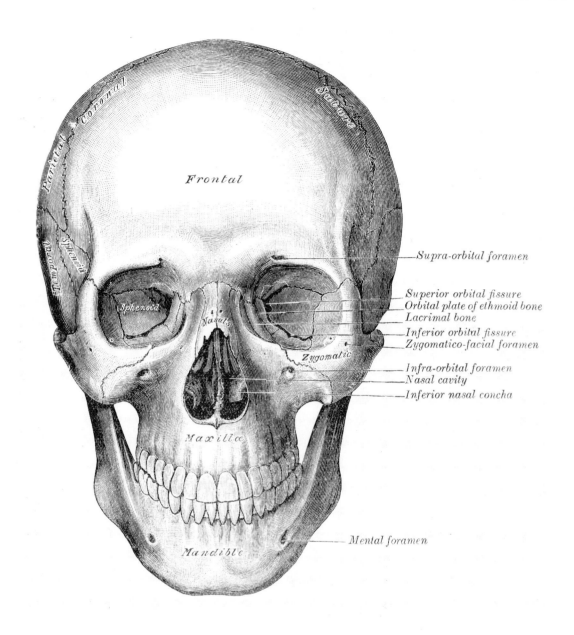

Dissections of the Eye in other Vertebrate Animals'. By the age of 25 he was elected a Fellow of the Royal Society, and the following year was awared the Astley Cooper Prize – then worth 300 guineas – for a thesis entitled 'On the Structure and Use of the Spleen'. Gray's *Anatomy* was compiled during the following years, the first edition appearing in 1858, followed by the second in 1860. In the following year, Gray took to attending a young nephew suffering from confluent smallpox and contracted the illness in its most virulent form. He died in 1861 when in line for the post of Assistant Surgeon to the St George's Hospital.

Gray's illustrator for the volume was H. Vandyke Carter, former Demonstrator of Anatomy at the hospital and a gifted draughtsman. The book came out at 750 pages with 363 engraved figures showing human anatomy with considerable realism. For all its rela-

GRAY'S *ANATOMY* – AN OBJECTIVE VISION OF MANKIND

Henry Gray (1827–1861) studied anatomy at St George's Hospital, London. His work was of exemplary standard, and he was elected a Fellow of the Royal Society in 1852 when aged 25. His great *Anatomy* was illustrated with vivid woodcuts. Their merit has endured, for in the current editions of the work (it has been continuously in print since it first appeared in 1858) several of the original woodcuts still appear. The style of the book was always impeccably detached and accurate, and the clarity of the illustrations brought anatomy into the realm of the exact sciences.

Gray, Henry, *Anatomy*, 1942

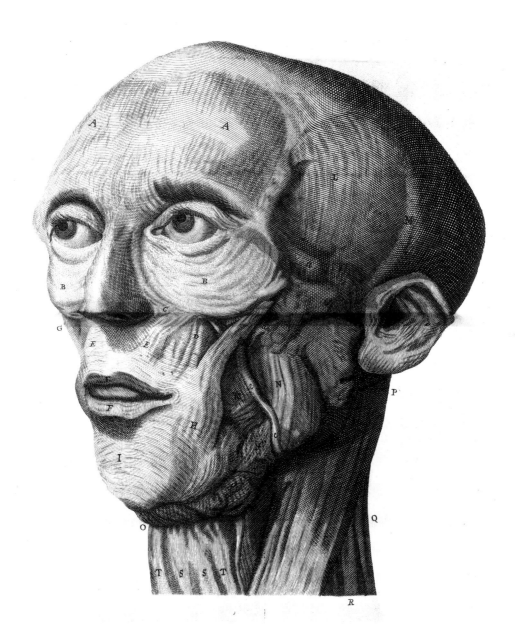

DISSECTIONS FROM THE *MYOTOMIA REFORMATA*

A great dissector and student of anatomy was William Cowper, after whom the Cowper's glands are named. In 1698 he published an *Anatomy of Human Bodies*. Most of the drawings were plagiarized from the work of Govert Bidloo, who protested loudly about the offence. Eventually, Cowper published an apology under the title *Eucharistia*. It now seems that the Cowper's glands were not a new discovery, either. Cowper announced their existence in 1702, but in 1687 they had been demonstrated to the French Academy of Medicine by Jean Mery.

Cowper, William, *Myotomia reformata*, 1694

tive antiquity, revised editions of Gray's *Anatomy* have remained in print continuously ever since, and students of the medical and nursing sciences refer to it to this day. It is a fitting memorial to an anatomist of consummate skill, and a tribute to the melding of observational science with artistic talent which has marked out the development of medical illustration. The fact that the artist is as often employed today – even in an era when computer-generated artwork and photography are sophisticated sciences in themselves – is a reminder of the need for cognitive interpretation of an image. The electronic image-processing technologics may assist the scientific illustrator in this field, but they have yet to replace the art of the scientific illustrator with science.

REFERENCES

[p.27] A series of representations of female forms from the palaeolithic is preserved at the Musée de l'Homme in Paris. A selection – the Venus of Vestoniče (Czechoslovakia), the carved stone Venus of Willendorf (Austria), the ivory lady of Brassempouy (France) and the stone relief Venus of Laussel (France) – are illustrated in:

Howell, F. C. *Early Man*, pp 162–163, Time-Life International, Netherlands, 1969.

[p.28] The earlier date of Galen's death is cited by E. A. Underwood in *A Biographical Dictionary of Scientists*, p 201, London, 1974; the greater longevity is ascribed by Nordenskiöld, E. *The History of Biology*, p 60, New York, 1928.

[p.37] The 'autopsy miniature' is one of a series of eight miniatures described by:

MacKinney, L. 'A Thirteenth-Century Medical Case History in Miniatures', *Speculum*, 35: 251–259, 1960.

The suggestion that the organs may have been a later addition was made by Walter Artelt in:

MacKinney, L. *Medical Illustrations in Medieval Manuscripts*, California and London, 1965 (*vide* p 101).

[p.38] Leonardo's studies of the heart are hailed, among others, by E. A. Underwood in the *Biographical Dictionary of Scientists*, p 324, 1974.

See also *Dictionary of Scientific Biography*, New York, 8: 192–245, 1973; and Kemp, M. *Leonardo da Vinci, the marvellous works of Man and Nature*, London, 1981.

But a discussion of his erroneous understanding of the cardiac septa is included in:

Cole, F. J. *A History of Comparative Anatomy from Aristotle to the Eighteenth Century*, p 53, London, 1944.

[p.40] William Harvey is set in his context by F. J. Cole, pp 126–131.

[p.43] The rising prominence of the technical scientist gave a lower profile to the limner who captured the illustrations on paper. Scattered throughout Home's papers are references to Franz Bauer's expertise and help:

1) E. Home – paper dated 27 February 1823, *On the Double Organs of Generation of the Lamprey, etc*, for *Philosophical Transactions*, 'I have taken advantage of Mr Bauer's superior skill in the use of the microscope.'
2) E. Home – *Croonian Lecture* dated 7 December 1820, *Microscopical Observations on the Structure of the Brain and Nerves ... etc*; contains coloured micrographs by Bauer.
3) E. Home – *Croonian Lecture* dated 4 December 1819, *A Further Investigation of the Component Parts of the Blood*, '(I) engaged Mr Bauer, whose microscopical observations have been too long put to the proof, to admit of the dispute (concerning the size of erythrocytes).'
'When the glass was laid across black paper, the globules appeared to be distinctly milk-white.'
4) E. Home – notes dated 1 June 1820: *Microscopical Observations on the Human Urethra*.
5) E. Home – Letter to John Herschel (Herschel Letters No 10), 'I have got Mr Bauer's measurements, and if you will take the trouble of calling in Sackville Street ... I will show them to you.'
6) E. Home, notes dated 14 January 1819:
'With the assistance of Mr Bauer I have traced the rise and progress of the Corpus Luteum to its full growth ... cells (were) met with in the ovaria.'
7) E. Home, notes dated 25 March 1819:
'To Mr Bauer's talents and microscopical observations ... we are indebted.'

The above documents are in the Royal Society Manuscripts, PT 16 1823, PT 15 1821, PT 13 1819, and the *Herschel Letters* collection, *q.v.*

[p.44] For all his influence, Henry Gray was not included in the authoritative *Dictionary of National Biography* reissued in 1975. A tribute to his work was published in the *St George's Hospital Gazette*, 21 May 1908.

Illustrating the animal world

AN EARLY VIEW OF ELEPHANTS
(*Left*.) Most scientific illustrations are drawn from earlier reference images, rather than from life. The creation of 'icons' – unrealistic images that pass down from one generation to the next – is a feature of science texts. An early example is the elephant. Familiar since Roman times, described by Pliny, this creature was caricatured for centuries. In these examples from *circa* 1230, we see elephants put to war (top) and gathering to tend a fallen friend (below). The tusks and trunk seem to bear more resemblance to those of pigs, rather than elephants.

British Library, Royal 12 FXIII f11v

AN ELEPHANT DRAWN FROM NATURE
This fine portrait of a captive elephant was a move towards realism in zoological art. The proportions are good, the trunk and tusks correctly observed. Matthew Paris, a monk of St Albans, made the drawing *circa* 1255. Yet the distorted, hog-like elephant persisted in manuscripts for a lengthy period subsequent to this.

British Library, Cotton Nero D 1 f169v

CAVE PAINTINGS OF ANIMALS seem remarkable today for their extraordinarily life-like quality. By comparison, Palaeolithic models of the human body are distorted and grotesque. Animal illustration began to move away from realism towards the realms of fantasy with the passage of time. Many of the medieval creatures bequeathed to us are legendary, or merely mythical – the unicorn, the phoenix and the dragon, for example. There are resonances of the trait in the illustrations of creatures believed to exist in more recent times. The Abominable Snowman, or Yeti, of the Himalayas, like the Big Foot of North America, are reputed to exist by a minority of travellers and appear in accounts of their encounters.

The earliest great student of zoology whose name has come down to us is Aristotle (384–322 BC) whom we have encountered as a founder of the scientific study of living organisms (*see* above p.17). Born in Chalcidice, he studied under Plato (427–347 BC), and learned much zoology through studies in Asia Minor before settling in Athens where he was appointed tutor to the future Alexander the Great. He founded the Lyceum, a form of university centre of learning and study in succession to Plato's Academy, about 335 BC.

Aristotle reportedly drew several diagrams of animal structure, though none are known to survive, even as copies. The earliest

Tab. XII.

Draco bipes apteros captus in Agro Bononiensi.

Draco alatus Apes ex Greuino Aldro.

record of the study of animals and their relationship to *Homo sapiens* dates from the records of the Hippocratic school in the fifth century BC, when the skeletons of mammals were compared to that of man. From the same period are reports that the head of a ram was dissected for study by Anaxagoras (*circa* 500–428 BC), while Empedocles (*circa* 490–350 BC) first recorded the cochlea on the basis of dissection and study in several species. An account that a full anatomical description of the chameleon – based on dissection – was made by Democritus (470/460–370 BC) is also noted, though scholars tend to doubt the authenticity of the report of Pliny the Elder.

Aristotle knew that the Cetaceans were mammals and not fish (a view reversed in 1551 by the French zoologist Pierre Belon): they

FANTASTIC DRAGONS

A doctor of medicine, Johann Johnston, produced works on the animal world in the mid-seventeenth century. Cloven-hoofed and bear-pawed versions of the hippopotamus appear in one plate together with a gryphon ready for take-off. In his work *De Serpentibus et Draconibus* of 1653 Johnston portrays a classification of dragons.

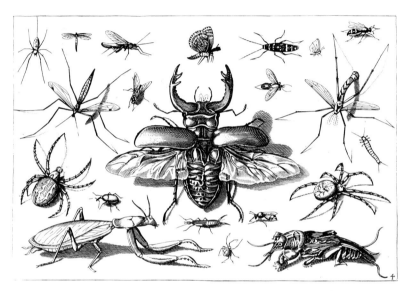

INSECT STUDIES FROM THE PRE-MICROSCOPIC ERA

Jacob Hoefnagel (1575–1640) was a leading Dutch engraver who learned the craft by engraving copies of his father's paintings (he was Joris Hoefnagel, 1545–1600).

Above This fine work on insects, *Insectarum Volitilium*, was published in 1630. Though insect studies had been published at an earlier date with the use of lenses, these illustrations by Hoefnagel represent the best of naked-eye observation.

Below This plate is tastefully decorated with a range of arthropoda, including a female earwig (lower middle) and the handsome stag beetle. Note too the silver-fish, later portrayed by Robert Hooke in his *Micrographia*. The attention to detail was considerable.

possessed hair, lungs, mammary glands, and mammalian bone, he wrote. His work on the reproductive anatomy of the Cephalopods was overlooked until the studies of C. T. E. von Siebold as late as 1852. In view of Aristotelian allusions to drawings, we may mark this canon of work as a landmark in the birth of the discipline, and regret the lack of surviving images all the more on that account. Galen (*see* above p.27 *et seq.*) studied a range of animal species. We learn this directly from his writings, and can detect the influence of animal studies through the descriptions in his work. His accounts of 'human' vertebrae, liver, the *rete mirabile* of the eye, the origin of the carotid arteries and the *os cordis* (non-existent in mankind, though present in cattle and horses) – these and other references betray Galen's reliance on animal dissection.

Representations of animal species portrayed as objects of art remained as a strand of decorative illustration for thousands of years. At Medum in Egypt, for example, survives a mural painted

CHRISTIAN SEPP AND THE SMALL TORTOISESHELL BUTTERFLY

The Dutch Sepp family of Christiaan, Jan, and Jan Christiaan, produced many works on entomology between them. The standard work, *Nederlandsche Insecten*, was compiled by Christiaan and published in 1762. The beautiful illustrations are well observed and particular attention was paid to the larvae.

The eye-catching beauty of the moth *Smerinthus ocellata* is well matched by the unique delicacy with which the larva is portrayed. These striking caterpillars live on sallow or apple, and when mature they drop to the ground and travel across the soil before burrowing down to pupate. The fine texture of the larval body is well shown by Sepp's engraving, and the use of tints to enhance the image gives it a remarkably life-like quality.

ELEAZAR ALBIN RECORDS THE PEACOCK AND TORTOISESHELL

(*Left.*) The principal occupation of Eleazar Albin (1713–1759) was as a water-colour painter and teacher of art. His beautiful butterfly studies were published in the name of his many sponsors. Hand-colouring was used with great effect, and the insects in this work would serve as exemplars in a modern work.

Albin, Eleazar, *Natural history of English insects*, 1720

5,000 years ago, in which a flock of (greylag?) geese are portrayed. Geese also feature in a Chinese scroll from 1,000 years ago, painted before AD 943, found at Dunhuang, Gansu (see p.57). There are clear lines of descent to the modern scientifically accurate portrayls of geese.

Images of fish are found in Ancient Egyptian sites, too; carvings on the walls of the temple at Deir-el-Bahri can be identified to species level, and so have many of the mosaics of sea-creatures that survive in the shadow of Vesuvius. From these descend the decorative portrayals that featured in Victorian works and remain with us to the present.

These continuous lines of endeavour stand in marked contrast to the vivid portrayal of non-existent and fantastic creatures that was a conspicuous strand in the medieval tradition, and the loss of scientific teaching in Europe for over a thousand years deprived us of any direct line of influence from the dawn of scientific zoological illustration.

Perhaps the earliest surviving manuscript in Europe from the investigative discipline is the 1150 *Anatomia Porci*, an account of

HISTORIA NATURALIS RANARUM AND
THE ART OF SCIENCE
Rarely has a book on natural history borne a
more pleasing frontispiece than this delightful
engraving. August Roesel von Rosenhof (1705–
1759) was a German naturalist and illustrator
who published on amphibia and insect life.
There is much careful observation and
considerable accuracy in this attractive plate, and
the hand-coloration is exquisitely controlled and
realistic.

von Rosenhof, August Roesel, *Historia Naturalis Ranarum*, 1758

the public dissection of a pig. As F. J. Cole has rightly surmised, its popularity (it was reprinted in eleven versions between 1502 and 1852) merely confirms the depressed state of zoology at the time.

From the era of Leonardo we may discern parallel strands of activity: a scientific line of investigation which set out to advance zoological understanding and to embody these findings in illustrations and descriptions of an ever-advancing accuracy, and a second school which reiterated received views of earlier eras and perpetuated them in ill-judged and inaccurate misrepresentations. As learning began its slow resurgence in Europe, Pliny's *Historia naturalis* was one of the earliest classical works to be published after the introduction of printing in the West. The first edition (Venice, 1469) was produced in a print-run of just 100 copies, making it a most rare incunabulum.

Some time between the second and fifth centuries, a work entitled *Physiologus* had been produced. It became widely known and the creatures in it were familiar to story-tellers: siren, unicorn, phoenix and others became popular as a result of the influence of this eponymous work of fiction. By the twelfth century *Physiologus* was the most popular picture-book of all, forming the basis of many bestiary manuscripts, and a later edition (renamed in Greek *Peri ton physiologon*) appeared in Rome in 1587.

But a break from the stranglehold of legend and dogma came with a work on falconry that was published about the middle of the thirteenth century. Entitled *De arte venandi cum avibus*, it was an attempt to document the life of birds based on observation, rather than superstition. Its author was Frederick II, Holy Roman Emperor and leader of the Fifth Crusade. Born of Sicilian and German parents he wrote perhaps the first work of scientific zoology. It was eventually typeset and printed in Augsburg in 1596.

A roughly contemporaneous endeavour was the *De animalibus* of Albertus Magnus, which celebrated its indebtedness to the teachings of Aristotle one-and-a-half millennia earlier. Albertus was a Dominican friar and his work on animals was first printed in 26 books by 1478. A pupil of his named Thomas of Cantimpré spent 15 years compiling an encyclopaedia of 19 books (more than a third concerned with animals) under the title *De natura rerum*. A German cleric, Konrad von Megenberg, translated and extended this work into his *Buch der Natur* which was published at Augsburg in 1475. It is the earliest printed book to contain figures of animal life. However its claim to a special position is diluted somewhat by the inclusion of many fantastic and mythological creatures, including mermaids and the centaur.

In England the son of an Oxford porter produced *De Differentiis Animalium*. He was Edward Wootton (1492–1555) who had studied to be a physician and then spent several decades of his spare time compiling an exposition of Aristotelian zoology, in which he starts to move away from the mythological creatures of

earlier works and towards more factual descriptions. His work heralded that of a new generation of students, and a scattering of zoologists across Europe discarded the mantle of Ancient Greece as the revival of learning took hold.

A vivid portrayal of a mammal from those days of change was the drawing of a rhinoceros made by Albrecht Dürer (1471–1528) in 1515 (*see* p.70). It was made from a sketch and a description of the animal exhibited in Lisbon that year – Dürer himself did not see the living rhinoceros. His portrayal is remarkably life-like none the less, and inspired a host of derivative images. Most are easily recognized through an error in the original. Dürer pictured his creature with an additional horn, set on the shoulder and forward-pointing. No such feature exists in reality, of course, and its regular appearance in later engravings is testimony to the influence of this fine portrayal. It has been said that German texts were derived from this image until the twentieth century!

Dürer was a gifted illustrator. He cut his own blocks directly from the wood, and so we can be clear that the images represented nature as the artist wished it to be portrayed. He also wrote on proportion, and his analysis of the techniques of representation

OLE WORM PUBLISHES THE LONG-EARED OWL

(*Left.*) Owls, long associated with mystical properties and evil intent, are common objects of the early works on natural history. This crude woodcut was published by the Danish collector Ole Worm. It shows the long-eared owl *Strix aluco*. But this is a typical 'icon': a picture distorted almost beyond recognition. It should be compared with the magnificent rendition of a diver, published in the same book (*see* p. 66).

ALDROVANDI'S BROODING TAWNY OWL

(*Right*) A fine and realistic woodcut of a tawny owl *Strix* was made for Ulisse's Aldrovandi's great work *Ornithologiae*, which was published in Bologna in 1599. Many of his pictures were fanciful and his text was laced with folklore, rather than natural philosophy. But comparison should be made with the woodcut by Worm. Many images were greatly inferior to the robust portrays of Aldrovandi, and some of them persisted for a long time.

ORNAMENTAL GEESE AND LOTUS PLANTS

There is a fluidity of line in oriental images which is often lacking from the more minutely observed studies of the west. These geese are vital and alive, and the use of line conveys a succulence to the lotus stems they hold. The scroll, written in Khotanese and Sanskrit, was found at Dunhuang, China.

British Library, OIOC CH.COOI Stein

influenced European art for many years after his death.

Konrad Gesner of Zürich (1516–1565) was not only the leading encyclopaedist of nature, but a founding figure of bibliography. He was the son of a Protestant fur dealer who was killed in war in 1531. With help from family and friends, the young Gesner studied in classics at Strasbourg and then spent time at Basle, Paris and Montpellier before graduating in medicine in 1541. He later settled in Zurich, and from this base made several visits to Austria and Italy. He died of the plague. Gesner's first major work was a bibliographical study, *Bibliotheca Universalis*, that was compiled between 1545 and 1549. It covered the work of Greek, Latin and Hebrew writers. His first great work of scientific merit was the *Historia Animalium* (1551–8) in five volumes. Only four were published during his life, the final volume appearing posthumously.

A 'BYRD OF AMERICA' PORTRAYED BY
MARY QUEEN OF SCOTS
A fine tapestry hangs at Oxburgh Hall in
Norfolk. The work was carried out in 1570 and
the central panel bears the Queen's initials, *MR*.
The 'byrd' is said to be very similar to the
yellow-shafted flicker found along the St
Lawrence River. Up till now it has not been
found in any contemporary woodcut. An answer
to this mystery may be offered; Gesner's fine
illustration of a toucan (illustrated below) is the
probable source of inspiration.
Victoria and Albert Museum

GESNER'S TOUCAN – THE QUEEN'S
INSPIRATION?
Konrad Gesner's *Historia Animalium* of 1555
included this sturdy portrayal of a toucan. The
book became popular amongst the wealthy of
Europe, and the Oxburgh tapestries are known
to contain other references to this work.

THE FLAMINGO FROM SIR WALTER RALEIGH'S EXPEDITION

John White, who flourished 1577–1590, was the first English artist to paint the wildlife of the new American colonies. This portrayal of a flamingo is one of the most sensitive portraits of a bird ever made. White was based at Roanoke, Virginia, with Walter Raleigh in 1585–1586. He disappeared on a return journey, and many of his wonderful paintings were lost, too.

British Museum, Department of Prints and Drawings 1906–5–9–1

The work was based on a system close to that of Pliny, with creatures described under separate headings in categories covering habits, capture, and use as food. It was lavishly illustrated, and the drawings represent a unique cross-section of what was known at the time. Gesner (he often spelled his own name 'Gessner') drew on earlier workers for his inspiration. Dürer, Olaus Magnus, Pierre Belon and others provided references for his images and some of the creatures that appear in his book are hard to relate to reality. His horned, toothed sea-creatures, for example, stand in stark contrast with his compellingly realistic depictions of porcupine and shore-crab. The illustrations are in the form of coarse woodcuts and are compelling, vivid, and memorable.

Gesner gained admirers at Court and was granted a monopoly over his writings within the Holy Roman Empire. The period of protection – equivalent to copyright in many ways – was for ten

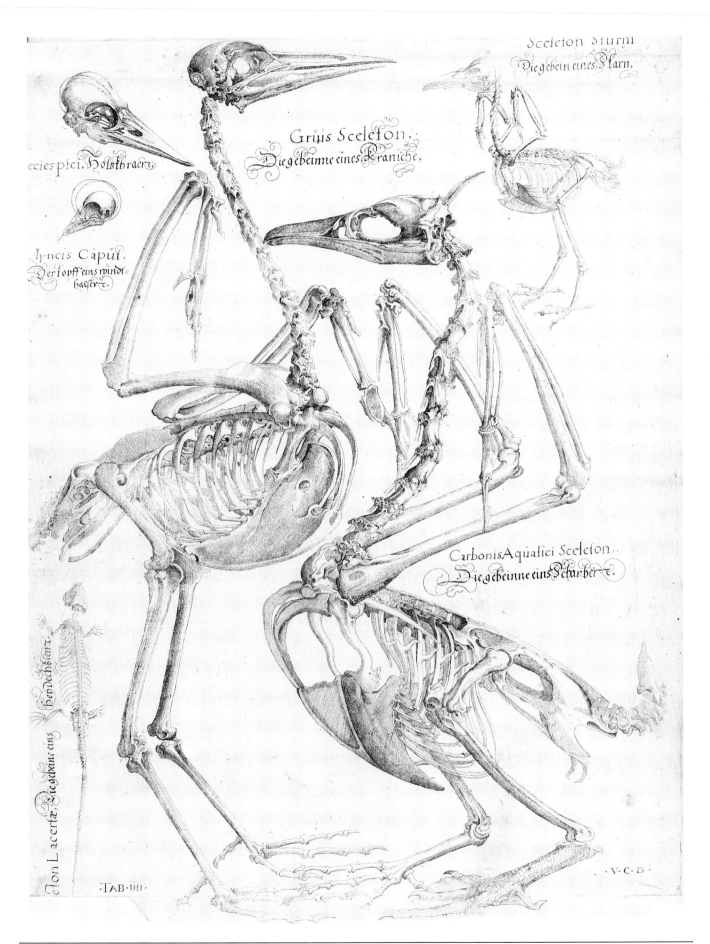

Sceleton Sturni
Die gebein eines Starn,

Gruis Sceleton.
Die gebeinne eines Kraniche,

ecies pici, Holtzhraem

Iyncis Caput,
Der kopff eins windt
halsers.

CarbonisAqualici Sceleton,
Die gebeinne eins Scharbers.

Ton Lacertæ, Die gebeine eins HeyDechhait,

TAB·IIII.

·V·C·D

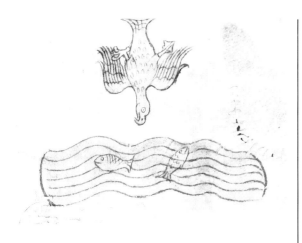

years. Yet his work was widely plagiarized from the time of its first publication. Edward Topsell's *History of Four-footed Beasts and Serpents* reproduced a host of cuts from Gesner, many of them reproduced directly, line for line, in 1558. Gaspar Scott used derivative copper engravings in his *Physica Curiosa* (3rd edition, 1693).

We may cross the Alps from Switzerland to Italy to find Ulisse Aldrovandi (1522–1605), first director of the Botanic Gardens of Bologna. His huge collections of specimens were amassed over 40 years and, in return for a promise that they would pass to the Government of Bologna, he was awarded a 100 per cent increase in pay. He compiled a 14-volume encyclopaedia of natural history, of which the first three on birds and one on insects appeared during his lifetime. The remaining ten volumes were edited and published over the following 50 years. His treatment of animals was similar to that of Gesner, but his figures were of higher quality. Aldrovani, in particular, liked to add anatomical details – the oviduct of a hen, the skeleton of a bird – when he considered this an aid to understanding. He broke open chicken eggs at different stages of incubation, to study what was going on within.

In France, two zoologists were at work in this period. Guillaume Rondelet (1507–1566) wrote a treatise on marine life, published in Lyons in 1554 under the title *De Piscibus Marinis*. It was followed in 1556 by a supplement, the whole being retitled *Universae Aquatilium Historiae*. The illustrations are of high quality, though nothing is known of the artist. Contemporary with Rondelet, though considerably more influential, was the prolific Pierre Belon (1517–1564). He began work as a botanist and is believed to have been responsible for the introduction into Europe of the Cedar of Lebanon, *Cedrus libani*. His first published work of zoology was a two-book treatise entitled *De Aquatilibus* published in 1551 and 1553. It included a range of mammals under the heading of 'fish', including the otter and beaver. He spent time in London with the great Venetian artist Daniel Barbaro (1528–1569) and is thought to have based his illustrations on studies made by his artist friend. 1555 saw the publication of Belon's major opus *L'Histoire de la Nature des Oyseaux*, with fine illustrations by Pierre Goudet. In this book we see the author working on birds from an essentially Aristotelian standpoint. He became a founder of comparative anatomy with his studies of human and avian skeletons. It is clear that he misunderstood the nature of the knee-joint in birds, for he gives his bird skeleton a non-existent pair of bones in the lower limb, analagous to the tibia and fibula in mammals. But the work is a landmark of anatomy, none the less.

A folio volume published by Ippolito Salviani (1514–1572) entitled *Aquatilium Animalium Historiae* (Rome, 1554–1557) also dealt with ichthyology. It is noteworthy that the pioneering works in these fields appeared in such a short space of time: Belon (1553), Rondelet (1553–1554) and Salviani (1554–1557). The plates by

MACROCERCUS ARACANGA.

Red and Yellow Macaaw.

⅓ Nat Size

E.Lear del et lith.

Printed by C.Hullmandel.

EDWARD LEAR: MASTER OF NONSENSE
VERSE, MASTER OF ILLUSTRATION
The name of Edward Lear (1812–1888) is
irrevocably linked to his outpouring of nonsense
verse. Yet this was an occupation forced on him
as his eyesight failed in later years, for Lear was,
first and foremost, an illustrator. His bird studies
were commissioned by many others, including
John Gould (1804–1881) whose *Birds of Europe*
contains nearly 70 of Lear's plates. Grotesque
creatures occur in Lear's later poetry, and in
some of them there is a hint of caricature. But in
his scientific illustrations he was a master of
observation.

Lear, Edward, *Illustrators of the family of Psittacidae*, 1832

Salviani were made at his home, and they are good examples of
early engravings on copper. In the main, they are based on original
investigation and they do not rely on the images established by
earlier workers. Salviani served as physician to three Popes, and
made a name as a poet as well as natural historian.

Mammalian anatomy took its next step with the work of Volcher
Coiter (1534–1576), born in the Frisian town of Gröningen,
Netherlands. He was taught by Rondelet at Montpellier and
studied under Eustachius in Rome and Fallopius in Padua. He
investigated the embryology of the chick in 1564 and published the
results in 1572. At the same time he worked on skeletal structure,
publishing accounts in 1566 and 1572. Coiter dissected a great
range of animal species, many of them under the direction of Ulisse

AUDUBON'S FLAMINGO
The flamingo is portrayed here as a strong and vital bird. It is the work of John James Audubon (1785–1851), who came to America at the age of eighteen. He was uneducated, and started adult life as a trader. Later his interests in birds took over and he set out as an explorer and collector, documenting the bird-life as he went. Audubon failed to find a publisher in America, and eventually came to England where work began on the production of his great work *The Birds of America* (1827–1838). These huge volumes are now the most expensive and sought-after works in natural history.

Aldrovandi at Bologna, and gave the most accurate descriptions of skeletons in birds, mammals and amphibia (a term he interprets loosely, it must be said).

Carlo Ruini of Bologna (*circa* 1530–1598) produced the first definitively illustrated work on the anatomy of any mammal – the horse. We do not know where he was born, and little is recorded of his life. His father was assassinated, and Ruini the son is said to have been poisoned (Belon, it may be noted, was also the victim of assassination in Paris in 1564). Ruini was a Senator at Bologna and his devotion to the study of the horse has some resonances of the clarity and style of Vesalius's work on human anatomy (*see* above, p.59). Vesalius wrote that he employed a draughtsman from the school of 'the divine Titian' to prepare illustrations of the human

The pet auk and its collar

Ole Worm (1588–1654) was an inveterate collector and spent much of his life amassing a great museum. A description was published under the title *Museum Wormianum* in 1655. His illustration of the great auk was widely plagiarized. Worm's auk was a pet, and bore a white collar. It shows clearly in this plate. But the white band was taken to be a characteristic of the bird in its natural state, and appeared in a host of derivative images thereafter.

Oliver Goldsmith

A History of the Earth and Animated Nature became a popular work of reference in Regency England. Its author was Oliver Goldsmith (1728–1774), best known as a poet and novelist, and as author of *The Vicar of Wakefield* (1776). A controversial figure, Goldsmith travelled widely in Europe and had aspirations to become a physician. His book was illustrated with plates with crowded images, a gesture towards economy of production. Many of the features were only millimetres in size, so the overcrowding was not helpful to the reader. However, the concept persisted, and was imitated by others for more than a century.

body ready for the engraver, and Ruini – who prepared his own original drawings – took great pains to avoid inaccuracy, too.

His research was published in five separate books:

BOOK I: Animal parts – the head
BOOK II: Spiritual parts – neck and thorax
BOOK III: Nutritive parts – abdomen and viscera
BOOK IV: Generative organs – genitalia
BOOK V: Distal parts – the limbs

Each was carefully documented with fine drawings and passed through 15 editions between 1598 and 1769. Many later writers plagiarized his work, and many of these portrayals were a travesty of the original. One of the latest was produced by G. Markham (1568–1637) under the modest title of *Markham's Maister-peece* (London, 1610).

THE BLACK-THROATED DIVER
As 'icons' were perpetuated in the works of
science, occasional new ground was broken by
engravers prepared to work from the specimen.
This stunningly realistic engraving of a black-
throated diver appears in Worm's book of 1665
alongside the caricature of a long-eared owl
(see p.56). This is clearly a portrayal of a dead
specimen. But that should not detract from the
innovative move towards representation at a time
when this was a nascent art.

Ruini had a minor counterpart in France. He was Jean Heroard
(1561–1627) who was personal physician to King Charles IX (and
the three following monarchs). His small book *Hippostologie* was
published in Paris in 1599, and is noted for its clear and concise
illustrations.

A considerable anatomist was Hieronymous Fabricius ab Aqua-
pendente (1533–1619) who succeeded Fallopius as Professor at
Padua in 1565. In 1594 he constructed a demonstration theatre at
Padua to facilitate instructional dissection of the human cadaver. It
was ingeniously designed with six galleries for spectators around
an oval dissecting theatre, in which spectators stood. This allowed
the furthest observer to be no more than 20 feet (seven metres)
from the subject. It has been preserved in original condition to the
present day (and indeed was in regular use until 1872).

Fabricius generated a stream of innovative work and his

Jewish artists reveal the leviathan

A great manuscript work entitled *Chummash et Mazchor Hebraice* was produced by Jewish scholars between 1278–1286 in northern France. Each of the 41 plates illustrating the manuscript was produced by a team of artists, and a range of (mostly mythical) creatures is depicted. The leviathan itself symbolizes the monstrous water monster over which God alone can triumph. There is no attempt here to observe and record: this is a religious or folkloric treatise and not a careful 'scientific' study.

British Library, OIOC Add 11639 f518v

Marcus Bloch and the supreme vision of *Dactylopterus*

Turning the pages of the *Icthylologie* is a remarkable experience. Marcus Bloch (1723–1799) wrote many books on fish, none finer than this set of vast volumes. Each engraving is beautifully hand-tinted, the images frequently highlighted with silver paint. *Dactylopterus volitans* (*Trigla volitans* at the time this work appeared, 1785–1797) has never been more vividly portrayed. (*See* also p.68).

Cambridge University Library MH 4.3

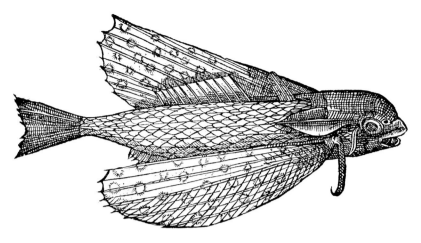

THE FLYING GURNARD
(*Left.*) Guillaume Rondelet (1506–1566) published many books on natural history. Their illustrations are of high quality and this study of *Dactylopterus volitans* from *L'Histoire Entière des Poissons* is clearly recognizable of the species. This standard of illustration was unsurpassed for more than a century.

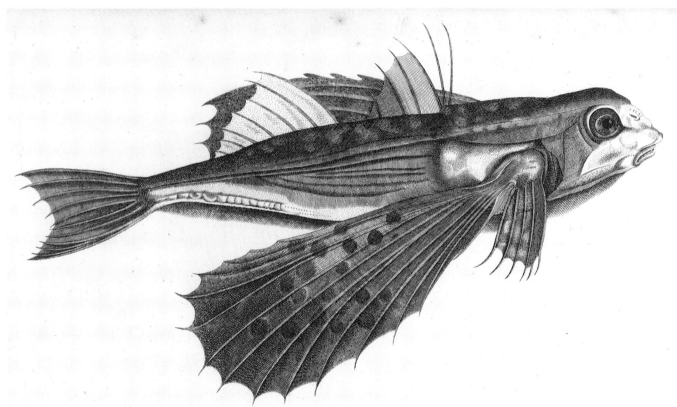

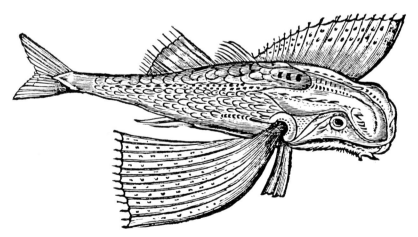

(*Above.*) Francis Willughby (1635–1672) cooperated with the great English naturalist John Ray in the production of much memorable work in natural history. The fourth book of the great *Historia Piscium* (1686) contained this skilful engraving, clearly drawn from nature.

(*Left.*) This flying gurnard is from the *Museum Wormianum* by Ole Worm (1655). Interestingly, the 'wings' are for display purposes only, for this species is incapable of the fluttering, gliding flight exhibited by the flying-fish. Though the drawing lacks the finesse of later images, it is clearly drawn from a specimen.

IMAGES OF SCIENCE

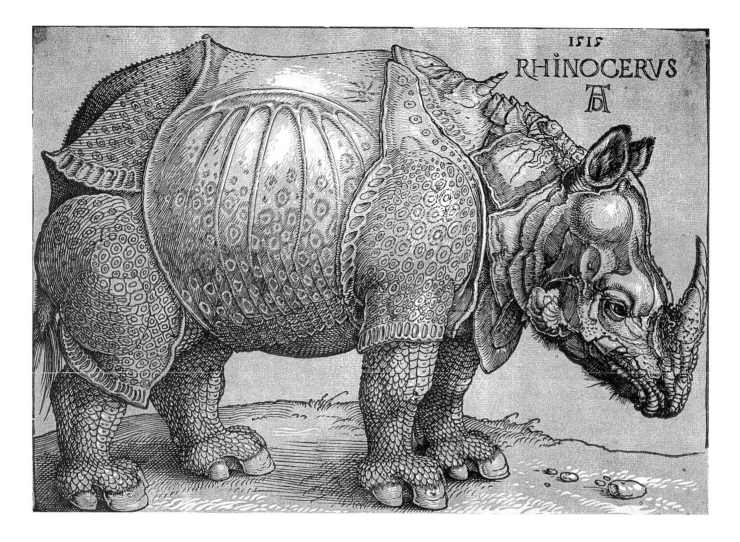

1515
RHINOCERVS
AD

THE RHINOCEROS
A woodcut by William Jannsen, after 1620,
based on Dürer's drawing of a century earlier
(reproduced overleaf).

British Museum, Department of Prints and Drawings

illustrations are painstaking and generally of high accuracy. His descriptions include the development of the mammalian foetus, the valvular structures that facilitate venous return, the compound stomach structures of ruminants, the eye (including its musculature) and ear, muscles and nerves; and he greatly advanced the study of comparative anatomy in a range of vertebrates.

His work on circulation inspired his most famous pupil, William Harvey (1578–1657) who was born in Folkestone, Kent and died in London – but who had much of his training under Fabricius at Padua. Harvey's only illustrations were copies of those by Fabricius. Harvey's investigations covered crustaceans, sponges, insects and molluscs; he dissected a range of fish, birds, reptiles and mammals, and is best known for his work on the circulation of the blood, published in 1628 as *De motu cordis et sanguinis in animalibus* (Frankfurt), followed by *De circulatione sanguinis* (Cambridge, 1649). But his *De generatione Animalium* (London, 1651) – translated into English by Martin Llewelyn in 1653 – was highly innovative. True, it lacks the sense of certainty of its predecessor. But the work on circulation confirmed observations from a widely

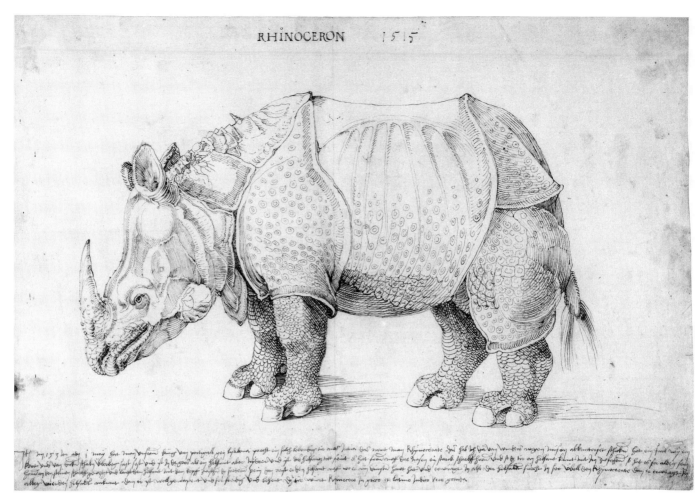

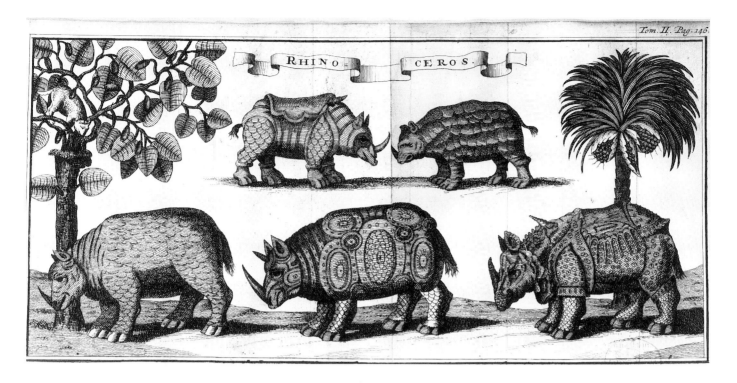

RHINOCEROS.

THE RHINOCEROS

Illustrated above is a plate from François Leguat's *Voyage et aventures* of 1708. He had travelled to the Cape of Good Hope in 1698, but evidently did not ever see a live animal.

The rhinoceros was an unfamiliar creature to the European eye until Albrecht Dürer made his magnificent drawing (*left, above*). Unlike most writers on natural history, Dürer not only made his own drawings but he made the woodcuts as well. We may be assured that the result is what Dürer himself intended. He never saw a rhinoceros, however: this fine study was based on a sketch of an animal that had been sent to Rome as a present for Pope Leo X, but which drowned when the homeward ship capsized.

British Museum, Department of Prints and Drawings

Dürer's image of the rhinoceros persisted over many generations. (*Left, below*) is a 1657 version by J. Johnston of a plate published in Gesner's *Historiae animalium*. The copying of the Gesner plate results from a mirror-image reproduction. (As the copy is laid face downwards during printing, this must be the case). The origin is plain, though Johnston's rhinoceros shows a subtle increase in size for the (non-existent) second horn shown on the shoulder.

investigated field, whereas his work on animal reproduction was breaking new ground.

Among the encyclopaedists who followed were Gerard Blasius (1625–1692), who lived and worked in the Netherlands, and the Italian Marco Aurelio Severino (1580–1656), both of whom published in anatomy and bibliography. Ole Worm (1588–1654) published an extensively illustrated account of his collections under the title *Musei Wormiani Historia* (1655). Clear descriptions of creatures large and small decorate the pages. The book provides an intriguing example of the dichotomy that exists between representational portrayal and the symbolic images that evolve for the purpose of decorating works of science. Some of the illustrations are caricatures, recognizable only because of their familiarity through previous misrepresentations; others are of fine quality and would fit well enough in a modern text. These clear and accurate portrayals heralded the expansion of scientific illustration which accompanied the new era of investigation and exploration. Thus, when Captain James Cook set off on his voyages of discovery in the *Endeavour* in 1768 he took scientific illustrators with him as a part of the team, confident in their ability to make faithful recordings of what was discovered as part of the process of science.

William Bartram (1739–1823) published *Travels Through North and South Carolina, Georgia, East and West Florida . . . etc*, at Philadelphia in 1791. He was the son of John Bartram – King George III's botanist in America – and the first American illustrator of natural history. His emphasis lay on the subtle interactions of the living community – plant and animal. For this reason he has been dubbed 'America's first ecologist'. His predecessor had been Mark

GESNER'S ORIGINAL PUBLICATION OF THE HYENA

This individualistic treatment of the hyena appears on page 76 of Gesner's 1560 volume in the *Icones Animalium Quadrepedum Viviparorum et Oviparorum*. It became, in the jargon of the illustrator, a 'reference' on which many later images were based. Gesner has been plagiarized more than perhaps any other author in zoology, with the possible exception of Dürer.

The Second kinde of *HYÆNA*, called *Papio* or *Dabuh*.

The Region and quantity. | This Beast aboundeth near *Cæsarea* in quantity refembling a Fox, but in wit and difpofition a Wolf; the fafhion is, being gathered together, for one of them to go before the flock finging, or howling, and all the reft, anfwering him with correfpondent tune: In hair it refembleth a Fox and

TOPSELL'S HYENA — RE-ENGRAVED FROM GESNER'S MASTER WORK

Edward Topsell produced two works, one on *Foure-footed Beastes* (1607) and the other his *Historie of Serpents* (1608). With the addition of some further material from France, he reprinted the entire collection as the *History of Four-footed Beasts and Serpents*. The result was a muddled and inaccurate book, based mostly (as the title page indicates) on the works of Thomas Mouffet, which none the less became a great commercial success. The bulk of its teachings are, however, fictitious.

Papio Pavion ı

THE REV. MR JOHNSTON'S HYENA
This time the hyena is seen in a different setting. In the distance lions, bears and leopards frolic as an elephant looks benevolently on. But for all the altered surroundings, the derivation, direct from the Gesner image, is entirely unmistakable.

Catesby (*circa* 1679–1749) who had published his *Natural History of Carolina, Florida and the Bahama Islands* in London in two volumes dated 1731/1743. Catesby was self-taught, and though born in England he worked for most of his life in the United States. His drawings were stylized rather than representational, but proved to generate great interest in the new species of the New World. A similarly rationalized style of interpretation had been used in the previous century, when Nehemiah Grew drew stylish diagrams of intestinal configurations in the starkly titled *Anatomy of Stomachs and Guts* published by subscription (organized by Grew himself) for the Royal Society in 1681.

But the summit of representational perfection may be exemplified by the body of work by John James Audubon (1785–1851) who began to publish his great books on the birds of North America in 1827. A romantic figure, Audubon was the illegitimate son of a French Navy officer and a local girl, was raised in France, and then emigrated to take charge of his father's Pennsylvania plantation in order to escape the draft into the Napoleonic army. He had started to draw birds at the age of fifteen, and after proving himself unsuccessful in the conduct of business affairs, he took up the task full-time when 35 years old. His wife supported him through her work as a governess, and – after failing to find an American publisher for his work – he settled for Robert Havell of London to publish the collection of studies.

The book is in elephant folio, a metre along the spine, and contains 435 hand-coloured aquatint plates. Only about 190 copies of *The Birds of America* in this grandiose format appear to have been produced, making this one of the supremely prized books in the history of scientific illustration.

IMAGES OF SCIENCE

A REALISTIC PORCUPINE WITH A HEDGEHOG ICON

(*Right.*) This intriguing plate is from Alexander Pitfield's *Natural History of Animals* (1702). The porcupine is an energetic creature as here portrayed, a worthy successor to Gesner's pioneering effort. But the hedgehog alongside seems redolent of a woodcut: it is stylized and un-lifelike. The upper portion of the plate shows the internal organs displayed in dissection.

VITALITY AND EARLY REALISM: THE PORCUPINE FROM *ICONES ANIMALIUM*

(*Left, above.*) Gesner taught many students of natural history, including Aldrovandi, and his woodcuts frequently embodied a sense of vitality and realism which marked them out as innovative. This memorable image of a porcupine appeared in later works and was not greatly improved upon until Alexander Pitfield published his *Natural History of Animals* in 1702.

THE PORCUPINE IN EDWARD TOPSELL'S BOOK

(*Left, below.*) Topsell's illustrations were direct copies of the originals published by earlier authors in other languages. His version of the porcupine has been derived directly from the portrayal by Gesner.

Topsell, Edward, *History of Four-footed Beasts*, 1658

The move from wood-cut to copper engraving heralded the later stages of evolution in the published images of animal life. Photography emerged as a force for illustration during the closing years of the Victorian era. It was followed by film in the inter-war years, and latterly by television. Each has made a contribution to zoological illustration, for each offers a permanent image of fleeting phenomena.

The basic purpose must always be didactic and instructional, an aid to recording and recognition. Illustration, in all its forms, is a statement of the state of human awareness. To the specialist it amounts to scientific publication, whilst to the public it is more often a question of incredulity and excitement – the sight of unimaginable creatures or events that seem strange in a world of convention. In those haunting cave paintings we may discern such threads, and the growth of representationalism brought images of life to a broader public.

Just as the hunter-explorers of the Victorian era returned with trophies to hang on the wall, so the television documentary maker

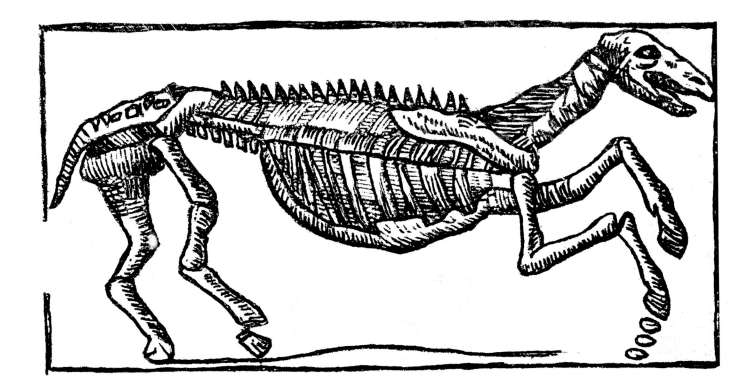

has immortalized many facets of animal behaviour. In each case the purpose is the same – to present nature to an audience uneducated in its ways. Previous generations must have wondered at the stupendous picture of a flea in Robert Hooke's *Micrographia* (1665), and at Dürer's stunning rhinoceros. The public of today hold comparably vivid images in the mind. The Orca which plucked a seal from the apparent safety of the shore; the group of pygmy hippopotamus running underwater across the lake-floor in Africa; diving seabirds snatching fish from the surface of the sea; these are the modern moving images that live on in the minds of everyone who witnessed, not the event, but the documentary programme.

There is an additional purpose of zoological illustration in this literal, broad sense. We are not merely recording life as it is, but as it has been. In zoology, the importance of scientific illustration lies in its ability to record events and animal behaviour of a kind which is, simply, disappearing in our lifetime. Oliver Goldsmith's *History of the Earth and Animated Nature* appeared in many editions, crammed with busy plates that illustrated the inestimable diversity of nature. It has decorated countless homes since the later years of the eighteenth century.

The first example of scientific illustration as a record of a species that had disappeared is the case of the Mauritian Dodo, *Raphus cucullatus*. The prolific French encyclopaedist George Louis Leclerc Buffon (1707–1788) described the creature in his 44-volume encyclopaedia entitled *Histoire Naturelle, générale et particulière*, published between 1749 and 1804. This vast enterprise was a landmark in scientific documentation. Of the Dodo, he wrote:

CRUDE ANATOMY
This caricature of the horse skeleton was published by Ferrari *circa* 1560. It shows a partly decayed body. The intercostal musculature is crudely shown and there is no attempt to probe the bone structure of the limbs.

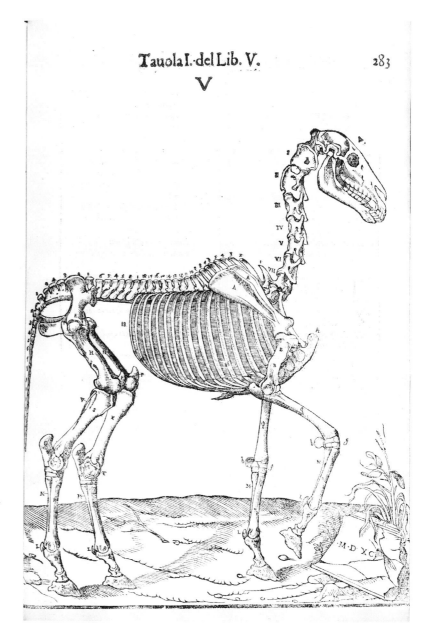

THE HORSE SKELETON EMERGES

Carlo Ruini (*circa* 1530–1598) was a Senator of
Bologna and an anatomist. His work on the
horse is the first on the anatomy of a mammal.
The illustrations took many years to complete,
and his great book *On the Anatomy and Infirmities
of the Horse* was published a month after he
died. He was widely plagiarized: Snape's
anatomy of the horse of 1683 is firmly founded
on Ruini, though Snape claims he was working
in an area where none had gone before. In turn,
Snape was plagiarized, too.

Ruini, Carlo, *Dell' Anatomia e dell' Infermità del Cavallo*, 1598

Lightness and liveliness are activities the Dodo could not claim. It
could in fact be taken for a tortoise covered with feathers . . its stupid-
ity is even more sickening by [nature] obliging us to admit that it truly
is a bird.

For all its familiarity, the Dodo is not typical of the many species
we have exterminated. It was clumsy and defenceless, depending
for its survival on its remoteness from predators (and not just
mankind). Many other species have existed in abundance, yet are
now lost from the earth for ever. The passenger pigeon *Ectopistes
migratorius*, for example, had been hunted by native North American Indians for thousands of years as an item of diet. They nested
in gigantic communities. One flock was estimated to contain
2,230,272,000 individuals. John James Audubon's calculation was

LE CORPS DES OS DV CHEVAL

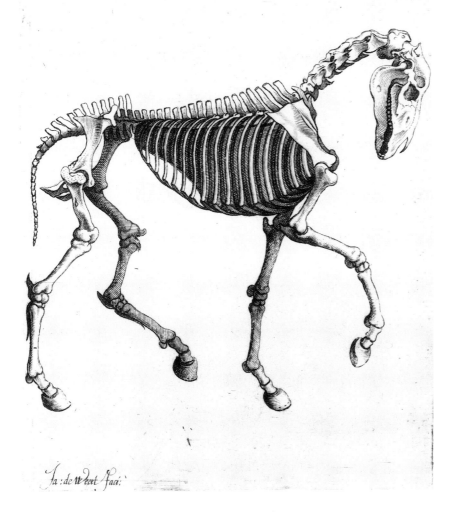

Ja : de Weert faci:

HEROARD'S INTERPRETATION
Jean Heroard (1561–1627) worked at the
same time as Ruini. His book appeared in
Paris in January 1599, a short while after
Ruini's treatise, and it is comparable in
accuracy and scientific merit. It now
appears that Heroard's work was done
earlier than Ruini's, though the two had no
contact and are unlikely to have known of
each other. Heroard, a physician, is said to
have planned a larger work, much of which
was said to have been lost in a shipwreck.

Heroard, Jean, *Hippostologie*, 1599

that a flock typically consumed a million tons of food per day. His
description of a passing flock as like a hard gale at sea, the branches
of trees breaking under their weight, the roar of guns as they
decimated the flock, is a vivid account which (like those television
images) lives on in the mind.

That was early in the nineteenth century. During the last year of
that same century came the sighting of the only wild specimen
remaining. The final bird in captivity died in the Cincinnati Zoo
on 1 September 1914. In the same year the last surviving Carolina
parrot, *Conuropsis carolinensis*, died in a nearby cage in the same
zoo. It is to the scientific illustrators of the past that we owe much
of our knowledge of the many species that have disappeared in the
last few centuries. *Bison priscus*, for instance, is known from cave
paintings left by the tribes who hunted it to extinction. Fashions

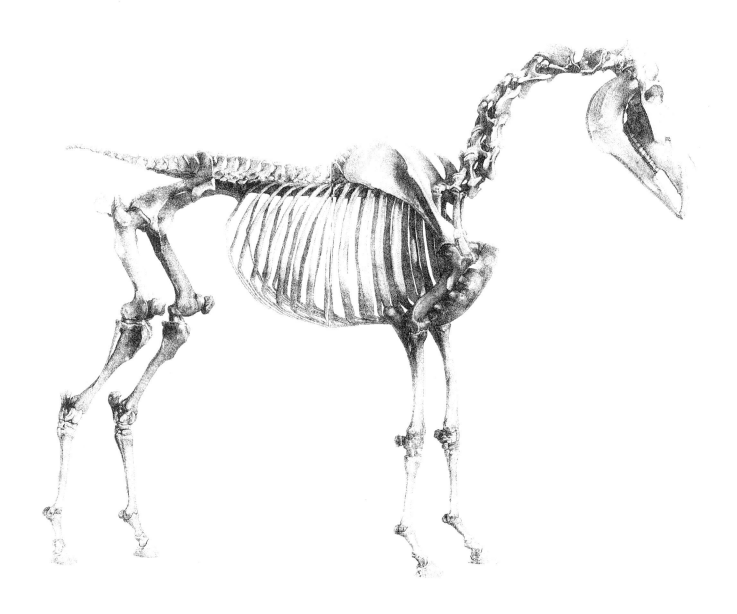

THE ART OF THE ANATOMIST

George Stubbs (1724–1806) was raised in close proximity to animal bodies, for his father was a leather dresser. The young Stubbs trained as an engraver and visited Italy in 1754. For the next 20 years he lived with a partner, Mary Spencer, in a lonely farmhouse in Lincolnshire and painstakingly dissected his way through countless horse cadavers. By 1776 he had finished *The Anatomy of the Horse*. It remains a classic interpretation of anatomy.

change. Species once derided, or hunted for pleasure, are now seen as objects worthy of preservation at all costs. The pressure of human society on natural cycles is inevitably leading to the loss of species. At the laboratory level we can now seek to preserve the genetic component of animals faced with extinction, in the hope that the future may provide an opportunity to restore them. And in the realm of scientific illustration we now have the capacity to preserve images of animal life. Optical storage is a fast-developing possibility, and high-definition television is another. It amounts to a considerable departure from the painstaking process of cutting and engraving of earlier centuries. But the pressure on nature lends an added urgency to the concept of archiving, for illustration – through every means available – may be the only way we have to document life before it is lost.

REFERENCES

[p.61] The possibility arises that mammals were included in a list of fish as a convention making it easier for Catholics to find a source of meat to eat on Fridays, when fish was ordained for the main meal. Consult: Bruno, L. C., *The Tradition of Science*, Washington, D.C., 1987.

[p.70] The story of the Dürer rhinoceros and its many plagiarists has been told in T. H. Clarke, *The Rhinoceros, 1515–1799*, Sotheby's Publications, London, 1986.

[p.79] A recent summary of extinct species is contained in the following volumes:

Balouet, J-C., and Alibter, A. *Extinct Species of the World*, Paris 1989, London 1990. It is said (Jean-Christophe Balouet, in a personal communication to the Author) that the many literal errors in the English language version are absent from the French edition.

Balouet, J-C., *Ces Espèces qui Disparaissent*, Paris, 1990.

Herbs, herbals and the birth of botany

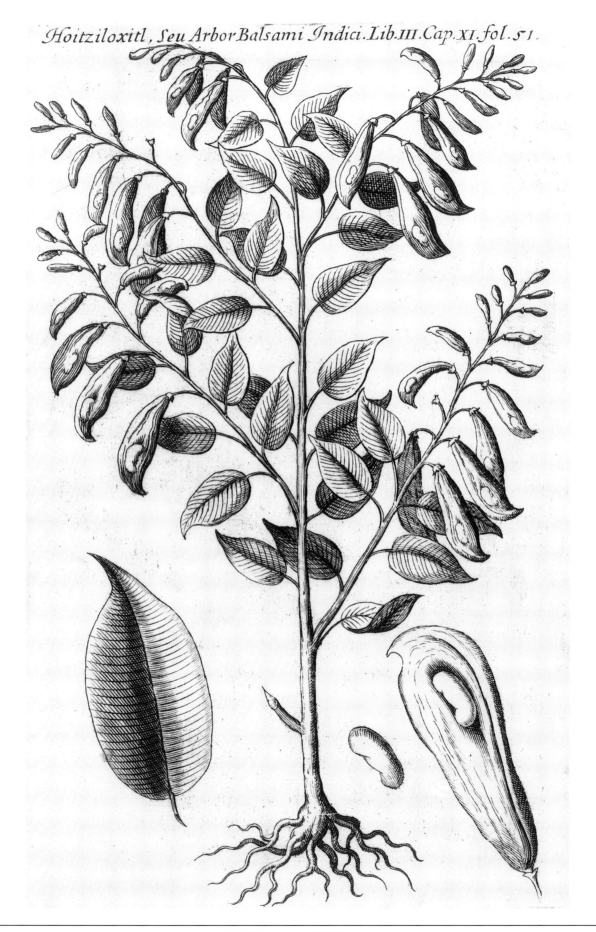

Familiar plants — rice, lotus, grape — appear in some of the earliest surviving paintings and wall reliefs from the ancient civilisations, those from the Far East and India tending to be more stylized than the images from ancient Egypt. Botanical painting has a lengthy history. But — just as it has an ancient origin — the discipline came to maturity earlier than other areas of scientific illustration. The theme that underpins our examination of the evolution of images is the dawn of accurate and representational scientific illustration — figures which would, for all their sophistication, fit well enough into a modern text without comment.

The art of plant illustration matured around 1400. The image of ripening grapes and ears of wheat in the Carrara Herbal was painted *circa* 1395, whilst the vivid composition of roses, vines, celandine, dandelion and daisy found in *The Adoration of the Lamb*, painted a little later by Hubert and Jan van Eyck, on display in the Cathedral of St Bavon, Ghent, shows these and other species in their most realistic portrayal. A crisp and accurate study of *Mandra-*

DIOSCORIDES AND THE MANDRAKE
The writings of Dioscorides featured the mandrake, which, because of the human form of its roots, attracted interest as a mystical object. Here the root is illustrated in a medieval Italian textbook, with emphasis on the real appearance of the plant. Dioscorides remained a revered authority, and an allusion to his teachings was a claim for scientific objectivity.

Dioscorides, P., *De Materia Medica*

WOODCUTS OF MEXICAN PLANTS FROM 1649
Philip II of Spain sent his physician, Francisco Hernández, to Mexico in the 1570s. His purpose was to collect and explore, and his work was later published as *Plantarum, Animalium et Mineralium Mexicanorum* in Rome, 1649. His woodcuts are among the earliest surviving views of plants as recorded by the first explorers of the newly-discovered American lands.

gora autumnalis painted around 1480 by Jacopo (or Giacomo) Ligozzi is preserved at the Uffizi Gallery, Florence, and exceeds in draughtsmanship many of the examples of botanical artwork published today.

As we have seen in the examination of zoological illustration (*see* Chapter 3), a crude and unrefined form of picture persisted long after these higher planes had been reached. The woodcuts of Fransisco Hernández in his *Plantarum, Animalium et Mineralium Mexicanorum Historia*, published in Rome as late as 1649, are little better than those of the herbals of two centuries earlier.

42

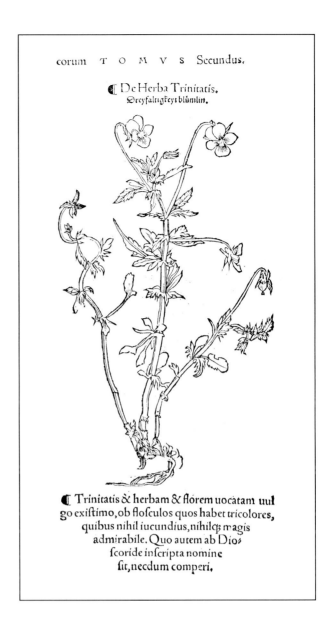

corum T O M V S Secundus.

❡ De Herba Trinitatis.
Dreyfaltigkeyt blůmlin.

❡ Trinitatis & herbam & flórem uocàtam uul
go exiſtimo, ob floſculos quos habet tricolores,
quibus nihil iucundius, nihilᴄᴣ magis
admirabile. Quo autem ab Dio-
ſcoride inſcripta nomine
ſit, necdum comperi.

THE *NOVI HERBARII* OF 1531
The publication in 1531 of Otto Brunfels's *Novi Herbarii* marked a move towards a representational strand of botanical illustration. Brunfels took pains to obtain woodcuts that were balanced in line and form, and which truly embodied some of the essence of the species concerned. The descriptive text set beneath each picture was centrally aligned, to produce a book of considerable artistic merit. This illustration is of the wild pansy.

ILLUSTRATION OF THE YARROW FROM *circa* 1050
(*Left.*) A great herbal was compiled about 400 AD from the works of Pliny and Dioscorides, and this copy was made in the middle of the eleventh century by an Anglo-Saxon artist. The original manuscript, compiled by Apuleius Barbarus (also known as Pseudo-Apuleius, to distinguish him from Lucius Apuleius) was rich with Mediterranean species, many of which also occur in the English copy. This plate features the yarrow *Achillea millefolium*, described as useful for treating bites, aches of the head and bowels, and toothache.

British Library, Cotton Vitellius C III f46

Aristotle and his pupil Theophrastus both described the plant world, though the only images that remain from the Greek civilizations of that era are on coins that date back to around 300 BC. The silphion *Ferula* species, the pomegranate *Punica granata* and the wild *Rosa* are examples. However, these are stylized images. Greek sculpture provides an indication of the artist's ability to represent objects accurately, and an apocryphal tale relates how representationialism was also recognized as a mark of attainment in the paintings of that era. The tale is told that in the fifth century BC a competition was held between Zeuxis of Heracleia and Parrhasius of Ephesus, to determine who could represent nature most accurately. When the time came to unveil the two pictures, Zeuxis revealed an illustration of *Vitis vinifera* so vivid that birds flew down to pluck the grapes. Believing that nothing could challenge this demonstration, he turned to Parrhasius and asked that he draw aside the curtains to reveal his own painting. But Parrhasius had no curtains; they were painted images. Zeuxis conceded that he had lost: 'I deceived the birds,' he said, 'but Parrhasius, you deceived the artist'. This leads us to feel that the ancient Greek students of plant life met high standards, though Pliny the Elder, four centuries earlier, recorded that the copying of images by artists employed by the producers of books left much to be desired. That the classical illustrations were influential cannot, however, be doubted. Studies by Crateuas in the first century B C became attached to the manuscript copies of the writings of Dioscorides,

THE VIOLET, FROM THE WORKS OF
SERAPION THE ARAB
(*Left*.) Serapion the Younger (who flourished about AD 800) wrote a detailed account of plants which was transcribed and illustated for Jacopo Filippo, a monk of Padua, in the 1390s. This picture of the violet *Viola odorata* is an extraordinary example of representational illustration.

British Library, Egerton 2020 f94

who flourished a century later, when he compiled his *De materia medica*. Though many of the descriptions came down to medieval scholars in a form that can no longer be recognized, some of the images from Crateuas were used to illustrate herbals. One example is Thomas Johnson's edition of Gerard's *Herball*, published in 1633, with a gap of almost 17 centuries between the first drawing and the date of publication.

We have encountered the Constantinople copy of the writings of Dioscorides (above, p.37), now at Vienna. The 127 parchment pages of this Codex Vindobonensis contain drawings of over 500 plants, drawn for their medicinal significance, and believed copied from the works of Crateuas. This is the oldest botanical manuscript known, though another copy from the eighth century is to be found at Naples, and there is a further example in the Pierpont Morgan Library, New York. Later versions of similar manuscripts exist both in French and Arabic. The figures which illustrate the

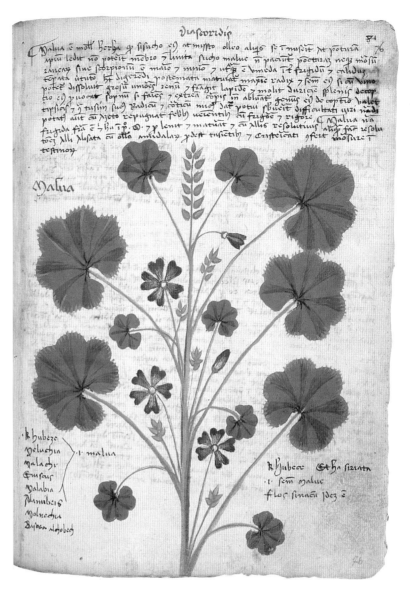

BRYONY AND MALLOW

These illustrations are from the Codex Bellunensis, a remarkable herbal made in Belluno around 1410–1430, with a text drawn from Dioscorides. It was produced in the Alps (Belluno is some 50 miles [80 km] north of Venice) and is the first work to include the eidelweiss *Leontopodium alpinum*. Depicted (*above*) is the bryony, and (*right*) the mallow.

British Library Additional 41623 f53v–4, 76

Codex Neopolitanus are clear and were not bettered for almost a thousand years.

Contemporaneous with these early endeavours was the work of the Arab physician Serapion the Younger (Ibn Sarabi) who produced a treatise on medicinal plants around A D 800. This too inspired many Western authorities. It is believed that the work was translated by Jacopo Filippo, a young Augustinian monk, who also transcribed the Carrara Herbal. It is not known who illustrated this work, although, as has been pointed out, the drawing has a naturalistic power that clearly derives from living specimens.

The realism of this Herbal and the Codex Vindobonensis stand as clear pointers to the dawning of scientific accuracy in botanical illustration, and can be compared with later images which accord more with the non-realism of the crude copyist who works from preconceived notions perpetrated by working, not from life, but from earlier (and degenerate) published works. A manuscript,

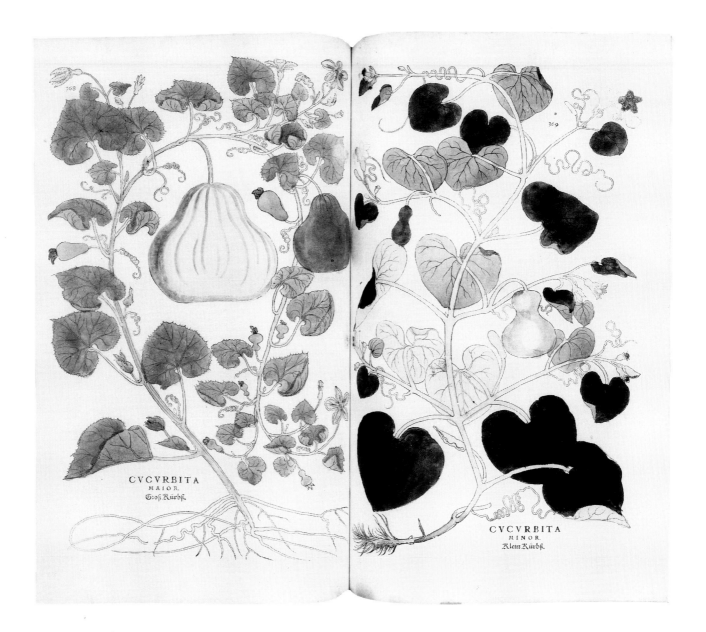

CVCVRBITA
MAIOR.
Groß Kürbß.

CVCVRBITA
MINOR.
Klein Kürbß.

dated *circa* 1450, now in the manuscript collections of the British Library typifies this second strand: the pictures (see page 89) are decorative cartoons, more suited, as one scholar has wryly asserted, for wallpaper manufacture.

It was about this time that printing with moveable type emerged in Western Europe, and the first book to contain woodcuts of plants appeared in 1475. Within a few years the illustrated herbal had become established. Though a herbal was printed in Naples as early as 1477 it did not acquire illustrations until a second edition of 1482. Meanwhile, the ninth-century manuscript copy of the *Herbarium* by Apuleius Platonicus (also known as Apuleius Barbaricus, depending on whose side you stood) – believed to date back to the fifth century – was printed in Rome during 1481. It was illustrated with woodcuts, crudely copied from decorations in the original manuscript in the monastery of Monte Cassino.

LEONHART FUCHS AND *DE HISTORIA STIRPUM*

Fuchs went a stage further than Brunfels when his *De Historia Stirpum* was published in 1542, 11 years later. His book was intended to be coloured, and the woodcuts were designed with this in mind. There is a sense of realism and vitality in the species he portrayed, though the coloration is none too careful. But this was the first such publication in botany.

Right The cannabis plant, *Cannabis sativa*.

Above These fine, almost juicy gourds appeared in the *Historia Stirpum* and are typical of the robust style of illustration employed by Fuchs. The large, folio pages make the book a magnificent object to handle, and the plates are reliably accurate for the period.

CANNABIS
SATIVA.

zamer Hanff.

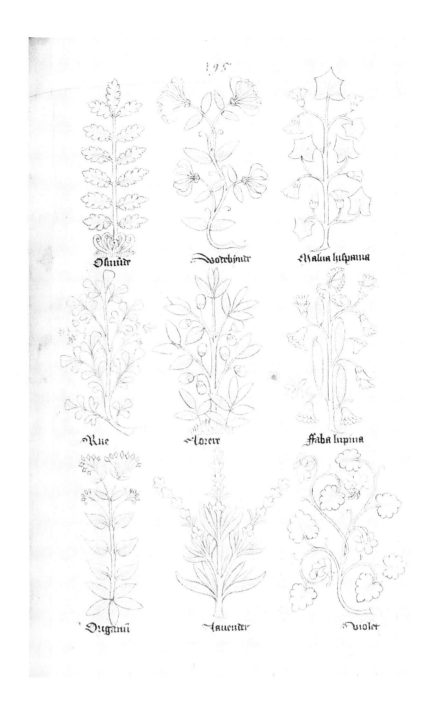

As zoology received its greatest stimulus from the work of
Gesner (*see* p.57), botany took its greatest step with the publication of the *Herbarum vivae eicones* (Strasbourg, 1530–1536). Its
author, Otto von Brunfels (1464–1534), derived most of his text
from traditional sources and much of it is inaccurate. The merit of
the book lay not in its text, however, but in the illustrations. They
were prepared from life by Hans Weiditz, who had been trained by
Albrecht Dürer. Many of the illustrations of biological books in the
early scientific period were taken directly from Dürer's work, and
he should be recognized as the first illustrator to devote time to
publishing the principles of scientific illustration. Weiditz set out to
record a single specimen, blemishes and all, and has been criticized

**JACOB VAN HUYSUM ENGRAVES FOR THE
CATALOGUS PLANTARUM
(*Right*.)** A pioneering book for horticulturalists
was the *Catalogus Plantarum* of 1730. It was
compiled by Philip Miller and Robert Furber.
The illustrations were engraved by Jacob van
Huysum (*c*.1687–1740), who was employed by
Horace Walpole but lost his post for his
intemperate and dissolute behaviour.

**A NEW REALISM
(*Left*.)** Whilst many herbals featured 'icons' so
often used in reference works – diagrams
composed for the textbooks, and unlike features
of nature – the unfettered illustrators of non-
botanical works portrayed plants with realism. A
common feature of wealthy homes was a Book of
Hours, a compilation of tracts and passages of
religious significance for personal taste. The
decoration was often surprisingly accurate. This
example, from the Hastings Hours, dating from
the late 1470s, features the speedwell *Veronica*
and the periwinkle *Vinca* with two butterflies.
The butterfly on the lower border, with closed
wings, is the small tortoiseshell, *Aglais utricae*.
British Library, Additional 54787 f49

for failing to distil the essence of a type species by studying many
specimens and drawing a synthesis. This was, however, the main
shortcoming of many earlier illustrators, and it is clear that the fresh
approach Weiditz brought to his work set in train the need for
original work in botanical drawing.

Leonard Fuchs (1501–1566) was responsible for bringing the
botanical textbook – as we would now recognize it – into existence. Born in Bavaria, he opened a private school in Wemding and
later took a degree in medicine. He was appointed Professor of
Medicine at the University of Tübingen where he worked for the
rest of his life. His herbal was not the only book to rival Brunfels;
Hieronymus Bock also produced a volume of his own. But
of the three, Fuchs was the only author to take trouble working
with the best artists and engravers he could find. He took on
Albrecht Meyer to draw the specimens under Fuchs's direct control, insisting that special attention be paid to accurate outlines and
botanical detail, whilst shadows and shading were extirpated.
Heinrich Fullmaurer copied the originals onto the wooden blocks
which Veit Speckle – whom Fuchs described as the best engraver
in Strasbourg – then engraved. The results were first published as

3 *Malum regale.*
The King of Apples.

4 *Malum reginale.*
The Quining, or Queene of Apples.

5 *Platomela ſiue Pyra æſtiua.*
The ſommer Pearemaine.

6 *Platarchapia ſiue Pyra hyemalia.*
The winter Pearemaine.

Of the Goose tree, Barnakle tree, or the tree bearing Geese. Chap.167.

Britannica Conchæ anatiferæ.
The breede of Barnakles.

❋ *The description.*

HAuing trauelled from the Graffes growing in the bottome of the fenny waters,
the woods, and mountaines, euen vnto
Libanus it felfe; and alfo the fea, and bowels of
the fame: we are arriued to the end of our Hiftorie, thinking it not impertinent to the conclufi-
on of the fame, to end with one of the maruels
of this land (we may fay of the world.) The Hiftorie whereof to fet foorth according to the
woorthines and raritie thereof, woulde not
onely require a large and peculiar volume, but
alfo a deeper fearch into the bowels of nature,
then my intended purpofe wil fuffer me to wade
into, my infufficiencie alfo confidered; leauing
the hiftorie thereof rough hewen, vnto fome
excellent men, learned in the fecrets of nature,
to be both fined and refined: in the meane fpace
take it as it falleth out, the naked and bare truth,
though vnpolifhed. There are founde in the
north parts of Scotland, & the Ilands adiacent,
called Orchades, certaine trees, whereon doe
growe certaine fhell fifhes, of a white colour
tending to ruffet; wherein are conteined little
liuing creatures: which fhels in time of maturi-
tie doe open, and out of them grow thofe little
liuing things; which falling into the water, doe
become foules, whom we call Barnakles, in the
north of England Brant Geefe, and in Lanca-

THE TREE BEARING GEESE
(*Above.*) A persistent legend was that the goose barnacle gave rise to adult geese, and was itself derived from a land plant. Gerard's *Historie of Plants* (1597) perpetuated the legend, with a full description of the 'plant' and its 'life story'. Gerard added that he had seen it all, and handled them with his own hands. The last account to appear in print was in Lonitzer's *Kreüterbuch* of 1783.

APPLES DEPICTED BY GERARD
(*Left.*) The historial significance of many earlier works lies in their ability to document the spread of plant varieties. John Gerard's book contains many varieties of apple, and these may be related to surviving strains today.

De historia stirpium (Basel, 1542), while a German version appeared the following year (with six additional illustrations) under the title *New Kreüterbuch*. Both were systematically plagiarized in the decades that followed. Fuchs is most familiar through the naming of the genus *Fuchsia* in his honour.

William Turner's *Herbal* of 1551–1562, printed in English with illustrations from Fuchs's woodcuts, gave him the title of the 'father of British botany', though the best known of the genre must be Gerard's *Herball* which first appeared in 1597. Many of the woodcuts came from earlier sources (Fuchs included). John Gerard (1545–1612) had an early interest in medicine and travelled extensively in Scandinavia, Russia and the Mediterranean lands. He supervised Lord Burghley's estate, and set up a garden of his own in London. In 1596 he published a catalogue of his garden plants, extending to more than a thousand species. Not only is it the first listing of any single plant collection but it provides an historically useful indicator of plants in cultivation at that time.

In 1618 William Lawson published his *Countrie Housewife's Garden*, the first account dedicated to women gardeners; in 1623

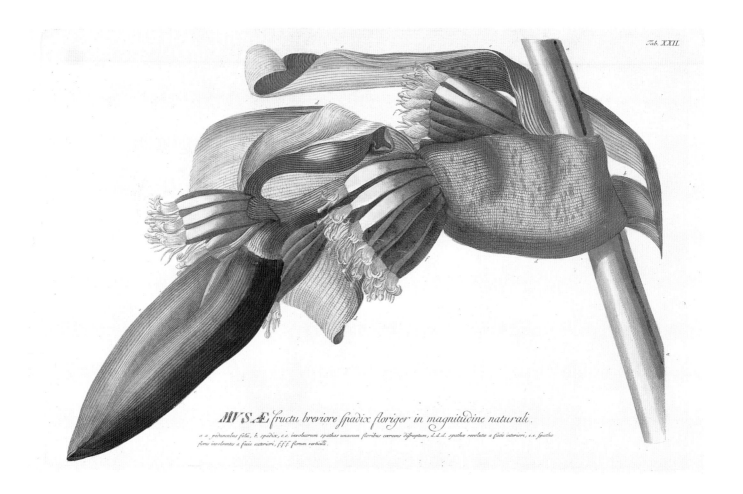

Tab. XXII.

MVSÆ fructu breviore spadix floriger in magnitudine naturali.

a a , pedunculus folii, b. spadix, c.c. involucrum spathas unacum floribus coercens disruptum, d. d. d. spathæ revolutæ a facie interiore, e.e. spathæ flores involventes a facie exteriori, f f f florum verticilli.

appeared Gaspard Bouhin's *Pinax theatri botanici*, now including 6,000 species (compared with the 260 described by Brunfels); and between 1686 and 1704 John Ray published his *Historica Plantarum* in three volumes. Ray (1628–1705) was the son of an Essex blacksmith, educated at Cambridge. He is East Anglia's greatest naturalist and has been called 'the English Aristotle'. With his companion Francis Willughby (1635–1672) he travelled widely through Europe and, after Willughby's death, Ray continued their great work of cataloguing and describing specimens from the world of natural history. Ray introduced a system of classification for plant species, and this in turn was extended and rationalized by Carl Linnaeus (1707–1778), whose work appeared in a series of books of incalculable importance: *Systema Naturae* (1735), *Genera Plantarum* (1737), and *Species Plantarum* (1753). The system developed by Linnaeus remains the basis of modern taxonomy.

As botanical expertise increased, printing techniques were changing: copperplate engraving was introduced shortly after 1550, and Pietro di Nobili published his *Herbal* (*circa* 1580) as one of the first plant texts to utilize this method of reproducing illustrations. In 1590 Adrian Collaert published his *Florilegium*, first of the plant books which featured beautiful illustrations rather than text; and in 1730 a volume on trees was published which pointed the

THE BANANA INFLORESCENCE ENGRAVED BY TREW

Christophe Jacob Trew was introduced to the great botanist Georg Dionysius Ehret by his nephew, a friend of Ehret's and an apothecary. Ehret travelled widely, he met Linnaeus, and worked later at the Chelsea Physic Garden in London. Trew used this magnificent hand-coloured engraving by Ehret to illustrate his *Plantae Selectae* (1750–1773). It is perhaps the definitive example of this medium at its best.

IRIS GERMANICA FROM *FLORA GRAECA*
Ferdinand Bauer, who, with his brother Franz, became famous for illustration in the early nineteenth century, produced this vivid portrayal of *Iris germanica* for the *Flora Graeca* (1806–1840). This work was compiled by John Sibthorp and J. E. Smith. The hand-coloured engravings are fine examples of their type.

way to the great age of botanical illustration. Its author was Jacob van Huysum (*circa* 1687–1740), and his book had been intended to be the first volume of a large *Catalogus plantarum*. What makes this work notable is that the illustrations were printed, from a single plate, in colour. Pigmented inks were used to render the otherwise undistinguished engravings in something approaching their hues in life. The first plants ever printed in this way had appeared in Holland in the late seventeenth century from the hand of Johann Teyler (1648–1699), but the van Huysum *Catalogus* was a pioneering attempt to introduce colour to the pages of books on botany.

Tab XLVIII

AZALEA *scapo nudo, flori-* *bus conferus terminatricibus, sta-*
minibus decli- *natis* *Linn. H. Cliff p. 69.*

a flore interior, b calyx brevissimus, c stamina declinata d. stylus cum stigmate abolysis e corolla defecta et resupinata, e flora interna, f. ovarium cui stylus insidet et stamina absunt, g. foetus nec fructu mature, h. h. gemma foliorum florumve, i. fructus quinquelocularis, k. idem maturus dehiscens, l. calyx persistens, m. locali tegumentum secedens, n. idem secedens, o. transverse sÿfectum, p. fructus transverse foetus, q.q.q. stylo rare persistens, rr. axis cum stylo continuus, ss. semina in naturali. tt. s. in eadem magnitudine.

In 1755 H. L. Duhamel de Monceau published his *Traité des arbres et des arbustes* – with old woodcuts as illustrations. This was the end of the woodcut in botanical publishing. Already active was George Dionysius Ehret (1708–1770), one of Germany's greatest botanical illustrators, whose excellence was widely acknowledged (Linneaus dubbed him a 'miracle'). Until Franz Bauer (1758–1840) came to Kew Gardens in 1790, Ehret was the leading botanical illustrator in Europe.

Bauer had been asked by Sir Joseph Banks to settle at Kew, and he stayed in England for the rest of his life, documenting new discoveries as they appeared. His brother Ferdinand (1756–1826) travelled far more widely collecting specimens and drawing them as he went. The two brothers reached the highest levels of accuracy and artistic beauty in botanical illustration, and in many instances it

AZALEA, BY EHRET
The backing of Trew gave Ehret the opportunity to prepare many fine studies of plant species. As this *Azalea* shows, his use of line and shading brings out the texture of the living plant in a remarkably realistic manner.

Trew, Christoph Jacob, *Plantae Selectae*, 1750–1773

FICUS, BY EHRET
Anatomical studies of the fruit add to the scientific interest of this study of the common fig, *Ficus carica*, by Ehret. He recognized the need to show, not just the structural features, but something of a plant's living appearance in nature.

Trew, Christoph Jacob, *Plantae Selectae*, 1750–1773

Overleaf: The plants shown on these pages are identifiable as follows:

First column: 'Sempuiuam' = *Sempervivum tectorum*, L., the houseleek. The crowded leaves of this succulent plant are unmistakable, and so are the three offsets. The main root shown is that of the parent plant.

Second column: 'Aneum' = *Anethum graveolens*, L., dill. The leaves of this culinary herb are finely divided, and a crude attempt to portray this is apparent. More easily recognisable is the umbellate inflorescence, though the discrete florets are shown fused into curved segments which does not occur in nature.

Third column, top: 'Origanum' = *Origanum vulgare*, Miller fennel, possesses finely divided leaves similar to those of dill. Here the umbellate inflorescence is shown with discrete flowers, closer to the true appearance of the plant.

Third column, below: 'Feniculum' = *Fœniculum vulgare*, Miller fennel, possesses finely divided leaves similar to those of dill. Here the umbellate inflorescence is shown with discrete flowers, closer to the true appearance of the plant.

Fourth column: 'Symphytu alba' = *Symphytum officinale*, L., the white-flowered comfrey. This unrealistic portrayal probably shows the basal leaves of this normally erect plant.

There is much to be said for the view that copiers of manuscripts moved further from reality with each generation of new images, but it is also apparent that the use of specialist imagery is used in science to restrict interference from outside. It may be that some of the distortion is a convention designed to confine the knowledge of herbs to the cognoscenti.

BL Sloane 1975 ff46v–47

has hard to tell their work apart. Franz (later known as Francis) became a fine microscopist and it is in this discipline that we have encountered his investigations (*see* p.43). Ferdinand took part in the expedition to Australia under the command of Captain Matthew Flinders, with William Westall, the landscape artist, and Robert Brown, the botanist. Their studies of plant life are inspiring, even to today's eyes.

Perhaps the most famous botanical artist was Pierre-Joseph Redouté (1759–1840), born at St Hubert in the Ardennes region of Belgium, and who trained in Paris. His first illustrations appeared in the *Stirpes Novae aut Minus Cognitae* (1784 and 1785) by Charles Louis l'Héritier de Brutelle (1746–1800), some of the plates being printed in colour. L'Héritier was a continuing influence on the young Redouté. In 1786, when they were working on a

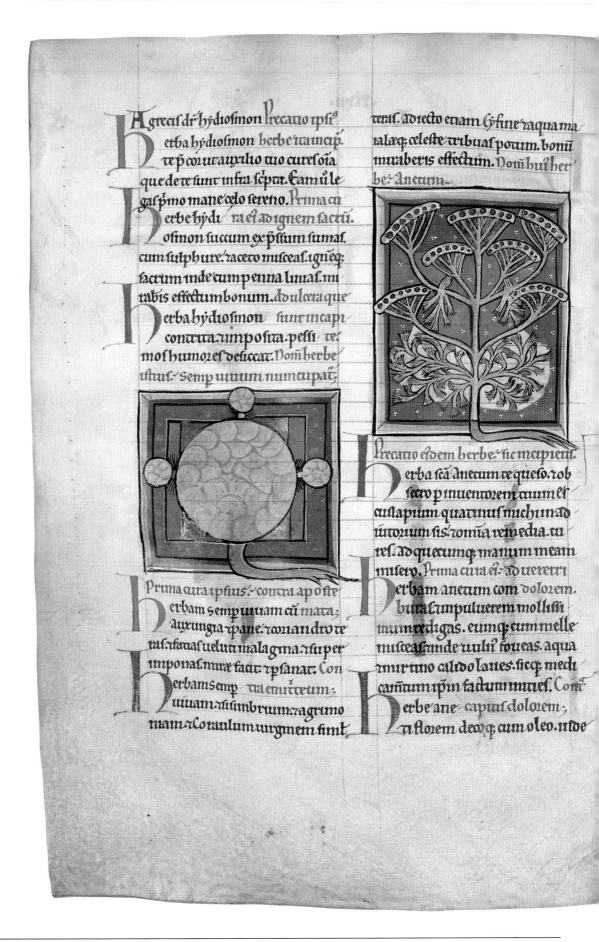

A greeis dr hydiosmon. Precatio ipse
erba hydiosmon herbe trā incip.
tpcorut auxilio tuo cures oīa
que de te sunt infra scpta. Eam ū le
gas pmo mane celo sereno. Prima cū
erbe hydi ra es ad ignem sacrū.
osmon succum ex pssum sumas.
cum sulphure. racevo misceas. ignieq
sacrum inde cum penna linias. mi
rabis effectum bonum. do ulcera que
erba hydiosmon sunt in capi
contrita. impostta. pessi te
mos humores desiccat. Dom herbe
istius. semp uiuum nuncupat.

teras. adiecto etiam cy fine raqua ma
talæq celeste tribuas potum. bonū
miraberis effectum. Dom hui her
be: Anetum..

Prima cura ipsius. contra apostē
erbam semp uiuam cū mata
auxungia rpane. rcouiandro te
ras. rfacias ueluti malagma. rr super
imponas. mira facit rpsanat. Con
erbam semp uia emitt eum
uiuam. rsi sumbrum. ragrimo
niam. rcotaulum uirginem simt

Precatio es dem herbe. sic incipient
erba sca Anetum te queso. rob
secto p inuentorem tuum et
culapium quatinus michi in ad
iutorium sis. romia remedia. tu
res. ad quecumq manum meam
misero. Prima cura es. ad uere trī
erbam anetum com dolorem.
buias. rī puluerem mollis
mum redigas. eumq cum melle
misceas. inde uulnī foueas. aqua
rmir tino calido laues. sicq medi
camnm ipm facturu inuties. Conī
erbe ane capius dolorem
rī florem decoq cum oleo. inde

caput punge. pfectiffime fanabi
tur: rdolor abfcedit. Nomen huuif
herbe: Origanum.

Yna cura eus contra tuffim gra
erbam Origanum tuffima.
impuluerem molliffimum
redige. mel autem uſq; ad tciam
deco q; illumq; cum eo puluerem
mifce. rro cuſos fanes exinde. rda
bis inaqua calida bibere. fanabit
mire.

Nom huuif herbe: feniculum. Pma
cura eus: contra Tuffim.

erbe feniculi radicel cum mero
tere. rieuno p dies nouem da
bis bibere. fanabitur mirifice. d
erbam fe uefice dolorem fanand
niculi uiridiſ: rlpii uiridis
radicem aſparagi agreftis immor
tario nouo mitte. raque fextariu
unum decoq; donec ad quartam
ueniat. ieuunoq; diebz feptem ut
plurimis dabis bibere. Balneo aute
utat. ita ut infrigida ñ defcendat.
neq; frigida bibat. ptauf fanabitur
pfectiffime.

Nomen iſtuf herbe: Symphyaı
albium. Yna ipfuif cura. Ad pro
erbam ſym fluuium mulie
phitum Albium deficca ris.
ta: ım puluerem molliffimum te

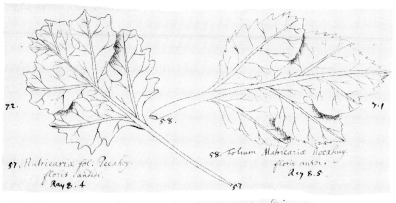

JOHN RAY'S *HISTORIA PLANTARUM*
(1700) (*Left* and *Right*)
John Ray (1628–1705) earned many titles in his
time, including the 'English Aristotle' and the
'Father of Natural History'. He was an East
Anglian naturalist, a conscientious collector who
prepared his drawings with speed and accuracy.
He travelled widely with Francis Willughby and
they prepared many volumes together. Ray's first
publication was in 1660, and in 1670 he
produced his catalogue of the English flora.
These pages are from his note-book, and reveal
the haste with which he prepared notes on his
travels.

collection of plants from the Spanish colonies, news came that the
Spanish ambassador to Paris was asking for their return before the
task was complete. L'Héritier and Redouté packed them away and
had them transported to Soho Square, London, where they were
placed in the care of Sir Joseph Banks. Redouté met many
botanists and artists in London and later became painter to the
Cabinet of Collections of Marie Antoinette. While Redouté was
largely unaffected by the French Revolution, l'Héritier himself was
murdered in the streets of Paris in 1800. Redouté continued his
work and produced some of the most stunning images in botany,
for authors including Augustin de Candolle and Philippe la
Payrouse. He became the *protégé* of Napoleon Bonaparte's wife,

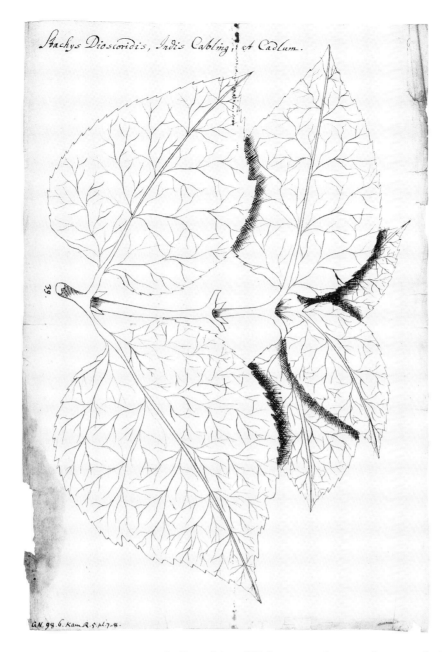

Josephine. With renewed vigour he recorded plant species, family by family, often finishing and colouring the plates himself. His *Les Liliacées* (Paris, 1802 1816) is perhaps the greatest botanical work of all.

Lithography, linear ancestor of today's offset printing, was invented by Alois Senefelder (1771–1874) in Germany during 1797. Lithography is not a relief printing process, where ink is held in depressions (as in engraving) or on projections (as in cold metal printing of a generation ago). Rather, it depends on the presence of oily substances on the image area of a stone or roller to attract ink, whilst non-printing regions are dampened with water to repel it. The first book containing plant illustrations and printed by lithography was Rudolph Ackermann's *Series of Thirty Studies from Nature* (1812). The idea was applied to zoology for Karl Schmidt's

TAB X

TURNERA e petiolo florens, foliis serratis. *Hort. Cliff.* 112. *fp* 1.
 1. *Ramus.*
 2. *Folium ad cujus bafin duae glandulae. Pedunculus e petiolo enatus cum calyce fructus, femine, ftylis, ftigmatibus.*

G. D. EHRET del.   J. WANDELAAR fecit.

HORTUS CLIFFORDIANUS, (1737)
George Clifford was a banker in Amsterdam
who became the employer of Carl Linnaeus.
The young Linnaeus prepared a catalogue to
Clifford's garden, the *Hortus Cliffordianus*
(1737). Twenty of the plates were prepared by
Ehret, and this fine example typifies the robust
use of line and form in these illustrations

REDOUTÉ AND THE BEAUTY OF THE LILY
The two Redouté brothers, Pierre-Joseph and
Henri-Joseph, were prominent botanical
illustrators, with P-J Redouté becoming the best-
known. This study is from *Les Liliacées* (Paris,
1802–1816), the work on lilies which is his finest
book. It contains 486 plates.

Beschreibung der Vögel (1818). The first book exclusively on botany
with lithographed illustrations was William Roscoe's *Monandrian
Plants*, published between 1824 and 1828. Drawing for lithography
became an art of its own. Indeed W. H. Fitch – who illustrated for
Sir William Hooker (1785–1865) and his son Sir Joseph Dalton
Hooker (1817–1911) – drew directly onto the stone, the specimen
at his side, omitting the need for a drawing on paper. His work for
the *Botanical Magazine* shows how proficient the experienced hand
could become.

The Hookers were the successive directors of the Botanic Gardens at Kew, which remains a centre for botanical study. In an
unprepossessing temple in the grounds is a vast collection of plant
paintings by Marianne North, who travelled the world to paint
exotic plants, often in dangerous conditions. And enthusiasts

CARLINA fulphurea.   224.

Redouté del.   Sellier Sc.

remain to this day, recording the hidden beauty of plant structure
that the camera may miss.

J. D. Hooker was an indefatigable traveller, and made his first
voyage of exploration at the age of 22. His travels in India gave rise
to an extensive body of knowledge, and Indian painters were
employed in teams to finish and copy drawings of new plants. It is
noteworthy, however, that Hooker's seven-volume *Flora of British
India* (1875–1897) was not illustrated. The use of verbal descriptions, rather than vivid illustrations, was seen as the principle of
objective science during the twentieth century. For this reason, the
579-page field guide by A. R. Clapham, T. G. Tutin and E. F. War-
burg, *Excursion Flora of the British Isles* (Cambridge, 1959) is also
entirely devoid of any plant illustrations.

In Australia, the first resident botanist was Sir Ferdinand Jakob

THE DAWN OF LITHOGRAPHY
Alois Senefelder (1771–1874) invented
lithography in Germany in 1797. It is based on
the drawing of an image by wax crayon on a
stone block later moistened with water. Ink is
attracted to the wax, but repelled by the
moisture; in this way the image is printed. The
first lithographs in botanical illustration were in
Rudolph Ackermann's A series of *Thirty Studies
from Nature* (1812), followed by William
Roscoe's *Monandrian Plants* (1824–1828), from
which this plate is reproduced.

Heinrich von Müller, a German *émigré* who wrote several works on the flora and fossils of that Continent. His *Plants Indigenous to the Colony of Victoria* (1860–1865) is illustrated with detailed lithographs by F. Schonfeld. The Far East meanwhile was being explored by the Russian Carl Maximovicz who spent two years in the Amur Valley travelling on board the frigate *Diana* commencing 1854 and published his *Primitiae Florae Amurensis* on his return. Père Armand David explored Eastern China and Tibet in the 1860s (a deer is named after him), and many of his findings appeared in Adrien-René Franchet's *Plantae Davidianae* (1884). His considerable efforts were dwarfed by the total of 200,000 specimens (including over 1,500 new species) sent to the Musée d'Histoire Naturelle in Paris by the explorer and naturalist Père Jean-Marie Delavay (1835–1895).

AUSTRALIAN FLORA FROM BANKS'S *FLORILEGIUM*

(*Opposite*.) An inflorescence and maturing seed-pod of *Castanospermum australe* are portrayed with graphical realism in this engraving from the 1770s. The plate was made at Sir Joseph Banks's behest for the *Florilegium* by G. Sibelius, after drawings by Sydney Parkinson and F. P. Nodder.

(*Above*.) The plate is here pulled two centuries later. Each plate was inked *à la poupée*, a process in which inks of differing colours are applied to specified areas of the engraved surface. The result is a vital and eye-catching rendition of a specimen in full colour.

By courtesy of Editions Alecto, London.

A SIDEWAYS CYCLAMEN
Charles de l'Ecluse was a French naturalist
known by his Latin name of Clusius (1526–
1609). He was a leading botanist and travelled
widely in Europe before publishing his *Rariorum
Plantarum Historiae* in 1601. Clusius included
many carefully-observed new plants in his
writings, including *Dracena*, the cabbage palm of
the Canary Islands, and the lily *Sprekelia
formosissima*. These woodcuts of cyclamens are
well-observed. The effect is spoiled somewhat by
the placing of the right-hand block in the wrong
orientation. The printer has set it sideways,
rather than upright.

Interest in botanical art continues unabated. Modern printing
has enabled the highest quality of reproduction to be attained, and
editions of works from plates engraved in previous eras have
become financially feasible. South Africa has proved to be an unexpected source of some modern floral printing, since the nation
combines a wealth of botanical material with wealth from the diamond and gold mines with which to support its publication. Span-
ning this developing era of botanical publishing has been the
Botanical Magazine, first published by William Curtis (1746–1799)
on 1 February 1787. The modern edition is produced by offset
lithography; but a link with the past lies in the fact that it was still
hand-coloured as recently as 1948.

REFERENCES

[p.86] Rix, M., *The Art of the Botanist* pp 8–9, London, 1981, contains a short account of early images of plants from the Hellenistic
traditions.

[p.88] The first printed book containing woodcuts of plants was
Megenberg, C. von, *Buch der Natur*, Hans Bämler, Augsburg, 1475.
This work was an adaptation of an earlier manuscript (see p.55),
Thomas de Cantimpré's *Natura rerum* dating from a century earlier.
The first herbal was: Floridus, M. *De viribus herbarum*, Naples 1477
(without illustrations); woodcut figures were added to the edition of
1482, published in Milan.

[p.94] The description published as:
de Bray, L. *The Art of Botanical Illustration, the Classical Illustrators
and their Achievements from 1550 to 1900*, London 1989, must be
viewed with caution, in view of the large number of inaccuracies in
the text. Bibliographical and chronological errors are frequent, and
names are given incorrectly, too. An indication of the extent of these
problems is provided by Ray Desmond in his review 'Pens and
Petals' (*Nature*, vol 342, 16 November 1989).

The non-living world

IMAGES OF SCIENCE

THE EARLIEST MATHEMATICAL illustrations are prehistoric. Some of the carvings in Palaeolithic caves may have a mathematical purpose (some are almost certainly calendars) and clay tablets from the Babylon of four millennia ago bear mathematical inscriptions. Pre-Columbian Incas in the Empire of Peru carried out calculations with maize grains on a grid similar to an abacus, and illustrated the result with a quipu, a series of knots tied to a woollen string. The Pueblo Indians of the south-west United States used a drawn swastika to calculate, with each arm representing unity; and geometric patterns with a mathematical precision are found in weaving in Central Africa and South America alike.

Many of the older traditions persist in modern mathematical notation. The ancient Mesopotamian sexagesimal system seems unmanageable, until we realize that our own calculations of the passage of time (60 seconds = 1 minute; 60 minutes = 1 hour) are also reckoned in sixties. Whereas ten can be divided only by one, two and five, 60 is divisible by 1, 2, 3, 4, 5, 6, 10, 12, 15, 20 and 30. The system was in use prior to 1700 BC and cuneiform tablets illustrate prodigious feats of mathematics carried out at that time. Conversely, many surviving Stone Age peoples of Brazil, New Guinea and Australia have no way of reckoning above two or three, and lack any means to express or illustrate their concepts.

The value of our modern system of notation is that it can be read by numerate individuals in any language. Numbers are pictographs, and any phoneme may be attached to them without altering their conceptual significance. Today's numerals are known generically as 'arabic' though they derive from Hindu numerals. Their introduction came in 773, when the Indian astronomer Kankah went to Baghdad to present the Caliph al-Mansur with a treatise in which the figures are used for astronomic calculations. The Caliph had the book translated into Arabic. The system was popularized by the Persian mathematician al-Khwarizmi (780–850) of Baghdad who wrote a famous book around AD 825, *Al Jabr Wal Muqabala* (Calculation and Reduction). The first few numerals have as many terminations as the numbers they represent (1 is one line, 2 is two, 3 has three 'points', 4 has four, *et cetera*). Some indication of today's notation was apparent in the Brahmin Hindu records about 300 BC, and by AD 876 most of the digits were recognizable in the Gwalior inscriptions.

In ancient Greece the philosophy of mathematical relationships gave rise to a school of geometrical analysis which was written up by the Alexandrian mathematician Euclid *circa* 300 BC. Of his 13 Books, the first six are devoted to elementary geometry; Books 7–9 deal with the theory of numbers; Book 10 is a geometrical treatment of the irrational roots known as surds; whilst Books 11–13 are concerned with solid geometry. Books 1–6 are the basis of geometry as still taught. Euclid's *Elementa geometria* represented the sum of knowledge since the time of Pythagoras (*circa* 572–497 BC).

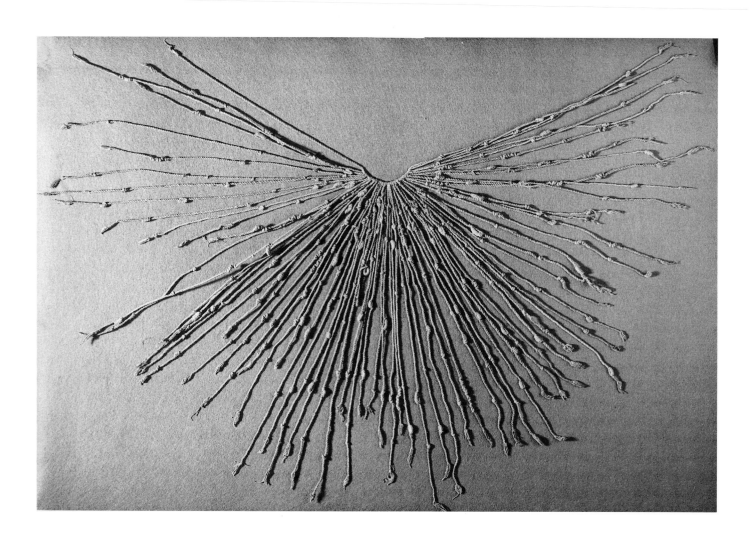

IMAGES OF SCIENCE

DATA STORAGE BY THE ANCIENT
PERUVIANS (*Above, left.*)
Knotted cords are widely used as *aides-mémoires*
for data or calculations. This example (a *quijon*)
is from Peru, where the Inca administrators
greatly depended on them, though others have
been recorded in China, Japan and Tibet; Africa;
the Californian Indians, and Polynesia. Beads on
a string are still used by Arabs, and are related to
the rosary of Catholicism.
British Museum, Museum of Mankind

A TALLY RECORD FROM THE TORRES
STRAIT (*Below, left.*)
Tallies have an ancient language. Often they take
the form of slivers of wood or stone, sometimes
being marked with notches that correspond with
mathematical amounts. This example is from the
Torres Strait islanders. Having been in regular
use in medieval times, a symbolic tally persisted
in England until 1826.
British Museum, Museum of Mankind

Whereas Euclid wrote in a strictly structured manner on the proof of mathematical reality, Archimedes (287–212 BC) wrote lucid and brilliant essays on mathematics, and was also an inventor.

The third great mathematician of the era was Apollonius of Perga (precise dates unknown, but flourished around 250–200 BC), who wrote on conical geometry. The work was ignored for centuries in the West, much of it surviving only in Arabic translation. Euclid's *Elements* edited by Campanus of Novara during the thirteenth century, who worked from an Arabic translation from the original Greek, was first printed in Venice during 1482. The printer, Ratdolt, used extraordinarily artistic border woodcuts to make this a most beautiful book.

The first full printed edition of Archimedes's works was the 1544 *Opera, quae quidem extant, omnia* produced in Basel. Apollonius received his break into print at the hands of Edmund Halley (1656–1742), discoverer of the periodicity of comets, who learnt Arabic in order to latinize the surviving text in full. The book was published in Oxford under the title *Conicorum Libri* in 1710, and is extensively illustrated.

One important European mathematician was Leonardo Fibonacci (also known as Leonardo da Pisa) who traded with Islamic North Africa where he learned Arabic from a tutor and became acquainted with Arabic numerals. In 1202 he completed his *oeuvre*, the 'Book of the Abacus', *Liber abaci*; it expounds algebra and introduces the benefits of Arabic numerals. It was this book which spelt the end of Roman numerals. Today they survive chiefly as the copyright date at the end of television documentaries and cinema films, where the sequence of letters may prevent too many in the audience from realizing quite how old the production truly is.

A further great work was written by a Franciscan monk Luca Paccioli. It was published in Venice during 1494 under the title *Somma di aritmetica, geometria, proporzione e proporzionalità* and, being written in Italian, it attained a wide readership. Paccioli was a friend of Leondardo da Vinci, and is several times mentioned in Leonardo's notebooks. The book is beautifully adorned, and represents the first printed work on mathematics and algebra. It contained nothing that significantly extended the teachings of that other Leonardo two centuries before, however.

Another Italian, Leon Battisa Alberti, wrote his great *Della pittura* in 1435 (not published until 1511), which contained the first mathematical analysis of perspective. This concept was extended by Albrecht Dürer, whose two volumes were *Underweysung der Messung* (1525) and *Bücher von menschlicher Proportion* (1528).

A practical application of mathematics is to be found in a curiously illustrated work by Leonard Digges (?–1571) which was completed for publication by his son Thomas. It was made up of several works together entitled *A Geometricall Practise, named*

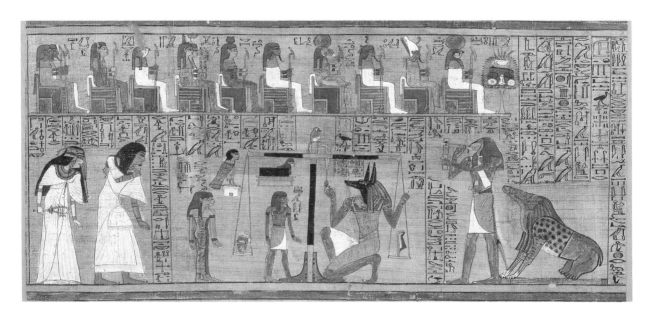

Pantometria, divided into three Bookes, Longimetria, Planimetria, and Stereometria, containing Rules manifolde for Mensuration, of all Lines, Superficies, and Solides, (London 1571). Many of the diagrams of measurement at a distance, through trigonometrical principles, reveal scenes of the time. Most intriguing is the allusion to the principles of magnification by compound lens systems which may be discerned in the text (*see* below, p.179).

The maturing of mathematics came with the prodigious output of René Descartes (latinized as Renatus Cartesius) who lived 1596–1650. His great work *Discours de la méthode pour bien conduire sa raison, & chercher la verité dans les sciences* appeared in 1637. It was unillustrated, unlike later work. A contemporary was Pierre Fermat (1601–1665) who came to mathematics in his thirties and anticipated much work on differential calculus and analytical geometry. His work was not appreciated during his lifetime, but was published posthumously by his son as *Varia opera mathematica* (Toulouse, 1679).

The unravelling of differential calculus was the work of two great men, Sir Isaac Newton (1642–1726) and Gottfried Wilhelm Leibniz (1646–1716). Newton, born in Lincolnshire, was by nature a somewhat solitary character. It was in the garden of his birthplace, where he took refuge from Cambridge as the plague ravaged London and the south, that he watched the apple fall which triggered his understanding of gravity. For nearly 30 years he was the Master of the Mint. Leibniz had the ear of the King of France and Peter the Great, and was a true socialite. Newton used the calculus as early as 1666, but did not publish an account until 1693; Leibniz, on the other hand, was in possession of calculus no earlier than 1675 but published it in 1684. The recognition of the power of calculus was due to the Swiss mathematician Jacques Bernoulli (1654–1705) and his brother Jean (1667–1748).

WEIGHING IN ANCIENT EGYPT
Toth, his head that of an ibis, watches over the weighing and judgement from the royal scribe Hunefer. This detailed illustration dates from *circa* 1250 BC and comes from Thebes. The design of the balance may be compared with that reproduced above, p.15.

British Museum, Department of Greek and Roman Antiquities

SUMERIAN CUNEIFORM AS A MATHEMATICAL RECORD
This text is written in Neo-Sumerian cuneiform, a complex and fully-developed written language. It is dated the 47th year of King Shulgi or Ur (2048 BC). This extract totals quantities of barley issued as pay and as loans to workmen. (This illustration is enlarged.)

British Museum, Department of Western Asiatic Antiquities

τῆ ϗ ξ. ὥστε ἢ ϗ ξ πρὸς ϗ τ ἐλάσσονα λόγον ἔχει, τουτέσιν ἢ πο πρὸς ῡ γ. ἢ ἢ μ ϗ πρὸς ϗ λ. ἔτι δὲ ἢ ϗ μ πρὸς ϗ λ ἐλάσσονα λόγον ἔχει, ἤπερ τὸ ᾱ πρὸς τὸ β̄. ϗ ἔτι μὲν πο πλευρὰ τ πόδιγ ρα ροδξίου πολυγώνου, ἥδε γ ν τ ἐγγραφομξίου· ὅπερ πρόκειτο εὑρεῖν.

Πάλιν δύο μεγέθων ἀνίσων ὄντων, καὶ τομέως, δυνατόν ὅτι πόδι τὸν ὁμέα πολύγωνον περ ἐγγράψαι, καὶ ἄλλο ἐγγράψαι. ὥστε τὴν τ ποδιγεγραμμξίου πλευρὰν, πρὸς τῇ ἐγγεγραμ μξίου πλευρὰν, ἐλάσσονα λόγον ἔχειν, ἢ τὸ μεῖζον μέγεθ⊙ πρὸς τὸ ἐλασσον. ἔσω γὰρ πάλιν δύο

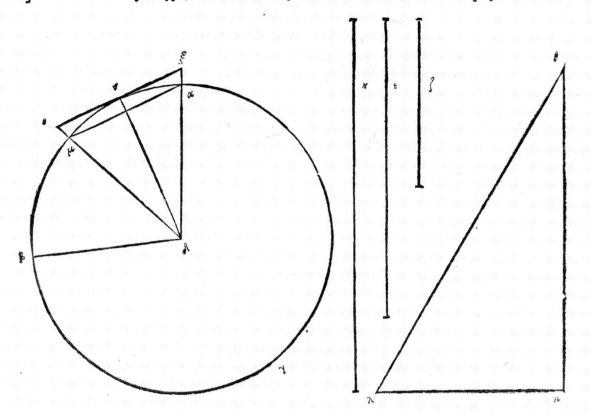

μεγέθη ἄνισα τὰ ε ζ. ὧν μεῖζον ἔσω τὸ ε, κύκλ⊙ δὲ ἴς ὁ αβ̄ γ, κέντρον ἔχων τὸ δ̄. καὶ πρὸς τὸ δ̄ ὁμεὺς συνεστάτω ὁ α δ̄ β. δεῖ δὴ ποδιγράψαι, καὶ ἐγγράψαι πολύγωνον περ τ αβ δ τομέα, ἴσας ἔχον τὰς πλευρὰς χωρὶς τῶν β δ ᾱ, ὅπως γχίνται τὸ ἐπίταγμα. εὑρήδωσαν γὰρ

Perhaps the final figure in the foundation of mathematics was Leonhard Euler (1707–1783), whose *Methodus inveniendi lineas curvas maximi minimive proprietate gaudentes* (Lausanne, 1744), came to influence every branch of physics, astronomy and mathematics. Not until 1911 did the editing begin of his *Opera omnia*: the work is still in progress.

Eye-catching illustrations were a feature of the era of experimentation. In 1650, Otto von Guericke (1602–1686) constructed the first vacuum pump and documented the properties of a vessel evacuated of air. He showed that an animal dies, a flame is extinguished, and a bell can no longer be heard. His most dramatic

ARCHIMEDES REPUBLISHED IN GREEK The use of typesetting of a high quality and fine woodcuts enhanced the publication of the works of Archimedes. This example from the *Adjecta . . . Eutochii* is dated 1544. It shows the care that was taken to ensure visual balance in the illustration of mathematical concepts.

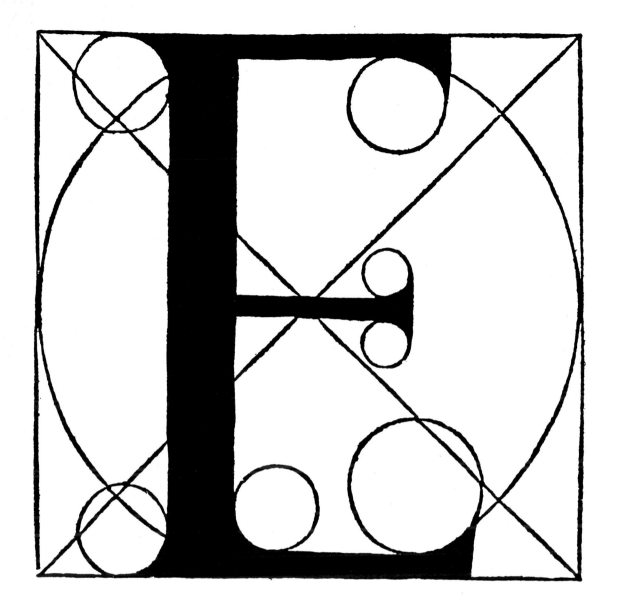

Quefta letrera. E fe caua del tondo e del fuo quadro . La
gamba groffa uol effer de le noue parti luna . La gamba
de fopra uol effe rper la mita de la gamba groffa quella de

An interest in proportion became evident during
the early Renaissance, and in 1509 Luca Paccioli
published his *Divina Proportione*. An example of
the care taken in the analysis of visual balance is
shown here. The upper-case 'E' is broken into its
components, and the underlying proportions are
revealed.

experiment was the demonstration before the Emperor Ferdinand
III. He evacuated two large metal hemispheres and had teams of
horses attempt to pull them apart. An engraving of the event featured in his *Experimenta nova Magdeburgica* of 1672 (*See* p.121).
Though this was intended to report a dramatic demonstration,
engravings were also being used to spread the word of a new
physical principle. One example was the modern clock escapement
developed by Christiaan Huygens in Holland and published in his
Horologium oscillatorium of 1673.

It is tempting to imagine that the study of electricity and magnetism was a feature only of the eighteenth and nineteenth centuries,

ΠΑΠΠΟΥ ΑΛΕΞΑΝΔΡΕΩΣ

ΛΗΜΜΑΤΑ

ΕΙΣ ΚΩΝΙΚΩΝ ΤΟ ΕΚΤΟΝ
ΑΠΟΛΛΩΝΙΟΥ ΠΕΡΓΑΙΟΥ.

PAPPI ALEXANDRINI

LEMMATA

IN SEXTUM LIBRUM CONICORUM
APOLLONII PERGÆI.

ΛΗΜΜΑ α´.

Ἔςω δύο τρίγωνα ἀμβλυγώνια τὰ ΑΒΓ, ΔΕΖ, ἀμβλείας ἔχοντα τὰς Γ, Ζ γωνίας, ἢ ἴσας τὰς Α, Δ ὀξείας. ὀρθαὶ τὰς ΒΓ, ΕΖ ἤχθωσαν αἱ ΓΗ, ΖΘ· ἔςω δὲ ὡς τὸ ὑπὸ τ͂ ΒΑΗ πρὸς τὸ ἀπὸ τ͂ ΑΓ τετράγωνον, ὕτω τὸ ὑπὸ τῶν ΕΔΘ πρὸς τὸ ἀπὸ τ͂ ΔΖ. λέγω ὅτι ὅμοιόν ἐςι τὸ ΑΒΓ τρίγωνον τῷ ΔΕΖ τριγώνω.

ΓΕΓΡΑΦΘΩ Ω ͞ ἐπὶ τ͂ ΗΒ, ΕΘ ἡμικύκλια, ἐλεύσεϑ᾽ δὴ ᾳᾳᾳ τ͂ Γ, Ζ. ἐρχέσϑω· ᾳ ἔςω τὰ ΗΓΒ, ΕΖΘ· ἤτοι δὴ ἐφάπτονται αἱ ΑΓ, ΔΖ τ͂ ἡμικυκλίων, ἢ γ᾽ ὔ. εἰ μὲν ἂν ἐφάπτονται, φανερὸν ὅτι μί νε᾽) ὅμοια τὰ ΑΒΓ, ΔΕΖ τρίγωνα. ἐὰν γὸ λάβω τὰ κέντρα τὰ Μ, Ν, ἢ ἐπιζεύξω τὰς ΜΓ, ΝΖ, ἔσον᾽) ὀρϑαὶ αἱ

LEMMA I.

Sint duo triangula obtufangula ΑΒΓ, ΔΕΖ, angulos habentia obtufos Γ, Ζ; acutos vero & æquales angulos Α, Δ. ipfis ΒΓ, ΕΖ ad angulos rectos fint ΓΗ, ΖΘ : rectangulum autem ΒΑΗ fit ad quadratum ex ΑΓ in eadem ratione quam habet rectangulum ΕΔΘ ad quadratum ex ΔΖ. Dico triangulum ΑΒΓ fimile effe triangulo ΔΕΖ.

DIAMETRIS ΗΒ, ΕΘ defcribantur femicirculi, quæ proinde tranfibunt per puncta Γ, Ζ; atque fint femicirculi ΒΓΗ, ΕΖΘ, quos vel tangunt rectæ ΑΓ, ΔΖ, vel non. Si vero tangant, manifeftum eft fimilia effe triangula ΑΒΓ, ΔΕΖ. Nam fi capiantur centra Μ, Ν ac jungantur ΜΓ, ΝΖ, erunt anguli ΜΓΑ, ΝΖΔ recti.

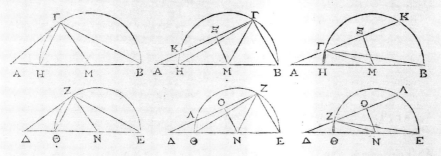

ὑπὸ ΜΓΑ, ΝΖΔ γωνίαι, ἢ εἰσὶν αἱ Α, Δ γωνίαι ἴσαι· ἢ ἡ ὑπὸ ΑΜΓ ἄρα τῇ ὑπὸ ΔΝΖ γωνία, ἢ τὰ ἡμίση· ἡ Β ἄρα γωνία τῇ Ε ὀξεῖν ἴση. ἀλλὰ ἢ ἡ Α τῇ Δ· ὅμοια ἄρα ἐςὶ τὰ τείγωνα.

Ἀλλὰ γὸ μὴ ἐφαπτέσθωσαν, ἀλλὰ τεμνέτωσαν τὰ ἡμικύκλια κατά τινα σημεῖα τὰ Κ, Λ, καὶ ἤχθωσαν κάϑετοι αἱ ΜΞ, ΝΟ· ἴση ἄρα ὀξὶν ἡ μ͂ ΚΞ τῇ ͂ ΞΓ, ἢ ἡ ΛΟ τῇ ΟΖ. ὅμοιον δὲ τὸ ΑΜΞ τῷ ΔΝΟ τειγώνω· ἔςιν ἄρα ὡς ἡ ΞΑ πρὸς ΑΜ ὕτως ἡ ΟΔ πρὸς ΔΝ. ἐπειδὴ ὀὖν ὡς τὸ ὑπὸ ΒΑΗ πρὸς τὸ ἀπὸ ΑΓ ὕτω τὸ ὑπὸ ΕΔΘ πρὸς τὸ ἀπὸ ΔΖ· ἢ ὡς ἄρα τὸ ὑπὸ ΚΑΓ πρὸς τὸ ἀπὸ ΑΓ, ττέςιν ὡς ἡ ΚΑ

& anguli Α, Δ funt æquales : angulus igitur ΑΜΓ angulo ΔΝΖ æqualis eft, unde & eorundem femiffes, nempe anguli ΑΒΓ, ΔΕΖ funt æquales. Sed anguli ad Α & Δ funt æquales : quocirca triangula funt fimilia.

Sed non tangant, fed occurrant femicirculis in punctis Κ, Λ, ac ducantur normales ΜΞ, ΝΟ : eft igitur ΚΞ ipfi ΞΓ æqualis, ut & ΛΟ ipfi ΟΖ. Simile autem eft triangulum ΑΜΞ triangulo ΔΝΟ, adeoque ΞΑ eft ad ΑΜ ficut ΟΔ ad ΔΝ. Cum vero rectangulum ΒΑΗ eft ad quadratum ex ΑΓ ficut rectangulum ΕΔΘ ad quadratum ex ΔΖ, erit etiam rectangulum ΚΑΓ ad quadratum ex ΑΓ, (five ΚΑ

P 2   ad

The.26.Chapter.

To meafure the diftance betvveene any tvvo markes lying in one
plaine leuell ground vvith your eie or ftation hovvre fo euer they
be fituate vvithout fupputation.

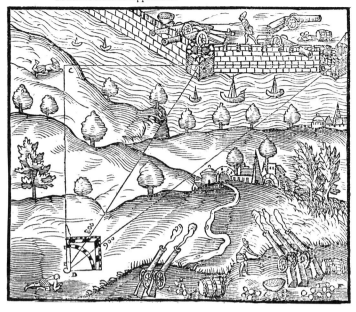

Ma piu nel anno MD XXXII effendo par Prefetto in Vero
na il Magnifico miffer Leonardo Iuftiniano. Vn capo de bombardie
ri amiciffimo di quel noftro amico. Vene in cócorrentia con un altro
(al prefente capo de bombardieri in padoa) et un giorno accadete che
fra loro fu propofto il medemo che a noi propoffe quel noftro amico,
cioe a che fegno fi doueffe affettare un pezzo de artegliaria che facef
fe il maggior tiro che far poffa fopra un piano. Quel amico di quel no
ftro amico gli conclufe con una fquadra in mani il medemo che da noi
fu terminato cioe come di fopra bauemo detto ($\mathbb{E}$ defignato in figura.

TARTAGLIA AIMS A CANNON WITH A
QUADRANT
(*Above, Right.*) The Italian philosopher Niccolò
Tartaglia (*d.* 1557) set out to explain the flight of
a cannonball on the basis of a straight trajectory
from the mouth of the gun, followed by a small
(circular) change of direction and a straight
downward path. His book *La Nova Scientifica*
(1550) reflects the growing Renaissance interest
in dynamic science, and was the first book
devoted to ballistics. Though his trajectory was
wrongly construed, his quadrant was widely used
in aiming a cannon.

but the first major work in this field was compiled by a contemporary of William Shakespeare named William Gilbert (1544–
1603). He graduated from Cambridge in arts and medicine, and in
1561 was elected a Fellow of St John's College. By 1599 he was
President of the College of Physicians in London and was subsequently appointed Personal Physician to Queen Elizabeth I (and
later to King James I). An earlier book on magnetism had been by
Petrus Peregrinus (1220–?) and was entitled *Epistola de Magnete*
(*circa* 1265). Gilbert – working with nothing more than natural
lodestone and bars of elemental iron – demonstrated magnetism
and concluded that the Earth is a natural magnet. He showed how
hammering an iron bar parallel to the Earth's lines of magnetic
force can increase the level of magnetism developed by the bar, and
he demonstrated how heating the bar red-hot can destroy the
effect. Gilbert's work, *De Magnete*, was published in 1600. As late
as 1822 it was being stated by Sir John Robinson (1778–1843)
that Gilbert had published 'virtually everything we know about
magnetism'.

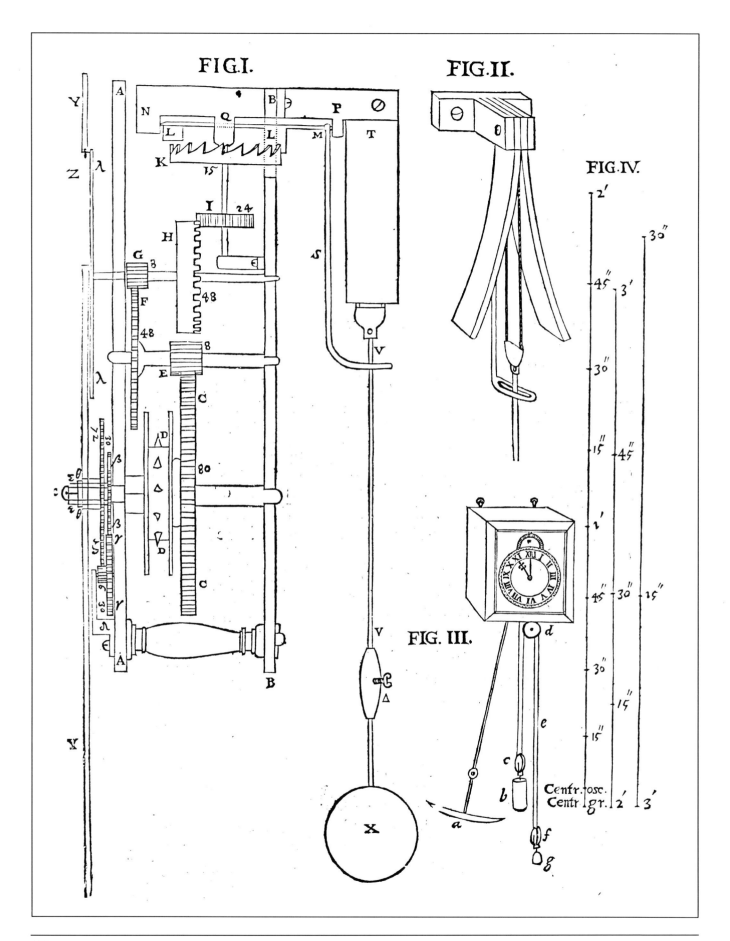

FIG. I.   FIG. II.

FIG. IV.

FIG. III.

EXPERIMENTS WITH A VACUUM AT MAGDEBURG, 1672
(*Above.*) Public demonstrations have marked the course of science. This remarkable engraving records an experiment by Otto van Guericke (1602–1686) at Magdeburg, Prussia. He showed that his newly-invented air pump could effectively evacuate the space between two metal hemispheres. The pressure on each would have been about three tonnes, more than two teams (each of 16 horses) could pull apart. The engraving showing the trial is from *Experimenta nova Magdeburgica* (1672).

British Library

THE CLOCK ESCAPEMENT OF CHRISTIAAN HUYGENS
(*Left.*) Christiaan Huygens (1629–1695) was a mathematical polymath. His abilities caught the attention of René Descartes, who predicted a great future for the young investigator. One of his innovations was the pendulum clock escapement. It appeared in *Horologium oscillatorium*, 1673.

The next individual to take up this topic was one of the first American scientists, Benjamin Franklin (1706–1790). Franklin was the tenth son of an immigrant English soap-boiler and began adult life as a newspaper proprietor in Philadelphia, Pennsylvania. His *Autobiography* is still read, for he was one of those who first drafted the Declaration of Independence (1776). His electrical experiments started in 1746 and concerned frictional ('static') electricity. In 1752 he carried out his famous experiment with a kite to show that lightning (as others had long suspected) was indeed an electrical phenomenon. He was elected a Fellow of the Royal Society of London, and an honorary graduate of Oxford University. He first communicated with Peter Collinson in London, and published his work in two volumes dated 1751 and 1753, *Experiments and observations on electricity made at Philadelphia in America*.

Remarkably vivid engravings illustrate the work of Luigi Galvani in Bologna (*De viribus electricitatis in motu musculari*, 1791), who observed the reflex jerking of a frog's muscle when brought into contact with a scalpel blade. Galvani (1737–1798) believed he had discovered 'animal electricity', though it is sensible to adduce that he did not fully comprehend the significance of his obser-

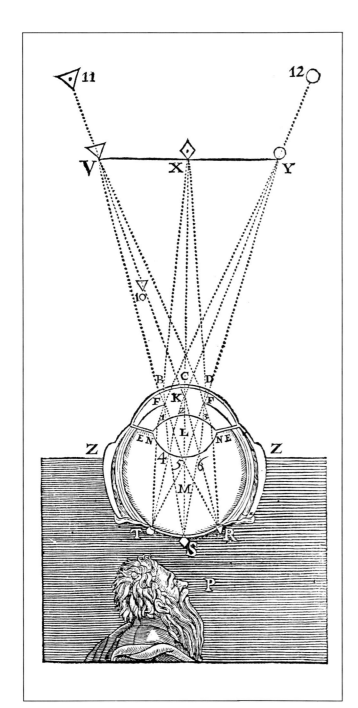

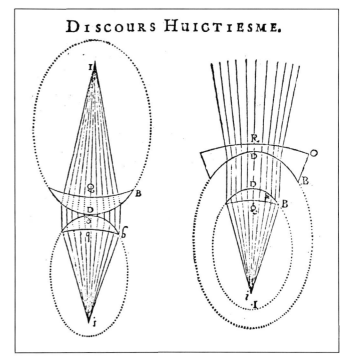

RAY DIAGRAMS FROM DESCARTES
(*Above.*) The first accurate ray diagrams of
convex and concave lenses were published by
Descartes. These admirably clear illustrations are
from his *Discours de la Méthode*, 1637, Eighth
Discourse, p. 99. Diagrams in some current texts
err in their depiction of the refractive process: in
optics we have 'icons' that take the place of
reality. Yet to Descartes, pioneering in the field,
accuracy was at premium.

(*Left.*) Reproducing a page of art-work has
always saved type-setting costs for the thrifty
publisher. In this example, from the Fifth
Chapter of *Dioptrice* by René Descartes, a
woodcut of the ray diagrams of human vision is
used to decorate the text. Such woodcuts have
often been repeated in early works in science.
One argument in favour of this convention was
that the reader could refer to an image without
having to turn back to its previous appearance in
the text. But here the concept is taken to
extremes – the same picture is repeated six times
in eleven pages.

It should be noted that Descartes considered
the front element of the cornea to act as a
refractive component of the eye. Though the lens
is normally thought to be the focussing element
of human vision, it is known that the cornea
itself is a leading refractive feature. In this sense
Descartes is anticipating modern interpretations
of visual function.

vations. The publication came to the attention of Alessandro Volta
(1745–1827) and encouraged him to write his account of the
Voltaic pile for the *Transactions of the Royal Society of London* in
1800. The communication was first sent to the President of the
Royal Society, Sir Joseph Banks, who recommended its expedient
publication. From this work came the later investigations of Hans
Christian Ørsted (1777–1851) who discovered that an electric current could be produced by magnetism, followed by the majestic
insights of Michael Faraday (1791–1867) who invented the
dynamo and also discovered benzene.

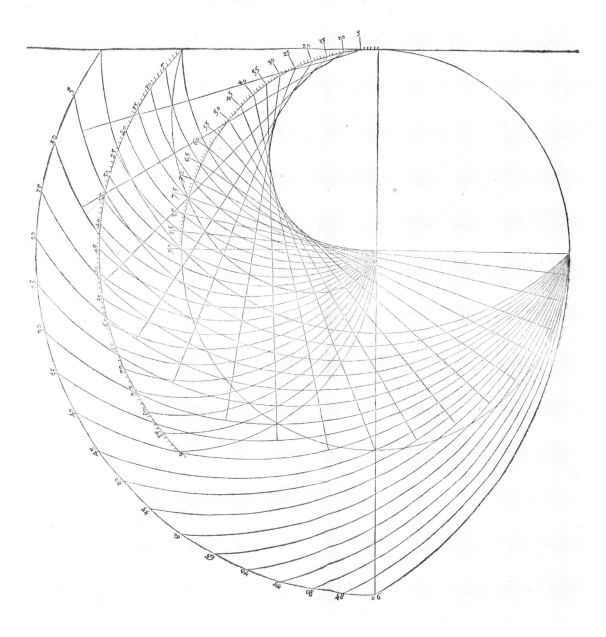

THE EARTH'S MAGNETISM ANALYSED IN THE 16TH CENTURY

The English physician William Gilbert (1546–1603) personally attended Queen Elizabeth I. He was a respected philosopher, and wrote the first English work on magnetism. Though there was some medieval influence in his text, his work on the Earth's magnetic field was sound and prophetic. Variation, inclination and magnetic delineation are all carefully explained in this sparsely illustrated book. It was published as *De Magnete* in 1600.

Later volumes in the field of physics embodied the new print technology, but it was not until the advent of photography that the full benefits of reportage could be obtained. Only when Röntgen published his first x-rays of the human body in 1895 did the existence of radiation begin to dawn on the world of science. With that final revelation the scene was set for today's understanding of physics in the broadest sense.

The notion that the Earth might comprise a dynamic system of interrelated forces seems to have been first expounded by the Greek philosopher Strabo (*circa* 63 BC–AD 20). His *Geographica*

AGRICOLA'S COMPENDIUM ON MINING
Georg Bauer (1490–1555) Latinized his name as
Agricola, and produced a book on mining and
metallurgy. It took the last 20 years of his life to
complete and was published as *De re metallica* in
the year following his death. The book contains
273 fine woodcuts, prepared by Hans Rudolf
Manuel Deutsch, all based on Agricola's
drawings of processes and phenomena he
personally observed. The separation of the ore
from the mined rock (above) appeared on p.261
of his book. The lower woodcut (from p.301)
reveals a clear understanding of perspective, and
depicts the large bellows used to heat the
furnace.

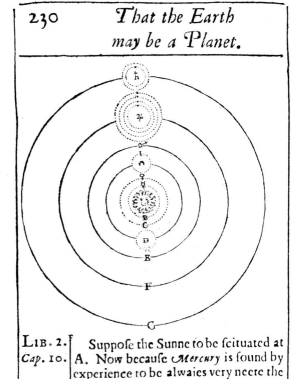

LIB. 2.
Cap. 10.

Suppofe the Sunne to be fcituated at A. Now becaufe *Mercury* is found by experience to be alwaies very neere the Sunne, fo that he do's for the moft part lye hid under his Raies. As alfo becaufe this Planet hath a more lively vigorous Light than any of the other ; therefore wee may inferre, that his Orbe is

MIGHT THE EARTH BE A PLANET? The mathematical considerations of earlier workers led the English writer J. Wilkins to compile a work entitled *Discovery of a New World*, 1640. In it he set the planets into a heliocentric universe. A number of clear illustrations were prepared for this book. In this plate the planetary system is set out – and note too how the orbits of the known planetary satellites are clearly shown.

was first printed in Venice in 1472, and can be related to the earlier work on stone by Theophrastus. Perhaps the most stimulating comment Strabo makes is his view that there remained many parts of the Earth yet to be discovered.

Agricola (in vernacular Georg Bauer (1494–1555) of Switzerland) became the 'father of mineralogy' through his several books. His greatest, a treatise on metals, appeared in twelve books covering mining and refining in his time. The magnificent and detailed illustrations (*see* opposite) were prepared over three years by Blasius Weffring. An elaboration of the chemistry of metals came from Lazarus Ercker (?–1593). His *Beschreibung aller fürnemisten mineralischen Ertz unnd Bergkwercks Arten* was published at Prague in 1574, and continued to advance scientific understanding in the practical aspects of chemical refining.

Such practical disciplines helped draw chemistry from the superstitious strictures of alchemy. At the time that Nicolaus Copernicus was publishing *De revolutionibus*, which largely founded heliocentric astronomy, and Andreas Vesalius produced his remarkable *De humana corporis fabrica*, set to advance medicine and anatomy (both works appeared in 1543), the best chemistry could offer was a book – believed to be by Ramón Lull (*d*. 1315), *De secretis naturae* (Venice, 1542), which described miracles in medicine and the transmutation of base into precious metals. Indeed alchemy was still being studied by Friedrich Roth-Stoltz (1687–1736) as late as 1719, when his *Bibliotechna chemica* was published in Nuremberg.

The birth of chemistry was effectively marked by Robert Boyle (1627–1691), the Irish-born son of the 'great' first Earl of Cork, educated at Eton and widely travelled. Among his early works was an extension of the experiments described by Guericke (above, p.116), but his revolutionary tome appeared in 1661. This, the *Sceptical Chymist*, attacked aspects of traditional alchemy, and was echoed by philosophers in many countries. Nicolas Lémery (1645–1715) popularized the subject in his *Cours de chymie* (Paris, 1675), published in London as *A Course of Chemistry* (1680), and he saw 13 editions appear in his life-time.

In 1771 oxygen was discovered by Karl Wilhelm Scheele (1742–1786), but his mentor T. O. Bergman (1735–1784) took so long writing his introduction to Scheele's book that the publication did not appear until 1777. By this time, Joseph Priestley (1733–1804) had made the same discovery (in 1774), and published all the work in three volumes entitled *Experiments and Observations on Different Kinds of Air* (London, 1774–1777). The illustrations of his work have charm as well as scientific accuracy.

In France, meanwhile, modern chemistry was set to emerge through the work of Antoine Laurent Lavoisier (1743–1794). He studied law at Paris and then, turning to geology, helped in the preparation of Guettard's map of France. In 1768 he was elected to

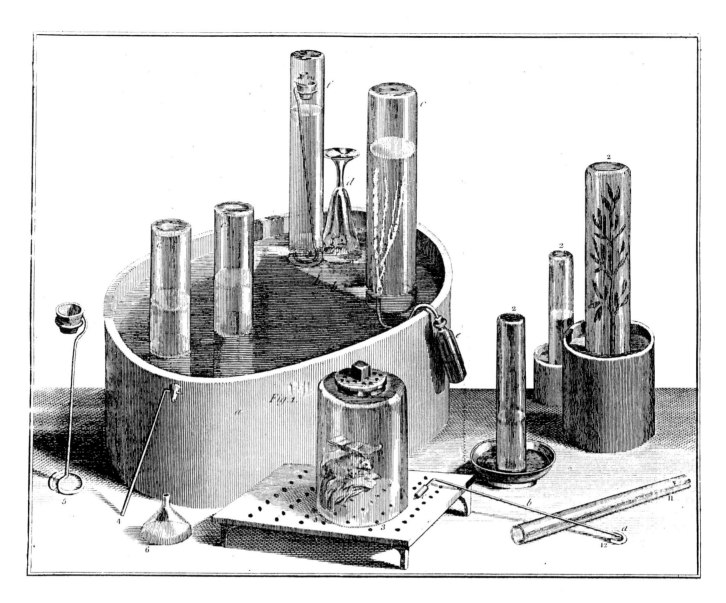

the Académie Royale des Sciences, and in 1771 he married the 14-year-old Marie-Anne Paulze, who assisted him greatly in his research. In his authoritative *Traité élémentaire de chimie* he set down a holistic view of chemistry, gave oxygen its name, overthrew finally the old theories of phlogiston, and synthesized the work of his predecessors into the discipline of chemistry as we now know it. The book, published in Paris (1789), appeared just as the Revolution began. This event brought in its train a peculiarly barbaric sequence of anti-intellectual executions, and Lavoisier was beheaded under the dogma that 'the Republic has no need of scientists'. The illustrations in his great book were all drawn by his wife, and they mark the dawn of laboratory investigations in chemistry. As the discipline moved towards atomic theory, the rôle of aesthetic illustration diminished.

If we move to the following century, clearly-designed and crowded engraved plates were used by another chemist to account for his work. In terms of graphic competence they are unremarkable:

EXPERIMENTS WITH OXYGEN
The English scientist Joseph Priestley (1733–1804) opened up the study of gases with a series of innovative experiments. Priestley showed that green plants *in vitro* gave off a gas which made respired air once more respirable. He also studied ammonia, sulphur dioxide, and a series of acids. He maintained adherence to the obsolescent phlogiston theory of combustion, which stood in the way of his full appreciation of the oxygen he had discovered. Many of his experiments appear in this eye-catching frontispiece to his *Experiments and Observations on Different Kinds of Air*, London, 1774–1777.

Madame Lavoisier illustrates her husband's experiments

The recognition of the true nature of oxygen was the work of Antoine Lavoisier (1743–1794). Among his 'elements' were 23 that we recognize today. His experiments were carried out with the assistance of his wife Marie-Anne (née Paulze) and it was she who drew the illustrations for publication. The engraving was by D. Lizars, and the resulting plates show clearly Lavoisier's apparatus in use. Lavoisier was effectively the father of modern chemistry. He had a wide circle of friends. These included Benjamin Franklin and Joseph Guillotin. It was the latter's invention which claimed Lavoisier's life in the French Revolution.

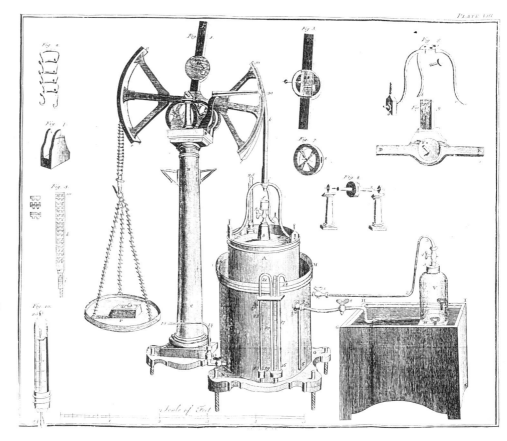

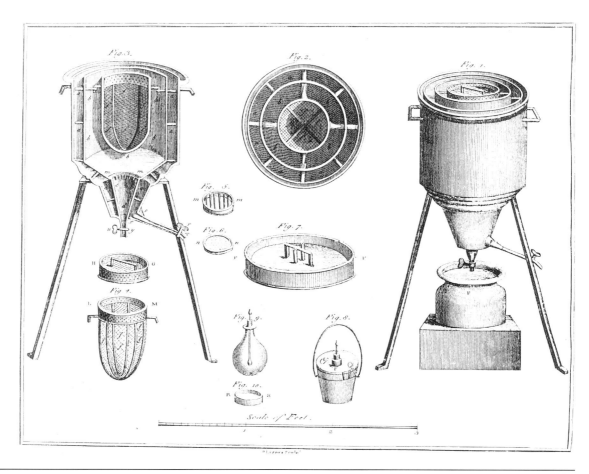

but this chemist had his eyes on a different discipline altogether. He was Louis Pasteur, and, though trained as a chemist, his destiny was to focus on mechanisms that remained a key to the preoccupations of an era in which biotechnology is at the forefront of knowledge. In those plates we may discern the move towards preoccupations due to surface fully in the 21st century.

REFERENCES

[p.113] It is said that other information systems based on knots in a cord have been found in Africa, the Californian Indian communities, China, Japan and Tibet, Siberia and the Polynesian Islands. They have been used for tallying taxes in Hawaii and a knotted-string system has been used to record current news in the Solomon Islands. The use of wampum and related data-storage systems is analysed by: Gaur, A., *A History of Writing*, London, 1984 and 1992.

[p.121] Ørsted, M. 'Experiments on the effect of a current of electricity on the magnetic needle', *Annals of Philosophy*, 16: 273–277, October 1820.
Volta, A. G. A. A., 'On the electricity excited by the mere contact of conducting substances of different kinds', *Philosophical Transactions of the Royal Society*, 90 (2): 403–431, 1800.
Faraday, M. *Experimental Researches in Electricity*, 3 vols, London, 1839–1855.

[p.123] Röntgen, W. Über eine neue Art von Strahlen, *Sitzungsberichte der Physikalisch-medizinische Gesellschaft*, 8: 132–141, 1895; 1: 11–19, 1896.

[p.123] For Strabo, see: Strabo, *Geographica*, Venice, 1472.
—*De situ orbis*, Venice, 1502.
See also:
Theophrastus, *Peri lithon*, (in) Aristoteles, *Opera*, 2: 254–260, Venice, 1497.
—*Traité des pierres*, Paris, 1754.

[p.125] For Agricola, see: Agricola, G. *De ortu & causis subterraneorum; De natura fossilium*, Basel, 1546.
—*De re metallica*, Basel, 1556 (note: this encyclopaedic work was published posthumously). A translation appeared as:
Hoover, H. C. and Hoover, L. H., 'Agricola on Metals', *Mining Magazine* (London), 31: 640 pp, 1912.

[p.128] Pasteur, L., 'Mémoire sur les corpuscles organisés qui existent dans l'atmosphere. Examen de la doctrine des générations spontanées', *Annales des sciences naturelles*, 16: 5–98, 1861; also *Annales des chimie et physique*, 64: 5–110, 1862.

6

Mankind in the world

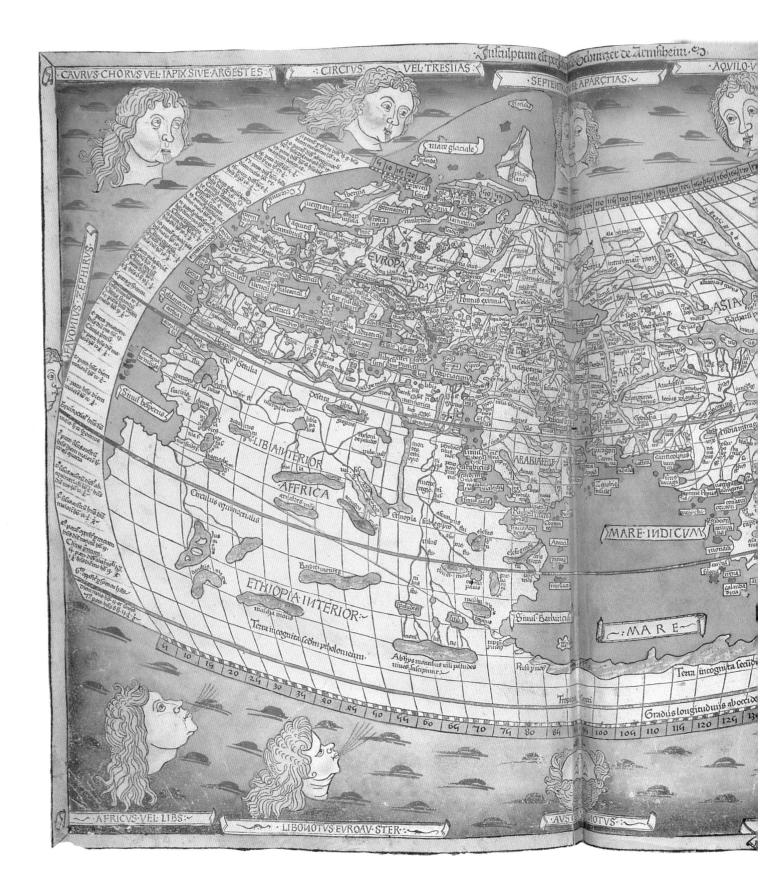

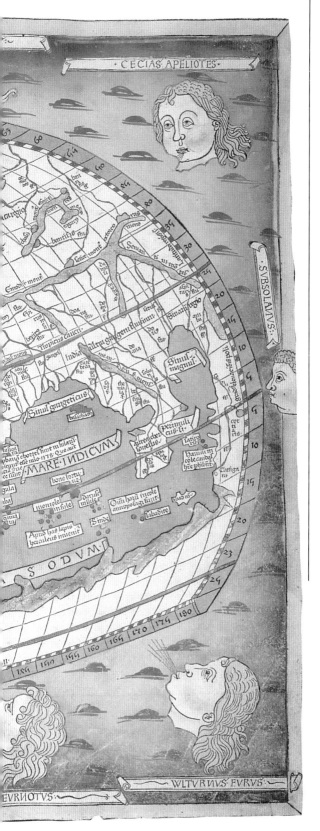

THE ETERNAL IMPONDERABLE for the early human investigator was the nature of the world. Circumscribed by the distance one can see, tempted by seemingly endless vistas above (oddly, only visible at night), taunted with tales of strange lands and unimaginable phenomena, threatened by mortality, and teased by the machinations of the mind, the philosopher of old found it hard to conceive of where he stood.

Once the philosophy of heaven and earth, water and the oceans had been assailed, an illustrative interpretation was a further order of magnitude. The earliest illustrations of the Earth depicted the simple division of earth and sea. The wheel map of Isidore, Bishop of Seville who died in AD 636 (published as part of his *Etymologiae* in 1472 and having the distinction of being the first printed map), epitomizes one medieval view of the world. Three land masses, Europe, Africa and Asia, stand separated by the 'great sea' of the Mediterranean (the name literally means 'at the Earth's centre'), the whole surrounded by an encircling oceanic belt. Little wonder navigators were frightened of falling off the edge.

To some extent it was the stoical attitude of a culture rooted in religious dogma which stood in the way of progress. St Augustine promulgated an adaptation of Platonism with all its implications of acceptance and contemplative inertia. The ancient notions of harmony were at odds with innovation. Attempts to situate the continents in some kind of spatial array were based on earlier teachings. The celebrated *Mappa mundi* at Hereford cathedral is one example, and the writings of Ptolemy (who flourished around 150 BC) inspired the earliest recognizable maps of the Renaissance era. A fifteenth-century German example from the British Library collections (illustrated, *left*) shows the Mediterranean area projected in modern form using curved reference lines of longitude and latitude.

As exploration increased, new outlines were progressively added. And new perspectives came, too. Leonardo drew a form of

A GERMAN MAP-MAKER RECREATES PTOLEMY'S VISION
In this extraordinary map of the Mediterranean, a German illustrator of the fifteenth century set out Ptolemy's understanding of geography. The map uses a form of projection in which longitude is fractions of hours measured east from the Fortunate Isles, and latitude is the number of hours in the longest day of the year. The curvature is easily reconciled with modern cartographical conventions.
British Library, Maps 1.d.2

A VIEW OF THE WORLD IN 1472
Medieval scholars were provided with a stereotyped view of the Earth as a body of land surrounded by sea. In this version of an Old Testament map by Isidore of Seville, east is at the top of the map, with north to the left. Bishop Isidore (560–636) compiled an encyclopedia of all the sciences under the title *Etymology*. The ideas were derived from the ancients (notably Pliny); Bede (English) 673–735 and Rabanus Maurus (German) 776–856, drew on this work for their own compilations.

map frequently employed in modern times (notably in guidebooks to mountain resorts), namely the aerial view. His version covered the Italian province of Arezzo. Early maps also served to perpetuate the anxieties and superstitions of the age, for mythological beasts of great ferocity adorn even the more accurate geographical representations of the Middle Ages, and these spilled over into Renaissance times, too.

The sophisticated understanding of Strabo took time to re-

AN EARTHQUAKE TOPPLES A TOWER
A dramatic woodcut of an earthquake in progress features in the ninth book of the *Margarita Philosophica Nova* (1503) by Gregor Reisch (*d*. 1525). His book was a pioneering attempt to account for the behaviour of the Earth. But the true nature of earth movements did not gain general acceptance until the nineteenth century.

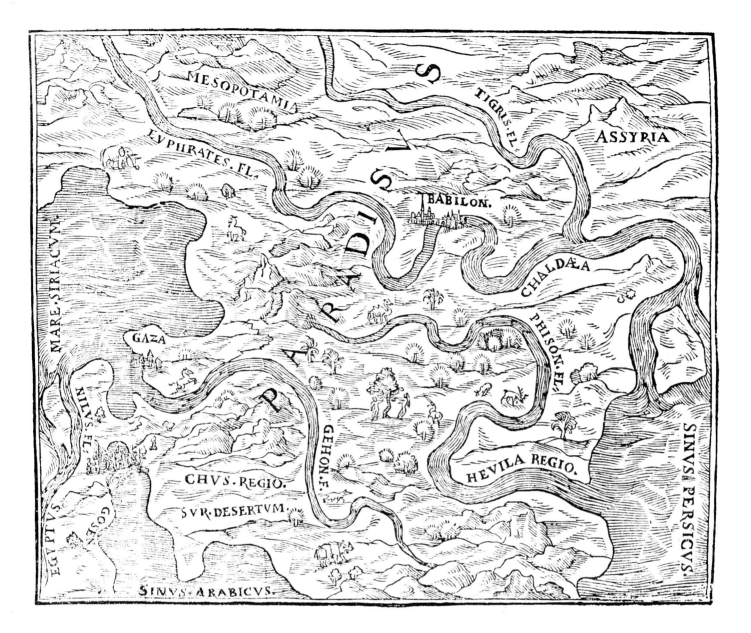

Map labels: MESOPOTAMIA · LVPHRATES.FL. · TIGRIS.FL. · ASSYRIA · PARADISVS · BABILON. · CHALDÆA · PHISON.FL. · MARE.SIRIACVM · GAZA · NILVS.FL. · EGYPTVS · GOSEN · CHVS.REGIO. · SVR.DESERTVM. · GEHON.F. · HEVILA REGIO. · SINVS.PERSICVS · SINVS.ARABICVS.

THE DEPICTION OF PARADISE
This woodcut, from Isidore's *Chronologia* (1577), portrays the Holy Land ('Paradisus'). The Gulfs of Arabia and Persia have retained their names to this day. Babylon (the ruins of which lie near to Baghdad on today's map of this area) is shown on the banks of the Euphrates. The Tree of Knowledge, with Adam and Eve (and unicorn?) close by, is precisely located, too.

emerge. On the occasions that great disasters were recorded, it was usual for them to be seen as the machinations of Heaven rather than the incessant turmoil of a restless globe. An earthquake is figured by Gregor Reisch (?–1525) in *Margarita philosophica*, Freiburg, 1503, but without any concept that this was the forces of the Earth at work. The hold of religious tradition remained firm. James Ussher, Archbishop of Armagh, Ireland (1581–1656), taking the chronology of the Old Testament as literal, calculated that the Earth had been created on the evening of 22 October 4004 BC, and this date was quickly passed around the Christian world and may be found written on the fly leaf of older Bibles. But fossils were becoming better known, and there was a drift towards the need for scientific insight, even if couched in comfortingly Christian terms. Thomas Burnet wrote a book which told how God had rent the Earth, causing floods and fissures, the results of which

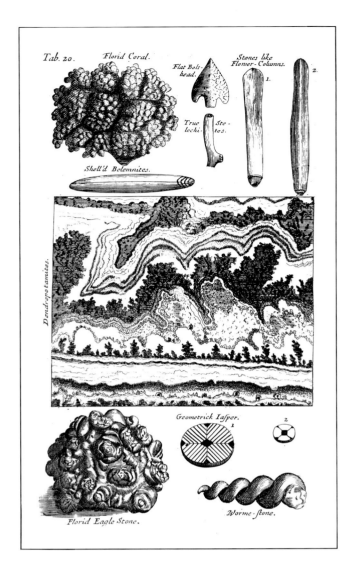

devastation had made the surface of the Earth the way it could now be seen. The book was entitled *The Sacred Theory of the Earth, Containing an Account of the Original of the Earth, and of All the General Changes Which it hath Already Undergone, or is to Undergo, Till the Consummation of All Things*, London, 1681. It became favourite reading for King Charles II.

In 1695, the Professor of Physick at Gresham College, John Woodward (1665–1728), published his *Essay Towards a Natural History of the Earth*. It was closely followed by William Whiston's *A New Theory of the Earth* . . . (London, 1696) which decreed that the Flood had caused the disruption of the Earth's surface. In response to Burnet, he too found a precise date: the cloudburst had begun on 18 November 2349 BC. Whiston (1667–1752) did have in his favour the belief that the creation 'days' might be figures of speech, not to be interpreted literally, and that the Earth itself might be of great antiquity.

But whilst this position held sway in Britain, a Danish geologist had already taken the first steps towards an understanding of how

MINERALS FROM THE COLLECTION OF THE ROYAL SOCIETY
The work of Nehemiah Grew (1641–1712) covered the microscopy of plants and a broader field of work in his capacity as curator of the Royal Society's collections. These fine engraved plates are from his *Catalogue of the Natural and Artificial Rarities belonging to the Royal Society* which he had privately published in 1681.

In this vivid plate George L.C.D.F. Cuvier (1769–1832), the most celebrated scientist in Europe in his time, restores the skeleton of the extinct sloth *Megatherium*, excavated in South America. The results appeared in his *Récherches sur les Ossements Fossiles*, published in Paris (1825).

the Earth's surface had been formed. Nicolaus Steno (1638–1686) was trained in medicine – the duct of the parotid gland has been known as the *ductus Stenorzianus* in his honour. Recognizing that fossil remains known as dragon's tongues were shark's teeth, he set about explaining how stratification might occur. The result was published as *De Solido intra Solidum naturalitur contento dissertionis Prodromus*, Florence, 1669, and appeared in English in 1671. Steno (originally Niels Steensen) became a priest in later life and did not return to the subject.

It may be wondered why such a thesis took so long to gain a foothold in Britain, more so when we reflect that the book was originally translated into English by Henry Oldenburg (1615–1677), then Secretary to the Royal Society. I can cite an even earlier publication which makes that wonderment increase. Robert Hooke (1635–1703) settled the origin of fossils, and the nature of activity in the Earth's crust, in his fascinating *Micrographia* of 1665 (*see* below, p.173). For all its title, this book became a current repository for much of Hooke's thinking. Tucked away in corners are short descriptions of his ideas from many other areas of activity,

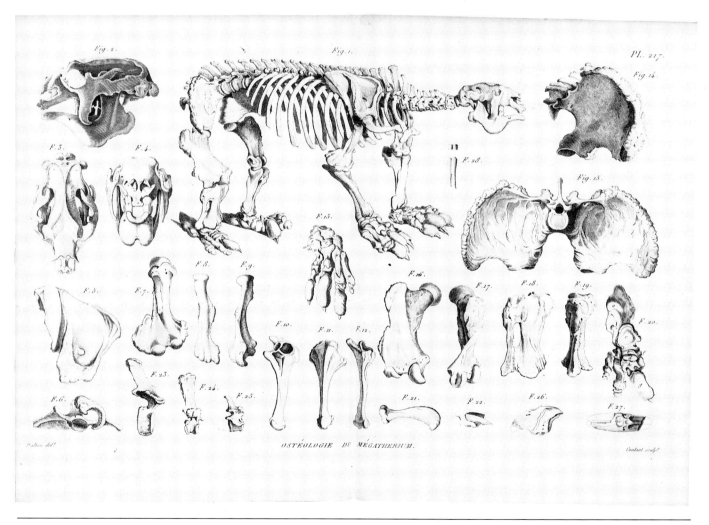

OSTÉOLOGIE DU MEGATHERIUM.

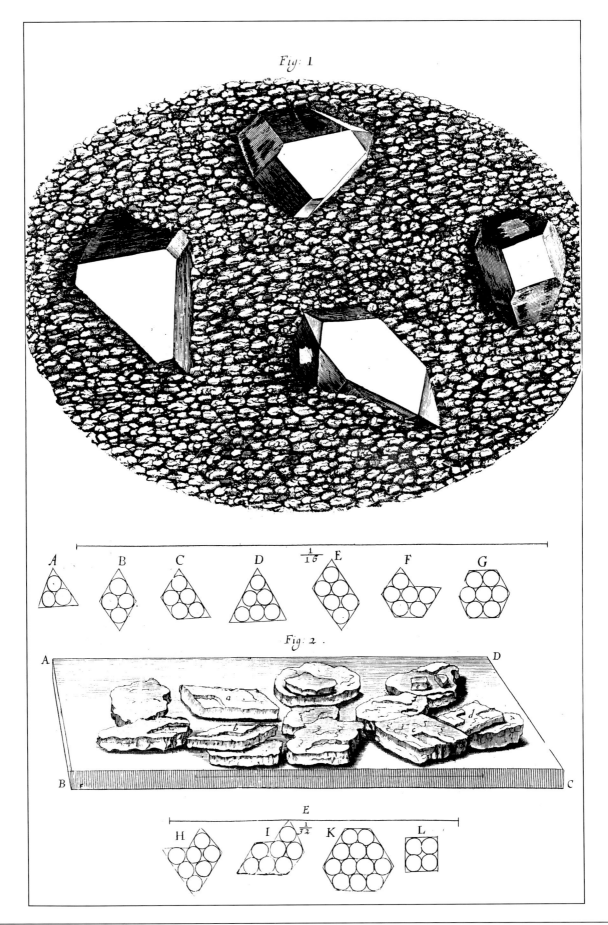

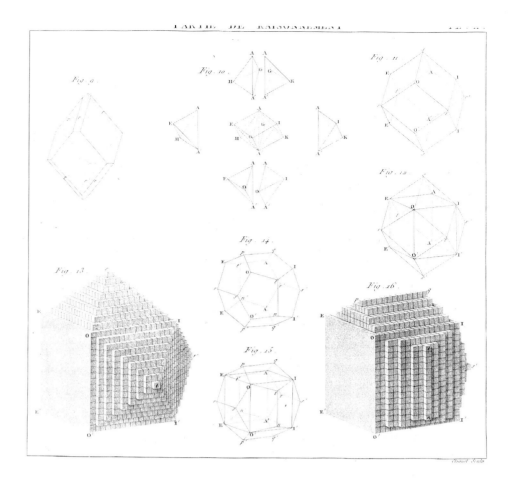

CRYSTALLOGRAPHY COMES OF AGE
(*Above.*) The work of René Just Haüy
(1743–1822) established the principles of
crystallography. It is said his interest was aroused
when he dropped and shattered a crystal of
calcite, and found that the rhombohedral
fragments were miniatures of the parent crystal
itself. He explained this in terms of mathematical
modelling. Haüy, a priest and amateur
mineralogist, published his *Essai d'une théorie sur
la structure des Crystaux* in 1784. His work was
clearly anticipated by the modelling concept of
Hooke over a century before.

THE ROOTS OF CRYSTALLOGRAPHY
(*Left.*) The predictable shape of crystals has
fascinated mankind since prehistoric times. It is
now known that the angles of the facets are
related to the molecular alignment within the
solid crystal, a concept first mooted in Robert
Hooke's *Micrographia* (1665). In this fine copper
engraving Hooke shows a series of what we
might now term 'molecular models', relating
their orientation to the facets that must result.

as a means of establishing precedent. His wide-ranging interests
gave him many insights that were ahead of their time, and which
served to stimulate the creative endeavours of others. His explanation of fossils begins on page 111 of *Micrographia*: 'Shells of certain
Shel-fishes . . . either by some Deluge, Inundation, Earthquake, or
some such means, come to be thrown to that place (and) by a long
continuance in that posture, been *petrify'd* and turn'd into the
nature of stone.' Later in the same book we find an indication of
the power that lies within the Earth, (p. 243 *et seq.*): 'The Earthquakes here with us seem to proceed . . . from some subterranean
fires, or heat, great quantities of vapours . . . which do not presently
find a passage through the ambient parts of the Earth, do at last
overpower, with their *elastick* properties, the resistance of the
incompassing Earth, and lifting it up, or cleaving it, (shatter) the
parts of the Earth above it . . .'. Yet as late as 1726, Johannes
Bartholomew Beringer (?–1740) published his *Lithographie Wir-
ceburgensis* (Würzburg, 1726) in which he revealed some startling
fossil discoveries in the hills near the University at which he was
Professor. The finds were false – some sardonic souls had carved
stones into fantastic shapes and planted them to fool the Professor.
When he realized he had been duped, he made strenuous efforts to
recall and destroy every copy of the book. It remains one of the

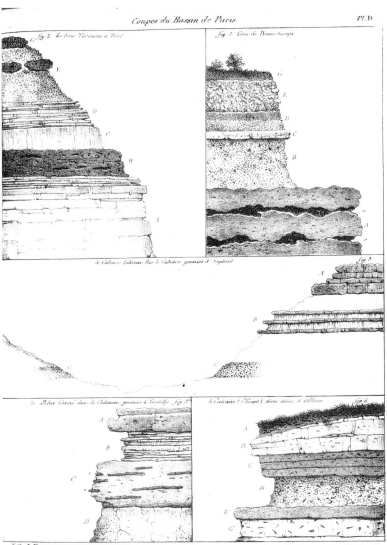

STRATIFICATION DELINEATED

This lithographic plate of vertical sections of
rocks near Paris was used to illustrate Cuvier and
Brongniart's *Essai sur la Géographie Minéralogique
des environs de Paris* (1811). A major
contribution of Cuvier's work was the concept
that the study of fossils could be used to place
geographical strata in chronological sequence.
For four years he worked with Alexandre
Brongniart on the geology of the Paris basin.
Their report of 1811 was a landmark in the
emergence of geology as a science.

rarest works in geology on that account.

The mapping project on which the young Lavoisier (*see* p.127)
was engaged was to become one of the finest pioneering geological
charts. It was the conception of Jean Étienne Guettard (1715–
1786) who realized that rock formations existed in vast bands or
layers that could be followed across the land. He thought nothing
of travelling 3,000 kilometres in order to follow some distinctive
strata, and drew his maps without regard for national boundaries.
His first mineralogical map appeared as a submission to a learned
journal. The quality of the illustrations (*see* p.141) remains
impressive.

The same regions of the Auvergne documented by Guettard
were studied later by Nicolas Desmarest (1725–1815) in greater
detail. His large-scale engraved maps revealed topographical features, and in the process he moved towards the style utilized by
modern map-makers aiming at a 'user-friendly' appearance.

A SURVEYOR UNVEILS THE GEOLOGY OF
ENGLAND

(*Right*.) The geology of southern England was
painstakingly unravelled by an educated and self-
taught surveyor, William Smith (1769–1839). A
farmer's son, he walked the width of Britain in
search of geological data, and produced his
results in the form of brilliantly constructed maps
in which different strata were carefully coloured.
His final work was *A Delineation of the Strata of
England and Wales with part of Scotland* (1815),
and these exciting maps proved a great stimulus
to the science of geology.

It was another French inspiration that gave rise to the major work on stratification. The project was that of the prolific Georges L. C. F. D. Cuvier (1769–1832), rightly regarded as the founder of palaeontology. In 1796 he discovered large bones during excavations in Paris, and recognized them as being from an elephant. This caused him to examine geological science, and he turned to

The revelation that glaciers were moving came in
the middle of a summer vacation that Louis
Agassiz (1807–1873) took in the Alps. He
realized that the glaciers were the remains of an
earlier ice-age, and he found that they moved.
His results appeared in *Études sur les Glaciers*
(1840). He was invited to lecture in the United
States and later became Professor of Zoology at
Harvard University.

Alexandre Brongniart, professor at the Museum of Natural History in Paris. They produced their first joint memoir in 1808 and
followed this in 1811 with *Essai sur la géographie minéralogique des
environs de Paris* (Paris, 1811). Cuvier's major solo publication was
Récherches sur les ossements fossiles des quadrupeds, (4 vols, Paris,
1812). Cuvier was a nobleman – wealthy, debonair and successful.
Yet a more beautiful work by far was to join the list. Its author
would seem to be no match for his illustrious counterpart, for
William Smith (1769–1839) was born into a farming family in rural
Oxfordshire, lost his father early, and was largely left to play. His
hobby was the collecting of fossils, and by 1791 he had settled in
Somerset to supervise the construction gangs building the network
of canals. He later travelled widely across Britain to see canals
under construction, and this stimulated him to keep notes on rock

DESMAREST AND EUROPE'S ANCIENT VOLCANOES

(*Right.*) Nicholas Desmarest (1725–1815) worked on smaller areas in studying geology. His most influential work built on one of the most startling conclusions of Guettard – that parts of France had once been volcanic. Desmarest worked in the Auvergne and produced a chronology of volcanic eras. Many people resisted his insights, but his far-reaching views set in train much modern thinking on evolution.

Histoire de l'Académie Royale des Sciences, 1774

THE NEW GEOLOGY

Great geological insights resulted from the work of Jean Étienne Guettard (1715–1786). His were the first true geological maps. They attracted considerable interest. Guettard was an inveterate traveller and was known to journey more than 3,000 kilometres to obtain data.

Guettard, Jean Étienne, *Atlas et description minéralogiques de la France*, 1780

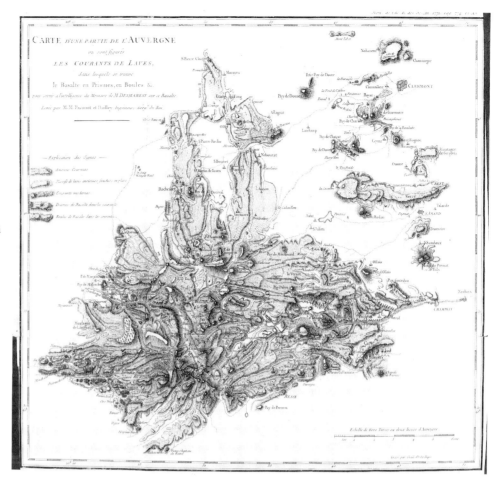

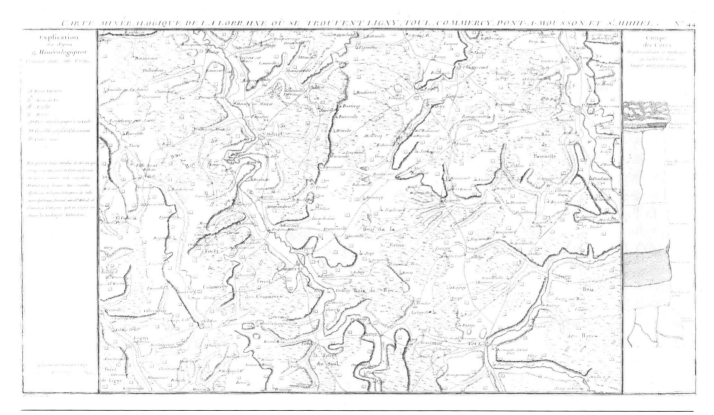

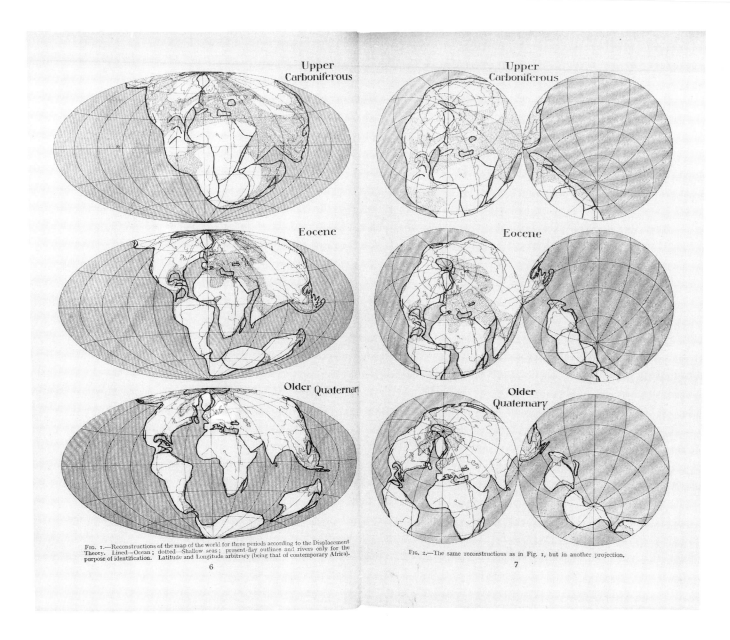

Upper Carboniferous

Eocene

Older Quaternary

Upper Carboniferous

Eocene

Older Quaternary

FIG. 1.—Reconstructions of the map of the world for three periods according to the Displacement Theory. Lined—Ocean; dotted—Shallow seas; present-day outlines and rivers only for the purpose of identification. Latitude and Longitude arbitrary (being that of contemporary Africa).

6

FIG. 2.—The same reconstructions as in Fig. 1, but in another projection.

7

formations and the stratification of fossil remains. He began to draw maps, to record geological data, and in 1815 he published *A Delineation of the Strata of England and Wales*, on a scale of five miles to the inch. With this project completed, he spent the next eight years publishing *Strata Identified by Organized Fossils*, and *Stratigraphical System of Organized Fossils*, together with the geological maps of 21 counties (intended as part of a complete atlas). Though Cuvier and Brongniart discovered the value of fossils in identifying strata in 1811, Smith had made that discovery in 1799.

Charles Lyell (1797–1875) was an indifferent scholar drawn to read the law; he was also an amateur geologist, and published the revolutionary *Principles of Geology* (3 vols, London, 1830–1833). It created a sensation; Charles Darwin took the book with him on his voyages, and Lyell saw 12 editions published during the following 45 years.

PLATE TECTONICS AND THE BIRTH OF GLOBAL GEOGRAPHY

The movement of the strata within the earth had been well established by the beginning of the twentieth century. It fell to a German geologist, Alfred Lothar Wegener (1880–1930), to show how the great plates of the earth's crust were capable of movement, too. His maps produced a storm of interest when they appeared. This plate is taken from the English edition of his book, *Origin of the Continents and Oceans* (1924).

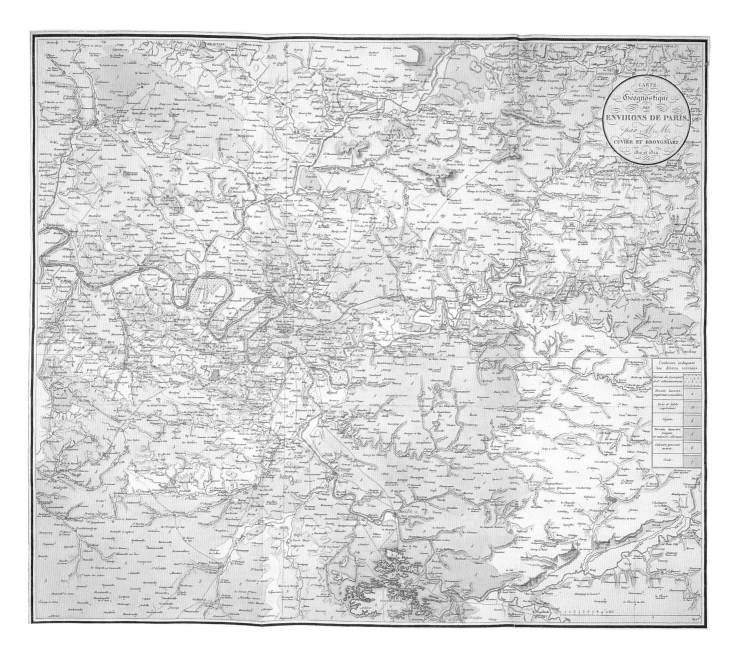

THE DOCUMENTATION OF THE DINOSAURS

The birth of the popularity of dinosaurs was due to the work of the French mineralogist, Georges Cuvier. He related fossils to the strata in which they were found, and published his results in his *Récherches sur les Ossements Fossiles*. His work on stratification with Alexander Brongniart did much to found that science. (*See* also p.138.)

Of later works we must refer to the eye-catching illustrations to Alfred Wegener's theory of continental drift. This far-reaching book appeared as *Die Entstehung der Kontinente und Ozeane* (Braunschweig, 1915). Alfred Lothar Wegener (1880–1930) was not the first to notice the way the continents seem to fit together, like pieces of a global jigsaw. That had been discussed by Baron Friedrich Heinrich Alexander von Humboldt (1769–1859) a century before. But whereas von Humboldt had concluded that the oceans had arisen by attrition and water erosion, Wegener postulated a slow process of drift. At the time he wrote, no such mechanism had been modelled; but his finely illustrated argument launched the theory of plate tectonics. That has been the underlying principle of global geology throughout recent years, and is the prime target of attention for students in the third millennium.

REFERENCES

[p.131] Ptolemy was believed to have been born at Alexandria, Egypt. He was the first great authority on geography. As is frequently the case, there are disputes and uncertainties over his involvement with all the works still extant. In his *Almagest*, for instance, he is understood to record the (since lost) major works of Hipparchus of Rhodes. The *Almagest* comprises 13 books:
1, 2: Outline of the Earth-centered Universe, chords, and the trigonometry of the celestial sphere.
3: Length of the year; movement of the Sun.
4: Months and the Moon, lunar inequalities.
5: Distances of Sun and Moon.
6: On Eclipses.
7, 8: Star catalogue, precession of the equinoxes.
9–13: Motions of the five major planets.
He also is reputed to have compiled an eight-volume *Geography*:
1: Mathematics of map-making.
2–7: Latitudes and longitudes of important sites; map of the known world (since lost).
8: Epilogue.
His third work, *Optics*, deals with reflection of light, mirrors, and tables of refraction (of little practical value, for they were not based on experimentation).

[p.133] Ussher, J. *Annales Veteris Testamenti*, London, 1650; the English translation appeared as *The Annals of the World*, London, 1658.

[p.137] René Just Haüy (1743–1822) was Professor of Mineralogy at the Museum of Natural History in Paris, and a colleague of Alexandre Brongniart. His two works on crystal structure were *Essai d'une theorie sur la structure des crystaux*, Paris, 1784; and *Traité de minéralogie*, 4 vols, Paris, 1801. Comparison of this theory may be made with Robert Hooke, *Micrographia*, p 82, scheme VII, London, 1665.

[p.137] Mention may be made of two other writers:
John Playfair (1748–1819) wrote a literary work extolling the theories of James Hutton (1726–1797). Hutton's paper, Theory of the Earth, had appeared as a paper in *Transactions of the Royal Society of Edinburgh*, 1 (2): 209–304, 1788; he argued that the formation of the continents was a gradual, rather than a cataclysmic, process. Playfair's lucid explanation of this view appeared as *Illustrations of the Huttonian Theory of the Earth* (Edinburgh, 1802) – the book is regarded as a landmark of clear exposition in science.
Horace B. de Saussure (1740–1799) was a Swiss traveller whose book *Voyage dans les Alpes*, 4 vols, Neuchâtel, 1779–1790, was the first to employ the term 'geology' – without apology – as a scientific term.

[p.137] A description of Hooke's diverse interests and his motivations in compiling the *Micrographia* may be found in:
Ford, Brian J., *The Revealing Lens – Mankind and the Microscope*, pp 36–48, London, 1973. See also Chapter Eight of the present volume.

[p.141] Guettard, J. E. 'Mémoire et carte minéralogique sur la nature & la situation des terrains qui traversent la France & l'Angleterre', *Mémoires de Mathématique, et de Physique*, Paris: 363–392, 1746.

Desmarest, N. Mémoire sur la détermination de trois époques de la nature par les produits des volcans, *Mémoires de l'Institut des sciences, lettres et arts*, 6: 219–289, 1806.
See also:
Werner, A. .G., *Von den äusserlichen Kennzeichen der Fossilien*, Leipzig, 1774.
Faujas de St-Fond, B. *Recherches sur les volcans éteints du Vivarais et du Velay*, Grenoble, 1778.

The world in space

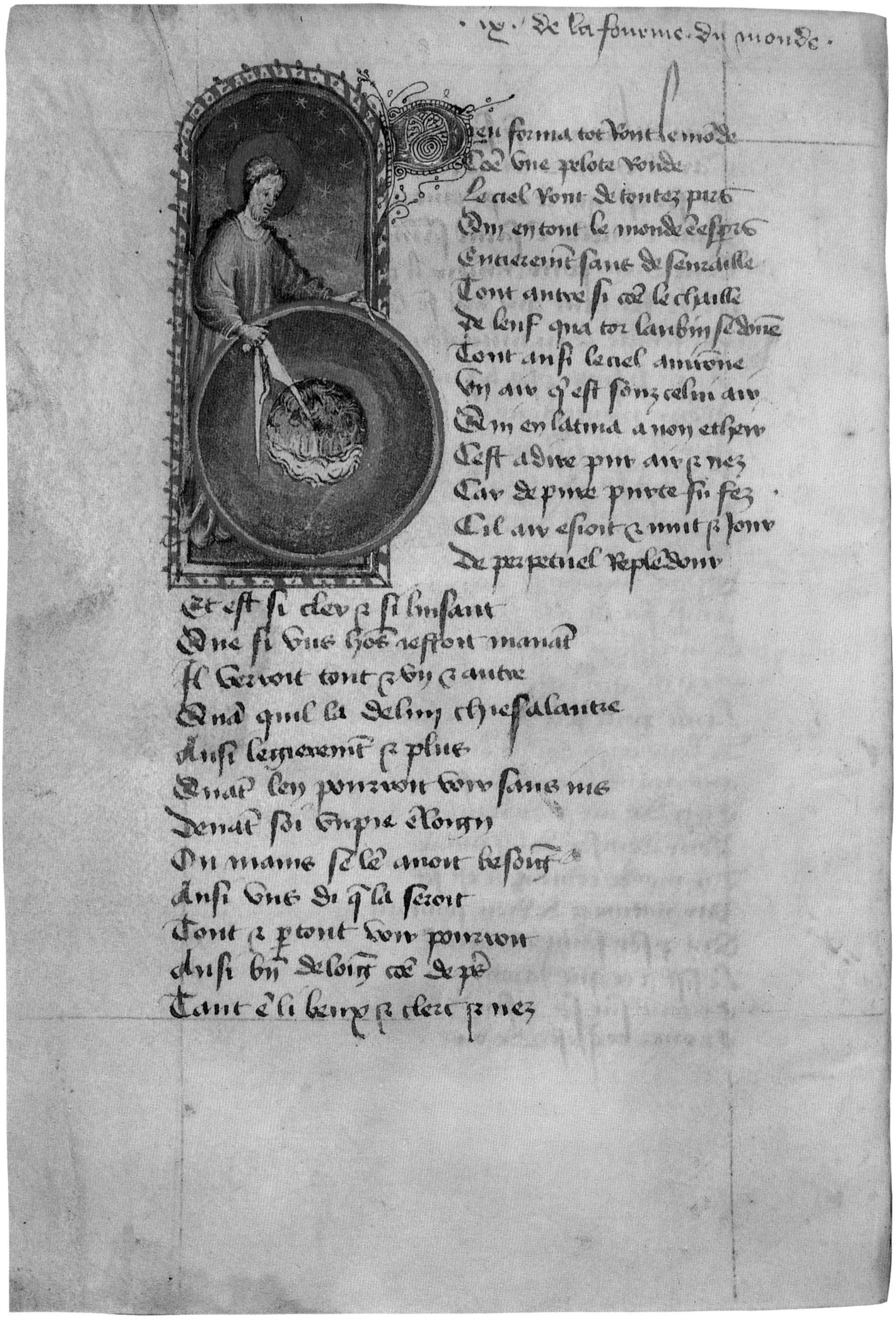
· x · De la fourme du monde ·
Deu forma tot ront le monde
Com une pelote ronde
Le ciel ront de toutez pars
Qui en tout le monde s'espars
Entierement sans desevraille
Tout autre si com le chaille
De l'euf qui tot l'aubun se done
Tout ansi le ciel avirone
Un air q'est sanz celui air
Qui en latin a non ether
C'est a dire pur air et nez
Car de pure purte fu fez
Cil air est tout et nuit et jour
De perpetuel resplendour
Et est si cler et si luisant
Que si uns hons reston manant
Il verroit tout et un et autre
Quanque il la de lui chies a l'autre
Ausi legierement et plus
Quant l'en porroit veoir sans nus
Denier soi orpie eloign
Ou mains se le avoit besoing
Ausi vues di que la seroit
Tout a partout voir porroit
Ausi bien de loing com de pres
Tant est li leus si clers et nez

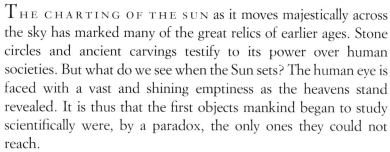

These fine images adorn a fifteenth-century English manuscript of *L'Image du Monde* by Gautier of Metz, who lived in the thirteenth century. The globe is seen floating in empty space, the Earth itself is seen clearly as a sphere, and there are reasoned explanations for the ellipses of the Moon and Sun.

British Library, Harley 334

THE CHARTING OF THE SUN as it moves majestically across the sky has marked many of the great relics of earlier ages. Stone circles and ancient carvings testify to its power over human societies. But what do we see when the Sun sets? The human eye is faced with a vast and shining emptiness as the heavens stand revealed. It is thus that the first objects mankind began to study scientifically were, by a paradox, the only ones they could not reach.

The length of the year had been known as 365 days as long ago as the fourth century BC and during the next century it was said that the planets revolved around the Sun, whilst our immense distance from the stars gave them their immobile appearance. The Greeks had found how to measure the angle of a star from the horizon by using an astrolabe. This is a simple device in which the vertical axis is found by using a plumb-line and the angles of stars may then be read from an engraved scale. The Arabs had always studied the stars, too; indeed some of their names (including Betelguese, Vega and Algol) are still used by modern astronomers. The Arabs took up the astrolabe and produced it in large numbers, and it was through them that the device was re-introduced to Europe. Arabs had visited China and India, and were experienced navigators. In turn, they passed to the developing Europeans their knowledge of the stars.

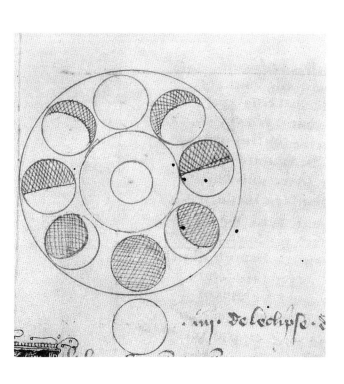

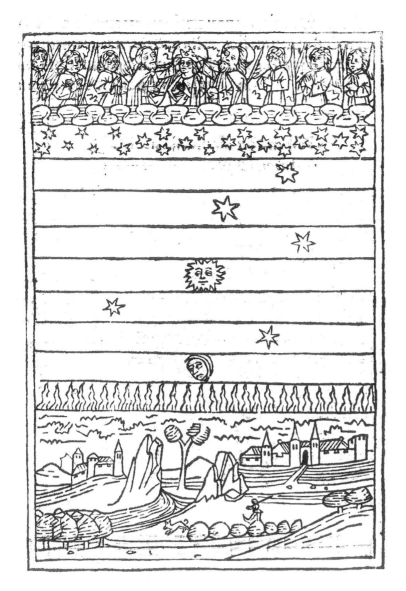

A MULTI-LAYERED COSMOS FROM THE 1400s
One section of Megenberg's *Buch der Natur* (1475) deals with the structure of the skies. His interpretation is a reflection of ancient beliefs. In this portrayal the planets lie in set strata in the heavens. Note the Moon (bottom) with two other bodies – Venus and Mercury – below the Sun.

The dawn of an era of scientific prophecy had been marked by the medieval scholar, the Franciscan, Roger Bacon (1214–1292). His planned encyclopaedia did not materialize, though he published three works: *Opus majus*, *Opus secondum*, and *Opus tertium*. His far-sightedness proved a considerable stimulus to speculative thought. For example –

'Machines for navigation can be made . . . so that the largest ships will be moved with a greater speed than if they were full of men. Cars can be made so that without animals they will move with unbelievable rapidity . . . also flying machines can be constructed. Machines can be made for walking in the sea and rivers, even to the bottom, without danger . . .'.

Many of the earliest printed books on astronomy reiterate ancient teachings – often based on a geocentric universe. The

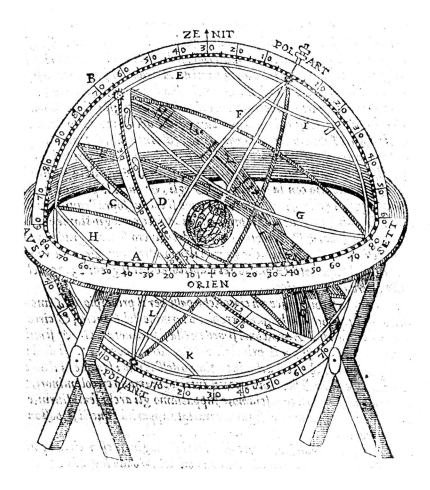

BRUNI'S *ARMONIA ASTRONOMICA* (1622)
Works on astronomy were often illustrated by
woodcuts – this example is from Part 1, page 9,
of *Armonia Astronomica & Geometrica* by the
Veronese philosopher Theophilus Bruni. The
armillary sphere in this illustration is not shown
with sufficient accuracy to enable readers to
construct their own. It serves only to act as a
guide to function.

diagrams published as illustrations are often perfunctorily produced. Konrad von Megenberg featured some artwork in his *Buch
der Natur* (*see* opposite), the stars in pre-ordained orbs like layers
in an onion.

But the first highly illustrated work of quality was by Petrus
Apianus (1495–1552); entitled *Astronomicum caesareum*, it was
printed in 1540 and contains many revolving volvelles among the
plates. The basis of discussion is that the Earth is centre of the
Universe, true; but Apianus correctly noted that the cometary tail
always points away from the Sun, and in any event the spectacular
extravagance of this book marks it out as the classical volume of
early astronomy.

For all the resurgence of interest in philosophical matters, little
progress was made in astronomy for 14 centuries following the
writing of Ptolemy's *Almagest* (the title is a blend of Arabic and Old
French). That step was taken by Nicolas Copernicus (1473–1543)
of Poland. His *De revolutionibus orbium coelestium libri V* of 1543
set out a stunning new synthesis: the Sun stood at the centre of the
solar system, and the planetary bodies moved in (circular) orbits.
The book had already existed in the form of notes for 30 years by
the time Copernicus found courage to publish, and his name
appears nowhere in the printed work. The author is anonymously

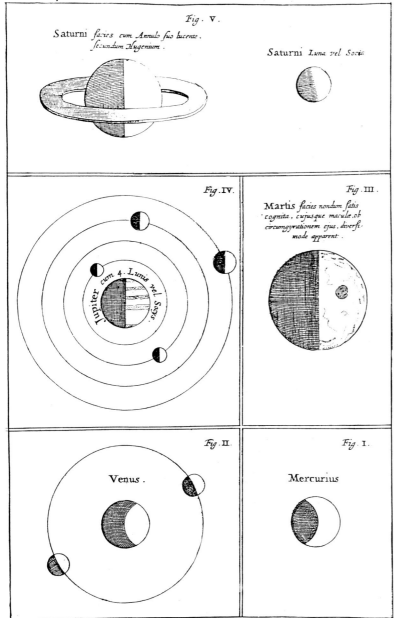

Fig. V.

Saturni *facies cum Annulo suo lucente.*
secundum Hugenium.

Saturni *Luna vel Socia*

Fig. IV.

Fig. III.

Martis *facies nondum satis*
cognita, cujusque maculæ, ob
circumgyrationem ejus, diversi-
mode apparent.

Jupiter cum 4. Lunis vel Sociis.

Fig. II.

Fig. I.

Venus.

Mercurius

THE PLANETS ILLUSTRATED BY KEPLER
IN 1611
(*Left*.) Johannes Kepler (1571–1630) has been
described as the most important discovery ever
made by Tycho Brahe (whose assistant Kepler
became in 1599). By 1609 he had – in
anticipation of Newton – recognized that a
falling body attracts the Earth, just as it is itself
attracted, and realized the elliptical nature of
orbits in space. His work put Aristotle in
perspective as a visionary whose model of the
heavens should now be discarded. Comparison
of this plate from *Dioptrice* with the modern view
of the planets demonstrates how prophetic
Kepler's work proved to be.

THE DUNHUANG STAR MAP OF 940 AD
(*Right*.) This manuscript star map has been
described by Joseph Needham as one of the
oldest star-charts in any civilisation. The Great
Bear may be recognized (left), whilst on the right
are constellations in Sagittarius and Capricornus,
drawn on a form of projection not unlike that of
Mercator. The use of white, black and yellow on
this illustration correspond with the three ancient
schools of astronomy (those of Shih Shen, Kan
Tê and Wu Hsien).

addressed as *domine praeceptor*, or 'master instructor'. For all its
importance, this great work exerted little immediate influence on
the conduct of investigation.

Tycho Brahe (1546–1601) was the son of a Danish nobleman
and the greatest observational astronomer prior to the invention of
the telescope. He was an extraordinary man. Having lost his nose
in a sabre duel he wore a metal replacement, and was entertained
by a metre-high court jester. His work was given a sense of urgency
by the supernova of 1572. It was a brilliant new star, brighter by far
than any star or planet, which took two years to subside. It caused a
good deal of comment amongst the public, for it was visible in
daylight. His account was published as *De nova stella*, Copenhagen,
1573. Brahe's other significant discovery was a young German

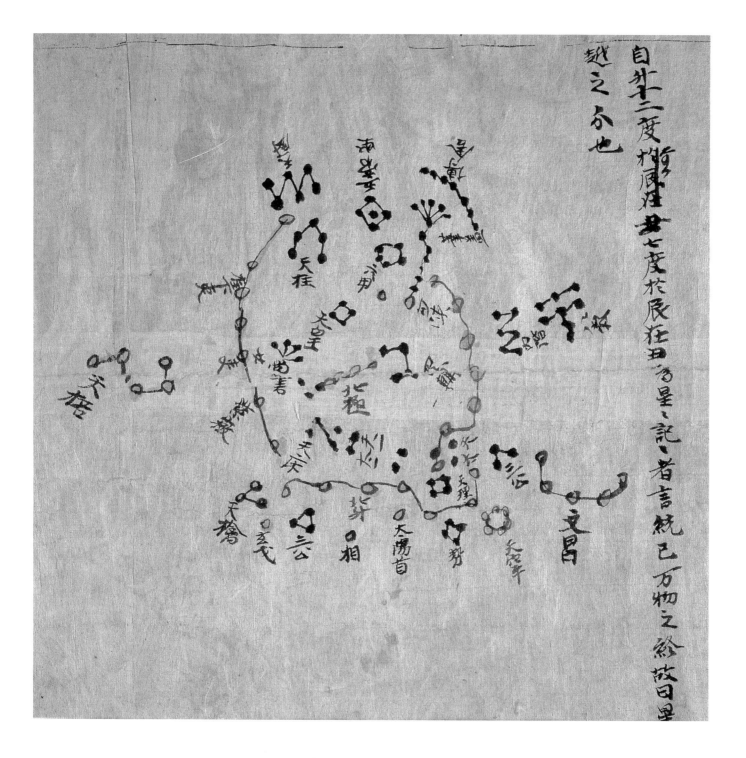

assistant, Johannes Kepler (1571–1630), who joined him in 1600. Tycho Brahe died suddenly in the following year and the young Kepler carried on the work alone. He published on refraction of light, founded a theory that explained the motion of the planets in elliptical orbits (he realized that the planet moved so as to sweep out equal areas of its orbit in a given unit of time – thus, they speeded up on approaching the Sun) and published several influential works. His orbital theories appeared in the *Astronomia nova* of 1609, and in the following year he obtained his first telescope.

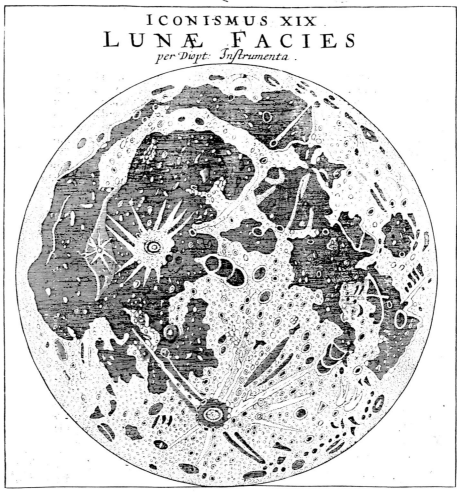

ICONISMUS XIX
LUNÆ FACIES
per Diopt: Instrumenta .

Within a year he published his *Dioptrice*, followed in 1619 by *De harmonice Mundi*, which hypothesized a range of harmonies in nature. The book also contained his third law of planetary motion (that the squares of the orbital periods of the planets vary with the cubes of their distance from the sun).

The telescope was first described in October 1608 and was first used in July 1609, according to most modern accounts. But an idea does not always arrive spontaneously: one may cite earlier references to the currency of the concept. For example, the *Longimetria* of Digges (*see* p.113) contains an intriguing reference to the telescope:

> 'But marvellous are the conclusions that may be performed by glasses concave and convex of a circular and parabolicall fourmes . . . by these kinde of glasses, or rather frames of them, placed in due angles, ye may not onely set out the proportion of an whole region, yea represent before your eye the lively image of every towne, village, etc . . . ye may be by due applycation of glasses in due proportion cause any peculiar house or roume thereof dilate and shew it selfe as in ample forme as

THE MOON ACCORDING TO JOHANNES KEPLER
This remarkable view of the full Moon appears in Book 5, page 176 of the *Dioptrice* of 1611. Kepler used telescopes with convex lenses as both objective and eyepiece. The Galilean telescope had a concave eyepiece lens. The advantage of Kepler's proposal is that the convex lenses offer a far wider field of view – but the disadvantage is that the image is inverted. Such telescopes are only of use for astronomy. Many of the features on this fine illustration can be reconciled with our present-day knowledge of the Moon.

GALILEO STUDIES THE MOON

In 1609 Galileo Galilei looked at the surface of the Moon and realized that its surface was hilly, irregular, and marked by mountains. Galileo drew the first illustrations of the lunar craters. He obtained his idea for the design of a telescope from the Netherlands, but went on to make his own instruments. Kepler, by contrast, admitted he was poor with his hands; he had his instruments made by local Bohemian or German craftsmen.

Galilei, Galileo, *Sidereus Nuncius*, 1610

the whole towne first appeared, so that ye may discerne any trifle, or reade any letter lying there open, especially if the sonne beames may come upon it.'

The use of lenses for the manufacture of a telescope is clearly set out here, but attention should be drawn to the phrase 'kinde of glasses, or rather *frames of them*,' to conclude that the lens elements were fitted into a telescope and not merely held in apposition. The writing of the Digges' account suggests that a telescope was available prior to 1571 (the date of publication) and it may therefore be presumed that the invention – discovery, perhaps – dates from the 1560s. The standard accounts might thus be modified (for instance Learner states: 'In the autumn of 1608 one of the spectacle-makers in . . . Middelburg in Holland realized that the lenses he held in his hands would make a useful telescope'). As for an earlier discovery, Bacon had written of being able to 'see thynges that were doon in other places'; but there is no hint here of anything other than futuristic guesswork on his part, and certainly no 'frame' or constructed telescope seems to have been in his mind.

A MANUSCRIPT ILLUSTRATION OF THE CONSTELLATIONS

(*Right.*) Here we see a fifteenth-century view of two major constellations, Libra and Scorpio. The linkage of stars into a recognizable pattern was a mnemonic used by navigators since prehistoric times. There is some correlation between Greek and Indian conventions, since explorers and traders connected the two cultures in antiquity. Chinese concepts remained entirely dissimilar to anything from further west.

British Library, Arundel 66, f. 41

A CAROLINGIAN COPY OF CICERO'S ARATEA

(*Left.*) This depiction of the heavens appears in a ninth-century manuscript of the *Aratea* of Cicero, which was derived from an earlier, late Antique, model. The manuscript had arrived in Canterbury by the late tenth century, where it was seen and copied by other scribes.

British Library, Harley MS 647, f.21v.

The drawings made by Galileo Galilei (1564–1642) revealed the craters on the moon, complexities around Saturn, sun-spots and the phases of Venus. The originals were made in pencil (preserved today at the National Library in Florence), with admirable wood-cuts that conveyed their essence being made for their publication in *Sidereus nuncius* ('starry messenger'), Venice, 1610. The *Opere di Galileo Galilei* appeared in Bologna (1655). The conclusions Galileo drew provoked a clash with religious authority and he agreed with Pope Urban VIII to publish his views under a neutralized title. *Dialogue on the Ebb and Flow of the Sea* was proposed by Galilei, but the Pope argued for the title *Dialogo ... sopra o due massimi sistemi del mondo, tolemaico e copernicano* (*Dialogue on two main systems of the world, Ptolemaic and Copernican*).

Although Galileo was granted his imprimatur, the book came out in Florence, rather than Rome, and when the Pope saw the resulting text he ordered the book to be withdrawn. Most of the

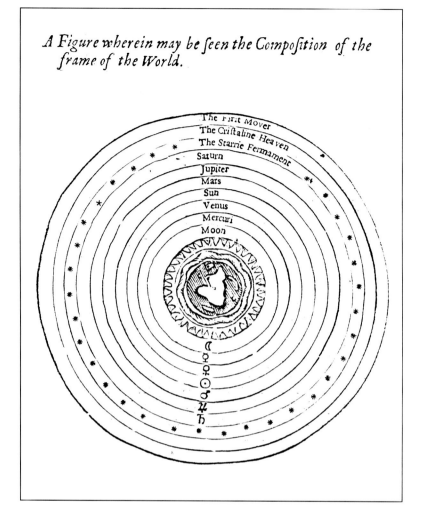

A Figure wherein may be seen the Compofition of the frame of the World.

The First Mover
The Criftaline Heaven
The Starrie Fermament
Saturn
Jupiter
Mars
Sun
Venus
Mercuri
Moon

THE PTOLEMAIC UNIVERSE
ILLUSTRATED IN 1661
Ptolemy's view of the Universe was essentially that of Aristotle, and both recapitulated the prehistoric view: the Earth lay in the middle of the Universe with the celestial bodies moving in their harmonious courses around it. Illustrated (*right*) are plates from the *Atlas Coelestis seu Harmonica Macrocosmica* by Andreas Cellarius published in 1661.

copies were burned by the Inquisition. This work, published in 1632, is in consequence one of the rarest in the history of astronomy. It contains a call for human reasoning to be the arbiter of realism and experimental observation to be the seat of truth.

The son of one of the most famous Dutch Renaissance figures Constantijn Huygens (1596–1687) became a natural successor to Galileo. He was Christiaan Huygens (1629–1695). The home of his parents was visited by such luminaries as René Descartes, whilst in adult life he met Newton and taught Leibniz. He postulated a wave front for the propagation of light, and delineated the irregular shape of Saturn's image as due to a ring system. Huygens's *Systema saturnium* appeared at The Hague in 1659.

Bearing in mind the relatively crude images recorded by Galileo – the shadows around the most prominent craters were used by him to attempt an estimate of the height of the crater walls – it is surprising to see the extraordinarily detailed maps of the moon published in 1647 by the German astronomer Johannes Hevel (who Latinized his surname to Hevelius) (1611–1687) which appeared as illustrations to his *Selenographia: sive, Lunae description*

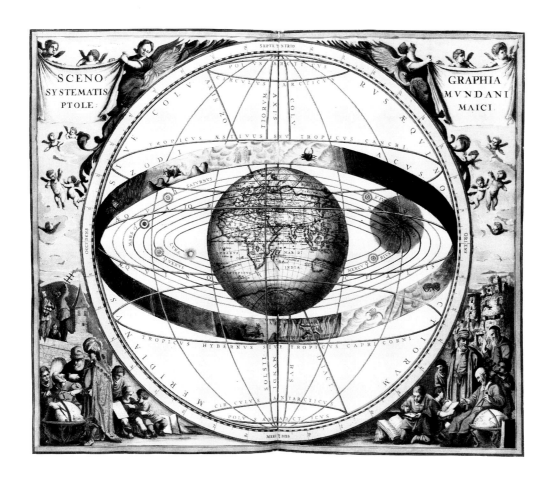

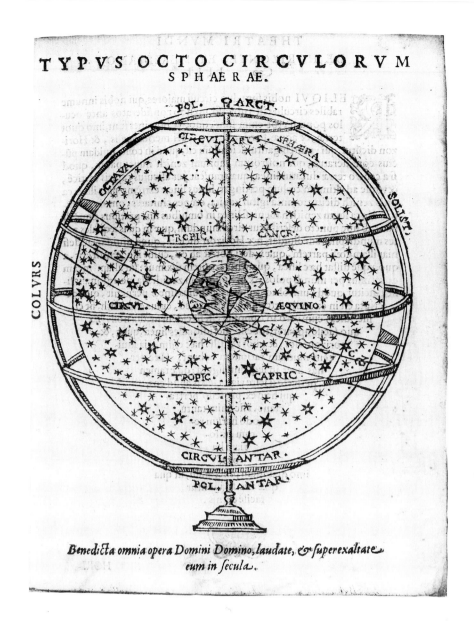

TYPVS OCTO CIRCVLORVM
SPHAE RAE.

Benedicta omnia opera Domini Domino, laudate, & superexaltate
eum in fecula.

Danzig, 1647. Ornamental illustrations decorated John Flamsteed's *British History of the Heavens*, 3 vols, London, 1725. Artistic delineations of mythological figures were woven through the star maps of the constellations.

William Herschel is known as the discoverer of the first new planet to be identified in recorded history (Uranus), but largely overlooked is his co-worker and sister Caroline, who prepared the lengthy and detailed tables in his works. Sir William Herschel (1738–1822) was a musician and was appointed organist at Bath, Somerset in 1766. In his spare time he began to study astronomy, and for this purpose ground his own 48-inch diameter reflecting telescope mirror. The discovery of Uranus – which at first he took to be a new comet – brought appointment as Royal Astronomer at a salary of £200 per annum. His largest telescope was 40 feet (12 metres) long and completed in 1789. It was not practically useful, however, and was last used for observation in 1815. F. W.

A STAR MAP FROM THE SIXTEENTH-CENTURY
This constellation map of the stars was published by Giovanni Paolo Gallucci in his *Theatrum mundi* (1588). The constellations themselves are well marked, but what makes this map historic is that it was the first time that stellar coordinates had been used in a chart of the heavens.

A PRIEST-ASTRONOMER IN THE CHINESE TRADITION
A European astronomer visited China and studied their ways. He was a Jesuit priest, Ferdinand Verbiest, whose Chinese name was Nan Huai-Jen. The illustration includes contemporaneous astronomical instruments, and was painted in 1675.

British Museum, Department of Japanese Antiquities
1906–12–20–1311

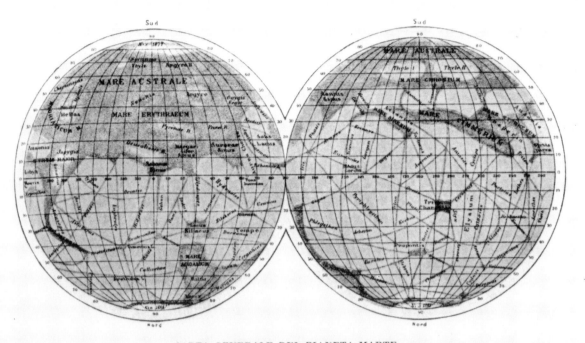

CARTA GENERALE DEL PIANETA MARTE

secondo le osservazioni fatte a Milano dal 1877 al presente.

NB. - *Le linee o strisce oscure che solcano i continenti sono in questa carta presentate nel loro stato semplice cioè come appaiono quando non sono geminate.*

II

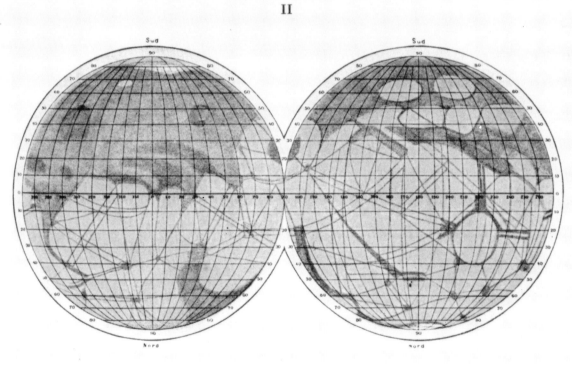

LE GEMINAZIONI DELLE LINEE OSCURE DEL PIANETA MARTE

quali furono osservate a Milano principalmente nel 1882 e nel 1888,

Herschel (his son) returned to the remains of the telescope in February 1839 and took a grainy photograph of it. The negative, on paper, and the notes which accompanied it, are now preserved in the Science Museum, London.

But this was a pointer to the way ahead, for photography was due to make a great impact on astronomy. The Daguerreotype had been invented in 1837, and by 1839 its inventor Daguerre himself tried to photograph the Moon using the process. The attempt failed: the plate was blackened by moonlight, but no image resulted. The first picture of the moon was taken during 1839–1840 in the United States, by John William Draper (1811–1882), Professor of Chemistry at the University of the City of New York. The sun was photographed by Hippolyte Fizeau and Léon Foucault at Paris in April 1845, and a total eclipse was successfully photographed in Sweden during July 1851. Detailed studies were made in 1877 by Giovanni Schiaparelli of the surface of Mars, the markings giving rise to the theory that intelligent beings on that planet had constructed a network of canals. As we now know, the appearance was due to the heavily cratered surface, details of which were not resolved by the telescope. Two years later, R. L. Maddox and Charles Bennett perfected the gelatine emulsion typical of more modern films, and during the 1880s many time-exposures of space showed heavenly bodies in a profusion invisible to the human eye. Observations of the small constellation known as the Pleiades were taken in Liverpool, England, by Isaac Roberts and in Paris, France, by Prosper and Paul Henry. The results showed more than 1400 stars in the cluster, whilst a later attempt by the Henrys increased the total to 2000. Six stars are normally visible to the naked eye; Galileo's telescope had increased that to 36; and as early as 1866 Rutherford had demonstrated 75 separate stars.

Photography was used to record spectra from the stars, an aid to chemical analysis. During the 1868 eclipse, the spectrum of the Sun was closely studied. Lines in the finely focussed spectrum of sunlight proved to correspond with known elements, and in this way the luminous gases could be associated with the elements they contained. The principle made it possible to analyse chemically distant bodies in space. After the eclipse, it occurred to several astronomers simultaneously that the light from the prominences on the Sun was sufficiently bright to be analysed whether there was an eclipse or not. One of these was Sir Joseph Lockyer (1836–1920) who showed that one of the lines did not correspond to any known element on Earth. Using the knowledge already available on the identity of the other elements whose lines were visible, Lockyer was able to calculate some of the properties of this unknown element. Edward Franklin, Professor of Chemistry at Imperial College, London, came up with a suitable name when Lockyer discussed the results with him. The Greek for 'sun' is *helios*, so Franklin offered the suggestion of 'helium' as the suitable name.

THE CANALS ON THE MARTIAN SURFACE

Observational astronomy continued apace once the telescope became popular in the seventeenth century. The belief that there might be life in other worlds was a continuing suspicion, and it was greatly encouraged by these studies of Mars by Giovanni Schiaparelli in 1877. He studied under F. G. W. Struve, and made his observations when the orbit of Mars brought it closer than normal to Earth. His careful drawings tended to unite what we now know as discrete structures into lines. This fed the body of opinion that there was life on Mars – clearly the lines were 'canals'. It is instructive to compare his Fig II with the etching published by Kepler (*see* page 150).

Schiaparelli, Giovanni, *Le Opere*, 1929

QVADRANS MVRALIS
SIVE TICHONICVS.

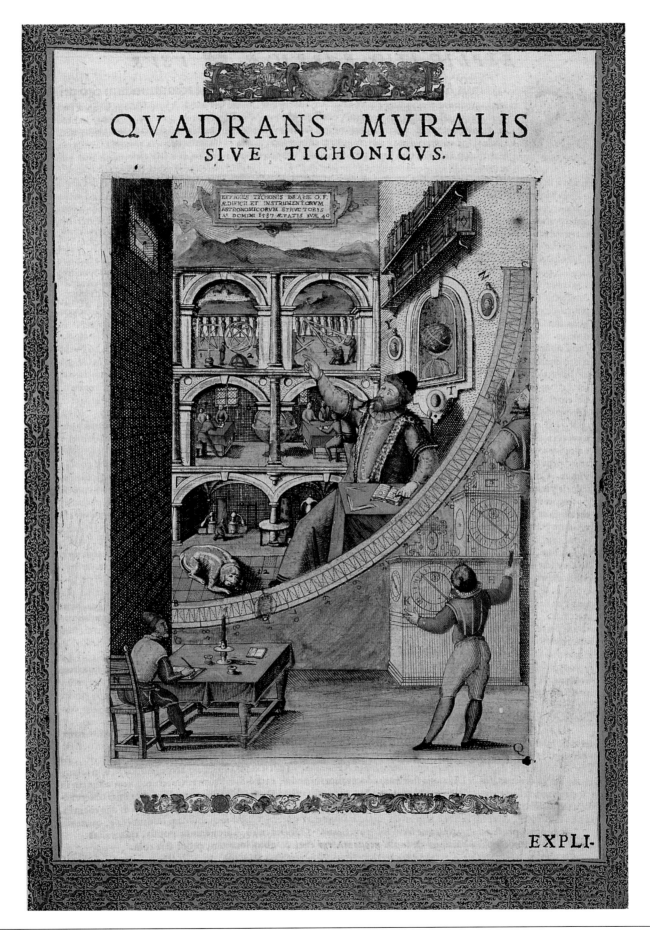

EFFIGIES TICHONIS BRAHE O. F.
ÆDIFICII ET INSTRUMENTORVM
ASTRONOMICORVM STRVCTORIS
AⁿDOMINI 1587 ÆTATIS SVÆ 40

EXPLI-

THE SURFACE OF THE MOON RECORDED BY A CAMERA
Experiments in the mid-nineteenth century showed that a photographic record of celestial objects might be possible. The most successful application of the technique was that of Warren de la Rue who produced a large number of pictures. The images were originated as colloidon positives, and copies were mounted on card for sale. This example is dated 22 September 1857 – it is signed to Sir John Herschel, the astronomer.
Science Museum, London

THE DANISH MASTER'S OBSERVATORY
(*Left.*) One of the greatest astronomers was Tycho Brahe (1546–1601) who lived and worked at Uraniborg, Denmark. This tinted engraving shows Brahe with his quadrant, installed in a room at his observatory. It was this instrument which enabled him to complete his great star catalogue (drawn up between 1575–1595). On Brahe's death in 1601 the work passed to his assistant, Kepler.
Brahe, Tycho, *Astronomiae Instaurata*, 1598

Later (in 1895) Sir William Ramsay (1852–1916) identified helium on Earth. An unidentified gas had been observed to be emitted from certain ores of uranium when they were heated. Ramsay, who had earlier discovered the inert gas argon, was approached about this problem in case the mystery gas was argon, too. In the event he found it was a new element, unknown to chemists. Its characteristics proved to match it with the unidentified gas whose spectrum Lockyer had detected on the Sun. Thus a new element was discovered through an image obtained in the course of astronomical research prior to its identification from any terrestrial source.

The final phase of astronomical illustration has been made possible by the use of wavelengths other than those of visible light, which have opened the windows on the radio astronomer's universe, and by telescopes above the atmosphere in space probes or satellites. The launch of the Hubble telescope in 1989 was heralded as a final stage in the exploration of space, but the mirror proved to have been wrongly shaped due to an elementary mechanical error. Though its images are helpful, there must be a certain wry satisfaction in knowing that, so late in our developing knowledge of the universe, a machinist's simple error can matter as much – and can occur as easily – as in the workshops where the study began a thousand years ago.

REFERENCE

[p.158] Learner, R. *Astronomy through the Telescope*, Van Nostrand Reinhold, 1981. Galileo's first use of a 9 × telescope is dated as 24 August, in a presentation to the Senate of Venice 1609; van Helden, A. 'Invention of the telescope', *Transactions of the American Philosophical Society*, 64 (4) 1977.

Hidden worlds,
hidden purposes

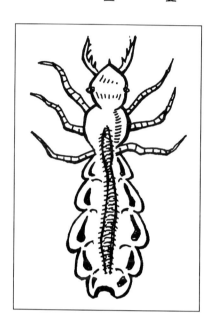

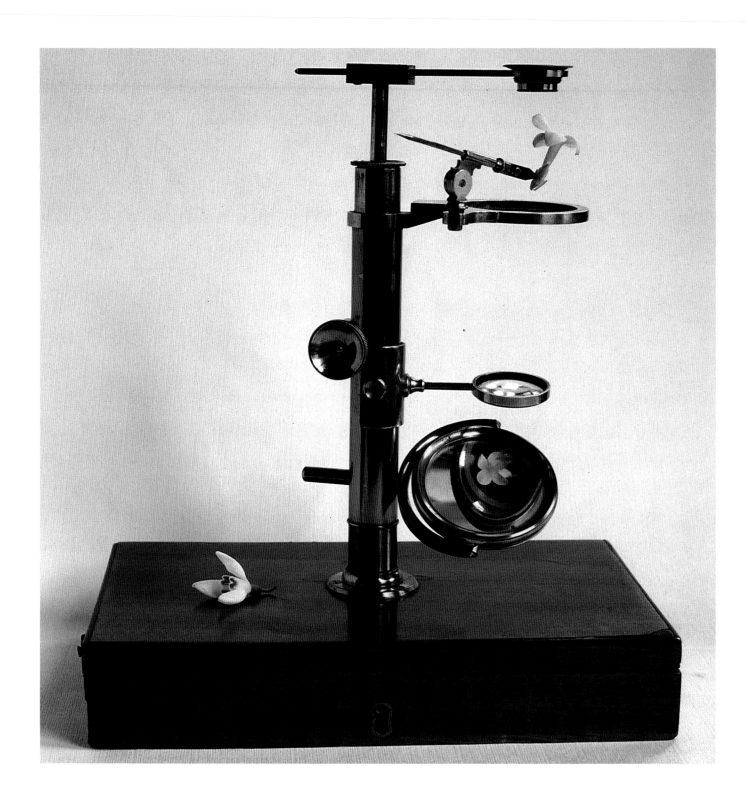

THE ILLUSTRATIONS OF SCIENTIFIC TEXTS show us the details of what lies around us. Only the microscope takes us within worlds we cannot otherwise know. Even the telescope, with its capacity to cut the distances between us and the recesses of space, leaves us tantalizingly far from the objects we wish to study. But even untutored peoples know that one makes a small object larger by bringing it closer to the eye. The only limiting factor is one's 8 inches or 20 cm would be a normal minimum for youthful eyes). The purpose of a microscope is to focus the image of the still-approaching specimen until it is, in effect, a tiny distance from the eye. The Victorian way of describing the power of a microscope objective lens was to cite its focal length in fractions of an inch. This was also the effective distance of the object. If a fly seemed intriguing at ten inches, think how much detail you might see with a $\frac{1}{12}$ inch objective!

The illustration of microscopic images was the most startling development of the scientific era, and the revelations offered to the specialist and to the public alike have been influential in almost every sphere of existence. Ancient maps and modern nuclear reactors; violin sounding-boards and the bacteria in a wound; the organs of sight in mammals, and the strangely similar organelles within the smallest of microbes; so many surprising sights have been presented to us through the use of microscopes to take us within the structures of our world. The development of micro-scopical illustration over more than four centuries perfectly paral-lels the systematic unravelling of scientific understanding.

Microscopical illustrations pose unique problems. The limits to resolution are strictures imposed by the physical nature of light. From the earliest days of microscopy, the available magnifications took investigators close to this ultimate barrier. Modern telescopes, printing processes, analytical machines and investigative apparatus from X-ray equipment to DNA electrophoresis devices, are all great improvements – in terms of efficiency – on their forerunners. This is uniquely different from the position occupied by the micro-scope, for some of the earliest instruments were close (in terms of optical performance) to the sophisticated optical microscopes of today.

Interpreting the image poses further difficulties unique to the discipline. Is a fine structure temporary, or a permanent feature? Is its colour real, or generated by defects in the lens? And when that has been successfully rationalized, we have the conceptual conun-drum of cause-and-effect. A microscopic organism may be demon-strated in a specific disease, and it may be assumed that it is the causative agent. But perhaps the disease produces an environment in which the micro-organisms can flourish. The supposed causa-tive agent may yet turn out to be a consequence of the condition.

We also lack artistic conventions that ally themselves with the singular structures of cells. Palaeolithic man used a range of

THE SIMPLE MICROSCOPE AS CONSTRUCTURED BY BANCKS
During the first three decades of the nineteenth century, the simple microscope reached its peak of development as an instrument of scientific research. This fine example was made by Bancks & Son of London for the Kew botanist George Bentham. Its focussing control and sub-stage condenser lens were antecedents of the design features of the achromatic compound microscopes which followed. The single lens produced remarkably little chromatic aberration (*see* p.194).

De variis figuris niuium.

pigments to portray creatures from the wild, just as a young child discovers how to utilize the artificiality of a line drawn on paper to circumscribe its own view of reality. But living cells are translucent, glistening, constantly in movement (sometimes the movement is barely apparent, other times a cell is moving rapidly and constantly changing its morphology). Though human bodies are composed of living cells, people as a rule do not know what they look like. Representing them on paper poses perceptual problems that make the 'canals on Mars' question seem simple in comparison.

The earliest illustrations featuring structures that are essentially microscopic appeared in 1555. The Bishop of Uppsala in Sweden, Olaus Magnus, produced a tome in that year which features a number of woodcuts, *Historia de Gentibus Septentrionalibus*. This book contains the first published pictures of skis and skates. Many of the pictures are crude, and there is little sense of fine artistry, but the first book features on page 37 a most historic illustration. The chapter is headed 'On the various forms of snow' and the illustration shows a scattered array of snowflakes. Some are fanciful, and may have their origins in the pre-Christian folklore of the Baltic lands: a small human hand and what looks like an eye are among them. But several of the shapes fit the categories of precipitation used today, and one is a clear and correctly proportioned hexagonal crystal of snow. The magnification of the image is approxi-

THE DAWN OF AWARENESS OF MICROSCOPICAL STRUCTURE

The earliest image of a microstructure known to the author is in the work of Olaus Magnus (1490–1557). He graduated at Rostock in 1513 and settled in his native Sweden until 1523 when he was exiled by the church to Rome. In 1555, in Rome, he published *Historia de Gentibus Septentrionalibus* – a survey of the people, climate and way of life in Sweden. Chapter xxII of the first book is decorated with this intriguing woodcut. Captioned *De variis figuris nivium* it shows a range of snowflake structures. Many are fictitious, but some can be related to the categories of structure recognized today. In contradiction to some recent accounts, Olaus Magnus clearly identified the six-pointed snowflake (near the bottom of the right-hand frame). It is the earliest known record of an essentially microscopic object.

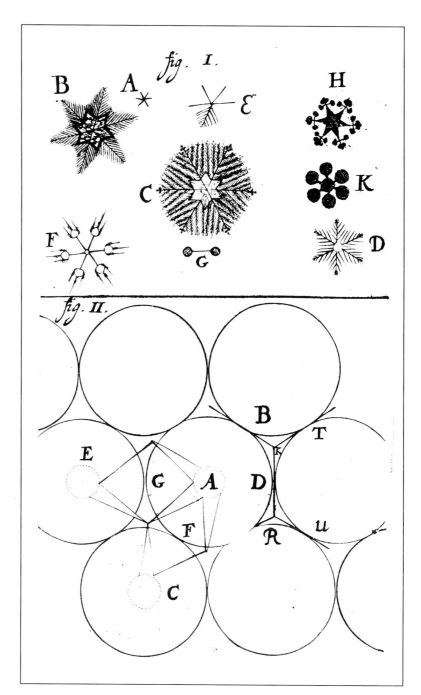

BARTHOLIN ESTABLISHES A LINEAGE
Thomas Bartholin (1616–1680) was a leading
Danish anatomist. He discovered the existence
of a separate lymphatic system. From his base in
Copenhagen – driven largely by a quest for a
cure for pulmonary tuberculosis – he travelled
south as far as Malta and wrote a number of
influential texts. In his *De Nivus usu Medico
Observationes Variae* (1661) this woodcut of
snowflakes appears. At 'A' appears a single flake,
life-size; but the rest are largely 'cartoons', unlike
flakes that exist in nature. These images and
their derivatives were destined to become 'icons'.
Their descendants decorate illustrations in the
twentieth century.

mately ten times. It is not known whether a lens was used to enlarge
the subject, for these snow crystals (many of which combine to
make a larger snowflake) can be discerned with the naked eye. The
lack of any feathery sub-structure inclines one to speculate that the
image was drawn directly from life. Whatever the truth of the
matter, here is an illustration of an essentially microscopic object in
a form one would recognize today.

Johannes Kepler wrote on the six-cornered snowflake in 1611.
During a snow flurry in Prague in 1610 he had noted single flakes
falling on his coat and his mind was drawn to this unexpected

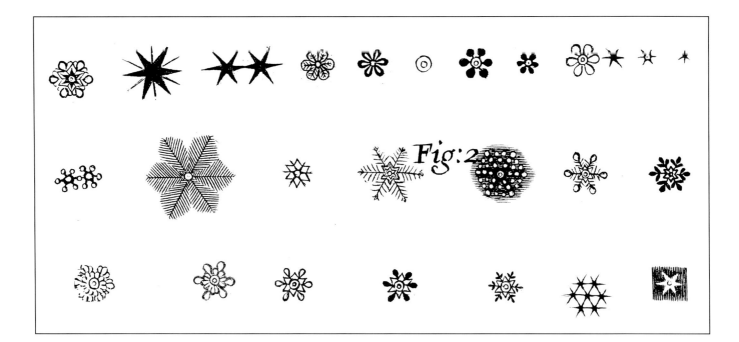

conformity: each had six branches, but why six? He had not been the first to note the phenomenon. Not only had the structure been published in 1551 but the ancient Chinese scholar Han Yin had noted that, whereas flowers had five petals, snowflakes had six; and his records date from the second century BC. Kepler's small book, *Seu De Nive Sexangula* (Frankfurt, 1611), contained a florid dissertation on the shape of snowflakes, though it was not illustrated.

The French philosopher René Descartes published the appearance of snowflakes at Amsterdam in 1635. They were intended to be representational, though the woodcuts show them as small images measuring 2–3 mm across and therefore not greatly larger than they are in reality. Interestingly, he did include at Fig. F two examples of crystals joined by a central column of ice. This is now known to be a recognized, though rare, variety of ice crystal.

The first illustration of snowflakes to give an indication of their structure and to present them in magnified form was published by Thomas Bartholin (1616–1680) in his *De Nivis usu Medico Observationes Variae* (Havniae, 1661) written in cooperation with his brother Erasmus (or Rasmus, 1625–1698). The illustration took the form of an engraving showing about six snow crystals magnified up to 20 times. The feathered nature of the crystalline branches of each crystal is clearly portrayed. At Fig. G, this illustration also shows a paired flake with a central column, as Descartes had earlier observed. So much for the good news, and now the bad: half of the examples shown are largely imaginary. Specimens B, C and D are accurate images of how snow appears under the microscope, whilst F, K and H are too fanciful to fit reality. Crystals like these do not occur in nature.

ROBERT HOOKE AS A PLAGIARIST OF BARTHOLIN

Robert Hooke's monumental work *Micrographia* includes these engravings of snowflakes. Hooke has been widely commended for his expertise in obtaining these pioneering studies. The snowflakes he shows, however, are not similar to snowflakes in life. Hooke had plagiarized Bartholin (whose own work was published four years earlier than Hooke's). In the process he perpetrated a series of images which influenced many succeeding studies.

A JAPANESE INTERPRETATION OF THE
HEXAGONAL SNOWFLAKE
(*Right.*) The earliest description of a six-pointed
snowflake dates from the Chinese philosopher
Han Ying about 135 BC. He wrote: 'Flowers . . .
of snow are always six-pointed'. These images
are from a Japanese publication *Sekka Zusetsu*
(1832) and are captioned: 'Illustrations of snow
blossoms'. There is much distortion in these
images, though they are clearly rooted in an
observation of snow specimens.

DESCARTES AND THE SNOWFLAKE
(*Below.*) René Descartes published these studies
of snowflakes based on research carried out in
1635. Some are eight-pointed, rather than six,
and many of the others are fanciful. The crystals
united by a central shaft (F) are a rare form of
crystallization familiar to modern meteorologists.
The examples at I, M and Z are inventions of the
imagination.

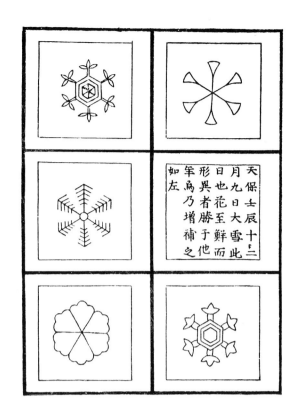

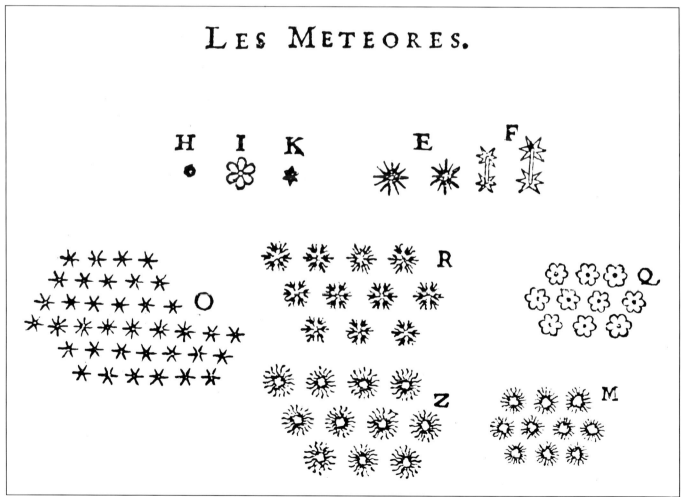

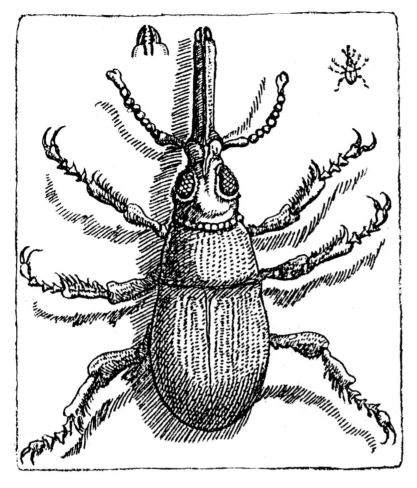

They do occur again, though, in Robert Hooke's folio volume
Micrographia (London, 1665, *see* above, p.170). Scheme VIII of this
impressive tome features studies of snow crystals drawn by Hooke
himself. We have no doubt of this, for the original drawing has
survived amongst Hooke's papers stored at the Royal Society –
unusually, since the others are believed to have been lost in the
Great Fire of London in 1666. There is a considerable degree of
clarity in Hooke's original study which has been cleverly contrived
in the engraver's interpretation. But the snowflakes that head the
figure are very different: wooden, solid, more like stylized blossoms
than crystals of snow, they are an assemblage of images which
Hooke has clearly plagiarized from the Bartholin engravings. Fig 4
of Hooke's Scheme VII clearly shows a single ray of a snow crystal
drawn from nature, just as Fig 3 portrays a melting specimen; but
the array of images that make up Fig 2 are a sorry selection alongside such clarity of illustration. Bartholin's Fig A is Hooke's No 12
(top line); Bartholin's B is Hooke's 4 (centre line); Bartholin's C is
Hooke's 2 (centre line); and the strange object of Bartholin's K is
Hooke's 7 & 8 (top line). Hooke is generally credited with publishing the first clear illustrations of snowflakes, and as he
frequently complained, his work was often plagiarized by others.

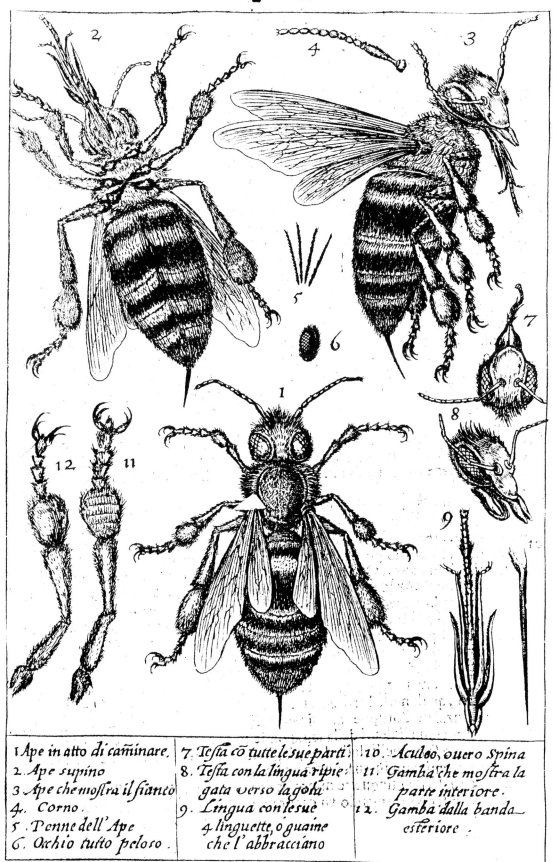

1.Ape in atto di caminare.	7. Teſta cō tutte le ſue parti	10. Aculeo, ouero Spina
2.Ape ſupino	8. Teſta con la linguà ripie	11. Gamba che moſtra la
3.Ape che moſtra il fianco	gata verſo lagolu	parte interiore.
4. Corno.	9. Lingua con le ſue	12. Gamba dalla banda
5.Penne dell'Ape	4 linguette, o guaine	esteriore.
6. Occhio tutto peloſo.	che l'abbracciano	

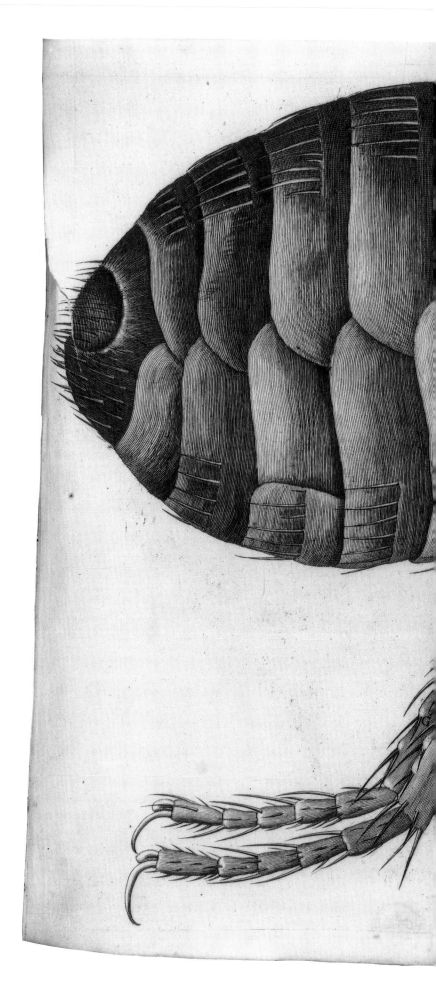

THE FLEA, FROM *MICROGRAPHIA*

This magnificent drawing of a flea is Plate 34 in
Robert Hooke's *Micrographia* (1665) The original
engraving was reproduced as a folded plate
measuring almost half a metre in length. The
plate was widely plagiarized in the next two
centuries. Hooke made his study by building up
a picture of the whole insect through a minute
examination of its separate regions. The
compound microscope he liked to use created a
distorted and indistinct image.

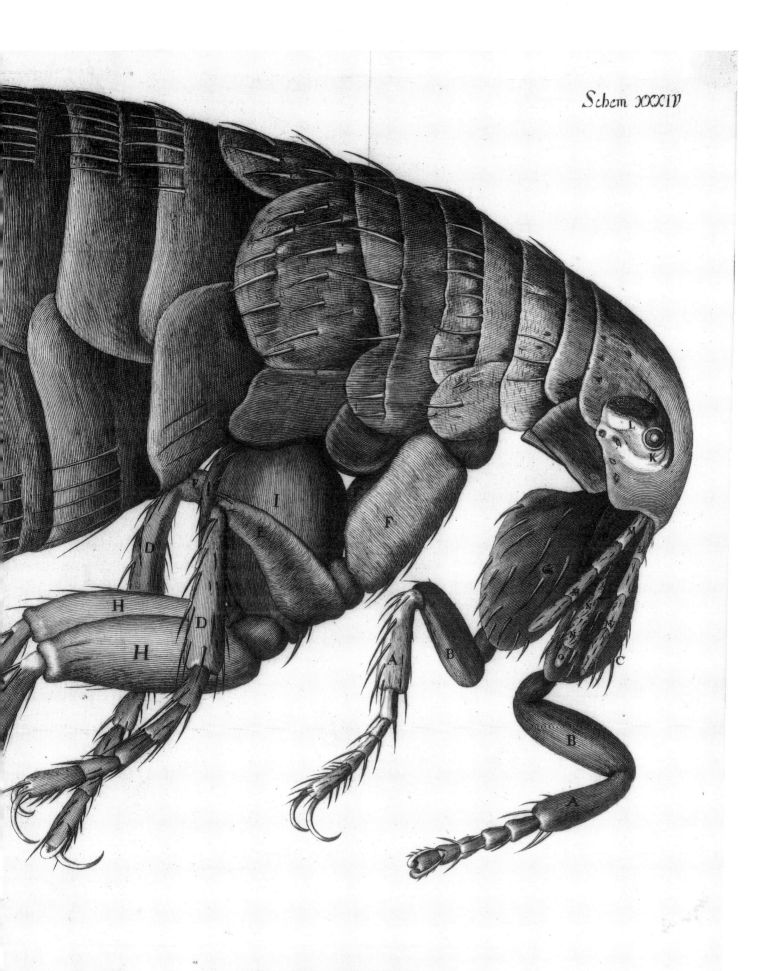

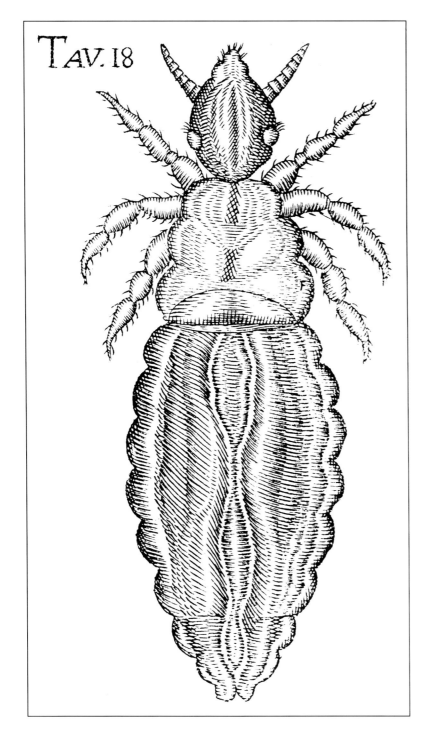

TAV. 18

Here we may turn the tables: Hooke was not breaking such new
ground with his studies after all, and in this instance he was the
plagiarist.

The first attempt at classification of snow crystals by shape was
made by Donato Rossetti at Revorno, Italy, in 1681, and an oriental
account was published by Toshitsura Oinokama – the feudal lord
of Koga, Japan – under the title *Sekka Zusetsu* (Pictures of Snow
Blossoms), 1832. As in Hooke's plate, the pictures are stylized and

PEDICULUS CAPITIS ENGRAVED BY
FRANCESCO REDI
(*Left.*) The head louse was featured by Francesco
Redi of Florence. His woodcut of 1668 is clearly
recognizable. In particular, the intestinal strand is
visible running the length of the abdomen. But
in terms of detail this plate is greatly inferior to
the study by Robert Hooke published several
years earlier.

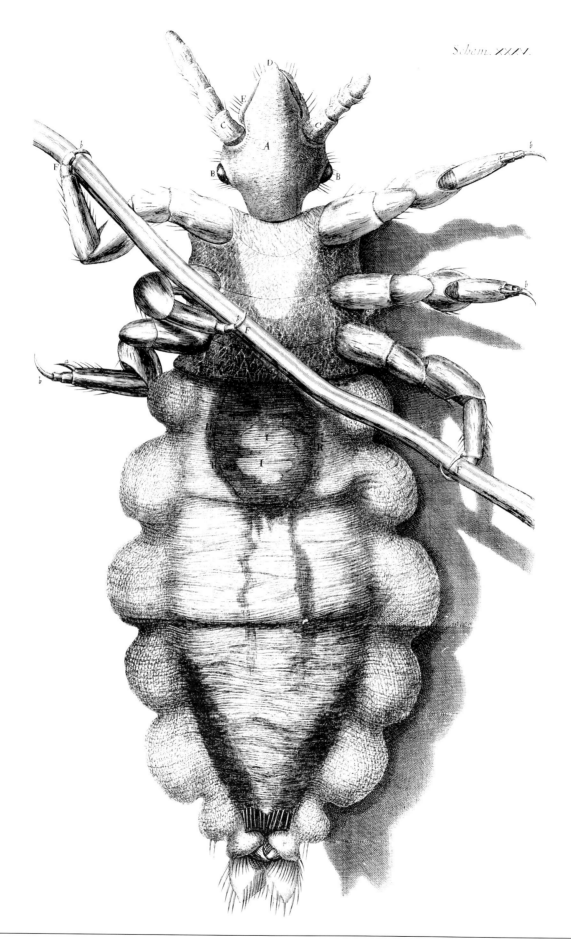

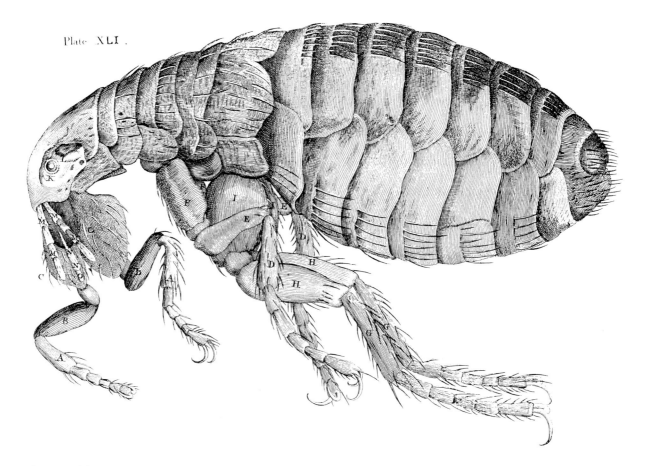

Plate XLI.

bear little resemblance to nature.

Yet the study of crystals made from ice is an uncomplicated strand of interest. There are none of the intricacies of interpretation, growth, life or death, that mark out the ground for dispute and misunderstanding in living organisms. It is in the realm of biological microscopy that the rôle of illustration becomes a crucial question of confidence.

The formal study of microscopy had its earliest impetus from Europe's oldest recorded 'scientific' organization, the Accademia Secretorum Naturae of Naples. It was founded in 1560 by Giambattista della Porta, a Neapolitan physician, and was formed of a group of like-minded enthusiasts who met at his home for discussion. Papal intervention led to its closure. But around 1602 a similar movement was founded in Rome by Prince Frederigo Cesi. It was the *Accademia dei Lincei*, the Academy of the Lynx. Attempts were made to close it down, but by 1609 it was firmly re-established with Giambattista della Porta and Galileo Galilei amongst the organizers. It continued to experience problems from the establishment, and when Galileo was indicted in 1633 it lost its will to survive. But its influence remained, and is marked by the author's description on the title-pages of the masterly *Dialogo* and the *Discorsi*; Galileo Galilei Linceo.

During the early years of its existence, the Academy of the Lynx

Plate XLII

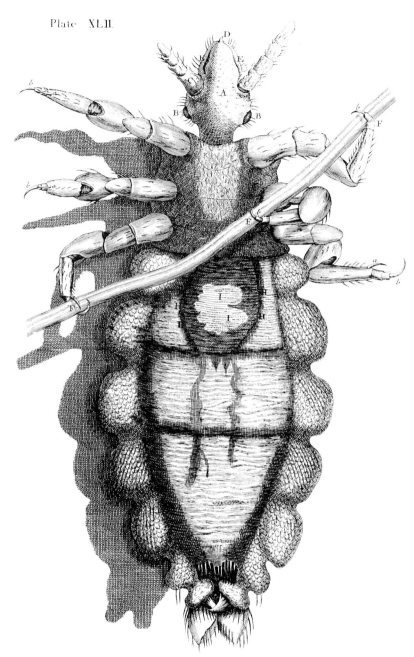

HOOKE'S ENGRAVINGS RESURFACE IN THE NINETEENTH CENTURY
Beautifully re-engraved versions of Hooke's flea (*left*) and louse (*right*) appeared in a popular reference work entitled *Blair's Prescription*, published in 1825. These are smaller images by far – one-quarter of the size of the original. But the skill of the engraver has been used to retain the detail of the Hooke plates.

conducted the first scientific investigations of objects through the microscope, and an active member of the group, Francesco Stelluti, published a sheet of engraved studies of the bee in 1625 (*see* p.173). He later produced a book of poems dedicated to the Cardinal Francesco Barberini entitled *Persio* and published in 1630. The Cardinal was nephew of Pope Urban VIII, and the family crest included three honey bees; so it seemed appropriate for Stelluti to re-use his engraved plate for the frontispiece of the book. This became the first published illustration of a biological specimen clearly magnified by a lens. Interestingly, the impressive images in Robert Hooke's *Micrographia* are not at a significantly higher magnification.

Illustrations of microscopes in use were first published in

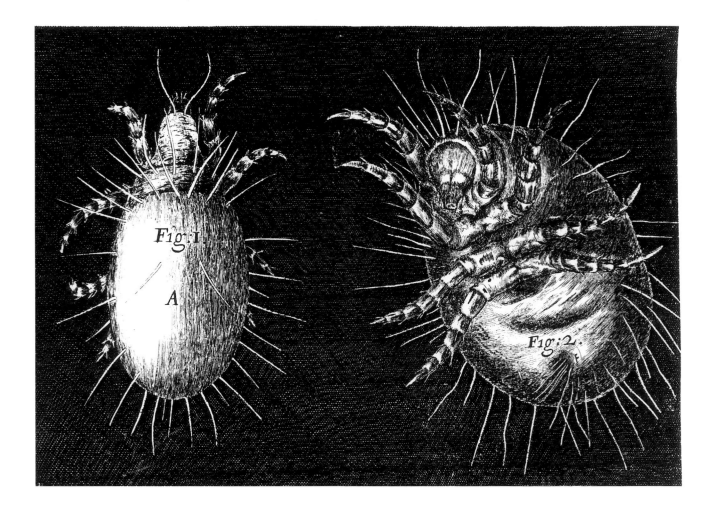

Descartes's *Dioptrique* of 1637, though they are restricted to diagrams, and they fail to include any examples of the results. Simple microscopes are also figured in the *Ars Magna Lucis et Umbrae*, (1646), though they are in the form of crude woodcuts and specimens are not shown. Some impression of the range of applications of microscopy is embodied in E. Gaspar Schott's book *Magia Universalis Naturae et artis* (1657) and F. Petrus Borellus devotes much of his *De Vero Telescopii Inventore* to descriptions of objects under the microscope. The first volume devoted to microscopy was a 24-page booklet, *L'Occhio della Mosca* ('The Eye of the Fly') published by Gioanbatista Hodierna in 1664. The illustrations are unremarkable – but all were made with the aid of a microscope.

Microscopical descriptions featured in one of the first books published through the newly formed Royal Society of London in 1663–1664. It was the *Experimental Philosophy in Three Books: Containing New Experiments Microscopical, Mercurial, Magnetical*, by Henry Power. But this was a slight work alongside Robert Hooke's great book. The illustrations in *Micrographia* are vivid and convey the three-dimensional clarity of the object with consider-

THE MITE OF ROBERT HOOKE'S *MICROGRAPHIA* (1665)

Many of Hooke's engravings were of insects shown at relatively low magnification. In this case he illustrates mites. These tiny arachnids are pictured at relatively high magnifications (150 times, perhaps) and are plainly seen through a simple microscope.

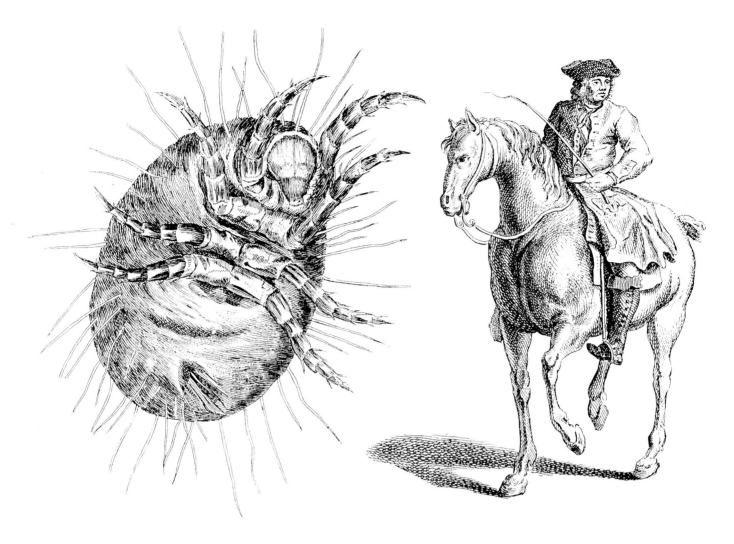

Albin borrows Hooke's illustration of a mite

In this illustration from 1720, each hair, each line, every detail is closely copied. The plate is from Eleazar Albin's *Natural History of English Insects*, published by Albin himself (seen here seated on his horse). The legend on the title page (as is usual with plagiarism of this sort) states: 'With Plates Curiously Engraven from Life'. Albin published valuable accounts of insect life, but was clearly not above plagiarizing the work of his predecessors·when he felt the need.

able accuracy. Hooke was involved with the preparation of the plates, and he paid much attention to the need to make the book fit the market – his first concern was to make sure nobody else was likely to produce a competing publication, his second was to include a host of subjects that were spectacular, rather than scientific (shavings from the beard, a louse and a flea, stinging hairs on a nettle leaf), and a third concern was the inclusion of a scattering of unrelated topics on which he had things to say. In consequence Hooke experienced some difficulties in finalizing arrangements for the publication, for there were many members of the Society who wished to disassociate themselves from his revolutionary views. However, the attractive nature of his illustrations drew admirers; Samual Pepys described his excitement over his purchase of the book in his *Diary*.

This book, more than any other, drew attention to the new era of scientific enquiry which was about to dawn. It was followed by Jan Swammerdam (1637–1680) whose work on insects revealed his ability to carry out fine dissection. The study of botanical microscopy was founded by the work of Nehemiah Grew (1641–

1712) who published several books on the subject, and also laid the groundwork for the discipline of comparative anatomy. His greatest work was the *Anatomy of Plants* (London, 1682) in which large plates explore the microscopic structure of a range of species. It followed an earlier quarto book of 1672, but – produced as a folio edition – featured the first extensive published illustrations in this field. Grew imposed a certain geometric precision on the distribution of cells which they lack in life, however; his figures lack the sense of realism found in Hooke.

Whereas Hooke was primarily concerned with magnifying the already visible (the stinging nettle *Urtica*, *Pediculus* the head louse, and *Pulex* the flea), the gifted Netherlands amateur Antony van Leeuwenhoek (1632–1723) discovered the new universe of microscopical life. The strength of his research lay largely in his unfettered ability to describe his observations and experiments, for Leeuwenhoek was unable to draw. Throughout his research career he used a limner to capture the details of what he observed. His drawings were of a high quality, not equalled until the Victorian era, and it is fair to say that some of the beauty of what he beheld is conveyed through the engraved plates prepared from the original drawings (made in red crayon or pencil on paper). The discovery of his specimens in 1981 provided me with a unique opportunity to compare his methods of microtechnique with his published

THE VIEW OF A FLEA OBTAINED BY HOOKE
Hooke utilized a microscope made by Christopher Cock in London. It offered a somewhat wider field of view than would be obtained with a simple (that is, single lens) microscope. But the distortion of the image is very clear in this recreation (by the author) of Hooke's demonstration. The quality of his published image is testimony to his diligence.

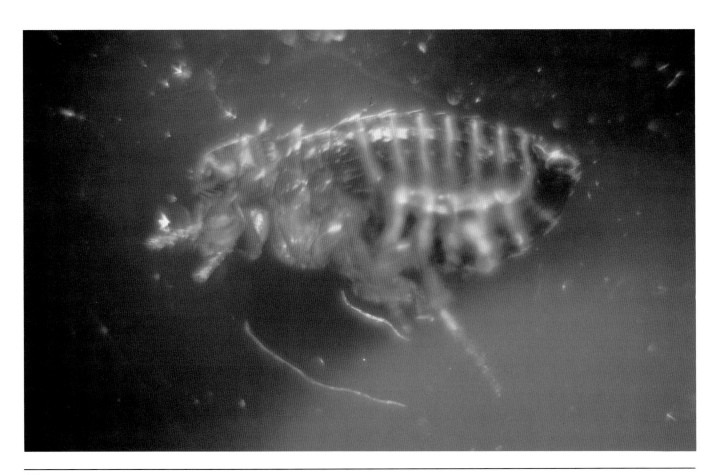

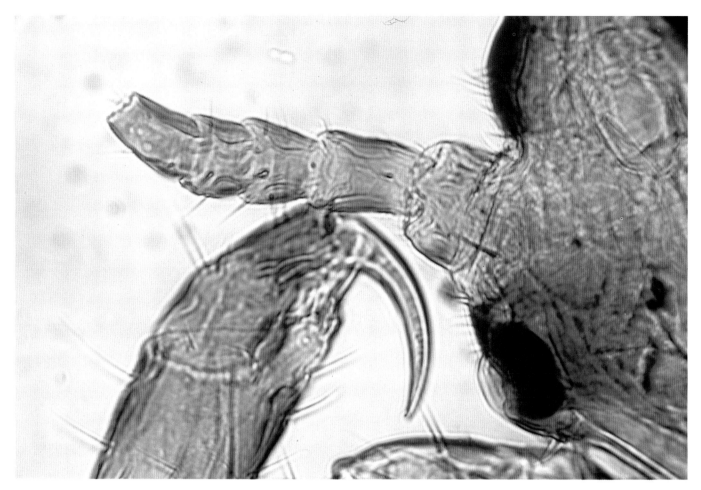

THE SIMPLE MICROSCOPE
DEMONSTRATES THE HEAD OF A LOUSE
Single lenses of short focal length are
inconvenient to use, as Hooke often wrote. But
they offered far more clarity of image than the
compound instrument could produce. In this
view we see the anterior portion of a louse
through a simple microscope of the kind used by
the seventeenth-century microscopist. The
increase in detail is clearly apparent.

accounts. Clifford Dobell published a list of Leeuwenhoek's publications in the biography he produced to mark the tercentenary of
Leeuwenhoek's birth in 1632.

A source of continuing controversy has been the ability of the
early microscopes to reveal as much as their users claimed.
Whereas Robert Hooke found a compound microscope useful for
his work because of its size, convenience and stability, the high-
magnification investigations were all carried out with simple microscopes, that is, instruments with a single magnifying lens. The small
biconvex lens remains the instrument of choice through to the
1840s and, for some people, even beyond that date.

Not that this meant the instruments were necessarily unsophisti
cated. George Adams the elder constructed a vast silver instrument
for King George III in 1761. It could be fitted with a range of
accessories (including simple lens systems for higher magnifications) but was clearly intended as a gesture of flamboyant gener-
osity – the instrument would be difficult to use with its sculptural
features in the way. The gradual evolution of the microscope gave
rise to the 'botanical' or 'aquatic' microscopes of the early nineteenth century. These were fitted with ingenious focussing mechanisms; some had a sub-stage condenser lens to focus light through
the specimen, even a mechanical stage to facilitate movement of the
preparation. With these the groundwork of modern microscopical

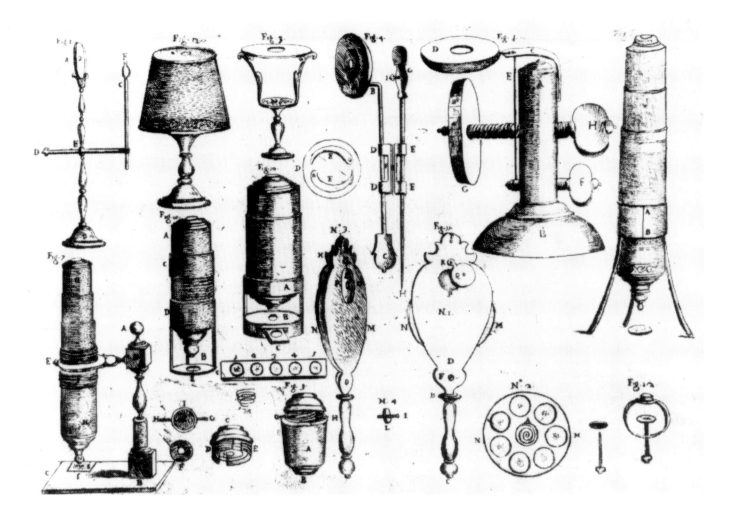

discovery was established. One of the manufacturers of these instruments in London was the family of Bancks, father and son. Microscopes were made by them for Robert Brown, who named the cell nucleus and after whom Brownian Movement is named; for the Hookers at Kew; for George Bentham the botanist (nephew of Jeremy Bentham, the lawyer and social reformer); for Charles Darwin – and were 'by appointment' to the Prince of Wales, later King George IV.

The clarity of image generated by these diminutive instruments is far greater than has been supposed. The literature of science abounds with the assertion that single lenses produce images that are 'distorted' and indistinct. But they embody only one significant drawback: chromatic aberration. This is the tendency of a lens to bring light of differing wavelengths (and therefore of different colours) to sharp focus at different distances from the lens. Red light is subject to less refraction than blue, and thus an image in blue light is brought to focus somewhat nearer the lens.

Commentators have therefore concluded that the images were blurred and fringed with rainbow hues. Sadly, such commentators have had a field day whereas microscopists interested in the re-

EARLY ITALIAN MICROSCOPES FROM 1686
A range of microscopes – compound (top right) and simple (lower middle) – are illustrated in this copper engraving. It was published in the *Nuove Inventioni di Tubi Ottici* of 1686. Note the disc of specimens (upper right) and the string-operated focussing control on a simple microscope.

SIMPLE MICROSCOPES IN USE IN 1800
A group of microscopes photographed by the
author at the Henri van Heurck Museum of the
Royal Zoological Society in Antwerp, Belgium.
They are typical of those in use around the end
of the eighteenth century. Each is a variation on
the Cuff microscope, and may be compared with
the instrument used by Brown (at the beginning
of this chapter) where the design came to its full
flowering. (*See* also p. 191.)

creation of these early experiments have been less in evidence. In
practice, chromatic aberration is less of a problem than might be
imagined. The image remains surprisingly clear when using a single
lens. The chromatism becomes manifest when small details are
inspected, for they sometimes acquire a tint of their own. Perhaps
they appear golden in colour, or lilac; clearly one is left wondering
whether this is the colour of the object or merely an optical artefact
of the lens. It was this preoccupation that led to the development of
compound lens systems which were corrected for the aberration.
With a fully corrected lens, colourless particles at the extreme range
of resolution were seen to generate colourless images, and the
spurious tint had gone. But this is not to decry the capacity of
simple microscopes for producing otherwise satisfactory images.
The limitations that seem so great to commentators who cannot use
them are much reduced when the instruments are put through
their paces under conditions analogous to those of the pioneers
who first employed them. Yet the scepticism remains: in 1991 an
independent consultant at Pasadena, California, was reported in
the prestigious magazine *Scientific American* to have made what he
later described as an important 'discovery': Brown could never

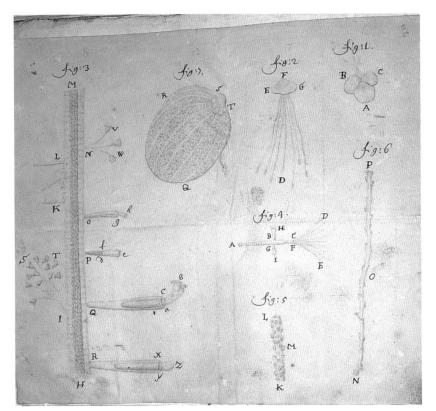

have observed the phenomenon, Brownian Movement, which now
bears his name. His microscope was too inefficient, the particles
too small. Had the writer of those words used the instruments
Brown himself employed, he would realize how unjustified is that
scepticism.

There is an historic reason that should confirm the belief that the
simple microscope played a crucial rôle in the history of science,
namely that most of the seminal discoveries (*le mot juste*) had been
made prior to the development of chromatically corrected lenses.
Leeuwenhoek himself had described spermatozoa, Hooke had
coined the term 'cell' (work carried out with his own simple microscope, of the kind later adopted by Leeuwenhoek), de Graaf had
discovered erythrocytes, the red blood cells or corpuscles, Brown
elicited the tenuous processes of fertilization in the gymnospermae
(the conifers); and by the time the chromatically corrected lens was
available for research, bacteria and protozoa, microscopic algae
and fungi, had been familiar sights for more than one and a half
centuries.

Although achromatic lenses had been produced experimentally
for some years before they were commercially available, they were
destined to restore the compound microscope to its position of
pre-eminence from the 1830s onwards. The microscope manufacturer Andrew Ross began to produce such a product in 1831, and

Plate IX.

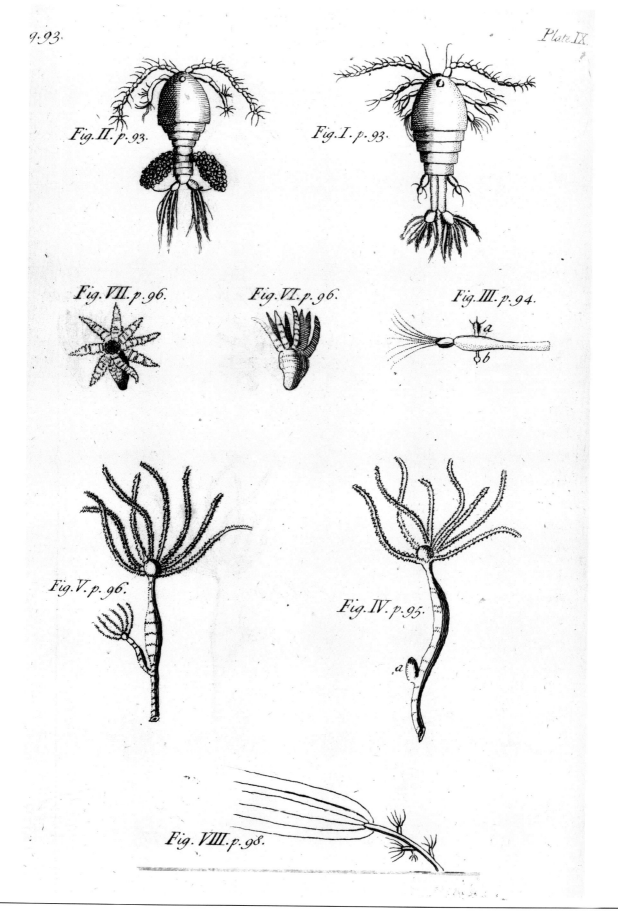

Fig.II. p.93.

Fig.I. p.93.

Fig.VII. p.96.

Fig.VI. p.96.

Fig.III. p.94.

Fig.V. p.96.

Fig.IV. p.95.

Fig.VIII. p.98.

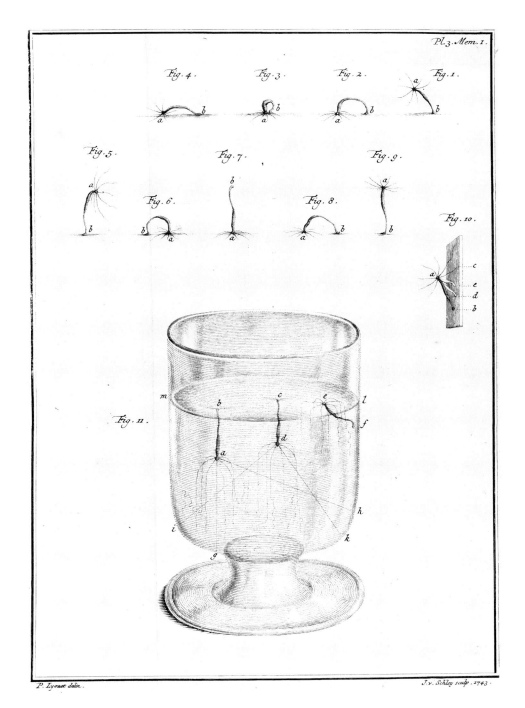

P. Lyonet delin.

J. v. Schley sculp. 1743.

THE HYDRA FROM TREMBLEY'S MASTER WORK

Abraham Trembley (1710–1784) was a Swiss tutor who studied *Hydra* whilst educating the children of the privileged in the Netherlands. The announcement of his discoveries was made in his *Mémoires . . . d'un genre des Polypes d'eau douce* of 1744. It created a great deal of interest. Partly this was because of the fantastic experiments he described – cutting, re-uniting, grafting the hydras – and also because *Hydra* itself is a common genus, and readers could easily obtain some for themselves.

by 1837 had made high-power achromatic objectives. In 1842 he revealed his first high aperture lens. By this time the concept was becoming popular; it had been about 1826 that the first practical achromatic microscope had been manufactured. The great era of 'brass and glass' erupted onto the commercial scene with manufacturers such as Andrew Ross, Hugh Powell and his partner P. H. Lealand, James Smith and Richard Beck. In 1866 Ernst Abbe was appointed as technical adviser to the German microscope manufacturers Carl Zeiss of Jena. He acted as adviser until 1875, when he was made a full partner in a company which prided

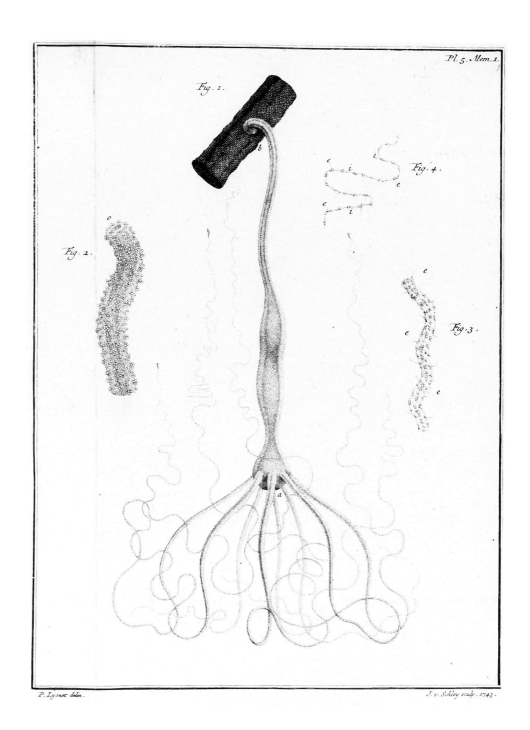

Pl. 5. Mem. 1.

Fig. 1.

Fig. 2.

Fig. 4.

Fig. 3.

P. Lyonet delin.

J. v. Schley sculp. 1743.

THE HYDROID TENTACLES EXTENDED

During his tuition activities, Trembley used the freshwater polyp *Hydra* for demonstration. He found it well matched for experimentation, and set in train a lengthy series of experiments. Both the plates reproduced here are from Trembley's *Mémoires* and have a vital quality that derives from study of the living creatures.

itself on the best possible working conditions for its workforce, and which pioneered the concept of social welfare on the shop floor. Abbe brought mathematical principles to the design of lenses. With his guidance, the science of lens production reached the limits imposed by the nature of light. With lenses manufactured in this manner, the range of microscopical investigations for professional and amateur became limitless, and many of the illustrations published in late nineteenth-century journals and textbooks were of a quality that exceeds that which is often seen today.

The studies of such organisms as the ciliated protozoa and

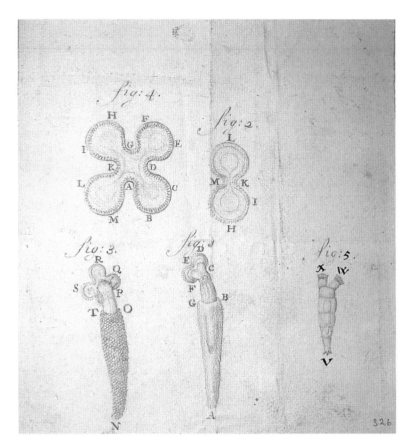

rotifers dating from this era are extraordinary examples of vivid
and accurate illustrations. Many were published as papers for the
journals of the Royal Microscopical Society and the Quekett
Microscopical Club, but a range of popular texts for the enthusiast
was also published. In these books, illustrations were at a premium. Jabez Hogg wrote the first edition of *The Microscope, its
History, Construction and Application* in 1854. It was still in production after the turn of the century (the 15th edition, 're-constructed,
re-written, revised and enlarged throughout' came out in 1898).
P. H. Gosse, a Fellow of the Royal Society, produced the first of his
*Evenings at the Microscope; or, Researches among the Minuter organs
and Forms of Animal Life*, in London during 1859; a 'new edition,
revised and annotated', came out in 1877. Lionel S. Beale (like
Gosse, a Fellow of the Royal Society) wrote *How to Work with the
Microscope*, which first appeared in 1857. By 1880 the fifth edition
was announced, 'revised throughout and much enlarged, with one
hundred plates, comprising more than six hundred engravings,
some printed in colours, and most of which have been drawn on
wood by the Author'. William Carpenter wrote *The Microscope and
its Revelations* (third edition 1862), and it became so successful that
it continued after his death with an 'Eighth Edition, the text
throughout reconstructed, enlarged, and revised by the Rev.
W. H. Dallinger, D.Sc., D.C.L., LL.D., F.R.S., &c, with XXII

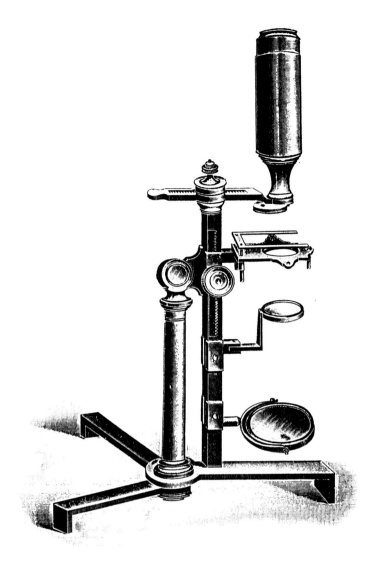

SCIENTIFIC INSTRUMENTS AND THE WOODEN BLOCK

The early method of making woodcuts extended past the middle of the eighteenth century, and were made by carving an image into the planed side of a softwood block. Towards the end of the 1700s, blocks were made from hardwood, and the image was engraved onto the end-grain. Detail was much finer, and the open vessels of the wood absorbed more ink. W. and S. Jones's 'Most Improved Microscope' dates from the end of the eighteenth century. This illustration appeared in the Royal Microscopical Society's *Catalogue of Instruments* published in 1928, when finely engraved wooden blocks were still widely used.

plates and nearly nine hundred wood engravings' in 1901. By this time the frontispiece took the form of photographic studies, pointing the way to the widespread use of the photomicrograph in microscopical textbooks.

These were all large and expansive tomes, aimed at the serious student. These great microscopes, often replete with accessories that most users would never utilize, were the 'executive toy' of the well-appointed Victorian household. They have their analogy in the personal computers of the modern era: every self-respecting successful individual would wish to own one, though few would know how to use them properly. They were objects of attainment. But the dilettante was catered for by smaller and less expensive works. The Honourable Mrs Ward wrote her book *The Microscope* (London, 1865) with the interest of 'every intelligent family' in mind, to quote from her Preface. It was based on her private study

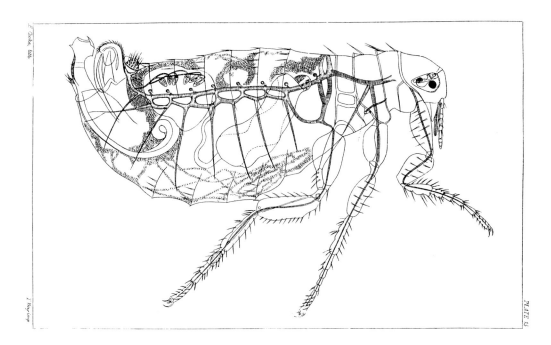

THE FLEA AS EXPLORED BY THE VICTORIAN MICROSCOPIST

(*Above*.) The flea remained an object of interest for microscopists. This delicately observed line drawing was published in the *Quekett Microscopical Journal*, 15: 15 (1870) and shows the high level of observational microscopy indulged in at the time by gentlemen microscopists. Study of the appendages reveals how Hooke was mistaken in his own published studies of the mouthparts of the flea.

DEGENERATION OF THE IMAGE IN INEXPERIENCED HANDS

(*Below*.) These portrayals of the flea and louse seem to be mere 'cartoons' – but they are not derived from earlier illustrations. Both represent the original work of J. H. Martin, who published *Microscopic Objects Figured and Described* in 1870. He used the best available compound instrument and was afforded the best of printing expertise. Yet his drawings are crude, flat, and lacking in detail. A comparison with Hooke's original studies almost exactly two centuries earlier shows how far Martin's view of realism had retreated back down the path.

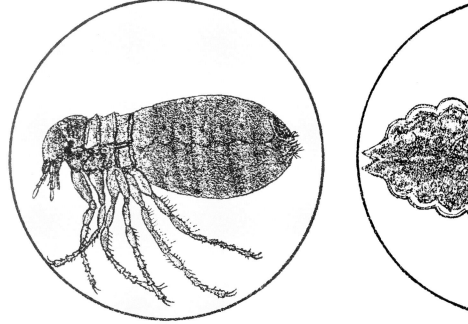

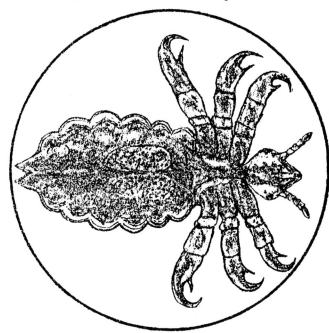

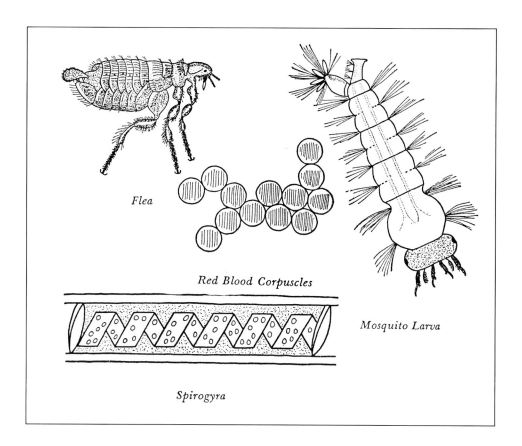

Flea

Red Blood Corpuscles

Mosquito Larva

Spirogyra

THE DEGENERATION OF OPTICAL MICROSCOPY

These sad and distorted images reveal the low level to which some more recent texts have sunk. Each of these images would compare poorly with those drawn by the pioneers in the seventeenth century (Robert Hooke and Antony van Leeuwenhoek produced greatly superior results for these specimens). The book from which they come is Richard Headstrom's *Adventures with a Microscope* (1941). The text of the book is a delight to read, and its enthusiasm for the subject thoroughly admirable. Yet some current texts on the optical microscope contain inferior images as illustrations. In a neglected science, the icon rules.

at her home in Moate, Ireland, and the 154 pages were illustrated by eight chromolithographic plates in full colour.

The 132-page *Common Objects of the Microscope* by the Rev. J. G. Wood, M.A., F.L.S., etc., ('twenty-first edition, 1896', though the editions were not dated in order to help sales), was a pocket-sized volume for the enthusiast. The plates were crowded with images printed in a pale grey ink, to encourage enthusiasts to colour in the objects as they observed them. Not all the works were of high quality, as must be anticipated in any mass-market sector of publishing. John H. Martin published *Microscopic Objects Figured and Described* in London during 1870. The 194 illustrations represent micrographs drawn in pencil and reproduced in circular borders to simulate the field of view. But the drawings are very poor and although the book represents the state of popular understanding at the time of publication its illustrations (*see* opposite) are far below the standard set by Hooke in 1665.

The turn of the century brought maturity to the illustration of works on microscopy. Half-tone reproduction of photomicrographs was becoming popular, and so was two- and three-colour printing of diagrams. The application of both technologies to microscopy is exemplified by the specialist work *Principles of Microscopy, being a Handbook to the Microscope* (London, 1906) by Sir A. E. Wright, M.D. (Dublin), F.R.S., Hon. D.Sc., (Dublin), Hon. F.R.C.S.I., which features half-tone micrographs with

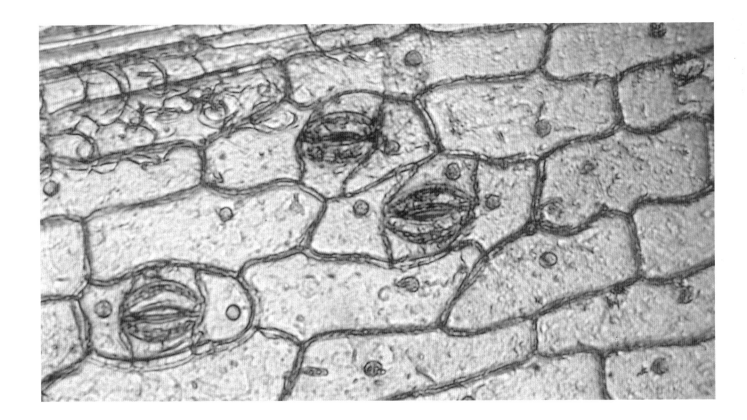

chromolithographic plates and woodcuts. Almroth Wright was a controversial figure. He was an opponent of the new political movement for feminism. And it was Wright who provided the gossip and anecdote that his good friend, Bernard Shaw, used in *The Doctor's Dilemma*. Wright was a proponent of serum therapy, believing that an injection could hold the answer to infectious diseases. The teaching had a profound effect on at least one young student, who went on to revolutionize modern medicine. The student was Alexander Fleming, discover of penicillin.

In more recent times, interest in optical microscopy has tended to wane. Microscopes were common enough in middle-class Victorian homes, but they are a domestic rarity now. The standard of microscopical illustration has reflected this change, for some of the representations in textbooks are hard to relate to reality. Once again, an orthodoxy has been created which bears little resemblances to the structures that exist in the specimen.

An example is Richard Headstrom's *Adventures with a Microscope* (Philadelphia, 1941). It is a wonderful text, filled with revelations and exciting to the mind. But its illustrations are a different matter. They take the form of crude ink diagrams and the few images that are truly representative of reality are plagiarized. Thus his illustration of *Allogramia*, though unattributed, is a rough copy of the beautiful illustration published many decades earlier by M. S. Schultze. Headstrom's text is carefully crafted and a delight to read, but the crude outlines and simplified diagrams are a

THE SIMPLE MICROSCOPE AND ORCHID EPIDERMIS

Robert Brown (1773–1858) was a most influential botanist. He documented Brownian Movement in 1828, named the plant nucleus, and described the naked ovule of the gymnospermae. He has often been accused of failure to see what he reported, largely because modern commentators are unable to concede that simple microscopes can generate high-quality images. This image shows orchid epidermis (the genus in which Brown made his momentous observations of a cell nucleus). The microscope used for this picture was Brown's own, now at the Linnean Society of London. In spite of the primitive nature of the lens, the image is remarkably good.

THE SEARCH FOR THE NATURE OF THE PROTOZOA

As the compound microscope became generally available during the nineteenth century, investigators pressed ahead with work on the amost diminutive animal organisms of all – the protozoa. This plate is from the book by C. G. Ehrenberg, *Die Infusionstierchen* (1838). It was the first major work to document these single-celled organisms since their discovery by Leeuwenhoek in 1674.

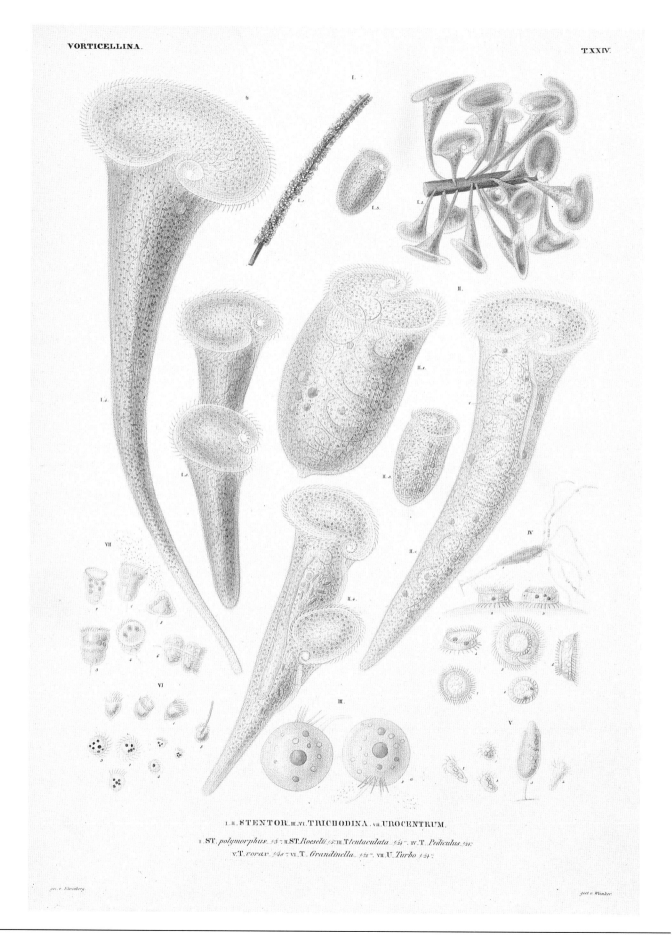

I.II. STENTOR. III.VI. TRICHODINA. VII. UROCENTRUM.

I. ST. polymorphus. 45 7. II. ST. Roeselii. 45. III. T. tentaculata. 44". IV. T. Pediculus. 49".

V. T. corax. 48 7. VI. T. Grandinella. 42". VII. U. Turbo 42 7.

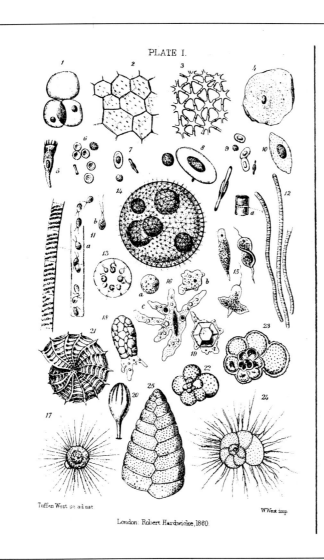

PLATE I.

HALF-HOURS

WITH

THE MICROSCOPE;

BEING A POPULAR GUIDE TO THE USE OF THE MICROSCOPE
AS A MEANS OF AMUSEMENT AND INSTRUCTION.

BY EDWIN LANKESTER, M.D.

ILLUSTRATED FROM NATURE,
BY
TUFFEN WEST.

A NEW EDITION.

LONDON:
ROBERT HARDWICKE, 192, PICCADILLY;
AND ALL BOOKSELLERS.

considerable step backwards from the standards of a previous century. Leeuwenhoek's rotifer studies from the seventeenth-century (the earliest in history) are far better than those in this still-used modern book.

More recent is the *World of the Microscope*, compiled by a team of eight scientists, writers and illustrators (Usborne, London, 1989). Rich with colour illustrations and lavishly designed, it is replete with grotesque images of cells, and the plant sections on pp.26–27 would compare poorly with the views that Nehemiah Grew published in the seventeenth century. Ray diagrams (p. 43) are inaccurate: the engravings in Descartes were of far higher quality.

We here see scientific illustration turning through a full circle. From the first revelations of microbial life in the seventeenth century we have moved to a peak of popularity – when illustrative standards were of a high order – and on to a stage of degeneration and lack of interest. A century ago, illustrations were clear and

A CROWDED FRONTISPIECE FOR A MICROSCOPICAL HANDBOOK
The late Victorian era was marked by a surge of popularity for microscopy. The home microscope was a direct antecedent to the home computer of more recent times. Pocketbooks became widespread, and it was normal for them to be illustrated with crowded plates containing as many images as possible. These specimens, gathered together as the frontispiece for Edwin Lankester's *Half-hours with the Microscope* (the first edition of which appeared in 1860) cover a typical range of preoccupations. Note *Volvox* (middle) and the red blood cells just above this spherical colony. The stellate cells of *Juncus* pith are visible (top) and so are the protozoa (lower middle). Interestingly, the amount of detail is not very much greater than that recorded by Leeuwenhoek in the seventeenth century.

Spiral bacteria: a triumph for the compound microscope

Spiral bacteria are larger than most bacterial cells, but their study demands critical illumination and a steady eye. These magnificent studies appeared in William B. Carpenter's *Microscope and its Revelations* (this from the eighth edition, edited by W. H. Dallinger, 1901). The fine flagella at each end of these tenuous cells are difficult to observe, and the sense of vitality in these active bacteria is well conveyed.

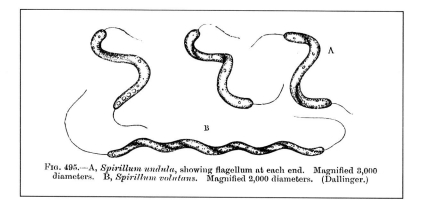

Fig. 495.—A, *Spirillum undula*, showing flagellum at each end. Magnified 3,000 diameters. B, *Spirillum volutans*. Magnified 2,000 diameters. (Dallinger.)

Jan Swammerdam documents aquatic insects

The free-swimming mosquito larva (left) and the pupa with its breathing tubes (right) were featured by Swammerdam in his celebrated book *Historia Insectorum Generalis* (1669), published while he was still in his twenties. The larva had been illustrated earlier, in Hooke's study of September 1663, but as isolated specimens on the slide. In young Swammerdam's study they were shown in a natural environment.

detailed. Only in the twentieth century have conference-goers regularly sat through images on a screen that have been obtained with a poorly focussed microscope, or were wrongly exposed.

Scientific images should represent the realities of discovery. When new phenomena are revealed by research, then the illustrations are the medium through which their appearance may be communicated, and its nature preserved in the literature of science. Since woodcuts and the era of the lithographic stone we have moved swiftly through photography and on towards compu-

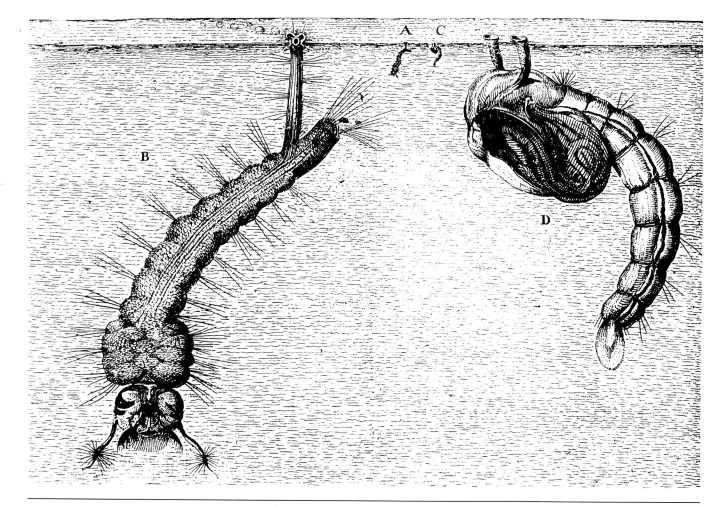

X. 550

R. Beck del.

ARACHNOIDISCUS JAPONICUS.

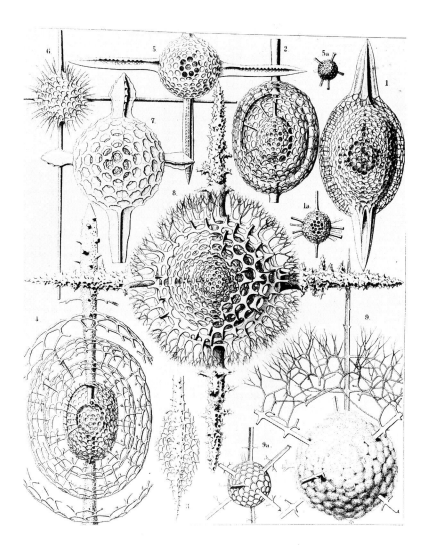

RADIOLARIAN SKELETONS FROM THE
SOUTH SEAS
Some of the Victorian illustrations of microscopic
life set standards few have since equalled. The
radiolarians in this plate are shown in careful
detail. It is from Ernst Haekel, *Reports on the
Scientific Results of* HMS Challenger, Zoology, vol
18 (1887). Microscopists were carried on
scientific expeditions since the time of Captain
James Cook in the 1720s.

THE CENTRIC DIATOM AND ITS
WOODCUT
These specimens of the discoid diatom identified
by Carpenter as *Arachnoidiscus japonicus*, is from
Microscope and its Revelations, reveal the diligence
with which woodcuts were prepared. Each of
these cells contains a siliceous network marked
with striae and microscopic pores. Each is
carefully cut into the surface, a task of immense
tedium and difficulty.

ter graphics and the use of false colour to dramatize an image.
Such, it is tempting to feel, is progress.

But when enthusiasms die and disciplines contract, no amount
of technical aid can restore reality to a degenerate image of science.
Authentic organisms are replaced by crude diagrams derived from
earlier orthodoxies, rather than from nature. Current attention to
the school and college curriculum in many nations is offering a new
opportunity to revive the excitement and the sense of wonder that
scientific revelation offers to the young mind. There are so many
opportunities for the public to witness the sights that science
reveals, as they strive to learn more about the world in which we
live. Optical microscopy should be a pinnacle of that process, and
not a poor relation. And it is certainly true that some of the exciting
drawings made by pioneers in a fervour of adventure and innovation many centuries ago are better, by far, than the dispirited and
uninspiring diagrams that we can find today.

Scientific illustration reveals more than we realize. The appearance of nature can surely be there. But so too is a resonance of
current preoccupations, and a commentary on the present state of

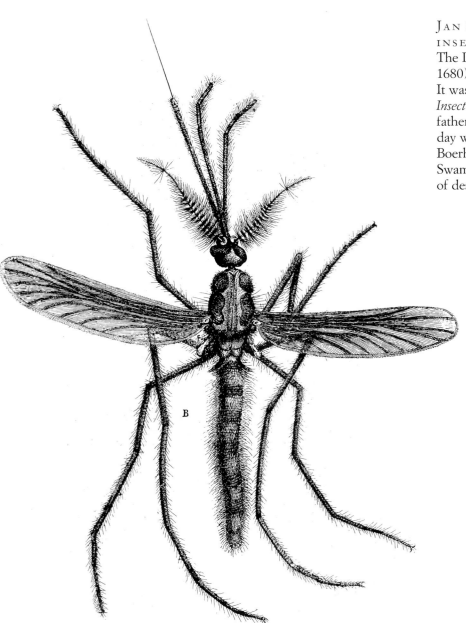

The Dutch naturalist Jan Swammerdam (1637–
1680) made this graphic portrayal of a mosquito.
It was published in his *Histoire Générale des
Insectes* of 1682. Swammerdam was reviled by his
father and his life's work only saw the light of
day when it was retrieved by Hermann
Boerhaave and published at his own expense.
Swammerdam is now remembered as the father
of descriptive entomology.

enthusiasms hidden within the scientific disciplines. As knowledge
develops, scientific illustration will record the state of human
understanding – not just what we know of science, of course; it says
as much about ourselves. The state of specialist art is a mirror of
self-image in the realm of science.

HOOKE COINS ONE OF THE GREAT TERMS
OF BIOLOGY (*right*)
On 12 April 1663, Robert Hooke presented to
the new Royal Society of London a study of cork
sections. They were enlarged with his compound
microscope, made by Christopher Cock, and
they revealed the porous structure of the tissue.
Because of their room-like nature Hooke named
them 'cells', and this usage has matured into the
present-day concept. This was not the first time
he had observed them, however. A week earlier
he had demonstrated a specimen of moss, and
Hooke's figure in Scheme 13 of *Micrographia*
(1665) shows that he first observed cells in that
specimen.

Fig:1.

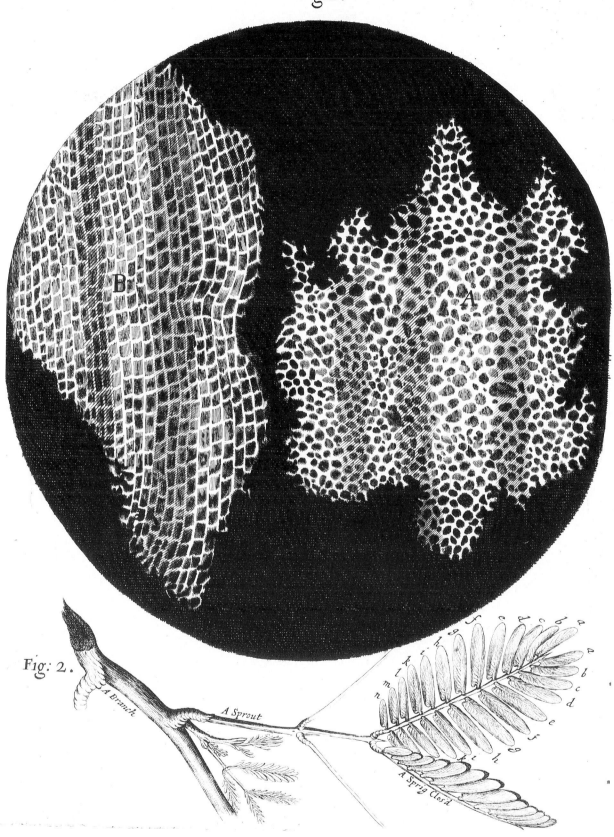

Fig:2.

REFERENCES

[p.168] Olao Magno Gotho, *Historia de gentibus septentrionalibus,* Liber Primus: De variis figuris nivium, Cap XXII p 37, 1555.

[p.172] Hooke's images have been discussed elsewhere:
Ford, Brian J. *The Leeuwenhoek Legacy,* pp 31–34, London and Bristol, 1991.

[p.171] Ukichiro Nakaya, *Snow Crystals, Natural and Artificial,* pp 1–5, Harvard, 1954.
The use of the camera gave rise to a definitive study of structure, Bentley, W. A., *Snow Crystals,* New York, 1931, and to Seligman, G., *Snow Structure and Ski Fields,* London 1936.
Snow crystals are also published for their aesthetic appeal as much as for scientific interest. See for example
LaChapelle, E. R., *Field Guide to Snow Crystals,* Seattle and London, 1970, and Ford, Brian J, 'Snowflakes', *New Knowledge,* 5 (5): 850, March 1966.

[p.173] Stelluti, F. *Persio Tradotto in verso sciolto* . . . Rome, 1630; features enlarged study of bee (p 52) and weevil (p 127).
It may be noted that Bonanni, in his *Micrographia Curiosa,* suggests that the fifty plates of George Hüfnagel's book of insects (Frankfurt, 1592) were also prepared with the aid of a microscope.

[p.181] Swammerdam, J. *Historia Insectorum Generalis, ofte Algemeene Verhandeling van de Bloedeloose Dierkens,* Utrecht, 1669 (translated into Latin by Henninius, 1682); and
—*Bybel der Natur of Historie der Insecten/Bilbiae Naturae, sive Historia Insectorum,* 2 folio vols, Leyden, 1737, 1738.
Grew, N. *The Anatomy of Vegetables Begun,* London, 1672.
—*Cosmologia Sacra,* etc, London, 1701.
—*Museum Regalis Societatis, or a Catalogue & Description of the Natural and Artificial Rarities belonging to the Royal Society,* London, 1681.
Grew also wrote a short account, adding little to the accounts of his predecessors, entitled 'Observations touching the Nature of Snow', published in *Philosophical Transactions,* 8 (92): 193–196, March 1673. See: LeFanu, W., *Nehemiah Grew M.D., F.R.S., a study and bibliography of his Writings,* Winchester and Detroit, 1990.

[p.182] Other pioneering works in microscopy include:
Redi, F., *Esperienze intorno alla Generazione degl'Insetti,* Florence, 1678.

—*Osservazioni intorno agli Animali Viventi che si trovano negli occhiali,* Florence, 1684.
de Graaf, R., *De mulierum organis generationi,* Amsterdam, 1672.
Cherubin d'Orleans, *La Vision Parfait,* Paris, 1677.
An extraordinary range of microscopes appeared in the illustrations to Johannes Zahn's *Oculus artificialis* . . . which was published first in Würzburg in 1685, but appeared in a grander guise at Nürnberg, 1702. Christiaan Huygens produced an impressive output of research, which was published in *Oeuvres Complètes,* The Hague, 1888–1916. The structure of wood, beautifully documented by Leeuwenhoek's limners, was described by John Hill in *The Construction of Timber from Its Early Growth,* London 1770, but he also brought together insect studies in his lesser-known *A Decade of Curious Insects . . . as they appear enlarg'd before the lucernal microscope* London 1773.

[p.183] Dobell, C. *Anthony van Leeuwenhoek and his Little Animals,* London, 1932.
Ford, Brian, J., *The Leeuwenhoek Legacy,* London & Bristol, 1991.

[p.184] The development of this instrument in its social context is examined in:
Ford, Brian J., *Single Lens, Story of the Simple Microscope,* London and New York, 1985.

[p.185] Rennie, J. 'A Small Disturbance: Did experimental obstacles leave Brown motionless?' *Scientific American,* p 10, August 1991; (cites) Deutsch, D. H., 'Did Brown Observe Brownian Motion: Probably Not', *Bulletin of the American Physical Society,* 36 (4): 1374, April 1991.
Ford, Brian J., In Defence of Robert Brown, (lecture) Inter Micro 91, Chicago; transcribed as: 'Robert Brown and Brownian Movement', *The Microscope* 39 (3): 161–173, 1991.

[p.188] The writings of Savile Bradbury should be consulted, notably:
Bradbury, S., *The Evolution of the Microscope,* Oxford, 1967; and *The Microscope past and present,* Oxford, 1968. See also:
Clay, R. S. and Court, T. .H., *The History of the Microscope,* London, 1932, and Disney, A. N., Hill, C. F., and Watson Baker, W. E., *Origin and Development of the Microscope,* London, 1928.
A recent survey may be considered for details of Victorian instruments:
Turner, G. L' E., *The Great Age of the Microscope,* Bristol and New York, 1989.

Select Bibliography

Aramata, H., *Fish of the World*, Heibonsha, Tokyo, 1989 (reissued by Portland House, New York, 1990)

Archer, M., *Natural History Drawings in the India Office Library*, HMSO, London, 1962

Barron, R., *Decorative Maps*, Crescent, New York, 1989

Blunt, W., *The Compleat Naturalist*, (Linnaeus), Collins, London, 1971

Blunt, W., and Raphael, S., *The Illustrated Herbal*, Frances Lincoln, London

Bridson, G., and Wakeman, G., *Printmaking and Picture Printing*, Plough, Oxford and Bookpress, Williamsburg USA, 1984

Bruno, L. C., *The Tradition of Science*, Library of Congress, Washington DC, 1987

Buchanan, H., *Nature into Art*, Weidenfeld & Nicolson, London, 1979

Bulloch, W., *The History of Bacteriology*, Oxford University Press, 1938

Challinor, J., *History of British Geology*, David and Charles, Newton Abbot, 1971

Coats, A., M., *The Book of Flowers*, Phaidon, London, 1973

Cole, F. J., *A History of Comparative Anatomy*, Macmillan, London, 1944

Dampier, Sir William, *A Shorter History of Science*, Cambridge University Press, 1945

Dance, S. P., *The Art of Natural History*, Bracken, London, 1989

Desmond, R., *Wonders of Creation, Natural History Drawings in the British Library*, The British Library, London, 1986

Dunthorne, G., *Flower and Fruit Prints*, published by the author, Washington DC, 1938

Dyson, A., *Pictures to Print*, Farrand, London, 1984

LeFanu, W., 'Some Illustrated Medical Books', *The Book Collector*, 21 (1): 19–28, Spring 1972

Finlay, D. (ed), *The Hunterian Society – A Catalogue*, London, 1990

Fournier, M., *The Fabric of Life*, Koninklijke Bibliotheek, The Hague, 1991

George, W. and Yapp, B., *The Naming of the Beasts*, Duckworth, London 1991

Gerard, J., *Gerard's Herbal*, (reprinted), Studio Editions, London, 1985

Harvey, P. D. A., *Medieval Maps*, The British Library, London, 1991

Hodges, E. R. S., *Scientific Illustration (Handbook)*, Van Nostrand Reinhold, New York, 1989

Hunter, M. and Schaffer, S., *Robert Hooke, New Studies*, Boydell, Woodbridge, 1989

Jackson, C. E., *Bird Illustrators*, Witherby, London 1975

Kastner, J., *The Bird Illustrated, 1550–1990*, Abrams, New York, 1988

Knight, D., *Zoological Illustration*, London 1977

Lambourne, M., *The Art of Botanical Illustration*, Collins, London, 1990

Lambourne, M. (ed), *John Gould's Birds of Great Britain*, Bloomsbury, London, 1979

Learner, R., *Astronomy Through the Telescope*, Van Nostrand Reinhold, New York, 1981

Lenhoff, H. & S., *Hydra and the Birth of Experimental Biology*, Boxwood Press, Pacific Grove, California, 1986

Lysaught, A. M., *The Book of Birds*, Phaidon, London, 1975

Margues, J. de, *Portraits of Plants 1533–1588*, Victoria and Albert Museum, London (1991)

Mitchell, P., (ed), *French Flower Painters of the Nineteenth Century*, Philip Wilson, London, 1989

Nordenskiöld, E., *The History of Biology*, Tudor, New York, 1928

Ravenswaay, C. van, *Drawn from Nature*, Smithsonian Institution, Washington DC, 1984

Rix, M., *The Art of the Botanist*, Lutterworth, London 1981 (reissued as *The Art of Botanical Illustration*, 1989)

Roberts, K. B. and Tomlinson, J. D. W., *The Fabric of the Body*, Oxford University Press, 1992

Rookmaaker, L. C., *The Zoological Exploration of South Africa 1650–1790*, Rotterdam, 1973

Simpson, I. *Anatomy of Humans*, Studio Editions, London, 1991

Smit, P., *History of the Life Sciences*, Asher, Amsterdam, 1974

Stearn, W. T., *Flower Artists of Kew*, Herbert Press, London, 1990

Stubbs, G., *Anatomy of the Horse*, Crescent Books, New York, 1990

Winsor, M. P., *Reading the Shape of Nature*, University of Chicago Press, 1991

Index

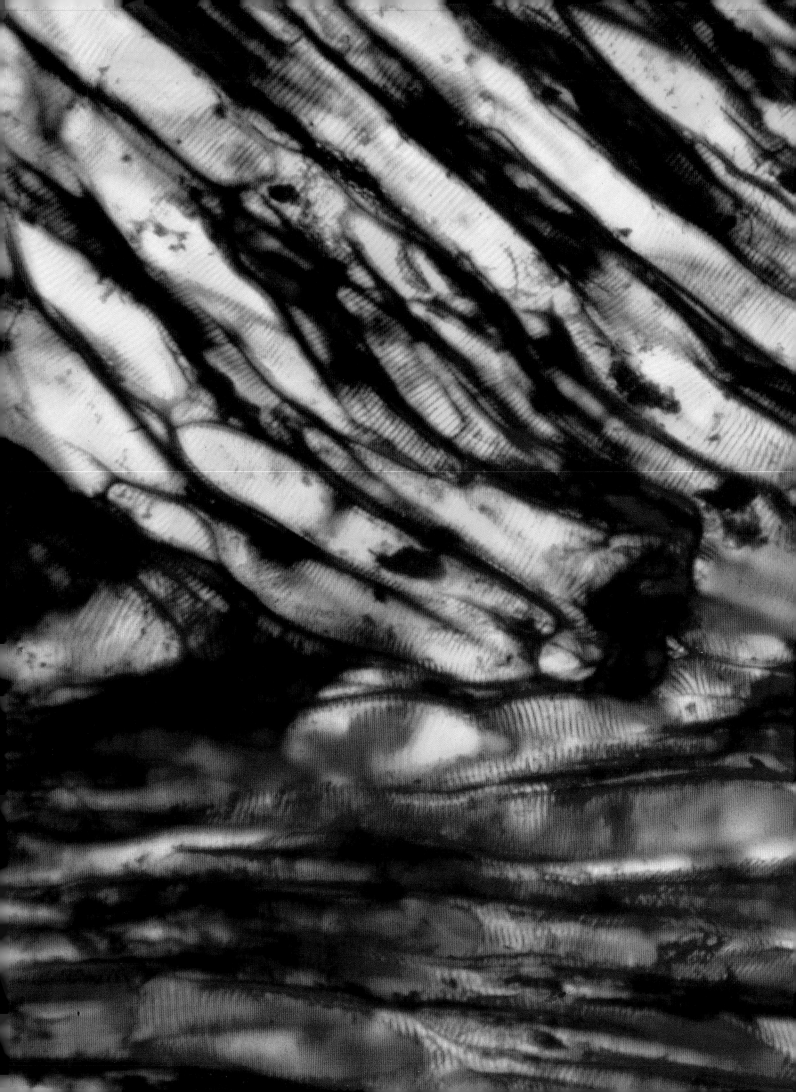